MALNUTRITION AND HUMAN BEHAVIOR

MALNUTRITION AND HUMAN BEHAVIOR

Experimental, Clinical, and Community Studies

Josef Brožek
Lehigh University

VNR VAN NOSTRAND REINHOLD COMPANY
———————————————————————— *New York*

Copyright © 1985 by **Van Nostrand Reinhold Company Inc.**
Library of Congress Catalog Card Number: 85-6135
ISBN: 0-442-21108-2

Manufactured in the United States of America.

Published by Van Nostrand Reinhold Company Inc.
135 West 50th Street
New York, New York 10020

Van Nostrand Reinhold Company Limited
Molly Millars Lane
Wokingham, Berkshire RG11 2PY, England

Van Nostrand Reinhold
480 Latrobe Street
Melbourne, Victoria 3000, Australia

Macmillan of Canada
Division of Gage Publishing Limited
164 Commander Boulevard
Agincourt, Ontario MIS 3C7, Canada

15 14 13 12 11 10 9 8 7 6 5 4 3 2 1

Library of Congress Cataloging in Publication Data
Main entry under title:
Malnutrition and human behavior.
   Bibliography: p.
   Includes Index.
   1. Malnutrition in children—Complications and sequelae.   2. Human behavior—
Nutritional aspects.   3. Child development.   4. Development psychology.
5. Malnutrition—Complications and sequelae.
I. Brožek, Josef M.
RJ399.M26M33   1985   616.3'9   85-6135
ISBN 0-442-21108-2

The author wishes to dedicate this volume
to four far-seeing scientists and administrators
who saw the need
in different places, different times, and different contexts
for the incorporation of scientific psychology
into nutritional research:

FRANCIS G. BENEDICT
Nutrition Laboratory, Boston
The Carnegie Institution of Washington
(1912, 1917)

ANCEL KEYS
Laboratory of Physiological Hygiene
School of Public Health
University of Minnesota, Minneapolis
(early 1940s)

R. F. A. DEAN
Group of Research on Infantile Malnutrition
(British) Medical Research Council
Mulago Hospital, Kampala, Uganda
(mid-1950s)

RICHARD M. BARNES
Graduate School of Nutrition
Cornell University, Ithaca, New York
(early 1960s, animal research)

CONTENTS

PART VI: GENERALIZED SUBCLINICAL MALNUTRITION: DESCRIPTIVE STUDIES

PART VII: GENERALIZED SUBCLINICAL MALNUTRITION: INTERVENTIONS

PART VIII: MALNUTRITION IN THE UNITED STATES

PREFACE

Information on the behavioral effects of the deficits of energy (calories derived from food) and of specific nutrients is of relevance to individuals concerned with the sciences of nutrition (clinical, public health, and laboratory oriented—human and animal) as well as to those interested in the sciences of behavior including physiological, clinical, and social psychology. However, the volume is of potential interest to a much wider range of disciplines, from child development and education through anthropology and sociology to pediatrics.

GENESIS OF THE BOOK

The adventure began with the assembly, over the years, of a large number of reprints and photocopies of journal articles and book chapters, books and monographs, and the proceedings of symposia and conferences. The feat of extracting from this impressive (and oppressive) supply the 30-odd publications that would merit reprinting was achieved by a painful process of successive reductions.

The first large area that had to be eliminated was that of animal research. According to the initial plan, this field was to be covered by Professor Thomas F. Massaro, but it became clear that the literature on animal studies would require a separate volume. The next step was the reduction of a detailed, comprehensive introduction, buttressed by appropriate papers, to a mini-introduction.

A dramatic event in the history of the volume was the disappearance, during travels, of a folder containing fresh translations with ample notes of the earliest work on the psychological effects of fasting, in Italian (Luciani, 1889) and in German (Weygandt, 1904). Eventually, this misfortune proved to be a boon because it greatly facilitated the shift from a chronological structure of the book to a perspective that became progressively more problem oriented. While the volume retains a historical flavor, it has no pretension of providing a systematic history of research on the psychological effects of malnutrition.

THE PORTRAIT

The volume begins with two papers on the behavioral consequences of malnutrition, studied in a community (World War I) and a laboratory (World War II). Part II deals with dietary deficits of micronutrients—thiamine, iodine, and iron. The body of the volume is devoted to generalized (energy-protein) malnutrition, both clinical (pioneering studies, rehabilitation, sequelae) and subclinical (descriptive studies, interventions).

The volume closes with an overview of research on developmental consequences of malnutrition in early childhood, and a multivolume book review places the behavioral research on malnutrition within a broader framework of research on nutrition and behavior. With focus on experimental research, investigations on the effects of dietary deficiencies on behavior, both human and animal, were reviewed elsewhere (Brožek and Vaes, 1961). This volume places emphasis on clinical and community studies on the psychological aspects of early generalized malnutrition, dominating the so-called psychonutritional research of the last 30 years.

The studies of the severe form of generalized malnutrition, requiring hospitalization of the affected children, were initiated in the mid-1950s in Mexico, East Africa (Uganda), and South Africa. The decade of the 1960s was a period of worldwide explorations and the early 1970s focused on retrospective studies.

The 1970s witnessed a shift of interest from the clinical, acute, severe forms of generalized malnutrition to subclinical, chronic energy-protein malnutrition. Two other features should be noted:

1. There was a growing awareness of the role of the socioeconomic macro-environment and, eventually, of the microenvironment of the family.
2. The 1970s were the years of *prospective,* logitudinal investigations, with and without behavioral interventions. The interventions varied in terms of the time when they were applied and in their nature—from clearly defined nutritional supplementation and psycho-affective, psycho-educational, and psychosocial stimulation to a broad intervention in the form of the adoption of Korean female infants by American families.

Throughout this period, human research was paralleled by animal investigations, although a genuine interaction between animal and human studies was altogether too rare.

INTENDED USES OF THE BOOK

It is the author's hope that this volume might serve a variety of constituencies at various levels of involvement in the subject matter. It should be interesting to a casual browser, a student, a beginning research worker (concerned with details, specific problems, methods, and references) as well as to the investigator who is asking questions related to the overall perspective, trends, significance, and the synthesis of information. Together with a systematic account (Galler, 1984) and a volume devoted to critical assessment (Brožek and Schürch, 1984), this book should be useful in upper undergraduate and graduate courses and seminars on behavioral aspects of nutrition and malnutrition, given in diverse contexts such as psychology, human nutrition, and public health.

Concern with the usefulness of the book is reflected in the inclusion of the section of comments labeled *Addendum* and following the reprinted papers. These comments are intended for use for further exploration and refer to additional papers on a particular topic that merited inclusion in the book had there been space. The introductory comments, preceding the reprints, aim to facilitate the understanding of the individual selections and to bring out their significance.

The incorporation of a separate section of papers on the research on malnutrition in the United States, closing with a paper on research needs and priorities, is another measure intended to broaden the appeal and usefulness of the book. In this spirit, the volume closes with an overview and a multipublication book review, supplemented with brief comments on the most recent additions to the literature of the field.

DEDICATION

The field of research on malnutrition and behavior, and the author, personally, owe thanks to many people and institutions. Thus, while the book is dedicated to a quartet of scientists and administrators who played an important role in facilitating research in this area, there were other, serious contenders:

1. A group of 36 young men, conscientious objectors in World War II, who served as volunteer subjects in the semistarvation-rehabilitation study carried out in 1944-1945 at the University of Minnesota (cf. Keys et al., 1950, p. XXXI);
2. Eunice Brožek, who some 10 years ago—half in jest, half in earnest— encouraged the author to switch from writing scientific papers to books;
3. Last, but not least, the author's maternal grandmother, Julia Hrdina Šourek, who in 1917—the hunger year in Bohemia—made available her food supplies, meager as they were, to the children of the neighborhood families and died, as a consequence, of starvation.

Looking at the dedication page, one could readily recall one of Rabindranath Tagore's *Fireflies* (1928, p. 51),

I have thanked the trees that have made my life fruitful,
but have failed to remember the grass
that has ever kept it green.

ACKNOWLEDGMENTS

Thank-you notes are due to the following persons and institutions:

My colleagues, Ernesto Pollitt (University of Texas, Houston) and Henry N. Ricciuti (Cornell University), for sharing with the author their ideas about what should be included in this volume, even though a variety of practical considerations, like availability of space, clipped the wings of our collective fancy.

The Nutrition Foundation, Washington, D.C., for financial assistance with the acquisition of some of the nonperiodic literature relevant to the preparation of this volume.

The *Annual Reviews* for giving the author permission to use freely his chapter (1978), covering primarily the literature of the decade 1967–1977. Marge Sawyers, whose careful typing and attention to detail helped immeasurably to make this book a reality.

JOSEF BROŽEK

REFERENCES

Brožek, J., 1978, Nutrition, Malnutrition and Behavior, *Annu. Rev. Psychol.* **29**:155-177.

Brožek, J., and B. Schürch, eds., 1984, *Malnutrition and Behavior: Critical Assessment of Key Issues,* Nestlé Foundation Publication Series, vol. 4, Lausanne, Switzerland, 656p.

Brožek, J., and G. Vaes, 1961, Experimental Investigations on the Effects of Dietary Deficiencies on Animal and Human Behavior, *Vitam. Horm.* **19**:43-94.

Galler, J. R., ed., 1984, *Nutrition and Behavior,* Plenum Press, New York, 514p.

Keys, A., J. Brožek, A. Henschel, O. Mickelsen, and H. L. Taylor, 1950, *The Biology of Human Starvation,* University of Minnesota Press, Minneapolis, 1386p.

Luciani, L., 1889, *Fisiologia del Digiuno: Studi sull' Uomo (Physiology of Fasting: Studies in Man),* Le Monnier, Firenze.

Tagore, R., 1928, *Fireflies,* Macmillan, New York.

Weygandt, W., 1904, Über die Beinflussung geistiger Leistungen durch Hungern (The Effects of Fasting on Mental Performance), *Psychol. Arb.* **4**:45-173.

CONTENTS BY AUTHOR

MALNUTRITION AND HUMAN BEHAVIOR

Introduction

Any time we go beyond the borders of our intellectual home territory, we feel perplexed by the body of novel concepts and technical terminology, methods and procedures, facts and theories. This happens when we are crossing the borders between any two disciplines belonging to different classes of sciences. The matter becomes still more complex and more perplexing when we deal with a multifaceted problem that calls for the pooling of competencies in a variety of disciplines. Human malnutrition represents just such a complex problem (cf. Brožek and Keys, 1944, 1945) and our collaborative monograph, *The Biology of Human Starvation* (Keys et al., 1950), has sections on morphology (including body composition studied *in vivo*), biochemistry, physiology, psychology, and special problems (mostly medical, such as edema, anorexia nervosa, and diets for nutritional rehabilitation). The appendixes include a section on the design of the study and methods of statistical analysis.

In the best of all worlds, an introduction to the study of malnutrition and behavior would constitute a separate book. Such a book, properly documented by seminal papers, would be divided into two roughly equal parts: one on nutrition, written for the benefit of readers whose specialization is in the area of the behavioral sciences, and one on behavior. This second part would keep in mind the information needs of readers with a nutritional and, more broadly, biomedical background. Such an introductory volume would be followed by three others: a volume on behavioral effects of human malnutrition, a parallel volume on animal studies, and a third one endeavoring to achieve a synthesis, critical and systematic, of the animal and the human literature. But the intellectual geography is more complex: Only in the laboratory can we put environment into brackets—though not without peril—and hope that all is well as long as we keep the environment constant. In the context of the societal reality within which human malnutrition breeds—the reality of poverty—cultural, social, and economic factors must receive consideration.

If we leave the realm of fantasy for the real world, it becomes clear that an introductory volume and a volume dealing with human environments must be compressed in the present book into a single chapter. It is not, and it cannot be, the aim of this introduction to teach biologically oriented readers, including nutritionists, all they need to know about the study of behavior; to make nutritionists out of psychologists; or to make social scientists, competent to deal with the complexities of the human environment, out of either psychologists or nutritionists.

Three sets of variables are considered: nutritional, behavioral, and environmental, with a postscript on research design, data analysis, and social (or substantive) versus statistical significance. Information about additional contributions of benchmark quality but not reprinted in this volume is given in the addenda that follow the reprinted papers in all parts of the book. Finally, comments on recent nonperiodical contributions are presented in the closing paragraphs of the book. We shall begin with a few references to overviews of the literature on malnutrition and behavior.

SOURCES OF INFORMATION

If an extreme economy of means were to be imposed in order to cover a span of 100 years of research on the effects of dietary deficits on human behavior, we would be forced to choose three communications: an extensive review of the early, primarily experimental phase (Brožek and Vaes, 1961) Galler's (1984b) survey of the evidence from human studies on the behavioral consequences of malnutrition in early life and Rush's supplementary chapter (1984).

Both Galler's and Rush's surveys are strong in tabular presentations of the literature and the data. Both accounts miss the 1954 pioneering Mexican report (reprinted in English translation in the present volume as Paper 6), as well as the first paper by Geber and Dean (1955). Also missing is a reference to the important study by Robles, Ramos Galván, and Cravioto (1959) on the psychological changes during the recovery of children hospitalized for advanced malnutrition (*desnutrición avanzada*) in which detailed data are reported for the subscales (Motor, Adaptive, Language, Personal-Social) of the Gesell Developmental Scale.

The technique of tabular summaries has also been used in the earlier reviews written by Lloyd-Still (1976), which focused on the early studies on the intellective performance of children who recovered from clinical malnutrition, and by Pollitt and Thomson (1977), who considered subclinical, chronic malnutrition as well (pp. 284–300). A welcome feature of the Pollitt-Thomson review is an appendix consisting of a brief glossary of the major tests of intelligence and developmental scales. Appropriately, the Caldwell Home Inventory Scale is included. The glossary's usefulness would have been increased by including, selectively, references to the papers in which a particular instrument is described in greater detail.

The early animal literature was included in the Brožek and Vaes (1961) review. Partial reviews of recent work became available, with reference to research in rodents (Levitsky and Barnes, 1973; Leathwood, 1979) and in primates (Riopelle, 1979), but we are not aware of a comprehensive, critical, synthesizing review of animal research on the effects of malnutrition and behavior. Original human studies carried out in Africa, Asia, and the Western Hemisphere were reported at international conferences (see Brožek, 1979).

NUTRITIONAL VARIABLES

Historical Perspective

At the very outset of her remarks in "Historical Landmarks in Nutrition," Todhunter (1984, p. 871) notes the complex background of the science of nutrition and provides references to selected publications dealing with development of the modern science of nutrition. A step of major significance in our understanding of the chemistry of life was Lavoisier's 1783 demonstration that respiration is a slow combustion. Six years later, with Seguin, Lavoisier measured, in humans, the twin processes of oxygen consumption and carbon dioxide exhalation under conditions of rest and work as well as following the ingestion of food. Thus, notes Todhunter (1984, p. 872), nutrition acquired a quantitative approach, and the foundations were laid for calculations of food energy requirements and caloric value of foods.

The realization that nutrients are chemicals that are essential for the support of life and for the maintenance of health and work capacity constituted another landmark. We wish to underscore the importance of the advances in our understanding of the nutritional etiology of disease syndromes with impaired behavior as an essential component—for example, deficits of energy and protein (kwashiorkor in infants, with complex behavioral changes), of vitamins (night blindness in vitamin A deficiency, the dementia of pellagra), and of minerals (cretinism, as a result of prenatal iodine deficiency, with a profound depression of the level of intellectual functioning).

A systematic history of behavioral research on the effects of nutrition (and, especially, of malnutrition) has not been written. The anchor point of psychonutrition is represented by the investigations carried out in Italy, Germany, and the United States (Langfeld, 1914), attempting to study not the effects of nutrition but of its absence—of fasting (cf. Brožek and Vaes, 1961, pp. 51-52). These developments were tied to the provision of appropriate methods by the use, adaptation, and expansion of procedures used by experimental physiologists for the study of the function of the sensory, motor, and central nervous systems. In time, measures of intellective functions and, finally, of personality were developed and used in the context of nutritional research. Concern with the behavioral effects of malnutrition was strongly reinforced by events related to World Wars I and II (see Part I).

Foods and Nutrients

Adequate food intake is a fundamental human need. Mixed diets provide a large number of nutrients, grouped into macronutrients (carbohydrates, fats, proteins and their components—fatty acids and amino acids), vitamins, and minerals. Nutrition Reviews' *Present Knowledge in Nutrition* (1984, pp. 79-618) provides up-to-date information on this subject.

Food Consumption

In a hospital or a laboratory, the food consumption of an individual can be monitored with substantial precision. In community studies, especially when we are concerned with quantitative information on the food consumption of individuals rather than households or larger social units, the task becomes very complex and discouraging. Thus, the Latin American longitudinal studies of the 1970s (see Part VII) were semi-experimental since only information about the *supplement* that was consumed was considered. The home consumption was either not studied at all or the information obtained was viewed as not being dependable enough to determine the total food intake. In one of the studies (Chávez and Martínez, 1982, pp. 28-33) heroic efforts were made to measure the consumption of breast milk.

For household dietary assessment Chávez and Hueneman (1984) list 11 methods, ranging from food frequency lists through the favorite 24-hour dietary recall to detailed quantitative record keeping, involving the weighing or measuring of food intake for varying periods of time.

Under certain conditions, especially when the studies are carried out in non-Western cultures (see Paper 21), not only food intake and practices of food preparation but also beliefs and attitudes toward specific foods, including weaning foods, deserve attention. These are anthropological rather than nutritional considerations.

Biomedical Measures of Malnutrition

In this volume, the reader will encounter primarily studies on the effects of generalized malnutrition due to deficits of food, with focus on energy and protein. Behavioral effects of the deficits of selected specific nutrients are covered in Part II. The volume does not deal with the behavioral effects of excessive food intake (obesity), of severe reduction of food intake in the midst of plenty (anorexia nervosa), or of the behavioral aspects of inborn errors of metabolism (phenylketonuria).

Generalized (energy-protein) clinical malnutrition occurs in three forms:

1. Nutritional marasmus—with severe underweight, no edema, minor disturbances of metabolism, chronic infections; typically occurs early in life (first year);
2. Kwashiorkor—with a less severe underweight than in marasmus but with edema, severe disturbances of metabolism; occurs in older infants and young children (2 to 4 years of age);
3. Marasmic kwashiorkor—a mixed form, combining a severe weight loss with the presence of edema.

Some authors view generalized clinical malnutrition as a single spectrum, with typical marasmus and typical kwashiorkor as the two ends of the spectrum.

The differentiation between generalized malnutrition and the forms of malnutrition due to the deficits of specific nutrients has a merit of simplicity. Unfortunately, the reality one encounters in field studies is not as simple as the schema would imply. Some authors (Good, Fernandes, and West, 1984, p. 696) go as far as to say that zinc deficiency, which has many physical manifestations similar to those of the generalized (energy-protein) malnutrition, "is a frequent if not virtually inevitable concomitant of protein-calorie malnutrition in humans."

In McLaren's view (1984, p. 43)—and who could disagree?—a clear understanding of the pathogenesis of clinical malnutrition is a prerequisite of a sound classification. Such an understanding is, however, not at hand. McLaren cites the Coward and Lunn (1981) model centered on the concept of adaptation, postulating partially successful adaptation to energy deficit in marasmus and a failure to adapt to protein deficit in kwashiorkor, with consequent metabolic and hormonal alterations accounting for major pathological changes. However, McLaren feels that the etiology of kwashiorkor is more complex and cites two points that support such a view. First, it appears that deficiency of other nutrients is more common in kwashiorkor than in marasmus; as noted by others, zinc appears to be one of the deficient microminerals, and it is plausible that, specifically, it may play a part in the skin changes so typical of kwashiorkor (Golden, Golden, and Jackson, 1980). Second, Golden (1982) reported that the edema of kwashiorkor was not uniformly corrected by increased protein intake and suggested that potassium deficiency may play a role.

McLaren's classification (1984) considers all forms of generalized (energy-protein) malnutrition. His criteria are *degree* (mild, moderate, severe [clinical]), *types* of clinical malnutrition (marasmus, marasmic kwashiorkor, kwashiorkor), *duration* (acute, subacute, chronic, acute superimposed on chronic), and *stage* (inactive, relapsing, in remission).

Earlier, McLaren and his colleagues (McLaren, Pellett, and Read, 1967; cf. McLaren, 1984, Table 2, p. 46) developed a simple scoring system based on symptoms (edema, dermatosis, edema plus dermatosis, hair change, enlarged liver) varying in the numerical value attached to them and on the level of serum albumin (or total serum protein). The sum of the points yields a total score that—supplemented by information on the child's estimated weight deficit (very low weight in marasmus)—places the child into one of the three categories of generalized malnutrition.

The schema, though not totally free of weaknesses, has the merit of simplicity and objectivity. Furthermore, it provides information on the severity of the condition within a given malnutrition category. However, it did not become standard practice. Another quantitative approach to the characterization of generalized clinical malnutrition was developed by Hoorweg (1976; cf. Paper 16).

Recently the topic of nutritional anthropometry was discussed in detail by Johnson and Lampl (1984), Waterlow (1984), and the commentators on their papers. Mora (1984) considered the issues of international versus local reference standards, biological (nutritional) meaning of the principal anthropometric indicators (weight for age, weight for height, height for age), and the choice of the cutoff points.

BEHAVIORAL VARIABLES

Behavior represents a complex of responses of organisms to internal and external stimuli. For complex human behavior the interaction with the sociocultural environment is of critical importance. Among the nutrients, only one is *behavior specific:* Vitamin A deficiency, if severe and prolonged enough, results in the impairment of dark adaptation (night blindness). We could also turn the tables around and say that impairment of dark adaptation is a nutrient-specific behavioral effect (cf. Brožek, 1974*b*). In general, simple sensory functions—

but not perception—are of little relevance in research on the effects of malnutrition. The relevance of the other facets of behavior—motor, intellective, socioemotional (personality)—varies with the characteristics of malnutrition: its nature, duration, and severity.

Elsewhere we have pointed out (Ricciuti and Brožek, 1984, p. 109) that behavior can be assessed in a multiplicity of ways and referred the reader to general sources of information on the methods of psychological measurement (cf. Allen, 1984). Brief comment was made on what to measure and on the fundamental requirements of all the behavioral measurements: reliability (consistency) and validity (cf. Yarbrough et al., 1974). Three meanings of the term *validity* were noted: predictive validity, construct validity, and ecological (real-world) validity.

A Brief Guide

A practically oriented review of methods used in published studies, yet not insensitive to the need for theoretically based methodological innovations, was contributed by Pollitt (1984) to the volume *Methods for the Evaluation of the Impact of Food and Nutrition Programs.* Since the behavioral methods are age specific, the primary grouping of the methods is in terms of age levels:

Infancy (birth to 24 months),
Preschool age (2 to 6 years),
School age (7 to 18 years).

Within each age group the methods refer to the following categories of behavior:

Activity and play behavior,
Motor development,
Social and emotional responses and development,
Cognition (general composite measures of intelligence, specific cognitive
    measures).

References are provided to original publications in which the use of a particular method is reported.

An omission occurred in the category *School age*, in which no information was made available about the methods for the study of motor development. Such information was provided by Hoorweg, whose 1976 monograph, in spite of its title, does contain a chapter on motor ability (pp. 80-87). The data were obtained by the Oseretsky scale, in the version developed by Sloan (1955) under the title "Lincoln-Oseretsky Motor Development Scale." The same test was used in South Africa (Bartel et al., 1978; Bartel, 1980, especially pp. 115-116; cf. also Griesel, 1984).

The second part of Pollitt's chapter (1984) is devoted to the description of a cognitive test battery developed in accord with the information-processing paradigm. The actual tests are described in the Appendix (pp. 198-200).

Categories of Behavior: A Systematic Account

The methods for the study of behavior were examined in extenso in "Part 2, Assessment of Function," of the volume *Malnutrition and Behavior* (Brožek and Schürch, 1984, pp. 116–336).

In his overview of psychometric methods, used or potentially useful for research on the effects of generalized (energy-protein) malnutrition in children, Hurwitz (1984) groups the procedures into six categories:

Development scales (Brazelton Neonatal Scale, Gesell Developmental Scale, Bayley Scales of Infant Development);

Tests of general intelligence (Stanford-Binet, Wechsler Intelligence Scales);

Neuropsychological test batteries (Halstead-Reitan, Luria-Nebraska);

Piagetian scales;

Measures of single dimensions of behavior (visual perception, language and speech competence, auditory discrimination, motor competence, and others);

Measures of Socioemotional Development (Vineland Social Maturity Scale).

As a rule, in behavioral research on the effects of malnutrition one applies behavioral methods that are available. At times one has to adapt the methods to a changed cultural setting or the special needs of longitudinal studies with their requirement for repeated administrations.

The development of an extensive test battery, adapted for use with Guatemalan infants and young children, was a major accomplishment of the Guatemalan project. In some of the earlier analyses (Irwin et al., 1979, p. 246) scores obtained on 8 of the subtests were used. A more comprehensive list of 15 tests, together with information on scoring methods, reliability, and ages at which the tests were administered, is appended (p. 176) to the Hurwitz (1984) account. An addendum to Hurwitz's chapter (Brožek, 1984a) takes up sensory integration (e.g., visual-kinesthetic comparisons of geometrical forms), behavioral observations in a naturalistic setting (the home), child's activities in standardized settings (in a room, in an open field), and educational outcomes (school marks, performance on standardized achievement tests including tests of reading and writing, and observations of actual behavior in the school room; cf. Paper 24).

Connolly (1984) covered the assessment of motor performance in children, while Brožek (1984b) dealt with motor functions measured in adults, with a brief comment on the measurement of general activity in children (cf. Pollitt and Amante, 1984). Barrett's chapter (Paper 23; see also Barrett, 1984a) deals with the socioemotional functioning in young school children (cf. Barrett, Radke-Yarrow, and Klein, 1982). The methods for the study of intra-organismic effects, using electrophysiological techniques, were described by Thatcher and Cantor (1984); the account was expanded by two addenda. Two other papers dealt with cross-cultural applicability of psychological measurements (Pollitt et al., 1984; Dasen, 1984).

ENVIRONMENTAL VARIABLES

Human organisms exist simultaneously in a variety of environments—atmospheric, geological, nutritional, socioeconomic, and cultural (Brožek, 1974*a*, p. 153). We may differentiate between the socioeconomic and cultural *macroenvironment*, characterizing the particular society as a whole, and the *microenvironment* of individual families (with their peculiarities reflected in the use of words, dietary practices, beliefs, and patterns of personal interaction).

For the purposes of first orientation, a simple schema can be used to indicate the synergistic effect of nutrition (N) and the socioeconomic and cultural environment (E) on behavior (B):

$$N \searrow \atop E \nearrow B$$

This is a triadic, not a dyadic (N→B), model (cf. Caldwell, 1974, p. 28).

In reference to malnutrition (M), we could replace E with P for poverty (cf. Pollitt, 1980):

$$M \searrow \atop P \nearrow B$$

These are extremely simplified schemata. For one, the relations between N and B as well as E and B are bidirectional, not unidirectional; this applies to M, P, and B as well. Furthermore, the factors N and E (and, even more clearly, M and P) interact as well.

In 1975 in Delhi, India, Gupta and co-workers (Paper 20) responded to "The Challenge of Nutrition and Environment as Determinants of Behavior" (Galler, 1984*a*). They established that, holding the degree of malnutrition constant, the children's mean IQs decreased with the decreasing level of socioeconomic status. Similarly, within a given social class, the mean IQs decreased in parallel to the increasing severity of chronic, subclinical malnutrition.

The data illustrate, in a simple and readily intelligible way, that in the given sample both the socioeconomic level of the family and the severity of chronic malnutrition influenced measured intelligence. The issue is so important that we would like to see the study repeated in other areas in which a wide range of variation in nutritional and socioeconomic status of the children is to be found, not so much to confirm the universality of the association but to learn more about the magnitude of the impact and the effect of variables such as the age of the children.

In a paper introducing a symposium on nutrition, brain, and behavior, Brožek (1981) reviewed studies on malnutrition, environment, and behavior with reference to both the subclinical (chronic) and the clinical malnutrition. In the first category, both the results of descriptive studies and of complex interventions were considered. In the second category, long-term effects of the socioeconomic environment on cognitive functioning and the effects of psychosocial stimulation on recovery were examined.

Socioeconomic Background of Childhood Malnutrition

The detailed review of this subject by Grantham-McGregor (1984) concentrates on the characteristics of the families that have malnourished children but urges us to place these families in a wider (national, regional, and local) societal context in which the families function. A failure to do so may readily lead us to blame the parents living in the poor areas of the Third World for the malnutrition of their children and to draw parallels between malnutrition in industrially underdeveloped countries and the child neglect in the developed countries. We are reminded that:

> The differences between developed and underdeveloped countries in factors such as infection rates and public amenities [such as health and educational facilities, garbage disposal, water supply, and sanitation as well as availability of steady employment and fair wages] are enormous [Grantham-McGregor, 1984, p. 359].

The author comments on the dearth of standard, valid, and reliable instruments for measuring the social background of malnourished children. She focuses on the available information rather than on specific methodological issues and procedures. The categories of characteristics that are discussed are as follows:

Physical and economic resources (income, housing, furniture, appliances, sanitation, possessions);

Family structure and size (stability of the family, type of family unit, number of family members, number and spacing of children);

Biological characteristics of parents (nutritional status, health, obstetric history, age);

Sociocultural characteristics of parents (literacy and education, occupation, ethnic origin, IQ, comprehension and verbal expression, media contact, modernity, taboos and superstitions);

Deaths of siblings;

Child-feeding practices;

Mother-child interaction (carrying time, time in crib, physical contact, maternal responsiveness to child, verbal communication, affection);

Stimulation in home (storytelling, playing, reading, availability of toys and books, trips and visits);

Schooling;

Characteristics of the child who becomes malnourished (constitution, level of nutrient requirements, feeding difficulties, season in which the child is born, gender).

The author's conclusions follow:

> Childhood malnutrition is related to a constellation of family disadvantages ranging over a wide area. These disadvantages are interrelated and interdependent. It is unwise to generalize from one location to another because the nature of the relationships is largely determined by the socio-cultural and economic conditions of the wider society in which the families live. [p. 371]

Socioeconomic Status: Physical and Economic Resources in the Home

In the study of a sample of Barbadian children hospitalized for nutritional marasmus during the first year of life and tested psychometrically at the age of 5 to 11 years (Galler et al., 1983), an interview schedule was used to assess the socioeconomic status of the families. The schedule (p. 11) consisted of 22 items and was administered to the child's primary caretaker by a public health nurse. By means of factor analysis, the characteristics were grouped into 7 clusters of related items.

Three factors differentiated between the families of the index children (hospitalized for marasmus) and comparison children (not hospitalized):

Factor 1, referring to conveniences available in the home (refrigerator, electricity, television, running water);

Factor 2, assessing the degree of crowding in the home (number of bedrooms, beds, and rooms);

Factor 5, bearing on the economic resources of the family (whether the father was employed or not and, if employed, what type of work he does).

The differentiating factors came as a surprise, and not a particularly welcome surprise, since the design of the study called for equalizing the groups of the index and the comparison families with reference to the physical and economic resources. This was to be achieved by selecting classmates and neighborhood children as members of the comparison group. The authors have failed in this regard, as demonstrated by the existence of statistically significant differences in favor of the comparison group on several indicators of socioeconomic status. What was learned is important, however.

It is of some interest to consider the factors that did not differentiate between the families of the index and the comparison children. Factor 3, intended to reflect the family's weekly income and the amount of money spent on food was apparently not assessed dependably. The assessment was based on the reported income (rather than on the observed evidence of relative wealth on which the scores for Factors 1, 2, and 5 were computed).

Factor 4 (presence of showers and running water) did not differentiate between the groups since, in fact, there were no differences among the families in this regard; these facilities are apparently uniformly available in Barbados. A genuine homogeneity may prevail also in regard to Factor 7 (means of transportation).

The failure of Factor 6 (referring to the work of the mother and the income she generates) to differentiate between the two groups is interpreted by the authors as demonstrating that on the island maternal outside work did not contribute significantly to the home income.

Basic Household Surveys: Household Organization and Composition

Anthropological methodologies for the assessment of households—the principal settings for the acquisition, preparation, and consumption of food—

were described by Pelto and Pelto (1984). Here we are interested in household characteristics as *intervening variables* to be taken into account in assessing the impact of a nutritional program. By contrast, in a sociological perspective, Christiansen (1984) examined the *social effects* of an intervention involving food supplementation and home stimulation such as money spent for food or change in the use of contraceptive methods.

The Basic Household Survey (Pelto and Pelto, 1984) is based on a face-to-face interview with one or more members of the household and addresses itself to specified characteristics of the household. The choice of the data to be collected depends importantly on the kinds of questions the investigators are asking. The authors point out that "preliminary ethnographic reconnaissance can often identify the key features of the household for research emphasis" (p. 205).

Four broad categories, relevant in nutritional studies, were considered:

Household composition,
Material resources and conditions,
Beliefs and attitudes (to food, nutrition, and health),
Household organization.

Special attention was given to the households as small-scale organizations that have a large number of tasks to accomplish. Three basic approaches can serve to characterize the activities of the individual household members in terms of the types and timing of the activities:

Direct observation,
Interviewing (such as a 24-hour recall of activities, based on a series of key questions),
Recording activities using time sampling (e.g., recording the presence of specified activities during the first 10 minutes of every half-hour for 2 hours) or noting in detail and timing a set of activities (like those related to infant feeding). In some areas it is feasible to request the members of the households to keep a personal record of their activities (activity diaries).

Observations of mother-child interaction are discussed at some length, and consideration is given to the potential use of videotapes.

Culture as a Factor

The behavior of human beings is codetermined by culture—the body of customs, ways of communicating, values, and attitudes. In Abel's phrasing, "Culture can be viewed as both a source and product of human behavior" (1984, p. 336). This is true of groups. For an individual child, culture is a source of the patterns of behavior; nevertheless, a child (including a malnourished child) codetermines the pattern of behavioral interaction in the family. Thus, Chávez and Martínez (1979) demonstrated that both mothers and fathers of supplemented and responsive children directed to the child a greater number of sentences per hour (p. 225, Fig. 9), and the members of the family provided a greater number of the forms of stimulation to such children (p. 227, Fig. 11) than was the case in the families of the unsupplemented children.

In the context of nutritional research, psychologists have been concerned primarily with the issue of the appropriateness of their tools in different cultures (Pollitt et al., 1984; Dasen, 1984; cf. Jensen, 1984; Alexander, 1984; McMillan, 1984). Substantially more is involved than a translation of Western verbal tests or of the instructions for the administration of the nonverbal tests into the language of the group in which a particular child has been growing up.

We shall dramatize the point by referring to a French scale of infant development. It could not be applied, without modifications, in a West African village since it included an item calling for the child to climb stairs. There simply were no stairs to climb in that village. Some of the critical issues emerging in cross-cultural studies are discussed in the comments preceding Paper 21 (Graves, 1979), and the directly relevant references are cited.

Caldwell's HOME Environment Inventory

The acronym HOME stands for *Home Observations for Measurement of the Environment,* a manual prepared by Caldwell and Bradley (1984; cf. Bradley and Caldwell, 1984, p. 316). The use of the inventory requires that families participating in a study be visited by a trained interviewer who is competent enough to observe properly the mother and child interacting at home. The child must be present and awake. The interview with the mother, using the HOME inventory, takes about an hour.

The 45 items of the inventory are grouped into 6 categories:

1. Emotional and verbal responsiveness of the mother;
2. Acceptance of the child (avoidance of restrictions and punishment);
3. Organization of the environment (e.g., safety of the child's play area);
4. Provision of appropriate play materials;
5. Maternal involvement with the child;
6. Variety in daily stimulation (daily activities).

Scores are obtained for each subscale as well as for the inventory as a whole. The total score represents the number of items recorded as facilitating the child's development. There are three versions of the inventory: for infants and toddlers (birth up to three years of age), for preschool children (3-6 years of age), and for elementary school children.

Chase and Martin (1970, p. 934) were first to use the inventory in connection with research on the psychological effects of malnutrition. They used an early version of the inventory (then called the Home Stimulation Inventory Scale and consisting of a total of 73 items and 8 subscales) as a tool for assessing the stimulation potential of the home (cf. Caldwell, 1967, p. 50). Data were obtained for 19 index children, hospitalized during the first year of life with the diagnosis of nutritional marasmus, and 19 comparison children with a similar socio-economic background. The mean total scores on the Caldwell inventory indicated that the index children were more disadvantaged than the comparison children.

A unique feature of the study, reported in 1972 by Cravioto and DeLicardie and reprinted in this volume as Paper 14, is that the data on social, emotional, and cognitive stimulation potential of the homes were obtained in a longitudinal study when the children were 6 months of age—that is, *prior* to the episode of severe malnutrition (except for one out of the 22 index children). At that time, as well as when the children were 48 months of age, the comparison children's families obtained higher home stimulation scores than the families of the index children, in accord with the findings of Chase and Martin (1970).

Elardo and Bradley (1981), whose paper begins with an overview of alternate aproaches to the assessment of home learning environments (pp. 113-117), comment on the Cravioto-DeLicardie data as follows: "The eventual appearance of malnutrition in apparently similar infants could have been *predicted* [editor's emphasis] by HOME scores" (p. 126).

The originator of the inventory feels that the instrument has its merits and that it represents improvement over a gross differentiation between subgroups of a population (such as middle and lower class) that, at best, provides actuarial estimates of what goes on in a child's environment (Caldwell, 1974, p. 30). However, she and her colleagues are humble about the analytical powers of the instrument: "It is . . . no electron microscope for looking at the social environment."

RESEARCH DESIGN, DATA ANALYSIS, AND SOCIAL VERSUS STATISTICAL SIGNIFICANCE

The issues of design and data analysis, common to scientists concerned with nutrition, behavior, and social environment, were considered by Martorell (1984) and the commentators on his presentation. The pressing problem of comprehensive data banks was examined by Read (1984), and Barrett (1984*c*) addressed himself to the issues of validity in research on the behavioral effects of malnutrition and to the merits and limitations of experimental versus nonexperimental designs (1984*b*).

While the basic theoretical considerations and procedures concerning design and data analyses are common to the biological, behavioral, and social sciences, some concepts, terms, and techniques are specific to a particular area or at least have a greater currency in one field than in another. This is true, for example, of quasi-experimentation (Cook and Campbell, 1979) or factor analysis (Dahlke, 1984). Factor analysis, used in several of the papers included in this volume, originated in the biometrics of Francis Galton and Karl Pearson, but the theory and the techniques blossomed in the context of psychometrics. It refers to statistical procedures designed to identify (hypothetical) principal dimensions, or factors, that underlie the relationships between a large number of variables such as items in an inventory of the characteristics of families or measures of socioeconomic status.

The concept of statistical significance (e.g., of an association between two variables or of a difference between two means) is universally accepted. But how about social significance of the findings on malnutrition and behavior? Here we are on a much less firm ground.

We (Keys et al., 1950, p. 917; cf. Brožek, 1984c) have estimated the magnitude of the socially relevant effects of semistarvation in terms of ensuing civil disorder and strife, capacity for prolonged physical work, and actual work performance. The percentages of body weight lost as a result of inadequate food intake, varying from 5 to 50% of the prestarvation weight, served as a criterion of the severity of starvation.

Pollitt (1981, pp. 268-269) raised the issue of social (real-life) significance versus statistical significance of the improvements in behavioral test performance observed in studies on nutritional supplementation in infancy and early childhood. In fact, there are two related issues to consider: First is the risk of the so-called washout effect—a gradual disappearance of the gains once the food supplementation comes to a stop. Second, even if the gains would last, in view of the fact that the improvements do not appear numerically impressive, it is "questionable whether the benefit will lead to behavioral changes in the recipients that will be meaningful in terms of adaptation to their own social systems." Gold stressed the need to pay attention to what Townsend called "substantive" significance in 1970. Townsend (1984, p. 615) is impressed (while most of us are apt to be depressed) by the sheer magnitude of the worldwide problem of generalized malnutrition, noting that "since 1970 nearly a billion people throughout the whole world have been victims of extreme poverty and chronic malnutrition."

The number of strategies of nutrition-related interventions that have been tried to solve the problem is large. Townsend's list includes food and nutrition planning, supplementary feeding programs, fortification of foods (such as salt, flour, and sugar), nutrition-oriented agricultural programs, marketing strategies, food and nutrition education, and integrated health and nutrition programs. Critical assessment of the social significance of these endeavors has been badly neglected.

Townsend reminds us that both the magnitude of the observed effect and the size of the sample (and we might add, the size of the population that is being considered) must be taken into account in assessing social significance. Thus, an effect of a given magnitude, which barely reaches a level of statistical significance in a small sample or samples, would become highly significant, both statistically and socially, on a national scale. The author refers to the effect of breastfeeding on delaying the onset of menstruation (and thus the possibility of conception) by two to three months. In an individual case it means next to nothing. In a small group the social impact is marginal. On a large scale it is relevant to population growth, and a shift away from breastfeeding, should it occur on a large scale, would bring about an increase in fertility—something the already overpopulated world surely does not need.

REFERENCES

Abel, T. M., 1984, Culture and Psychotherapy, in *Encyclopedia of Psychology,* vol. 1, R. J. Corsini, ed., John Wiley, New York, pp. 336-337.

Alexander, T., 1984, Cultural Differences, in *Encyclopedia of Psychology,* vol. 1, R. J. Corsini, ed., John Wiley, New York, pp. 332-333.

Allen, M. J., 1984, Testing Methods, in *Encyclopedia of Psychology*, vol. 3, R. J. Corsini, ed., John Wiley, New York, pp. 413-414.

Barrett, D. E., 1984*a*, Malnutrition and Child Behavior: Conceptualization, Assessment and an Empirical Study of Social-Emotional Functioning, in *Malnutrition and Behavior: Critical Assessment of Key Issues*, J. Brožek and B. Schürch, eds., Nestlé Foundation Publication Series, vol. 4, Lausanne, Switzerland, pp. 280-306 (with comments by D. A. Frank on pp. 307-326 and C. M. Super on pp. 327-336).

Barrett, D. E., 1984*b*, Methodological Issues in Nutritional Intervention Research, in *Malnutrition and Behavior: Critical Assessment of Key Issues*, J. Brožek and B. Schürch, eds., Nestlé Foundation Publication Series, vol. 4, Lausanne, Switzerland, pp. 585-596.

Barrett, D. E., 1984*c*, Methodological Requirements for Conceptually Valid Research Studies on the Behavioral Effects of Malnutrition, in *Nutrition and Behavior*, J. R. Galler, ed., Human Nutrition: A Comprehensive Treatise, vol. 5, Plenum Press, New York, pp. 9-36.

Barrett, D. E., M. Radke-Yarrow, and R. E. Klein, 1982, Chronic Malnutrition and Child Behavior: Effects of Early Caloric Supplementation on Social-Emotional Functioning at School Age, *Dev. Psychol.* **18**:541-556.

Bartel, P. R., 1980, Findings on EEG and Psychomotor Studies on Malnourished Children, in *Malnutrition in Southern Africa*, University of South Africa, Pretoria, pp. 111-116.

Bartel, P. R., D. R. Griesel, L. S. Burnett, I. Freiman, E. U. Rosen, and J. Geefhuysen, 1978, Long-Term Effects of Kwashiorkor on Psychomotor Development, *S. Afr. Med. J.* **53**:360-362.

Bradley, R. H., and B. M. Caldwell, 1984, The HOME Inventory and Family Demographics, *Dev. Psychol.* **20**:315-320.

Brožek, J., 1974*a*, From QUAC Stick to a Compositional Assessment of Man's Nutritional Status, in *Nutrition and Malnutrition: Identification and Measurement*, A. F. Roche and F. Falkner, eds., Plenum Press, New York, pp. 151-164.

Brožek, J., 1974*b*, Sensory Functions, in *Methodology in Studies of Early Malnutrition and Mental Development*, WHO Workshop, Swedish Nutrition Foundation, Uppsala, Sweden, pp. 17-20.

Brožek, J., ed., 1979, *Behavioral Effects of Energy and Protein Deficits*, NIH Publication Number 79-1906, U.S. Government Printing Office, Washington, D.C., 366p.

Brožek, J., 1981, Nutrition, Brain, and Behavior: An Introduction, in *Nutrition in Health and Disease and International Development: Symposia from the XII International Congress of Nutrition*, Alan R. Liss, New York, pp. 371-382.

Brožek, J., 1984*a*, Psychometric Methods: An Addendum, in *Malnutrition and Behavior: Critical Assessment of Key Issues*, J. Brožek and B. Schürch, eds., Nestlé Foundation Publication Series, vol. 4, Lausanne, Switzerland, pp. 177-185.

Brožek, J., 1984*b*, The Assessment of Motor Functions in Adults, in *Malnutrition and Behavior: Critical Assessment of Key Issues*, J. Brožek and B. Schürch, eds., Nestlé Foundation Publication Series, vol. 4, Lausanne, Switzerland, pp. 268-279.

Brožek, J., 1984*c*, Criteria of Significance: Dependability, Magnitude, and Impact, in *Malnutrition and Behavior: Critical Assessment of Key Issues*, J. Brožek and B. Schürch, eds., Nestlé Foundation Publication Series, vol. 4, Lausanne, Switzerland, pp. 608-614.

Brožek, J., and A. Keys, 1944, General Aspects of Interdisciplinary Research in Experimental Human Biology, *Science* **100**:507-512.

Brožek, J., and A. Keys, 1945, Interdisciplinary Research in Human Biology, with Special Reference to Behavior Studies, *Am. Sci.* **33**:103-111.

Brožek, J., and B. Schürch, eds., 1984, *Malnutrition and Behavior: Critical Assessment of Key Issues*, Nestlé Foundation Publication Series, vol. 4, Lausanne, Switzerland, 656p.

Brozek, J., and G. Vaes, 1961, Experimental Investigations on the Effects of Dietary Deficiencies on Animal and Human Behavior, *Vitam. Horm.* **19:**43-94.

Caldwell, B. M., 1967, Descriptive Evaluations of Child Development and Developmental Settings, *Pediatrics* **40:**46-54.

Caldwell, B. M., 1974, The Malnourished Environment, in *Methodology in Studies of Early Malnutrition and Mental Development,* WHO Workshop, Swedish Nutrition Foundation, Uppsala, Sweden, pp. 28-34.

Caldwell, B. M., R. H. Bradley, and Staff, 1984, *Home Observations for Measurement of the Environment,* rev. ed., Center for Child Development and Education, University of Arkansas, Little Rock, 131p.

Chase, H. P., and H. P. Martin, 1970, Undernutrition and Child Development, *New Engl. J. Med.* **282:**933-939.

Chávez, A., and C. Martínez, 1979, Behavioral Effects of Undernutrition and Food Supplementation, in *Behavioral Effects of Energy and Protein Deficits,* NIH Publication Number 79-1906, U.S. Government Printing Office, Washington, D.C., pp. 216-228.

Chávez, A., and C. Martínez, 1982, *Growing Up in a Developing Community,* Instituto Nacional de Nutrición, Mexico City, 155p.

Chávez, M., and R. Hueneman, 1984, Measuring Impact by Assessing Dietary Intake and Food Consumption, in *Methods for Evaluation of the Impact of Food and Nutrition Programs,* D. E. Sahn, R. Lockwood, and N. S. Scrimshaw, eds., The United Nations University, Tokyo, pp. 127-143.

Christiansen, N., 1984, Social Effects of a Family Food Supplementation and Home Stimulation Program, in *Malnutrition and Behavior: Critical Assessment of Key Issues,* J. Brožek and B. Schürch, eds., Nestlé Foundation Publication Series, vol. 4, Lausanne, Switzerland, pp. 520-530.

Connolly, K. J., 1984, The Assessment of Motor Performance in Children, in *Malnutrition and Behavior: Critical Assessment of Key Issues,* J. Brožek and B. Schürch, eds., Nestlé Foundation Publication Series, vol. 4, Lausanne, Switzerland, pp. 230-259.

Cook, T. D., and D. T. Campbell, 1979, *Quasi-Experimentation: Design and Analysis Issues for Field Settings,* Rand-McNally, Chicago, 405p.

Coward, W. A., and P. G. Lunn, 1981, The Biochemistry and Physiology of Kwashiorkor and Marasmus, *Br. Med. Bull.* **37:**19-24.

Dahlke, A. E., 1984, Factor Analysis, in *Encyclopedia of Psychology,* vol. 2, R. J. Corsini, ed., John Wiley, New York, pp. 2-3.

Dasen, P. R., 1984, Cross-Cultural Uses of Piagetian Methodology, in *Malnutrition and Behavior: Critical Assessment of Key Issues,* J. Brožek and B. Schürch, eds., Nestlé Foundation Publication Series, vol. 4, Lausanne, Switzerland, pp. 203-229.

Elardo, R., and R. H. Bradley, 1981, The Home Observation for Measurement of the Environment (HOME) Scale: A Review of Research, *Dev. Rev.* **1:**113-145.

Galler, J. R., 1984a, Introduction: The Challenge of Nutrition and Environment as Determinants of Behavioral Development, in *Nutrition and Behavior,* J. R. Galler, ed., Human Nutrition: A Comprehensive Treatise, vol. 5, Plenum Press, New York, pp. 1-5.

Galler, J. R., 1984b, Behavioral Consequences of Malnutrition Early in Life, in *Nutrition and Behavior,* J. R. Galler, ed., Human Nutrition: A Comprehensive Treatise, vol. 5, Plenum Press, New York, pp. 63-117.

Galler, J. R., F. Ramsey, G. Solimano, W. E. Lowell, and E. Mason, 1983, The Influence of Early Malnutrition on Subsequent Behavioral Development, I., Degree of Impairment in Intellectual Performance, *J. Child Psychiatry* **22:**8-15.

Geber, M., and R. F. A. Dean, 1955, Psychological Factors in the Etiology of Kwashiorkor, *WHO Bull.* **12:**471-475.

Gold, D., 1970, Statistical Tests and Substantive Significance, in *Significance Test Controversy,* D. E. Morrison and R. E. Henkel, eds., Aldine, Chicago, pp. 172-181.

Golden, M. N. H., 1982, Protein Deficiency, Energy Deficiency, and the Oedema of Undernutrition, *Lancet* **1:**1261-1265.

Golden, M. N. H., B. E. Golden, and A. A. Jackson, 1980, Skin Breakdown in Kwashiorkor Responds to Zinc, *Lancet* **1:**1256.

Good, R. A., G. Fernandes, and A. West, 1984, Nutrition and Immunity in *Present Knowledge in Nutrition,* 5th ed., The Nutrition Foundation, Washington, D.C., pp. 693-710.

Grantham-McGregor, S., 1984, Social Background of Childhood Malnutrition, in *Malnutrition and Behavior: Critical Assessment of Key Issues,* J. Brožek and B. Schürch, eds., Nestlé Foundation Publication Series, vol. 4, Lausanne, Switzerland, pp. 358-374 (with comments by I. E. López, J. M. Celedón, and M. Colombo on pp. 375-377, S. A. Richardson on pp. 378-382, and G. Sellers on pp. 383-388).

Graves, P. L., 1979, Cross-Cultural Comparisons of Mothers and Their Malnourished Children in Asia, in *Behavioral Effects of Energy and Protein Deficits,* J. Brožek, ed., NIH Publication Number 79-1906, U.S. Government Printing Office, Washington, D.C., pp. 100-108.

Griesel, R. D., 1984, Psychomotor Development of Malnourished African Children, in *Malnutrition and Behavior: Critical Assessment of Key Issues,* J. Brožek and B. Schürch, eds., Nestlé Foundation Publication Series, vol. 4, Lausanne, Switzerland, pp. 260-267.

Hoorweg, J. C., 1976, *Protein-Energy Malnutrition and Intellectual Abilities: A Study of Teenage Uganda Children,* Mouton, The Hague, 148p.

Hurwitz, I., 1984, Psychometric Methods, in *Malnutrition and Behavior: Critical Assessment of Key Issues,* J. Brožek and B. Schürch, eds., Nestlé Foundation Publication Series, vol. 4, Lausanne, Switzerland, pp. 164-176.

Irwin, M., R. E. Klein, J. W. Townsend, W. Owens, P. L. Engle, A. Lechtig, R. Martorell, Ch. Yarbrough, R. E. Lasky, and R. L. Delgado, 1979, The Effects of Food Supplementation on Cognitive Development and Behavior among Rural Guatemalan Children, in *Behavioral Effects of Energy and Protein Deficits,* J. Brožek ed., NIH Publication Number 79-1906, U.S. Government Printing Office, Washington, D.C., pp. 239-254.

Jensen, A. R., 1984, Cultural Bias in Tests, in *Encyclopedia of Psychology,* vol. 1, R. J. Corsini, ed., John Wiley, New York, pp. 331-332.

Johnston, E. F., and M. Lampl, 1984, Anthropometry in Studies of Malnutrition and Behavior, in *Malnutrition and Behavior: Critical Assessment of Key Issues,* J. Brožek and B. Schürch, eds., Nestlé Foundation Publication Series, vol. 4, Lausanne, Switzerland, pp. 51-70 (with comments by R. Martorell on pp. 71-76).

Keys, A., J. Brožek, A. Henschel, O. Mickelsen, and H. L. Taylor, 1950, *The Biology of Human Starvation,* University of Minnesota Press, Minneapolis, 1385p.

Langfeld, H. S., 1914, On the Psychophysiology of Prolonged Fast, *Psychol. Monogr.* **16**(5):1-50 (plus appendixes).

Leathwood, P. D., 1979, Early Nutrition and Behavior in Rodents, in *Behavioral Effects of Energy and Protein Deficits,* J. Brožek, ed., NIH Publication Number 79-1906, U.S. Government Printing Office, Washington, D.C., pp. 5-11.

Levitsky, D. A., and R. H. Barnes, 1973, Malnutrition and Behavior, in *Nutrition, Development, and Social Behavior,* D. J. Kallen, ed., NIH Publication Number 73-242, U.S. Government Printing Office, Washington, D.C., pp. 3-16.

Lloyd-Still, J. D., 1976, Clinical Studies on the Effects of Malnutrition during Infancy on Subsequent Physical and Intellectual Development, in *Malnutrition and Intellectual Development,* J. D. Still, ed., Publishing Sciences Group, Littletown, Mass., pp. 103-159.

McLaren, D. S., 1984, Forms and Degrees of Energy-Protein Deficits, in *Malnutrition and Behavior: Critical Assessment of Key Issues,* J. Brožek and B. Schürch, eds., Nestlé Foundation Publication Series, vol. 4, Lausanne, Switzerland, pp. 42-50.

McLaren, D. S., P. L. Pellett, and W. W. C. Read, 1967, A Simple Scoring for Classifying the Severe Forms of Protein-Calorie Malnutrition in Early Childhood, *Lancet* **1:**533-535.

McMillan, J. H., 1984, Culture-Fair Tests, in *Encyclopedia of Psychology,* vol. 1, R. J. Corsini, ed., John Wiley, New York, pp. 353-356.

Martorell, R., 1984, Design and Data Analysis, in *Malnutrition and Behavior: Critical Assessment of Key Issues,* J. Brožek and B. Schürch, eds., Nestlé Foundation Publication Series, vol. 4, Lausanne, Switzerland, pp. 556-575 (with comments by R. E. Lasky on pp. 576-578 and B. J. Kaplan on pp. 579-584).

Mora, J. O., 1984, Nutritional Assessment by Anthropometry: Prevalence Studies, in *Malnutrition and Behavior: Critical Assessment of Key Issues,* J. Brožek and B. Schürch, eds., Nestlé Foundation Publication Series, vol. 4, Lausanne, Switzerland, pp. 98-106.

Nutrition Reviews, 1984, *Present Knowledge in Nutrition,* 5th ed., The Nutrition Foundation, Washington, D.C., 900p.

Pelto, G., and P. Pelto, 1984, Anthropological Methodologies for Assessing Household Organization and Structure, in *Methods for Evaluation of the Impact of Food and Nutrition Programs,* D. E. Sahn, R. Lockwood, and N. S. Scrimshaw, eds., The United Nations University, Tokyo, pp. 204-225.

Pollitt, E., 1980, *Poverty and Malnutrition in Latin America: Early Childhood Intervention Programs,* Praeger, New York, 162p.

Pollitt, E., 1981, Effects of Nutritional Supplementation on the Behavioral Development of Infants and Children, in *Textbook of Pediatric Nutrition,* R. M. Suskind, ed., Raven Press, New York, pp. 263-269.

Pollitt, E., 1984, Methods for Behavioral Assessment of the Consequences of Malnutrition, in *Methods for Evaluation of the Impact of Food and Nutrition Programs,* D. E. Sahn, R. Lockwood, and N. S. Scrimshaw, eds., The United Nations University, Tokyo, pp. 179-203.

Pollitt, E., and P. Amante, eds., 1984, *Energy Intake and Activity,* Alan R. Liss for the United Nations University, New York, 418p.

Pollitt, E., and C. Thomson, 1977, Protein-Calorie Malnutrition and Behavior: A View from Psychology, in *Nutrition and the Brain,* vol. 2, R. J. Wurtman and J. J. Wurtman, eds., Raven Press, New York, pp. 261-306.

Pollitt, E., D. B. Greenfield, C. Saco-Pollitt, and S. Joos, 1984, Validation of Attention-Retention Tests in Two Cultures, in *Malnutrition and Behavior: Critical Assessment of Key Issues,* J. Brožek and B. Schürch, eds., Nestlé Foundation Publication Series, vol. 4, Lausanne, Switzerland, pp. 186-202.

Read, M. S., 1984, The Need for Comprehensive Data Banks, in *Malnutrition and Behavior: Critical Assessment of Key Issues,* J. Brožek and B. Schürch, eds., Nestlé Foundation Publication Series, vol. 4, Lausanne, Switzerland, pp. 597-602 (with comments by D. B. Greenfield on pp. 603-606).

Ricciuti, H. N., and J. Brožek, 1984, Measuring Outcomes, in *Malnutrition and Behavior: Critical Assessment of Key Issues,* J. Brožek and B. Schürch, eds., Nestlé Foundation Publication Series, vol. 4, Lausanne, Switzerland, pp. 108-115.

Riopelle, A. J., 1979, Protein-Energy Malnutrition in Primates, in *Behavioral Effects of Energy and Protein Deficits,* J. Brožek, ed., NIH Publication Number 79-1906, U.S. Government Printing Office, Washington, D.C., pp. 43-54.

Robles, B., R. Ramos Galván, and J. Cravioto, 1959, Valoración de la Conducta del Niño con Desnutrición Avanzada y de sus Modificaciones durante la Recuperación, *Méd. Hosp. Infant. (Méx.) Ból.* **16:**317-341.

Rush, D., 1984, The Behavioral Consequences of Protein-Energy Deprivation and Supplementation in Early Life: An Epidemiological Perspective, in *Nutrition and Behavior,* J. R. Galler, ed., Human Nutrition: A Comprehensive Treatise, vol. 5, Plenum Press, New York, pp. 119-157.

Sloan, W., 1955, The Lincoln-Oseretsky Motor Development Scale, *Genet. Psychol. Monogr.* **51:**183-252.

Thatcher, R. W., and D. S. Cantor, 1984, Electrophysiological Techniques in the Assessment of Malnutrition, in *Malnutrition and Behavior: Critical Assessment of Key Issues,* Nestlé Foundation Publication Series, vol. 4, Lausanne, Switzerland, pp. 116-136.

Todhunter, E. N., 1984, Historical Landmarks in Nutrition, in *Present Knowledge in Nutrition,* 5th ed., The Nutrition Foundation, Washington, D.C., pp. 871-882.

Townsend, J. W., 1984, Significance of Nutrition-Related Programs, in *Malnutrition and Behavior: Critical Assessment of Key Issues,* J. Brožek and B. Schürch, eds. Nestlé Foundation Publication Series, vol. 4, Lausanne, Switzerland, pp. 615-629.

Waterlow, J. C., 1984, Current Issues in Nutritional Assessment by Anthropometry, in *Malnutrition and Behavior: Critical Assessment of Key Issues,* Nestlé Foundation Publication Series, vol. 4, Lausanne, Switzerland, pp. 77-90 (with comments by J. D. L. Hanson on pp. 91-97).

Yarbrough, Ch., R. E. Lasky, J.-P. Habicht, and R. E. Klein, 1974, Testing for Mental Development, in *Methodology in Studies of Early Malnutrition,* WHO Workshop, Swedish Nutrition Foundation, Uppsala, Sweden, pp. 7-12.

Part I

Effects of Food Deficits:
World Wars I and II

Papers 1, 2, and 3: Commentary

1 **BLANTON**
Excerpts from *Mental and Nervous Changes in the
Children of the Volksschulen of Trier, Germany, Caused
by Malnutrition*

2 **BROŽEK**
Excerpt from *Food as an Essential: Experimental Studies
on Behavioral Fitness*

3 **LEYTON**
Excerpts from *Effects of Slow Starvation*

Severe food deficits have plagued humankind since time immemorial, either as a result of natural disasters interfering with food production and distribution or of man-made disasters associated with wars. An account entitled "Behavior and Complaints in Natural Starvation" was incorporated into the collaborative treatise on *The Biology of Human Starvation* (Keys et al., 1950, pp. 783-818).

Paper 1 constitutes perhaps the earliest, nonanecdotal report on the effects of prolonged inadequate diet on the mental functioning of school children. Only the parts relevant to malnutrition have been reproduced. The study was carried out in the wake of World War I in Trier, in the western part of Germany, close to Luxembourg. The nutrition of the children was rated as good, fair, poor, and very poor, but the criteria were not specified and the results of psychological tests that were made were not reported.

The author, Smiley Blanton, served as a captain in the Medical Corps, U.S. Army of Occupation. He had an M.D. from Cornell University. We were unable to establish the time at which he received a diploma of psychological medicine from the London College of Physicians and Surgeons, indicated on the title page of a volume on *Child Guidance* (Blanton and Blanton, 1927). Blanton noted the following effects of inadequate diet: a low level of energy, lack of attention in school, poor comprehension, poor memory, and restlessness in the classroom.

Paper 2 summarizes studies on the effects of restricted food intake, carried out in the Laboratory of Physiological Hygiene, School of Public Health, University of Minnesota, in the 1940s and the early 1950s. Only the section dealing with a prolonged (six months) severe food restriction, followed by nutritional rehabilitation, is reprinted in this volume.

The laboratory's nutritional research grew out of the staff's interest in human fitness (Taylor and Brožek, 1944; cf. Brožek, 1964), which is viewed as an integral of many features and functions of the organism—morphological, metabolic, physiological, and behavioral. Accordingly, research on human nutrition was viewed and practiced as an area of an experimentally oriented human biology (Brožek and Keys, 1945).

The semistarvation-rehabilitation study was presented in extenso in a two-volume, collaborative monograph (Keys et al., 1950). The design of the rehabilitation phase of the study was complex, with four levels of energy (calories), two levels of protein, and two levels of vitamin supplements. This phase of the study may be viewed as the applied part in contrast to the semistarvation phase. It is this basic study that receives emphasis in the re-printed paper.

In volume 1 of the book (Keys et al., 1950), the behavioral aspects of the study are considered in the chapters on special senses and on neuromuscular functions and motor performance. Volume 2, in the section on psychology (pp. 767–918), contains seven chapters: "Psychological Problems in Starvation," "Behavior and Complaints in Natural Starvation," "Behavior and Complaints in Experimental Starvation and Rehabilitation," "Intellective functions," "Personality," "Psychological Case Studies," and "Psychological Effects— Interpretation and Synthesis."

Supplementary journal articles are cited in the reference section of Paper 2. They serve to illustrate and summarize the results of a quantitative (ref. 3) and a qualitative (ref. 4) case study and provide additional data on personality obtained by methods such as an item analysis of the psychoneurotic scales of the Minnesota Multiphasic Personality Inventory (ref. 9), the study of perception and association (ref. 11), the Rosenzweig P-F test (ref. 18), systematic observation (ref. 19), and the Rorschach test (ref. 33). Reference 34 deals with the concept of experimental neurosis in the context of the semistarvation study.

In terms of the comprehensiveness of the methods used for the study of behavior in nutritional context, the Minnesota semistarvation study is unique (see Keys et al., 1950, pp. 1094–1104).

The aim of the study was to examine the effects of severe prolonged reduction in food intake free from the complications typical of countries suffering from famine, besieged cities, or concentration camps. The degree of weight loss obtained in the Minnesota study parallels the weight loss experienced in many instances of natural starvation and thus assures the realism of the study. The absence of the stresses of life typically accompanying severe food shortages is both a merit and an inescapable limitation of the study.

In summary, what were the behavioral effects of the loss of one-quarter of the prestarvation (control) weight in normal-weight young men? The sensory functions as well as the capacity for intellective performance showed little or no indication of impairment. By contrast to measured intelligence, however, self-initiated intellective activities such as letter writing, intellectual discussions, or participation in a special course on the rehabilitation of postwar Europe were affected profoundly or withered away altogether. Strength, as measured by the hand-grip and back-lift tests, was markedly reduced. While all the motor functions were impaired, speed and coordination suffered least. The greatest decrement was observed in the test of endurance in hard physical work, involving running on an inclined treadmill, with the average running time being reduced from 242 seconds in the control period to 50 seconds at the end of 6 months of semistarvation. Changes in the feeling of well-being and in personality were also marked. Tiredness, awareness of the desire for food, muscle soreness, muscle cramps, apathy, and dizziness were prominent. There was an increase in irritability, especially in the sensitivity to noise. Decreases were noted in ambition, concentration, sex drive, self-discipline, mental alertness, and drive to activity. In the Minnesota Multiphasic Personality Inventory the largest average score increment was obtained for the Depression scale.

The alterations in personality and in other behavioral variables were reversed in the course of nutritional rehabilitation. By the thirty-third week after the end of the semistarvation phase of the study, the scores on the personality scales returned to the preexperimental, normal, levels.

G. B. Leyton, a British medical officer, was captured early in World War II and had an unusual opportunity to observe the effects of severe food deprivation, mostly combined with hard physical work, in German camps for the prisoners of war in Libya, Italy, and Germany. An important part of these observations dealt with behavior. The relevant sections of his report are contained in Paper 3. The paper, based on extensive field observations, usefully supplements Paper 2, which reports the data of an experimental study.

REFERENCES

Blanton, S., and M. G. Blanton, 1927, *Child Guidance,* The Century Company, New York, 335p.

Brožek, J., 1950, Psychology of Human Starvation and Rehabilitation, *Sci. Mon.* **70:** 270-274.

Brožek, J., 1954, Physical/read: Psychological/Performance, in *Methods for Evaluation of Nutritional Adequacy and Status,* H. Spector, M. S. Peterson, and T. E. Friedeman, eds., National Academy of Sciences-National Research Council, Washington, D.C., pp. 204-221.

Brožek, J., 1964, Experimental Investigations on Nutrition and Human Behavior: A Postscript, in *Science in Progress,* ser. 14, W. E. Brode, ed., Yale University Press, New Haven, Conn., pp. 1-37.

Brožek, J., and A. Keys, 1945, Interdisciplinary Research in Human Biology, with Special Reference to Behavior Studies, *Am. Sci.* **33:**103-111.

Keys, A., J. Brožek, A. Henschel, O. Mickelsen, and H. L. Taylor, 1950, *The Biology of Human Starvation,* vols. 1 and 2, University of Minnesota Press, Minneapolis, 1385p.

Taylor, H. L., and J. Brožek, 1944, Evaluation of fitness, *Fed. Proc.* **3:**216-222.

1: MENTAL AND NERVOUS CHANGES IN THE CHILDREN OF THE VOLKSSCHULEN OF TRIER, GERMANY, CAUSED BY MALNUTRITION

S. Blanton

THE medical officers of the Department of Sanitation and Public Health, Civil Affairs, Advanced General Head-quarters, under the direction of Colonel Henry A. Shaw, M. C., while studying the physical changes occurring in the school children of Trier, Germany, due to malnutrition caused by war conditions encountered so many complaints from teachers and school officials concerning the great mental deterioration of the children as shown by their poor school work, and the number of nervous disorders occurring, that it was decided to supplement the physical examination by a psychiatric study to determine, as far as possible, just what the conditions were. It was also desired to take advantage of the unusual opportunity, probably never offered before, to make a psychiatric and psychological study of several thousand children forced to subsist for three years upon a rigid and inadequate diet. Moreover, such a survey would make it possible to substitute for the necessarily biased and emotionally influenced judgments of the German teachers and officials the facts obtained from an analysis of all the factors in the case.

The psychiatric study was restricted to the children of the *Volksschulen*, numbering about 6,500, between five and a half and fourteen years of age, for it was between these ages that the

Reprinted from *Mental Hygiene* **3**:343-344, 362, 385-386 (1919); *Copyright © 1919 by the National Mental Health Association, Inc.*

changes in school children caused by malnutrition were found to be greatest. First it was necessary to discover the obvious changes,—the number of children who had failed to pass their grades one or more times, and the extent of mental deficiency, nervous and conduct disorders of all kinds; this would free the field for a closer study of the less obvious but nevertheless quite definite changes occurring in children who did not attract the attention of teachers because of retardation or some abnormality. Then it was desired to determine to what extent all these changes were caused by malnutrition due primarily to war conditions.

It was soon seen that the problem was primarily one for careful clinical observation rather than for psychological tests. Even had it been possible to give each one of the 6,500 children a psychological test this would have given only the degree of retardation and not the underlying causes; nor would such tests have shown the emotional changes or the extent of the neuroses and nervous diseases. Investigations along the following lines were carried out:

1. The *Rektors* of the *Volksschulen* were asked to pick out and send for examination, as follows:

 (a) All children who were retarded in their grades one year or more

 (b) Children who were abnormally "nervous"

 (c) Children who had any organic nervous disease

 (d) Children with serious conduct disorders,—i. e., persistent lying, stealing, etc.

 (e) Children suffering from symptoms of psychoses or neuroses,—i. e., children who acted queerly or seemed emotionally abnormal in some way.

2. Interviews with teachers and *Rektors* concerning mental and nervous changes occurring in the children during the war.

3. Observation of the children in the school, on the playground and in their homes, together with interviews with parents.

4. A survey to determine the number and type of speech defects occurring in the school children.

5. Psychological tests given to those children suffering primarily from malnutrition, to determine the specific changes in mental abilities such as comprehension, learning ability, memory span and quickness of the associations.

[*Editor's Note:* Material has been omitted at this point.]

The effect of malnutrition on the physical and mental abilities of children, as shown by the survey, depends on two factors: on the severity of the malnutrition and the mental status of the child —whether a dull type or possessor of average intelligence or superior intelligence. Since the summer of 1916 the population has been subjected to a diet which has not possessed sufficient fats or easily digestible proteins. The children of well-to-do families had access to food supplies beyond the reach of the poorer classes and did not suffer. There were also variations in the malnutrition of children subjected to the same diet. Some children because of poor health or individual make-up were less able to assimilate the proteins—the coarse bread and the watery vegetables—and hence they suffered from a severer grade of malnutrition. Others became ill and after recovery did not get food suited to their condition and therefore fell permanently into a lower grade of malnutrition.

For these reasons this malnutrition varied among children:

1. Children of rich or well-to-do parents were able to buy much extra food.

2. Some children due to a physical weakness or individual make-up were less able to assimilate the coarse bread and watery vegetables.

3. Children who were convalescing after illness, unable to get food suited to their condition, dropped permanently into a lower grade of malnutrition.

[*Editor's Note:* Material has been omitted at this point.]

CONCLUSIONS

The chief conclusions and findings of the whole study may be briefly summarized as follows:

1. At least forty per cent of the children in the *Volksschulen* of Trier, Germany, are suffering from malnutrition to such a degree as to cause a loss of nervous energy.

2. There has been no increase in the percentage of cases normally found of neuroses, psychoses, abnormal "nervousness," organic nervous diseases, tics or conduct disorders.

3. There has been an increase of the number of border line defectives totaling not more than one per cent of the total school population.

4. There has been no increase in the percentage of speech defects, especially stuttering, normally found; but there has been a marked increase in poor, lisping, slurring speech due to the retardation or interference of the fine coordinations necessary for good speech, caused chiefly by malnutrition.

5. The percentage of children failing to pass their grades has increased from an average of eight per cent in pre-war years to fifteen per cent in 1917 and 1918. It is estimated about half of this seven per cent increase in retardation has been due to malnutrition, the other half has been due to war conditions.

6. There has been a lowering of the whole standard of school work caused chiefly by malnutrition but partly by war conditions in general; half of the children who in pre-war times did superior work now do average work, and the percentage of children who do inferior work has been increased from twenty to more than thirty per cent.

7. The specific changes noted in the children caused by malnutrition are:

    (a) A lack of nervous and physical energy
    (b) Inattention during school hours
    (c) Poor and slow comprehension for school tasks
    (d) Poor memory for school work
    (e) A general nervous restlessness while in school.

[*Editor's Note:* Material has been omitted at this point.]

2: FOOD AS AN ESSENTIAL: EXPERIMENTAL STUDIES ON BEHAVIORAL FITNESS

J. Brožek

[*Editor's Note:* In the original, material precedes this excerpt.]

Reprinted from pages 49-60 of *Food and Civilization,* S. M. Farber, N. L. Wilson, and R. H. L. Wilson, eds., Charles C Thomas, Springfield, Ill., 1966; Courtesy of Charles C Thomas; *Copyright © 1966 by Charles C Thomas.*

The condition in which food is totally absent but water is unlimited is referred to as acute starvation. When the energy equivalent of the food intake is moderately below the physiological requirements, we may speak of calorie restriction. When the calorie deficit is prolonged and fairly severe, we refer to it as semi-starvation. Actually, we deal with continua, both of time and of energy deficit. More important than the verbal label is, of course, a precise specification of the conditions of food intake and energy expenditure.

Famine is a semi-starvation under "natural conditions" and differs from experimental studies in the onset of the food deficit (which is usually gradual), in the uncertainty regarding the outcome and availability of eventual relief, and in the disruption of economics and of communal hygienic facilities. Famines have been one of mankind's worst scourges, ranking with epidemic diseases (plagues) and war, with which famine was frequently associated.

There is a large volume of incidental observations on the behavioral effects of famines that affected whole populations[37] and on the experiences of travelers and explorers, of sailors and soldiers who ran out of food, for one reason or another and for varying periods of time. The Second World War, with its infamous concentration camps, besieged cities, and whole areas subjected to man-made famine, provided voluminous and frightening documentation concerning the profound effects of qualitative malnutrition and quantitative undernutrition on the human organism.

The Second World War provided also the background for a systematic, experimental study on the biological impact of prolonged, severe calorie deficit and on the course of the subsequent nutritional rehabilitation.[29] The study was carried out on thirty-six volunteers, conscientious objectors, at the University of Minnesota in 1944-1945, with some follow-up observations in 1946. The focus of the study was on the evaluation of the effectiveness of rehabilitation diets varying in calories, protein, and vitamins. This was the "applied" aspect of the study. The large array of morphological, biochemical, physiological, and psychological observations made during the semi-starvation phase of the experiment provides basic information on the effects of severe semi-starvation, not complicated by the stresses typically accompanying famines. Only this material will be considered here, except for brief reference to the general trends and degree of recovery upon rehabilitation.

In regard to psychological aspects, the general character of the changes in behavior in semi-starvation and refeeding was described,[19, 35] a quantitative[3] and qualitative[14] case study of a typical subject was reported, and the results obtained by personality inventories[9, 12] and projective tests[11, 18, 33] were examined. The monograph, *The Biology of Human Starvation*,[29] contains a comprehensive survey of the literature on behavior and complaints under conditions of natural, nonexperimental starvation and famine.

What were the dietary conditions and the principal findings? During the twelve weeks of the control period, the basic diet provided about 3,500 calories daily, with 112 gm of protein, 124 gm of fat and 482 gm of carbohydrate; quantitative adjustments, upward or downward, were made on individual basis according to body size and relative underweight. At the start of the semi-starvation period, the mean actual caloric intake was decreased from 3,492 calories to 1,658 calories with the grand mean of 1,570 calories per day for the twenty-four weeks of semi-starvation.

Sensory functions remained largely unaffected.[29] Visual thresholds, measured with illumination intensities of 1- and 100-foot-candles at the level of the test patch, were unaltered. The rate of perceptual fluctuations showed a negligible, statistically non-significant decrement. The mean value of the flicker-fusion frequency decreased from 36.3 to 35.3 flickers per second after six months of semi-starvation. The change, though small in absolute terms, was consistent and significant statistically.

The acuity of hearing not only did not deteriorate in semi-starvation, but it actually improved. This change was statistically significant in the lower range of the sound frequencies. For the biological interpretation of the significance of these changes the single, most relevant fact is that the changes were reversed in the course of nutritional rehabilitation. Thus, though small in absolute terms, they probably represent a genuine alteration, nutritionally induced. The mechanism involved is not clear. The enlargement of the free lumen of the external auditory canal by reduced production of earwax and by some thinning out of the soft tissues constituting the walls of the canal was suggested[29] as a possible mechanical explanation in the absence of other evidence.

In general, neurological examinations revealed no abnormalities. The sense of vibration was not impaired. Skin sensitivity remained normal, except for three men who developed sensory disturbances in the form of mild paresthesias. The tendon reflexes (patellar and ankle reflex) were definitely diminished. These neuromuscular functions were discussed together with the motor performance.[29] The changes in strength, speed, and coordination are summarized in Table II-VI.

TABLE II-VI

CHANGES IN PSYCHOMOTOR FUNCTIONS AFTER TWENTY-FOUR WEEKS OF SEMI-STARVATION: N = 32

Performance Tests	Control (C) Mean SD	Semi-starvation (S) Mean SD	Difference (Δ) $\frac{\Delta}{SD_c}$
Strength			
Hand grip (kg)	58.2 7.6	41.8 6.3	−16.4 2.2
Back pull (kg)	165.4 27.8	116.1 17.8	−49.3 1.8
Speed			
Gross body reaction time (1/100 sec)	42.3 3.7	45.6 4.7	+3.3 0.9
Hand and arm movements (units/min)	75.3 5.7	71.4 6.5	−3.9 0.7
Tapping (taps/10 sec)	66.6 5.5	63.2 5.1	−3.4 0.6
Coordination			
Pattern tracing (No. of error contacts)	115.3 13.7	135.9 13.4	+20.6 1.5

Statistically, the changes in all six scores were highly significant and were in the direction of deterioration throughout. They were reversed by refeeding. Two points should be made in regard to the data in Table II-VI. First, there was a very large absolute change in strength. Prolonged semi-starvation, with its significant decrease in body musculature, was the only nutritional stress that in our experience resulted in significant loss in the measured strength. Secondly, there were large differences in the relative amount of deterioration as expressed by the "displacement ratios" (last column of Table II-VI), relating the semi-starvation changes to the standard deviations of the control scores.

In the area of gross motor performance (locomotion), dramatic decrement was observed in the endurance test, which involved running on an inclined treadmill to exhaustion. The mean duration of the run decreased from 242 seconds to 50 seconds. The course of the changes in semi-starvation and during the first twenty weeks of rehabilitation is indicated in Figure II-I.

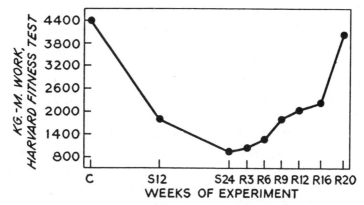

Figure II-1. Total work, as kilogram-meters, performed in the Harvard Fitness Test during semistarvation and rehabilitation. The values represent the averages for twelve subjects. C = control, S = semi-starvation, R = rehabilitation.

Measured intellective performance[29] did not show important changes, even though the subjects complained about inability to concentrate and to maintain a trend of thought. Also, spontaneous mental effort and achievement declined remarkably during semi-starvation. Performance on the six short tests of intellective functions (perception of spatial relations, word fluency, memory, number facility, inductive reasoning, and perceptual speed) showed no significant changes in starvation. There was a consistent but minimal change in the mean total raw score on the extensive CAVD tests, with no time limits. The average time to complete the test was eight to nine hours. The mean raw scores were 137.9 in the control period, 135.6 at the end of twelve weeks, and 133.5 in the twenty-fourth week of starvation. The psychometric data, together with the clinical observations, indicate that intellective capacity was certainly not profoundly affected by the loss of one-quarter of body weight.

The impact of semi-starvation on behavior, as it was expressed in the self-ratings, is portrayed in Table II-VII. The items are arranged in the order of subjectively appraised severity. This list is headed by "Tiredness" and "Appetite" (interpreted as felt need for food). A few characteristics, clearly brought out in the interviews, were represented not at all or at least not adequately in the self-ratings. Of these the most important were weakness and lack of energy, general slowing down of all activities, sensitivity to cold, gnawing concern with thoughts about food expressed in such activities as collecting recipes, and decrease in sociability.

Perhaps it will be useful to supplement the self-ratings by a few illustrative results obtained by the use of inventories in which the subjects simply noted the presence or the absence of a symptom. For purposes of comparison the percentages referring to the prestarvation control will be given in parenthesis, when applicable. Thus at the end of semi-starvation 97 per cent of the subjects tired quickly, 94 per cent felt unsteady in walking, and 81 per cent had sensations of being "weak all over." The more psychological symptoms were somewhat less prominent. Nevertheless, they were definitely present. Thus 66 per cent of the subjects found it hard to keep their mind on the job at hand (12 per cent in Control), 62 per cent were frequently bored with people (6 per cent at C), and 62 per cent frequently felt down-hearted (3 per cent at C). For 62 per cent the "guinea pig" life seemed to be a strain much of the time, whereas at the end of three months of the strenuous standardization (control) period not one subject answered the item affirmatively. Fifty per cent preferred to be left alone (6 per cent at C).

Sensations of faintness and light-headedness are commonly associated with "natural" semi-starvation. In the Minnesota study the phenomenon was confirmed. More importantly, information was obtained on some of the factors involved.[29] Some degree of faintness immediately after rising up from bed or

TABLE II-VII

AVERAGE INTENSITY OF SYMPTOMS OF DETERIORATION AFTER SIX
MONTHS OF SEMI-STARVATION. THE ITEMS WERE RATED ON A
SCALE EXTENDING FROM 0 (NORMAL) TO 5 (EXTREME):
N = 32

Symptom	Average Value	Direction of Change
Tiredness	3.5	+
Appetite	3.1	+
Muscle soreness	2.1	+
Sensitivity to noise	1.8	+
Irritability	1.8	+
Apathy	1.8	+
Hunger pain	1.8	+
Ambition	1.8	−
Concentration	1.7	−
Sex drive	1.6	−
Self-discipline	1.5	−
Mental alertness	1.5	−
Moodiness	1.5	+
Depression	1.4	+
Drive to activity	1.3	−
Muscle cramps	1.3	+
Dizziness	1.3	+
Comprehension	1.0	−
Salt craving	0.8	+
Apprehension	0.4	+
Fainting	0.3	+
Nausea	0.3	+

standing up from a chair was experienced almost universally by the semi-starvation subjects. The experience of faintness was transitory and varied in intensity from a slight sensation of dizziness to a dimming of vision and "blacking out," causing the subject to reach for a temporary support. The faintness during these episodes has never progressed to a complete loss of consciousness.

In addition to the type of faintness present upon arising suddenly, a number of the subjects registered complaints of light-headedness, dizziness, and weakness. These symptoms tended to occur near the end of starvation while the men were on their feet doing a variety of chores. One man fainted and remained unconscious for two or three minutes while waiting in line for his supper.

The trend of changes in the Minnesota Multiphasic Personality Inventory is indicated in Figure II-2. The data refer

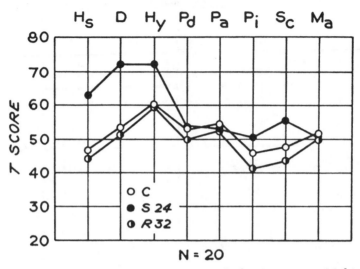

Figure II-2. Mean scores on the scales of the Minnesota Multiphasic Personality Inventory during the control period (C), at the end of twenty-four weeks of semi-starvation (S 24), and after thirty-two weeks of refeeding (= 32). Hs = Hypochondriasis, D = Depression, Hy = Hysteria, Pd = Psychopathic Deviation, Pa = Paranoia, Pt = Psychasthenia, Sc = Schizophrenia, Ma = Hypomania.

to twenty men who were retested thirty-two weeks after the end of semi-starvation. The mean profile obtained at this time was very close to the prestarvation profile.

In the whole group of thirty-two men, the largest increments during semi-starvation took place on the scales of "hypochondriasis" (45.7 to 63.0, $\Delta = 17.3$), "Depression" (54.2 to 73.9, $\Delta = 19.7$), and "Hysteria" (59.0 to 70.0, $\Delta = 11.0$). In regard to the "psychotic" scales there was no change in the mean scores in "Psychopathic Deviation," "Paranoia," and "Hypomania." There was a small rise in "Psychasthenia" (45.7 to 51.9, $\Delta = 6.2$) and "Schizophrenia" (47.5 to 55.1, $\Delta = 7.6$). The absence of changes on the "Psychopathic Deviation" scale indicates the absence of a tendency to develop aggressive antisocial reactions or "character neuroses." Several factors may account for this. For one, two subjects who could not adhere to the diet were eliminated early in the semi-starvation period and two others were shifted to non-subject duties and their data were not used. The monograph[29] contains detailed psychological case studies of these men and of several other subjects who showed unusual behavioral reactions, superimposed on the common (and therefore, in this sense, "normal") responses to semi-starvation. The absence or rare occurrence of symptoms interpretable as "character neuroses" is due, also, to the rigorous selection of the subjects, their motivational structure, the conditions of the experiment, the general atmosphere of seriousness of purpose in which the experiment was carried out, and the knowledge that the stress would end within specified time.

The alterations in behavior, observed clinically documented and psychometrically, were induced by the semi-starvation dietary regimen and were reversed by diet therapy. Consequently, they may be regarded as a form of "experimental neurosis." This applies, also, to the effects of acute vitamin deprivation. These alterations, studied in the context of morphological, biochemical, and physiological changes, clearly demonstrate the potential significance of the biochemical factors (food, in these instances) in behavior.

REFERENCES

1. BROZEK, J.: A new group test of manual skill, *J Gen Psychol*, *31*:125-128, 1944.
2. ————: Quantitative criteria of oculomotor performance and fatigue, *J Appl Physiol*, 2:247-260, 1949.
3. ————: Starvation and nutritional rehabilitation: A quantitative case study, *J Amer Dietet Ass*, 28:917-926, 1952.
4. ————: Semi-starvation and nutritional rehabilitation, *J Amer Clin Nutr*, 1:107-118, 1953.
5. ————: Nutrition and behavior: Psychologic changes in acute starvation with hard physical work, *J Amer Dietet Ass*, 31:703-707, 1955.

6. ——————: Psychologic effects of thiamine restriction and deprivation in normal young men, *Amer J Clin Nutr, 5*:109-120, 1957.

7. ——————: Soviet studies on nutrition and higher nervous activity, *Ann N Y Acad Sci,* Art. 15, 665-714, 1962.

8. ——————: Experimental investigations on nutrition and human behavior: A postscript, *Amer Scientist, 51*:139-163, 1963.

9. BROZEK, J., AND ERICKSON, N. K.: Item analysis of the psychoneurotic scales on the Minnesota Multiphasic Personality Inventory in experimental semi-starvation, *J Consult Psychol, 12*:403-411, 1948.

10. BROZEK, J., GRANDE, F., TAYLOR, H. L., ANDERSON, J. T., BUSKIRK, E. R., AND KEYS A.: Changes in body weight and body dimensions in men performing work on a low-calorie carbohydrate diet, *J Appl Physiol, 10*:412-420, 1957.

11. BROZEK, J., GUETZKOW, H., AND BALDWIN, M. V.: A quantitative study of perception and association in experimental semi-starvation, *J Personality, 19*:245-264, 1951.

12. BROZEK, J., AND SCHIELE, B. C.: Clinical significance of the Minnesota Multiphasic F scale evaluated in experimental neurosis, *Amer J Psychiat, 105*:259-266, 1948.

13. BROZEK, J., SIMONSEN, E., AND KEYS, A.: A work test for quantitative study of visual performance and fatigue, *J Appl Psychol, 31*:519-532, 1947.

14. BROZEK, J., SIMONSEN, E., AND KEYS, A.: A test of speed of leg and arm movements, *J Appl Physiol, 4*:753-760, 1952.

15. BROZEK, J., AND TAYLOR, H. L.: Tests of motor functions in investigations on fitness, *Amer J Psychol, 67*:590-611, 1954.

16. BROZEK, J., AND TAYLOR, H. L.: Psychological effects of maintenance on survival rations, *Amer J Psychol, 71*:517-528, 1958.

17. BROZEK, J., AND VAES, G.: Experimental investigations on the effects of dietary deficiencies on animal and human behavior, *Vitamins Hormones, 19*:43-94, 1961.

18. FRANKLIN, J. C., AND BROZEK, J.: The Rosenzweig P-F Test as a measure of frustration response in semi-starvation, *J Consult Psychol, 13*:293-301, 1949.

19. FRANKLIN, J. C., SCHIELE, B. C., BROZEK, J., AND KEYS, A.: Observations on human behavior in experimental starvation and rehabilitation, *J Clin Psychol, 4*:28-45, 1948.

20. GUETZKOW, H., AND BROZEK, J.: Intellective tests for longitudinal experiments on adults, *Amer J Psychol, 60*:350-366, 1947.

21. GUETZKOW, H., TAYLOR, H. L., BROZEK, J., AND KEYS, A.: Relationship of speed of motor reaction to blood sugar level during acute starvation in man, *Federation Proc, 4*:28, 1945.

22. HANFORD, S. A. (trans.): *Fables of Aesop*, Baltimore: Penguin Books, Inc., 1961

23. HARRIS, S. J., BROZEK, J., AND SMITH, K. U.: The effects of caloric restriction on the travel and manipulation components of human motion, *Int Z Angew Physiol, 17*:34-41, 1958.

24. HATHAWAY, S. R., AND McKINLEY, J. C.: *The Minnesota Multiphasic Personality Inventory* (rev. ed.), Minneapolis, University of Minnesota Press, 1943.

25. HENSCHEL, A., TAYLOR, H. L., AND KEYS, A.: Performance capacity in acute starvation with hard work, *J. Appl Physiol, 6*:624-633, 1954.

26. HUME, E. M., AND KREBS, H. S. (eds.): *Vitamin A Requirements of Human Adults*, London, His Majesty's Stationery Office, 1949.

27. INSTITUTE OF EDUCATIONAL RESEARCH: *The I.E.R. Intelligence Scale CAVD*, New York, Teachers College, Columbia University, 1933.

28. KETY, S. S., POLIS, B. D., NADLER, C. S., AND SCHMIDT, C. F.: Blood flow and oxygen consumption of human brain in diabetic acidosis and coma, *J Clin Invest, 27*:500-510, 1948.

29. KEYS, A., BROZEK, J., HENSCHEL, A., MICKELSEN, O., AND TAYLOR, H. L.: *The Biology of Human Starvation*, Minneapolis, University of Minnesota Press, 1950.

30. KEYS, A., AND HENSCHEL, A.: Vitamin supplementation of U. S. Army rations in relation to fatigue and the ability to do muscular work, *J Nutr, 23*:259-269, 1942.

31. KEYS, A., HENSCHEL, A., MICKELSEN, O., AND BROZEK, J.: The performance of normal young men on controlled thiamine intakes, *J Nutr, 26*:399-415, 1943.

32. KEYS, A., HENSCHEL, A., MICKELSEN, O., BROZEK, J., AND CRAWFORD, J. H.: Physiological and biochemical functions in normal young men on a diet restricted in riboflavin, *J Nutr, 27*:165-178, 1944.

33. KJENAAS, N. K., AND BROZEK, J.: Personality in experimental starvation: a Rorschach study, *Psychosom Med, 14*:115-128, 1952.

34. LANGFELD, H. S.: On the psychophysiology of a prolonged fast, *Psychol Monogr*, (71), 1914.

35. SCHIELE, B. C., AND BROZEK, J.: Experimental neurosis resulting from semi-starvation in man, *Psychosom Med*, *10*:31-50, 1948.

36. SIMONSON, E., BROZEK, J., AND KEYS, A.: Effect of meals on visual performance and fatigue, *J Appl Physiol*, *1*:270-278, 1948.

37. SOROKIN, P. A.: *Man and Society in Calamity*, New York, Dutton & Co., Inc., 1942.

38. SPECTOR, H., BROZEK, J., AND PETERSON, M. S. (eds.): *Performance Capacity: A Symposium*, Washington, D. C., National Academy Science, National Research Council, 1960.

39. SPILLANE, J. D.: *Nutritional Disorders of the Nervous System*, Baltimore, The Williams & Wilkins Company, 1947.

40. TAYLOR, H. L., BUSKIRK, E. R., BROZEK, J., ANDERSON, J. T., AND GRANDE, F.: Performance capacity and effects of caloric restriction with hard physical labor on young men, *J Appl Physiol*, *10*:421-429, 1957.

41. TAYLOR, H. L., HENSCHEL, A., MICKELSEN O., AND KEYS, A.: Some effects of acute starvation with hard work on body weight, body fluids and metabolism, *J Appl Physiol*, *6*:613-623, 1954.

42. TAYLOR, H. L., AND KEYS, A.: Criteria for fitness and comments on negative nitrogen balance, *Ann N Y Acad Sci*, *73*:465-475, 1958.

43. THURSTONE, L. L., AND THURSTONE, T. G.: *Factorial Studies of Intelligence*, Chicago, The University of Chicago Press, 1941.

44. WILDER, R. M.: Experimental induction of psychoneuroses through restriction of intake of thiamine. In: *The Biology of Mental Health and Disease*, New York, P B. Hoeber, Inc., 1952, pp. 531-538.

3: EFFECTS OF SLOW STARVATION

G. B. Leyton

[*Editor's Note:* In the original, material precedes this excerpt.]

GENERAL EFFECTS OF STARVATION

The following observations were made in camps in Libya, Italy, and Germany, but the majority were made and the others confirmed at the prisoner-of-war hospital at Tost, in Germany. This establishment was equipped with beds for 1000 Russians, 250 British, and 250 other nationalities, and also had an outpatient department caring for over 15,000 prisoners. Thus it gave ample clinical material for this investigation.

The reactions to the reduction of diet from that of a front-line soldier to that in table II can be divided into many stages. First, there was the loss of the natural feeling of well-being. A growing feeling of hunger followed and gradually increased in intensity until, after about three weeks, the whole thought of the prisoner-of-war was concentrated on his food. His chief concern was how long it was to the next meal, and by what means he could supplement the meagre rations. This insistent feeling of hunger remained even after years of a low diet. It appeared even to increase with time, with the result that the half-starved man would go to the greatest lengths of ingenuity and dishonesty to obtain small amounts of extra nourishment. Only when death was imminent did the desire for food slowly vanish and the grossly emaciated prisoner become resigned to his fate, of which he seemed to be aware some weeks before it happened.

The next notable abnormality was a progressive mental and physical lethargy. The desire for sleep would increase; the number of hours that an adult male would wish to remain in bed, partly dozing but for the most part in genuine deep sleep, steadily rose from the normal eight hours to sixteen or more out of the twenty-four. Finally the only way to rouse a man from his bed was by the mention of food. Shortly after this came rapid fatigue in mental and physical effort. The experienced card-player, for instance, would forget the cards that had been played. Part of this was certainly lack of power of concentration, but the major portion was a lack of memory for recent events, though the memory for distant ones was still normal. The young athlete trying to keep fit found that he could no longer run; even walking left him exhausted and faint. Loss of consciousness from this cause, however, was never observed. The ability to make and maintain even severe physical exertion, when life depended on it, was still present.

[*Editor's Note:* Material has been omitted at this point.]

FULLY DEVELOPED PICTURE OF STARVATION

Muscular action became progressively slower, and the reaction times (which could not be measured owing to lack of apparatus) increased. Patients in the X-ray room, when told in their own language to place their hands on their head, showed a long lag, as though the order had not been heard or would not be obeyed, but in the end, very slowly and one movement at a time, the arms would be raised and placed in the required position. The rate at which conversation was carried out was equally slow, very often minutes would pass before the answer to a question could be obtained. Frequently the question would be repeated when, after a long pause, the patient said he had heard it the first time. This exceedingly slow cerebration was always present in advanced cases of inanition.

The gait, instead of being smart and military, became a shuffle. The feet seemed to be pushed forward over the ground rather than lifted and placed down again. This was particularly obvious on rough ground, where the patients would stumble over the smallest obstruction. There was a perceptible pause between each step, as if it were too much of an effort for the man to lift his feet and move forward. The whole performance was very similar to a slow-motion picture, except that the feet slid forward instead of being lifted.

At work these men were particularly prone to accidents ; for, though they could see that a fall of rock or of a branch of a tree was imminent, their actions were too slow to enable them to move out of danger.

At this stage all were completely apathetic and more or less resigned to a feeling of constant weakness, though they all said they would soon be fit if they could only get enough to eat. Their only thought was food. Sexual desire was reduced but seldom completely lost, and in a few cases it became all-absorbing, though the man was to all appearances in the last stages of inanition. The longing for books, games, and other recreational pleasures slowly vanished, but the desire for alcohol remained and that for tobacco was greatly increased. Many men would sell even their meagre rations for a small quantity of tobacco. Moral standards were completely in abeyance, for a man would steal his best friend's rations or sell his overcoat for food or tobacco. The whole attitude was strongly reminiscent of hungry animals waiting for food. Standards of cleanliness were far below normal, and any pride in personal appearance was entirely lost.

PHYSICAL EXAMINATION

Little was found on physical examination except extreme emaciation. The tongue was occasionally atrophic but seldom glazed. Sight was good, only the exceptional cases having even mild night-blindness. Hearing was normal or very acute.

[*Editor's Note:* Material has been omitted at this point.]

Nervous System.—All the reflexes were sluggish, but complete absence of knee or ankle jerks was never observed. The eyes reacted normally to light and convergence. Sensation of touch and of temperature was normal.

[*Editor's Note:* Material has been omitted at this point.]

SUBJECTIVE AND TEMPERAMENTAL EFFECTS

The sensation of persistent *hunger* is the body's answer to lack of sufficient nourishment. It is almost always present when too little food is being ingested, but it can generally be said to disappear after the first few days of complete fasting. Although not commented on in the early writings, the longing for food of the chronically undernourished people was clearly present. Whether the desire for food causes the secretion of the digestive juices, or the continued secretion of the juices without adequate food intake propagates the feeling of hunger, must at present remain a matter of speculation ; but it is evident from the test-meals that the secretory power of the stomach is well maintained. It is certain that this persistent hunger, which is of a different intensity from that normally felt before meals, completely alters the character and outlook of the starving man and is perhaps the chief cause of his moral degeneration.

The changes in the *nervous system* were constant and uniform. The loss of memory, the confused and unco-operative state, the slowness of mental reactions, the lack of power of concentration, the rapid fatigue of the mind, the slowed movement. and the sluggish reflexes, can all be explained by a depression of the vital activity of the nerve-cell. Similar effects have been observed in severe anæmia (Wolff 1936) and among people exposed to a reduced oxygen tension at high altitudes. It has been proved that in these conditions the cause is poor oxygenation of the tissues (Leedham 1938). Though some of the effects of starvation on the nervous system can be explained in this way (the slower heart-rate would not improve matters), neither cyanosis nor dyspnœa is present in undernourishment. May it not be that the reduction in the plasma-protein level only indicates that all the body tissues are suffering from part of a general protein-starvation, and that this is the underlying cause of the depression of the nervous system ? This depression cannot be explained by an abnormal blood-calcium level, since this is normal or reduced in starvation and not increased.

The effect of starvation on the *mental outlook* of the patient can roughly be assessed according to his outlook before starvation. His power of self-control and his conduct as a civilised being last just so long as he can maintain the veneer he has developed in society. None of the other hardships suffered by fighting men observed by me brought about such a rapid or complete degeneration of character as chronic starvation, and it seems that the silent areas of the brain which control the character suffer very early from deficient nutrition. Besides this it must be remembered that the instinct of self-preservation is one of the most powerful in animal life, and modern civilised man's existence is seldom threatened by lack of food ; hence it is not surprising that the half-starved man will go to any lengths, even stealing from his friends, to obtain food when his life is endangered by starvation. Once the first barriers are broken down, deterioration proceeds rapidly, especially when he sees others behave like him.

[*Editor's Note:* Material has been omitted at this point.]

CONCLUSIONS

By combining previous reports with my own investigation, it is possible to present a moderately clear picture of the effects of chronic starvation and to correlate the clinical condition with some of the changes in the blood. Thus the main clinical features of starvation are, in order of their appearance, loss of feeling of well-being, rapid physical and mental fatigue, increased desire for sleep, and loss of memory for recent events. The next stage produces clinical signs, of which the most important are bouts of polyuria, decreased pulse-rate, lowered blood-pressure, lowered basal metabolic rate, and reduction in temperature. Œdema as a direct result of lack of food is a late sign. The change in the mental outlook is part of the syndrome and develops concomitantly with the physical changes.

[*Editor's Note:* Material has been omitted at this point.]

The recovery from chronic starvation in the absence of organic disease or vitamin deficiencies is excellent and complete, provided the patient is not moribund before further rations become available.

REFERENCES

Aldred-Brown, G. R. P., Munro, J. M. H. (1935) *Quart. J. Med.* 4, 269.
Bruckman, F. S., D'Esopo, L. M., Peters, J. P. (1930) *J. clin. Invest.* 8, 577.
Budzynski, B., Chelchowski, K. (1916) *J. trop. Med.* 19, 141.
Enright, W. (1920) *Lancet*, i, 314.
Falta, W. (1917a) *Wien. klin. Wschr.* 30, 1637.
— (1917b) *Münch. med. Wschr.* 64, 1539.
Gordon, C. M., Wardley, J. R. (1943) *Biochem. J.* 37, 393.
Hawke, P. B., Bergeim, O. (1938) Practical Physiological Chemistry, London.
Hehir, P. (1922) *Brit. med. J.* i, 865.
Hülse, W. (1917) *Münch. med. Wschr.* 64, 921.
Jansen, W. H. (1917) *Dtsch. Arch. klin. Med.* 74, 1.
Leedham, C. L. (1938) *J. Aviation Med.* 9, 150.
Levy, M. (1906) *Z. klin. Med.* 9, 177.
Liu, S. H., Chu, H. I., Li, R. C., Fan, C. (1931a) *Proc. Soc. exp. Biol., N.Y.* 29, 252.
— — Wang, S. H., Chung, H. L. (1931b) *Ibid*, 29, 250.
Mitchell, H. H. (1924) *Physiol. Rev.* 4, 424.
Moore, N. S., Van Slyke, D. D. (1930) *J. clin. Invest.* 8, 337.
Schittenhelm, A., Schlect, H. (1918) *Berl. klin. Wschr.* 55, 1138.
Weech, A. A. (1936) *Int. Clin.* 2, 223.
Wolff, H. G. (1936) *Physiol. Rev.* 16, 545.
Zuntz, N., Loewy, A. (1918) *Biochem. Z.* 90, 244.

Addendum to Part I

AN EXPERIMENTAL HUMAN STUDY

W. R. Miles participated as a psychologist in a laboratory study on the effects of calorie restriction on initially normal young men (Benedict et al., 1919). Two groups of subjects were used, each consisting of 12 men: Squad A was maintained on a quantitatively reduced diet for 120 days, and Squad B was submitted to dietary restriction for 20 days. Our comments are limited to Squad A, which lost, over a period of 4 months, about 11% of their initial body weight.

The subjects, students at the YMCA College in Springfield, Massachusetts, came periodically to the Carnegie Nutrition Laboratory in Boston where they underwent a series of investigations, including physiological work tests and psychological measurements. The latter involved motor functions (strength, speed, endurance in static work), sensory thresholds (visual acuity, pitch discrimination, electrical shock), and intellective functions. A systematic account of the Boston study is provided in Chapter 3 of the treatise by Keys et al. (1950, pp. 34-62).

The study's fatal weakness was the lack of a prerestriction practice period during which the functions that are altered through repeated testing (practice) would have attained a stable plateau. The moderate decrement in grip strength (about 8 to 9%) and the reduction in the number of chin-ups represent the most dependable measured behavioral effects of moderately reduced intake of energy (calories). Weakness in the legs was a frequent complaint, and some increase in irritability and decrease in sex drive were noted.

It may be appropriate to note the earliest U.S. psychodietetic-study-before-psychodietetics, Langfeld's (1914) investigation of a prolonged fast. The work was done in 1912. Langfeld cites the relevant European literature, especially Luciani's 1889 monograph known to Langfeld in the German translation of 1890. The physiological aspects of the Boston study of a man living for 31 days without food and drinking only distilled water were described, in extenso, by Benedict (1915).

HUNGER IN RUSSIA

P. A. Sorokin's *Golod kak Faktor* (The Effects of Hunger), set in print in 1922 in Petrograd (today's Leningrad), but not published, is a unique contribution to the world literature on massive hunger. One reason for its uniqueness is bibliographic and historical: The work, in the original Russian, exists in only one copy — in fact, a set of page proofs — which the author was able to take along when fleeing for his life to the West. It took more than 50 years before the book became available in English translation (Sorokin, 1975).

Chapter 1 contains some eminently quotable passages:

> Like the work of a machine, which depends on the quality and quantity of fuel, the work (behavior) of a man-machine depends directly or indirectly on the quantity and quality of energy [food] received from without.

> It was said long ago that "the whole history of mankind rotates around hunger (and love)." How this "hunger" (for food, water, and air) affects the behavior of people, what effects it produces in social life, what events are functionally connected with it, and finally which independent variables condition it — all this has received little systematic study. This work attempts to fill this gap to some extent. [pp. 4-5]

The term *hunger* is defined objectively, without reference to human subjective experience, in terms of a "cessation or decrease, or change in content or frequency of delivery of food to the human mouth or inadequate assimilation of food by the organism." This is the independent variable. The question to which the author addresses himself reads, then, as follows: "What changes occur in physiological functions, psychological experiences, and behavior of this organism as a result of . . . variations in the 'independent variable'?" (p. 14).

Chapter 2 is entitled "Changes in the Structure of Physiological and Psychological Processes." It was fascinating to compare Sorokin's observations in Russia (made available to us during a work visit to Harvard University around 1946) with what we had the opportunity to observe in the context of an experimental study described in Paper 2.

Referring to the conditions prevailing in Russia from 1918 to 1921, the years of severely inadequate food supply, at least in some areas and some periods, Sorokin writes:

> The principal topic of conversation at that time were rations, bread, and food in general. Irrespective of where you went and regardless of the initial topic of conversation, the talk turned eventually to the problems of food, ration cards, black markets, the cost of the edibles, and the ways of procuring them. [p. 75]

Reference is made to the deterioration of memory in the adults and the decline of mental capacity of the children:

> During these years [1918-1921] the general productivity of labor decreased everywhere in the USSR, particularly in the centers where famine prevailed. This was true not only for the physical laborers, but also for the semi-intellectual occupations (printers, clerks, accountants, etc.). The attention, speed, energy, etc., once prevailing all disappeared. [p. 84]

Earlier, the decrease in the mental energy and capacity for work among the university professors and intellectual workers in Petrograd was noted.

In the present context, of central importance is Chapter 3, entitled "Changes in Human Behavior." It deals with the changes in the time budget (with much of the time and effort being devoted to the procurement of food), expenditures (with the largest fraction of the expenses going for food), activities intended to assure self-preservation (such as stealing food, dangerous searches for food in the countryside, or severe violations of the allegiancies to one's group and ideals), the weakening of sexual appetite, and alterations in behavior in a variety of areas (religion, law, morality, and customs; esthetic values; professional commitments).

In summary:

> To hunger nothing is sacred. It is blind and it . . . crushes everything, large and small, convictions and norms, when they are opposed to its satisfaction. When satisfied, we preach "the sanctity of property," but when starving we can steal without the smallest hesitation. When satisfied we are convinced of the impossibility that we will kill, rob, rape, deceive, defraud, engage in prostitution, etc. When starving we can perform all these acts. [pp. 148-149]

A chapter titled "How Famine Influences our Behavior," based in a large measure on Sorokin's 1922 monograph, is included in *Man and Society in Calamity* (Sorokin, 1942, pp. 50-82). A tabular presentation of activities induced by starvation and the percentages of the population succumbing to the pressure of starvation is given on page 80.

REFERENCES

Benedict, G. F., 1915, *A Study of Prolonged Fast,* Carnegie Institution of Washington, Washington, D.C., 416p.

Benedict, G. F., W. R. Miles, P. Roth, and M. M. Smith, 1919, *Human Vitality and Efficiency under Prolonged Restricted Diet,* Carnegie Institution of Washington Publication Number 280, Washington, D.C., 701p.

Keys, A., J. Brožek, A. Henschel, O. Mickelsen, and H. L. Taylor, 1950, *The Biology of Human Starvation,* University of Minnesota Press, Minneapolis, 1385p.

Langfeld, H. S., 1914, On the Psychophysiology of Prolonged Fast, *Psychol. Monogr.* **16**(5):1-50 (plus appendixes).

Luciani, L., 1889, *Fisiologia del Digiuno: Studi sull'Uomo (Physiology of Fasting: Human Studies),* Le Monnier, Florence, Italy, 157p. (In Italian.)

Luciani, L., 1890, *Das Hungern: Studien und Experimente am Menschen,* M. O. Frankel, trans., L. Voss, Hamburg and Leipzig, 239p. (In German.)

Sorokin, P. A., 1942, *Man and Society in Calamity: The Effects of War, Revolution, Famine, and Pestilence upon Human Mind, Behavior, Social Organization and Cultural Life,* Dutton, New York, 352p.

Sorokin, P. A., 1975, *Hunger as a Factor in Human Affairs,* E. P. Sorokin, trans., University Presses of Florida, Gainesville, 319p.

Part II

Dietary Deficits of Micronutrients

Papers 4 and 5: Commentary

4 BROŽEK
Psychologic Effects of Thiamine Restriction and Deprivation in Normal Young Men

5 GREENE
Iodine Malnutrition and Behavior in Highland Ecuador

Vitamins, especially vitamins of the B complex (Brožek and Vaes, 1961, pp. 59-70) as a whole and their components (like thiamine [pp. 63-68]) and vitamin A (pp. 70-73), were among the earliest micronutrients, the dietary deficits of which were studied in terms of behavioral impact.

Paper 4 is a link in the chain of studies on the effects of enhanced and restricted intake of vitamins carried out in the early 1940s in the Laboratory of Physiological Hygiene, University of Minnesota. An overview of this work makes up the body of a paper presented at a symposium on stress (Brožek, 1965, pp. 219-235).

The significance of the study lies, in part, in its contribution to our knowledge of the thiamine requirement of normal young men. The special merit of the study (and of the Paper 4) has to do with the comprehensiveness with which the psychological changes associated with acute thiamine deficiency were characterized. The effects of thiamine deficiency were reversed by means of thiamine supplements. The recovery was dramatic both in terms of speed and degree. The effects are described briefly in the summary of the paper.

Iodine is essential for the biosynthesis of thyroid hormones that are required, in turn, for normal physical and mental growth and development during embryonal life and childhood (Matovinovic, 1984, pp. 596-604). Iodine deficiency is the dominant cause of endemic goiter and of the behaviorally more dramatic disorders—for example, cretinism, with its very low level of intellective functioning, and deaf-mutism. In 1938 the editor of this volume encountered a substantially lowered measured intelligence in a group of adults originating from a mountain area of Czechoslovakia in which cretinism and deaf-mutism indicated the presence of endemic iodine deficiency.

Paper 5 is the first communication to come to our attention that stresses and documents the presence of a broad continuum of functional impairment in the areas characterized by endemic iodine deficiency. There is an overlap in the distribution of error scores obtained in the Bender-Gestalt test for the normal group and the group of deaf-mute cretins, even though the average scores show striking differences between the two groups. The study was carried out in the highlands of Ecuador.

REFERENCES

Brožek, J., 1965, Sleep Deprivation, Nutritional Deficit, and Some Soviet Work on Stress, in *Symposium on Medical Aspects of Stress in the Military Climate,* Walter Reed Army Institute of Research, Washington, D.C., pp. 215-242.

Brožek, J., and G. Vaes, 1961, Experimental Investigations on the Effects of Dietary Deficiencies on Animal and Human Behavior, *Vitam. Horm.* **19:**43-94.

Matovinovic, J., 1984, Iodine, in *Nutrition Reviews' Present Knowledge in Nutrition,* 5th ed., The Nutrition Foundation, Washington, D.C., pp. 587-606.

4: PSYCHOLOGIC EFFECTS OF THIAMINE RESTRICTION AND DEPRIVATION IN NORMAL YOUNG MEN

J. Brožek*

With the technical assistance of Harold Guetzkow,† Ph. D.

THE present report is concerned with selected aspects of an interdisciplinary study on the relation of thiamine intake to "fitness." The study represented a logical sequel to the earlier work of this Laboratory,[1-4] including restriction of the vitamins of the B-complex for 161 days followed by 23 days of acute deprivation and 10 days of supplementation with thiamine alone.[5-8] The provision of thiamine was followed by a rapid return of appetite and regression of other symptoms and functional abnormalities. This indicated that thiamine was the crucial component. Consequently, in the present investigation the dietary restriction and terminal deprivation was limited to thiamine alone, other dietary components being provided in adequate amounts.

From the Laboratory of Physiological Hygiene, School of Public Health, University of Minnesota, Minneapolis, Minn.

* Professor, School of Public Health, University of Minnesota, Minneapolis, Minn.

† Present address: Graduate School of Industrial Administration, Carnegie Institute of Technology, Pittsburgh, Pa.

The data were collected under the terms of a contract with the Office of Scientific Research and Development. Important financial assistance was also provided by the Nutrition Foundation, Inc., the U. S. Cane Sugar Refiners' Association, N. Y., the Corn Industries Research Foundation, N. Y., Swift and Co., Chicago, the National Confectioners' Association, Chicago, the National Dairy Council, Chicago, and the Graduate Medical Research Fund, University of Minnesota. Merck and Co., Inc., provided a generous supply of pure vitamins. Most of the food materials were supplied by the Subsistence Branch, Office of the Quartermaster General, U. S. Army. The present report was prepared in the framework of investigations jointly supported, in part, by the Quartermaster General and the Surgeon General of the Department of the Army under Contract No. DA44-109-qm-1526.

Presented at a Symposium on Nutrition and Behavior held at the Laboratory of Physiological Hygiene, University of Minnesota, April 27, 1956, with the cooperation of the National Vitamin Foundation, Inc., New York and under the sponsorship of the School of Public Health, University of Minnesota.

DESIGN OF THE EXPERIMENT

The effects of a prolonged restriction and of a brief but acute deprivation of thiamine were investigated in a group of ten young men, clinically normal at the start of the experiment.

During the *standardization* period, about one month in duration, all men were maintained on an identical adequate diet and training schedule. The subjects became thoroughly familiar with the routine of "guinea-pig" life and a wide variety of test procedures. In those areas, such as motor functions, in which practice affects the test scores concerted effort was made to reach stable plateaus. The data obtained at the end of the standardization period served as "control" values for the evaluation of the effects of partial *restriction* (referred to as R in the text).

In this period a standard diet was served, consisting of ten daily menus served in rotation. The average daily caloric intake was about 3300 cal with carbohydrates, protein and fat contributing 54, 11, and 35 per cent of the total, respectively. The thiamine content of the standard diet was determined at frequent intervals and was found to vary only within narrow limits. Averaging mean values of the ten diets yields 0.612 mg as the daily dietary thiamine intake. As indicated in Table I, men in the "L" (low) group received placebos while the "M" (medium) and "H" (high) groups were given supplements of synthetic thiamine bringing their total daily intakes up to 1.01

TABLE I

Design of the Experiment. Size of Groups and Thiamine Intake During 6 Months of Partial Restriction.

Group	N	Mean thiamine intake, *mg/day*
L ("Low")	4	0.61 (Basal diet plus placebos)
M ("Middle")	4	1.01 (Basal diet plus 0.4 mg supplement)
H ("High")	2	1.81 (Basal diet plus 1.2 mg supplement)

NOTE: During subsequent acute deprivation the thiamine intake of all subjects was near zero. During supplementation 5 mg of thiamine were given per day to each man.

and 1.81 mg, respectively. The National Research Council recommended allowance of thiamine (1945 revision) was 1.5 mg vitamin B_1 for moderately active men (3000 cal) of average weight, or 0.5 mg per 1000 cal. The 1953 revision of the recommended allowance specifies 1.6 mg vitamin B_1 per day for young, moderately active (3200 cal) young men or, again, 0.5 mg/1000 cal.

The dietary supplement for all the subjects throughout the whole experimental period (restriction, deprivation, supplementation) contained: 2 mg riboflavin; 10 mg nicotinamide; 2 mg pyridoxine; 1 capsule containing vitamins A (5000 I.U.), and D (170 I.U.); 50 mg ascorbic acid; 5 mg calcium pantothenate; 1.3 g autoclaved yeast; 1 g choline hydrochloride, and a salt mixture. In partial restriction the subjects walked daily for two half-hour periods on a motor-driven treadmill (3.5 m.p.h., 10% grade). Additional exercise was provided by walking out of doors over a prescribed course, thus bringing the total daily energy expenditure to about 3300 cal.

Partial restriction was followed by a period of *acute deprivation* (D) during which all men were maintained on a diet considered adequate in all respects except for thiamine. The thiamine intake was decreased to the extremely low value of only 0.050 mg per day (0.015 mg per 1,000 cal). The period of deprivation varied from 15 to 27 days, according to individual resistance to this dietary stress. A good deal of effort went into making the thiamine-

free diet of maximum palatability.[9] Four daily menus were prepared and served in rotation.

Before the acute deprivation period the thiamine excretion in the low-thiamine (no-supplement) group was close to zero. In the middle group (0.4 mg vitamin B_1 supplement) the average daily excretion for the 163rd and 164th day of restriction was 25 μg per day, in the high group (1.2 mg supplement) 188 μg per day. On the withdrawal of the supplements and of practically all the dietary thiamine, the thiamine excretion decreased to the average of 8 μg within 24 hours in the middle group and to near-zero in 48 hours. In the high thiamine group the average values of the two men decreased from 43 to 10 μg during the first four days of thiamine deficiency and zero or near-zero for the rest of the experimental period.

The scheduled physical work involved walking for two hours on the treadmill. As was true during the preceding months, there were occasional brief periods of anaerobic work associated with measurements of maximum oxygen intake or the Harvard Fitness Test involving running on the treadmill (8.5 per cent grade, 7 m.p.h.) until exhaustion or a maximum of five minutes.

In the period of *supplementation* (S) the same diet was continued but the men were given oral supplements of 5 mg thiamine per day.

METHODS

The methods used in this study followed the general pattern developed in previous work.[10] Observations will be reported on measurements of sensory functions, motor and intellective performance, and personality. The psychologic observations were carried out along with the study of biochemical and physiologic aspects of fitness. Parenthetically, it may be added that it is our general experience that performance in tests of sensory and intellective functions is surprisingly resistant to deterioration in nutritional stresses.

Items making up the self-ratings questionnaire are:

(1) Ability to concentrate
(2) Headache

(3) Patience with group members
(4) Ability to sleep at night
(5) Sense of humor
(6) General muscular weakness
(7) Mental alertness
(8) Ambition
(9) Apprehension
(10) Fatigability
(11) Interest in the project
(12) Nervousness
(13) Feeling of well-being
(14) Backache
(15) Numbness
(16) Irritability with project work
(17) Loss of appetite
(18) Burning sensations
(19) Forgetfulness
(20) Dizziness
(21) Muscle or joint pains
(22) Nausea
(23) Irritated by staff members

During the period of acute thiamine deprivation the questionnaires were filled out every four days and the ratings were based on the situation present during the preceding four-day period. The items were rated on a scale extending from 0 (normal; symptom absent) to +3 (very much more) and −3 (very much less than usual). In computing the scores as weighted sums of the items, all ratings indicating changes in the direction of deterioration were given a negative sign.

The Minnesota Multiphasic Personality Inventory (MMPI)[11,12] was developed in the framework of psychiatric diagnosis but it has also proven useful in experimental nutritional studies.[13,14] It may be scored with reference to a large number of scales, with transformed scores having a "normal" mean value of 50 and a standard deviation equal to 10. The scales constituting the "psychoneurotic triad"—hypochondriasis, depression and hysteria—have been shown to be particularly sensitive to experimentally induced nutritional deficiencies.

Cattell's Cursive Miniature Situations (CMS) personality test[15] consists of a moving strip, visible through a narrow opening and containing a variety of tasks. The speed of movement was 52.5 sec per strip. Eight strips were combined into a single unit, 176 in. long. The performance was evaluated in terms of a general score and two of the specific scores. The general score represents the number of correct responses (using the "wholistic" scoring, the maximum possible score was 136). The "emotionality" score is obtained as the number of errors (slanting lines crossed; the maximum was 269). The second specific measure, the "timidity" score, represents the ratio of points made in comparable tasks before and after the insertion of a surprise situation; a score above 1.00 indicates that the performance just after the "surprise" was poorer.

Intelligence was measured both by tests which took several hours to complete as well as by a battery of brief tests repeated at intervals of four days throughout the period of acute deprivation.[16] The C.A.V.D. intelligence scale belongs in the first category.[17] It consists of four subtests (Completions, Arithmetic, Vocabulary; Directions). There are 17 forms of the test, graded according to the difficulty of the items. In the present study the upper five levels (M,N,O,P,Q) were used, yielding a maximum possible score of 200.

In the area of sensory functions, determinations of flicker fusion frequency were included as a measure of sensitivity of the retino-cortical system.[18] A beam of light directed onto an opal glass plate was interrupted by a perforated rotating disc (Ref. 10, p. 1094). The rate of flicker was increased at a slow, constant rate until fusion was reported. An ambiguous cube, i.e., a cube design with a reversible perspective, was used in the test of perceptual fluctuation (ibid). Blinks were permitted at the 15th, 30th, and 45th sec during a one-minute period of fixation. Score is the average number of involuntary fluctuations of perspective obtained in three one-minute fixation periods separated by half-minute rest periods.

Auditory acuity was determined with a Maico D-5 audiometer, for the right ear. The average of three ascending threshold determinations was computed and used as a score. The measurements were made with tones of different pitch. Only the values obtained for tones with frequencies of 128, 2048, and 8192 d.v./sec were analyzed in greater detail.

The vibratory sensitivity was determined at two sites (external malleolus and sole of the foot, on the spot immediately posterior to the ball) using the "bone conduction" unit of the audiometer. The frequency of 256 d.v./sec was used consistently except for one subject who was always tested at 128 d.v./sec. The contact point of the vibrator, 0.65 cm in diameter, was applied each time at approximately the same spot with a pressure of 700 ± 100 g. The values, obtained as the average of three determinations, were expressed in terms of the bone-conduction figures of the hearing-loss dial. The pressure-pain threshold was determined by applying pressure to the calf by means of a sphygmomanometer. The scores, in mm of Hg, are averages of three successive determinations.

Capacity for motor performance is an important facet of "fitness." It is generally more sensitive to nutritional stresses than are intellective performance and sensory functions,[19,20] and was examined in considerable detail (Ref. 10, p. 1095 ff.). Except for those psychomotor tests in which specific reference is made to the frequency of determinations carried out during each testing session, the individual scores were obtained as the averages of two successive determinations.

Motor coordination was tested by having the subjects trace a grooved pattern while walking on the treadmill. This represents a complex task involving the coordination of eyes, hands and feet. The path was traced at a constant speed (one path unit per one sec). Performance was evaluated in terms of two scores: (1) the total number of errors, i.e., contact between the stylus and the sides of the path, and (2) the total duration of the contacts.

In the test of manual steadiness the subject was seated and held a stylus (0.5 cm in diameter) in a small opening (1.7 cm in diameter) in a metal plate. The amount of involuntary hand movement was recorded in terms of the number of contacts between the stylus and the metal plate. At each trial three 30-second testing periods separated by one minute of rest were used and the number of contacts was averaged.

In measuring body sway the subject stood erect for two minutes, with feet together and parallel, and with the eyes closed. The score for the ataxiometer represents the amount of anteroposterior movement, in cm.

Eye movements in reading were recorded by means of an ophthalmograph.[21] Equivalent 50-word passages were used in different testing periods. The performance was analyzed in terms of two scores: (1) the number of regressive eye movements per 100 words (regression score) and (2) the number of words read per 1/100 minute (speed score).

In the ball-pipe test of motor speed and coordination the score indicates the number of times a steel ball (marble) was passed through a 1-foot conduit pipe in 60 sec. In the 2-plate tapping test of motor speed the number of taps by a stylus during a 10-sec period was recorded.

In another test measuring the speed of movements, gross body-reaction times to visual stimuli while walking were determined. The response to the three stimuli, appearing in an irregular order and at irregular intervals, involved bending down and depressing the right the left, and both telegraphic keys. The reaction times were recorded in 1/100 sec. A score was obtained as the average of 50 reactions. It should be noted that this test as well as pattern tracing, ball-pipe, and tapping tests were performed while the subject walked on a motor-driven treadmill. The toe-reaction time to a simple auditory stimulus was measured with the subject seated. Again, 50 determinations were made and averaged, with the times recorded in 1/100 sec.

"Static" strength was measured by handgrip and back-lift dynamometers. The score, in kg, at a given testing session was obtained as the average of the two highest of three successive determinations.

Only data obtained prior, during, and following the period of acute thiamine deprivation will be presented here. The subjects were maintained on the thiamine-free diet until general debilitation and personality disturbances approached a critical level.

RESULTS

In general, the appearance of subjective symptoms and objective signs of deficiency

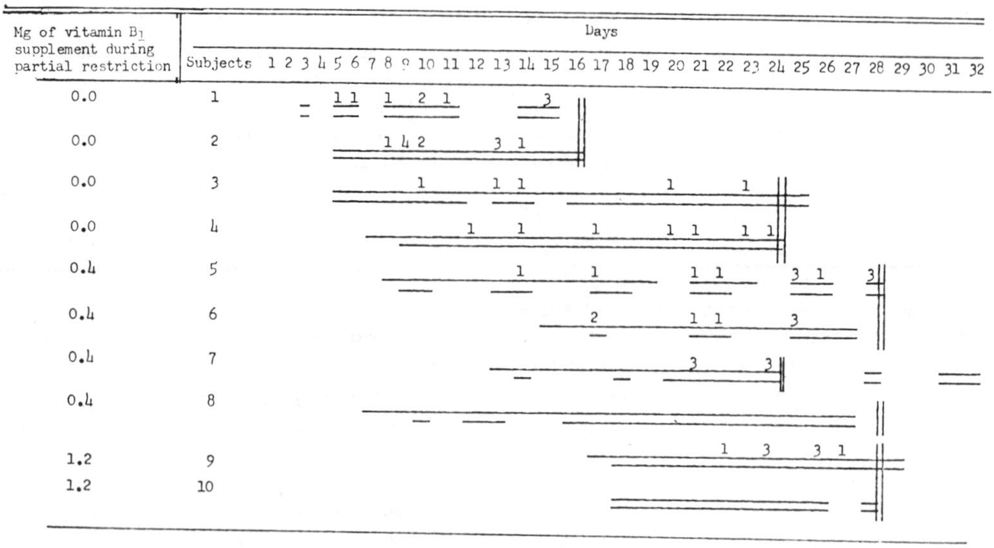

Fig. 1. Nausea and vomiting during acute thiamine deprivation and subsequent supplementation. Single horizontal lines indicate a slight nausea, double horizontal lines indicate a severe nausea (subject's ratings). The numbers above the lines refer to the frequency of vomiting on a particular day. The vertical lines indicate the start of thiamine supplementation (5 mg per day).

reflected the level of thiamine intake during the period of partial restriction. The men maintained previously on the highest intake were "protected" (i.e. did not develop symptoms of deficiency) longer (27 days) in comparison with those who were previously on the lowest thiamine intake (19 days). The men on the intermediary intake were also intermediary in reference to the onset of the symptoms but were closer to the high thiamine group (26 days). The course of the deficiency symptoms was much the same for all men.

The first signs of deficiency were anorexia and nausea. Vomiting first occurred in the previously lowest thiamine group on the 5th day, in the intermediary group on the 14th day, and in the high group on the 22nd day (Figure 1).

Results of neuropsychiatric examinations were summarized by Dr. B. C. Schiele on the basis of records available for nine subjects and are presented in Table II. Weakness, paresthesias, peripheral nerve involvement (including nerve trunk and muscle tenderness) and a change in mood were outstanding characteristics. Muscle weakness in one man (Number 4 in Table II) reached such a degree that he was unable to stand up from a squatting posi-

TABLE II

Neuropsychiatric Findings. Presence of a Symptom is Indicated by Letter X.

Subject Group Day of deprivation	1 L 10	2 L 13	3 L 22	4 L 22	5 M 23	6 M 26	7 M 26	8 M 25	9 H 25
Generalized weakness	X	X		X		X	X	X	X
Paresthesias		X	X	X	X		X		
Peripheral nerve involvement	X	X	X	XX	?			?	
Headache			X		X				
Feeling of being cold			X	X					
Marked irritability and depression	X	X	X	X	X				

TABLE III

Symptoms of "Neurasthenia" (Self-Ratings).   The Score for Each Individual was Obtained as the Weighted Sum of 23 Items.   Minus Sign Indicates Deterioration, Plus Sign Indicates Improvement.   F = F.   Tests of Statistical Significance of the Mean Changes During Deprivation (F_D) and Supplementation (F_S).

Group	R	D	S	Δ_D	F_D	Δ_S	F_S
L	−12	−28	+2	−16		+30	
M	− 8	−27	−8	−19		+19	
H	− 4	−10	−4	− 6		+ 6	
TOTAL	− 9	−24	−3	−15	10.8**	+21	17.6**

R   = mean scores obtained at the end of *partial restriction*
D   = mean scores at the end of maintenance on the thiamine-free diet (*deprivation*)
S   = mean scores at the end of *supplementation*
Δ = mean change during deprivation (Δ_D) and supplementation (Δ_S)
F   = test of statistical significance of the mean change during deprivation (F_D) and supplementation (F_S)
*   = significance at the 5% level (reference value $F_{0.05} = 5.12$)
** = significance at the 1% level (reference value $F_{0.01} = 10.56$)

tion without help.   This, plus other symptoms, including peripheral nerve involvement, indicated that we were dealing with an experimentally induced beri-beri.   One man (Number 5), who showed a marked deterioration on some psychomotor tests involving timed responses, was characterized as "shaky and dizzy."

Self-ratings, referring to symptoms of "neurasthenia," showed a marked deterioration (Table III).   Statistical tests indicate a highly significant negative change during thiamine deprivation and a remarkable recovery at the end of supplementation with this vitamin. This refers to the changes in the group as a whole (N = 10).   However, the subscores of the men maintained on different supplement levels during the preceding period of partial restriction are of some interest, with the "low" group showing a larger change than the "high" group.   The differences are even more striking when the recovery scores are considered as the reference point.   Yet the uncertainties inherent in quantitative ratings of subjective symptoms cannot be disregarded, making interindividual comparisons difficult.

TABLE IV

Mean Scores on Selected Scales of the Minnesota Multiphasic Personality Inventory.   Increment = "Deterioration," Decrement = "Improvement."   See Table III for explanation of symbols.

Group	R	D	S	Δ_D	F_D	Δ_S	F_S
			Scale: "Hypochondriasis"				
L	52	84	50	32		−34	
M	48	75	49	27		−26	
H	48	62	43	14		−19	
TOTAL	50	76	48	26	38.9**	−28	38.7**
			Scale: "Depression"				
L	73	93	54	20		−39	
M	57	73	62	16		−11	
H	70	75	62	5		−13	
TOTAL	66	82	59	16	6.9*	−23	14.9**
			Scale: "Hysteria"				
L	68	85	63	17		−22	
M	64	79	65	15		−14	
H	62	66	56	4		−10	
TOTAL	65	79	62	14	13.7**	−17	26.5**

NOTE: On all these scales "normal" mean = 50, 1 standard deviation = 10.

The Minnesota Multiphasic Personality Inventory requires the respondent to answer in terms of "yes," "no," or "cannot say." The scores are based on a larger pool of items and their diagnostic significance was validated objectively. In acute thiamine deprivation there were large increments on the scales of the "psychoneurotic triad"—Hypochondriasis, Depression, and Hysteria (Table IV). The significance of the mean changes was examined in reference to the group as a whole (N = 10), with the result that both the increments (deterioration) in acute thiamine deficiency and the decrements (improvement) in the period of supplementation exceeded the 1 per cent level of statistical significance. The startling magnitude of some of these changes will be appreciated more keenly if the values of the "normal" mean (=50) and the standard deviation (=10) are kept in mind. There is a definite tendency for the men who had received no supplements in the period of partial restriction to show a greater degree of deterioration than the groups receiving supplements of 0.4 and 1.2 mg. of thiamine per day, respectively. The differences between the two supplemented groups suggest some advantage for the higher supplement but the differences are for the most part small and not completely consistent.

In contrast to the marked changes obtained on the MMPI, the performance in Cattell's Cursive Miniature Situations test (Table V) was essentially not altered. The general score showed a negligible decrement during thiamine deprivation, with the increment (recovery) during supplementation barely reaching the 5 per cent level of significance (the reference value $F_{0.05} = 5.12$). The "emotionality" score showed a small average increment at the end of deprivation, with a further increment at the end of supplementation. However, individual responses varied a good deal and the mean change in neither period was significant. Similarly, no significant increment was observed in "timidity."

Measured intellective functions remained surprisingly stable and free from deterioration, whether we used long tests (Thorndike's C.A.V.D.) or brief tests administered at four-day intervals, such as the battery measuring six "factors" (spatial perception, verbal fluency, perceptual speed, rote memory, number facility and inductive reasoning.) The only change reaching the 5 per cent level significance during supplementation was the improvement in the test of spatial perception which may be interpreted as reflecting a continuing practice trend.

There was a small decrement in flicker fusion frequency (Table VI) during deprivation followed by a larger and statistically highly significant increment during the recovery period. A slowing down was observed in the rate of perceptual fluctuations in the ambig-

TABLE V

Performance in Cattell's Cursive Miniature Situations Test of Character-Temperament for the Total Group (N = 10). For units see text (Methods). See Table III for explanation of symbols.

	R	D	S	Δ_D	F_D	Δ_S	F_S
General score	91	89	95	−2	0.38	+6	5.18*
"Emotionality"	23	27	30	+4	0.88	+3	0.82
"Timidity"	1.06	1.13	1.12	+0.07	0.38	−0.01	0.04

TABLE VI

Sensory Functions (N = 10)

	R	D	S	Δ_D	F_D	Δ_S	F_S
Flicker fusion frequency	43.6	43.0	44.4	−0.6	1.59	+1.4	9.45*
Perceptual fluctuation	23	19	23	−4	13.82**	+4	3.13
Vibratory sensitivity, malleolus	25	24	25	−1	0.39	+1	0.17
Vibratory sensitivity, sole	25	26	23	+1	1.17	−3	10.56**
Pressure pain threshold	180	153	168	−27	8.52*	+15	9.94*

TABLE VII

Motor Functions (N = 10)

	R	D	S	Δ_D	F_D	Δ_S	F_S
Eye-hand coordination, number of errors	39	44	31	+5	1.28	-13	21.12**
Eye-hand coordination, length of contacts	271	359	254	+88	4.70	-105	8.36*
Manual steadiness	15	20	13	+5	2.62	-7	8.59*
Body sway	21.0	25.4	19.3	+4.4	1.16	-6.1	1.65
Eye movements, regressions	16	14	13	-2	0.83	-1	0.25
Eye movements, speed score	3.1	3.3	3.6	+0.2	0.16	+0.3	1.97

TABLE VIII

Motor Functions (N = 10)

	R	D	S	Δ_D	F_D	Δ_S	F_S
Manual speed and coordination	75.6	68.6	77.0	-7.0	6.56*	+8.4	13.91**
Motor speed (tapping)	66.2	63.0	71.3	-3.2	4.30	+8.3	11.69**
Body reaction time †	46.3	51.1	48.2	+4.8	12.82**	-2.9	11.91**
Toe reaction time	28.1	31.3	28.7	+3.2	10.10*	-2.6	11.68**
Grip strength	58	56	55	-2	5.18*	-1	0.14
Lift strength	158	157	153	-1	0.15	-4	0.96

† N = 9 (omitting subject No. 5 with atypically long reaction times).   Reference value of $F_{0.01}$ = 11.26.

uous-cube test, with a reversal of trend on supplementation. The mean size of the change was the same but the decrements during deprivation were more consistent.

Auditory acuity, at any of the three frequency levels of the stimulus that were examined in greater detail, and the vibratory sensitivity measured at the malleolus, were not affected. The vibration threshold determined at the sole of the foot showed negligible increment during deprivation. The change in recovery was somewhat larger and fairly consistent. It is not clear whether this should be considered as an indication of a real change, be it a small one, or a chance effect of random fluctuation. There is no doubt that the pressure-pain threshold decreased in thiamine deprivation. At the end of supplementation the recovery was not complete but it was statistically highly significant.

The means and F tests of significance of the changes in motor functions for the 10 men are given in Tables VII and VIII. The changes in eye-hand coordination during movement (pattern tracing) and in manual steadiness are in the direction of deterioration and there is a significant improvement on thiamine supple-

mentation. Body sway increases during deprivation and is reduced during recovery but individual responses were highly variable. In one man, who may have suffered a spell of dizziness, a grossly atypical score (159 displacement units) was obtained. This value was not considered in calculating the group means in Table VII. With his score included the means for the three periods are 25.1, 38.8, and 21.6 units respectively. The F tests remain insignificant (F_D=1.88, F_S=2.10) because of the large interindividual variability.

Analysis of ophthalmographic records yielded no consistent changes, when either the number of regressive movements or the speed of reading was considered. The apparent trend toward a greater speed of reading, associated with a decrease in the number of regressions, is independent of the changing nutritional status.

There was a definite deterioration in the measurements involving speed of motion (Table VIII) whether one considers repetitive movements of the upper arm and hand (test of manual speed and coordination) or the tests of reaction time. In two-plate tapping the change in deprivation is also in the direction of deterioration but only the recovery during supplementation is significant statistically.

In agreement with previous experience, but contrary to possible *a priori* expectations, there was minimal or no change in simple strength as measured by the hand-grip and the back-lift dynamometer. The decrement in grip strength during thiamine deprivation is negligible in terms of biologic importance and barely reaches the 5 per cent level of statistical significance.

The subgroups consisting of four men who received placebos during the period of partial restriction and six men who prior to acute thiamine deprivation had been given supplements (at the levels of 0.4 and 1.2 mg of thiamine per day) are too small for a detailed statistical analysis. Nevertheless, it may be noted that the changes in psychomotor functions tended to be larger in the "placebo" group. During thiamine deprivation in this group the increase in number and total duration of error contacts on the test of eye-hand coordination, decrements in the speed of tapping, and lengthening of the toe reaction time exceeded the 5 per cent level of the F test. In the "previously supplemented" the changes were for the most part in the same direction but did not approach statistical significance.

SUMMARY AND CONCLUSIONS

This study forms a link in a series of investigations of the impact of dietary variations on man's "fitness." The independent variables that were examined included vitamins, especially vitamins of the B-complex, calories[22] and—more recently—water.

The present study is concerned with the impact of a thiamine-free diet. It consisted of four periods: (1) a month devoted to standardization and collection of control measurements; (2) 168 days of partial restriction of thiamine, with respective daily intakes of 0.61 (N=4), 1.01 (N=4) or 1.81 mg (N=2), and energy expenditure of about 3300 cal; (3) a period of acute thiamine deprivation, lasting 15 to 27 days during which all men received a thiamine-free diet and no thiamine supplements; and (4) a period of thiamine supplementation (5 mg per day for 9 to 21 days).

With other vitamins of the B-complex available in adequate amounts, the intake of 0.2 mg of thiamine per 1000 cal in our subjects, healthy young men, was at the borderline of deficiency.

In acute deprivation definite signs of deficiency developed in a matter of days or weeks. When the previously "thiamine-restricted," unsupplemented subjects were subsequently placed on a practically zero intake of thiamine, they exhibited a poor resistance to thiamine deficiency. This is an additional argument for considering the intake of about 0.2 mg of thiamine per 1000 cal as bordering on the inadequacy level.

Oral administration of thiamine was started for each man when it appeared that the deficiency had progressed as far as we considered safe. At this time general weakness and incoordination of the legs was very pronounced, anorexia was extreme, and hyperpyruvinemia was present. Thiamine supplements restored appetite and brought about a dramatic change in the attitudes of the subjects. The signs of peripheral neuropathy were more refractory. In one man definite residues, in the form of a peculiar gait, remained for several months.

Large changes in the direction of deterioration were observed during thiamine deprivation on the "psychoneurotic" scales of the Minnesota Multiphasic Personality Inventory; later these changes were reversed through thiamine supplements.

Within the limits of the experimental conditions, performance on tests of intelligence was not affected adversely by thiamine deprivation. There was a marginal decrement in flicker fusion frequency and the rate of perceptual fluctuations. In the sensory area the most consistent change, with statistically significant decrement in deprivation and return toward "normal" on supplementation, was observed in the pressure-pain threshold.

Manual speed and coordination, complex body reaction time and toe-reaction time exhibited a similar pattern of statistically significant changes. Motor speed (tapping), eye-hand co-ordination, manual steadiness, and body sway also exhibited deterioration in thiamine deprivation and recovery upon supplementation but only one or the other change was statistically significant.

The nutritional status during the period of partial restriction was reflected in the tendency toward larger changes, in the direction of deterioration, among men receiving only the basal diet plus placebos prior to acute thiamine deprivation in comparison with the subjects who were given supplements (0.4 mg and 1.2 mg of thiamine, respectively). This differentiation was especially noticeable in the selected scales of the Minnesota Multiphasic Personality Inventory ("Hypochondriasis," "Depression," and "Hysteria"), and in several aspects of motor performance.

The significance of the present report is in its contribution to our information on the thiamine requirements of normal young men, and, in particular, in a comprehensive characterization of the psychologic changes associated with acute thiamine deficiency, reversed by means of nutritional supplementation. The effects of supplementation were dramatic both in the speed and degree of recovery.

REFERENCES

1. KEYS, A., and HENSCHEL, A.: Vitamin supplementation of U. S. Army rations in relation to fatigue and the ability to do muscular work. *J. Nutrition* 23: 259, 1942.

2. KEYS, A., HENSCHEL, A., MICKELSEN, O., and BROŽEK, J.: The performance of normal young men on controlled thiamine intakes. *J. Nutrition* 26: 399, 1943.

2a. KEYS, A., HENSCHEL, A., MICKELSEN, O., BROŽEK, J., AND CRAWFORD, H. H.: Physiological and biochemical functions in normal young men on a diet restricted in riboflavin. *J. Nutrition* 27: 165, 1944.

3. KEYS, A., HENSCHEL, A., TAYLOR, H. L., MICKELSEN, O., and BROŽEK, J.: Absence of rapid deterioration in men doing hard physical work on a restricted intake of vitamins of the B complex. *J. Nutrition* 27: 485, 1944.

4. HENSCHEL, A., TAYLOR, H. L., BROŽEK, J., MICKELSEN, O., and KEYS, A.: Vitamin C and ability to work in hot environments. *Am. J. Trop. Med.* 27: 259, 1944.

5. KEYS, A., HENSCHEL, A., TAYLOR, H. L., MICKELSEN, O., AND BROŽEK, J.: Experimental studies on men with restricted intake of the B vitamins. *Am. J. Physiol.* 144: 5, 1945.

6. BROŽEK, J., GUETZKOW, H., AND KEYS, A.: A study of personality of normal young men maintained on restricted intakes of vitamins of the B complex. *Psychosom. Med.* 8: 98, 1946.

7. GUETZKOW, H., AND BROŽEK, J.: Intellectual functions with restricted intakes of B-complex vitamins. *Am. J. Psychol.* 59: 358, 1946.

8. BROŽEK, J., GUETZKOW, H., MICKELSEN, O., AND KEYS, A.: Motor performance of normal young men maintained on restricted intakes of vitamin B complex. *J. Appl. Psychol.* 30: 359, 1946.

9. ANDERSON, MARIETTA, MICKELSEN, O., AND KEYS, A.: Diets and food items for the experimental production of thiamine deficiency in man. *J. Am. Diet. Assoc.* 22: 1, 1946.

10. KEYS, A., BROŽEK, J., HENSCHEL, A., MICKELSEN, O., AND TAYLOR, H. L.: *The Biology of Human Starvation*. University of Minnesota Press, Minneapolis, 1950.

11. HATHAWAY, S. R., AND MCKINLEY, J. C.: A multiphasic personality schedule (Minnesota). I. Construction of the schedule. *J. Psychol.* 10: 249, 1940.

12. WELCH, G. S., AND DAHLSTROM, W. G., *Basic Readings on the MMPI in Psychology and Medicine*. University of Minnesota Press, Minneapolis, 1956.

13. SCHIELE, B. C., AND BROŽEK, J.: "Experimental neurosis" resulting from semi-starvation in man. *Psychosom. Med.* 10: 31, 1948.

14. BROŽEK, J., AND ERICKSON, NANCY K.: Item analysis of the psychoneurotic scales on the MMPI in experimental starvation. *J. of Consulting Psychol.* 12: 403, 1948.

15. CATTELL, R. B.: An objective test of character—temperament. *J. Gen. Psychol.* 25: 59, 1941.

16. GUETZKOW, H., AND BROŽEK, J.: Intellective tests for longitudinal experiments on adults. *Am. J. Psychol.* 60: 350, 1947.

17. THORNDIKE, E. L., WOODGARD, ELLA, AND LORGE, I.: Four new forms of the I.E.R. Intelligence Scale for use on the college or higher levels. *School and Society* 42: 271, 1935.

18. SIMONSON, E., AND BROŽEK, J.: Flicker fusion frequency: Background and applications. *Physiol. Rev.* 32: 349, 1952.

19. BROŽEK, J., AND TAYLOR, H. L.: Tests of motor functions in investigations on fitness. *Am. J. of Psychol.* 67: 590, 1954.

20. BROŽEK, J.: Physical performance. In *Methods for Evaluation of Nutritional Adequacy and Status*. H. Spector, M. S. Peterson and T. E. Friedman, eds. National Research Council, Washington, D. C., 1954, pp. 204–211.

21. Bureau of Visual Science. *The Ophthalm-o-graph. The Metron-o-scope: Manual for Controlled Reading.* American Optical Co., Southbridge, Mass., 1937.

22. BROŽEK, J., AND TAYLOR, H. L.: Psychological effects of maintenance on survival rations (carbohydrate diet, 1010 calories per day, water *ad libitum*). *Am. J. Psychol.* 1957 (in press).

ADDENDUM: SOME BIOCHEMICAL DATA*

It may be useful to present some additional biochemical information concerning the diet and the metabolic state of the subjects. Data on the thiamine content of the individual diets and their variability, as determined by chemical analysis,[1] indicate that the mean of the 10 diet means is 0.612 mg, with average $\sigma_{within\ diets}$ = 0.105 mg and $\sigma_{between\ diets}$ = 0.070 mg All subjects were maintained during the first six months on this dietary regimen and received capsules containing 0, 0.4, or 1.2 mg of thiamine per day, respectively.

The average urinary excretions of thiamine and pyramin, the pyrimidine end-product of thiamine metabolism normally present in human urine,[2] are indicated in Table I. While

In trying to assess the metabolic state of the three groups of men at any particular time, a critical question arises as to how close they have come into equilibrium with their respective levels of thiamine intake. It is known that: (a) body reserves of thiamine are not large, and (b) severe deficiency signs occur within a few days when men are placed on a zero intake of this vitamin. These facts have been taken as evidence of a rapid metabolic adjustment to alterations in the intake. When thiamine intake is changed in the intake range between 1.0 and 2.0 mg per day, the thiamine and pyramin excretion levels adjust in such a way that in each successive ten-day period the mean excretion level changes by half of the remaining distance toward the new equilibrium

TABLE I

Thiamine and Pyramin Excretion, mcg/24 hrs, in the Three Groups Maintained on Different Levels of Thiamine Intake*

Group	No. of subjects	Thiamine intake, mg	Thiamine excretion mean σ within days		Pyramin excretion mean σ within days	
Low (L)	4	0.61	4.6	6.3	125.5	21.0
Medium (M)	4	1.01	26.2	15.9	171.5	22.9
High (H)	2	1.81	195.4	35.8	267.4	27.7

* The excretion levels refer to values obtained after a stabilization in excretion was reached following the change from a thiamine intake common to all subjects during the control period.

thiamine excretion may be considered as an amount of vitamin wasted by the body, pyramin excretion presumably is more directly related to the metabolic utilization of this vitamin in the body. At daily thiamine intakes above 0.7 mg. per day, the thiamine excretion is linearly related to intake. Below 0.7 mg per day, the values are very close to zero. The small amounts reported in the urine may be due, in part to extraneous fluorescent materials in the urine. Thus, thiamine excretion data are of little value at these low intake levels. Pyramin excretion data, on the other hand, are of special importance under conditions of low thiamine intake. They approach a nearly constant excretion level at thiamine intakes above 2 mg per day.

*This material was obtained in cooperation with Dr. Olaf Mickelsen and Mr. Howard Condiff in the Laboratory of Physiological Hygiene, University of Minnesota by W. O. Caster.

level.[2] From this, one would expect approximately 90 per cent equilibration to be attained within a month on the new intake. One to two months should provide substantially complete equilibration. In the present experiment, it may be recalled the subjects were maintained on constant levels of 0.6, 1.0 and 1.8 mg/day for some six months before being placed on a zero-thiamine diet.

The problem of adaptation to this new level is of special interest in reference to the rate at which deficiency symptoms developed in the three groups (L, M, and H) when all men were placed on a zero intake of thiamine. Did increased levels of thiamine intake during the preceding six-month period provide a substantial degree of protection against the effects of the acute deficiency stress? The answer, in general, seems to be that there were no appreciable differences between the responses of the M (1.0 mg/day) and H(1.8 -mg/day) groups.

The L(0.6 mg/day) group, on the other hand, deteriorated much more rapidly than either of these higher intake groups. This can be seen, for example, in the blood pyruvate data (Table II). There were no significant differences be-

TABLE II

Average Plasma Pyruvate Levels, in mg per 100 ml Measured One Hour After Oral Administration of 100 g of Glucose

Group	Partial restriction		Acute deficiency	
	Thiamine intake, mg/day	Pyruvate in 6th mo	Thiamine intake, mg/day	Pyruvate on 10th day
L	0.61	1.3	0.05	2.0
M	1.01	0.9	0.05	1.5
H	1.81	0.9	0.05	1.3

tween the 1.0 and 1.8 mg/day groups either in the six-month restriction period or in acute deficiency. The blood pyruvate level of the 0.6 mg group, on the other hand, was somewhat elevated even during the restriction period, and it rose sharply in acute deficiency. On the tenth day of thiamine deprivation, pyruvate levels of the M and H groups were not far from those characteristic of the L(0.6 mg/day) group prior to the acute deficiency stress.

There is a good correspondence between the picture emerging from these data and the changes in motor functions, personality, and general condition of the subjects.

All of these data seem to lead to two conclusions: (1) The intake of 0.6 mg of thiamine per day seems to be a suboptimal level for this group of men as shown by (a) their rapid deterioration when placed on a zero thiamine intake, (b) their elevated blood pyruvate levels, and (c) their substantially zero thiamine excretion levels. (2) Raising the level of thiamine intake above 1.0 mg/day provided, at best, only a few days of added protection.

REFERENCES

1. MICKELSEN, O., CONDIFF, H., and KEYS, A.: The determination of thiamine in urine by means of the thiochrome technique. *J. Biol. Chem.* 160: 361, 1945.
2. MICKELSEN, O., CASTER, W. O., and KEYS, A.: A statistical evaluation of the thiamine and pyramin excretions of normal young men on controlled intakes of thiamine. *J. Biol. Chem.* 108: 415, 1947.

5: IODINE MALNUTRITION AND BEHAVIOR IN HIGHLAND ECUADOR

L. S. Greene

Nutrition is an important component of the environment of human communities. Although the proceedings of this meeting are primarily concerned with the behavioral effects of energy and protein deficits, it is instructive to consider the influence of other types of malnutrition on behavior. This is particularly true since specific nutritional deficiencies are often accompanied and complicated by varying degrees of energy-protein malnutrition. Such is the case with iodine deficiency which we studied in highland Eduador.

OBJECTIVES AND BACKGROUND

Our studies, motivated by a desire to examine the effects of nutritional factors on inter- and intra-population variability in the morphological, neurological and behavioral characteristics of human populations, were focused on three specific goals. First, we wished to test the hypothesis that there is a broad continuum of neurological and behavioral deficits in populations living under conditions in which malnutrition is endemic (28,30, 31), i.e., that the effects are not limited to a small number of severely affected individuals. The second goal was to determine which social, biological and nutritional factors were the major determinants of physical growth and neurological maturation among children in these communities (30,33). The third goal was to describe the effects produced by the presence of a large number of behaviorally limited individuals on the socio-cultural characteristics of the community under study, and to develop an heuristic model which would show the interrelationships between environmental, biological, and socio-cultural systems (28,30,31,32).

The study of the developmental effects of iodine malnutrition offers certain methodological advantages over one in which energy-protein deficits predominate. Iodine deficiency is easily quantifiable and affects almost all individuals in areas where goiter and cretinism are hyperendemic. This dietary deficiency is primarily a consequence of geochemical characteristics of the environment that show little variation over long periods of time; thus, in retrospective studies, behavioral deficits observed in adults can reasonably be imputed to iodine malnutrition experienced early in life. Another advantage in working with populations in which goiter and cretinism are endemic is that there is an easily definable group of individuals who are severely deficient neurologically (deaf mute cretins).

To evaluate the effects of this nutritional stress, we chose to work in the parroquias of Tocachi and La Esperanza in the Andean region of Ecuador. In this area the iodine intake is extremely

Reprinted from pages 278-295 of *Behavioral Effects of Energy and Protein Deficits*, J. Brožek, ed., NIH Publication Number 79-1906, U.S. Government Printing Office, Washington, D.C., 1979, 370p.

low, due to geochemical factors; naturally-occurring goitrogens
of plant origin appear to be interfering with the utilization of
the small amounts of iodine being ingested; energy-protein malnutrition is common; and the prevalence of goiter and cretinism
is extremely high.

The data for this report were collected by the author
between 1970 and 1972, in the context of a larger public health
program directed by Rodrigo Fierro-Benítez (Escuela Politécnica
Nacional, in Quito) and John B. Stanbury (Department of Nutrition
and Food Science at the Massachusetts Institute of Technology).
The program concerned the effect of depot iodine supplementation on physical growth and neuro-motor development (21,22,
23, 24).

IODINE AND THE THYROID GLAND

External Iodine Cycle

Most of the earth's iodine is concentrated in ocean waters,
from where it evaporates as gaseous iodine or hydrogen iodide,
is carried inland in the gaseous state or affixed to dust parti-
cles, and enters terrestrial soils via rain or snow. Soils differ in their iodine content as a function of a number of factors:
less air-borne iodine reaches areas more distant from the ocean;
soils subject to late Pleistocene glaciations are usually iodine
deficient for tens of thousands of years; and soils that are
highly eroded are also usually iodine poor (27). Populations
living at a distance from the sea have limited access to sea products (both plant and animal) which have high iodine content.
Dietary factors may also interfere with iodine utilization. The
ingestion of certain plants containing naturally-occurring antithyroid compounds (goitrogens) and some organic water pollutants
may interfere with the uptake and binding of iodine within the
thyroid gland.

As a consequence of the factors listed above, iodine deficiency tends to be most severe in mountainous areas of the world
where the soils have been highly eroded and have been subjected
to the effect of late Pleistocene alpine glaciations. The Pyre-
nees, Swiss and Italian Alps, Himalayas, highland New Guinea, and
the Andean region of South America are all areas where severe
iodine malnutrition and its sequelae -- hypothyroidism, goiter,
and cretinism -- have been common. In many of these regions energy-protein malnutrition also has been, or still is, widespread.

Thyroid Hormones

Iodine is of nutritional significance in that it is necessary
for the production of thyroid hormones: thyroxine (T_4) containing
four atoms of iodine; and 3, 5, 3' - triiodothyronine (T_3), containing three. These hormones are necessary for normal physical

growth, nervous system development, temperature regulation, nerve conduction, and a variety of other important processes (11,34). Reverse T_3 (rT_3, 3, 3', 5' - triiodothyronine) is also normally produced in small amounts by the thyroid gland, but is metabolically inactive.

The blood level of thyroid hormones is dependent on the dietary intake of iodine and the trapping and synthesizing capacity of the thyroid gland. "Free" thyroid hormone affects secretion by the hypothalamus of the thyrotropic hormone-releasing factor (TRF) and release of the thyroid-stimulating hormone (TSH) from the adenohypophysis. Insufficient dietary iodine lowers the blood level of thyroid hormones, thereby stimulating an increased secretion of TSH by the adenohypophysis. The increased secretion of TSH produces a cellular hypertrophy of the thyroid gland with a concomitant increase in the secretion and release of thyroid hormones (11,17). An enlarged thyroid gland is referred to as a "goiter" if the enlargement exceeds two to five times its normal size of 25 gm. The enlarged thyroid gland (goiter) is more efficient in trapping the small amount of available iodine and in synthesizing thyroid hormone, and is thus a positive adaptation. Goiter is considered endemic if more than 10% of the population manifest thyroid enlargement (12). The prevalence of goiter in the communities under study was 69.7% in Tocachi and 52.8% in La Esperanza.

Nutritional factors also have an effect on the metabolism of thyroid hormones. In energy-protein malnutrition and under conditions of systemic illness there is a decrease in serum T_3 and an increase in serum levels of rT_3 (44). This is a consequence of a shift in the peripheral monodeiodination of T_4 away from metabolically active T_3 and toward the metabolically inactive rT_3 form (8,38). This shift appears to be an important biological adaptation to a limited protein and energy supply; however, it suggests that alterations in thyroid function may be a significant factor in the etiology of the developmental abnormalities associated with severe energy-protein malnutrition. Conversely, energy-protein malnutrition may hamper the thyroidal response to low iodine availability. This is so because the increased blood level of metabolically inactive rT_3 does not lead to an increase in TSH secretion by the adenohypophysis (38). Thus, the thyroid gland does not enlarge under conditions of nutritional or disease stress even though the blood level of metabolically active hormone is decreased. We would therefore expect to see an extremely high prevalence of developmental abnormalities in populations living under the dual stress of iodine and energy-protein malnutrition, a situation which is the case in the communities we studied in highland Ecuador.

In addition to low iodine availability, a large number of food crops, especially those of the _Brassica_ genus (cabbage, kale, brussel sprouts, rutabaga, turnip), contain small amounts of antithyroid compounds (goitrogens) which interfere with thyroid function. One group of these goitrogens are monovalent anions (such as thiocyanate) which compete with iodide for uptake into the thyroid gland. A second group are the thiocarbamides which interfere with the binding of iodine to thyroglobulin within the thyroid gland (45).

Consequences of Insufficient Thyroid Function (Hypothyroidism)
    Hypothyroidism induced in experimental animals during the neonatal period leads to marked deficits in linear growth (18,20, 40) and neurological development. Brain size and dendritic interconnectivity are decreased (20,39). amino acid incorporation into the immature brain is hampered (26,42). brain neurochemistry is altered (4,5), and there is a significant deficit in adult brain cell numbers as measured by total brain DNA (2,3).

    The effect of hypothyroidism is time-dependent, especially with respect to the nervous system. The somatic effects appear to be largely reversible (if iodine or thyroid hormone is later supplied), but the neurological consequences of hypothyroidism within a critical period of the first 24 days in the rat and with in the first 18 to 24 months in the human infant are generally less alterable or are irreversible (19,41). The effect of hypothyroidism on human neurological development thus appears to be similar to that produced by energy-protein malnutrition, with the period of greatest vulnerability occurring during the time of rapid brain growth (13,14,15,46,47).

THE COMMUNITIES UNDER STUDY

    The parroquías of Tocachi and La Esperanza are located in the province of Pichincha in the Andean region of Ecuador, approximately 2 km north of the equator at an altitude ranging from 2500 to 3300 m. The population size as determined by a household census is 1100 in Tocachi and 1600 in La Esperanza. The ethnic composition of the populations are 22% blanco and mestizo and 73% indígena in La Esperanza, and 37% blanco and mestizo and 63% indígena in Tocachi. Most householders are semi-subsistence agriculturalists -- pastoralists who grow corn, potatoes, peas, beans and squash for domestic consumption, and barley and wheat for both domestic consumption and as a cash crop, if there is a surplus. Six large haciendas (over 1500 acres) and a smaller one (150 acres) are located on the best lands and account for over one-half of all arable land.

    At the time of the study 42% of the households surveyed in La Esperanza owned no land. Opportunities for wage labor were extremely limited. In La Esperanza in 1971, approximately 70 indigenas had full-time positions on the haciendas earning the equivalent of 60-68 cents daily. This was then considered a desirable wage and was approximately that paid by the blanco and mestizo small landowners. A more extensive discussion of the community of La Esperanza has been presented elsewhere (31,31).

The prevalence of goiter was 69.7% in Tocachi and 52.8% in La Esperanza; 8.2% of the inhabitants of Tocachi and 6.0% of the population of La Esperanza were deaf-mute cretins (21,22). Energy-protein malnutrition, common among children, had not been studied systematically. As a consequence of nutritional stresses, adult stature (as an indicator of the cumulative effect of an individual's nutritional history) was extremely short in these communities compared to other Andean populations (21,28,30).

NEUROLOGICAL DEFICITS IN ADULTS

The Bender-Gestalt Test
This portion of the study involved 276 individuals, 15 to 54 years of age, from the community of La Esperanza. The Bender-Gestalt test (6), scored by Koppitz' system (35), was utilized to evaluate visual-motor perceptive functioning. This simple, un-timed, relatively "culture-free" paper-and-pencil test is consi-dered a sensitive measure of neurological deficit (35). In terms of error scores, maturation in visual-motor perception reaches an asymptote of 1.5 errors at 10 years of age among North American children. Those subjects in La Esperanza who made six or more errors were considered to have deficits in visual-motor perception. These individuals would fall below the fifth percentile of the reference group and near the mean Bender error scores of 9 to 10 year-old children in their own community. The rationale for the use of the Bender-Gestalt test, sampling procedure, and test ad-ministration is discussed at greater length elsewhere (28,30).

Deficits in Deaf-Mute Cretins
Table 1 gives the mean Bender error scores of a sample of 45 deaf-mute cretins and of the "normal" adults, 15 to 54 years of age. As expected, the dear-mute individuals show impairment of age. As expected, the deaf-mute individuals showed impairment of visual-motor perceptive functioning that was as profound as their obvious deficits in audition and language development. These deficits tended to be greater in the female than in the male cretins.

Table 1. Mean number of errors on the Bender-Gestalt test.

| | Deaf-Mute Cretins | | "Normal" Adults | |
	Males	Females	Males	Females
X̄	9.8	15.9	1.8	3.8
SD	5.7	4.6	2.1	2.9
N	25	20	111	165

Variations in "Normal" Adults
    1. Sex differences - The data in Table 1 document a marked
difference in the "normal" adult sample (F = 40.3, df = 1/268,
p < .001), with the females having mean error score (3.8) more
than twice as large as the males (1.8). This sex difference in
visual-motor development is a consequence of endocrine-mediated
 difference in adaptation to low iodine availability, and co-vary
with sex differences in goiter prevalence (28,30,33). Similar
sex effects existed among children 6 to 15 years of age in La
Esperanza, but were absent among children in Tocachi who had been
receiving supplemental injections of iodine in oil (30).

    2. Neurological deficits - Among the "normal" adults, 17.4%
had Bender-Gestalt error scores greater than 6 and were considered
likely to have neurological deficit affecting visual-motor perception. Of the 31 scoring criteria used in the Koppitz Developmental Bender Scoring System, 10 are considered to be "highly
significant" indications of brain damage. According to these 10
indicators, the deaf-mute group had a mean "brain damage" score
of 1.9; the segment of the "normal" group considered likely to be
cerebrally injured (on the basis of their high total error score),
1.5; and the remainder of the "normal" population, 0.25. Thus
the individuals suspect of cerebral injury on the basis of total
number of errors had "brain damage" scores that closely approxi-
mated those of the deaf-mute groups, and were considerably greater than those of the remainder of the "normal" population.

The Continuum of Neurological Deficit:
    Table 2 presents distributions of Bender-Gestalt scores in
the "normal" population and the deaf-mute group. Although all of
the individuals with extreme visual-motor deficits (> 15 errors)
are "cretins," there is a considerable degree of overlap in the
6-15 error range. About 70% of the individuals in the 6-12 error

Table 2. Deaf-mute cretins and "normal" adult individuals
          in each Bender-Gestalt test error score category.
          Sexes combined.

Score Category (no. errors)	Normal	Cretins	% "Normals"
0-5	228	5	97.9
6-9	39	16	70.9
10-12	8	4	66.7
13-15	1	4	20.0
15	0	16	0

range are not deaf-mutes and 20% of the scores falling in the 13-15 error range belong to "normal" individuals. These data demonstrate quite conclusively that there is a broad continuum of neurological deficit that affects a rather large portion of the population of La Esperanza. The deaf-mute cretins were distinguished only by the severity of their language, auditory, and in some case, neuro-motor deficits. A large segment of the "normal" population showed deficits in visual-motor perception (error scores of 6-15) that were comparable to those shown by the majority of the deaf-mutes.

SOCIAL AND BIOLOGICAL PREDICTORS OF DEVELOPMENT

Inbreeding:
        Being concerned that in addition to nutritional stress, inbreeding might have a significant negative effect on development in these communities (7), we estimated the average inbreeding coefficient (f) in Tocachi and La Esperanza on the basis of isonymy, the frequency of marriages between persons of the same surname (9). Average inbreeding coefficients were .0179 in Tocachi and .0222 in La Esperanza. This was well below the average inbreeding coefficient, as estimated by isonymy, of .0445 in the Hutterite population (9) and within the range of figures reported on "genetic isolates" in coastal Peru (36), two Italian alpine populations (37), and a Swiss alpine community (25). None of these other communities showed the high rates of developmental retardation that were observed in Tocachi and La Esperanza. It is thus unlikely that inbreeding is a signficant cause of the developmental deficits in the communities under study.

        Furthermore, we compared inbreeding and development in adults among the three moderately endogamous social segments (barrios and anejos) of La Esperanza. If anything, inbreeding in La Esperanza appears to be associated with a lower prevalence of developmental deficits. Among indigenous adults, those living in the upper altitudinal-ecological zone (above 2950 m) were significantly taller (F = 6.54, df = 2/143, p < .01) and scored significantly better on the Bender-Gestalt test (F = 3.27, df = 2/176, p < .05) than indígenas living in the middle (2700-2950 m.) and lower (2500-2700 m) altitudinal-ecological zones. However, inbreeding is much greater in the indigenous social units of the upper zone (f = .0437) than in those of the middle (f = .0214) and lower (f = .0029) zones. Micro-environmental and economic differences across these three zones, rather than inbreeding, appear to account for the developmental differences (33).

Developmental Predictors:
        In this portion of our study we have attempted to evaluate the relative importance of a number of factors affecting growth and behavioral development in Tocachi and La Esperanza. The data are based on 348 children 6 to 15 years of age. Half of the children were from Tocachi and the other half from La Esperanza, with

approximately equal numbers of male and female children in both populations at all age levels. The samples were drawn from all ethnic, socio economic, and altitudinal segments of the two communities.

We shall report on two dependent developmental variables. The child's stature is used as a reflection of the cumulative effect of nutritional stress on physical growth, while the Bender-Gestalt test scores give an indication of how nutritional factors may affect the maturation in visual-motor perception. Table 3 lists the social, nutritional, and biological factors (independent variables) that were evaluated as predictors of stature and visual-motor development (dependent variables) in this sample of children. The relationships between the independent and dependent variables were evaluated through a stepwise multiple regression analysis using the Data-Text statistical package (1).

1. Physical growth - The result of the analysis of multiple regression of the independent variables on stature is shown in Table 4. After age, ethnicity is the best predictor, with

Table 3. Independent variables evaluated as predictors of physical growth and visual-motor development.

Social	Nutritional	Biological
Amount of travel	Total Resource Index	Thyroid size
SES rating*	Age at weaning	Sex
Marital status of	Type of salt used	Age
mother	Altitudinal zone	Birth order
		PTC taste
		sensitivity**
		Ethnic group

*Socio-economic status rating.
**Phenylthiocarbamide taste sensitivity.

Table 4. Independent variables which are significant predictors of stature among childen 6 to 15 years of age in Tocachi and La Esperanza.

Variable	Standardized Partial Regressions Coefficient	t-test	DF	P
Age	0.86	33.30	343	< .001
Ethnic Group	0.14	5.49	343	< .001
SES Rating*	0.09	3.28	343	< .002

*Socio-economic status rating.   R = .88; R^2 = .78

indigena children being smaller than blanco and mestizo children. The rating of the socio--economic status (SES) is a significant, but weak, predictor of stature, with children from wealthier households being taller.

The standardized partial regression coefficients are adjusted for differences in the scale of measurement of each of the independent variables and can be compared to one another to assess the relative predictive power of each independent variable with the others held constant (1).

2. Visual-motor development - Table 5 shows those variables which account statistically for a significant portion of the total variance in the Bender Gestalt scores of the 348 children, 6 to 15 years of age, from both populations. In addition to age, the analysis identifies two indepedent variables -- one the socio-economic status (SES) rating, and the other a biological rating of phenylthiocarbamide (PTC) taste sensitivity -- as the major statistical predictors of the Bender scores. Sex, the second biological variable, accounts for somewhat less of the variation. Thus, children from households with a higher (better) SES rating scored better than those from households with low ratings; sensitive tasters of PTC scored better than less sensitive tasters and non-tasters of PTC; and males scored better than females.

Table 5. Independent variables which are signficant predictors of the Bender-Gestalt Test score of children 6 to 15 years of age in Tocachi and La Esperanza.

Variable	Standardized Partial Regressions Coefficient	t-test	DF	P	Unique Variance
Age	− 0.55	13.27	341	<.001	.293
SES Rating*	0.19	4.66	341	<.001	.036
PTC Taste Threshold**	0.18	4.40	341	<.001	.032
Sex	− 0.14	3.30	341	<.002	.018

*Socio-economic status rating. $R = .66$; $R^2 = .43$
**Phenylthiocarbamide taste threshold.

The fact that PTC taste sensitivity is not a predictor of
stature, but of visual-motor maturation, is undoubtedly associated with the relative irreversibility of neurological deficits
incurred during early critical phases of brain growth, compared
to the ease of reversibility of statural deficits ("catch-up"
growth) throughout growth and development.

(a) PTC (phenylthiocarbamide) taste sensitivity: In previous
publications (29,30) we have noted that PTC is structurally similar to a large number of bitter-tasting, naturally-occuring antithyroid compounds (goitrogens) that are hydrolysis products of
thioglucosides contained in many edible plants, especially those
of the _Brassica_ genus. PTC is itself an antithyroid compound. We
have suggested that PTC taste sensitivity, a well-known genetic
polymorphism, is an oral defense mechanism functioning to reject
or modify (through washing and boiling) these goitrogenic goods.
We reasoned that in areas where iodine intake is low and these
foods are consumed in significant quantities (as is the case in
Tocachi and La Esperanza), that non-tasters and less sensitive
tasters of PTC (individuals with higher taste thresholds)
would eat more goitrogens, be under greater thyroid stress (which
is probably intermittent), and consequently be more likely to show
neurological deficits. These data support that hypothesis.

The finding that PTC taste sensitivity is a significant predictor of visual-motor development contributes to an understanding
of one of the central conceptual issues posed by the problem of
endemic goiter and cretinism. The question is why, in a population where iodine deficiency is uniformly present due to low environmental availability, some individuals become deaf-mute cretins, others are only moderately affected, and still others are
apparently free of nerological impairment? An individual's gene-
tically determined ability to detect and reject or modify the
bitter-tasting antithyroid compounds appear to be a significant
determinant of who is or is not likely to develop neurological
deficits under given environmental circumstances.

(b) Socioeconomic status rating: This variable is a product
of a rating of the household of each child by our main informants,
two respected adult individuals who had lived their entire lives
in these communities. The rating was on a six-point scale (muy
rico, rico, corriente, medio pobre, pobre, muy pobre). The numerical equivalent of "very rich" was 1, of "very poor," 6. The
scale is basically economic and in these communities the children
from poorer households are more likely to have experienced energy-
protein malnutrition than children from wealthier households.
Therefore, this rating probably measures some portion of the effect of energy-protein malnutrition on neurological maturation.
The scale also involves social judgments and thus incorporates
behavioral evaluations of the children's parents. These experimental factors in a child's environment may have a significant
effect on neurological development (32).

We were surprised that our informants' subjective evaluation of socioeconomic status had such a high predictive value for the Bender error scores, while the more quantitative Total Resource Index (determined on the basis of a household's wealth in animals, annual wage income, and worth of harvest) had no predictive value. Possible low reliability of the data composing this measure and the lack of its stability over time appear to limit its utility. The finding that the subjective SES rating was a better developmental predictor than the "objective," quantitative Total Resource Index should alert investigators to the potential utility of such a measure when made by a suitable person from within the community.

(c) Sex: Sex is a significant predictor of visual-motor development in these children, with males scoring better than females at all ages. A similar sex effect was noted earlier among the La Esperanza adults where possible differences in rates of development cannot obscure the comparisons. The sex effects are a consequence of the female's greater vulnerability to low iodine intake as a consequence of hormonal factors. Estrogen causes a marked increase in thyroxine-binding globulin (TBG) levels. With more binding sites to saturate, it is more difficult for the female to maintain adequate blood levels of "free" T_3 and T_4 when iodine intake is low. This results in a markedly higher prevalence of goiter in females than males, and apparently a higher prevalence of neurological deficits under these environmental conditions.

The finding that the blanco children are significantly taller than the indígena children when socio-economic status is controlled is interesting since it is frequently suggested that population differences in the parameter are more likely to be a consequence of differential nutritional and disease experience than of genetic factors. This observation is a bit perplexing since data on the La Esperanza adults suggests that ethnic and altitudinal differences in stature and in visual-motor performance are largely a function of economic circumstances (33).

3. Association between the dependent variables- Height for age is a useful index of the cumulative effect of nutritional stress on the child and is frequently used to differentiate well- from poorly-nourished children in studies done retrospectively. Children with poor nutritional histories (as reflected in low height for age) are more likely to show neurological deficits as a consequence of this stress than are better-nourished children.

Table 6 shows the coefficients of partial correlations between height and Bender-Gestalt score in both sexes in Tocachi and La Esperanza. When age is controlled, shorter children perform more poorly than taller children in both sexes in both populations. The correlation coefficients are fairly large and statistically highly significant. These data indicate that children

Table 6. Partial correlation between stature and Bender-Gestalt Error Score controlling for age among children 6 to 15 years of age in Tocachi and La Esperanza.

| | Tocachi | | La Esperanza | |
	Males	Females	Males	Females
r	-.36	-.44	-.33	-.25
N	85	85	85	79
P	<.001	<.001	<.001	.01

who are smaller (most likely as a consequence of lifelong nutritional and disease stress) lag significantly behind better nourished children in visual-motor development. Although there is a wide range of normal variation in rate of visual-motor maturation, it is likely that some portion of the retardation among the smaller children reflects the consequence of nutritional stress.

The correlation between stature and a measure of neurological maturation is useful as an indication of how individuals who have been malnourished may show both statural and neurological deficits. However, these correlations generally underestimate the effect of malnutrition on neurological development since neurological deficits are relatively irreversible while statural deficits can be greatly ameliorated if the child is subsequently well nourished. Consequently, some of those children who are operationally defined as being "malnourished" on the basis of height for age may not have sustained significant neurological deficits, while others with profound impairment may be of average height. Thus, in a population where malnutrition is endemic, the prediction of neurological development from height for age will always be less than perfect.

4. Iodine vs. energy-protein malnutrition- It is extremely difficult to evaluate the relative impact of iodine and energy-protein malnutrition on development in these communities. In the multiple regression on the Bender-Gestalt scores, we took the standardized partial regression coefficients for PTC taste sensitivity (.18) and sex (.14) as reflecting the measurable effect of iodine malnutrition, and the SES rating (.19) as an indication of the influence of energy-protein malnutrition on neurological development (Table 5). The unique variance in the Bender scores accounted for by these three variables is shown in Table 5. These data indicate that the two variables (PTC taste sensitivity and sex) reflecting the effect of iodine malnutrition account for a larger fraction (0.068) of the variance of the Bender scores than does the SES rating (0.-18), a variable which we believe is asso-

ciated with the effect of energy-protein malnutrition.

We noted above that under conditions of energy-protein deprivation the peripheral monoiodination of T_4 shifts away from the highly metabolically active T_3 form to the metabolically inactive rT_3. Even though there is a lower blood level of metabolically active hormone, the high level of rT_3 prevents an increase in secretion of TSH. Consequently, we would expect that TSH secretion and thyroid enlargement (a positive adaptation to increase the iodide-trapping and hormone-synthesizing capacity of the gland) would be impeded in iodine-deficient individuals who were also experiencing energy-protein malnutrition. Therefore, energy-protein malnutrition would exacerbate the effects of severe iodine malnutrition. This may account, importantly, for the geographic pattern of endemic cretinism as well as intra-population variability in developmental deficits in areas where goiter and cretinism are endemic.

BEHAVIORAL DEFICITS AND SOCIAL ORGANIZATION

In the community of La Esperanza 5.7% of the adults were deaf-mute cretins, and another 17.4% of the "normal" adult population showed moderate neurological deficits that overlapped in degree of severity with those manifested by many of the deaf-mutes. To the anthropologist, endemic malnutrition poses a question of great theoretical interest. If all of the deaf-mutes and most of the moderately-affected individuals have some limitations in behavioral capacity (30,31), then the nigh frequency of such individuals (over 20% in La Esperanza) should have some effect on the socio-cultural characteristics of the community in which they reside. Previous publications have discussed these effects in La Esperanza (30.31.32). We are suggesting that a similar continuum of neurological and behavioral deficit (perhaps not quite as severe as in La Esperanza) will exist in populations where energy-protein malnutrition is endemic and that it will produce comparable social and cultural effects.

It is extremely important to remember that what we call human culture and human social structure does not have an independent existence, but reflects information that is carried in the heads of members of human communities. The ability to carry and manipulate the cognitive representations of cultural and social structures depends on an intact cerebral cortex. If large numbers of individuals in a population have neurological deficits as a consequence of moderate-to-severe malnutrition, then we would expect that the culture-carrying capacity of the population would be greatly reduced. Not only is cultural information likely to be lost, but, more importantly, there would be fewer individuals who are capable of manipulating, or transforming, cognitive representations of social structures. Consequently, these societies or segments of societies would be much less capable of generating new social structures to deal with new problems. Such societies

would be at an adaptive disadvantage and face the prospect of social dissolution when they encounter an environmental stress with
which they cannot cope (10).

Further, within stratified societies, the differential division of environmental resources may impose a socially-produced
form of endemic malnutrition on the subordinate strata. This may
represent a form of social control which, by limiting cognitive
ability among members of the subordinate strata, guarantees the
perpetuation of a docile pool of laborers.

From this perspective, any analysis of socio-cultural dynamics and change must include a careful consideration of the effects of nutrition and disease stress on the biologically-based
behavioral characteristics of human populations and sub-popula-
tions.

CONCLUSION

The data presented in this paper indicate that there is a
broad spectrum of neurological deficit among the members of the
two populations living under conditions of severe iodine and moderate energy-protein malnutrition. Inbreeding does not account
for these developmental deficits while several social and biological factors were found to be significant predictors of visual-
motor maturation under these environmental circumstances. We
believe that there is a similar spectrum of neurological and behavioral deficits in most areas where energy-protein malnutrition
is endemic and that the social consequences are comparable to
those which we have described.

REFERENCES

1. Armor, D. J. and Couch, A. J. Data-Test Primer. New York:
    Free Press, 1972.

2. Bass, N. H. and Netsky, M. G. Microchemical pathology of
    adult rat cerebrum following neonatal nutritional deprivation
    and hypothyroidism. Transact. Amer. Neurolog. Assoc., 94:
    216-219, 1969.

3. Bass, N. H. and Young, E. Effects of hypothyroidism on the
    differentiation of neurons and glia in developing rat cere-
    brum. J. Neurolog. Sciences, 18:155-173, 1973.

4. Balázs, R., Kovács, S., Cocks, W. A., Johnson, A. L. and
    Eayrs, J. T. Effect of thyroid hormone on the biochemical
    maturation of the rat brain: Postnatal cell formation.
    Brain Res., 25:555-570, 1971.

5. Balázs, R., Kovács, S., Treichgraber, P., Cocks, W. A. and
    Eayrs, J. T. Biochemical effects of thyroid deficiency on

the developing brain. <u>J. Neurochem.</u>, 15:1335-1349, 1968.

6. Bender, L. <u>A Visual Motor Gestalt Test and its Clinical</u>
<u>Use</u>. American Orthopsychiatric Association, Research Mono-
graph No. 3, 1938.

7. Cavalli-Sforza, L. L. and Bodmer, W. F. <u>The Genetics of</u>
<u>Human Populations</u>. San Francisco: Freeman, 1971.

8. Chopra, I. J. An assessment of daily production and significance of thyroidal secretion of 3,3',5'-triiodothyronine
(reverse T_3) in man. <u>J. Clin. Invest.</u>, 58:32-40, 1976.

9. Crow, J. F. and Mange, A. P. Measurement of inbreeding from
the frequency of marriages between persons of the same surname. <u>Eugen. Quart.</u>, 12:199-203, 1965.

10. d'Aquili, E. B. and Mihalik, G. J. Malnutrition: Its effect
on psychological development and cultural evolution. In
L. S. Greene, Ed., <u>Malnutrition, Behavior, and Social Orga-</u>
<u>nization</u>. New York: Academic Press, pp. 233-252, 1977.

11. De Groot, L. J. and Stanbury, J. B. <u>The Thyroid and its</u>
<u>Diseases</u>, 4th ed. New York: Wiley, 1975.

12. De Smet, M. P. Pathological anatomy of endemic goitre. In
<u>Endemic Goitre</u>. World Health Organization Monograph No. 44.
Geneva: World Health Organization, 1960.

13. Dobbing, J. Vulnerable periods of brain development. In
<u>Lipids, Malnutrition and the Developing Brain</u>. Ciba Foun-
dation Symposium No. 3. Amsterdam: Elsevier, pp. 9-29,
1972.

14. Dobbing, J. T. Nutrition and the developing brain.
<u>Lancet</u>, 1:48, 1973.

15. Dobbing, J. T. and Sands, J. Vulnerability of developing
brain. 9. The effect of nutritional growth retardation on
the timing of the brain growth-spurt. <u>Biologia Neonator</u>,
19:363-378. 1971.

16. Dumont, J. E., Delange, F. and Ermans, A. M. Endemic cretinism. In J. B. Stanbury, Ed., <u>Endemic Goiter</u>. Pan American Health Organization Scientific Publication No. 193.
Washington, D. C.: World Health Organization, pp. 91-98,
1969.

17. Dumont, J. E., Neve, P. and Otten, J. Recent advances in
the knowledge of the control of thyroid growth and function.
In J. B. Stanbury, Ed., <u>Endemic Goiter.</u> Pan American Health

Organization Scientific Publication No. 193. Washington, D. C.: World Health Organization, pp. 14-29, 1969.

18. Dye, J. A. and Maughan, G. H. Further studies of the thyroid gland. 5. The thyroid gland as a growth promoting and form-determining factor in the development of the animal body. Amer. J. Anat., 44:331-368, 1929.

19. Eayrs, J. T. Age as a factor determining the severity and reversibility of the effects of thyroid deprivation in the rat. J. Endocrinol., 22:409-419, 1961.

20. Eayrs, J. T. and Taylor, S. H. The effect of thyroid deficiency induced by methyl thiouracil on the maturation of the central nervous system. J. Anat., 85:350-358, 1951.

21. Fierro-Benítez, R., Penafiel, W., De Groot, L. J. and Ramírez, I. Endemic goiter and endemic cretinism in the Andean region. New Eng. J. Med., 280:296-302(a), 1969.

22. Fierro-Benítez, R., Ramírez, I., Estrella, E., Jaramillo, C., Díaz, C. and Urresta, J. Iodized oil in the prevention of endemic goiter in the Andean region of Ecuador. I. Program design, effects on goiter prevalence, thyroid function, and iodine secretion. In J. B. Stanbury, Ed., Endemic Goiter. Pan American Health Organization Scientific Publication No. 193. Washington, D.C.: World Health Organization, pp. 306-340 (b), 1969.

23. Fierro-Benítez, R., Ramírez, I., Garcés, J., Jaramillo, C., Moncayo, F. and Stanbury, J. B. The clinical pattern of cretinism as seen in highland Ecuador. Amer. J. Clin. Nutr., 27:531-543, 1974.

24. Fierro-Benítez, R., Ramírez, I. and Suárez, J. Effect of iodine correction early in fetal life on intelligence quotient. A preliminary report. In J. B. Stanbury and R. L. Kroc, Eds., Human Development and the Thyroid Gland. Relation to Endemic Cretinism. New York: Plenum Press, pp. 239-247, 1972.

25. Friedl, J. and Ellis, W. Inbreeding, isonymy, and isolation in a Swiss community. Human Biol., 46:699-712, 1974.

26. Gelber, S., Campbell, P., Diebler, G. E. and Solokoff, L. Effects of 1-thyroxine one amino acid incorporation into protein in mature and immature rat brain. J. Neurochem., 11:221-229, 1964.

27. Goldschmidt, V. M. Geochemistry. New York: Oxford University Press (Clarendon), 1958.

28. Greene, L. S. Physical growth and development, neurological maturation and behavioral functioning in two Ecuadorian Andean communities in which goiter is endemic. I. Outline of the problem of endemic goiter and cretinism. Physical growth and neurological maturation in the adult population of La Esperanza. Amer. J. Phys. Anthropol., 38:119-134, 1973.

29. Greene, L. S. Physical growth and development, neurological maturation and behavioral functioning in two Ecuadorian Andean communities in which goiter is endemic. II. PTC taste sensitivity and neurological maturation. Amer. J. Phys. Anthropol., 41:139-152, 1974.

30. Greene, L. S. Nutrition and behavior in highland Ecuador. (Doctoral dissertation, University of Pennsylvania,1976). Ann Arbor: University Microfilms, No. 76-695, 1976.

31. Greene, L. S. Hyperendemic goiter, cretinism, and social organization in highland Ecuador. In L. S. Greene, Ed., Malnutrition, Behavior, and Social Organization. New York: Academic Press, pp. 55-94(a), 1977.

32. Greene, L. S. Toward an appreciation of the biological bases of behavioral variation and its influence on social organization. In L. S. Greene, Ed., Malnutrition, Behavior, and Social Organization. New York: Academic Press, pp. 267-291 (b), 1977.

33. Greene, L. S., Fierro-Benítez, R. and Stanbury, J. B. The effect of iodine and protein-energy malnutrition on physical growth and neurological development in highland Ecuador. In L. S. Greene and F. E. Johnston, Eds., Social and Biological Predictors of Nutritional Status, Physical Growth, and Behavioral Development. New York: Academic Press, 1979.

34. Hoch, F. L. Biochemistry of hyperthyroidism and hypothyroidism. Postgrad. Med. J., 44:347-362, 1968.

35. Koppitz, E. M. The Bender Gestalt Test for Young Children. New York: Grune & Stratton, 1964.

36. Lasker, G. The occurrence of identical (isonymous) surnames in various relationships in pedigrees: A preliminary analysis of the relation of surname combinations to inbreeding. Amer. J. Human Genet., 20:250-257, 1968.

37. Lasker, G., Chiarelli, B , Masali, M., Fedele, F. and Kaplan, B. A. Degree of human genetic isolation measured by isonymy and marital distances in two communities in an Italian alpine valley. Human Biol., 44:351-360, 1972.

38. Merimee, T. J. and Fineberg, E. S. Starvation-induced alter-
     ations circulating thyroid hormone concentrations in man.
     Metabolism, 25:79-83, 1976.

39. Nicholson, J. L. and Altman, J. The effects of early hypo-
     and hyper-thyroidism on the development of the rat cerebellar
     cortex. II. Synaptogenesis in the molecular layers. Brain
     Res., 44:25-46, 1972.

40. Scow, R. O. and Simpson, M. E. Thyroidectomy in the newborn
     rat. Anatom. Rec., 91:209-226, 1945.

41. Smith, D. W., Blizzard, R. M. and Wilkins, L. The mental
     prognosis in hypothyroidism of infancy and childhood. Pedi-
     atr., 19:1011-1022, 1957.

42. Solokoff, L. Action of thyroid hormones and cerebral deve-
     lopment. Amer. J. Dis. Children, 114:448-503, 1967.

43. Stanbury, J. T. The role of the thyroid in the development
     of the human nervous system. In L. S. Greene, Ed., Malnutri-
     tion, Behavior, and Social Organization. New York: Academic
     Press, pp. 39-54, 1977.

44. Vagenakis, A. G., Burger, A., Portnay, G. I., Rudolph, M.,
     O'Brian, J. T., Azizi, F., Arky, A., Nicod, P., Ingbar, S.
     H. and Braverman, L. E. Diversion of peripheral thyroxine
     metabolism from activating to inactivating pathways during
     complete fasting. J. Clin. Endocrinol. Metab., 41:191-194,
     1975.

45. Van Etten, C. H. Goitrogens. In L. Liener, Ed., Toxic Con-
     stituents of Plant Food Stuffs. New York: Academic Press,
     1969.

46. Winick, M. and Russo, P. The effect of severe early malnutri-
     tion on cellular growth of human brain. Pediatr. Res., 3:
     181-184, 1969.

47. Winick, M., Russo, P. and Brasel, J. Malnutrition and cel-
     lular growth in the brain: Existence of critical periods.
     In Lipids, Malnutrition, and the Developing Brain. Ciba
     Foundation Symposium, No. 3. Amsterdam: Elsevier, 1972.

Addendum to Part II

DARK ADAPTATION IN VITAMIN A DEPRIVATION

When we step from a brightly lit space into a darkened room, at first we can barely perceive any details of our surroundings. After a lapse of time, the visual system adapts to the low environmental illumination, our light sensitivity increases, and we can get around in the darkened room quite effectively.

The process of dark adaptation is affected unfavorably by severe Vitamin A deficiency, and this part of the volume would be incomplete without a reference to this subject. The account of the progress in our understanding of the role of vitamin A in vision, on a molecular level, is presented in Moore's comprehensive treatise (1957, pp. 270-276), which also contains a section (pp. 365-374) on the photometric tests of the efficiency of dark adaptation and the effects of vitamin A deprivation on this function.

This addendum considers the British classical study of prolonged dietary deprivation of vitamin A carried out at the Sorby Research Institute in Sheffield, England (Hume and Krebs, 1949), with the volunteer participation of conscientious objectors. The focus of the study was on vitamin A requirements of young human adults. The research design called for the use of two groups, both maintained on a diet virtually devoid of vitamin A and carotene (a vitamin A precursor). The control group received a prophylactic supplement of either vitamin A or carotene. The experimental group was to be maintained on the experimental diet "until unmistakable signs of deficiency appear, and then to determine what dose of vitamin A or carotene was needed to ensure recovery to normal" (p. 2).

In the present context we shall be concerned only with a facet of the study bearing on the deterioration of the capacity for dark adaptation measured by the Wald adaptometer (Hume and Krebs, 1949, pp. 102-109), using the rise in the *final rod threshold* as the criterion of the deterioration of the capacity for dark adaptation. Definitive, large changes in this criterion were observed in only 3 out of the 16 experimental subjects: one after 10, one after 12, and one after 20 months of maintenance on the experimental diet. At that time, the vitamin A content of the blood of the 3 subjects dropped from the initial level of about 100 International Units (IU) per 100 ml to below 40 IU.

At present, the major problem is methodological: to devise a sensitive and dependable technique that could be used in the field with young children for early identification of the presence of vitamin A deficiency. Solomons and

Allen (1983, p. 40) report that a new rapid test of dark adaptation has been proposed (Thornton, 1977) and that it is being validated (Vinton and Russell, 1981; Schlossman et al., 1982).

BEHAVIORAL EFFECTS OF IRON DEFICIENCY IN INFANTS

Iron deficiency is regarded as the most common deficiency disorder in the world (Halberg, 1984, p. 460), including the industrialized countries. Iron deficiency anemia is indicated by the depletion of the iron store in the body, reflected in the low concentration of serum ferritin (an iron-storing protein) and by the fall in the blood level of hemoglobin (involved in the transport of oxygen). A World Health Organization report (1975, p. 7) registered that severe anemia impairs the capacity for heavy (near-maximum) physical work by placing limits on oxygen transport to the tissues, but it was noted that it was not known whether milder degrees of anemia affect performance in less strenuous work.

In recent years the interest in the behavioral effects of iron deficiency has been on the increase (cf. Edgerton et al., 1982; Pollitt et al., 1982; Tucker and Sandstead, 1982). More than that, the editors of the proceedings of the conference in Houston on brain chemistry and behavior, with special reference to iron deficiency, hope that these studies may aid in the development of a general model for the study of nutrition-behavior interaction (Pollitt and Leibel, 1982, p. VII; cf. Leibel et al., 1982). The paper by Lozoff et al. (1982*a*; cf. also 1982*b* and 1982*c*), on which we shall comment, is one of the studies on the behavioral effects of iron deficiency contributed to the conference. The study was carried out in Guatemala.

A brief review of the literature indicates that while earlier clinical studies of anemic infants suggest the presence of lethargy and apathy combined with irritability, some controlled behavioral studies (Honig and Oski, 1978; Oski and Honig, 1978) appear inconclusive. In a double-blind study with random assignment of treatment involving urban Guatemalan infants from 6 to 24 months of age, Lozoff et al. (1982*a*, Table 2, p. 188) observed that the anemic infants were initially (prior to treatment) significantly more tense, fearful, withdrawn or hesitant, and less reactive to usual stimuli than the nonanemic infants. There was also a tendency toward decreased bodily activity and a lack of persistence. In the authors' view, "These results provide further evidence for behavioral correlates of iron deficiency anemia in human infants" (p. 189).

There were also large differences in the infants' development scores, based on the Bayley Scales. The initial Mental Development Index of the anemic group was 86.6 and of the nonanemic group, 100.4; the initial values of the Psychomotor Development Index were 85.6 versus 94.4, and the differences were statistically highly significant.

However, it should be noted that short-term (one-week) oral iron therapy did not improve significantly either the behavioral ratings or the developmental scores. Several possible explanations of the failure of the anemic infants to improve significantly with oral iron treatment were examined.

REFERENCES

Edgerton, V. R., Y. Ohira, G. W. Gardner, and B. Seneviratne, 1982, Effects of Iron Deficiency Anemia on Voluntary Activities in Rats and Humans, in *Iron Deficiency, Brain Chemistry and Behavior,* E. Pollitt and R. L. Leibel, eds., Raven Press, New York, pp. 141-160.

Halberg, L., 1984, Iron, in *Nutrition Reviews' Present Knowledge in Nutrition,* 5th ed., The Nutrition Foundation, Washington, D.C., pp. 459-478.

Honig, A. S., and F. A. Oski, 1978, Development Scores of Iron-Deficient Infants and the Effects of Therapy, *Infant Behav. Dev.* **1:**168-176.

Hume, E. M., and H. A. Krebs, comp., 1949, *Vitamin A Requirements of Human Adults: An Experimental Study of Vitamin A Deprivation in Man,* Medical Research Council Special Report Series Number 264, His Majesty's Stationery Office, London, 145p.

Leibel, R. L., E. Pollitt, I. Kim, and F. Viteri, 1982, Studies Regarding the Impact of Micronutrient Status on Behavior in Man: Iron Deficiency as a Model, *Am. J. Clin. Nutr.* **35:**1211-1221.

Lozoff, B., G. M. Brittenham, F. E. Viteri, and J. J. Urrutia, 1982*a,* Behavioral Abnormalities in Infants with Iron Deficiency Anemia, in *Iron Deficiency, Brain Chemistry and Behavior,* E. Pollitt and R. L. Leibel, eds., Raven Press, New York, pp. 183-194.

Lozoff, B., G. M. Brittenham, F. Viteri, A. W. Wolff, and J. J. Urrutia, 1982*b,* The Effects of Short-term Oral Iron Therapy on Developmental Deficits in Iron-Deficient Anemic Infants, *J. Pediatr.* **100:**351-357.

Lozoff, B., G. M. Brittenham, F. Viteri, A. W. Wolff, and J. J. Urrutia, 1982*c,* Developmental Deficits in Iron-Deficient Infants: Effects of Age and Severity of Iron Lack, *J. Pediatr.* **101:**948-951.

Moore, T., 1957, *Vitamin A,* Elsevier Publishing Company, Amsterdam, 645p.

Oski, F. A., and A. S. Honig, 1978, The Effects of Therapy on the Development Score of Iron-Deficient Infants, *J. Pediatr.* **92:**21-25.

Pollitt, E., and R. L. Leibel, eds., 1982, *Iron Deficiency: Brain Biochemistry and Behavior,* Raven Press, New York, 214p.

Pollitt, E., F. E. Viteri, C. Saco-Pollitt, and R. L. Leibel, 1982, Behavioral Effects of Iron Deficiency Anemia in Children, in *Iron Deficiency: Brain Biochemistry and Behavior,* E. Pollitt and R. L. Leibel, eds., Raven Press, New York, pp. 195-208.

Schlossman, N., N. Solomons, A.-M. Guerrero, L. Meija, O. Pineda, D. Bankson, and B. A. Underwood, 1982, The Rapid Dark Adaptation Test: Performance with Relation to Circulating Zinc Levels, *Fed. Proc.* **41:**349.

Solomons, N. W., and L. H. Allen, 1983, The Functional Assessment of Nutritional Status: Principles, Practice, and Potential, *Nutr. Rev.* **41:**33-39.

Thornton, S. P., 1977, A Rapid Test for Dark Adaptation, *Ann. Ophthalmol.* **9:**731-734.

Tucker, D. M., and H. H. Sandstead, 1982, Body Iron Stores and Cortical Arousal, in *Iron Deficiency: Brain Biochemistry and Behavior,* E. Pollitt and R. L. Leibel, eds., Raven Press, New York, pp. 161-181.

Vinton, N. E., and R. M. Russell, 1981, Evaluation of a Rapid Test of Dark Adaptation, *Am. J. Clin. Nutr.* **34:**1961-1966.

World Health Organization, 1975, *Control of Nutritional Anemia, with Special Reference to Iron Deficiency,* WHO Technical Report Series Number 580, Geneva, 71p.

Part III

Generalized Clinical Malnutrition: Pioneering Studies

Papers 6 and 7: Commentary

6 GÓMEZ et al.
Studies on Malnourished Children: XVII. Psychological Manifestations

7 GEBER and DEAN
The Psychological Changes Accompanying Kwashiorkor

Cravioto and Robles (1965, p. 449) credit Brock and Autret's report (1952) with making the scientific world conscious of kwashiorkor, so-called wet form—characterized by the presence of edema—of severe (clinical) generalized malnutrition. The Brock-Autret publication may well have served as the common root, involving also concern with the infant's behavior, of the pioneering work by the Group for the Study of Malnutrition in the Child (*Grupo para el Estudio de la Desnutrición en el Niño*) at the Children's Hospital of Mexico (*Hospital Infantil de México*) in Mexico City, and the Group for Research in Infantile Malnutrition, at the Mulago Hospital in Kampala, Uganda.

We do not know precisely the date and the circumstances under which the Mexican unit was constituted. The Kampala group was established in 1953, with the support of the (British) Medical Research Council (Hoorweg and Stanfield, 1972, p. 55), with R. A. F. Dean as director. The psychological studies in Kampala were initiated in 1955. While there is some uncertainty about the year in which Paper 6 appeared in print, a footnote in the Mexican publication specifies that the paper had been read on 27 October 1954 at the *Academia Nacional de Medicina* in Mexico City. Thus, Paper 6 represents the first extensive, systematic account of the psychological manifestations of malnutrition that is advancing in severity.

The group associated with the Nutrition Service (subsequently, the Department of Nutrition) of the *Hospital Infantil de México* published, in English, an early, extensive overview of severe generalized malnutrition (Gómez et al., 1955). Among the children with third-degree malnutrition seen at the Hospital Infantil, edema was present in 71% of the children and was absent in the remaining 29%. Thus, the kwashiorkor-like form of malnutrition accounted for about three-fourths and the marasmus-like form accounted for about one-fourth of the cases of severe malnutrition. No reference was made in that publication to the psychological aspects, except for a very brief comment in the discussion of the course of successful treatment of malnutrition: "Psychomotor activity, which in third-degree malnutrition is minimal, reappears. . . . There is also a progressive improvement in intelligence" (p. 159).

The broad view of the etiology of severe malnutrition is remarkably contemporary: "Malnutrition, one of the gravest medical and social problems of our time, is caused by a combination of a number of factors—social, economic, educational—including the problems of food production, transportation and population growth" (Gómez et al., 1955, p. 163). Elsewhere (Brožek, 1984, p. 39) we have provided a schematic "macroportrait" of the web of factors related to world hunger. More specific and more closely focused on food production, availability, consumption, and utilization is the schema of factors determining the state of nutrition, presented in the monograph summarizing some 20 years of labor by the staff of the Department of Nutrition, Children's Hospital of Mexico (Ramos Galván et al., 1969, p. 8). The monograph contains a large chapter on mental development (pp. 317-331), based on a variety of tests. However, we must go back to the beginnings.

Paper 6 represents the yield of the initial phase of work dealing with the psychological aspect of malnutrition. The paper is not based on the study of a concrete sample or samples of malnourished children but represents a mosaic that reflects the authors' pooled experience.

It is noted that the psychological alterations tend to appear earlier than the clinical (medical) symptoms and that their severity increases with the increasing severity of the physical changes. The report stresses the importance of the awareness and correct interpretation of the early behavioral manifestations of malnutrition for a timely and effective treatment of generalized infant malnutrition and recognizes the crucial role of the family and the cultural setting. In the Mexican peasant culture of the 1950s, the early psychological changes were frequently ascribed to nonnutritional factors such as teething, "evil eye," or the presence of evil spirits in the child, thus deflecting the mother's attention to inappropriate remedial measures. In the comments appended to the report, the authors pointed out that the psychological symptoms of the child have an impact on the mother's personality and that her responses, in turn, affect the child.

Paper 6 is characterized by the authors as a preliminary report on observations of psychological changes accompanying malnutrition, made in a variety of contexts but primarily in the Nutrition Ward of the *Hospital Infantil de México*. In the summary and once in the text, reference is made to the use of the Gesell Developmental Scale, but no specific data are given or even discussed. It may be assumed that at the time the report was written sufficient data were not available. In this respect Paper 6 differs radically from the report from Kampala, Uganda (Paper 7).

There are other differences between the two papers as well. One important difference is that the Kampala study is based on 25 infants admitted to the hospital with a diagnosis of kwashiorkor. By contrast, the Mexican paper traces the development of generalized malnutrition and its psychological manifestations through what might be called mild, moderate, and severe (clinical) forms of malnutrition. The Mexican group used the Gómez classification, with its three degrees of malnutrition, based on the weight of a given child, expressed as a percentage of the reference weight for age (75-85%, grade I; 60-75%, grade II;

below 60%, grade III). In infants with edema, the accumulated extracellular fluid would tend to decrease the estimated severity of the child's condition.

Paper 7 stands out as the first report of a study in which, in addition to direct observations of the infants and young children, technical psychological tools (the Gesell tests, to be specific) were used to assess the developmental status of the children under observation, most of whom were between the ages of one and three years. When feasible, the first testing was done at the time of admission of a child to the hospital or shortly thereafter. The tests were repeated a week later and, again, about a month later when the children were to be released from the hospital. The scores were reported, in the form of ranges, for five subscales: Locomotion, Manual ability, Adaptive behavior, Language, and Personal-social behavior. The overall development quotients (DQs) were not reported. All the tests were administered by Marcelle Geber.

It is most unfortunate, and all but incredible, that the test scores were reported only for the first (upon admission) and the second (a week later) administration but not for the final testing. Thus, the very purpose of the study—to document quantitatively the functional recovery after kwashiorkor— was not achieved, and the reader is left with the imprecise verbal statement that the quantitative results improved.

The present editor's discomfort is heightened by Grantham-McGregor's comment (1984, p. 531) that "Available data suggest programmes in hospitals are insufficient and that long-term ones are required. These programmes should include both nutritional and educational inputs." Had the events in Kampala been documented quantitatively, it is questionable whether the statements would hold up that, at the end of five or six weeks of therapy, the children "no longer appeared retarded" and "compared well with normal African children of the same age" (p. 10 in Paper 7).

One would also like to see objective support for the comment relating different rates of recovery to the quality of the mother-child relationship—a statement that need not be doubted, in principle: "If the [mother-child] relationship was good, the recovery was rapid; if it was bad, the improvement in physique might be good but the return to a satisfactory psychological state was likely to be slow and difficult" (p. 12 in Paper 7). Two points should be noted for clarification. First, typically, the very young African child is in very close contact with the mother. Second, the overwhelming majority of the children were brought to the hospital by their mothers, who remained in the ward with their children.

REFERENCES

Brock, J. F., and M. Autret, 1952, *Kwashiorkor in Africa,* WHO Monograph Series Number 8, Geneva. Switzerland, 71p.

Brožek, J., 1984, The Web of Causes and Consequences, in *Malnutrition and Behavior: Critical Assessment of Key Issues,* J. Brožek and B. Schürch, eds., Nestlé Foundation Publication Series, vol. 4, Lausanne, Switzerland, pp. 34-40.

Cravioto, J., and B. Robles, 1965, Evolution of Adaptive and Motor Behavior during Rehabilitation from Kwashiorkor, *Am. J. Orthopsychiatry* **35:**449-464.

Gómez, F., R. Ramos Galván, J. Cravioto, and S. Frenk, 1955, Malnutrition in Infancy and Childhood with Special Reference to Kwashiorkor, *Adv. Pediatr.* **7:**131-169.

Grantham-McGregor, S., 1984, Rehabilitation Following Clinical Malnutrition, in *Malnutrition and Behavior: Critical Assessment of Key Issues,* J. Brožek and B. Schürch, eds., Nestlé Foundation Publication Series, vol. 4, Lausanne, Switzerland, pp. 531-554.

Hoorweg, J. C. and P. Stanfield, 1972, The Influence of Malnutrition on Psychologic and Neurologic Development: Preliminary Communication, in *Nutrition, the Nervous System, and Behavior,* Pan American Health Organization Scientific Publication Number 251, Washington, D.C., pp. 55-63.

Ramos Galván, R., A. Mariscal, C. Viniegra, and B. Pérez Ortiz, 1969, *Desnutrición en el Niño* (Malnutrition of the Child), Hospital Infantil de México, 596p. plus appendixes.

6: STUDIES ON MALNOURISHED CHILDREN: XVII. PSYCHOLOGICAL MANIFESTATIONS

S. F. Gómez, J. Velasco Alzaga, R. Ramos Galván, J. Cravioto, and S. Frenk

Among the many aspects of malnutrition in childhood, the psychological disturbances have been explored least thoroughly, even though they are extremely important.

Some attempts to describe psychological disturbances of malnutrition have been made both in Mexico (1, 2) and abroad (3-8) but without the depth the subject deserves.

The group in the Division of Nutrition, Children's Hospital of Mexico, has given serious thought to the matter, being convinced that the knowledge of the facts and a correct interpretation of the role of the psychological factors operating in the etiology and the pathology of malnutrition, involving the child, its mother, and the home environment, are essential for a comprehensive understanding of malnutrition.

The information obtained at the Children's Hospital of Mexico will enable us to develop new ideas for therapy and to pursue new directions in the management of malnourished children. The psychological disturbances develop slowly and grow in severity as the child's nutritional status continues to deteriorate, and they decrease during the course of physical recovery. In a child suffering from chronic undernutrition, the psychological alterations appear before the clinical manifestations. Whereas the psychological changes begin to manifest themselves as soon as the food inadequacy starts, the clinical signs and symptoms are barely perceptible until the exhaustion of the body's reserves has progressed substantially.

The incorrect perception of many mothers and of many physicians makes them ignore or wrongly interpret the first psychological manifestations of malnutrition and ascribe them to such causes as cutting teeth, the "evil eye," the fallen fontanel (*caída de la mollera*), fussiness (*chipilez*), jealousy, emotional shock, or infection.

The repeated frustration of the child, unable to satisfy its need for food and to meet the pressing demands of the organism, gives rise to symptoms which are in general misinterpreted. This is due primarily to the difficulty of assessing quantitatively and understanding the child's reactions. Its restlessness, anxiety, tension, anguish, and malaise tend to be viewed as related to other causes and not to deficient nutrition.

Since the psychological manifestations differ according to the severity of malnutrition, we shall describe them separately for three degrees of malnutrition corresponding to 75-80% (first degree), 60-75% (second degree), and less than 60% (third degree) of the reference weight for age.

DATA AND METHODS

The data analyzed in this report were derived from different groups of malnourished children: private patients, nursery children, children seen in out-patient depart-

---

*Read on 27 October 1954 at the Academia Nacional de Medicina in Mexico City.

This article is translated by J. Brožek of Lehigh University from Méd. Hosp. Infant. (Méx.) Ból. 11:631-641 (1954).

ments, and hospitalized children cared for by the Nutrition Service of the Children's Hospital of Mexico. Studies of the mothers' attitudes and of the alterations in the behavior of malnourished children have been carried on for some time in the Nutritional Ward of the Hospital and constitute a large part of the material on which this preliminary paper is based. The studies became more systematic when, recently, a medical specialist in mental hygiene was added to our team.

In general, the procedure has been as follows: When a child is admitted, the routine clinical and laboratory tests and examinations are carried out. The child is carefully observed, from the outset, in reference to its attitudes, reactions, and habits, and a psychological examination using the Gesell development schedule is made. The mother is interviewed repeatedly and observed while she is interacting with the malnourished child. In addition, the family, social, and community environment are taken into account, together with the analysis of the family's economic situation and a personality assessment of the mother. We are beginning to use motion pictures in order to register the child's behavior in different stages of malnutrition and during recovery. The clinical and psychological observations are repeated periodically in order to obtain a comprehensive portrait of the child's recovery, with special reference to the child's interaction with the external environment, the relatives that visit the child, and the other children on the ward.

Even though we do not have at this time a motion-picture documentation ample enough to draw conclusions, the data have proved to be of great value for the formulation of a future research program; in this preliminary communication we shall refer only to the procedures currently in use.

The nursing and medical personnel of the Nutrition Ward, with their kind and humane approach, create an ambience radically different from the child's home environment: in contrast to the mother's anxiety, the child encounters an atmosphere of calm security; in contrast to the fearfulness and tension seen in the faces of the members of the family, affected by the seriousness of the condition of severe malnutrition, the child is greeted with kind words and smiles. Instead of forcing the child aggressively to eat, the child is permitted to eat or not to eat what is offered to it, without negative comment and hostile or sugar-sweet (*meloso*) attitudes. In contrast to a monotonous and meager diet the child was given at home, the diet that is offered on the Nutrition Ward is attractive and varied, and food is provided on the child's demand.

The total dependence of the child at home contrasts with a reasonable degree of independence, according to its condition and physical ability: the child can choose what it wishes to eat and it is encouraged to use its own hands for managing the food, in the atmosphere of non-interference. In addition the child is offered dishes that it did not see at home for a long time, since a physician may have prohibited them or because the mother, out of fear, drastically reduced such components of the diet as beans, milk, tortillas, hot sauce, liver, meat, plantane, bread, and cookies.

As soon as the child gets over its exhaustion and adjusts to the environment, children recovering from malnutrition or ready to go home visit the new arrival, smile at him, stimulate him, and bring him toys.

When the child becomes strong enough to maintain a seated position, it is placed near the children that eat well and with gusto. From its seat and with a plate in front of it, without any help or pressure on the part of the nurse, the child sees the other children putting their hands into the soup, meat, and beans, trying to feed themselves. The child learns quickly to imitate them. Leaving the malnourished child to shift for itself, even though the child may still be weak, and select the food at will rather than having the food given to it by the nurse and placed in its mouth, generates an attitude encouraging the child to reach out for the food. In the Nutrition Ward we view such behavior as a healthy sign of independence and a valuable strategy that the child will take along when it leaves the hospital and that will permit the child to search for food and protect itself from the privations to which it will be subjected.

PSYCHOLOGICAL MANIFESTATIONS OF THE
FIRST DEGREE OF MALNUTRITION

At this level of malnutrition (75-80% of the reference weight for age), the psychological changes are minor, since the child is barely beginning to experience the effects of the unsatisfied demands of its appetite.

In order to better understand the behavior of this group of malnourished children, we shall note the behavior of a well nourished, satisfied, and healthy child. Such a child is happy, feels well, laughs readily, engages in a great deal of spontaneous activity, sleeps deeply, is amused by minor stimuli, has a positive attachment to its mother, enjoys its environment, and exhibits a healthy appetite.

At the beginning of food deprivation, the psychological changes are barely perceptible since the organism manages to cope with a brief stress. However, if the food deficiency persists, the child begins to cry frequently and be unhappy without any apparent reason, and the characteristics of the feeling of well-being begin to vanish. The child is unhappy, cries frequently, falls asleep with difficulty, and wakes up at the slightest noise, bites its mother's breast, is readily distracted when it is being breastfed, and the siblings bother it. For brief periods it may recover good humor but loses skills it has acquired so readily. The child sleeps poorly, preferably in the arms of the mother who has difficulty to separate herself from the child without upsetting it.

If the mother and the physician become aware that the child's body weight has become stationary for several weeks or that the child has actually lost weight, and if they realize that this is due to undernourishment, the provision of adequate supplementary food leads quickly to the recovery of the weight; in a few weeks the child becomes happy and feels well again.

If, however, the restlessness, poor humor, poor sleep, and loss of weight and good habits are attributed to teething, head cold, infection, or any of the absurd factors postulated in our country, without carefully analyzing the diet, the fall of the weight becomes more steep, a prolonged denial of an essential biological need increases the psychological stress, and the behavioral manifestations of malnutrition become exacerbated.

On the whole, in Mexico the mother that breastfeeds her child begins to fail to provide adequate amounts of breast milk between five and six months of the child's age. When we analyze carefully the clinical history of a malnourished child, it becomes evident, according to the mother's recall, that around that time the child's feeling of well-being begins to deteriorate. However, typically, the mother does not realize that this is due to the insufficiency of nourishment, since she "feels" that she has had plenty of breast milk. As a rule, a Mexican mother whose economic and cultural status is low, is indifferent to the illnesses and accidents of her children, and is incapable of comprehending and interpreting the psychological effects of malnutrition unless they are very clear and far advanced.

Relating the psychological changes to the etiological and pathogenic schema that enables us to understand severe malnutrition better, we can say that the changes correspond to a period in which body reserves begin to be consumed and the depletion of tissues is initiated. At this time some biochemical alterations take place, such as the increase in the extracellular space (as a measure of excess hydration); and there is a marked retardation of growth and development.

PSYCHOLOGICAL MANIFESTATIONS OF THE
SECOND DEGREE OF MALNUTRITION

When the psychological manifestations and the clinical signs present in a child receiving an inadequate diet are not understood by the mother or the physician or when the child is not cured for other reasons, it reaches the second degree of malnutrition (60-75% of the reference weight for age) and the psychological symptoms become more alarming.

The mother, until now indifferent and unconcerned about the child, becomes inescapably an active participant in the malnutrition drama, since the child's illness becomes more readily perceptible. The child is perceived as definitely being ill. It becomes very thin and the weight loss continues; frequently the child suffers from diarrhea and no food is tolerated. The child becomes an easy prey for infections.

Diarrhea, vomiting, and infections make the ignorant mother or the uninformed physician give the child a diet that becomes steadily less nutritious. The ingestion of food is reduced and assimilation impaired. The monotony of a thin corn-flour gruel, vegetable broth, or various inappropriate concoctions exacerbates the malnourished child's unsatisfied need for food, and the mother becomes afraid to give the child the food it wants and needs. All of this induces in the child an attitude of negativism. The child's refusal of food is viewed by the mother as a consequence of the loss of appetite and is attributed to the child's illness. This is the beginning of an anorexia that for a long time tenaciously accompanies the child with advanced malnutrition.

The mother, previously indifferent, is now overcome by anxiety and concern when she sees the child's condition worsens steadily. Some mothers turn first to "home remedies," then to the folk doctor (*curandero*). As the disease progresses, the mother begins to visit physicians, beginning with the homeopaths, then the free medical services and Centers of Assistance to the Child and, finally, at enormous cost, turns to private medical offices. All of these efforts fail, since the child at this stage requires, in order to recover, replacement of the anxious and disturbed environment of the home by an environment that is peaceful, that can understand and properly manage the patient—the environment of a hospital.

This odyssey seriously affects the mother who has journeyed from here to there in vain: the mother is anxious, desperate, impatient, and frequently suffers from a bitter feeling of guilt that makes her neurotic. All her attitudes, actions, and remarks have a direct (and negative) effect on the severely malnourished child.

At this stage all kinds of faulty notions come into play; all the neighbors and relatives offer their advice and the mother is the target of these misleading comments.

The sick child and the sick mother disrupt the home life and the whole family shares the tragedy of the child that is becoming thinner and thinner, suffers from diarrhea, does not want to eat, has edema of the legs and the face, blotchy skin, loss of hair, and receives no medication that could bring about improvement of its health. The child, with retardation of its physical development, enters into a phase of regression and its behavior shows profound personality disturbances and perversion of habits.

In regard to the spheres of motor functions and language, the alterations can be readily perceived but their evaluation is complicated by the fact that second-degree (and especially third-degree) malnutrition is frequently associated with polyneuritis, varying in severity and distribution. In this condition a child that has been walking ceases to do so and later is unable to stand on its feet; a child that ate with a spoon now accepts only liquid nutrition and the nipple of the bottle has to be placed in its mouth. The child is sad, does not talk or move. The "useless activity" of the well-fed child disappears, words are "forgotten," and a 3- or 5-year old child is unable to express itself. A child that had control of the sphincters loses this ability, and a child that did not learn to control the sphincters does not acquire this ability even if it is older than 18 months. Even at 24 months it will not eat using its own hands, and it is unable to use a spoon. At times the child holds a cracker in its hand, without eating it.

Frequently there is a severe emotional maladjustment between the severely malnourished child and its family: the child may "hate" the siblings, manifest attitudes of mistrust, defensiveness, or fear in front of adults, sulkiness (*berrinches*) in the presence of its mother and, most of all, anorexia and rejection of any and all food that is offered to it.

Anorexia is present, in severe form, in many children with second-degree malnutrition. In addition to perseverations and mannerisms, true perversions of appetite may be seen: some children obstinately tear out their hair or pick skin scabs and eat them; others keep their hands in the mouth or put the fingers into the nostrils and bring to the mouth the particle of mucous that they are able to extract. Some children eat threads of fragments of the tissue of the bed clothes, or become coprophagous.

Occasionally there are perseverations of movements or speech: moans, words, or brief phrases are repeated monotonously and with low intensity—an endless monotonous wailing; the head may swing up and down for minutes at a time. Even at the level of second-degree malnutrition, the behavior may appear psychotic, although this is rare.

Finally, in order to evaluate the symptoms of severely malnourished children, we have to keep in mind Gesell's view that personal behavior is profoundly influenced both by the personality of the child and by the social conditions of the child's home. The range of individual variability is large.

PSYCHOLOGICAL MANIFESTATIONS OF THE THIRD DEGREE OF MALNUTRITION

When a child reaches this advanced stage of deprivation (below 60% of the reference weight for age), its psychological state may be described as "fatalistic resignation."

Prior to this the patient struggled, cried, was restless, even violent, slept poorly, manifested tenacious hunger. It ate earth, threads, animal and vegetable waste and, at time, fecal matter. However, all of this effort was useless since the organism, deprived of adequate nutrition, continued to consume such body reserves as still remained, without stopping nutritional deterioration. As an inescapable result of the use of its body tissue, the child reaches the final stage of its life. The only defense is the avoidance of all motion, total indifference to its environment, prolonged sleep—be it apparent or real, hypothermia, and a complete isolation from the environment. In this way the metabolic needs are reduced to a minimum, and the bare existence is prolonged for a while. It is as if the organism descended into a stage of spontaneous hibernation, as the ultimate lowest limit of the organism's energy metabolism.

The severely malnourished child, a "pile of skin and bones," lays in bed with the arms and legs bent, in a curled-up position with the eyes closed—not always as a result of a photophobia due to xerophthalmia but as an aversion to looking at things that move around the child. It pays no attention to the environment, is immobile, and only desperately wishes that its rest not be interrupted. The child rejects any food that may be offered, clenching the teeth. If food is forced into the child's mouth, it is retained there and is not swallowed or, if the food reaches the stomach, it is regurgitated. Some children manage to cover their face body with a sheet or a bedspread so as to isolate themselves even more completely.

At times these children cry without tears, with weak and monotonous moaning, mumbling a syllable or an unintelligible word that they repeat and repeat. When they are examined, they respond with weak reactions of defense against the discomfort or the pain. They remain in the same position for hours and days, unless they are moved.

The weak reactions they display to auditory, gustatory, or tactile stimuli manifest systematic negation and rejection. Many children dislike the mother's presence. Some reject the mother outright while others tolerate her presence but ignore her. A few seek mother's hand or finger and continue to rub their own hand against her's.

At times we find that they adjust better to the hospital environment if the mother is absent, even though the hospital environment must appear to them at first as strange and hostile due to medical examinations, laboratory tests, intravenous administration of nutrients, and transfusions.

Extreme prostration and helplessness, together with extreme emaciation, typical of the very advanced stages of malnutrition, represent a grave prognostic sign, even in the absence of infection.

REFERENCES

1. Gómez, F.: *Bol. Méd. Hosp. Infantil Méx.* 3:543, 1946.
2. Gómez, F.: *Rev. Esp. de Pediatría* 8:165, 1953.
3. Gómez, F.: *Bol. Méd. Hosp. Infantil Méx.* 7:479, 1950.
4. Gómez, F.; Ramos Galván, R.; Cravioto, J.; and Frenk, S.: *Acta Pediatr. Scand.* 43, Suppl. 100, 1954.
5. Trowell, H. C.: *Brit. Med. J.* 1:789, 1952.
6. Williams, C. D.: *Lancet* 2:1051, 1935.
7. Meneghello, J.: *Desnutrición del Lactante Menor,* Ed. Central, Santiago de Chile, 1950.
8. Clark, M. E.: *Afr. Med. J.* 28:229, 1951.

7: THE PSYCHOLOGICAL CHANGES ACCOMPANYING KWASHIORKOR

M. Geber and R. F. A. Dean

ERRATUM

In the Introduction, line six should read "came from Africa, and Brock and Autret (1952) . . . ." In footnote 1, line 3 should read "objects—a coloured ring, ...

Reprinted from pages 295-311 of *Readings in African Psychology from French Language Sources,* Frederic R. Wickert, ed., African Studies Center, Michigan State University, East Lansing, 1967, 381p.; *Copyright © 1956 by Human Sciences Press.*
(Originally published in 1956 in *Courrier,* vol. 6, no. 1.)

From pages 3-13, The psychological changes accompanying Kwashiorkor. <u>Courrier</u>, 1956, 6 (1).

Editor's Introduction. This classical articles demonstrates clearly that a condition, apparently a purely medical (physiological) matter, actually has a large psychological component. The proof of the psychological component is nicely shown as the reader follows the various phases through which the research proceeded. He sees how highly systematic test performance supplements and sharpens less standardized and less systematic clinical-type observation. He comes to respect the neat, simple tool that imaginative psychological testing can be.

Introduction

The psychological changes accompanying the disease known as kwashiorkor, and by many other names, have long been recognised. Irritability has been noticed many times: for example, by Williams (1933), Purcell (1939) and Russell (1946) on the Gold Coast, Hughes (1945-46) in Nigeria, Gelfand (1946) in Southern Rhodesia, Hanafy (1948) in Egypt, and Clark (1951) in Kenya. These reports came from Africa, and Brock and Autret (1951), after their tour of that Continent, recorded that the mental changes were well known to all who had seen kwashiorkor. They occurred or were recognised, in variable degrees. Gelfand and Russell mentioned how easily the child was upset, and cried at the slightest provocation: Purcell said the children were "bad-tempered and cried much, . . . listless and indifferent, never buoyant, not disposed to play; the eyes . . . dull": Doucet (1946), from a central province of the Belgian Congo, wrote "Les gros troubles psychiques ou nerveux . . . manquent chez les malades" but went on to say "Apparemment ils ont un esprit un peu moins alerte, une apathie plus prononcée. Indiscutablement il existe un retard sinon un arrêt total de tout développement intellectuel".

Outside Africa, irritability was described in India by Ramalingaswami, Menon and Venkatachalam (1948) writing from Coonoor, in Indonesia by Oomen (1953) and by Meneghello (1949) in Chile. He gave Scroggie (1942) credit for having first drawn attention to the changes in <u>distrofia policarencial</u> in Chilean children and said that they were very common. The experienced doctor could recognise at once the child's lack of interest in his surroundings, and in the toys that might be brought to him or put on his bed, his indifference to other children and his apathy. He would be somnolent, but would wake easily and then react in a hostile way, weeping and distressed, to anyone who came to bring him food or to examine him and he had a long monotonous cry. Meneghello made also the important point that the child's condition was not merely a reaction to the hospital environment, because the mother nearly always reported that the child had behaved in the same way at home, and because the condition might persist for many weeks in hospital. The cry is of particular interest. Hanafy wrote of "a pathegnomonic long peevish cry," Clark of "a low miserable whimper." Peña Chavarria (quoted by Autret and Behar, 1954) of Costa Rican children who are "indifferent to their surroundings and remain immobile for hours with open eyes and expressionless features, suggesting a mask rather than a human face. This immobility without tears, and the children refuse all food and whimper at the least touch." The anorexia here mentioned is another constant feature of kwashiorkor: it complicates hospital treatment and in severe cases has usually been overcome by intra-gastric drips or by other methods of unnatural or forced feeding.

A preliminary report of a study being undertaken in Mexico City on cases of "malnutrition" ("third degree malnutrition" probably corresponds to kwashiorkor) has recently appeared (Gomez, Alzaga, Galvan, Cravioto and Frenk, 1954). "Emotional maladjustment" between the child and his family, loss of sphincter control, inability to stand, unwillingness to take any food that is not liquid, and "perseverations of motions, attitudes and spoken word" are said to be observed in the penultimate stages of the disease. In the final stages, there is "an absolute quietness" and "a full withdrawal from (the) environment." The child lies with his eyes closed "reluctant to watch the things that move about"; reactions to "auditive, gustative and tactile stimuli" are slight, and consist of "systematic negation and refusal." The changes are attributed partly to polyneuritis, and partly to the frustration of the emotional and biological needs of the child, which brings "non-specific reactions of the whole personality towards the external medium." Anorexia, which is severe, is considered to be the result of the child's daily "frustrations to the satisfaction of its most imperative demands." The full account of this study should be of great interest as in the work to be described here, Gesell tests are being used.

It might be expected that profound psychological changes of the kind described would be associated with disturbances in the electrical activity of the brain. Encephalographic records were made of twelve children in Algiers by Sarrouy, Saint-Jean and Clausse (1953). Abnormalities in the form, frequency and amplitude of the waves were found during the first days after admission for treatment, and often persisted for many months: some abnormalities have also been found in a study that will be reported at a later date by members of the Infantile Malnutrition Group in association with the South African National Institute for Personnel Research.

The aetiology of kwashiorkor has been the subject of much controversy, which has been fully reviewed elsewhere (Trowell, Davies and Dean, 1954) but in recent years opinion has become more and more unanimous: a deficiency of protein in the diet in the second or third year is believed to be the chief factor. That is certainly the opinion at Kampala, but there are some puzzling features of the incidence of the disease. It has often been found that only one of several children in the same family has been affected, although no change in family circumstances, or of diet, can be discovered. It has been notable, too, that the families affected were not necessarily the poorest, or the most ignorant, or those that had the greatest difficulty in getting food to which they were accustomed. Although the local name of the disease, like local names elsewhere, implies something of the deposition of one child by the next following, the only child was sometimes attacked. The explanations offered have never been entirely satisfactory, and it has for a long time been clear that the problem of aetiology is not simple.

There can be no doubt at all that malnutrition is in part of a sociological problem, and that a knowledge of living conditions, of local prohibitions and of customs, is necessary to the complete understanding of aetiology. The child in Africa, like children everywhere, needs happiness and security if he is to develop as well as possible, and usually derives them from his mother. Williams (1938) in the course of a description of the lives of children in the Gold Coast, referred to the possibility that permanent injury might be done by the sudden complete withdrawal of maternal care, at the age of about two years, and later in the same paper gave a description of kwashiorkor in children of that age. The connection was more implicitly stated by Davies (1951) during a discussion in which the opinion was expressed that the injury might have serious social consequences.

In 1937, Trowell wrote of the "wretchedness and irritability" of children in Kampala. "They refused to play and sat sadly . . . In bed they lay curled up and covered by bedclothes . . . were petulent, were continuously crying. They presented a constant picture of misery." Today at Kampala the picture is the same and the present investigation was undertaken to try to define exactly the changes, and to analyse their cause.

The Children

The number of children investigated was 25: they were unselected consecutive admissions with the diagnosis of kwashiorkor. One was under one year
old, and one over three; all the rest were between these ages. Fourteen were
boys and eleven were girls. Most were of the autochthonous Bantu tribe, the
Ganda; some were from other tribes, but tribal distinction did not appear to
be important. They had all been breast fed but none was at the breast at the
time of the investigation.

The children conformed to the description already given of kwashiorkor as
it is seen in Kampala (Trowell, Davies, and Dean, 1952) and were without any
serious complicating disease except that in two cases pulmonary tuberculosis
was demonstrated by the clinical findings, the Mantoux reaction, and the X-ray
examinations of the chest. They were all treated with a high-protein diet
based on milk protein (Dean, 1952; 1953). On this diet, it is usual to obtain
a rapid recovery, and at the end of a week the appetite has improved, the skin
has begun to heal, the oedema has largely disappeared, the serum albumen has
increased by about 1 g./100 ml. and the serum cholesterol by about 50 mg./100
ml., and enzymes of various kinds have become more active (Dean and Schwartz,
1953). At the same time the general demeanour should have changed, and the
child should appear to be interested in his surroundings, in his attendants,
and indeed in life in general. It has been noticed, however, that the improvement in behaviour does not always parallel exactly the other improvements:
in some children the physical condition may obviously change for the better,
and the change may be correlated with alterations in the chemical findings,
but misery and unfriendliness remain; in other children although the physical
condition is bad, the behaviour is more or less normal, strangers are accepted
easily and the hospital regime is tolerated without apparent difficulty. Even
in such children, however, it is usual for the appetite to be poor at first,
and to need much coaxing.

In nearly all the cases studied, the child was brought to hospital by the
mother, who stayed in the ward and was encouraged to help in the treatment to
the best of her ability or inclinations. She left the child for such purposes
as eating her meals, and her own toilet; at night she slept on the floor near
the cot and, if she so desired, had the child on the floor with her.

Two children were brought by their fathers, who did not stay with them;
the mothers had recently died.

Methods

For all children who are admitted to the Group's wards, a history is
carefully taken by an African doctor, that is intended not only to provide the
necessary medical details, but also to show the social and nutritional milieu
in which the child has become ill. The mile-stones of development--the age at
which the child sat, stood, talked, and so on--are recorded, although it is
known that in a community where calendars are rarely used, the information obtained cannot always be accurate. Anthropological measurements are also taken,
and the bone age is assessed by X-ray examination. The psychological observations have in fact been made in conjunction with a study of physical and
psycho-motor development that will be reported at a later date. For the children now to be described, special emphasis was placed on the collection, from
any available source, of data that might help in an assessment of the mental
condition: the father, if he appeared, or any other friend or relative, could
usually yield new or confirmatory facts, or at least help to define the social
and economic status of the family.

The methods of investigation consisted of daily psychological observation,
and Gesell tests.

The main ward of the Group building has two smaller wards adjacent to it.
From one, which is used as the Sister's Office, it is possible to see through
large wall windows into the main ward in which the children and their mothers
live: from the other the occupants of the main ward can be observed without
the observer being seen. Some observations were made from the small wards;
others were made by being in the same room as the mothers and their children.

They were made at all hours of the day, and all activities could therefore be watched. Stress was laid on the necessity for defining the mother-child relationship, known to be so important in young European children.

The Gesell tests[1] were carried out in a quiet room, in which distraction from outside could be avoided. One of us (M.G.) conducted all the tests.

The mother was always present and all the ordinary material was employed; as usual, the tester was at the side of the child and slightly behind him, so that the child could use her or not, as he preferred. The Gesell scheme was modified in only one way, in adaptation to the conditions of African life: the mother, the child and the tester all sat on a mat on the ground. A photographic record, of most of the tests, was made by a member of the Group, with electronic equipment giving a silent flash of very short duration. The children paid hardly any attention to the camera or the light, and were quite undisturbed by them.

For most of the children, the test was repeated three times: on the day of admission to hospital or the day after, a week later, and a month later. The last test was, in some instances, done in the child's own home.

Results

a) The history

The histories of the 25 children were similar to those of the much larger number of cases of kwashiorkor that one of us (R.F.A.D.) has observed during five years in Uganda. As long as breast feeding lasted, the child grew well and appeared to be developing normally. When, at the end of about a year, he was fully weaned, his diet rarely contained any cow's milk except a little said to have been given in tea, and consisted almost entirely of cooked bananas (plantains), sweet potatoes, and cassava (manioc) with sauces made from beans and groundnuts; meat was included in the family's food once or twice a week, but it was unlikely that the child received more than a little of the gravy. For a time, progress continued to be uneventful, but sooner or later--the interval after weaning varying from a few months to many--there appeared some febrile or gastro-intestinal illness. Nearly every informant thought that the illness was the beginning of the child's decline; it seems likely, however, from observations that have been made at Child Welfare Clinics and elsewhere in Uganda, that the decline had begun earlier in most cases, but had passed unnoticed. Within a few weeks of the illness, it had been observed that the child's appetite became poor, his skin dry and his hair pale in colour and altered in texture. Finally, the general condition became worse, the skin began to peel, and the feet and legs, and sometimes the face and hands, began to swell. At this stage medical advice was usually sought, but home treatment with native remedies was usually tried before the child was brought to hospital. As such remedies are usually purgative, they were probably not beneficial

---

[1]Some explanation of these tests may be desirable. They are primarily intended to measure psycho-motor development. The child is offered, in a prearranged order, a series of objects--a colured ring, a small bell, cubes, tablets and a glass bottle, and various other devices that will interest him. According to his state of development, he will examine or manipulate the objects, arrange them, and invent ways of using them. Finally he is invited to play with the ball, to mount a short staircase and to see himself in a mirror. His manual ability, his preferences, his willingness to change his occupation, and all the other details of his behaviour yield, to the experienced observer, information on the stage of development that has been attained. A quantitative estimate, based on the performance of individual tests, can be made for tests that can be grouped under headings such as Locomotion, Manual ability, Adaptive behaviour, Language, Personal-social behaviour. On the scale used, 100 represents the performance of the "normal" child in Europe or the U.S.A. at the age of the child being tested.

One father and one mother said that the first indication of ill-health had been a change in their children's behaviour. The father was a widower, and the change had occurred about two months after the mother had died. No other parents volunteered any similar remark, but information obtained during the questioning suggested that in nearly every child there had been some alteration in behaviour. The duration of marked changes, such as apathy and irritability, was usually set at about two weeks.

In the histories of 13 of the 25 children, there was a remarkable feature. It was the separation of the child from his mother, to live, in accordance with local custom, with a grandparent or some other relative. The custom is believed by some mothers to be a necessary part of the education (or self-education) of the child, and to others, is a way of honouring the grandparent. In some cases the separation was arranged because the mother was pregnant and knew that the first child would be a worry and a nuisance when the new child was born. In several cases, it coincided with weaning: the child was weaned on a date fixed more or less arbitrarily, sometimes the first birthday, either because the mother thought it was time that the child made an advance in development, or because she thought she deserved relief from the incessant demand for the breast. Whatever the reason, the weaning, and the separation, appear to have been decided without any consideration of their possible effects on the child. The separation was nearly complete. Some mothers went to see the child each month, but others did not go at all for the first three or even six months. Sometimes as early as the first month a mother found the child less well, but thought he would get used to the new home: more often the child got worse and worse, lost his appetite, and became listless. Finally, a state of ill-health was recognized, and the mother had taken away the child. In other cases she had only gone to see the child when she was told that he was ill.

Two mothers, one of whom has already been mentioned, were dead. In two other cases, the history was of special importance, because the mothers were obviously anxious. The anxiety in one may have arisen when it became necessary to wean the child at one month. The second was more complex: the anxiety may have been due partly to a lymphangitis (the mother had lost another child some days after weaning because of a lymphangitis) and partly to the father having sent the mother away, with the child, when he took another wife.

b) Results of observation.

In the first days after admission, a severely ill child would lay inert in his bed, completely apathetic, but crying monotonously for long periods, especially if he had been disturbed for an examination or for treatment of any kind. Examination, or any interference, was often resented with an intensity that was unexpected in its violence. There was usually great difficulty in feeding and much patience was needed. No child could be induced to take anything except a thin liquid feed. At this time the child slept relatively little, and usually had his eyes fully open, looking at nothing.

When, after some days of treatment, the state of the child improved, he would remain sitting immobile, in the middle of his bed, his face always sad and vacant. He took no notice of the life going on around him, allowed himself to be fed or taken up, and when returned to the bed stayed in the position in which he was put. Sometimes he aroused himself to call for his mother.

The period of inertia lasted sometimes only a day or two, sometimes for more than a week. It was followed by a period in which there was great physical improvement; the oedema disappeared, the skin healed, weight was regained, and the child began to eat willingly and no longer merely accepted food passively.

Whilst he was emerging from the state of inertia, he had great need for the considerate care of his mother. He wanted to have her always close by, called her at the slightest pretext, and cried in despair when she went away. He accepted anyone else very badly, and usually refused to be distracted by toys, or by any person other than the mother who tried to make contact with him. It was very important to analyse the relation of the mother to the

child, because it appeared that the prognosis of recovery depended on her behaviour. Some mothers were very attentive to the needs and desires of their
children, and were always on hand to feed them, to change them and to bathe
them. Some were even more active, and tried to entertain the children, talking to them and playing with them happily. Four children who were at one time
utterly miserable, but who recovered with extraordinary rapidity, had mothers
of the latter kind.

The behaviour of 4 of the mothers was especially remarkable. In the
first days after admission, they passed in and out of the ward on their own
affairs--their meals, their toilet, and so on--but hardly looked at the children when they passed their cots. If they sat by the cots, they faced away
from them. During a ward round, they went away. As the children's condition
improved, the behaviour changed. They became more interested in the children,
but although they would help them to sit up, or would watch their toilet, they
still preferred to entrust the feeding to one of the nurses. Despite their
revived interest, they stayed very little with the children and did not reply
when they called. One of the children recovered rapidly, one fairly slowly,
one extremely slowly, and one died.

Two other mothers, from the moment of admission, occupied themselves
ceaselessly in necessary and unnecessary attentions to their children. In
each case, the child had been separated from the mother. One child died, and
the other recovered.

c) Results of the Gesell tests.

The first test. i. General.--The test was usually very slow and very
difficult to carry out successfully. It often seemed to be too much for the
child. In spite of the need to try to obtain some kind of performance, it was
necessary to be extremely watchful of his behaviour, and to understand his
limitations.

Most of the children were extremely apathetic. They remained seated on
the mother's knees, huddled up, pressed against her bosom, not looking at the
tester, and having no interest in the objects presented (Fig. 1 to 4). The
child was a kind of pendant to his mother, relying on her completely. He remained on her knees because he was put there but this passive "parcel" attitude was more than anything else an attitude of self-protection. He not only
showed his need of contact with his mother, but also behaved as though he
realized that only by making a demonstration of his misery, and his need for
solace, could he hope to obtain comfort from her. Usually, he was interested
in the tester, following her movements and watching her if she moved a little
distance away, but only if she made no attempt at communication. In some very
ill children, the interest was feeble, but it could always be elicited except
in the two cases in which there was an associated tuberculosis.

Usually the children refused most of the objects, either passively, looking at them with a far-away expression, or somewhat more actively, looking at
them whilst they were being arranged, touching them perhaps, but then taking
their hands away when the objects were offered several times. Two objects
gave especially interesting results: the tablet and the mirror. The tablet
was the only object that several children would pick up. It was small and
relatively colourless and it made no noise; the children took it and kept it
clutched tightly. The mirror produced an obvious refusal in all the children,
even the most apathetic turning away as though they found their own reflection
unbearable.

It was noticed that the children who took an interest in the test held
the objects close and would make many efforts to pick up and to keep all the
ten cubes in their hands although, of course, the hands were far too small.
The test would not be allowed to go on unless the objects presented all remained within reach, or at least within sight.

With such behaviour the quantitative results were necessarily very low.
Of the twenty-five children, eight did not give any results that could be
measured at the first test. The eight included the two with tuberculosis who
refused completely and passively and two whose refusal was violent (Figs. 5

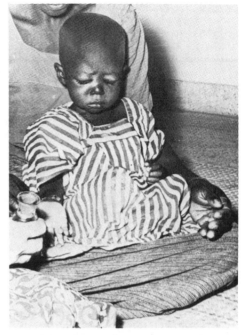
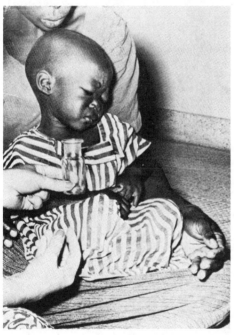
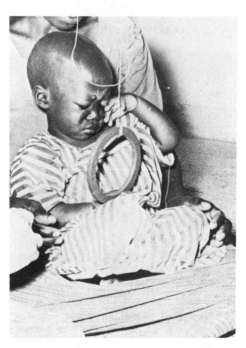

Figs. 1 to 4. --The typical behaviour of refusal of a child suffering from
acute kwashiorkor. In Fig. 1 refusal is expressed in a look of fury;
in Fig. 2 the child is showing some interest in the tablet, but is
allowing it to fall from his open hand; in Fig. 3 he is pressed against
his mother, his left arm drawn back towards her and his head turned
away from the bottle presented by the tester; in Fig. 4 he has covered
his eyes against the sight of the ring. The child died.

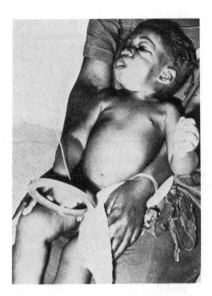

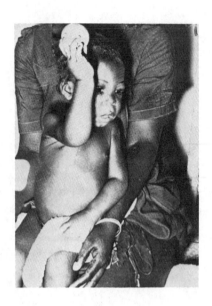

Fig. 5 --A child expressing his refusal by making an arc of his body against his mother.

Fig. 6 --The same child throwing the ball violently as far as he can away from the tester.

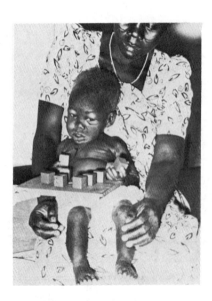

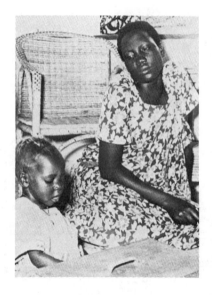

Fig. 7. --This mother is almost encir- cling the child with her arms, giv- ing him security, and watching him attentively and lovingly. Although the child was very ill when he was admitted to hospital (rhagades, skin changes and oedema can be seen in the original photograph) he made a very rapid recovery.

Fig. 8. --A mother whose whole attitude expresses her boredom and lack of interest. In another test she went to sleep. The photograph shows the child a few days before discharge from hospital. He recovered fairly well physically, but his mental con- dition remained bad. It was impos- sible to make any contact with him, even after two months of treatment.

and). At the beginning of the test these two like the other children, were inert, and their faces were sad and inanimate, but when the attempts at arousing interest were repeated, they hurled the objects in the direction of the tester. When the objects were brought back and again presented, they seized them quickly and angrily threw them into an opposite corner of the room. The objects being presented once more, they refused this time completely, holding themselves tensely still, all their fury expressed in their look. The four others remained inert but showed their opposition, when the test was continued, by hiding their eyes. All four took the tablet and of those, who took the cubes, but all did nothing with either tablet or cubes except hold them tightly.

The children who carried out the tests moved very slowly and carefully, as if they were afraid to move at all and wanted to hide their movements. Some put out their hands two or three times in the direction of an object before taking it.

For all the children, the score was particularly low for locomotion and language. A finding that seemed to be important was that adaptivity was comparatively high.

ii. Locomotion. None of the children walked at the first test and if attempts were made to force them to walk they defeated the attempts by drawing up their legs. Some had been walking for several months, but had then presumably become so weak or so apathetic that they refused to walk. When the oedema disappeared, the muscular wasting and the extreme slenderness of the legs was very noticeable. The scores ranged from 50 to 67.

iii. Manual ability was better conserved. The two children with tuberculosis did not take up any object. The other children, even if they merely took the objects mechanically without making use of them, or angrily to throw them away, at least showed some manual dexterity. The scores were from 77 to 92.

iv. Adaptive behaviour was relatively good. In spite of the apparent apathy and inertness, some performances were carried out perfectly. The adaptivity was often very unequal: an infant in a very low category for most tests would sometimes succeed in one or two tests of a remarkably high calibre, in which success was not to be expected at that age. The child did not want to utilize everything put within his reach, but if one object particularly interested him, he carried out the test intelligently, and made good use of the motor and sensory possibilities it offered. The scores were from 75 to 91.

v. Language, communication with the external world, was very poor, in both expression and comprehension. The child's only wish was to be with his mother, and to cut himself off from any contact with things around; he would not understand, and he would not express himself. The refusal of expression was translated by feeble moans and monotonous cries. The scores for expression ranged from 53 to 81, and for comprehension from 53 to 88.

vi. Personal-social behaviour was, like adaptivity, relatively good, but here too the inequality was very marked. The intelligence and the powers of observation of the child enabled him to have the social behaviour that might please the mother. The scores were from 61 to 89.

vii. Summary. It was at this first test that we realized the intense need of the child for the mother and his total dependence on her--a dependence so necessary that he had to refuse anything that might lead to a loss of contact. He refused to walk even if he was physically able, and he refused any communication with the external world; he had become an infant again, and wanted to remain infantile. The behaviour of the mother gave the most information about the mother-child relationship (Figs. 7 and 8). Some mothers remained quite passive during the test and one even stretched herself out on the mat and went to sleep; others were essentially occupied with themselves, pushed themselves forward when the child was asked to do something and when the child was shown the mirror, looked at themselves and at nothing else. Others were attentive and watchful, ready to help the child but content to leave him to try alone (Fig. 7).

The second test. i. General. --An astonishing degree of recovery was

shown by nearly all the children in this test. About half allowed themselves
to be seated beside the mother; the others remained sitting on her knees, but
instead of being merely inert, showed actively their need to remain in physical contact with her and protested vigorously if attempts were made to dis-
lodge them. They were obviously still very dependent on their mothers.

In general the children were interested in the objects, taking them and
looking at them intently on all sides, but their behaviour was a function of
the mother's attitude: if she took no interest, they seized the objects and
held them close, and did very little with them: if on the contrary the children saw the mother was watching carefully, and if she responded to their need
for encouragement, their interest was lively and they tried to do well in the
tests. The children who were most insecure again showed their special interest in the tablets and often had to be allowed to play with them for 10 to 15
minutes before attention could be distracted to other objects. At this second
test, all the children, except two who were the most severe cases of kwashiorkor, were interested in their reflection in the mirror and some even laughed
at it.

The quantitative results were much better than in the first test. All
the children made a reasonable score, but two categories of scores and of behaviour could be distinguished. Some children were secure: they were no longer very ill and their mothers were nearly always with them, ready to attend
their needs. They accepted the test situation with pleasure. At the start
they made many exchanges with the mother, but they were also interested in the
tester and were pleased to communicate with her. The exchanges were mostly
in looks and in works: only rarely would any of the objects be handed over.
They made use of the objects happily, and accepted easily one object after the
other. The test could be carried out fairly quickly (in about three quarters
of an hour) and the results were markedly superior to those of the first test.
Other children did not find themselves secure enough to accept the test situation. They remained close to their mothers, could not communicate with the
tester and were very slow in anything they did. If they took any of the objects, it was only to hold them close. The test was slow, with little action,
and usually it lasted about an hour and a half.

   ii. Locomotion was still retarded. Some children refused to walk,
clinging tightly to their mothers: they would stand for a time, then suddenly
collapse to the floor. Others crawled, or tried to stand and to take a few
steps, looking at their mothers, or even to the tester, for approval. The
scores could be assessed for all the children and were between 51 and 87.

   iii. Manual ability was considerably improved, and even at this stage
it was possible to see in some of the children the precocity of motor development that is so remarkable in Africans (Geber, 1955). The scores were from
77 to 126.

   iv. Adaptive behaviour, which expresses both the interest of the child
and his intelligence, was less scattered than in the first test. The scores
were between 75 and 105.

   v. The results for language showed how the child had begun to take part
in the life around him. The change was demonstrated by communication with the
mother--by talking to her, and showing her and giving her the objects--and
also by some of the children inviting the tester to take part in their play.
Expression was very different from that observed in the first test and the
total scores for language were between 60 and 100.

   vi. There was good progress in personal-social behaviour, the child not
only wanting to give the mother pleasure, but wanting also to take part in a
more extensive social life. The scores were from 66 to 107.

   vii. Summary of the second test. The test showed an important degree of
improvement in those children to whom the mothers, by their attentiveness and
care, had been able to give security. Despite the physical improvement
brought about by the medical treatment, there was less evident progress in
children whose mothers could not make them feel that they were safe. The
quantitative results were better than those in the first test because the
children were less apathetic, but locomotion and language remained at a stage

of development very inferior to that usual for the real age, and the quality of the results showed how little advance towards independence had been made. The children could not establish any relationship with anyone except their mothers, and the children's interest for the test objects depended on the degree of interest the mothers showed in the children.

The mother-child relationship was exactly the same as it was in the first test. Some of the mothers were attentive, as they had been before, and others were still indifferent, with the result that their children wanted nothing so much as to attract their attention.

The third test. This test, made about a month after the first, and for five of the children made at home, confirmed the result of the second. The children in whom progress had been so considerable in one week had continued to progress; they no longer appeared to be retarded and compared well with normal African children of the same age (Geber, 1955). They accepted the test with pleasure and the results were good quantitatively. The children in whom the quality of behaviour had shown the depth of their psychological disturbance, still presented the same difficulties: the test was usually not very active. The interest in the objects was only moderate and the exchanges with the tester were restrained.

Summary of the Gesell tests.

The three tests spanned the period of recovery, and a broad view showed how closely recovery was bound to the mother-child relationship. At the first test, all the children showed their need for their mothers' care: at the second, some children had become independent: at the third, the children's behaviour was not much different, but the quantitative results were improved; because some degree of happiness had been recovered better use could be made of the material of the Gesell test, and of the world around.

The quality of the mother-child relationship could be accurately judged even at the first test. The quality did not alter, and therefore the prognosis of the psychological condition could also be judged. On the other hand, the behaviour of the mother when the child was very ill was no sure guide to the security and comfort she would provide later. The three mothers who refused to take part in the nursing, and whose children survived (see page 301, last paragraph), bestirred themselves on behalf of the children when the period of acute danger had passed, but the amount of nursing they were prepared to do was not the dominating factor in the children's recovery.

a) Correlation with biochemical findings.

In the acute stage of the first days after admission, the psychological changes in the present series of cases followed closely the results of the biochemical tests that were made at the same time: the children most affected were almost without exception those whose blood chemistry was most abnormal. During recovery, however, the blood chemistry improved consistently but the psychological condition did not always alter correspondingly; in some cases, appetite remained capricious and strangers were not readily accepted. For the moment, further correlation is not practicable, and must await the collection of a larger series.

Discussion.

We have attempted to describe the psychological changes seen in Kampala as the accompaniment of acute kwashiorkor. They appear to be similar to those described by Meneghello (1949) in Chile and by Gomez et al. (1954) in Mexico but may not be exactly like those seen elsewhere, and one of us (RFAD) who has travelled to several African and American countries, has formed the impression that in Kampala the changes may be more constant, and more severe, than they are in many other places. Such an impression could only be verified, of course, by undertaking psychological investigations in those places.

Kwashiorkor is almost world-wide, but the profound changes may not be universal; it might be argued that they occur in some countries, but have not been recorded, but it seems unlikely that an observer such an Frontali in

Italy, who has discussed the close resemblance of distrofia da carboitrate to kwashiorkor (Frontali, 1952-53) could have failed to notice in Italian children changes so great as those we have seen in Kampala.

Two of the questions that will immediately be asked are: to what extent are the psychological changes described specific to kwashiorkor, and can acute kwashiorkor be related to any antecedent psychological trauma? The first question can be answered in two ways. To anyone who is familiar with African children, the appearance and behaviour described are not like those of any other illness: admittedly, that is not conclusive, because no other illness seen in Kampala produces the multiplicity of physical deformities that may accompany kwashiorkor, but the misery of kwashiorkor is more constant than any of the obvious physical lesions and its degree cannot be correlated with their extent. In some diseases, of which meningitis is an example, the child may be very irritable, but the irritability usually has a close connection with certain stimuli and particularly with stimuli that may evoke pain: it lacks the quality of hopelessness and despair that is characteristic of kwashiorkor. It is more physical, less psychic. Gesell tests were made on a few ill children who had malaria, or pneumonia and were pyrexial. These children were not unduly miserable, and their performances seemed to be very little affected. Experience with European children is similar; illness, with the possible exception of severe chronic tuberculosis, has very little effect on the tests, except that the child may tire more easily.

The second question cannot be answered at present. There are undoubtedly many ways of arriving at the state of severe and obvious kwashiorkor. In every case there is probably an unsatisfactory dietary background: the child grows slowly until some event occurs that turns his progress downhill. The event may be an infection, or it may be anything that in effect reduces his protein intake or makes the intake temporarily or permanently inadequate. If any other proof were needed, the results of the appropriate dietary treatment would alone show the importance of the nutritional factor, but it does not seem unreasonable to suggest that faults in the psychology of the child may favour the development of the disease, and acute psychological trauma may precipitate the development: the trauma may enact the part of the infection or the other cause.

The possible mechanisms of development of psychological injury.

It would certainly be wrong to place too much emphasis on separation as the cause of the onset of kwashiorkor in our cases, because it was not possible to determine exactly the part that separation played. The 4 children who died, and all the rest of the children who were judged on clinical grounds, on the biochemical findings and on the psychological tests, to be most severely affected, had been separated, but 3 of the separated children were considered to be mild cases. It was not practicable to make a complete enquiry into the lives of the families; such an enquiry might have shown on the one hand factors additional to the separation that were important, on the other how separation could occur without serious consequences. We are hoping to undertake a further study of cases of kwashiorkor in which there is no history of separation, and we hope that other workers in centres where kwashiorkor is common many think it worth while to assess the importance, in the aetiology of the disease, of the lack of maternal care. According to our information, the custom of sending the child away from the mother soon after weaning is not very widespread, even in Africa, but separation of a kind occurs in other ways. Particularly in South Africa, in the native "locations" around the big towns, there is an increasing tendency for the mother to leave the child whilst she goes out to work. She often has to be absent from home for nearly all the child's waking hours, and to leave the minding of the child to a relative or friend. In those circumstances, everything will depend on the relationship that the child achieves with the mother-substitute. If that is satisfactory, so that the child is secure and happy, there is no reason to expect that any special harm will ensue; if, however, it is unsatisfactory, and the child is unable to make the necessary compromise between love and isola-

tion, it does not seem too fanciful to suggest that he may suffer in such a
way that his state of nutrition is affected, even if he is presented with food
that should be fairly adequate in quantity and (but this is less certain) in
quality.

In more than half of all the cases of kwashiorkor that have been admitted
to the wards of the Infantile Malnutrition Group, there has been a history of
separation. The effects cannot be judged exactly, but it is worth remembering
that the child deprived of maternal care has become a well-recognised pathological entity as an outcast from European society; Bowlby (1952) has described
him perfectly. One of the first and most important reactions to deprivation
is nutritional, and the child is described as expressing his distress by an
alteration in his way of eating, usually a refusal to eat usual food and a demand for the more exotic. If the European and the African child happen to react in the same way to deprivation, the consequences may be even more specta-
cular for the African. He may get kwashiorkor.

We may perhaps reasonably suggest that in some of the Kampala cases, separation may have precipitated the onset of the disease, but we can be less
sure that it bore any relation to the severity of the child's condition when
he was seen in hospital. Although the information available about the families
was imperfect and incomplete, the daily observations in the intimacy of the
conditions described enabled the quality of the relationship between the mother and the child to be assessed with some degree of confidence. Nothing was
found to suggest that the relationship was any less important in African
children than it is in European children but it was invariably noticed that in
the severest cases, the relationship was not good: the child was obviously insecure and his behaviour was consistent in other ways with rejection. It
seemed likely therefore that the quality of the relationship might determine
to some extent the degree of severity. There were two children whose relationship with their mothers was bad, and were not, clinically or psychologically, severe cases; for one the mother had evidently been fortunately replaced
by the grandmother, and the other had adapted himself by refusing to develop
from a state of infantile dependence. This child, examined a year after his
discharge from hospital, was found not only to have failed completely to advance in psycho-motor development, but to have made little increase in either
height or weight. During the year he had been admitted three times to the
Group's wards for the treatment of very slight recurrences of his original
illness, but he was never very ill, and no medical reason had been found for
his failure to thrive.

Six children were thought to have excellent relationships with their
mothers. None of them showed any considerable degree of psychological upset,
but two were certainly very ill; one had an associated anaemia caused by overwhelming malaria, and the other was one of the few children in the series who
had been breast-fed for only a few weeks. He was one year old when he was admitted for treatment.

Although the behaviour of the mother might change, in the way that has
been described, as the child recovered, the quality of the mother-child relationship did not alter: as might be expected, if it was good or bad when the
child was first seen, it remained so at the end of treatment. Perhaps the
most striking proofs of the importance of the relationship were to be found in
the different rates of recovery. If the relationship was good, the recovery
was rapid: if it was bad, the improvement in physique might be good, but the
return to a satisfactory psychological state was likely to be slow and difficult. The extreme case was a child whose young mother was married, as the
second wife, to a man who was not the child's father and who refused to have
him in his home. The apathy and misery of the child were entirely typical of
severe kwashiorkor when the child was admitted, and when he was discharged,
about 6 weeks later, they were almost unchanged. A year later, when the child
was seen in the home of his grandmother, it was obvious that recovery was still
incomplete.

The importance of the mother-child relationship can hardly be denied,
even by those who are the most distrustful of what they regard as psycholo-

gical "explanations". It may be permissible, therefore, to examine some of
the features of African life, as exemplified by our cases, that may have a
bearing on the relationship.

It is difficult for the European to realise the degree of intimacy in
which the young African child lives with his mother. From birth, he is always in the closest possible contact with her, constantly carried by her,
either in her arms or held against her back by a fold of dress, and at night
he sleeps with her: the physical union is so close that it is almost no ex-
aggeration to say that he lives as part of her. Even more, she complies with
all his desires and feeds him at every demand. Weaning is usually gradual,
and sudden, brutal, measures like the coating of the nipples with aloes--the
practice in Natal and elsewhere--are not employed in Uganda: nevertheless,
there comes a time when the breast is finally denied, and the denial, even if
it is not reinforced by sending the child away, is marked by a considerable
alteration in the mother's behaviour. She no longer passes her whole life
with the child; she carries him less often and she does not sleep with him.
The child cannot be prepared for the loss: his extreme dependence can hardly
allow him to conceive of a separate existence. But a separate existence becomes a necessity.

Some of our children behaved as though they were profoundly distressed
at losing their mothers' care. In those children, many signs of distress were
to be found: the apathy, the lack of interest in things and in people, the
vacant look, the strange cry, the desire for a kind of non-existence that
showed in immobility and the choice of the smallest of all the objects that
were offered. The children did all they could to recapture their former state
of total dependence on the mother, and succeeded to some extent because their
adaptivity was good.

The mental structure of the child must be of importance in deciding
whether kwashiorkor occurs. The consequences of psychological trauma are
likely to be all the more severe the more the child is under-developed. The
child who has been given security by maternal care and is therefore developing
satisfactorily may for a time be intensely distressed by separation, but the
quality of the bond established with the mother will enable him to recover his
balance as soon as he finds her again. Such a child might even find a way of
profiting from a mother-substitute--the grandmother or the aunt to whom custom
sends him. On the other hand, the child who has never been sure of his mother
will remain haunted by the fear of losing her: he will be so insecure that he
is incapable of profiting by anything that can be done to help him. If the
mother returns to the child but she continues to maintain his insecurity by
her behaviour, he must feel more and more rejected.

It may be that a change in the attitude of the mother, and a prolongation
of the child's stay with her, is responsible for a curious feature of the
child's progress after he has left hospital. The children return to conditions of diet that cannot be greatly different from those in which kwashiorkor
was contracted, and yet relapses are very uncommon. It is true that whilst
the mothers are in hospital attempts are made to educate them, by example, in
the ration feeding of their children: it is also true that the active follow-
up of discharged children has only recently begun: but most of those children
who have been seen after discharge, either at hospital or in a few instances,
at home, have been strikingly healthy. Nearly all have remained with their
mothers, and it is tempting to believe that their good condition can be ascribed to that circumstance, examples have already been quoted of children who
have not remained with their mothers and who have not thrived, either physically or psychologically. Nowadays, children admitted to the Group's wards are
taken to their homes whenever possible and are visited there regularly if they
do not re-appear for out-patient examination. In a few years, information may
have been accumulated that will make clear the part played by the restoration
of maternal care.

Treatment and implications.

The prognosis of the recovery from kwashiorkor has usually been considered in terms such as the restoration of the protein-depleted body, the removal of fat from the liver, and the re-starting of enzymatic activity. If there is any validity in the thesis that has been advanced it is necessary also to consider the mind of the child and his mother. The same defect that may provide a favourable ground for the development of the disease may retard recovery even in the best circumstances. We believe that in hospital treatment the child's psychological needs must be taken into account, and that everything possible must be done to gain and maintain his confidence, especially if the mother is unable to do so. Since the establishment of that principle, it has been possible to abolish tube feeding except, of course, for children who are comatose: great patience is often needed, because the anorexia is often extreme, but the successful results have shown us and our nursing staff the value of gentle and intelligent persistence. We believe also that the admission of the mother with the child, usually considered to be a nuisance, must be regarded as a vital part of treatment: it would be senseless to take the child and to refuse to admit the one person whom the child needs more than any other. In the same way, the mother who wants the child to sleep in her arms at night should not be discouraged unless there are strong, not merely conventional, reasons for thinking it would be bad for the child.

Scrimshaw (1955: personal communication) has recently told us that children in a hospital in Guatemala City who are receiving what appears to be a full and adequate diet during convalescence from kwashiorkor consistently fail to gain weight. The same failure occurs only very occasionally in Kampala. There are, of course, several possible explanations, but it would be of interest to know if the constant presence of the mother--at present mothers are not admitted to the Guatemalan hospital as they are in Kampala--made for better recovery.

One more speculation remains. The final fate of the child who suffers in his early life from kwashiorkor is unknown: his liver may be permanently damaged, as some believe, and he may die young of cirrhosis or primary hepatic carcinoma, or he may recover completely and live to a happy old age. No one can tell, but there is slightly better statistical evidence for the first alternative. The final fate must include his psychological development. In the cases described, the child that made a rapid recovery into mental well-being probably did so because he had established the necessary relationship with his mother. What will be the later fate of those unfortunate children for whom the relationship was only established temporarily, or was never perfectly established? Will they survive into adult life intact, or will they suffer another profound illness? Will it be possible, one day, to survey these cases, and to complete the series of which Kwashiorkor was the first term? The answer seems to place a heavy responsibility on the parents, but in fairness to them, we should admit that we have very little knowledge of the circumstances that have determined their attitude. All we know is that the life of the African is often hazardous and uncertain, and that for many reasons disturbances of family life are common. We have need of much more understanding before we can suggest any effective method of preventing the psychological damage that we believe to be so important.

REFERENCES

1. Aubry, J. (1955). La carence de soins maternels. International Children's Centre, Paris.

2. Autret, M. and Behar, M. (1954). Sindrome policarencial infantil (kwashiorkor) and its prevention F.A.O. Nutritional Studies, No. 2, Rome.

3. Bowlby, J. (1952). Maternal care and child health. W.H.O. Monograph Series, No. 2, Geneva.

4. Brock, J.F. and Autret, M. (1952). Kwashiorkor in Africa. W.H.O. Monograph Series, No. 8, Geneva.

5.   Clark, M. (1951). Kwashiorkor. E. Afr. Med. J., 28, 22·.

6.   Davies, J.N.P. (1951). Trans. 9th Conference on Liver Injury. Josiah
     Macy, Jr. Foundation, New York.

7.   Dean, R.F.A. (1952). The treatment of kwashiorkor with mild and vegtable
     proteins. Brit. Med. J., 2, 791.

8.   Dean, R.F.A. (1953). Treatment and prevention of kwashiorkor. Bull. Wld.
     Hlth. Org., 9, 767.

9.   Dean, R.F.A. and Schwartz, R. (1953). The serum chemistry in uncompli-
     cated kwashiorkor. Brit. J. Nutr., 7, 131.

10. Doucet, G. (1945). Le "mbuaki" ou maladie de carence observée au Kwango.
     Rec. Sci. Med. Congo Belge, 5, 261.

11. Frontali, G. (1952-53). Quasciorcor o distrofia da farine. Boll. Accad.
     Med. Roma, 61.

12. Geber, M. (1955). Développement psycho-moteur de l'enfant africain.
     Courrier, 6, 17.

13. Gelfand, M. (1946). Kwashiorkor. Clin. Proc., 5, 135.

14. Gomez, F., Alzaga, J.V., Galvan, R.R., Cravioto, J. and Frenk, S. (1954).
     Studies on the Malnourished child. XVII--Psychological manifestations.
     Bol. méd. Hosp. infant. (Méx.), 11, 631.

15. Hanafy, M. (1948). The subacute subnutritional syndrome in infants.
     Acta Paediat. (Uppsala), 36, 316.

16. Hughes, W. (1945-46). Kwashiorkor and ariboflavinosis. Trans. Roy. Soc.
     Trop. Med. Hyg., 39, 437.

17. Meneghello, J. (1949). Desnutricion en el lactante major (Distrofia
     policarencial). Central de Publicaciones, Santiago.

18. Oomen, H.A.P.C. (1953). A survey on malignant malnutrition in Djakarta
     toddlers. Docum. Med. Geog. Trop., 5, 128.

19. Purcell, F.M. (1939). Diet and ill-health in the forest country of the
     Gold Coast. H.K. Lewis and Co., Ltd., London.

20. Ramalingaswami, V., Menon, P.S. and Venkatachalam, P.S. (1948). Infantile
     pellagra. Indian Physician, 7, 228.

21. Russell, B.A.S. (1946). Malnutrition in children under 3 years of age in
     Ashanti, West Africa. Arch. Dis. Childh., 21, 110.

22. Sarrouy, C., Saint-Jean, -. and Clausse, -. (1953). L'électroencéphalo-
     gramme au cours de la dystrophie nutritionnelle œdémateuse. Algérie
     Méd., 57, 584.

23. Scrimshaw, N. (1955, personal communication). I.N.C.A.P., Guatemala City,
     Guatemala.

24. Scroggie, A. (1942). Sindromes policarenciales en la infancia. Rev. Chil.
     Pediat., 13, 945.

25. Trowell, H.C. (1937). Pellagra in African children. Arch. Dis. Childh.,
     12, 193.

26. Trowell, H.C., Davies, J.N.P. and Dean, R.F.A. (1952). Kwashiorkor.
     II. Clinical picture, pathology and differential diagnosis. Brit. Med.
     J., 2, 798.

27. Trowell, H.C., Davies, J.N.P. and Dean, R.F.A. (1954). Kwashiorkor,
     Edward Arnold (Publishers) Ltd., London.

28. Williams, C.D. (1933). A nutritional disease of childhood associated with
     maize diet. Arch. Dis. Childh., 8, 423.

29. Williams, C.D. (1938). Child health in the Gold Coast. Lancet, 1, 97.

Addendum to Part III

EAST AFRICA (UGANDA)

The editor of this volume struggled with the issue of whether to reprint the first but brief paper by Geber and Dean (1955) dealing with psychological aspects of kwashiorkor—a communication all but lost to the subsequent generation of investigators—or the more detailed account published a few months later in 1956. In the end he chose the latter communication, reprinted here as Paper 7.

However, the earlier Geber-Dean paper is not without interest. For one, it refers to the study itself as "a *preliminary* study of the psychological changes associated with kwashiorkor" (p. 471). As far as we know, Marcelle Geber, a young French physician interested in child psychology and child psychiatry, returned to Uganda on several occasions, but no other communication(s) devoted to the subject and reporting the results of a more comprehensive psychological study of kwashiorkor could be found in the literature (except for the 1956 paper that deals with other aspects of the same study). It would have been particularly useful to have available comparative data on children suffering from kwashiorkor and children ill with malaria, pneumonia, and anemia, especially since the authors suggest that it seems possible to demonstrate a difference between the mentality of these children.

While the use of quantifying instruments (tests) has its unique merits, this does not mean that qualitative observation lacks value. Other observers would confirm the comment (Geber and Dean, 1955, p. 471) that "When the child is responding well to treatment, an improvement in the mental state is one of the most hopeful signs, and when the child can be induced to smile, he is out of danger." The improvement in appetite is noted as another important sign of recovery.

Paper 7 stresses the relevance of the mother-child relationship. The 1955 report goes on to say (p. 472): "we have become convinced that the attitude of the mother must play an important role in the *causation* [emphasis added] of the disease." The author supports this statement, in part, by pointing out that "About half of the children admitted for treatment have been sent away from their mothers for one of a variety of reasons, and while away have contracted the disease."

This, we believe, is a culture-bound phenomenon, not an essential feature of the etiology of kwashiorkor. Barrera Moncada (1963, p. 47) noted, specifically, that in the Venezuelan study, "there have been no cases in which the development of kwashiorkor was preceded by a separation of the mother from the child."

SOUTH AFRICA

The South African study of the sequelae of an episode of generalized clinical malnutrition in infancy is impressive and, in fact, unique in the world literature in terms of length of time—a full 20 years—during which the children were followed, with periodic, repeated observations and measurements.

The study was initiated in 1955, in close contact with R. A. F. Dean, the moving spirit of the Group for Research in Infantile Malnutrition, in Kampala, Uganda. The results were reported for the periods of 5, 10, 15, and 20 years of follow-up (Stoch and Smythe, 1963, 1967, 1968, 1976; Stoch et al., 1982). The 20 subjects assembled between 1955 and 1959 were described in the 1967 report (p. 1027) as "twenty of the most grossly undernourished Cape Colored infants who could be found" but we are not told how they were located. The authors refer to these children as "severe cases of marasmus" (Stoch and Smyth, 1976, p. 335). The comparison group, matched for age and sex, were "selected from a creche-cum-nursery school serving a subpopulation of the same social class as the index group" (p. 327).

Unfortunately, this is a very misleading statement. The two groups differed substantially in the social conditions of the families: "The disparity of their living conditions was very marked. Alcoholism, illegitimacy and broken homes were the rule in the undernourished group, whereas the control group lived under more stable home conditions" (Stock and Smythe, 1967, p. 1027). At the beginning, only six parents of the severely undernourished children were gainfully employed. The initial disparity in the living conditions of the index children and the controls constitutes a critical limitation of a study carried out with remarkable dedication. This is so even though the reader of the reports is informed that over the years the home environment of the index children has steadily improved.

The initial, large differences in the social conditions of the families of the two groups of children throw a long and heavy shadow of doubt regarding the validity of the tremendous amount of labor involved in the follow-up examinations.

Scrimshaw and Gordon (1968), editors of the proceedings of an international conference on malnutrition, learning, and behavior, commented on the paper by Stoch and Smythe (1968) as follows:

> There is no way of knowing how much of the poorer performance, as determined by a great variety of tests, depended upon early malnutrition and how much was due to the exceedingly adverse social circumstances of their early childhood. This question should have had greater attention. (pp. 288-289)

MEXICO

The first published report in which detailed information was provided on changes registered by the Gesell scales during recovery from clinical malnutrition was presented, in Spanish, by Robles, Ramos Galván, and Cravioto (1959). It fully deserves to be placed in the category of pioneering studies.

The study involved eight children recovering from severe malnutrition in the ward of the Nutrition Service of the Children's Hospital of Mexico and was carried out in the framework of the activities of the Group for the Study of Malnutrition in Children. It represents a substantial technical advance over Paper 6 in the sense that detailed information is provided on the changes in four of the Gesell scales during the period of hospitalization, varying in individual children from 6 to 18 weeks.

The Gesell scales were administered for the first time as soon as any acute infection was brought under control and the acute disequilibrium of the electrolytes was corrected. Subsequently, the testing was repeated at intervals of two weeks.

The body weights of the children at admission were very low, varying from 44 to 75% of the reference weight for age. The initial means (calculated by the editor of this volume) of the Developmental Quotients, DQs, for the four scales are as follows:

Motor, 39.9 (10-75);
Adaptive, 37.1 (3-75);
Personal-social, 34.2 (7-75);
Language, 29.1 (5-65).

The values given in the parentheses refer to the ranges.

The interindividual variability of the DQs for the four scales is very large so that little confidence can be placed in the differences between the scales. In absolute terms, the performance level is affected most on the Language scale and least on the Motor scale. More important is the fact that all four areas of development were severely depressed.

The individual recovery data, obtained during repeated administrations of the Gesell scales, were presented in the forms of tables and graphs. Since the number of test periods varied widely (from three to eight) in different individuals and since, in addition, some data are missing, it is difficult to summarize the information effectively. By averaging the final values for each child and comparing the means with the values obtained for the first administration, one obtains a general notion of the degree of recovery that was attained prior to the child's release from the hospital. The mean DQs and the increase in the mean values for the four scales are as follows:

Motor, 60.4 (+21.5);
Adaptive, 68.5 (+25.7);
Personal-social, 62.8 (+28.6);
Language, 51.1 (+29.1).

It should be stressed that these values are averages of DQs obtained after widely different lengths of the period of hospitalization (and, thus, of treatment). However, when we examine the data for two of the patients for whom the data are available for the eighth testing, the picture is not radically different from that obtained by averaging the final scores of the individual children.

The 1959 paper just reviewed was designated as preliminary. It was followed by the study of a larger sample ($N = 20$) in which the same testing procedure and study design was used (Cravioto and Robles, 1965). Paper 8 graphically presents some of the results.

VENEZUELA

Barrera Moncada was a Venezuelan pediatrician interested in the physical growth of infants and in comprehensive study and preventive care of preschool children. These topics were examined in a sizable monograph published in 1954. As indicated by citations in the bibliography, the author was aware of the monograph on kwashiorkor by Trowell, Davies, and Dean (1954); of the report by Geber and Dean (Paper 7) on psychological changes accompanying kwashiorkor; and of the paper by Robles, Ramos Galván, and Cravioto (1959), in Spanish, entitled "Evaluation of the Behavior of Children with Advanced Malnutrition and Its Modifications during Recovery."

Barrera Moncada's work, reported in the 1963 monograph, was carried out from 1955 to 1957 in the *J. M. de los Rios* Children's Hospital and continued until 1962 at the University Hospital in Caracas, Venezuela. The psychological aspects of kwashiorkor are presented in Part 3 (pp. 43-82) of the book.

In a prior analysis of over 1,200 cases of multideficiency syndrome (kwashiorkor), treated in the Caracas Children's Hospital, the following physical symptoms were most prominent: growth retardation (present in 95% of the cases studied), edema (90%), skin changes (86%), and hair changes (73%). Psychological changes (*alteraciones del psiquismo*) were also noted with a very high frequency (86%).

In an earlier study (Zubillaga and Barrera Moncada, 1953, originally published in 1944), the psychological changes were described as involving deep apathy, immobility, and statuelike appearance. At times the child manifested uncontrollable irritability. Barrera Moncada was interested in the acute phase of the illness and the course of recovery. He made psychological studies on 60 infants with severe multideficiency syndrome, using two sets of criteria:

1. Special forms (cards) for the daily recording of systematic observations of different aspects of the child's behavior such as eating, mobility, emotional responses, or communications;
2. The Gesell scales, used to evaluate the infants' psychological development, in common with the Ugandan and the Mexican studies but on a substantially larger sample.

The author was trained in the use of the Gesell scales in the 1940s at Yale University's Clinic of Child Development, where the scales were developed. In Caracas the Gesell scales were administered during the acute phase of the illness (when possible) and during recovery, prior to the child's leaving the hospital. In six cases the tests were given semiannually for the next two years and, in four cases, up to about six years beyond hospitalization.

Four behavioral phases of illness and recovery were distinguished: (1)

intense apathy, (2) passive receptivity, (3) active receptivity, and (4) genuine recovery. A detailed description (Barrera Moncada, 1954, pp. 48-63), documented photographically, of the changes in the children's behavior constitutes a particularly valuable feature of the study. The author wondered what long-term effects a severe malnutrition in infancy might have on the communities of which the child would become a member as an adult (Barrera Moncada, 1963, p. 44).

REFERENCES

Barrera Moncada, G., 1954, *La Edad Prescolar: Ensayo sobre su Estudio Integral y Programa de Protección (Preschool Age: An Essay on a Comprehensive Study of the Child and Preventive Care)*, Imprenta Nacional, Caracas, 377p.

Barrera Moncada, G., 1963, *Estudios sobre Alteraciones del Crecimiento y del Dearrollo Psicológico del Síndrome Pluricarencial (Studies on the Alterations of Physical Growth and Psychological Development Associated with the Multi-Deficiency Syndrome)*, Editora Grafos, Caracas, 94p.

Cravioto, J., and B. Robles, 1965, Evolution of Adaptive and Motor Behavior during Rehabilitation from Kwashiorkor, *Am. J. Orthopsychiatry* **35:**449-464.

Geber, M., and R. F. A. Dean, 1955, Psychological Factors in the Etiology of Kwashiorkor, *World Health Organ. Bull.* **12:**471-475.

Robles, B., R. Ramos Galván, and J. Cravioto, 1959, Valoración de la Conducta del Nĩno con Desnutrición Avanzada y de sus Modificaciones durante la Recuperación (Assessment of the Behavior of Children in an Advanced Stage of Malnutrition and Its Modifications during Recovery), *Méd. Hosp. Infant. (Méx.) Ból.* **16:**317-341.

Scrimshaw, N. S., and J. E. Gordon, eds., 1968, *Malnutrition, Learning, and Behavior,* MIT Press, Cambridge, Mass., pp. 288-289.

Stoch, M., and P. M. Smythe, 1963, Does Undernutrition during Infancy Inhibit Brain Growth and Subsequent Intellectual Development?, *Arch. Dis. Child.* **38:**546-552.

Stoch, M., and P. M. Smythe, 1967, The Effect of Undernutrition during Infancy on Subsequent Brain Growth and Intellectual Development, *S. Afr. Med. J.* **41:**1027-1030.

Stoch, M., and P. M. Smythe, 1968, Undernutrition during Infancy, and Subsequent Brain Growth and Intellectual Development, in *Malnutrition, Learning, and Behavior,* N. S. Scrimshaw and J. G. Gordon, eds., MIT Press, Cambridge, Mass., pp. 278-288.

Stoch, M., and P. M. Smythe, 1976, 15-Year Developmental Study on Effects of Severe Undernutrition during Infancy on Subsequent Physical Growth and Intellectual Functioning, *Arch. Dis. Child.* **51:**327-336.

Stoch, M., P. M. Smythe, A. D. Moodie, and D. Bradshaw, 1982, Psychological Outcome and CT Findings after Gross Undernourishment during Infancy: A 20-year Development Study, *J. Dev. Med. Child Neurol.* **24:**419-436.

Trowell, H. C., J. N. P. Davies, and R. F. A. Dean, 1954, *Kwashiorkor,* Edward Arnold Publishing, London, 308p.

Zubillaga, A., and G. Barrera Moncada, 1953, Sindromes policarenciales en la infancia (Multiple-deficiency Syndromes in Infancy), *Archiv. Venezolanos Puericultura Pediatría* **16:**473-536. (Reprinted from *Memorias Primeras Jornadas Venezolanas Puericultura Pediatría* **4:**203-276, 1944.)

Part IV

Generalized Clinical Malnutrition: Rehabilitation

Papers 8 Through 11: Commentary

Paper 8 is the first communication in the English language on a study that examined in detail the course of behavioral recovery after severe (clinical), generalized (energy-protein) malnutrition, using biweekly administrations of the Gesell scales. A comprehensive account of the study was made two years later (Cravioto and Robles, 1965). The study was reported in Spanish by Robles, Ramos Galván, and Cravioto (1959).

Three age groups were studied, Group I, up to 6 months of age, $N = 6$; Group II, 15 to 29 months, $N = 9$; and Group III, 37 to 41 months, $N = 5$.

The length of the observation period and, consequently, the number of testing periods per child, varied widely. In order to combine the data, regression equations were calculated for each of the four scales (Psychomotor, Adaptive, Language, Social-personal) at each age level. The equations (see Table 3 in Paper 8) relate the developmental ages in months (Y) to days of treatment (X). A regression line was superimposed upon each set of graphs in Paper 8 portraying the developmental ages of individual children, attained in a particular area of behavior at successive testing sessions. In each graph the upper line refers to normal (theoretical) levels and rates of development.

For all age groups and for all Gesell scales, the observed (empirical) values were below the normal values. Figure 13 in Paper 8 clearly indicates that in their psychomotor development the children in the age group of 15 to 29 months were "catching up." Their developmental ages were coming closer to their chronological ages, and the normal and the calculated regression lines were convergent. By contrast, in the youngest group, below 6 months of age at the beginning of the treatment period, no true recovery could be demonstrated for either psychomotor development (Fig. 11 in Paper 8) or for adaptive behavior (Fig. 12 in Paper 8). Data reported elsewhere indicated that in Group II (15-29 months) the rate of recovery was highest for Adaptive development and lowest for the Language area.

Paper 9 was the first report of a follow-up (prospective) study on the effects of psycho-social stimulation ("rich environment and warm nurse-child relationship," p. 26), when added to medical care and diet therapy, on recovery from severe nutritional marasmus (wasting). At admission the children, born to Arab Lebanese families, ranged in age from 2.5 to 16 months. They were cared for in the Clinical Nutrition Unit of the American University of Beirut.

At the beginning of the study, the mean relative weight (actual weight expressed as percentage of the reference standard) was 53.0 for the children included in the stimulated group and 52.9 for the unstimulated group, indicating a severe weight deficit. The mean ages were also similar (32.9 and 30.0 weeks, respectively), and the differences between the mean general DQs were not statistically significant.

In the Beirut study, a Griffiths Mental Development Scale (not the Gesell scales, as in the earlier studies) was used. It yields a general DQ and DQs for five subscales.

Both groups showed substantial behavioral recovery in the course of the four months of rehabilitation during which the tests were administered at two-week intervals. In the stimulated group ($N = 17$) the general DQ rose from 51 to about 78; in the unstimulated group ($N = 13$), from 46 to about 67. Taking into account the data for all eight test sessions (Table 2, p. 28), the analysis of variance indicated that the stimulated group obtained higher general DQs, with the difference being significant at the .05 level.

The authors note (p. 30)—and the point deserves emphasis— that the children failed, by a substantial margin, to reach normal levels of behavioral functioning by the end of the fourth month of rehabilitation.

In a later paper (Yaktin, Kanawati, and Sabbagh, 1971) the authors reported that by the end of one year after the discharge of the children from the Nutrition Unit, no difference was found between the previously stimulated and the unstimulated groups in terms of the IQs obtained using the Stanford-Binet test of intelligence adapted for local use. Two years later (McLaren et al., 1973), the performance of the previously stimulated group actually dropped below that of the unstimulated comparison group—a change that the authors found difficult to interpret.

Paper 10 reports on an innovative response to the need for more ample, less expensive, and more effective facilities for the treatment of Chilean children suffering from severe malnutrition. This alternative solution—that is, alternative to admission to a hospital—was provided in the form of special centers. These centers were to be provided with a small, interdisciplinary professional staff and were to offer not only medical and nutritional care but also three other ingredients of therapy, namely, psychosensory stimulation, physical exercise, and affective stimulation provided by trained volunteers.

The study compared the effectiveness of the standard treatment in a pediatric hospital and a special center for the rehabilitation of severely malnourished children. The size of the two groups was substantial ($N = 80$ in each case), and the groups were matched in birth weight, body weight upon admission, and psychomotor DQ (56 for the hospital group, 55 for the center). At the end of the treatment period of four months, the DQs rose to 65 and 85, respectively, yielding a statistically highly significant mean difference between the two groups. In contrast to several other studies, the younger children (under six months of age) did better than those who were over six months of age at admission. Clearly, the effect of age is a complex and unresolved issue.

Paper 11 reports the results of a study, the design of which provided for two malnourished groups treated in a hospital: one malnourished group receiving standard hospital care and one malnourished group whose members participated daily in sessions of structured play during their stay in the hospital and weekly for six months after discharge. In addition, an adequately nourished group, admitted to the hospital for reasons other than malnutrition, served as a comparison group.

A brief report on the effects of stimulation was published in *The Lancet* as a letter to the editor (Grantham-McGregor et al., 1979), followed by a communication from Cravioto and Arieta (1979) and a reply (Grantham-McGregor et al., 1980). The incorporation of a nonmalnourished comparison group had been introduced earlier (Grantham-McGregor, Stewart, and Desai, 1978).

The stimulation program provided in the hospital proved to be effective. At discharge, the mean DQ based on the Griffiths test was 77 for the nonstimulated children recovering from severe malnutrition and 86 for the stimulated children. One month after discharge, the mean DQ values were 83 and 93 respectively. The comparison group, free of malnutrition, recovered rapidly and reached a near-normal level of performance (with a mean DQ of 96) in the second test, administered one week after admission to the hospital.

Grantham-McGregor (1984, p. 55) closed her review paper by noting that

> We need [additional] information on the type, site, and cost effectiveness of programmes, as well as the type, intensity, and duration of the curricula. Available data suggest that both educational and nutritional inputs are required over a long period of time and that, given adequate programmes, marked improvements can occur in the children.

REFERENCES

Cravioto, J., and R. Arieta, 1979, Stimulation and Mental Development of Malnourished Infants, *Lancet* **2:**899.

Cravioto, J., and B. Robles, 1965, Evolution of Adaptive and Motor Behavior during Rehabilitation from Kwashiorkor, *Am. J. Orthopsychiatry* **35:**449-464.

Grantham-McGregor, S., 1984, Rehabilitation Following Clinical Malnutrition, in *Malnutrition and Behavior: Critical Assessment of Key Issues,* J. Brožek and B. Schürch, eds., Nestlé Foundation Publication Series, vol. 4, Lausanne, Switzerland, pp. 531-554.

Grantham-McGregor, S., M. Stewart, and P. Desai, 1978, A New Look at the Assessment of Mental Development in Young Children Recovering from Severe Malnutrition, *J. Dev. Med. Child Neurol.* **20:**773-778.

Grantham-McGregor, S., M. Stewart, C. Powell, and N. W. Schofield, 1979, Effect of Stimulation on Mental Development of Malnourished Children, *Lancet* **2:**200-201.

Grantham-McGregor, S., M. E. Stewart, C. Powell, and N. W. Schofield, 1980, Stimulation and Mental Development of Malnourished Infants, *Lancet* **1:**89.

McLaren, D. S., U. S. Yaktin, A. A. Kanawati, S. Sabbagh, and Z. Kadi, 1973, The Subsequent Mental and Physical Development of Rehabilitated Marasmus Infants, *J. Ment. Defic. Res.* **17:**273-281.

Robles, B., R. Ramos Galván, and J. Cravioto, 1959, Valoración de la Conducta del Niño con Desnutrición Avanzada y de sus Modificaciones durante la Recuperación (Evaluation of the Behavior of Children with Advanced Malnutrition and the Modification of Behavior during Recovery), *Méd. Hosp. Infant. (Méx.) Ból.* **16:** 317-341.

Yaktin, U. S., A. A. Kanawati, and S. Sabbagh, 1971, Effect of Undernutrition in Early Life on Subsequent Behavioral Development, in *Proceedings of the 13th International Congress of Pediatrics (Vienna),* part 2, sect. 15, Vienna Medical Academy, p. 71.

8: THE INFLUENCE OF PROTEIN-CALORIE MALNUTRITION ON PSYCHOLOGICAL TEST BEHAVIOR

J. Cravioto and B. Robles

[*Editor's Note:* In the original, material precedes these excerpts. Figures 1 through 10 and Tables 1 and 2 are not included in these excerpts.]

4. THE MALNOURISHED CHILD

Gesell tests were administered to a group of 30 children suffering from severe kwashiorkor, just after the acute episode of infection or electrolyte disturbance had been corrected. All of them gave very low scores, but the different fields of behavior explored, motor, adaptative, language, and personal-social, were not equally affected. In general, language development showed the lowest score and motor response was the least retarded (Robles, Ramos-Galván and Cravioto, 1959).

The mental performance of these kwashiorkor cases was tested at two-week intervals during their stay in the hospital. As recovery took place, the difference between their chronological and mental ages, computed on the basis of their psychological behavior, diminished in all the children except in those less than six months of age on admittance to the hospital whose increment in mental age was equal to the number of months of treatment. In other words, in the less than 6 months-old group the initial deficit held constant throughout the observation period which in some cases was extended up to six and one-half months (Table 3, Figs. 11, 12, 13) (Cravioto, Robles and Ramos-Galván, 1962).

TABLE 3. *Regression equations for the relation between psychological test behaviour (Y) and days of successful treatment (X) in three groups of children recovering from severe protein-calorie malnutrition.*

Field of behaviour	Age group (months)		
	3–6	15–29	37–41
Motor	$2.18 + 0.03\,X$	$12\ \ +0.06\,X$	$14 + 0.10\,X$
Adaptative	$2.30 + 0.03\,X$	$12\ \ +0.08\,X$	$15 + 0.11\,X$
Language	$2.0\ \ +0.03\,X$	$9\ \ +0.05\,X$	$15 + 0.07\,X$
Social–personal	$2.11 + 0.03\,X$	$10.5 + 0.07\,X$	$16 + 0.11\,X$

Reprinted from pages 121-122, 123, 124, and 125 of *Mild-Moderate Forms of Protein-Calorie Malnutrition,* G. Blix, ed., Symposia of the Swedish Nutrition Foundation, vol. 1, Uppsala, Sweden, 1963; *Copyright © 1963 by the Swedish Nutrition Foundation.*

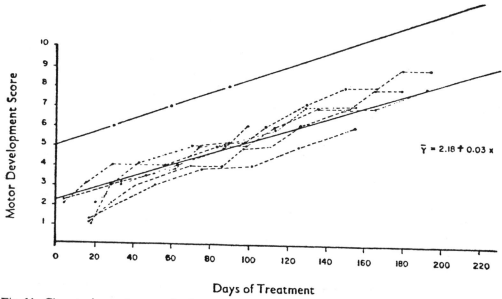

Fig. 11. Changes in psychmotor development of infants less than six months of age during recovery from severe protein-caloric malnutrition.

[*Editor's Note:* Material has been omitted at this point.]

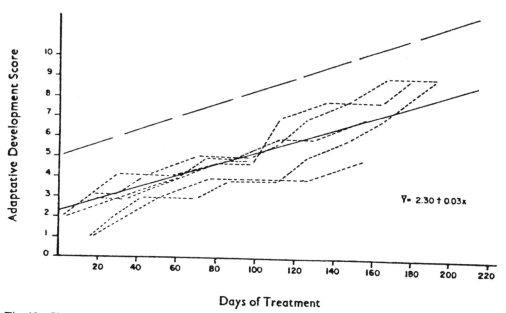

Fig. 12. Changes in adaptative development of infants less than six months of age during recovery from severe protein-caloric malnutrition.

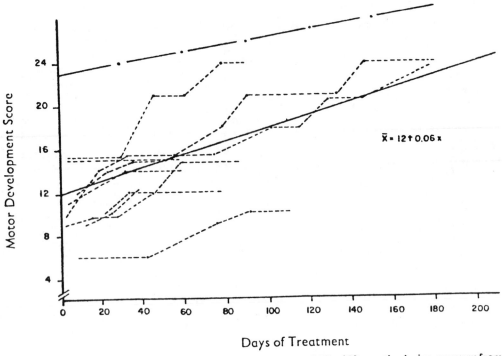

$\bar{X} = 12 + 0.06x$

Days of Treatment

Fig. 13. Changes in psychomotor development of children aged 15 to 29 months during recovery from severe protein-calorie malnutrition.

LITERATURE CITED

AUTRET, M. and BÉHAR, M. (1955) Síndrome Pluricarencial Infantil (Kwashiorkor) y su Prevención en América Central. Rome, Italy. FAO-Estudios sobre Nutrición No. 13.

CRAVIOTO, J. (1958) *Bol. Med. Hosp. Infantil Mex.* 15, 925.

— (1962) *Am. J. Clin. Nutrit.* 11, 484.

CRAVIOTO, J., ROBLES, B. and RAMOS-GALVÁN, R. (1962) *Bol. Med. Hosp. Infantil Mex.* (In press.)

— (1962) *Bol. Med. Hosp. Infantil Mex.* (In press.)

DAVIES, J. N. P. (1952) *Ann. Rev. Med.* 3, 99.

FALADÉ, S. (1955) Le développement psychomoteur du jeune africaine originaire du Senegal au cours de sa première année. R. Foulon, Paris.

GEBER, M. and DEAN, R. F. A (1957) *Pediatrics,* 20, 1055.

GESELL, A. and AMATRUDA, C. (1951) Developmental Diagnosis. Normal and Abnormal Child Development. Hoeber, New York.

KEYS. A., BROZEK, J., HENSCHEL. A., MICKELSON, O., and TAYLOR, H. L. (1950) The Biology of Human Starvation, v. II, p. 767. Univ. of Minnesota Press, Minneapolis, Minnesota, U.S.A.

KNOBLOCH, H. and PASAMANICK, B. (1960) *Pediatrics,* 26, 210.

KUBALA, A. L. and KATZ, M. M. (1960) *J. Genet. Psychol.,* 96, 343.

LLOPIS, DE PEINADO, L. (1956) *Bol. Med. Centro Materno Infantil,* 7, 73.

RAMOS-GALVÁN, R. and CRAVIOTO, J. (1958) *Bol. Med. Hosp. Infantil Mex.* 15, 855.

RAMOS-GALVÁN, R., CRAVIOTO, J. and VEGA, L. (1959) Operación Zacatepec VII. La prueba de Goodenough. Reporte preliminar del estudio de 850 dibujos realizados por escolares del poblado de Tlaltizapan. Mor. Proc. 9th Meeting. Mex. Soc. Pediat. Research. Cuernavaca, Mexico.

ROBLES, B. and CRAVIOTO, J. (1959) Operación Zacatepec. VI. Influencia de ciertos factores ecológicos sobre la conducta del niño en el medio rural Mexicano. Proc. 9th Meeting. Mex. Soc. Pediat. Research. Cuernavaca, México.

ROBLES, B., RAMOS-GALVÁN, R. and CRAVIOTO, J. (1959) *Bol. Med. Hosp. Infantil Mex.* 16, 317.

SÉNÉCAL, J. (1958) *Ann. N. Y. Acad. Sci.* 69, 916.

SCRIMSHAW, N. (1959) *In* Amino Acid and Protein Metabolism. Report of the 13th Ross. Conference on Pediatric Research. Fomon, S. J. ed. Columbus Ross Laboratories, p. 27.

WATERLOW, J. C. (1948) Med. Res. Council (Brit.) Spec. Rept. No. 263. Fatty Liver Disease in Infants in the British West Indies.

[*Editor's Note:* The Discussion has been omitted.]

9: THE BEHAVIOURAL DEVELOPMENT OF INFANTS RECOVERING FROM SEVERE MALNUTRITION

U. S. Yaktin and D. S. McLaren

The relationship between malnutrition in early life and behavioural development has been investigated in man and animals. The results suggest that malnutrition in early life retards both physical and mental growth, and has been shown to result in long lasting or even permanent retardation in the development of learning behaviour (Stoch and Smythe, 1963, 1967; Cowley and Griesel, 1963; Cravioto and Robles, 1963). The learning behavioural responses already established before the onset of malnutrition are depressed or abolished and the capacity to elaborate new ones is affected. As a result of nutritional rehabilitation the re-establishment of these responses is slow. Cravioto, Goana and Birch (1967) concluded from their results with an auditory-visual integration test applied to older children, that malnutrition in earlier life could impair the intersensory organization, thus contributing to inadequate learning and consequently causing these children to become potential school failures.

Most of the studies reported to date have suffered from methodological problems because of the many variables that have to be considered and controlled. The investigators have generally failed to study the children systematically during their malnourished state and during follow-up after nutritional recovery. In one study, cross-sectional comparison was made of primary school children who were living in a rural community of small farmers and were assumed to have been undernourished, with 'healthy' children in an urban community of middle and upper class parents (Cravioto, De Licardie and Birch, 1966). Cultural deprivation factors that affect behavioural development were not taken into account. Caldwell (1967) studying the development of two groups of children of middle and lower class background, found that a change in the environment of a young child from a deprived background can help to counteract the detrimental effect of the poor environment.

Other studies have measured the subsequent mental development of children who had suffered from kwashiorkor (Champakam, Srikantia and Gopalan, 1968) and marasmus (Botha-Antoun, Babayan and Harfouche, 1968) in early childhood. Sometimes children were selected because they showed poor physical growth and were assumed to have been previously malnourished (Cravioto, De Licardie and Birch 1966; Nutrition Reviews 1968). In these instances a clear picture of the child prior to his entry into the study was not provided. Frequently the age at which malnutrition manifested itself has not been taken into account. The work of Kugelmass, Poull and Samuel (1944) and Cravioto and Robles (1963, 1965) in man, and

Reprinted from *J. Ment. Defic. Res.* **14**:25-32 (1970); *Copyright © 1970 by Blackwell Scientific Publications Ltd.*

of Cowley and Griesel (1959) and Barnes and co-workers (1966 and 1967) in animals, have pointed out the importance of the period of life at which malnutrition starts. Cowley and Griesel (1959, 1963) showed that protein deficiency in the mother can cause measurable retardation in the learning behaviour, growth and development of young rats.

In children recovering from malnutrition the quality and duration of care may also be important factors. The crucial rôle played by maternal-infant interaction in influencing the rate and the degree of somatic and mental recovery has been stressed (Stoch and Smythe 1963; Cravioto, De Licardie and Birch 1966, and Nutrition Reviews 1968). Bowlby (1954), Dennis (1960), and Levine (1957, 1958) have all shown the adverse effect of lack of stimulation on mental, motor and emotional development. In marasmus, lack of emotional and physical stimulation could be expected to have this effect. Lack of curiosity and activity of the marasmic child has been noticed by a number of investigators. It has been suggested that these emotional changes may be partly due to malnutrition and partly to the sudden separation from the mother (Eichenwald and Crooke, 1969).

The present study has been designed to take into account as many variables as possible and it is therefore hoped that it will throw some new light on this very complex but obviously important subject.

MATERIAL AND METHODS

The experimental group consisted of thirty severely malnourished Arab children. They were admitted from a general hospital to our own Clinical Nutrition Unit in Beirut of ten paediatric beds. Their physical condition was one of acute and severe marasmus or wasting (McLaren, Pellett and Read, 1967). Only those in whom the malnutrition was primary were included. Marasmus secondary to genetic metabolic defects, chronic wasting diseases etc. was excluded from the study. The patients were between $2\frac{1}{2}$ and 16 months of age on admission and remained in the unit for at least 4 months. They all came from a low socio-economic class, with a family income of about 150 Lebanese pounds per month or less (about £20) and the majority of the fathers and almost all of the mothers were illiterate. On admission to the unit each child was cared for in one or other of two 5-bed wards throughout its entire stay. The two experimental groups thus produced were matched for age and sex and will be referred to hereafter as the stimulated and unstimulated groups respectively. The stimulated group was provided with a rich environment and a warm nurse-child relationship. They lived in a colourful 5-bed ward which was decorated with animal pictures, red patterned curtains and bright coloured linoleum on the floor. A variety of toys, baby chairs, a pram, a play pen, and music were provided for the children. The nursing staff spent part of their time playing with, singing to, and nursing these children. The unstimulated group were cared for in a room of the same size furnished as an ordinary small hospital ward. From the point of view of nursing and medical care the two groups were treated similarly. The high-protein, high-calorie cow's milk-based diet was similar for all patients and there was no significant difference in the mean intake of protein/kg body weight/day or of calories/kg body weight/day between the two groups.

During their stay in hospital the children were assessed every 2 weeks for 8 testing sessions on the 1955 revision of the Griffiths Mental Development Scale. This scale gives a general development quotient (D.Q.) made up of five mental functions : locomotor, personal-social, hearing and speech, eye and hand, and performance.

RESULTS AND DISCUSSION

In Table 1 are shown the composition of the groups and some findings at the beginning of the study. The differences between the stimulated and unstimulated groups in terms of age, weight and D.Q., are not significant. The severe degree of mental retardation in both groups is evident.

Table 1

The sample at the beginning of the study.

	Sex			Age in weeks		Mean	Mean*
Groups	M	F	Total	Mean	(Range)	D.Q.	Weight
Stimulated	11	6	17	32.9	11-72	51	53.0
Unstimulated	8	5	13	30.0	13-56	46	52.9
Total	19	11	30	31.6	11-72	49	53.0

*Expressed as percentage of the 50th percentile of the Boston standard.

An analysis of variance was carried out in order to study the effect of nutritional improvement on behavioural development (Table 2). This analysis requires equal numbers of subjects in each sub-group. A total of five subjects from each sub-group; stimulated male, stimulated female, unstimulated male, unstimulated female, were randomly selected for the analysis, making a total of twenty subjects. The factor of sex did not have any significant effect on performance.

The stimulated group obtained significantly higher scores than the unstimulated group ($p < 0.05$) (Table 2 and Fig. 1). The difference between test sessions within subjects was found to be significant ($p < 0.01$). The interaction between conditions and test sessions was not significant. This means that both experimental groups improved regardless of environmental conditions but the stimulated group did so to a significantly greater extent than the unstimulated group.

The Newman-Keuls procedure (Winer, 1962) was carried out to find out in which test sessions significant improvement occurred. Table 3 shows that improvement in mental growth occurred during the first three test sessions i.e. during the first five weeks that the child spent in hospital, although he kept on improving steadily throughout the four months. The correlations between D.Q. and weight and D.Q. and head circumference (expressed as per cent of expected value for age) at the initial and final examinations were tested by the Pearson product-moment

Table 2

Analysis of variance of sample throughout the study.

Source	M.S.	d.f.	F.	P.
Between Subjects	1718.7	19	1.22	N.S.
Sex (S)	1363	1	0.97	N.S.
Environmental conditions (C)	8366.5	1	5.9	<0.05
S × C	393.8	1	0.28	N.S.
Errors	1408.3	16		
Within Subjects	206.9	140	1.29	N.S.
Test sessions (T)	1428.5	7	8.9	<0.01
T × S	56.7	7	0.35	N.S.
T × C	53.3	7	0.33	N.S.
T × S × C	38.6	7	0.24	N.S.
Errors	160.1	112		
Total		159		

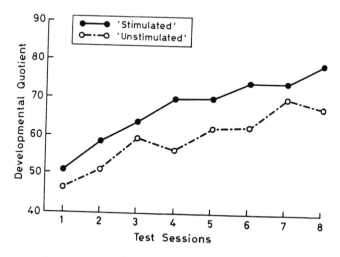

Fig. 1. Development quotient during recovery in stimulated and unstimulated groups.

Table 3

Newman-Keuls procedure between the 8 test sessions.

	1.	2.	3.	4.	5.	6.	7.	8.
1.	( )	N.S.	*	**	**	**	**	**
2.		( )	N.S.	*	**	**	**	**
3.			( )	N.S.	N.S.	N.S.	*	*
4.				( )	N.S.	N.S.	N.S.	N.S.
5.					( )	N.S.	N.S.	N.S.
6.						( )	N.S.	N.S.
7.							( )	N.S.
8.								( )

* $p < 0.05$

** $p < 0.01$

correlation. There was a significant correlation between D.Q. and weight ($r = 0.289$, $p < 0.01$) and a more highly significant correlation between D.Q. and head circumference ($r = 0.433$, $p < 0.01$). Thus, improvement in mental development takes place *pari passu* with physical recovery and is especially closely reflected by change in head circumference.

Analysis of the five mental functions separately revealed that improvement takes place in each of the areas studied during the recovery of the marasmic infant (Fig 2). The pattern of improvement can be seen to vary considerably for the different functions and is clearly related to the degree to which the physical condition of the child is involved. Over the entire period of recovery the greatest improvement occurred in the personal-social mental function. That this alone did not account for the results in Table 2 was shown by the fact that omitting the personal-social function did not alter materially the results of the analysis of variance. It is the area of hearing and speech which seems to be the most retarded in the long run (Cravioto and Robles, 1963).

On admission there was no significant difference between the stimulated and unstimulated groups in any of the five mental functions. However, throughout the entire period of recovery the stimulated group performed consistently better in each of these areas. These differences reached significant levels on six occasions [test session 4 : personal-social ($p < 0.05$), hearing and speech ($p < 0.05$), eye and hand ($p < 0.05$; test session 5 : eye and hand ($p < 0.05$); test session 6 : hearing and speech ($p < 0.01$), eye and hand ($p < 0.05$)].

That the Griffiths test is appropriate for Arab children is suggested by a mean D.Q. of about 100 obtained in preliminary testing of a group of healthy low income children.

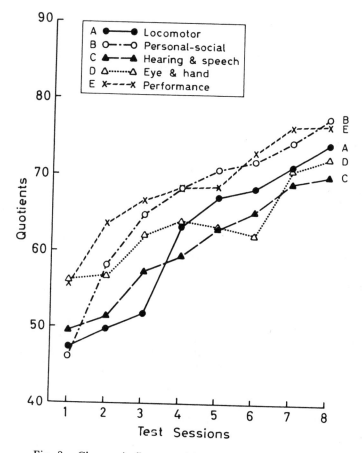

Fig. 2.   Changes in five mental functions during recovery.

SUMMARY

The relationship of nutritional status and behavioural development was investigated in two experimental groups of infants recovering from severe marasmus. Stimulated and unstimulated groups differed in their environmental conditions of hospitalisation during recovery but received the same medical and nutritional care. The degree of responsiveness to the environment was assessed eight times by the Griffiths Mental Development Scale applied every two weeks throughout the hospitalisation period of four months.

The results show that an improvement in the nutritional state is associated with marked and steady increase in Developmental Quotient (D.Q.). The stimulated group showed a significantly greater improvement than the non-stimulated group. Both groups, however, failed to attain the normal quotients by the end of rehabilitation. Thus while malnutrition during early childhood may cause profound retardation in development and behaviour, it is clear that the environmental stimulation, as well as the medical and nutritional care provided during hospitalization, is an important factor in the speed and degree of recovery. Significant correlations were found between D.Q. and weight (p<0.01) and D.Q. and head circumference (p<0.001).

The five mental functions composing the D.Q. improved to varying degrees, with hearing and speech most affected at discharge. The superior performance of the stimulated group involved each of the five mental functions.

ACKNOWLEDGEMENTS

This work was supported by U.S.P.H.S. Grant AM-05285 to the Institute of Nutrition Sciences, Columbia University, New York. The patients were under the medical care of Dr. Nadra Haddad Abu-Faisal and nursing care of Mrs. Mary Gheublikian and Miss Sirarpi Khalarian.

REFERENCES

BARNES, R. H., CUNNOLD, S. R., ZIMMERMANN, R. R., SIMMONS, H., McLOED, R. B. and KROOK, L. (1966) Influence of nutritional deprivations in early life on learning behavior of rats as measured by performance in a water maze. *J. Nutr.*, **89**, 399.

BARNES, R. H., MOORE, A. U., REID, I. M. and POND, W. G. (1967) Learning behavior following nutritional deprivations in early life. *J. Amer. diet. Ass.*, **51**, 34.

BOTHA-ANTOUN, E., BABAYAN, S. and HARFOUCHE, J. K. (1968) Intellectual development related to nutritional status. *J. trop. Pediat.* **14**, 112.

BOWLBY, J. (1954) *Maternal care and mental health.* W.H.O. monograph series, No. 2 Geneva: W.H.O.

CALDWELL, B. M. (1967) Descriptive evaluations of child development and of developmental settings. *Pediatrics*, **40**, 46.

CHAMPAKAM, S., SRIKANTIA, S. G. and GOPALAN, G. (1968) Kwashiorkor and mental development. *Amer. J. clin. Nutr.*, **21**, 844.

COWLEY, J. J. and GRIESEL, R. D. (1959) Some effects of a low protein diet on a first filial generation of white rats. *J. genet. Psychol.*, **95**, 187.

COWLEY, J. J. and GRIESEL, R. D. (1963) The development of second generation low protein rats. *J. genet. Psychol.*, **103**, 233.

CRAVIOTO, J. and ROBLES, B. (1965) Evolution of adaptive and motor behaviour during rehabilitation from kwashiorkor. *Amer. J. Orthop.*, **35**, 449.

CRAVIOTO, J., DE LICARDIE, E. R. and BIRCH, H. G. (1966) Nutrition, growth and neuro-integrative development: An experimental and ecologic study. *Pediatrics*, **38**, 319.

CRAVIOTO, J. and ROBLES, B. (1963) The influence of protein-calorie malnutrition on psychological test behavior. In *Mild-moderate forms of protein-calorie malnutrition.* Ed. G. Blix. pp. 115-126. Uppsala: Swedish Nutrition Foundation.

CRAVIOTO, J., GOANA, C. E. and BIRCH, H. G. (1967) Early malnutrition and auditory-visual integration in school age children. *J. spec. Educ.*, **2**, 75.

DENNIS, W. (1960) Causes of retardation among institutional children: Iran. *J. genet. Psychol.*, **96**, 47.

EICHENWALD, H. F. and FRY, P. C. (1969) Nutrition and learning. *Science*, **163**, 644.

KUGELMASS, I. N., POULL, L. E. and SAMUEL, E. L. (1944) Nutritional improvement of child mentality. *Amer. J. med. Sci.*, **208**, 631.

LEVINE, S. (1957) Infantile experience and consummatory behavior in adulthood. *J. Comp. Physiol. Psychol.*, **50**, 609.

LEVINE, S. (1958) Noxious stimulation in infant and adult rats and consummatory behavior. *J. comp physiol. Psychol.*, **51**, 230.

McLaren, D. S., Pellett, P. L. and Read, W. W. C. (1967) A simple scoring system for classifying the severe forms of protein-calorie malnutrition of early childhood. *Lancet* **1**, 533.

Nutrition Reviews (1968) Undernutrition in children and subsequent brain growth and intellectual development. **26**, 197.

Stoch, M. B. and Smythe, P. M. (1963) Does undernutrition during infancy inhibit brain growth and subsequent intellectual development? *Arch. Dis. Childh.*, **38**, 546.

Stoch, M. B. and Smythe, P. M. (1967) The effect of undernutrition during infancy on subsequent brain growth and intellectual development. *S. Afr. med. J.*, **41**, 1027.

Winer, B. J. (1962) *Statistical principles in experimental design.* New York: McGraw Hill.

10: RECOVERY OF SEVERELY MALNOURISHED INFANTS: EFFECTS OF EARLY SENSORY-AFFECTIVE STIMULATION

F. Monckeberg

During the last 10 years Chile has made notable progress in the fight against infant malnutrition. In 1967 as much as 68% of rural children under 6 years of age in a rural province had some degree of malnutrition (6). Currently the overall malnutrition rate for the country is 15.9%. A marked reduction has been observed in the indices of infant and preschool mortality. In 1967, the infant mortality was 94 per 1,000 live births; in 1976, 54. The corresponding figures for preschool child mortality were 4% and 2% (7).

There has also been a change in the clinical characteristics of malnutrition. In 1940, 65% of the children with severe malnutrition could be classified clinically as having kwashiorkor. Subsequently, kwashiorkor has almost disappeared and now nearly all of the children with severe malnutrition are typically marasmic.

Several factors account for the observed changes in the pattern of infant malnutrition. Perhaps the most important of these is the recent rapid increase in urban population, together with the formation of poverty belts around the large cities, and a marked reduction of breast feeding. In 1940, 78% of the women breast fed their children for 6 months or more. Currently, only 8% of the population does so (4). Under normal socio-economic conditions such a change in infant feeding practices would not produce malnutrition. However, under poverty conditions it can be a dominant factor.

The families with children that develop clinical malnutrition belong to very low socio-economic strata. The educational and cultural levels are low, and the sanitary conditions are unsatisfactory.

A recent national survey (1) has shown that approximately 7,000 infants suffer from severe marasmic malnutrition in Chile. Many of these children die from respiratory infections (bronchopneumonias) or intestinal infections (diarrheas, dehydration). This constitutes a serious problem for the health services; hospitalization is long and intra-hospital mortality is very high (30%).

In the pediatric hospitals of Chile there is a total of 1,500 beds for children under 2 years of age. A high percentage of these are occupied by children with severe malnutrition and

Reprinted from pages 121-130 of *Behavioral Effects of Energy and Protein Deficits,* J. Brožek, ed., NIH Publication Number 79-1906, U.S. Government Printing Office, Washington, D.C., 1979, 370p.

frequently, the children are released from a hospital without having fully recovered, due to a shortage of hospital beds.

Even though the children receive an adequate diet, the recuperation of the patients is slow. In our experience, 30% of the children who suffer from severe malnutrition require at least 6 months of hospitalization before they begin to show signs of a real recovery (8). A follow-up of survivors shows that important sequelae can be found up to 15 years later (8): reduced height, other anthropometric alterations, and low IQ. Ambulatory treatment presents even more problems, due to metabolic fragility (3) and high susceptibility to infections (8).

For these reasons, a modified treatment program was proposed which could deal effectively with severely malnourished children. A pilot program began with establishing a treatment center equipped with 30 beds. The objective was to offer a more efficient treatment, at lower cost than in the hospitals, while as the same time incorporating the family into the treatment process in order to prevent subsequent relapses.

Traditional hospital treatment has been focused exclusively on medical and nutritional aspects, without providing sensory stimulation and affection. The proposed treatment program not only considers nutritional factors but psychosensory stimulation and affection as well.

MATERIALS AND METHODS

Strict sanitary norms were followed in the Center, with special attention to hygienic preparation of nursing bottles. A multidisciplinary professional staff was assembled, consisting of a pediatrician (chief of staff), a psychologist, a nutritionist, a kinesiologist, a nurse, a social assistant, and nurses aides. In addition, a group of 80 volunteers were trained. The staff performed two types of activities: activities directed at the malnourished child in the Center, and activities directed at the family unit.

Activities involving the malnourished child included

1. Adequate feeding, utilizing cows' milk.

2. Early psychosensory stimulation, based on the concepts developed by Piaget and by Weikert; a regimen of 1/2 hour of stimulation was provided to each child two times a day (Figure 1c).

3. Physical exercise, given for 1/2 hour twice each day (Figure 1a).

4. Affective stimulation, provided by volunteers throughout the day (Figure 1b).

(a)

(b)

(c)

Figure 1. Activities directed at the malnourished child:
(a) physical exercise,
(b) affective stimulation, and
(c) early psychosensory stimulation.

Work with the family unit included

1. Integration of the mother into the treatment program.

2. Training of the mother in care and stimulation of the child.

3. Rehabilitation of the family through efforts to improve living and sanitary conditions, to provide educational programs and job training, to provide counseling in the area of family planning, to treat and prevent alcoholism and, in general, to enhance the self-esteem of the parents.

This program was begun in April 1975. The results presented here were obtained with the first 80 infants admitted for severe malnutrition. The infants remained in the Center for an average period of 140 days. They were subsequently followed in their homes for an additional period of 6 months or longer.

RESULTS

Clinical Progress in the Center

The recovery of the 80 infants with severe malnutrition, treated in accordance with the described program, is compared with that achieved by traditional treatment techniques in a Santiago hospital. Table 1 shows the age and weight at admission, birth weight, and psychomotor development quotient at admission. Group A refers to children admitted to a pediatric hospital; group B consists of children admitted to the Center. The characteristics of the two groups are low average birth weight, severe malnutrition which begins early in the first semester of life, and retardation of psychomotor development.

Table 1. Admission characteristics of severely malnourished infants.

GROUP	AGE AT ADMISSION days	WEIGHT AT ADMISSION kg	BIRTH WEIGHT kg	PSYCHOMOTOR DEVELOPMENT QUOTIENT
A. Admitted to pediatric hospital (n = 80)	154 ± 32	3.6 ± 1.2	2.8 ± 0.3	$56 \pm 8*$
B. Admitted to treatment center (n = 80)	148 ± 36	3.5 ± 1.3	2.7 ± 0.5	55 ± 16

*Average of 25 children.

The weight recovery during the 4 months of treatment is quite
different for the two groups. While at the end of 4 months weight
increased by only 10% in group A, in group B it increased by 65%.
This difference is highly significant (P < 0.001). Height recovery
in the two groups was also quite different. At the end of 4 months
there was still a deficit of 65% in group A; in group B the deficit
had been reduced to 25%. The differences were significant by the
50th day of treatment (Table 2, Figure 2).

Table 2. Clinical progress of severely malnourished infants during 4 months of treatment.

	On admission	50th day	100th day	150th day
% Weight deficit	A: 56 ± 8 B: 55 ± 5	A: 54 ± 13 B: 36 ± 8 p 0.001	A: 48 ± 12 B: 21 ± 6 p 0.001	A: 40 ± 13 B: 16 ± 3 p 0.001
% Height deficit	A: 76 ± 10 B: 82 ± 13	A: 70 ± 17 B: 50 ± 14 p 0.001	A: 65 ± 16 B: 32 ± 6 p 0.001	A: 65 ± 14 B: 21 ± 7 p 0.001
Psychomotor D.Q.	A: 56 ± 8 B: 55 ± 5	A: 60 ± 11 B: 71 ± 10 p 0.01	A: 64 ± 14 B: 80 ± 8 p 0.001	A: 65 ± 12 B: 85 ± 7 p 0.001

* A represents group of 80 treated at pediatric hospital.
 B represents group of 80 treated at treatment center.

The psychomotor quotient exhibits a similar pattern. While
for group A the quotient was 65 ±12 at 150 days of treatment, for
group B it was 85 ±7.

However, not all of the children who received the integral
treatment responded equally. In Table 3, the severely malnourished
children are divided into two subgroups according to the age
at which they were admitted to the Center, a division which to
some degree separates them according to the duration of malnutrition. Those who were less than 6 months old at admission recovered significantly more than those who were between 6 and 12
months at admission. A similar difference was observed in body
weight, with those who were more than 6 months of age at admission
gaining more weight than the younger subgroup.

Table 3. Age-related difference of the psychomotor development
quotient in severely malnourished infants on admission
and on discharge following treatment.

AGE GROUP	PSYCHOMOTOR DEVELOPMENT QUOTIENT	
	Admission	Discharge
Under 6 months old	0.58	0.82
Over 6 months old	0.55	0.67

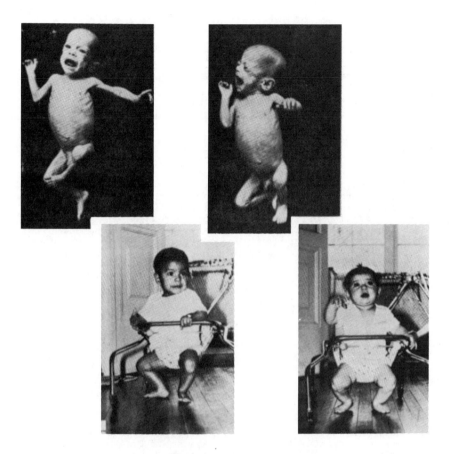

Figure 2. Malnourished infants before and after 120 days
of treatment.

     The frequency of intercurrent infections during treatment is
also very different, "infection" being defined as any clinical
syndrome which produced fever over 38° C for 4 or more days
(Table 4). The average for group A was 4.5 episodes during treatment, while for group B it was only 0.3 episodes. Mortality during treatment was also strikingly different: 29% in group A,
and 0% in group B.

Table 4. Incidence of intercurrent infections and mortality
          among severely malnourished infants.

GROUP	INFECTIONS (No. of episodes)	MORTALITY
A. Pediatric hospital	4.5 + .2	29%
B. Treatment center	0.3 + 0.6	0%

Development after Discharge from the Center
      After discharge, the children in group B were seen regularly
in their homes where the care and stimulation provided by the mother was monitored. The children in group A were not followed up.
Data on psychomotor development quotient, weight, and height at
250 days after discharge are given in Table 5. Weight continued
to increase satisfactorily. Height also increased but the deficit of height for age remained stationary at 20%. Psychomotor
performance also progressed with age but did not return any closer
to normal levels. Figure 3 contains pictures of an infant before
treatment, after 120 days of treatment, and 6 months later at
home.

Figure 5. Mean values of weight, height, and psychomotor
           development quotient (DQ) in 80 infants recovered
           from severe malnutrition at time of discharge
           from center and 250 days later.

	ON DISCHARGE	250 DAYS LATER
% Weight deficit for age	16%	8%
% Height deficit for age	25%	20%
Psychomotor DQ	81	81

DISCUSSION

      Serious malnutrition is difficult to treat in small infants.
In practice, many children die within hospitals or afterwards in
their homes. This study tested a new system of treatment, with
surprisingly favorable results. Two factors appear to have been
essential in achieving these results: sensory stimulation and
affection, and an environment free of pathogenic microorganisms.

      A standard pediatric hospital is not an ideal place for the
treatment of malnourished infants. In the first place, the hospital regimen fails to provide adequate psychological stimulation
and affection. Furthermore, the hospital ward in general is highly
contaminated, which explains the high frequency of intra-hospital
infections among seriously malnourished children. Both factors
can be controlled in specialized centers where volunteer personnel
provide sensory stimulation and affection, and hygienic conditions
are maintained.

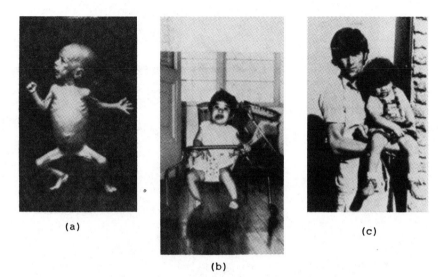

(a)

(b)

(c)

Figure 3.   Severely malnourished infant (a) before and (b)
            after 120 days of treatment. (c) Infant 6 months
            later at home.

Such centers are justified not only because of the effectiveness of the treatment but also on account of differences in cost.
The pediatric hospital bed costs $27(U.S.) per day while in a 60-
bed center this cost was reduced to about $5.50(U.S.) per bed day.

Early psychosensory and affective stimulation appears beneficial, not only in terms of psychomotor recuperation but also with
reference to physical recovery. Stimulation may promote an earlier initiation of the recovery processes. Psychomotor development
progresses at a normal rate but the development quotient (Table 5)
remains stationary during the period of observation. There is some
recovery in physical growth but neither height nor weight reaches
normal levels.

Initial data from nitrogen balance studies indicate a large
difference in nitrogen retention when psychosensory stimulation
is provided simultaneously with feeding. The malnourished infants who received only feeding absorbed nitrogen well but more
of it was eliminated in the urine.(Table 6). This fact suggests
the possibility of   hypothalamic regulation restarting growth
and development (3).

Table 6. Comparison of nitrogen balance in 18 marasmic children
on admission and after 30 days of treatment.

NITROGEN SOURCE	GROUP A* (mg/kg/day)		GROUP B* (mg/kg/day)	
	ADMISSION	30 DAYS LATER	ADMISSION	30 DAYS LATER
INGESTED FOOD	842 + 36	850 + 29	880 + 40	910 + 40
URINE	648 + 41	620 + 38	635 + 42	520 + 46
FECES	78 + 18	73 + 22	96 + 33	78 + 28
% RETENTION	31.8%	18.5%	17.0%	34.3%

*Pediatric hospital admissions (10)
**Treatment center admissions (8)

The degree of recovery appears to be related inversely to
the duration of the malnutrition. Specifically, in those cases
where treatment is begun after the first 6 months of life, recovery is significantly less than in cases where rehabilitation
begins before 6 months of life.

The results obtained in this pilot project have led to an
extension of the program to a national level. In order to carry
out the national program, a non-profit foundation to implement
the centers and to direct their operation and motivate the communities has been formed. During 1977, 18 centers were established
and 26 were to be completed by the end of the year, with a capacity of nearly 1,000 beds; the program for 1978 envisions 16
more centers. To date, over 300 infants have been discharged
from the centers. Results of their treatment have been very similar to those obtained in the pilot project (2).

REFERENCES

1. INUAL: El Impacto de los Desnutridos Graves en el Servicio
    Nacional de Salud y Estudio de una Solución Alternativa.
    Report for CONPAN, Santiago, Chile, 1975.

2. Monckeberg, R. Effect of early marasmic malnutrition on
    subsequent psychological development. In N. S. Scrimshaw
    and J. E. Gordon, Eds., Malnutrition, Learning and Behavior.
    Cambridge, Mass.: MIT Press, pp. 269-278, 1967.

3. Monckeberg, F. Adaptation to caloric and protein restriction
    in infants. In R. A. McCance and E. M. Widdowson, Eds.,
    Caloric Deficiencies and Protein Deficiencies. London: J.
    A. Churchill, pp. 91-108, 1968.

4. Monckeberg, F. Shortened breast feeding: A health risk
    factor in developing countries. Rev. Nutrición, Educación y
    Salud, CONPAN, Santiago, Chile, p. 25, 1976.

5. Monckeberg, F., Donoso, G., Oxman, S., Pak, N. and Meneghello, J. Human growth hormone in infant malnutrition. Pediatrics, 31:58-64, 1963.

6. Monckeberg, F., Donoso, G., Valiente, S., Arteaga, A., Maccioni, A., Merchak, N., Oxman, S. and Lacassie, Y. Estudio del estado nutritivo de las condiciones de vida de la población infantil de la provincia de Curicó, Rev. Chil. Ped., 30:491, 1967.

7. National Council for Food and Nutrition. Food and Nutrition Policy in Chile. Santiago, Chile: Editorial Gabriela Mistral, 1976.

8. Schlesinger, L., Ohlbaum, A., Grez, I. and Stekel, A. Cell-mediated immune studies in marasmic children from Chile: Delayed hypersensitivity, lymphocyte transformation and interperon production. In R. M. Suskind, Ed., Malnutrition and the Immune Response. New York: Raven Press, pp. 91-98, 1977.

11: EFFECT OF LONG-TERM PSYCHOSOCIAL STIMULATION ON MENTAL DEVELOPMENT OF SEVERELY MALNOURISHED CHILDREN

S. Grantham-McGregor, M. E. Stewart,
and W. N. Schofield

Reprinted from *Lancet* **2:**785-789 (1980); *Copyright © 1980 by The Lancet Ltd.*

Summary   The effect of adding psychosocial stimulation to the treatment of severely malnourished children was studied by comparing the developmental levels (DQs) of the children with those of two other groups of children—an adequately nourished group with diseases other than malnutrition and a second malnourished group who received standard hospital care only. The intervention children underwent structured play sessions daily in hospital and weekly for 6 months after discharge; mothers were also shown how to play with them. The non-intervention malnourished group showed a marked deficit in DQ compared with the adequately nourished group throughout the study period. The intervention group made significant improvements in DQ in hospital and continued to do so after discharge. By 6 months they were significantly ahead of the non-intervention malnourished group, and were no longer significantly behind the adequately nourished group.

INTRODUCTION

CHILDREN who have had severe protein-energy malnutrition (PEM) in early childhood usually retain a marked deficit in mental development several years later.[1-4] Although there is much uncertainty about the precise role of PEM in the ætiology of this deficit,[5,6] impaired mental development is perhaps the most serious long-term handicap associated with early childhood malnutrition. Prospective studies of children from communities where the general level of nutrition is poor and PEM is endemic—for example, in Guatemala[7] and in Mexico[8] —showed that nutritional supplements given to pregnant women and subsequently to their offspring were associated with improved levels of mental functioning in the children. Little work has been done on therapy for children who have already had severe PEM.

Children in Lebanon[9] and Mexico[10] who underwent programmes of increased stimulation while recovering from severe PEM in hospital showed significant improvement in developmental levels (DQ) by the time they left hospital, compared with other malnourished children not exposed to such programmes. The programmes were not continued after discharge, and 1 year later the benefits gained had been lost;[11] the advantages gained from "stimulation during rehabilitation were evanescent,"[12] but longer term intervention with maternal education and home visiting might be more successful.[13] The intelligence scores of several malnourished young Korean children who were subsequently adopted by middle class North American families reached or exceeded mean values of North American children several years later.[14] These adopted children were presumably exposed to vast improvements in most aspects of their environments including health, nutrition, and stimulation, improvements that would probably be unavailable to many children in third world countries.

We have shown that the mental development of children recovering from severe PEM in hospital was severely delayed compared with that of adequately nourished children; this impairment was still present six months after discharge.[15,16] We also observed a lack of stimulation in the hospital that was unlikely to facilitate improvement in mental development.[17] Here we report the early results of a low-cost, long-term intervention programme of increased stimulation for another group of children recovering from severe PEM.

SUBJECTS AND METHODS

The three groups of children in the study had been admitted to the pædiatric medical wards of the University Hospital of the West Indies. The first comprised 18 children with severe malnutrition according to the Wellcome classification[18] (the non-intervention group), and the second comprised 15 adequately nourished children with diseases other than malnutrition (the comparison group); both groups were admitted between June, 1975, and July, 1976. 1 child in the comparison group was lost and was dropped from the analysis. Both these groups received standard care that was being offered by the hospital. A third group, admitted to the hospital between September, 1976, and November, 1977, comprised 21 severely malnourished[18] children who received hospital care similar to that of the other malnourished group, but who also participated in an intervention programme of increased stimulation (the intervention group).

Children were selected for the study on admission to hospital according to the following criteria—all were singletons aged 6-24 months; none had a birth-weight below 2.3 kg, had a physical handicap, or had had any disease other than malnutrition which might have affected their mental development. All the children lived in or around Kingston, in houses below pre-defined standards of amenities and overcrowding, and no mother had completed secondary education. After selection of the children, their mothers' (or guardians') verbal IQ was tested by the Peabody Picture Vocabulary Test (PPVT)[19] when they visited hospital. After discharge children were visited, and the standard of housing was rated on an eight-point scale.[20]

INTERVENTION

The intervention programme was designed to be inexpensive so that it could be repeated on a larger scale. Toys were made from used household materials, and personnel had limited training. The programme consisted of structured play with the children 1h a day for 6 days each week while they were in hospital. A nurse or a community health aide (CHA, a Jamaican government-employed para-professional who had completed primary education and had a short course in health care) worked directly with the children, and whenever the mother visited she was included in the play sessions. After discharge a nurse or CHA visited the child at home for an hour every week, and the mother was shown how to play with the children in ways which encouraged optimum development in her child.

The cognitively oriented curriculum designed for play with the children was based largely on Piagetian theory and included modified items from the Infant Psychological Development Scale[21] and from intervention programmes for disadvantaged children in the United States.[22,23]

MEASUREMENTS

Development was assessed throughout the study by the Griffiths Mental Development Scales for Babies and Young Children.[24-26] We used four subscales of the test (locomotor, hearing and speech, eye and hand coordination, and performance). The assessments were done by either S.G.-McG. or M.E.S. Test-retest correlations between these two testers over a 5 month period on 20 children were high ($r = 0.92$). All the children were first assessed 48-72h after admission to hospital unless they were considered unfit to be tested by pre-defined criteria such as dyspnœa and fever.[15] As soon as these conditions were remedied the children were tested. They were retested 1 week later, then again when they were ready to go home, providing that this was at least 1 week after the second test. At 1 and 6 months after discharge, the children were brought back to the hospital and tested in the presence of their mothers. All children had all of the scheduled tests, except 8 comparison children who left hospital after the second test session, which consequently provides their discharge data.

The interval between tests varied in individual children because of different durations of hospital stay, inability of working mothers to accompany their children to hospital for tests, temporary absence of families from Kingston, or illness of children at the time of a scheduled test.

Head circumferences, lengths, and weights of the children were measured twice weekly in hospital and then at the time of developmental assessments.

ANALYSIS

The main hypotheses of the experiment were tested in a series of repeated-measures analyses of covariance. These had one grouping factor with three levels (comparison, intervention, and non-intervention) and one trial factor with four levels (test on admission, discharge, and 1 and 6 months after discharge).

For this report there were two covariates. The first was age on admission to hospital. The second had four levels varying across the trials; these were the difference in days between admission and each test point for each child. The objective here was to remove variance due to differences in the spacing of the test sessions to see if any effect attributable to the intervention held after these were taken into account. The interval betweeen admission to hospital and first test was an indicator of severity of illness, and, in addition to use of the present covariate, separate analyses were made to confirm that this, and length of stay in hospital, did not affect the results.

The model for the analyses followed Winer[27] as developed for computer solution.[28] This model assumes that the regression coefficients for the separate groups in the analysis of covariance do not differ significantly and this was confirmed. All individual comparisons were made by an appropriate post-analysis of covariance method.[29]

RESULTS

The two malnourished groups were very similar in standard of housing and maternal verbal IQ (PPVT) (table I). The comparison group was better in both these indices. All groups were similar in age at first test.

The malnourished children (intervention and non-intervention) had marasmus (weights below 60% of expected weight for age, without œdema), marasmic-kwashiorkor (weights below 60% of expected weight for age, with œdema), or kwashiorkor (weights below 80% of expected weight for age, with œdema). All the comparison children had weights above 80% of the expected weight for age and did not have œdema.

Table II shows anthropometric data for the three groups, expressed as percentages of international standards for age and sex.[30] The degree of stunting is usually accepted as a good indication of the duration of malnutrition, whereas deficit in weight for height is a measure of wasting and an indication of current malnutrition.[31] Both malnourished groups were very similar in the degree of both stunting and wasting. The intervention group had more children with œdema.

Table III gives the unadjusted mean DQ scores of the three groups at each session. The analysis of covariance for DQ scores (see table VA) showed a highly significant main effect on group, and the age on admission to hospital covariate was highly significant. The second covariate did not make a significant contribution to this effect. The main effect on test session was significant, and so was the interaction between test session and group. The overall pattern of the mean scores was examined. For all groups there was a considerable improvement between admission and discharge but not thereafter, and this quadratic trend was highly significant. However, there was also a significant linear trend in the mean scores due largely to the intervention group which alone continued to improve at every test point.

Individual comparisons were made and on admission to hospital there was no significant difference in DQs between

TABLE I—DESCRIPTION OF THE THREE GROUPS

	Malnourished groups		Comparison group
	Non-intervened (n = 18)	Intervened (n = 21)	(n = 14)
Males	7	13	9
Females	11	8	5
Age at 1st test (MO)	12·9± 4·5	12·7± 3·0	12·7± 4·8
Housing index	6·4± 1·7	6·5± 1·6	8·6± 1·3
Mother's PPVT (raw score)	60·0±14·6	60·9±14·4	68·1±10·6

Findings are given as mean ± SD

TABLE II—NUTRITIONAL STATUS TO HOSPITAL

Variable	Malnourished group		Comparison group
	Non-intervened (n = 18)	Intervened (n = 21)	(n = 14)
Nos. with œdema	4	10	0
On admission: % expected weight for age	55·1±8·1	57·9±10·1	88·7±8·2
% expected height for age	88·0±5·1	88·7± 4·6	101·6±3·5
% expected head circ. for age	91·3±3·5	91·8± 3·8	99·5±3·7
% expected weight for height	73·2±9·9	74·8± 8·5	86·6±8·9

Findings given as mean ± SD

TABLE III—MEAN DEVELOPMENT QUOTIENTS ON GRIFFITHS TEST

Time of test	Malnourished		Comparison
	Non-intervention (n = 18)	Intervention (n = 21)	(n = 14)
Admission to hospital	61±19·6	64±20·3	86±15·4
1 week later*	72±14·9	76±14·5	96±15·9†
At discharge	77±12·0	86±12·7	98±14.8
1 mo after discharge	83±11·7	93±12·7	107±11·4
6 mo after discharge	82±12·1	96±11·3	105±11·2

DQ given as mean ± SD
* not included in present analyses
† 100±14.1 if 8 subjects for whom this forms discharge data are excluded

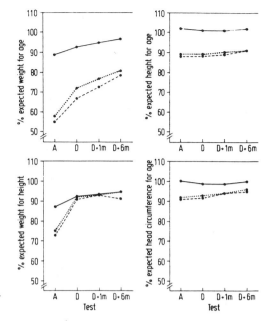

Anthropometric measurements expressed as a percent of expected value for age and sex,

Unbroken line = comparison group;
Dotted line = malnourished intervention group;
Broken line = malnourished non-intervention group.

A = admission;
D = discharge.

the intervention and non-intervention groups, but both groups were significantly behind the comparison subjects ($p<0.001$, see table VB). By discharge all three groups had improved, the greatest improvement being made by the intervention children who by then were significantly ahead of the non-intervention children ($p<0.05$) and were behind, but not significantly behind, the comparisons ($p<0.01$). The non-intervention children remained significantly behind the comparison group ($p<0.0005$). This position was largely maintained at 1 month after discharge since each group improved by approximately the same amount. By 6 months after discharge the adjusted mean for the intervention group did not differ significantly from that of the comparison group ($p<0.1$), but it did differ significantly from the non-intervention group ($p<0.001$), who remained significantly behind the comparisons ($p<0.001$).

The mean scores for the four subscales are shown in table IV. The results of the analyses of covariance made on the four subscales of the Griffiths test were very similar to those made on the full scale. For each of them, group and test session, and the fixed-age covariate were all highly significant

($p<0.001$). Differences for the group and test session interaction were significant for the hearing and speech scale ($p<0.05$); hand and eye coordination ($p<0.05$); and performance ($p<0.05$). It was not significant for the locomotor

TABLE IV—DEVELOPMENTAL QUOTIENTS IN EACH SUBSCALE OF THE GRIFFITHS TEST

Subscale	Time of Test	Malnourished		Comparison
		Non-intervention	Intervention	
Locomotor	Admission	72·2±14·6	71·9±21·3	102·0±23·3
	Discharge	82·5±15·4	84·9±19·6	110·6±20·2
	1 mo after discharge	91·2±15·2	92·9±18·9	119·1±13·8
	6 mo after discharge	89·8±15·6	97·5±17·4	119·5±20·5
Hearing & speech	Admission	39·1±23·9	44·0±21·3	47·3±17·8
	Discharge	57·7±16·7	71·3±14·2	67·5±22·6
	1 mo after discharge	69·9±13·6	92·7±15·3	94·1±10·9
	6 mo after discharge	74·1±13·5	96·5±17·6	93·2± 8·2
Hand & eye	Admission	64·6±25·5	68·6±22·2	93·9±17·1
	Discharge	80·3±14·4	95·2±13·2	103·1±14·2
	1 mo after discharge	83·6±11·6	96·5±14·1	106·2±16·2
	6 mo after discharge	85·0±14·6	100·5±10·4	104·5±13·0
Performance	Admission	67·0±26·5	70·1±29·5	99·9±19·3
	Discharge	87·4±12·0	94·8±15·1	110·4±12·6
	1 mo after discharge	85·9±16·6	90·6±14·2	106·6± 9·7
	6 mo after discharge	78·2±14·2	90·5±10·6	101·6±11·0

DQ given as mean ± SD

TABLE V—SUMMARY OF STATISTICAL FINDINGS

(A) Analysis of covariance, DQs	F	df	p
Group effect	17·03	2, 48	<0.001
Covariate 1	29·30	2, 48	<0.001
Covariate 2	0·16	2, 48	NS
Test session	50·59	3, 149	<0.001
Test session x group	2·98	6, 149	<0.01
Quadratic trend	97·93	2, 49	<0.001
Linear trend	5·12	2, 49	<0.01
(B) Post-analysis of covariance comparisons, DQs	t	df	p
I vs C (admission)	4·71	54	<0.0001
Non-I vs C (admission)	4·78	54	<0.0001
I vs non-I (discharge)	2·24	54	<0.05
I vs C (discharge)	1·82	54	NS
Non-I vs C (discharge)	3·95	54	<0.001
I vs non-I (6 mo)	4·43	54	<0.0001
I vs C (6 mo)	1·85	54	NS
Non-I vs C (6 mo)	5·83	54	<0.0001
(C) Anlaysis of covariance, anthropometry*	F	df	p
Group effect (weight)	25·07	2, 48	<0.001
Group effect (height)	32.72	2, 48	<0.001
Group effect (head)	13·08	2, 48	<0.001
Test session (weight)	39·22	3, 149	<0.001
Test session (height)	2·07	3, 149	NS
Test session (head)	4·99	3, 149	<0.001
Group x test (weight)	6·81	6, 149	<0.001
Group x test (height)	2·14	6, 149	NS
Group x test (head)	7·55	6, 149	<0.001

I = intervention group, non-I = non-intervention group, and C = comparison group.
* weight = % expected weight for age
  height = % expected height for age
  head = % expected head circumference for age

scale. The changing covariate age to test session made a highly significant contribution to the test session effect for the locomotor scale (p<0.005) and to the cubic components of performance (p<0.01), but not to the other subscales. This covariate removed among other things variation related to length of stay in hospital, which might affect aspects of development measured by the performance and locomotor subscales.

By 6 months the intervention and comparison groups had more or less the same scores for hearing and speech and also for hand and eye coordination, whereas the non-intervention children lagged significantly behind both of these groups (p<0.01). The intervention children did not do so well on the performance subscale, but by 6 months after discharge they had improved, although they remained significantly behind the comparisons (p<0.05); however, they had moved significantly ahead of the non-intervention group (p<0.0005). The intervention children, considered as a group, remained well behind the comparison children on the locomotor subscale (p<0.01). They finished ahead of the non-intervention group, but not significantly, since both malnourished groups made similar gains.

The accompanying figure shows the anthropometric data at each test session for the three groups. Analysis of covariance (see table VC) showed a significant group effect for % expected weight for age; % expected height for age; and % expected head circumference for age. The main test session effect was significant for % expected weight for age and for % expected head circumference for age, but not for % height for age.

The interaction between group and test session was significant for % weight for age and for % head circumference for age. It was close to the 5% level for % height for age.

For the indicator of wasting (% expected weight for height) the malnourished children caught up completely with the controls as can be seen by the highly significant interaction between group and test session and the lack of a significant main effect for group. It was also found that all groups improved significantly across the test sessions (p<0.001).

The discharge testing was the third in hospital for all subjects in both malnourished had groups, but for only 6 comparison children since the remaining 8 were discharged after the second test. Further analyses established that although there was some differences between these two components of the comparison group these in no way affected the findings reported.

DISCUSSION

The main finding is that the intervention group began catching up with the comparison group in DQs while in hospital and continued to do so after discharge. 6 months after discharge they were no longer significantly behind the comparisons and were significantly ahead of the non-intervention group. This improvement in mental development in the intervention group in hospital is in keeping with the findings in Mexico[10] and Lebanon.[9]

We had initially doubted whether the malnourished children would respond to a home visiting intervention programme because the success of a home visiting programme depends upon the cooperation of the mothers or guardians. The malnourished group came from extremely poor families and had mothers with very low verbal IQ scores. Moreover, other investigators in Jamaica had described mothers of children with severe PEM as having chronically disrupted lives and resenting their children.[32] The continued improvement of the children's DQ after their return home suggests that despite their many handicaps these mothers were still able to help improve the mental development of their children. It seems unlikely that the weekly play sessions with child, mother, and visiting nurse or community health aide would be sufficient to produce the DQ gains recorded, although this remains a possibility.

The observation that improvement was best in language development and hand and eye coordination, but less so in performance, and absent in locomotor development may reflect a bias in the project's curriculum in which particular emphasis was put on improving verbal communication between mothers and children in a similar fashion to that described by Levenstein in the United States.[33] Also, after severe PEM certain areas of development may be more resistant to improvement by this type of intervention than others.

Mora[34] in Bogota, Colombia, reported that nutritional supplementation in deprived, undernourished children had more benefit on locomotor development than increased stimulation, and, conversely, stimulation had a greater effect on language development than locomotor development. We could not provide nutritional supplementation, but nutritional advice was given to both malnourished groups. It can be seen that both malnourished groups remained stunted, with small head circumferences, and were lighter than comparison children (see accompanying figure). The failure to catch up in locomotor development may have been related to the failure to catch up nutritionally.

Continued intervention may result in further improvements. There were no signs of the DQ scores of the intervention group levelling off, and a preliminary look at the data after another 6 months' intervention shows the improvement in development continues.[35]

McKay and colleagues[36] in a carefully conducted study in Cali, Colombia, showed that the longer the intervention the greater the benefits. However, the children in their study entered the programme at a later age than those in ours, and, although they were undernourished, had not necessarily had severe PEM. We intend to continue the Jamaican intervention project for a total of three years. An important question is whether the gains will be maintained after intervention is stopped.

There are many theories on the ætiology of the mental deficit following severe PEM.[6] The improvement shown by these children in no way excludes the possibility that they may have brain damage. What happens to them when intervention stops should add some further insight into the ætiology.

We thank Mrs E. Buchanan, Mrs C. James, Ms I. Halstead and Ms M. Johansen; the Ministry of Health, Jamaica for providing Community Health Aides; and the late Professor J. Tizard of the Thomas Coram Research Unit, University of London, for advice and encouragement.

The project was funded by the Medical Research Council of the U.K.

REFERENCES

1. Stoch MB, Smythe PM. 15-year developmental study on effects of severe undernutrition during infancy on subsequent physical growth and intellectual functioning. *Arch Dis Childh* 1976; **51**: 327-36.
2. Hertzig ME, Birch HG, Richardson SA, Tizard J. Intellectual levels of school children severely malnourished during the first two years of life. *Pediatrics* 1972; **49**: 814-24.
3. Hoorweg J. Stanfield JP. The effects of protein energy malnutrition in early childhood on intellectual and motor abilities in later childhood and adolescence. *Devl Med Child Neurol* 1976; **18**: 330-50.
4. Pollitt E. Early childhood intervention programs in Latin America: a selective review. Unpublished report presented to the Office of Latin America and the Caribbean, International Division, The Ford Foundation. January 1979.
5. Richardson SA. The relation of severe malnutrition in infancy to the intelligence of school children with differing life histories. *Pediat Res* 1976; **10**: 57-61.
6. Lloyd-Still JD. Clinical studies on the effects of malnutrition during infancy on subsequent physical and intellectual development. In: Lloyd-Still JD, ed. Malnutrition and intellectual development. Lancaster: MTP Press, 1976: 103-59.
7. Klein RE, Irwin M, Townsend JW, et al. The effects of food supplementation on cognitive development and behavior among rural Guatemalan children. Paper presented to the International Conference on Behavioral Effects of Energy and Proteins Deficits, Washington D.C., November 30-December 2, 1977.
8. Chavez A, Martinez C, Yaschine T. Nutrition, behavioral development and mother-child interaction in young rural children. *Fed Proc* 1975; **34**: 1574-82.
9. Yaktin US, McLaren DS. The behavioural development of infants recovering from severe malnutrition. *J Ment Defic Res* 1970; **14**: 25-32.
10. Cravioto J. Not by bread alone: effect of early malnutrition and stimuli deprivation on mental development. In: Ghai OP, ed. Perspectives in pediatrics. New Delhi: Interprint, 1977: 87-104.
11. McLaren DS, Yaktin US, Kanawati AA, Sabbagh S, Kadi Z. The subsequent mental and physical development of rehabilitated marasmic infants. *J Ment Defic Res* 1973; **17**: 173-81.
12. McLaren DS. Role of stimulation in recovery from marasmus. In: Chavez A, Bourges H, Basta S, ed. Proceedings of the 9th International Congress of Nutrition, Mexico 1972; **2**: 335-37. Karger, Basel 1975.
13. Bronfenbrenner U. A report on longitudinal evaluations of preschool programs, Vol. II. Is early intervention effective? DHEW publication (OHD) 76-30025, 1974.
14. Winick M, Meyer KK, Harris RC. Malnutrition and environmental enrichment by early adoption. *Science* 1975; **190**: 1174-75.
15. Grantham-McGregor SM, Stewart ME, Desai P. A new look at the assessment of mental development in young children recovering from severe protein-energy malnutrition. *Devl Med Child Neurol* 1978; **20**: 773-78.
16. Grantham-McGregor SM, Stewart ME, Desaid P. Mental development of young children recovering from severe protein energy malnutrition. In: Brozek J, Proceedings of International Conference on Behavioral Effects of Energy and Protein Deficits. DHEW Publ (NIH) 79-1906, 1979.
17. Stewart ME, Grantham-McGregor SM. The experiences of young children in a Kingston hospital, Jamaica. *W I Med J* 1979; **28**: 30-35.
18. Editorial: Classification of infantile malnutrition, *Lancet* 1970; **i**: 302.
19. Dunn LM. Peabody Picture Vocabulary Test. Nashville, Tennessee. American Guidance Service, 1965.
20. Grantham-McGregor SM, Stewart ME, Desai P. The relationship between hospitalisation, social background, severe protein energy malnutrition and mental development in young Jamaican children. *Ecol Food Nutr* (in press).
21. Uzgiris IC, Hunt J McV. Assessment in infancy. Ordinal scales of psychological development. Urbana, Chicago and London: University of Illinois Press, 1975.
22. Jason LA. A behavioral approach in enhancing disadvantaged children's academic abilities. *Am J Comm Psychol* 1977; **5**: 413-21.
23. Palmer F. Concept training curriculum for children ages two to five. Vol. I-V, State University New York, Stony Brook 1971.
24. Griffiths R. The abilities of babies. London: University of London Press, 1970.
25. Griffiths R. The abilities of young children. London: Child Development Research Centre, 1970.
26. Grantham-McGregor SM, Desai P. A home-visiting intervention programme with Jamaican mothers and children. *Devl Med Child Neurol* 1975; **17**: 605-13.
27. Winer BJ. Statistical principles in experimental design. New York: McGraw-Hill, 1971.
28. Dixon WJ, Brown MB. Biomedical computer programs P-series. Berkeley, California: University of California Press, 1977.
29. Kerlinger FE, Pedhazar LJ. Multiple regression in behavioral research. New York: Holt, Rinehart, and Winstan Inc, 1973.
30. Stuart HC, Stevenson SS. Physical growth and development. In: Nelson WE ed. Textbook of pediatrics, 7th ed. Philadelphia: WB Saunders 1959: 48-58.
31. Waterlow JC, Ritishauser HE. Malnutrition in man. In: Cravioto J, Hambreus L, Valhquist B eds. Early malnutrition and mental development. Uppsala: Almquist and Wiksel, 1974; 13-25.
32. Kerr MAD, Landman-Bogues J, Kerr DS. Psychosocial functioning of mothers of malnourished children. *Pediatrics* 1978; **62**: 778-84.
33. Levenstein P. The mother-child home program. In: Day MC, Parker RK, eds. The Preschool in action, 2nd ed. Boston: Allyn & Bacon (in press).
34. Mora JO, Waber D, Herrera MG, et al. Effects of nutritional supplementation and early home stimulation on infant's intellectual development. XI International Congress of Nutrition, Rio de Janeiro (Brazil) Aug 27-Sept 1, 1978.
35. Grantham-McGregor SM, Stewart ME, Powell C, Schofield WN. Effect of stimulation on mental development of malnourished child. *Lancet* 1979; **ii**: 200-01.
36. McKay H, Sinisterra L, McKay A, Gomez H, Lloreda P. Improving cognitive ability in chronically deprived children. *Science* 1978; **200**: 270-78.

Addendum to Part IV

AGE FACTOR IN MARASMIC INFANTS

The age of infants hospitalized with the diagnosis of generalized malnutrition (kwashiorkor) as a factor influencing the effectiveness of rehabilitation was considered by Cravioto and Robles (1965, p. 463; see also Paper 8). They noted that in the group of children whose chronological age on admission was below 6 months of age, the initial behavioral deficits did not decrease in the course of nutritional treatment, even in children who remained on the ward for over 6 months. The relative weight (percentage of the reference weight for age) of this group of children was severely depressed, with a mean of 45.7% — in contrast to the normal value of 100% — and a narrow range from 35 to 57%. This suggests that we are dealing with marasmic (or at least "marasmoid") children. In the older age group (15 to 29 months) the weight on admission was higher (with a mean of 57% and a range from 45 to 82%).

Celedón and co-workers (1980) refer to a group of children treated and studied in the metabolic ward of the Institute of Nutrition and Food Technology, University of Chile, Santiago, specifically as "severely marasmic infants." At admission their ages ranged from 3 to 13 months, with Ns of 20 (males) and 15 (females). The treatment included, in addition to medical and nutritional care, sensory-motor and cognitive stimulation and a positive relationship between the therapists and the infants.

The behavioral assessment was made using the Bayley scales (Bayley, 1969), yielding a Mental and a Psychomotor Development Index. At admission their average relative weights were 58% of the reference values. At discharge, 160 days later, it reached 86%. However, their average values of the Mental Development Index (79.1 versus 80.3 at discharge) and the Psychomotor Index (76.5 versus 76) remained stationary.

This is true for the group as a whole. What is the effect of splitting up the group according to the age at admission? In regard to the motor area, the infants below six months of age at admission showed actually an *impairment* while those above six months *improved*. The difference is statistically significant at the .01 level.

The Mental Development Index exhibited similar trends, but the difference between the changes observed in the two age groups of infants did not reach a level of statistical significance. The author interprets the results, although tentatively, as being in agreement with the so-called vulnerable period hypothesis (Dobbing and Sands, 1979), specifying that the insult of inadequate nutrition has severer and more permanent consequences if it coincides with a period of rapid brain growth.

REFERENCES

Bayley, N., 1969, *Manual for Bayley Scale of Infant Development,* Psychological Corporation, New York, 178p.

Celedón, J. M., D. Csaszar, J. Middleton, and I. de Andraca, 1980, The Effect of Treatment on Mental and Psychomotor Development of Marasmic Infants According to the Age of Admission, *J. Ment. Defic. Res.* **24:**27-35.

Cravioto, J., and B. Robles, 1965, Evolution of Adaptive and Motor Behavior during Rehabilitation from Kwashiorkor, *Am. J. Orthopsychiatry* **35:**449-464.

Dobbing, J., and J. Sands, 1979, Comparative Aspects of the Brain Growth Spurt, *Early Hum. Dev.* **3:**79-83.

Part V

Generalized Clinical Malnutrition: Sequelae

Papers 12 Through 17: Commentary

Early in the days of research on malnutrition and behavior, the issue of long-term consequences of generalized clinical malnutrition appeared simple, as did the etiology of malnutrition. The papers included in this part illustrate and document the increasing sophistication in the definition and use of comparison groups, diversity of psychometric tools, definition and quantification of the severity of kwashiorkor-like and marasmus-like varieties of generalized clinical malnutrition, and the awareness of the significance of biological (nutritional status, health) and social conditions under which the survivors of infantile malnutrition live.

Paper 12 is significant, historically, as the first retrospective study of the sequelae of infantile generalized (energy-protein) clinical malnutrition. While the data (and the authors, associated with the city's pediatric clinic) come from Sarajevo, Yugoslavia, the intellectual roots of the paper go to England and, more specifically, to the University of Cambridge where the senior author participated in the epoch-making studies, initiated by R. A. McCance. This work dealt with the differential effects of three dietary conditions (severe calorie deficiency, protein deficiency, and ad libitum food intake) on the morphology of the pig (Čabak, Gresham, and McCance, 1962), but it included also studies on animal behavior, and the paper by Lat, Widdowson, and McCance (1960) is cited by the Sarajevo authors. Čabak acknowledged Professor McCance's encouragement and help in connection with the preparation of the paper for publication.

Čabak and Najdanović cite also the initial report of the South African prospective study on the long-term effects of severe undernutrition experienced in infancy (Stoch and Smythe, 1963) but, strangely enough, do not refer to the work of Geber and Dean (Paper 7), even though prior to the establishment of the research unit at Kampala, Uganda (in 1953), Dean was associated with Professor McCance in the Department of Medicine, Cambridge University Medical School (cf. McCance and Dean, 1951), and the two groups maintained close contacts.

The children studied by Čabak and Najdanović (Paper 12) were identified in the records of a Sarajevo hospital as having experienced generalized malnutrition of the marasmus type in infancy. When the children were of school age (with a range from 7 to 14 years—mean age is not reported), they were tested by the Binet-Simon scale of intelligence, adapted for use with children speaking Serbo-Croatian. No control group was tested, but a comparison with the distribution of IQs in the normative population indicated that the survivors of marasmus had an excess of IQs in the range of 71 to 90. Their mean IQ was not given.

In the study reported in Paper 13, the psychometric data were obtained, as in the Sarajevo study, using the Stanford-Binet test of intelligence. The group had experienced severe under-nutrition in infancy, as had the Yugoslav children. But here the similarities between the two studies end.

In the Lebanese sample studied in Paper 13, both the index and comparison children were part of a large group of children born in the University Hospital in Beirut and enrolled in a longitudinal study. When tested at the age of four to five years, they showed dramatic effects of differential nutritional experience in infancy, with mean IQs of 79.5 for the index children and 103.0 for the control group; the difference was highly significant in statistical terms.

The study has several interesting, positive features. For one, it is the earliest and one of the very few studies in which the children were observed before some of them became severely malnourished. While no psychometric evidence is available, the authors believe that there is no reason to believe that the two groups differed initially in intelligence level. While this is a weak argument, it is a fact—a welcome piece of information—that there were no statistically significant differences in the mean intelligence scores of the two sets of parents, using the Raven Progressive Matrices Test.

Paper 14 shares with Paper 13 the uncommon feature that the children who developed clinical malnutrition in infancy and early childhood had been studied from their birth on. In the Mexican project (Paper 14) a large amount of information is available on the children and their families prior to the incidence of clinical malnutrition.

The paper is one of the early reports on a facet of a comprehensive ecological, noninterventive, longitudinal study of a Mexican rural community. The prevalence of chronic undernutrition in the preschool children of "The Land of White Dust" was high, and other factors affecting the children's lives varied within a range that was sufficiently large to make possible analyses of the effects of nutritional, health-related, and socioeconomic variables on the children's physical growth and mental development.

The first part of Cravioto and DeLicardie's (1973) paper (pp. 73-84), not reproduced in this volume, describes the aims of the project as a whole, the setting of the study, the cohort, and an impressive collection of variables to be studied. Among some 300 children, born in the community within a calendar year (1 March 1966 to 28 February 1967), 22 children developed clinical malnutrition before the age of 5 years. Eighteen of them were available for study. The body of the paper reprinted here is devoted to the language development in the subsample constituted by the survivors of severe malnutrition.

The retardation of the children who had experienced clinical malnutrition is reflected in the Language subscale of the Gesell Developmental Schedule. At the age of 1,080 days, the average language development scores were 657 for the index children and 947 for a comparison group, matched for gestational age, body length, and body weight at birth. The difference in language development is highly significant statistically. The children who recovered from clinical malnutrition differed significantly also in terms of the acquisition of bipolar concepts (such as long-short), with the mean scores of 17.2 and 20.1 at the age of 58 months. The styles of responses to cognitive demands (DeLicardie and Cravioto, 1974) and the development of intersensory integration (Cravioto, 1980) were examined in later publications.

The closing part of Paper 14 is devoted to the biological and social characteristics of the families. An important finding was that the comparison children had higher scores on the Caldwell Inventory of Home Stimulation. This encouraged the investigators to undertake a more detailed study of the microenvironment.

A substantial amount of research on malnutrition and behavior was carried out in Africa—East, West, and South (Brožek, 1980). Paper 15 bears on one facet of a South African retrospective study on the sequelae of kwashiorkor, dealing with the results obtained in selected subtests of the Halstead and Reitan Neuropsychological Test Batteries. It is paralleled and supplemented by a communication on psychomotor functions (Bartel et al., 1978).

The index group consisted of 31 urban black children who had been hospitalized and received treatment for kwashiorkor or marasmic kwashiorkor during the first 27 months of their life, recovered, and were tested 5 to 10 years later when they were 6 to 14 years of age. Their performance was compared with the test scores obtained in two comparison groups: a group of siblings and a group of yard mates, both free of acute (clinical) infantile malnutrition. It may be assumed that the mean ages of the three groups were similar, but the values were not reported.

The four neuropsychological tests involved tactile form discrimination, intersensory comparisons (visual recognition of the form of objects that were first examined by touch), concept formation, and tracing mazes.

Only in one comparison (out of 18) of the performance of the three groups, concerning short-term memory, did the differences reach a level of statistical significance, with scores of 1.38 for the index children, 2.52 for siblings, and 1.72 for the yard mates.

The measures of the psychomotor functions included the Lincoln-Oseretsky motor development scale, covering a wide range of motor skills, and the tests of two additional functions: grip strength and fine motor speed measured by a finger-tapping test (included in the Halstead and Reitan Neuropsychological Test Batteries).

Throughout, the mean scores of the index children were somewhat lower than the scores of the comparison groups. Thus, the total raw scores for the Lincoln-Oseretsky scale were 80.7 for the index children, 91.2 for siblings, and 82.5 for the yard mates. The corresponding mean values of grip strength, in kilograms, for the dominant hand were 14.8, 16.6, and 15.2. None of the *F*-tests of the group differences reached or even approached a level of statistical significance.

The authors considered several alternate interpretations of their negative results. They favor the hypothesis that the kwashiorkor group made up any deficits due to clinical malnutrition in infancy.

In the editor's view, the principal contribution of the study reported in Paper 16, a preliminary account (Hoorweg and Stanfield, 1972), and a monograph (Hoorweg, 1976) is a sophisticated reinforcement of the idea, expressed by others, that it is highly desirable to specify the nature of generalized clinical malnutrition experienced in infancy when we are asking whether or not such an event has long-term consequences.

This retrospective study, based on data obtained in Kampala, Uganda, is similar in a variety of ways to the South African study referred to in Paper 15. The children were hospitalized for generalized (energy-protein) malnutrition at the same age (range from 8 to 27 months). They and their peer controls were tested when they were in their teens (range, 11 to 17 years; mean, 14 years).

A distinctive feature of the Uganda study was the quantitative characterization of clinical malnutrition experienced by the index children and the identification of two dimensions (principal components) on the basis of a factorial analysis of the features of generalized clinical malnutrition. The author speaks of *acute malnutrition* and *chronic malnutrition*. The present editor prefers to label them the *K*-component (where *K* stands for kwashiorkor) and the *M*-component (*M* for marasmus).

For each child a severity score was computed for each component and used as a point of reference for the analysis of the test scores obtained when the children reached their teens. The *K*-component is characterized by the presence of edema and by skin changes; the *M*-component, by a severe underweight at admission. We may argue about the optimal label for the components, but one cannot deny the usefulness, at least for some situations, of the classification system.

Interestingly enough, the correlations of the *K* values with scores obtained on nine psychological (cognitive) tests were not statistically significant; furthermore, the coefficients of correlation were random in direction, five having a plus sign and four being negative. By contrast, the greater the *M* value, the lower the performance in tests of numerical ability, reasoning, spatial-perceptual ability, and memory. The correlations for these variables are significant statistically and, for the most part, highly significant. The correlations are negative for scores on all the tests. The construction or adaptation of the tests is described, in detail, in the monograph (Hoorweg, 1976, pp. 53-65).

The total score on the Lincoln-Oseretsky scale of motor development also correlates negatively with the M values ($r = -0.25$, significant at the .05 level). Children with a high M value rested more during the day, were less active, slower, and were more docile as well (Hoorweg, 1976, Table 24, p. 95).

The data on which Paper 17 is based were obtained in Jamaica, West Indies, and refer to boys within the age range of 6 to 24 months who were hospitalized for malnutrition and tested at school age (6 to 10 years). The results were reported in several earlier communications, cited in Paper 17. These studies brought out that, as a group, at school age the index children were significantly smaller in height (but not in weight) and head circumference than their unrelated classmates and neighbors matched for age and sex. They also had a lower level of intelligence, did significantly less well in school, and tended to be rated by their parents more often as backward, withdrawn, and unsociable.

It is important to note that there were differences in the socioeconomic characteristics of the families of the index and comparison children—for example, the caretakers' level of ability, the quality of home furnishings and appliances, and the intellectual stimulation provided to the children. These differences indicated that the index children came from more disadvantaged backgrounds than the peer comparison group.

Of critical importance is the next stage in the analysis of the factors influencing the level of intellectual functioning of the index and comparison children. These data are presented on page 172 of Paper 17 in a table and figure (cf. Richardson, 1976, p. 60). The data are compatible with a model according to which an episode of clinical malnutrition in infancy has different consequences for the intellectual functioning of the child depending on the social background and on nutrition (and health) in the years following recovery from clinical malnutrition (cf. Rossetti Ferreira, 1979, p. 39; Brožek, 1984, p. 345).

In the Jamaica study (Paper 17), the members of the comparison group who had a relatively favorable social background and who were relatively tall had an index of mental functioning of 71; for shorter children, the index dropped to 65; for unfavorable social background combined with a relatively good nutrition (measured as stature), the value was 62; for comparison children who had an unfavorable social background and were short, the mean of the index of intellectual functioning reached the low value of 58.

What was the impact of social background and chronic nutritional status on the level of mental functioning of the index children? For the four combinations just described, the means were 69, 62, 55, and 49. The differences between the comparison and the index children were 2, 3, 7, and 9, showing the progressive impact of the cumulation of stresses. The data provide additional, empirical support for the thesis that there is no single, simple answer to the question Does clinical malnutrition in infancy have permanent effects on intellective functioning?

REFERENCES

Bartel, P. R., R. D. Griesel, L. S. Burnett, I. Freiman, E. U. Rosen, and J. Geefhuysen, 1978, Long-Term Effect of Kwashiorkor on Psychomotor Development, *S. Afr. Med. J.* **53:**360-362.

Brožek, J., 1980, Recent Africana on Malnutrition, in *Malnutrition in Southern Africa,* R. D. Griesel, ed., University of South Africa, Pretoria, pp. 59-73.

Brožek, J., 1984, Why Theories? in *Malnutrition and Behavior: Critical Assessment of Key Issues,* J. Brožek and B. Schürch, eds., Nestlé Foundation Publication Series, vol. 4, Lausanne, Switzerland, pp. 338-347.

Čabak, V., G. A. Gresham, and R. A. McCance, 1962, Severe Undernutrition in Growing and Adult Animals—Part 10. The Skin and Hair of Pigs, *Br. J. Nutr.* **16:**635-640.

Cravioto, J., 1980, Intersensory Development in Survivors of Early Malnutrition and Stimuli Deprivation, in *Nutrition, Food, and Man: An Interdisciplinary Perspective,* P. B. Pearson and J. R. Greenwell, eds., University of Arizona Press, Tucson, pp. 46-64.

Cravioto, J., and E. R. DeLicardie, 1973, Environmental Correlates of Severe Clinical Malnutrition and Language Development in Survivors of Kwashiorkor or Marasmus, *Of. Sanit. Panam. Bol.* (English ed.), **7:**73-84.

DeLicardie, E. R., and J. Cravioto, 1974, Behavioral Responsiveness of Survivors of Clinical Severe Malnutrition to Cognitive Demands, in *Early Malnutrition and Mental Development,* J. Cravioto, L. Hambraeus, and B. Vahlquist, eds., Symposia of the Swedish Nutrition Foundation, vol. 12, Uppsala, Sweden, pp. 134-153.

Hoorweg, J. C., 1976, *Protein-Energy Malnutrition and Intellectual Abilities,* Mouton, The Hague, 148p.

Hoorweg, J. C., and J. P. Stanfield, 1972, The Influence of Malnutrition on Psychologic and Neurologic Development: Preliminary Communication, in *Nutrition, the Nervous System, and Behavior,* Pan American Health Organization Scientific Publication Number 251, Washington, D.C., pp. 55-63.

Lat, J., E. M. Widdowson, and R. A. McCance, 1960, Some Effects on Accelerating Growth. III. Behaviour and Nervous Activity, *R. Soc. Proc.,* ser. B, **156:**326-327.

McCance, R. A., and A. F. R. Dean, 1951, Neuromuscular System: Tendon Reflexes and Galvanic Responses, in *Studies in Undernutrition, Wuppertal, 1946-1949,* Members of the Department of Experimental Medicine, Cambridge, Medical Research Council Special Report Series Number 275, His Majesty's Stationery Office, London, pp. 140-146.

Richardson, S. A., 1976, The Relation of Severe Malnutrition in Infancy to the Intelligence of School Children with Differing Life Histories, *Pediatr. Res.* **10:**57-61.

Rossetti-Ferreira, M. C., 1979, Interação entre Factores Biologicos, Socioeconomicos e Culturais no Desenvolvimento Mental e Desempenho Escolar na Criança Desnutrida (Interaction between the Biological, Socioeconomic, and Cultural Factors in Mental Development and School Performance of Malnourished Children), *Cuadernos de Pesquisa* (São Paulo), **29:**37-48.

Stoch, M. B., and P. M. Smythe, 1963, Does Undernutrition during Infancy Inhibit Brain Growth and Subsequent Mental Development? *Arch. Dis. Child.* **38:**546-552.

12: EFFECT OF UNDERNUTRITION IN EARLY LIFE ON PHYSICAL AND MENTAL DEVELOPMENT

V. Čabak and R. Najdanović

It was pointed out by Trowell, Davis, and Dean (1954) that, 'Nothing is known about the completeness of recovery from severe kwashiorkor', and this is to a large extent still true. An increase in the body weight is admittedly a sign of recovery, and indeed a very important criterion of it, but unless the final weight and height attained are also known it is impossible to say whether it has been complete. The experiments on animals give some information about this problem. McCance and Widdowson (1962) showed that the body weights of rats undernourished during suckling never reached those of their controls in spite of subsequent unlimited food. Undernutrition for the first six months of life can also affect the final stature of cockerels (Pratt and McCance, 1961), but this has not been found to be true of all species and for these differences references should be made to Aron (1911), Moulton, Trowbridge, and Haigh (1921), Jackson (1925), Clarke and Smith (1938), Crichton, Aitken, and Boyne (1959), and McCance (1962). The extent of the undernutrition and the age at which it affects the animal are also certainly important (Widdowson and McCance, 1963).

Even less is known about the mental than about the physical development of children after a period of undernutrition (Stoch and Smythe, 1963; Graham, 1964). Attention has been drawn to defects in their ability to learn a language (Waterlow, Cravioto, and Stephen, 1960), which is one of the most important ways of estimating the intelligence of a child (Stevanović, 1937). Jersild (1955) has stated that, 'A positive relationship is usually found between language ability and mental ability.' Many authors, moreover (Porter, 1895a, b; Boas, 1940; Tanner, 1955), have found that children who are physically advanced for their age score higher in mental tests than those who are less mature, but of the same chronological age. Lat, Widdowson, and McCance (1960) showed this to be true also of rats.

Material and Methods

Children were selected from the records who had been admitted for malnutrition (marasmus) to the Hospital for sick children in Sarajevo between 1951 and 1957. Though slight oedema was present in a few, there were no other signs of kwashiorkor. Their ages at the time were between 4 and 24 months. At the time of admission they had all been 27% or more below the correct weight for their age, according to the tables of Lust, Pfaundler, and Husler (1953). Children suffering from chronic diseases such as tuberculosis or diseases of the central nervous system were excluded from the investigation and, for financial reasons, only children from the town of Sarajevo were invited to attend. This restricted the numbers and, for various reasons, some did not come, so that finally only 36 children were available. The history of the health and development of these children after discharge was taken, the body weight and height were measured, the intelligence was tested by Binet-Simon scale as adapted by Stevanović (1937), and finally their grade at school was recorded. At the time of the follow-up assessment their ages were between 7 and 14 years. The parents of these children were mainly unskilled and skilled workers, but about one-third was drawn from the professions or were army officers.

Results

Fig. 1 shows the deficits in the expected weight for age at the time of admission plotted against the age. Most of the cases were less than 12 months old and all the most serious were below this age.

The body weights of these children at the time of interview are shown in Fig. 2 in comparison with the weights of the healthy schoolchildren of Sarajevo (Jelisavčić-Mihal, 1961). More of the children were below the standard curve at 7 or 8 years of age than later, but the mean values and the standards were not significantly different at any age by the 't' test.

Fig. 3 shows the heights of the 36 children, also in comparison with local standards. The results are similar to those for weights.

Reprinted from *Arch. Dis. Child.* **40:**532-534 (1965); *Copyright © 1965 by the British Medical Association.*

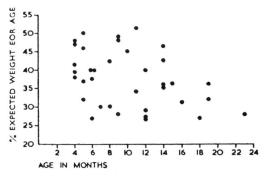

FIG. 1.—Deficit in body weight of the undernourished children, expressed as a percentage of the weight to be expected at that age, plotted against their age on admission.

The results of the intelligence tests are shown in Fig. 4. Only 18 were within the normal IQ limits (91-110), 12 were 'stupid', with IQs between 71 and 90, and the remaining 6 children had IQs of 70 or below. None showed an IQ greater than 110. In other words, half the children were below the limit of normal intelligence, and this difference between normal and subnormal intelligence was highly significant by the Kolmogorov Smirnov test (p = 0·01).

There are no local standards for the dispersion of the intelligence quotient, so the present results have been compared with those for Serbian children (Stevanović, 1957). Of the Serbian children, 21% were below normal intelligence as against 50% of the previously undernourished children, and 32% of the Serbian children were above the range of the under-

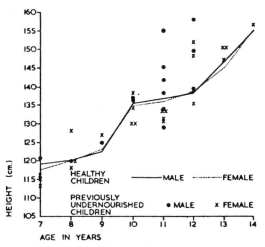

FIG. 3.—The heights of the 36 previously undernourished school-children when they attended for interview compared with the heights of healthy schoolchildren in Sarajevo.

nourished children. The mean IQ of the under-nourished series was 88, in contrast to 101 for children from Mostar, 80 miles from Sarajevo, and 109 for children from Beograd. It is well known that socio-economic factors influence the IQ but even if all the undernourished children had come from families of 'non-qualified' workers their IQ was below the mean value of 93 for this group.

No correlation was found using the Spearman test (Siegel, 1956) between the age of the children when they were ill and undernourished and their subsequent

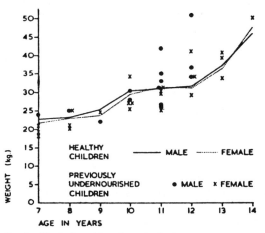

FIG. 2.—The body weights of the 36 previously undernourished children when they attended for interview compared with the weights of healthy schoolchildren in Sarajevo.

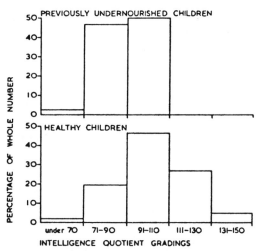

FIG. 4.—The distribution of quotients of intelligence shown by the 36 undernourished children compared with the standards established for Serbian children.

mental development and IQ. A correlation, however, was found between the deficit in the expected weight for age on the original admission and the IQ on subsequent re-examination. The school grades of these children were in good agreement with their rating by IQ tests, and this confirms the experience of others.

Summary

Serbian children who had been seriously undernourished in infancy were found at school-age to have normal physical characteristics but subnormal mental capacity.

I am grateful to Dr. E. Serstnev for his assistance with the statistical analysis of the results and to Dr. L. Skoric for help in the appraisal of the results of the intelligence tests. Professor R. A. McCance encouraged me to write this paper, and advised and helped me over its presentation. I would like to thank him for all he has done.

REFERENCES

Aron, H. (1911). Nutrition and growth. *Philipp. J. Sci. B.*, 6, 1.

Boas, F. (1940). *Race, Language and Culture*. MacMillan, New York.

Clarke, M. F., and Smith, A. H. (1938). Recovery following suppression of growth in the rat. *J. Nutr.*, 15, 245.

Crichton, J. A., Aitken, J. N., and Boyne, A. W. (1959). The effect of plane of nutrition during rearing on growth, production, reproduction and health of dairy cattle: 1. Growth to 24 months. *Anim. Prod.*, 1, 145.

Graham, G. (1964). *Diet and Bodily Constitution. Ciba Foundation Study Group No. 17*, p. 11. J. & A. Churchill, London.

Jackson, C. M. (1925). *The Effects of Inanition and Malnutrition Upon Growth and Structure*. J. & A. Churchill, London.

Jelisavčić-Mihal, M. (1961). Prilog antropometrijkom ispitivanju školske omladine. *Biltin Rep. Z. za Zdrav. zaštitu br.*, 1-2, 78.

Jersild, T. A. (1955). *Child Psychology*, 4th ed., p. 417. Staples Press, London.

Lat, J., Widdowson, E. M., and McCance, R. A. (1960). Some effects of accelerating growth: III. Behaviour and nervous activity. *Proc. roy. Soc. B*, 153, 347.

Lust, F., Pfaundler, M. von, and Husler, J. (1953). *Krankheiten des Kindesalters*. Urban & Schwarzenberg, Munich.

McCance, R. A. (1962). Food, growth, and time. *Lancet*, 2, 621, 671.

——, and Widdowson, E. M. (1962). Nutrition and growth. *Proc. roy. Soc. B*, 156, 326.

Moulton, C. R., Trowbridge, P. F., and Haigh, L. D. (1921). Studies in animal nutrition: 1. Changes in form and weight on different planes of nutrition. *Res. Bull. Mo. agric. Exp. Sta.*, 43, 73.

Porter, W. T. (1895a). The physical basis of precocity and dullness. *Trans. Acad. Sci. St Louis*, 6, 161.

—— (1895b). The relation between the growth of children and their deviation from the physical type of their sex and age. *ibid.*, 6, 233.

Pratt, C. W. M., and McCance, R. A. (1961). Severe undernutrition in growing and adult animals: 6. Changes in the long bones during the rehabilitation of cockerels. *Brit. J. Nutr.*, 15, 121.

Siegel, S. (1956). *Nonparametric Statistics: for the Behavioral Sciences*. McGraw Hill, New York.

Stevanović, B. (1937). *Merenje Inteligencije*. Ed. Drag. Gregorić, Belgrade.

—— (1957). *Pedagoška psihologija*. Ed. Naučna Knjiga, Belgrade.

Stoch, M. B., and Smythe, P. M. (1963). Does undernutrition during infancy inhibit brain growth and subsequent intellectual development? *Arch. Dis. Childh.*, 38, 546.

Tanner, J. M. (1955). *Growth at Adolescence*. Blackwell, Oxford.

Trowell, H. C., Davis, J. N. P., and Dean, R. F. A. (1954). *Kwashiorkor*, p. 225. Edward Arnold, London.

Waterlow, J. C., Cravioto, J., and Stephen, J. M. L. (1960). Protein malnutrition in man. *Advanc. Protein Chem.*, 15, 131.

Widdowson, E. M., and McCance, R. A. (1963). The effect of finite periods of undernutrition at different ages on the composition and subsequent development of the rat. *Proc. roy. Soc. B*, 158, 329.

13: INTELLECTUAL DEVELOPMENT RELATED TO NUTRITIONAL STATUS

E. Botha-Antoun, S. Babayan, and J. K. Harfouche

Several recent investigations have been concerned with the possible permanent effects of undernutrition in early childhood on mental development (KUGELMASS, 1943; STOCH and SMYTHE, 1963; CRAVIOTO, 1963). In view of the knowledge that the greatest effects of undernutrition on physical development may be produced at periods of maximal growth and the fact that most brain growth and much mental development take place in the first two years of life, it is probable that adverse effects on mental functioning during that period will not disappear as a consequence of later adequate diets.

This paper presents an attempt to study the relationship of low nutritional status in the first 18 months of life to intellectual performance at the age period 4-5 years.

METHODS

(1) *Subjects.* A sample of 22 Lebanese children in the age group 4-5 years who were of low nutritional status during the first 18 months of life were matched with a control group of adequately nourished children of the same age, sex, and ethnic group. (Mean age of both groups was 4 years and 6 months).

The children of both groups were taken from a larger sample of 316 who took part in a longitudinal study at the Out-patient Department of the American University Hospital in Beirut. The children were all born at the maternity ward of the University Hospital. Their growth patterns were studied at birth, at the end of the first and third months of life, and at regular three monthly intervals thereafter. The children were all fullterm, normal neonates. No prematurely born children were included in the group; none weighed less than 2,500 grams at birth; none with congenital, natal or neonatal defects were included in the group. Clinical observations at birth, and at periodic intervals revealed no neural malfunctioning prior to the nutritional deficiency state.

The nutritional status of most of these children was relatively good during the first three months while they were completely breast-fed, but from the third month onward when complete breast feeding was declining and the children were partially or completely weaned nutritional deficiency states made their appearance. The most common cause of low nutritional status in this group was protein calorie deficiency associated with illness e.g. stomatitis, combination of respiratory and diarrheal diseases, diarrhea alone and measles.

The children in the experimental group all at some time during the 18 month period fell below the tenth percentile in weight and length compared with Stuart's charts. With the exception of two, all at some stage, usually shortly after weaning, fell below the third percentile on both of these parameters. (The average scores of normal Lebanese children appear to be similar to those of American infants. WOODRUFF, 1966). None of the control group during this period scored below the 25th percentile in weight and length.

The experimental group also exhibited other symptoms of undernutrition, for example, decrements in skinfold thickness, extreme pallor, poor muscle tone; hair and skin changes, augular lesions, flat buttocks and large abdomen in varying degrees.   The severely affected had also pitting edema, cyanosis and coldness of their extremities with liver enlargement in the recovery stage.   Total serum protein and its fractions were determined, but were not of much help in assessing the degree of severity of the nutritional deficiency state (HARFOUCHE, 1966).

The mean birth weight of the experimental group was 3,324 grams and that of the control group 3,333 grams.   The difference was not statistically significant (t = .095, p > .05) their weights at 18 months, however, differed significantly, the mean weight of the experimental group being 9,482 grams and that of the control group, 10,849 grams (t = 5.19, p < .05).   At 18 months the average weights for girls and boys in the experimental group were between the 3rd and the 10th percentiles although at this time the nutritional state had improved and they were all gaining weight.   The average weights of boys and girls in the control group separately were between the 25th and 50th percentiles at 18 months.

The parents of both groups were matched for age, intellectual performance and educational level.   The mean age of the experimental group mothers was 31 years 2 months and that of the control mothers 29 years 6 months (t = .860, p. > .05).   The mean age of the experimental group fathers was 36 years 8 months and that of the control fathers 35 years 3 months (t = .915, p > .05).

Data about the educational level of the mothers only, were available.   The groups were very similar in this respect.   Eleven of the experimental group mothers had a few years of elementary school and 12 of the control group mothers.   Seven experimental group mothers completed elementary school and 5 control group mothers.   Three experimental group mothers had some high school education and five control group mothers. Only one mother in the experimental group was illiterate.

(2)   *Tests.*   I.   The parents' intellectual level was assessed by means of the Raven's Standard Progressive Matrices Test which is considered to be unaffected by nationality, education and literacy.   An analysis of variance showed no significant differences between the intelligence scores of the two sets of parents ($F < 1$, $p > .05$).

II.   To test the hypothesis that children who had been undernourished in early infancy are likely to have retarded mental development at the 4-5 year age level, the Stanford Binet Intelligence test as modified for a Lebanese population was administered to both groups.   The investigator at the time of testing did not know to which group the individual children belonged.

RESULTS

The mean IQ of the experimental group was found to be 79.5 and that of the control group 103.   This difference is statistically significant (t = 10.28, $p < .01$).

Since it has been found that undernutrition retards physical growth and development (DREIZEN, 1953; MANN, 1947) it was decided to compare the ages of onset of walking and talking in the two groups as well as their scores on the performance and verbal items of the intelligence test, separately.

The mean age at onset of walking for the undernourished group was 13.5 months and that of the control group 11.8 months.   This difference is statistically significant (t = 2.24, $p < .05$).   The mean age at onset of talking for the undernourished group was 16.7 months and that of the control group 14.4 months.   This difference is also statistically significant (t = 3.05, p<.01). Both sets of scores were however, within the normal age range as compared with Gesell's developmental scale (GESELL and AMATRUDA, 1947). (The data were obtained from the pediatric clinic which both groups attended.)

On the intelligence test, it was expected that there might be a greater difference on the "performance" than on the "verbal" items between the experimental group and the control group in view of the known effects of undernutrition on physical development. The results did not confirm this expectation; both the performance and verbal scores of the experimental group were significantly lower than those of the control group ("performance" t = 8.45, p<.01); ("verbal" t = 10.2; p<.01). Moreover, the differences expressed as proportions of the total performance and verbal scores do not differ ("performance" .51, "verbal" .49). Other investigators (BARRERA-MONCADA, 1963) have found greater differences on language than on performance development between malnourished and well nourished children. This finding seems to point more to maternal attitudes toward intellectual development than to specific effects of malnutrition.

All Measurements are summarized in Table I below.

TABLE I.

	Unnderourished group Means	Control group Means		
Birthweight	3324.77 gms.	3332.73 gms.	t = .095	p>.10
Weight at 18 months	9482.22 gms.	10849.00 gms.	t = 5.193	p<.001
Mother's age	31.2 gms.	29.6 years	t = .860	p>.10
Father's age	36.8 years	35.3 years	t = .915	p>.10
Mother's IQ (percentile rank)	18.6	17.9	t = .740	p>.10
Father's IQ (percentile rank)	21.7	22.5	t = .233	p>.10
Children's IQ	79.5	103.00	t = 10.28	p<.001
Age at onset of walking	13.5 months	11.8 months	t = 2.24	p<.05
Age at onset of talking	16.7 months	14.4 months	t = 3.05	p<.01
Scores on 'Performance' items	3.68	9.28	t = 8.45	p<.001
Scores on 'Verbal' items	5.54	14.00	t = 10.2	p<.001

CONCLUSION

The main finding of this study was that a group of children who had been undernourished before 18 months had significantly lower IQ's than an adequately nourished group at the age level of 4-5 years with no evidence for an original difference in IQ's. This result supports findings in other countries (STOCH and SMYTHE, 1963). To the writers' knowledge, this is the only study in which the children were observed before nutritional deficiencies occurred.

However, some factors still remain to be considered. The children of low nutritional status in this study, for example, were not placed in different, and perhaps more favourable environments. They remained with the mothers through whose neglect they might in the first place have acquired the nutritional deficiency states. This same neglectful attitude may constitute a deficiency in intellectual stimulation. We only know that intelligence scores of the two groups of parents did not differ significantly, the means of both sets being low, as in other studies, (below the 25th percentile) but we still do not know much about attitude differences.

REFERENCES

Barrera-Moncada, G. (1963).   Estudios Sobre Alteraciones del Crecimiento y del Desarrollo Psicologico
    del Sindrome Pluricarencial (Kwashiorkor).   Editora Grafos, Caracas, Venezuela.
Cravioto, J. (1963).   *Amer. J. Publ. Hlth.*, **53,** 1803.
Dreizen, S. (1953).   *Child Develop.*, **24,** 189.
Gesell, A. and Amatruda, C. (1947).   *Developmental diagnosis.*   New York, Paul B. Hoeber, In.
Harfouche, J. K. (1966).   *Growth and illness patterns of Lebanese infants.*   Beirut Khayats.
Kugelmass, I. (1944).   *Amer. J. Med. Sci.*, **208,** 631.
Mann, A (1947).   *J. Ped.*, **31,** 27.
Stoch, M. and Smythe, P. (1963).   *Arch. Dis. Childh.*, **38,** 546.
Woodruff, C. W. (1966).   An analysis of the ICNND data on physical growth of the Pre-school child.
    In: *Pre-school Child Malnutrition.*   Washington D.C.

14: ENVIRONMENTAL CORRELATES OF SEVERE CLINICAL MALNUTRITION AND LANGUAGE DEVELOPMENT IN SURVIVORS OF KWASHIORKOR OR MARASMUS

J. Cravioto and E. DeLicardie

[*Editor's Note:* In the original, material precedes this excerpt.]

Language Development and Malnutrition

Having described in detail the setting of the study and the birth cohort, we wish to present the preliminary results of a study of certain language features in a group of children who developed severe clinical malnutrition.

During the first five years of life of the cohort, 22 children—14 girls and eight boys—were found to be suffering from severe clinical malnutrition. It must be said that such cases appeared despite all medical efforts to prevent them. The patients' ages at the time of diagnosis ranged from four to 53 months. Only one child was below one year of age, nine were between one and two years, eight were between two and three years, three were between three and four years, and one was 53 months old.

Fifteen of the 22 cases matched the clinical picture of kwashiorkor; the other seven cases were of the marasmic variety (1). The proportion of marasmus in girls and boys was 4:3, but the number of girls with kwashiorkor was twice the number of boys. Because of the small number of cases, these differences are not of statistical significance.

Ten children, six with kwashiorkor and four with marasmus, were treated at home; nine children with kwashiorkor and three with marasmus were treated in the hospital. The average duration of each hospital stay was 30 days, and none of the children stayed longer than 60 days. No deaths occurred in the hospital-treated group. In contrast, three of the 10 children treated at home died. Of the latter, two had kwashiorkor and one had marasmus; their respective ages at the time of diagnosis were 12, 14, and 22 months. All three patients who died did so within 15 to 60 days of diagnosis. Of the 19 survivors, one child emigrated from the village after his discharge from the hospital, leaving a total of 18 cases for study.

The present report compares perceived language development in the 19 children who developed severe clinical malnutrition before the age of 39 months with the language development of a group of children from the same birth cohort who were never considered as severely malnourished and who were matched at birth for gestational age, body weight, and total body length.

As may be seen in Table 6 and Figure 17, mean language development, as measured by the Gesell method (14), was very similar in the malnourished group and the controls during the first year of life. Only one case of severe

Reprinted from pages 63-70 of *Of. Sanit. Panam. Bol.* (English ed.), **7**:50-70 (1973);
Copyright © 1973 by the Pan American Health Organization.

TABLE 6–Language development scores, measured in day equivalents, of severely malnourished children and matched controls.

Age (days)	Birth	180	360	540	720	900	1,080
Past or present severe malnutrition	27 ±3.2	167 ±14.4	289 ±47.2	385 ±86.0	467 ±102.7	534 ±103.0	657 ±119.5
Control group	28 ±1	177 ±21.2	334 ±55.4	490 ± 73.3	633 ± 93.4	785 ±143.1	947 ±135.2
"t" test	1.37	1.69	2.69[a]	3.90[a]	4.80[a]	5.80[a]	6.53[a]

[a]Significant at less than 0.01.

malnutrition was diagnosed during this period. As time elapsed and more children came down with severe malnutrition, a difference in language performance favorable to the matched controls became evident. The difference was more pronounced at each successive age tested.

Not only were mean values significantly lower in the malnourished group, but the distribution of individual scores was also markedly different from that obtained in the control group. Thus, for example, at three years of age (Figure 18) 11 children of the control group had language scores above 1,021 days' equivalent and only one child scored below 720 days'

equivalent. In contrast, none of the children with past malnutrition scored above 960 days' equivalent, 12 children had values below 720 days' equivalent, and three of the latter had language performances six months behind those of the control children with the lowest scores.

Concept development, particularly the emergence of verbal concepts, has long been viewed as a basic factor in the development of human intelligence. The emergence of the concept of opposites, and with it bipolar labelling, represents an early and readily measured aspect of concept development in young children.

As a consequence of their concern with

FIGURE 17.–Mean language development as a function of age in severely malnourished children and matched controls.

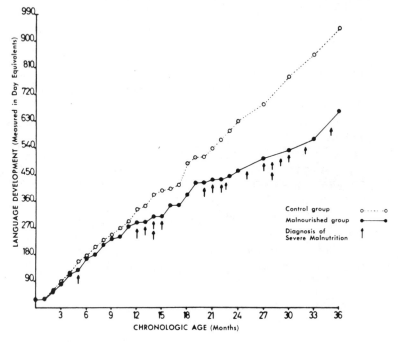

FIGURE 18—Distribution of language scores at 1,080 days of life of malnourished children and controls matched at birth for sex and body length.

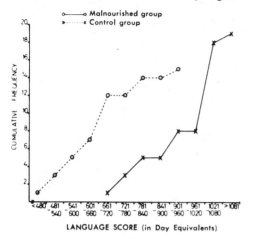

improving the school performance of disadvantaged children, Francis H. Palmer and his colleagues at the Institute for Child Development and Experimental Education of the City University of New York evolved the view that development of a progressively more difficult series of bipolar concepts could be used for systematic training and enrichment of language experience. Accordingly, as part of their studies on the effects of intervention programs started at age two, they developed a test covering both "poles" of 23 concepts (e.g., big-little, long-short, in-out) in two different situations. The score derived from the test provides a measure of the child's knowledge of various conceptual categories that are commonly used in organizing sensory experience.

Although Palmer and his associates had not designed the series of bipolar concepts that were developed to be a language test, it is implicit that the progressively more difficult training series could be used by itself, without training, as a way of assessing the natural acquisition of bipolar concepts in young children.

To test this hypothesis, we administered 22 of the 23 concepts selected by Palmer as a repeated test of bipolar concept acquisition at ages 26, 31, 34, and 38 months to the total cohort of 229 children living in a preindustrial society (9). All items were presented to the children at all ages, independently of the number of successes or failures. In all instances the order of presentation was the same, beginning with the first item contained in Form I. Data obtained at the successive ages tested clearly demonstrated a developmental course of competence in response to tasks involving the utilization of bipolar concepts.

Data on bipolar concept acquisition in children with past or present severe malnutrition, as compared with matched controls, is presented in Table 7 and Figure 19. As may be seen, the mean number of bipolar concepts acquired by the malnourished children was significantly lower than the mean number of concepts grasped by the control group.

It is important to remember that after 40 months all the children included in the malnourished group represented cases rehabilitated from severe clinical malnutrition, i.e., survivors considered cured of the disease. It may be noted in this respect that the mean test score of the malnourished group at 46 months was almost twice the score obtained at 38 months. Nonetheless, the increase is not enough to bring the previously malnourished children up to the level of the controls. In other words, the lag in

TABLE 7—Mean number of bipolar concepts in children with past or present severe malnutrition and in matched controls.

Age (months)	26	31	34	38	46	52	58
Past or present malnutrition	1.61 ±1.26	3.92 ±2.56	4.85 ±3.15	6.07 ±2.94	12.16 ±4.13	15.35 ±3.05	17.21 ±2.60
Control group	3.54 ±2.11	5.46 ±2.96	8.92 ±3.26	13.42 ±3.56	16.92 ±3.26	18.42 ±3.29	20.07 ±1.38
"t" test	2.68[a]	1.42	3.36[b]	5.97[b]	3.23[b]	2.57[a]	3.66[b]

[a] Significant at less than 0.05.
[b] Significant at less than 0.01.

FIGURE 19–Number of bipolar language concepts n children with and without antecedents of severe clinical malnutrition.

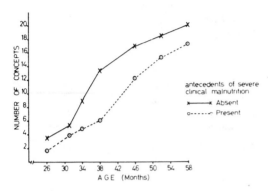

antecedents of severe clinical malnutrition

×———× Absent

o------o Present

language development found in severely malnourished children continued to be present after clinical recovery had taken place.

It has been repeatedly stated that human malnutrition does not occur in a vacuum, and that it is the outcome of an ecological situation characteristic of preindustrial societies (8). Because of this multiple causation, before interpreting our findings as due simply to severe malnutrition, it is necessary to try to sort out what other factors besides the nutritional deficiency may have been interfering with the normal development of these children. In trying to answer this question we have compared the family macroenvironments and some features of the family microenvironments of the severely malnourished children with those of the matched control group.

Environmental Factors

Broadly speaking, there are three kinds of macroenvironmental factors. These relate first to the parents as biologic and social organisms; second to the family structure; and third to objective circumstances of life such as sources of family income, income per capita, and sanitary facilities present in the household. Since a detailed description of these factors has already been presented, the association of each one with the presence or absence of severe malnutrition can now be considered.

Biological Characteristics of the Parents

Differences in the age, height, or weight of either parent; in the mother's number of pregnancies; or in the number of live children in the family failed to distinguish between families with and without severely malnourished children.

Sociocultural Characteristics

No significant relationship was found between the presence or absence of severe clinical malnutrition and the variables of personal cleanliness, literacy, and educational level.

Contact with mass media was explored through literate parents' newspaper reading and radio listening. The number of mothers or fathers of malnourished children who were regular newspaper readers was not significantly different from the number in the matched control group. Similarly, the number of fathers who listened regularly to the radio was similar in both the malnourished group and the control group.

As may be seen in Table 8, the case of the mothers was different. There were almost equal numbers of radio listeners and nonlisteners in the malnourished group, but the number of listeners among the matched control group was more than three times the number of nonlisteners. The difference is significant at the 0.05 level of statistical confidence (Chi square = 4.20; Df = 1; p < 0.05).

Family Structure and Economic Status

No significant differences between the mal-

TABLE 8–Radio listening by mothers of severely malnourished children and matched controls.

Mother of	Radio listening		
	Yes	No	Total
Severely malnourished children	8	10	18
Matched controls	14	4	18
Total	22	14	36

$X^2 = 4.20$; Df = 1; p < 0.05.

nourished and control groups were found with respect to family size or type of family (nuclear or extended).

The socioeconomic status of the families was estimated using four indicators: main source of family income, sanitary facilities in the household, annual income per capita, and percentage of total expenditures spent on food. No significant associations were found between any of these four indicators and the presence or absence of severe malnutrition.

In summary, considering all features of the macroencironment, the only differential between severely malnourished children and controls—matched at birth for gestational age, body weight, and total body length—was the mother's contact with the world outside the village through regular radio listening. None of the other characteristics of the parents (biological, social, or cultural) or family circumstances (including per capita income, main source of income, and family size) were significantly associated with the presence or absence of severe malnourishment.

The Microenvironment

Since the features of the macroenvironment could not explain severe malnutrition, our attention was directed toward analysis of the microenvironments of the two sets of children. We selected the potential stimulation of the home as our first general indicator of the quality of child care, and the mother as the principal stimulating agent for young children.

The instrument used for estimating home stimulation was the inventory developed by Beattye Caldwell (*3*). This inventory was designed to sample certain aspects of the quantity (and in some ways the quality) of social, emotional, and cognitive stimulation available to a young child within his home. Two forms of the inventory were used, one designed for infants up to three years of age and the other for children three to six years old. In both versions the selection of items included has been guided by a set of assumptions about conditions that foster development.

Accordingly, the inventory describes and quantifies the following eight areas of the home environment: (1) frequency and stability of adult contact; (2) vocal stimulation; (3) need gratification; (4) emotional climate; (5) avoidance of restriction; (6) breadth of experience; (7) aspects of the physical environment; and (8) available play materials. In each of these areas almost all items receive binary scores; no attempt is made to rate finer gradations. The total score is the number of items recorded as positive for the child's development. If desired, each area may be scored separately and related to specific features of development.

A trained pshychologist recorded the inventory of home stimulation for every child in the cohort at six-month intervals during the first three years of life and at yearly intervals thereafter. At the time of data collection and scoring, the psychologist was unaware of the nutritional antecedents of the children.

Figures 20 and 21 show the distribution of total home stimulation scores obtained by malnourished and control children at six and 48 months of age. As may be noted even at six months, when only one case of severe clinical malnutrition was present, the control children

FIGURE 20—Proportion of malnourished and control children showing different home stimulation scores at six months of age.

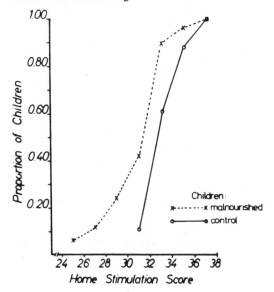

FIGURE 21—Proportion of malnourished and control children showing different home stimulation scores at 48 months of age.

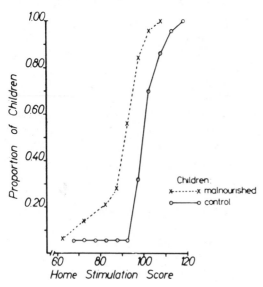

FIGURE 21—Proportion of malnourished and control children showing different home stimulation scores at 48 months of age.

had significantly higher home stimulation scores. Thus, while none of the control children's homes scored less than 30 points, almost one-fourth of the homes of the future malnourished children scored below 30 and almost one-half had scores below 32 points. Similarly, at 48 months of age, children who had recovered from malnutrition were living in homes whose scores were well below those in which the control children were living. With scores ranging from 60 to 120, about one-half of the survivors of severe clinical malnutrition had home stimulation scores below 94 points, and only one had a home that scored between 105 and 109. This distribution of scores is markedly different from that shown by the homes of the control children. Only one of these homes had a score below 95 while four reached values between 110 and 120. These differences are statistically significant at the 0.01 level of confidence.

The difference found in the quality of the home environment points toward the value of analyzing other features of the microenvironment. Associations between the presence of severe clinical malnutrition and the mother's psychological profile, maternal attitudes, proclivity for change, concepts of health and disease, concepts of food and feeding, and family visiting pattern are now under analysis.

Malnutrition, Language Development, and Home Stimulation

Since the presence of severe malnutrition had been significantly associated with home stimulation, and since survivors of severe malnutrition showed a significant lag in language bipolar concept formation, it seemed logical to investigate the interrelations among these three factors. As a first approach to this matter a technique of partial correlation was used to look at the degree of association between two variables "holding constant" the influence of the third variable. Since the number of cases of malnutrition was rather small, we decided to test for interrelationships in the total birth cohort.

The coefficients of correlation product moment among home stimulation scores, total body height, and number of bipolar concepts present at 46 months of age in the total cohort (229 children) were:

Home stimulation score:
 Number of bipolar concepts = 0.20
Home stimulation score:
 Total body height = 0.23
Total body height:
 Number of bipolar concepts = 0.26

There are various approaches to this matter of relative contributions by several variables to both the presence of malnutrition and the presence of somatic and mental lags in survivors (such as regression analyses and multivariate analysis of variance). Such approaches should be used in order to obtain a more quantitative answer to this question.

Conclusions

With the results now available, one can fairly state the following conclusions:

1) Susceptible infants cannot be identified before the development of severe clinical mal-

nutrition, since they do not differ from the rest of their birth cohort somatically or behaviorally.

2) The appearance of severe clinical malnutrition seems to be associated, in some preindustrial communities, with features of the microenvironment.

3) Children who have recovered from severe clinical malnutrition lag behind controls in language development, but poor microenvironmental conditions are not sufficient to fully explain the behavioral lag.

4) How long the survivors will perform more poorly than the matched controls is a question which has not yet been adequately answered.

SUMMARY

The authors have selected a specific group or "cohort" of Mexican children born over a one-year period and have observed them for a number of years in order to study their nutritional status. The cohort selected was composed of 300 children born in a rural village between 1 March 1966 and 28 February 1967. The study is expected to run seven years, though only five years of observations are covered in the report presented here.

The village in question is primarily agricultural and in 1965 was inhabited by roughly 5,600 persons ranging in age from 0 to 85 years old. Fifty per cent of these people were less than 15 years old, indicating low life expectancy at birth. Agriculture was the villagers' main activity, though relatively small numbers of people were engaged principally in factory work, crafts, commerce, or the professions. The social and economic status of those with agricultural occupations varied considerably.

The cohort contained equal numbers of girls and boys, with the children's social origins closely matching those of the village as a whole. The mean birth weight of cohort children was 2,848 + 444 grams and their median body length was 48.5 cm. As would be expected, the boys had a higher mean weight and greater median length at birth than did the girls.

The height, weight, and age of cohort mothers varied widely (the mean values being 148.2 ± 2.8 cm, 53.0 ± 4.8 kg, and 25.6 ± 6.8 years). Nearly half of the mothers had been pregnant three or more times before, and over 46 per cent were completely illiterate. Few had any contact with television and half had little or no regular contact with radio. Sanitary characteristics of their households varied widely, but a considerable number of the homes had good to excellent sanitary conditions and facilities.

Twenty-three of the 300 infants delivered failed to survive a month; four were stillborn, seven died the first week after birth, three died during the remainder of the first month, and nine died during the remainder of the first year. Those that died tended to be shorter and weigh less than the survivors. Though this may have been due to prematurity in some cases, only three of the 23 dead infants had a body length equal to or greater than the median of the cohort as a whole. Ten deaths occurred in cohort children between the ages of one and five years. Seven of these were directly related to infectious disease accompanied in most cases by severe malnutrition.

During the first five years a total of 22 cohort children were found to be suffering from severe clinical malnutriton—despite medical efforts to prevent such cases. Twelve of the children were given hospital treatment and ten were treated at home. All the hospitalized cases recovered, but three of those treated at home died.

For purposes of subsequent study, the 19 survivors were matched with other cohort children who had never been considered severely malnourished. The matching was done with respect to birth data—including gestational age, body weight, and total body length.

Tests of the two groups showed that on the average the malnourished children were less able to develop certain types of mental concepts than their counterparts in the control group. This lag continued long after the once malnourished children had recovered their health. However, it is unclear whether the lag was the direct result of malnutrition or whether other ecological factors played a major role.

Data concerning the children's parents; family structure; sources and amounts of family income; sanitary facilities in each household; and the mother's personal cleanliness, literacy, and educational level failed to indicate statistically significant relationships between any of these variables and the malnourished children.

The only statistically significant factor of this kind discovered was radio listening by the child's mother. There were almost equal numbers of listeners and nonlisteners among mothers of the malnourished group, but the number of listeners among control group mothers was more than three times the number of nonlisteners.

These generally negative findings directed attention to the "microenvironment," in particular the stimulation received by the child within its home. Tests using the inventory developed by Beattye Caldwell showed that members of the malnourished group tended to receive significantly less home stimulation than control group members. This indicates that other microenvironmental factors should be investigated. At the present time the authors are analyzing possible associations between malnutrition and such factors as the mother's psychological profile, maternal attitudes, proclivity for change, concepts of health and disease, and concepts of food and feeding—as well as the family's visiting pattern.

REFERENCES

(1) Autret, M., and Moises Behar. *Sindrome Pluricarencial Infantil (Kwashiorkor) and its Prevention in Central America.* Food and Agriculture Organization, Rome, 1954. (FAO Nutrition Series No. 13.)

(2) Botha-Antoun, E., et al. "Intellectual Development Related to Nutritional Status." *J Trop Pediatr 14:* 112-115, 1968.

(3) Caldwell, B. M. "Descriptive Evaluations of Child Development and of Developmental Settings." *Pediatrics 40:* 46-54, 1967.

(4) Champakam, S., et al. "Kwashiorkor and Mental Development." *Am J Clin Nutr 21:* 844-852, 1968.

(5) Chase, H. P., and H. P. Martin. "Undernutrition and Child Development." *New Engl J Med 282:* 933-939, 1970.

(6) Cravioto, Joaquín, and Beatriz Robles. "The Influence of Protein-Calorie Malnutrition on Psychological Test Behavior." Proceedings of the First Symposium of the Swedish Nutrition Foundation on Mild-Moderate Forms of Protein-Calorie Malnutrition. Bastad and Göteborg, 1962, pp. 115-125.

(7) Cravioto, J., et al. "Nutrition, Growth and Neurointegrative Development: an Experimental and Ecologic Study." *Pediatrics 38:* 319-372, 1966.

(8) Cravioto, J., et al. "The Ecology of Infant Weight Gain in a Preindustrial Society." *Acta Paediatr Scand 56:* 71-84, 1967.

(9) Cravioto, J., et al. "The Ecology of Growth and Development in a Mexican Preindustrial Community. 1. Method and Findings from Birth to One Month of Age." *Monogr Soc Res Child Dev 34:* 1-76, 1969.

(10) Cravioto, J. and E. R. DeLicardie. "Mental Performance in School Age Children: Findings After Recovery from Early Severe Malnutrition." *Am J Dis Child 120:* 404-410, 1970.

(11) Cravioto, J. "The Complexity of Factors Involved in Protein-Calorie Malnutrition." *Bibliotheca Nutritio et Dieta 14:* 7-22, 1970.

(12) Cravioto, J. and E. R. DeLicardie. "The Long-Term Consequences of Protein-Calorie Malnutrition." *Nutr Rev 29:* 107-111, 1971.

(13) Cravioto, J. and E. R. DeLicardie. "Infant Malnutrition and Later Learning." In S. Margen and N. L. Wilson (eds.), *Progress in Human Nutrition,* Vol. 1, Avi Publishing Co., Westport, Conn., 1971, pp. 80-96.

(14) Gesell, A. L., and C. S. Amatruda. *Developmental Diagnosis; Normal and Abnormal Child Development, Clinical Methods and Practical Applications.* Second edition, Hoeber, New York, 1947.

(15) Liang, P. H., et al. "Evaluation of Mental Development in Relation to Early Malnutrition." *Am J Clin Nutr 20:* 1290-1294, 1967.

(16) Mönckeberg, Fernando. "Effect of Early Marasmic Malnutrition on Subsequent Physical and Psychological Development." In N. S. Scrimshaw and J. E. Gordon (eds.), *Malnutrition, Learning, and Behavior,* M.I.T. Press, Cambridge, Massachusetts, 1968, pp. 269-278.

(17) Pollitt, E., and D. M. Granoff. "Mental and Motor Development of Peruvian Children Treated for Severe Malnutrition." *Rev Interam Psicol 1:* 93-102, 1967.

(18) Yaktin, U. S., and D. S. McLaren. "The Behavioural Development of Infants Recovering from Severe Malnutrition." *J Ment Defic Res 14:* 25-32, 1970.

15: THE EFFECTS OF KWASHIORKOR ON PERFORMANCE ON TESTS OF NEUROPSYCHOLOGICAL FUNCTION

P. R. Bartel, L. S. Burnett, R. D. Griesel, I. Freiman,
E. U. Rosen, and J. Geefhuysen

In an attempt to quantify the long-term effects of malnutrition on human development, many investigators have regarded cognitive test performance as an indicator of the integrity of the brain (e.g. Stoch and Smythe, 1968; Kaplan, 1972).

A pioneering longitudinal study of the effects of marasmus (i.e. a more severe form of malnutrition than kwashiorkor in terms of retardation of physical growth) on cognitive test performance was commenced in Cape Town in 1955. Markedly lower IQ scores were reported for the malnourished group as compared to the control group throughout the 11-year follow-up period (Stoch and Smythe, 1963, 1967).

Several other investigators, using a cross-sectional approach have reported significant deficits in cognitive test performance of school-age children who had survived an episode of acute infantile protein-calorie malnutrition (PCM) (Champakam et al., 1968; Chase and Martin, 1970; Hertzig et al., 1972).

Evans et al. (1971) failed to find any significant differences in the cognitive test performance of a group of Cape Coloured children and their acutely malnourished siblings.

In a very important study, Valman (1974) compared the cognitive test scores of a group of children who had survived a period of malnutrition, during the neonatal period, following extensive resection of the ileum and a group of normal controls from the same upper socio-economic group. This is possibly the first study of the effects of malnutrition in a relatively non-deprived high socio-economic group. No significant group differences were found.

Employing a unique experimental design Evans (1973) compared the cognitive test performance of four groups of children, one in each group, from the same family, but having experienced different qualities of nutrition during infancy. The results suggested that malnutrition was associated with specific deficits in abstract reasoning and learning ability.

Several investigators have related deficits in intersensory integration functioning (i.e. the integration of information from different sensory modalities) to malnutrition (Cravioto et al., 1966; Cravioto and De Licardie, 1970; Champakam et al., 1968). Champakam et al. (1968) reported that the deficit tended to be reduced in older children suggesting some recovery over time.

The aim of the present study was to assess any effects of PCM found 4–12 years after the acute phase, using testing instruments likely to be culture-free. Much attention was paid to the selection of the experimental and control groups following the procedure of Richardson et al. (1972) in an attempt to avoid some of the more damaging criticism levelled at earlier studies.

Method

Subjects

The malnourished group of subjects consisted of 31 black children 6–14 years of age who had been hospitalized 5–10 years before the commencement of the study during the first 27 months of life. They were diagnosed as having kwashiorkor or marasmic kwashiorkor on the basis of criteria described by Freiman (1975).

The hospital records of potential subjects were carefully examined by a paediatrician and any indication of neurological involvement, i.e. brain damage, fits, birth trauma, coma while in hospital, or of hypoglycaemia, led to exclusion of the potential subject from the investigation. Once the subject had been located and parental permission obtained for participation in the study a further requirement had to be met. A sibling, reasonably close in age, who had not suffered from acute PCM (i.e. kwashiorkor or marasmus), had to be available for inclusion in the study. A second control group was constituted from yardmates of the probands and were of similar age. Parents were closely cross-examined and hospital records were carefully scrutinized to ensure that the controls had not been hospitalized for the treatment of infantile malnutrition. The latter criterion was regarded as particularly reliable in view of the fact that the hospital is the only one serving the area in which the subjects live.

A number of subtests from the Reitan-Indiana Neuropsychological Test Battery (RINTB) for children aged 5–8 years and from the Halstead Neuropsychological Test Battery (HNTB) for children aged 9–14 years, were selected on a logical *a priori* basis as being relatively culture-free.

The four tests administered in this study were:

(1) *Tactual Performance test* which utilises a modification of the Seguin Goddard form board. This test measures the subject's ability to fit 6 blocks into their correct spaces on the board while blindfolded. A memory for localization component is provided by the subject's drawing of the board after he/she has attempted to place the blocks. This is a complex test in terms of its requirements, successful completion of which depends upon tactile form discrimination, co-ordination of movement of the upper extremities, manual dexterity and visuo-spatial ability.

(2) *Tactile Form Recognition test*. Four flat plastic objects are placed in the subject's hand behind a wooden board and must then be matched visually against a set of diagrams of the stimulus figures. This test provides a measure of sensory-motor functioning and corresponds to an intersensory intergration task.

(3) *The Category test*. Stimulus figures are projected onto a milkglass screen and the subject responds by depressing one of four levers situated below the screen. If the response is correct a gong sounds, while a wrong answer results in a harsh buzzing noise. At the start of the test the subject can only guess with regard to the correct answer but feedback allows the subject to test various principles with respect to the relation of the levers to properties of the stimuli such as size, form, order, colour, etc. This procedure is repeated until an hypothesis is arrived at which receives consistent positive reinforcement. This test is a relatively complex concept formation task requiring competence in abstraction ability. The Category test alone has been shown to be almost as sensitive in the prediction of brain damage as the impairment index derived from the entire test battery of 10 items (Reitan, 1955). One study has suggested that the children's version of the Category Test reflects a level of intellectual ability similar to that assessed by standard measures of cognitive function (Knights and Tymchuk, 1968).

(4) *The WISC Maze test* (Wechsler, 1949) measures visuo-spatial and visual sequential ability (Reitan and Davison, 1974).

Procedure

Testing took place in a well-ventilated and illuminated mobile laboratory. The children were tested individually by the same experimenter. An interpreter was available to explain the requirements of each test in the child's home language. Information regarding the handedness and footedness of each subject was obtained prior to testing by means of the Reitan-Klove Lateral Dominance Examination (Reitan and Davison, 1974).

The tests were administered and scored according to instructions in the test manuals (Anon., 1968; Reitan, no date). In the testing of subjects and scoring and analysis of results a 'blind' approach was employed throughout so that the group identities of individual subjects were not known.

Data were gathered on a wide range of biographical variables relating to the child's developmental history, the child's family background and socio-economic status, the child's school performance and the child's physical status at the time of testing. These data have been described in detail elsewhere (Bartel, 1976).

The scores of the three groups for each test item were compared by using a one-way analysis of variance incorporating Bartlett's test for homogeneity of variances (Guilford, 1956). Where the analysis of variance indicated a statistically significant difference ($p < 0,05$) among the groups, pairs of group means were compared by using Scheffé's multiple comparison test (Scheffé, 1959).

Table 1

Test scores for each group and analysis of variance results

Test	Item	Kwashiorkor		Siblings		Yardmates		F
		Mean	SD	Mean	SD	Mean	SD	
Tactual Performance No. of Blocks Correct	Memory for Blocks	4,15	1,22	4,60	1,19	4,77	1,23	1,69
	Location of Blocks	1,38	1,38	2,52	1,61	1,72	1,88	3,25*
Time in Minutes	Total Time	13,24	5,46	10,97	4,85	12,30	6,55	1,05
	Time for DH	5,89	2,48	5,17	2,71	6,45	3,12	1,50
	Time for NDH	4,68	2,50	4,00	1,96	4,67	2,97	0,60
	Time for Both Hands	2,83	1,88	2,37	1,71	2,07	1,25	1,28
	DH–NDH	1,06	2,77	0,47	1,97	0,75	2,34	0,38
	DH–Both Hands	2,88	2,86	2,21	1,88	3,57	2,45	1,80
	NDH–Both Hands	1,85	2,31	1,62	2,16	2,69	2,98	1,19
Tactile Form Recognition (time in s)	Time for RH	21,75	6,16	19,16	6,18	19,77	5,45	1,55
	Time for LH	18,24	6,17	16,19	5,77	18,85	5,63	1,75
	RH–LH	3,44	5,40	2,96	4,74	1,37	5,25	1,36
	Total Time	40,00	11,10	35,35	10,99	38,30	9,96	1,46
Category Test	Total Errors	42,60	25,32	41,00	29,69	37,30	19,91	0,10
	Errors in Sub 3	18,63	11,06	18,07	9,51	14,80	10,25	1,04
	No. of Concepts Correct	2,13	0,69	2,17	0,94	2,17	1,07	0,02
Mazes (No. of Errors)	Raw Score	9,20	4,90	10,48	5,48	10,40	4,68	0,59
	Scaled Score	6,45	2,40	6,87	3,04	7,29	2,35	0,79

* $p < 0,05$

DH	= Dominant Hand	RH	= Right Hand
NDH	= Non-Dominant Hand	LH	= Left Hand
DH-NDH	= Difference in scores for the two hands	RH–LH	= Difference in scores for the two hands

Results

The three groups were similar in terms of all the biographical variables assessed. No significant differences were found among the groups in respect of the child's developmental history, .tribal affiliation, family background, family's socio-economic status, living conditions at the time of the study, school achievement and level of competence in the classroom, physical status and age at time of testing. The groups did not differ significantly with respect to sex and handedness (Bartel, 1976).

Means, SDs and F-ratios for each test item are presented in Table 1. The one-way analysis of variance revealed a statistically significant difference among the groups for only one variable, namely memory for location of blocks in the Tactual Performance test. Scheffé's multiple comparison test failed to reveal any statistically significant differences between pairs of group means.

Discussion

The biographical results showed a striking similarity among the groups in respect of the wide range of variables assessed. All studies investigating the effects of malnutrition on human development have failed to control for many relevant intervening social variables. It is acknowledged that to control variables such as maternal attitudes towards the child and the degree of social and maternal deprivation experienced by the malnourished child is virtually impossible (Scrimshaw and Gordon, 1968). However, many previous studies have apparently neglected to consider social factors. The present study has investigated a malnourished group and two control groups who, to some extent, have experienced similar family situations and whose families appeared to have virtually the same socio-economic status. This largely circumvented the problem encountered by Stoch and Smythe (1967) whose control group had a vastly different family background to that of the malnourished group (Bartel, 1976).

Although a significant inter-group variance was found for the memory of location of blocks in the Tactual Performance test, an isolated statistically significant result against a background of so many variables must be viewed with caution. Furthermore, Scheffé's test failed to reveal any significant differences between pairs of means for the groups on this variable. In addition, the majority of scores on the TPT do not differ significantly among the groups.

The groups did not differ significantly in performance on the Tactile Form Recognition test. These results are interesting in view of previous reports of marked deficits in the sensory-integration ability of previously malnourished subjects (Champakam *et al.*, 1968; Cravioto and De Licardie, 1970). Champakam *et al.* (1968) reported that the deficits were particularly severe in 'visual-haptic' ability, which was also assessed by the Tactile Form Recognition test in the present experiment.

The three groups did not differ in performance on the Category test. This finding suggested an equivalence among the groups in complex concept formation and abstraction ability. Furthermore, as this test is a sensitive indicator of brain damage (Reitan,

1955), the performance of the kwashiorkor group is of great significance in view of claims that PCM may result in organic brain damage (Stoch and Smythe, 1967). If the contention of Knights and Tymchuk (1968) is valid that the children's version of the Category test reflects intellectual ability similar to that assessed by standard cognitive measures, then the results of the present study contradict several previous studies associating lowered IQ test scores with PCM (Stoch and Smythe, 1963, 1967; Champakam *et al.*, 1968; Chase and Martin, 1970; Hertzig *et al.*, 1972). However, the Category test results would support the findings of Evans *et al.* (1971) and Valman (1974) of no significant differences between the IQ test performance of previously malnourished and control subjects.

The WISC Maze test performance of the three groups was not significantly different indicating equivalence among the groups in visual sequential ability.

The results of the present study can be interpreted in at least three ways:

(1) The test performance of the three groups was not significantly different because they had all been exposed to some degree of PCM; the kwashiorkor group to acute PCM and the two control groups to subclinical PCM. Therefore, the experimental group on the one had, and the two control groups on the other, were not sufficiently different in terms of nutritional status. This interpretation is considerably weakened by electrophysiological findings reported elsewhere (Bartel, 1976). The sibling and yardmate groups failed to differ significantly from a high socio-economic white control group, in the face of several significant differences between these groups and the kwashiorkor group, e.g. the amount of alpha present in the electroencephalogram. On the other hand, if the original contention is accepted, the present investigation, at the very least, suggests no differences in the longterm effects of acute and sub-clinical PCM.

(2) The tests used in the present study were not sufficiently sensitive to detect subtle behavioural deficits caused by kwashiorkor. This remains to be answered by future research. However, these tests have been shown to be sensitive enough to detect such dysfunctions as subsumed under the rubric "minimal cerebral dysfunction" (Reitan and Davison, 1974). Thus the functional significance of deficits not reflected in these test scores is not likely to be great. In the light of this it appears that children recover from kwashiorkor to a far greater extent than has frequently been claimed (See Lewin, 1975).

(3) The kwashiorkor group had made-up the deficits assessed by the tests used in the present experiment. This interpretation is in line with the findings of two previous studies (Keet *et al.*, 1971; Evans *et al.*, 1971) showing the apparent recuperative ability of humans treated for kwashiorkor. Keet *et al.'s* (1971) claim that "it is clearly worthwhile to give every malnourished child the benefit of active clinical treatment" (p. 1448) has been strengthened. The exceptional redundancy factor protecting the human brain cannot be relied on alone since untreated PCM inevitably leads to the demise of the individual before this factor can be detected behaviourally.

ACKNOWLEDGEMENTS

The study was authorized and guided by Dr. G. K. Nelson, Director of the National Institute for Personnel Research. We would like to thank Prof. J. D. L. Hansen, Professor of Paediatrics and Mrs. S. Mashigo, Social Worker, both of the University of the Witwatersrand and Mr. B. D. Murdoch, Head of the Division of Neuropsychology, NIPR, for their invaluable assistance with the planning and carrying out of this project.

REFERENCES

1. ANON (1968) *Neuropsychology Test Manual* (Revised), Topeka, Kansas, Topeka Veteran's Administration Hospital.
2. BARTEL, P. R. (1976) *Long-Term Electrocerebral Sequelae of Kwashiorkor*. CSIR Special Report PERS 244, NIPR, Johannesburg.
3. CHAMPAKAM, S., SRIKANTIA, S. G. *and* C. GOPALAN (1968) Kwashiorkor and mental development. *Am. J. clin. Nutr.*, 21, 844–852.
4. CHASE, H. P. *and* H. P. MARTIN (1970) Undernutrition and child development. *New Engl. J. Med.*, 282, 933–939.
5. CRAVIOTO, J. *and* E. R. DE LICARDIE (1970) Mental performance in school age children. Findings after recovery from early severe malnutrition. *Am. J. Dis. Child*, 120, 404–410.
6. CRAVIOTO, J., DE LICARDIE, E. R. *and* H. G. BIRCH (1966) Nutrition, growth and neurointegrative development: an experimental and ecologic study. *Pediatrics*, 38, 319–372.
7. EVANS, D. E. (1973) *Malnutrition and Intellectual Development*. Ph.D. Thesis, University of Cape Town.
8. EVANS, D. E., MOODIE, A. D. and J. D. L. HANSEN (1971) Kwashiorkor and intellectual development. *S. Afr. med. J.*, 45, 1412–1426.
9. FREIMAN, I. (1975) Protein energy malnutrition and its treatment. A review. *S. Afr. med. J.*, 49, 898–902.
10. GUILFORD, J. P. (1956) *Fundamental Statistics in Psychology and Education*. New York, McGraw Hill.
11. HERTZIG, M. E., BIRCH, H. G., RICHARDSON, S. A. and J. TIZARD (1972) Intellectual levels of school children severely malnourished during the first two years of life. *Pediatrics*, 49, 814–824.
12. KAPLAN, B. J. (1972) Malnutrition and mental deficiency. *Psychol. Bull.*, 78, 321–334.
13. KEET, M. P., MOODIE, A. D., WITTMANN, W. *and* J. D. L. HANSEN (1971) Kwashiorkor: a prospective ten-year follow-up study. *S. Afr. med. J.*, 45, 1427–1449.
14. KNIGHTS, R. M., *and* A. J. TYMCHUK. (1968) An evaluation of the Halstead-Reitan Category Tests for children. *Cortex*, 4, 402–414.
15. LEWIN, R. (1975) Starved brains. *Psychol. Today*, 9, 29–33.
16. REITAN, R. M. (no date) *Manual for Administration of Neuropsychological Test Batteries for Adults and Older Children*. Indianapolis, Indiana, Indiana University Medical Center.
17. REITAN, R. M. (1955) Certain differential effects of left and right cerebral lesions in human adults. *J. comp. Physiol. Psychol.*, 48, 474–477.
18. REITAN, R. M. *and* L. A. DAVISON. (1974) *Clinical Neuropsychology: Current Status and Applications*. New York, Wiley.
19. RICHARDSON, S. A., BIRCH, H. G., GRABIE, E. *and* K. YODER. (1972) The behavior of children in school who were severely malnourished in the first two years of life. *J. Health & soc. Behav.*, 13, 276–284.
20. SCHEFFÉ, H. (1959) *The Analysis of Variance*. New York, Wiley.
21. SCRIMSHAW, N. S. *and* J. E. GORDON, *eds.* (1968) *Malnutrition, Learning and Behavior*. Cambridge, Mass., MIT Press.

22. STOCH, M. B. *and* P. M. SMYTHE. (1967) Does undernutrition in infancy inhibit brain growth and subsequent intellectual development? *Arch. Dis. Child.* 38, 546–552.
23. STOCH, M. B. *and* P. M. SMYTHE. (1967) The effect of undernutrition during infancy on subsequent brain growth and intellectual development. *S. Afr. med. J.*, 41, 1027–1031.
24. STOCH, M. B. *and* P. M. SMYTHE. (1968) Undernutrition during infancy, and subsequent brain growth and intellectual development. *In*: SCRIMSHAW, N. S. *and* J. E. GORDON, *eds. Malnutrition, Learning and Behavior.* Cambridge, Mass., MIT Press.
25. VALMAN, H. B. (1974) Intelligence after malnutrition caused by neonatal resection of ileum. *Lancet* (March 16), 425–427.
26. WECHSLER, D. (1949) *Manual: Wechsler Intelligence Scale for Children.* New York, The Psychological Corporation.

16: INTELLECTUAL ABILITIES AND PROTEIN-ENERGY MALNUTRITION: ACUTE MALNUTRITION VS. CHRONIC UNDERNUTRITION

J. Hoorweg and J. P. Stanfield

INTRODUCTION

The question whether energy-protein malnutrition during
early childhood has a lasting influence on intellectual abilities
carries grave social implications. Despite increasing evidence
of such a relationship, many reviewers are hesitant to draw definite conclusions about the damage caused by childhood malnutrition. Warren in 1973 still regarded the "influence of malnutrition on mental development ... a rather open question" (25) and
one conclusion after a high-powered symposium in 1974 was that
"despite the widely held and widely publicized opinion that malnutrition in early life jeopardizes mental development the evidence to support this opinion -- especially from studies in man --
is scanty" (29). The reasons for this hesitancy are several.

The findings from animal studies are not easily generalized
to man because of the extreme conditions to which laboratory
animals often are exposed and because the development of the
human brain in relation to birth is different from that in most
animals. Studies of the relation between energy-protein malnutrition and intellectual abilities in humans are bedevilled by
problems of design and measurement, both of nutritional status
and intellectual abilities. All investigations -- whether they
are called follow-up, longitudinal or intervention studies --
have inherent weaknesses of design. Although many of the studies
have been carried out in countries of the developing world, the
problems of measuring intellectual abilities among these populations have often received little attention.

There has also been relatively little effort to investigate
the role of different aspects of malnutrition. Energy-protein
malnutrition of early childhood is a complex of elements, the
most important of which pertain to severity, duration and the
nature of metabolic disturbances. The forms of energy-protein
malnutrition may be subclinical or overt; acute, chronic or relapsing; oedematous (hypoproteinaemic) or marasmic. Children suffer
from malnutrition at different ages, and the food deficit often
coincides with infections or other nutritional deficiencies.
Many of these aspects are interrelated. In the typical case,
malnutrition starts during the first year of life, with growth
faltering because of an insufficiency of calories and protein.
As this condition continues, the child becomes increasingly
marasmic. At any time a variety of acute stresses, including
infections and further reduction in intake of proteins and

Reprinted from pages 148-163 of *Behavioral Effects of Energy and Protein Deficits.*
J. Brožek, ed., NIH Publication Number 79-1906, U.S. Government Printing Office,
Washington, D.C., 1979, 370p.

calories, may precipitate an acute metabolic imbalance in the child and result in kwashiorkor. One can therefore distinguish in any severely affected child a mixture of chronic undernutrition and acute malnutrition. The first is mainly reflected in stunting of somatic growth, the second in metabolic abnormalities, the chief of which are hypoproteinaemia and oedema. That a distinction should be drawn between undernutrition persisting over time and an acute condition arising over a short period has also been suggested by Waterlow and Rutishauser (26). Others regard acute malnutrition as a metabolic imbalance superimposed on long-term growth failure (20). Clearly energy-protein malnutrition cannot be regarded as a single entity, and it is to some of the distinctions outlined above that the present study addresses itself, notably the age at which children suffer from malnutrition and the differential effects of acute malnutrition and chronic undernutrition.

The present study was carried out in Uganda between 1970 and 1971. From 1953 to 1973 the British Medical Research Council operated a child nutrition research unit in Kampala. Most of the acutely malnourished children admitted to this unit were first seen and thereafter followed in a rural clinic some 12 miles north of Kampala. Many healthy children were also regularly seen at this rural clinic. The records of both groups of children were carefully kept throughout their attendance and offered the opportunity to investigate:

1. the existence of a long-term effect of malnutrition on (a) physical, (b) mental, and (c) motor development; and if so,

2. the influence of the age at which malnutrition occurs;

3. the influence of the type and severity of the malnutrition; and

4. the nature of the effect.

This paper will concentrate on the questions raised under (1b), (2) and (3).

METHOD

Design of Study
    Three groups of 20 children (the index children), admitted to the Kampala unit because of energy-protein malnutrition at least 10 years earlier, were selected for this follow-up study. Their ages on admission to the Unit fell between 8 and 15 months (group 1), 16 and 21 months (group 2), and 22 and 27 months (group 3). A comparison group of 20 children (group 4) who had not suffered from clinical malnutrition in infancy was selected from those attending the rural clinic. A design (6) was used in which the children constituting the four groups of children were individually matched. Only Baganda children were included.

Table 1. Study design: sample characteristics, education and
          socio-economic variables (means and standard deviations
          in parentheses).*

Group Number / Variable	1 Age 8-15 months	2 Age 16-21 months	3 Age 22-27 months	4 Comparison Group
Child's age at testing (years)	14.1 (1.3)	14.0 (1.5)	13.8 (1.4)	13.9 (1.5)
Child's education (years)	4.6 (1.6)	4.5 (1.3)	4.4 (1.2)	4.4 (1.4)
Male guardian's education (years)	3.1 (3.3)	5.4 (2.5)	4.9 (3.3)	5.7 (3.0)
Female guardian's education (years)	3.2 (2.8)	3.6 (2.5)	1.4 (2.3)	3.5 (2.1)
Socio-economic status: modern expenditures	3.6 (2.2)	2.6 (1.2)	2.3 (1.7)	2.7 (2.4)
Traditional sources	2.7 (1.7)	2.2 (0.9)	1.8 (1.1)	1.9 (1.6)

*Each group includes 20 children: 11 boys and 9 girls.

   The Baganda are the largest tribe in Uganda numbering about
one million people. They speak Luganda and live in the province
of Buganda, where the capital of the country, Kampala, is situated.
The children were matched for age, sex, education and social environment. Social environment took into account education of the
parents and various household characteristics combined into Gutt-
man scales for modern expenditures and for traditional resources,
respectively. The results of the matching are presented in Table 1.

   The sex composition of the groups is identical as are, for
all practical purposes, the average age and education of the children. Although there are some differences in the environmental
variables, they do not consistently favour one group.

   The ages of the children at the time of the study ranged from
11 to 17 years. The index children had suffered from acute malnutrition 10 to 16 years previously. Each child's date of birth
was checked against the village birth registers when necessary and
a child was excluded from the study if there was any doubt or discrepancy about the date of birth. Children with any indication of
possible brain insult (such as convulsions or respiratory infections with anoxia) were also excluded, as were those with long-
term chronic infections such as tuberculosis. Severe anaemia did
not exclude a child unless there was a record of a disturbance of
consciousness or convulsions.

Status of the Malnourished Children upon Admission (1954-1961)
The admission records contained data about the type and severity of the symptoms of malnutrition in the index children.
From these data seven indicators of the condition of each child
at admission were selected.

Many children lost some weight immediately after admission,
mainly as a result of loss of oedema fluid. This initial weight
loss was expressed as a percentage of the weight on admission.
The weight recorded on admission was expressed as a percentage of
the expected weight-for-age of each child, using Baganda standards.
The lowest haemoglobin level on admission and the serum protein
level on admission were recorded. Oedema and over-all clinical
severity was rated from 1 to 5 (severe), and skin changes were
rated from 1 to 4 (severe) by the attendant doctor at the time
of admission (Table 2).

After being admitted to the ward, the children lost an average of 8.4% of their weight. The lowest weight, on the average,
was 70% of the Baganda standard; none was above 90%, and only
seven children remained above 80% of this standard. The comparison children, whose weights had not fallen below the Boston
10th percentile, remained well above 90% of the Baganda standard
throughout the period of observation.

Serum protein levels of the index children averaged 4.2 g/
100 ml, considerably below normal values. Haemoglobin levels
on admission were also low, the average being 6.7 g/100ml. No
biochemical tests were available for the comparison children.
On admission the index children showed other signs of malnutrition
not seen in the comparison children. Some degree of oedema,
ranging from mild to severe,was present in all the index children,
and skin changes were observed in 87% of the cases.

Psychological Examinations (1970-1971)
A broad spectrum of indicators of mental development was examined, including general reasoning, verbal-educational abilities,
spatial-perceptual abilities, memory, and learning. The following
tests were used:

1. Board form of coloured progressive matrices (21)
2. Luganda vocabulary especially contructed for this purpose
3. Arithmetic test adapted from the WISC (27)
4. Shortened version of the Porteus mazes (1)
5. Memory-for-designs test (13)
6. Memory-for-designs test (13)
7. Knox cubes (1)
8. Rote-learning test in which associations had to be memorized
9. Incidental learning on the previous test.

A detailed description of the tests, their construction,
adaptation, reliabiltiy, and validity can be found elsewhere (15).

In the presentation of Knox cubes two speeds, normal and quick, were used following a suggestion by Klein (17). Since the normal and quick versions produced similar results and since no other indications were found that the two versions assessed different abilities a combination of the two scores is used throughout.

Table 2. Condition of index children at admission (N= 60).

Medical Indicators at Admission	Mean	Standard deviation
Percentage of expected weight for age[a,b]	69.7%	9.7
Percentage of weight lost after admission	8.4%	6.1
Haemoglobin level[b]	6.7g	2.1
Serum protein level	4.2g	0.7
Oedema[d]	3.8	0.8
Skin changes[e]	2.7	1.0
Overall clinical severity[c,d]	3.3	0.9

[a] Baganda standards (]0,26).
[b] lowest level during hospitalization.
[c] as judged by the attending doctor.
[d] rated on ordinal scale from 1 to 5 (severe).
[e] rated on ordinal scale from 1 to 4 (severe).

The psychological examination took place near the child's home in a converted VW bus. All tests were given individually and did not rely on written instructions or questions. They were all conducted in the child's own language, Luganda, with the help of a female interpreter. Because African children are particularly at a disadvantage with speed tests, speed bonusses were abolished for all tests and time limits doubled.

Reliability estimates of the individual tests fall between .80 and .90 except for vocabulary (between .70 and .80), and Porteus mazes and incidental learning (both between .50 and .60). Factor analysis of the tests revealed three principal dimensions. The first dimension represents general reasoning and education. It is predominantly loaded by Raven matrices, vocabulary and arithmetic. The second, spatial-perceptual dimension, is identified mainly by block design and Porteus mazes, while memory-for-designs also loads on this component. The third component consists primarily of the memory and learning tests.

Additional Examinations

In addition to the psychological tests various other examinations were carried out. These included:

1. A clinical medical examination
2. An anthropometric assessment.

The findings from these examinations have been presented elsewhere (4,5,16).

RESULTS

Malnourished vs. Comparison Children:

The mean test scores for the four groups under study are presented in Table 3. The three groups of malnourished children scored significantly lower on the Raven matrices, block design, memory-for-designs, and incidental learning (Table 4).

The memory-for-designs test has a skewed distribution of scores and the scores were dichotomized for purposes of correlational analysis. An error score of 5 or higher was recorded as 0, and a score of 4 or lower, as 1. Furthermore, wherever analysis of variance was used, Wilcoxon's signed ranks tests for matched pairs was utilized for this test.

Many studies have reported that the intellectual abilities of previously malnourished children are affected, including studies which have seriously attempted to eliminate the influence of external variables (2,3, 8,14,17,19). Two studies report contrary findings. The first found differences in IQ between malnourished children and matched controls, differences that were not significant although they were of a magnitude similar to those found in other studies (12). Evans, Moodie and Hansen (11) failed to find differences in IQ between formerly malnourished children and their siblings. The general picture is that malnourished children show impairment.

None of these investigations studies adults and the possibility remains that the malnourished children can still catch up by one or both of the twin processes of accelerated development or delayed maturation allowing for a longer period of development in the malnourished children. If catch-up occurs among the malnourished children, this means that over the years their test scores should improve more than that of better nourished children. This should be reflected in a higher correlation between age and test scores among the malnourished children. Because education will also influence test performance, partial correlations, independent of education, were calculated (Table 5). The partial correlations of age with test scores are neither positive nor significant, with a mean of -.12 among the malnourished children and -.08 in the comparison group, excepting the correlation between vocabulary and age which is positive as well as higher among the malnourished children. On the whole this evidence does not support the idea of a diminishing deficit. With the exception of the mastery of Luganda, both groups of children have reached their full mental development and the deficits of the malnourished children are likely to be permanent.

Table 3. Mean test scores for malnourished children and comparison group.

Group Number	1	2	3	4
Test	Age 8-15 months	Age 16-21 months	Age 22-27 months	Comparison Group
Raven matrices	22.8	21.9	21.5	24.1
Vocabulary	7.2	8.6	8.7	9.0
Arithmetic	8.8	9.7	9.6	9.3
Porteus mazes	6.4	6.3	6.2	7.0
Block design	16.7	15.7	16.4	21.9
Memory-for-design (errors)	7.1	8.7	4.4	4.7
Knox cubes	37.5	38.7	40.7	39.6
Learning	3.8	4.5	4.8	5.1
Incidental learning	4.0	5.1	4.6	5.9

Table 4. Analysis of variance: randomized block design (df = 1,57). F-values resulting from comparison of group 4 (comparison children) with groups 1, 2, and 3 (malnourished children).

TEST	F-VALUES % VARIANCE
Raven matrices	F = 4.24*
Vocabulary	F = 0.78
Arithmetic	F = 0.03
Porteus mazes	F = 2.66
Block design	F = 8.28**
Memory for designs	T = 48.5*[a]
Knox cubes	F = 0.18
Learning	F = 1.17
Incidental learning	F = 5.94*

[a]Wilcoxon matched-pair signed-ranks test.
*$p < .05$
**$p < .01$

Table 5. Partial correlations of age with test scores (education constant).

TESTS	MALNOURISHED GROUP (N = 3 x 20) *	COMPARISON GROUP (N = 20)
Raven matrices	-.14	-.01
Vocabulary	.46**	.25
Arithmetic	-.17	-.15
Porteus mazes	-.08	-.10
Block design	-.28	-.10
Memory for designs	-.11	-.19
Knox cubes	-.09	.07
Learning	-.03	-.17
Incidental learning	-.08	.05

*pooled results
**$p < .01$

Malnourished Children: Age at Hospitalization

The idea that a critical period in brain development exists not only in animals but also in man has given rise to the hypothesis that the younger the child when energy-protein malnutrition occurs, the more severe the ultimate effect. Findings from an early study by Cravioto and Robles (9) seemed to support this idea. Other studies, however, have failed to find a relation between the age at which malnutrition occurs and later intellectual abilities (7,14,19,22). One study which compared children hospitalized for malnutrition between 10 and 15 months of age with children admitted between 16 and 48 months, in fact, reported the opposite. When tested after the age of 9 years, the groups which had suffered earlier in life did considerably better than the group which had been admitted later in life (11).

All malnourished children in the present study had been admitted before the age of 28 months. Analysis of variance shows that there are no significant differences between the children admitted before 16 months of age and the children admitted at later ages (Table 6). In regard to the four tests which showed significant differences between the malnourished and comparison children, the group admitted at the younger age scored slightly higher on Raven matrices and block design, but slightly lower on memory-for-designs and incidental learning than the children admitted at later ages.

In the studies discussed above, the children were usually older than 6 months on admission. This is conceivably past the age of greatest vulnerability. Chase and Martin (8) compared nine children who were admitted for malnutrition before 4 months

of age, with ten children who were admitted between the ages of
5 and 12 months. These groups were identical in their social
background. At the age of $3\frac{1}{2}$-$4\frac{1}{2}$ years, the groups which had suffered early were only slightly behind a matched control group of
normal children in development. Contrary to what might be expected, the group of children admitted late, between 5 and 12 months,
scored far below the group which was admitted early, and below
the comparison group.

There is almost no convincing evidence that malnutrition
occurring after 6 months of age, or even after 12-18 months of
age, is less damaging than earlier malnutrition. However, we
face a fundamental problem of interpretation. The age of the
child at first treatment is usually taken to be synonymous with
the age at onset of malnutrition. This seems justified with
regard to acute malnutrition since the time elapsed between onset
and first treatment will be short. The age at first treatment,
however, does not correspond to the onset of chronic undernutrition, which may antedate the admission by varying amounts of time.
In the next section we shall take a closer look at these two aspects of malnutrition.

Table 6.   Analysis of variance: randomized block design
           (df = 1,57). F-values resulting from compa-
           rison of groups 2 and 3 (late admissions) with
           group 1 (early admissions).

TEST	F-VALUES
Raven matrices	F = 1.10
Vocabulary	F = 2.44
Arithmetic	F = 2.33
Porteus mazes	F = 0.14
Block design	F = 0.10
Memory for designs	T = 74.5[a]
Knox cubes	F = 1.96
Learning	F = 1.35
Incidental learning	F = 2.53

[a]Wilcoxon matched-pairs signed ranks test, n.s.

Dimensions of Malnutrition: Acute vs. Chronic
     As noted before, from the data in the admission records
seven indicators of the condition of each child were selected:
weight, weight loss after admission, hemoglobin and serum protein
level, and the degrees of oedema, skin changes, and over-all
clinical severity as rated at the time of admission by the attending physician. The correlations between these seven indicators

were computed for each of the malnourished groups and the three
resulting correlation matrices were pooled into one matrix subjected to principal component analysis in order to obtain as
systematic and economic a description of observed data as possible. This analysis yielded two independent dimensions of malnutrition (Table 7) which, to a greater or lesser extent, were
present in each child. The first dimension is composed of those
variables which are predominant in kwashiorkor, i.e., metabolic
abnormality (low serum-protein levels giving rise to oedema and
initial weight-loss during treatment after admission), skin
changes and the doctor's judgment of severity of the condition
on admission.

The dominant element in the second dimension is the weight
deficit characteristic of marasmus, with stunting of somatic
growth. Haemoglobin deficit also is an important element in this
component.

We have called these components "acute malnutrition" and
"chronic undernutrition," respectively. Together they determine
the type of clinical malnutrition a child exhibits. Kwashiorkor
and marasmus are used clinically as diagnostic terms for the total syndrome, and it would be confusing to apply them to its
component parts. Furthermore, the variables in each of the two
dimensions tend to evolve over different periods of time. The
first dimension reflects acute changes, usually developing over
a short time and precipitating admission to hospital.   The second, consisting of weight deficit and haemoglobin deficit, usually
develops over a longer period and thus reflects the chronicity of

Table 7. Medical indicators at admission: varimax rotation of
first two principal components (malnourished groups
pooled; N = 3 x 20).

MEDICAL INDICATORS AT ADMISSION	DIMENSION 1	DIMENSION 2
% of expected weight for age[a,b]	.07	-.80
% of weight lost after admission	.58	-.55
Haemoglobin level[b]	-.28	-.66
Serum protein level	-.59	-.10
Oedema	.73	-.17
Skin changes	.69	.00
Overall clinical severity[c]	.73	.23

[a] Baganda standards (10,26).
[b] lowest level during hospitalization.
[c] as judged by the attending doctor.

the malnutrition. Initial loss of weight during early treatment is
characteristic of the acute condition. In contrast, the smaller
the weight loss the more severe is the chronic condition.

For each child the severity of acute malnutrition and
chronic undernutrition was computed as a weighted index, with
a standard deviation of 1.0, based on the original seven variables.

The correlations between the magnitude of these two components
of malnutrition as observed early in life and the test scores
obtained more than 10 years later are presented in Table 8.
Acute malnutrition shows no consistent correlations with the
tests. Five of the nine correlations do not exceed ±0.06, while
four of the correlations are positive and five are negative. The
correlations of chronic undernutrition with the tests are consistently negative; that is, the children do less well on the
tests the greater the degree of chronic undernutrition in early
childhood. For five of the tests the correlations are significant;
and although not significant for vocabulary, Porteus mazes, and
learning, they are still negative and larger than 0.15.

Table 8. Correlations of two independent dimensions of
malnutrition, acute malnutrition and chronic
undernutrition, with tests (results of
malnourished groups pooled; N = 3 x 20).

TEST	ACUTE MALNUTRITION	CHRONIC MALNUTRITION
Raven matrices	.02	-.40*
Vocabulary	-.12	-.17
Arithmetic	-.05	-.44*
Porteus mazes	-.06	-.18
Block design	-.02	-.34*
Memory-for-designs	-.02	-.33*
Knox cubes	.17	-.27**
Learning	.13	-.21
Incidental learning	.13	-.03

*p < .01, one-tailed test.
**p < .05, one-tailed test.

Other studies have also reported a relation between the degree of wasting or chronic undernutrition, and test performance
(5,7,17). As previously discussed, Chase and Martin (8) found
that children who had been admitted between 5 and 12 months of
age showed much greater retardation than children who had been
admitted before 4 months of age. The authors attribute this to

the longer duration of chronic undernutrition in the older children, assuming that the malnutrition commenced shortly after birth. These studies, however, did not exclude the possibility of the acute episode also having an effect. The results of the present study indicate that chronic undernutrition is the factor responsible for lowered intellectual abilities later in life and not acute malnutrition, which shows no evidence of having an impairing effect. This offers an explanation why in one important study no differences in test performance were found between formerly malnourished children and their siblings when they were between 8 and 15 years of age (11). Siblings share the same environment and presumably experience similar nutritional circumstances. In fact, in this particular study the comparison group of siblings was also not different in respect to somatic growth. Apparently these children, although having escaped an episode of acute malnutrition, had suffered similar degrees of chronic undernutrition and were therefore equally intellectually affected.

CONCLUSION

The present study has explored the relation between malnutrition and intellectual abilities in two ways: first, by comparison with a matched group of children who were not severely malnourished during the first years of life; and second, by relating present intellectual abilities to the condition of each child on admission to the hospital.

The previously malnourished children show signs of (permanent) impairment when compared, at the ages of 11-17 years, with children of the same sex, age, and education coming from a comparable environment. Since the pattern of malnutrition occurring in Buganda is rather uniform (weight deficit together with frequent infections commences at the time of weaning, usually between 6 and 12 months of age), it follows that the child is still vulnerable at **weaning**. The impairment exhibited by the previously malnourished children shows a strong relation with an index, composed of weighted medical indicators, measuring the degree of chronic undernutrition at admission. No such relation exists with a similar index assessing the degree of acute malnutrition or metabolic **imbalance** at admission. This fits in with the finding that the impairment is independent of the age at which the children were admitted to the hospital.

The limitations of this study are that certain information, such as height, was not recorded at admission and that no systematic observations were made of these children prior and after their episode of malnutrition. On the one hand this reflects the limited knowledge about the condition at the time. On the other hand, it is through the foresight of Dr. Dean, the late director of this unit, that systematic observations were recorded and carefully kept from 1954 onwards. The combination of data in admission records with later test performance has enabled us to identify **chronic undernutrition as the damaging process.**

Chronic undernutrition has two components, the degree of faltering and the duration of such faltering. There is little evidence that one of these two is the more important. Furthermore, in retrospective studies it is usually not possible to distinguish between the respective contributions of these two aspects of the final condition of the child. The lack of positive findings among children in Western countries who for strictly medical reasons become malnourished suggests that duration is important (18,24). After the age of 5 years these children showed no difference in test performance when compared with their siblings. Although both studies have certain weaknesses they recall similar findings in a study (8) where no effects were observed among children who had been malnourished before the age of 4 months. This suggests that children who become severely malnourished early in life suffer relatively little damage as regards their later intellectual abilities. This could be explained by a greater plasticity of the infantile nervous system during the early months of life. It is also possible that in very young children malnutrition simply has not lasted long enough to have measurable long-term effects. Another possible explanation is that malnutrition impairs intellectual abilities by way of experiential deprivation, which possibly becomes important only after 6 months of age.

Whatever the answers to these last questions, two inferences can be drawn. First, since chronic undernutrition plays the crucial role, treatment of acute cases is insufficient to prevent intellectual impairment. Secondly, the intellectual abilities of children who suffer from chronic undernutrition but who never experience an acute episode, a far more numerous group, are likely to be similarly impaired.

SUMMARY

Three groups of Ugandan children (20 in each group) and one comparison group of 20 children were examined between 11 and 17 years of age. The children in the first three groups had suffered from energy-protein malnutrition 10 to 16 years previously when they were hospitalized at different ages (between 8-15 months, 16-21 months, and 22-27 months). The comparison group consists of of children who had not suffered from clinical malnutrition during infancy. All the children came from one tribe and were individually matched for sex, age, education and home environment.

The three groups malnourished in infancy fell significantly below the comparison group in test performance at the later age. Further analysis showed that the deficit is not related to the severity of acute malnutrition, but rather to the degree of chronic undernutrition at admission. No evidence was found for a relationship between impairment and the age at admission.

ACKNOWLEDGEMENT

This study was supported and financed by the Medical Research Council, Child Nutrition Unit, Kampala; Makerere University, Kampala; and African Studies Centre, Leyden.

REFERENCES

1. Arthur, G. A Point Scale of Performance Tests. New York: Psychological Corporation, 1947.

2. Birch, H. G., Pineiro, C., Alcalde, E., Toca, T. and Cravioto, J. Relation of kwashiorkor in early childhood and intelligence at school age. Pediatr. Res., 5:579-585, 1971.

3. Botha-Antoun, E., Babayan, S. and Harfouche, J. K. Intellectual development related to nutritional status. J. Trop. Pediatr., 14:112-115, 1968.

4. Briers, P. J., Hoorweg, J. and Stanfield, J. P. The long term effects of protein energy malnutrition in early childhood on bone age, bone cortical thickness and height. Acta Paediatr. Scandin., 64:853-858, 1975.

5. Brockman, L. M. and Ricciuti, H. N. Severe protein-calorie malnutrition and cognitive development in infancy and early childhood. Dev. Psych., 4:312-319, 1971.

6. Brownlee, K. A. Statistical Theory and Methodology in Science and Engineering. New York: John Wiley, 1965.

7. Cabak, V. and Najdanvic, R. Effect of undernutrition in early on physical and mental development. Arch. Dis. Child., 40: 532-534, 1965.

8. Chase, H. P. and Martin, H. P. Undernutrition and child development. New Eng. J. Med., 282:933-939, 1970.

9. Cravioto, J. and Robles, B. Evolution of adaptive and motor behaviour during rehabilitation from kwashiorkor. Am. J. Orthopsychiatr., 35:449-464, 1965.

10. Dean, R.F.A. Standards for African children and the influence of nutrition. J. Trop. Med. Hyg., 57:283-289, 1954.

11. Evans, D. E., Moodie, A. D. and Hansen, J. D. L. Kwashiorkor and intellectual development. S. Afr. Med. J., 45:1413-1426, 1971.

12. Ghai, O. P., Ratna, K., Ramachandran, K. and Neki, J. S. Effect of early marasmic malnutrition on subsequent mental development. Ind. Pediatr., 10:155-159, 1973.

13. Graham, F. K. and Kendall, B. S. Memory-for-designs test: Revised general manual. Percep. Mot. Skills, 11:147-188, 1960.

14. Hertzig, M. E., Birch, H. G., Richardson, S. A. and Tizard, J. Intellectual levels of school children severely malnourished during the first two years of life. Pediatrics, 49:814-824, 1972.

15. Hoorweg, J. Protein-energy Malnutrition and Intellectual Development. The Hague: Mouton, 1976.

16. Hoorweg, J. and Stanfield, J. P. Protein-energy malnutrition of early childhood as it affects intellectual and motor abilities in the older child and adolescent. Dev. Med. Ch. Neurol., 18:330-350, 1976.

17. Klein, R. E., Lester, B. M., Yarbrough, C. and Habicht, J. P. On malnutrition and mental development: Some preliminary findings. In A. Chavez, H. Bourges and S. Basta, Eds., Nutrition: Proceedings of the IXth International Congress of Nutrition, Mexico, 1972. Vol. 2. Basel: Karger, pp. 315-321, 1975.

18. Lloyd-Still, J. D., Hurwitz, L., Wolff, P. H. and Schwachman, H. Intellectual development after severe malnutrition in infancy. Pediatrics, 54:306-311, 1974.

19. McLaren, D. S., Yaktin, U. S., Kanawati, A. A., Sabbagh, S. and Kadi, Z. The subsequent mental and physical development of rehabilitated marasmic infants. J. Men. Def. Res., 17: 273-281, 1973.

20. Rao, K. S. J. Evolution of kwashiorkor and marasmus. Lancet, 1:709-711, 1974.

21. Raven, J. C. Guide to the Coloured Progressive Matrices. London: Lewis, 1965.

22. Richardson, S. A., Birch, H. G. and Hertzig, M. E. School performance of children who were severely malnourished in infancy. Am. J. Ment. Def., 77:623-632, 1973.

23. Rutishauser, I. H. E. The heights and weights of middle class Baganda children. Lancet, 2:565-567, 1965.

24. Valman, H. B. Intelligence after malnutrition caused by neonatal resection of ileum. Lancet, 1:425-427, 1974.

25. Warren, N. Malnutrition and mental development. Psych. Bul., 80:324-328, 1973.

26. Waterlow, J. C. and Rutishauser, I. H. E. Malnutrition in man. In *Symposia of the Swedish Nutrition Foundation XII*, Pt.1, Uppsala: Almquist and Wiksell, 1974.

27. Wechsler, D. *Wechsler Intelligence Scale for Children*. New York: Psychological Corporation, 1949.

28. Wechsler, D. *Wechsler Adult Intelligence Scale*. New York: Psychological Corporation, 1955.

29. World Health Organization. Malnutrition and mental development. *WHO Chronicle*, 28:95-102, 1974.

ERRATUM

In the section *Psychological Examinations (1970-1971)*, item 5 should read "Block design."

17: THE LONG RANGE CONSEQUENCES OF MALNUTRITION IN INFANCY: A STUDY OF CHILDREN IN JAMAICA, WEST INDIES

S. A. Richardson

The purpose of this paper is to describe some research into the question: Does malnutrition during infancy cause permanent intellectual impairment?

Until the latter half of this century, the question was academic because infants with marasmus and kwashiorkor often died. With the introduction of antibiotics and increased knowledge about the control of fluid loss and electrolyte imbalance, the effectiveness of medical treatment of malnutrition improved and an increasing number of malnourished young children survived. The question of whether survivors were permanently intellectually impaired then became a practical issue and an important one for social policy.

Two views published three years apart in the 1970's illustrate the spread in the interpretation of research relating to the long term consequences of malnutrition during infancy: —

"There is overwhelming evidence that severe malnutrition during the early years of life, especially the first two years, leads to retarded brain growth, permanent reduction in brain size, and defective intellectual development. Malnutrition has, therefore, been rightly blamed as one of the main causes of mental retardation [1]."

"Our review of knowledge about the effects of postnatal nutrition on later mental development suggests to us that such effects do exist but that they are not large or easily detected. There are many areas of ambiguity. There is as yet no evidence to support the hypothesis that nutritional deprivation not only retards development but that its effects persist into adulthood and prevents the full realisation of potential mental competence [2]."

Other Studies

A brief review of the designs of the studies of the long term effects of early malnutrition may help in understanding why two such different conclusions were

Reprinted from pages 163-176 of *Topics in Pediatrics 2, Nutrition in Childhood,* B. Wharton, ed., Pitman Publishing Ltd, Tunbridge Wells, England, 1980; *Copyright © 1980 by Pitman Publishing Ltd.*

reached by the reviewers. It will also help explain the design of our study which stemmed from questions arising from previous studies.

Most of the studies of humans have been of two kinds. One has been to infer malnutrition from measurements of height for age and judge short children to have been at greater nutritional risk than taller children of the same age. A number of variables other than nutrition account for differences in height, so stature provides only an approximate measure of nutrition. The other kind of study has been of children with histories of malnutrition. In these studies, the strongest evidence of malnutrition was where children had been treated in hospital and there was evidence of kwashiorkor or marasmus.

In both approaches it was necessary to compare previously malnourished with non-malnourished children to determine whether they were similar or different in functioning some years after malnutrition occurred. To obtain similarity between the two sets of children on non-nutritional variables, the comparisons were selected through matching on some of the characteristics of the malnourished children. Variables used in matching have included age, sex, attending the same class in school, socio-economic status, religion and being a sibling. No one or combination of these matching variables, however, comes close to meeting the requirements of a rigorous experimental design.

Once the study subjects were selected, measures of intellectual functioning were obtained, generally using some intelligence test. The results of most studies showed the malnourished children to have lower intelligence than the comparisons who were not malnourished. These results could not be interpreted because the requirements of an experimental design had not been met. Yet, with varying degrees of caution, investigators did interpret their results as showing that malnutrition caused intellectual impairment. In part, the temptation to make this interpretation may stem from the widespread inappropriate use of the term 'controls' for the non-malnourished, making it easy to begin to assume that they met the requirements of an experimental design.

Once it is accepted that an experimental design is not feasible for the study of the long term consequences of malnutrition in humans, other approaches can be considered. Instead of asking, 'Does malnutrition cause mental impairment?', a more general question may be asked. 'What are the range of factors which influence the intellectual development of children, and to what extent is malnutrition a contributing factor?' This question suggests a more ecological research approach in which a variety of biological and social factors are included which may contribute to the later level of functioning of children.

The Jamaican Study

The study that I shall now describe began in 1970. Professor John Waterlow, Director of the Metabolic Research Unit of the Medical Research Council in Jamaica, invited the late Dr Herbert Birch and me to investigate the effects of early malnutrition by following up infants who had been treated in his research unit for a primary diagnosis of severe malnutrition and who, by then, were of school age. We accepted the invitation and worked with the close cooperation of Professor Waterlow and his staff, and also with Dr William Miall, the Director of the adjoining Epidemiological Research Unit of the MRC in Jamaica and his staff. The late Professor Jack Tizard was a valuable consultant and participated in the intellectual assessment of the children. The study was designed to examine the following questions:

1. At school age are children malnourished during infancy functioning less well than children not malnourished during infancy? Almost the only functional measure used in previous studies was level of intelligence. The reason for concern about the development of children malnourished in early life is the fear that malnutrition causes permanent impairment to the central nervous system. It is unlikely that such impairment would be restricted to skills needed in taking an intelligence test, and likely that impairment would be more broadly manifested in school work and various forms of behaviour related to school and home activities. For this reason a variety of school performance and behaviour measures were included in our study, to determine whether the index boys were more generally functionally impaired than the comparisons.

2. In addition to experiencing malnutrition, do the index boys experience more disadvantageous environmental circumstances for the development of their social and intellectual skills? Only through examining this question will it be possible to begin to assess what factors may contribute to differences, if the index boys are found to be more functionally impaired.

3. Does the age at which malnutrition occurs within the first two years relate to whether and to what extent functional impairment is found in the index children at follow-up? In 1971 data from animal experiments indicated that during the time of most rapid brain growth, severe malnutrition is more likely to cause central nervous system impairment than during periods of life when the brain is growing less rapidly. It was suggested that the most rapid period of brain growth in humans was up to nine months of age [3]. By selecting cases who had experienced malnutrition at different times during the first two years of life, we could determine whether different levels of functioning are associated with the time the malnutrition was experienced.

The subjects for the study were seventy-one boys in Jamaica, West Indies, who had been admitted to hospital with a primary diagnosis of severe malnutrition at some time during their first two years of life (hereafter referred to as index boys). Malnutrition took the form of marasmus, kwashiorkor, or marasmic-kwashiorkor. Fifty-nine of the boys had been patients in the Tropical Metabolism Research Unit. The remaining twelve were added in order to have fuller representation of malnutrition over the first two years of life. They were obtained from the Pediatric Ward of the University Hospital, at the University of the West Indies,

Mona, Jamaica. Children received, on the average, eight weeks of in-patient care. In general, follow-up visits in the home were conducted for the two years following discharge. Approximately half of the index boys lived in the city of Kingston and the remainder came from other smaller towns, villages and rural districts, in some cases more than 100 miles from Kingston.

For each index boy attending school a classmate of the same sex and nearest in age was selected as a comparison. For those boys not attending school at the time of the study or for whom no classmate met the age requirement, a comparison case was chosen by finding the nearest neighbouring child who was not a relative and who was within six months of the index boy's age. None of the comparison cases had been in hospital for severe malnutrition.

Throughout, those collecting the data were not told whether a boy was an index or comparison case. The differences in functioning to be reported were all tested to determine level of significance. All results to be described here were at the 5% level of probability or better. The kinds of tests used and the levels of significance are reported in the papers cited.

Intelligence Test Performance

We used the WISC I.Q. test even though the results are clearly not comparable to those of children on whom the test was standardised. The test is useful for comparing children within a culture provided it discriminates across the children tested. For the Full Scale, Verbal and Performance measures of I.Q., the index boys were seven to nine points lower than the comparison boys [4].

School Performance and Behaviour

The I.Q. test does not measure the full range of a child's cognitive abilities. An evaluation of school performance provides culturally relevant estimates of cognitive behaviour in Jamaica and complements information obtained from the I.Q. test. In school performance the index boys scored lower in reading, spelling and arithmetic on the Wide Range Achievement Test [5].

The teachers' evaluations of school performance are perhaps more relevant in terms of their influence on the child's future education and vocation. Teachers will vary in their standards for evaluating children. This was a reason why the class at school was one of the matching variables used to select comparisons. In this way the same teacher judged each pair of boys. Index boys were given a lower overall evaluation of their school work and had lower marks on school subjects. Index boys were judged by their teachers to have poorer attention and memory, to be more easily distracted, offer fewer suggestions and talk less in the classroom. In social relations the index boys were judged to get on less well with peers, cooperate less with the teacher and have more behaviour problems, including shyness, being withdrawn and hard to reach, being unresponsive and lacking in communication.

We also used the boys' classmates as judges of the study subjects' behaviour at school. Each boy in the class was asked who were the three boys he played with most often. The index boys were selected less often by classmates than the comparisons [6].

Behaviour at Home

To obtain information about the functioning of the study subjects in a different setting from the school, we obtained an assessment from their parents or guardians on their functioning at home [7]. Here it was not possible to obtain direct comparisons by the same judge for an index case and the matched comparison. Instead, each parent or guardian had to judge their child against their general standards of child behaviour. This information was obtained in an interview at each boy's home and included the boys who were not attending school at the time of the study. According to the parents or guardians, the index boys were less liked by their siblings and were more often unhappy or having trouble at school. The index boys were judged more often immature as indicated by more often having a bad temper, not being able to stand still when told, and more often having enuresis. In co-ordination, the index boys were judged to be more awkward and clumsy.

In summary, then, the findings at this point were in the same direction as other studies of children malnourished during infancy in that at school age they functioned less well than peers who had not been malnourished. However, we cannot make causal inferences from these results.

Critical Periods

We examined the issue of whether there are critical periods within the first two years of life when malnutrition has more serious long term consequences. No differences were found in the various measures of functioning just described relating to age at which the index boys were hospitalised.

Home Environment

Our next step was to examine the background histories of the index and comparison boys. We feld that malnutrition could well be an indicator of a set of family conditions and upbringing experiences that are disadvantageous for a child's social and intellectual development. We developed a home interview, supplemented by interviewer observations of the home environment and of the informant, which would provide information on the social and biological conditions of the lives of the children and their families. The selection of these background factors was based on a review of variables that have been shown or hypothesised to influence the functional development of children. Many were derived from literature related

TABLE   Ecological Factors Which May Influence the Functional Development of Children

Child's Biologic Mother

Reproductive history
Health history

Mother's or Caretaker's Capabilities and Activities

Verbal ability
Values
Exposure to ideas
Activities and affiliations
Human resources
Training and upbringing of the child
Aspirations for the child
Mother as teacher of the child

Father or Adult Male

Presence of adult male role model in the household
Existence of affectionate ongoing relationship with the child
Joint activities of husband and wife with the child
Degree of conflict or cooperation between husband and wife in childrearing

Family

Composition
Stability
Extended family
Social relations between family, friends, and neighbours
Alternative caretakers available for the child

Physical and Economic Resources of the Family

Income in cash and kind
Type and size of dwelling
Water supply
Availability of electricity
Appliances
Type of fuel used
Transportation

Area of Residence

Spectrum ranging from isolated rural location to large urban centre

Child's Background History

Pregnancy number and ordinal position
Birth weight and general health history (other than malnutrition)
Feeding during the first two years of life
Continuity in prime caretaker
Continuity in composition of family
Relationships with adults
Relationships with other children
Exposure to ideas and language
Activities and experiences outside the home
School history

to 'cultural deprivation' and 'social disadvantage'.

An indication of the types of variables considered is summarised in Table I [8]. These variables had to be translated from concepts to operational measures derived from our interview and observation data; the details of this procedure are given elsewhere [9]. Here I shall illustrate some of the variables on which the index cases differed significantly from their comparisons in the direction of their histories being more unfavourable. The mother or caretaker had a less favourable upbringing and education, was judged to have a lower level of capability, had less contact with mass media, and fewer human resources she could turn to for help and support. The mothers had a less favourable general reproductive history. The economic and housing variables were more unfavourable for the families of the index children as indicated by the structure and condition of the house, the home furnishings and appliances, and the amount of crowding in the house. The mortality among siblings was higher for the index boys and the index boys received less intellectual stimulation.

The evidence then supports our expectation that the index boys come from more disadvantageous social and biological backgrounds than the comparisons.

Having found the index and comparisons differ on background as well as nutritional history, our next step was to determine which of the factors accounted for differences in level of functioning. An early analysis we did can serve as an introduction.

The measure of the boy's early intellectual stimulation was based on responses to a series of questions about whether the child had any toys, books or magazines, whether he was told stories or read to, whether he listened to the radio or watched television, and whether he was taken on trips.

Index and comparison boys were classified according to whether they scored above or below the median on the measure of intellectual stimulation, and for each of the four resulting sets of boys, the average I.Q. score was obtained. The results are shown in Table II. It shows, as might be anticipated, that the boys who

TABLE II. Average I.Q. Score for Index and Comparison Boys Who Scored Above and Below Median Score on Measure of Intellectural Stimulation

Measure of Intellectual Stimulation	Hospitalised for Malnutrition	
	Yes (index)	No (comparison)
Below Median Score	mean I.Q. = 53	mean I.Q. = 61
Above Median Score	mean I.Q. = 63	mean I.Q. = 71

were both malnourished and were below the median score on intellectual stimulation have the lowest average I.Q., and those who were not malnourished and were above the median score on intellectual stimulation had the highest average score. What is crucial in the Table is that malnourished boys with more intellectual stimulation have as high I.Q. scores as the non-malnourished boys who received less intellectual stimulation. Clearly, the effect of malnutrition on the boys is not so dominant that it outweighs or masks the effect of the intellectual stimulation they received in early childhood.

We then developed a composite measure of the boys' social background histories. From all the background variables, three general variables were selected: the caretaker's level of capability, a socio-economic measure based on the home furnishings and appliances, and the intellectual stimulation measure already described. Each of the three variables shown (see Table III) was given equal weight to obtain a composite background history score, and the scores were divided into deciles. As would be expected, a high or advantageous score was significantly associated with a higher I.Q. score ($p < 0.005$) (see Table IV) [10].

TABLE III. Three Social Background Variables Used to Make a Composite Score

1. *Caretaker's level of capability derived from:*

   a. How the caretaker used her spare time
   b. The caretaker's level of ability in reading and writing
   c. Whether others sought out the caretaker as a source of help or advice
   d. The state of the neatness and organisation of the house
   e. How well the caretaker understood the questions in the interview, how well she responded, and an interviewer rating of her intelligence

2. *A socio-econimic measure, using home furnishing and appliances, derived from:*

   a. If electric power, the presence of a refrigerator
   b. If electric power, the number of other electrical appliances
   c. If no electricity, the presence of a sewing machine
   d. The type of fuel used for cooking
   e. The presence of a transistor radio
   f. Person/bed ratio

3. *Intellectual stimulation derived from:*

   a. Whether child had any toys
   b. Whether child had any books or magazines
   c. Whether child listened to the radio
   d. Whether child watched Television
   e. Whether child was taken on trips
   f. Whether child was told stories
   g. Whether child was read to

TABLE IV. Index and Comparison Boys Combined by I.Q. and Social Background History*

Social background score	Full scale I.Q.		
	< 55	$55-65$	> 66
Lowest 3 deciles	31	9	5
Middle 4 deciles	20	22	14
Highest 3 deciles	5	10	29

* $x^2 = 45.2$; $p < 0.0005$

Height at Follow-up

The episode of hospitalisation provides information about the nutritional status of the boys for part of the first two years of life only. To provide some indication of the child's overall history of nutrition, the heights of the boys at follow-up were used. The distribution of heights was divided into three categories of tall, medium and short. There was an association between height and I.Q., with the taller boys having higher I.Q.'s (see Table V) [10].

TABLE V. Index and Comparison Boys Combined by I.Q. and Height*

Height	Full scale I.Q.		
	< 55	56–65	> 66
Short: > 0.5 SD below mean	26	12	9
Medium: 0.5 SD below mean to			
0.5 SD above mean	20	15	13
Tall: > 0.5 SD above mean	10	14	26

* x^2 = 16.88; $p < 0.01$

Having found that malnutrition in infancy, height at follow-up and the composite social history measure are each associated with I.Q. in the expected direction, our next step was to determine the relative contribution of each variable to I.Q. Using a multiple regression, we found the largest contributor to I.Q. was the social background measure, the smallest contributor was malnutrition, and height at follow-up was intermediate (see Table VI). The magnitude of the beta weights

TABLE VI. Multiple Regression Using Measures of Malnutrition, Percent Height/Age, and Environment to Predict I.Q.

Multiple R = 0.673
R^2 = 0.453
F = 38.85 df = 3, 141
$p < 0.005$

Independent variables	Beta weights	F	p
Malnutrition	− 0.153	5.42	$p < 0.05$
Height	0.271	17.98	$p < 0.005$
Environment	0.502	60.98	$p < 0.005$

show the ordering of the contribution to the outcome of I.Q. The probability levels show whether the beta weights of the independent variables differ significantly from zero.

It is possible that the effects of malnutrition may vary depending on the particular circumstances and conditions of the life experiences of the child. We can examine this possibility by comparing the I.Q. scores of sub-sets of index and comparison boys who have similar stature at follow-up and similar social background experiences. Table VII and Figure 1 show that under the most favourable

TABLE VII. Mean I.Q. of Index and Comparison Boys Holding Constant Height at Follow-up and Social Background

Social Background	Height at follow-up	Whether hospitalised for malnutrition				Difference in mean I.Q. between index and comparisons
		No (comparisons)		Yes (index)		
		mean I.Q.	n	mean I.Q.	n	
Advantaged	Tall	71	13	69	6	2
Advantaged	Short	65	4	62	8	3
Disadvantaged	Tall	62	6	55	8	7
Disadvantaged	Short	58	7	49	14	9

Disadvantaged = lowest 4 deciles of social background scores
Advantaged = 7th, 8th and 9th deciles of social background scores
Tall = > 0.05 S.D. above mean standard height
Short = > 0.05 S.D. below mean standard height

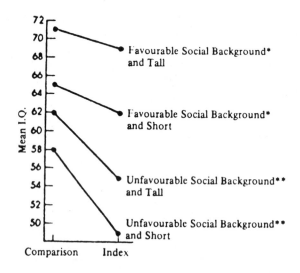

Figure 1. Mean I.Q.'s of index and comparison of boys when social background and height are held constant. * 7th, 8th and 9th deciles. ** Lowest 4 deciles

conditions of an advantageous social background and tall stature at follow-up there is only a two point difference in average I.Q. between index and comparison boys. At the other extreme of a disadvantageous social background and short stature at follow-up, the difference in average I.Q. is nine points. Under conditions of short stature and advantageous social background, and of tall stature and disadvantageous social background, the average I.Q. difference between index and comparison cases is three and seven points respectively. This evidence suggests that when malnutrition occurs under the conditions of an unfavourable social background and for children who achieve poor physical growth at school age, the malnutrition may play a contributory role in intellectual impairment, but not under conditions of favourable physical growth and social background.

Type and Severity of Malnutrition

So far the results reported have compared boys who were and were not hospitalised for malnutrition in the first two years of life. We also wanted to find out whether for the index cases the more severely malnourished would be more likely to later show mental impairment than the less severely malnourished [11]. This question has received little attention. To obtain measures of degrees and types of malnutrition, we adopted the measures suggested by Waterlow and Rutishauer [12]. They proposed, following a review of measures of malnutrition, that below a certain percent of weight for height, an acute episode of malnutrition, usually associated with a diagnosis of kwashiorkor can be inferred. Further, they proposed that below a certain percent of height for age, chronic malnutrition and the clinical diagnosis of marasmus and marasmic-kwashiorkor may be indicated. They suggest the chances of permanent mental impairment may be greater for the child with a background of chronic, rather than acute malnutrition.

Among the Jamaican index boys, information on height and weight at admission to hospital for malnutrition was available for fifty-nine cases. Measures of percentage of height for age and weight for height were calculated for each boy. Using Boston standards, percentage height for age is expressed as a percentage of the 50th percentile of height for each boy's age. The percent of weight for height was derived from the same standards. The social background measure is the same as already described.

The simple correlations between the two nutrition measures, the social background measure and I.Q. showed that percentage height for age (the measure of chronic malnutrition) and social background were both significantly correlated with I.Q. in the expected direction. To examine the effect of each variable in the presence of the others, we used a multiple regression to determine how well percent height for age, percent weight for height and the social background measure predicted I.Q., and to find the relative contribution of each of the three background variables to the outcome of I.Q. The only variable which made a significant contribution to I.Q. was the social background measure (see Table VIII). An analysis of variance produced the same result.

This finding provides no evidence in support of the hypothesis that differing degrees and types of malnutrition cause different degrees of intellectual impairment. Lack of supporting evidence may be a function of the measures of nutrition

TABLE VIII. Multiple Regression Using Percent Height/Age, Percent Weight/Height, and Social Background to Predict I.Q.*

	Multiple R = 0.57 R^2 = 0.32 F = 8.70 df = 3,55 p < 0.005		
Independent variables	Beta Weights	F	p
Social background	0.52	20.68	< 0.005
Percent height/age	0.15	1.80	NS
Percent weight/height	− 0.05	0.22	NS

Predicted I.Q. = 24.82 + 0.09 (Social Background) + 0.27 (% H/A) − 0.06 (% W/H)

* The SPSS computer package was used to obtain the multiple regression

used for the anlysis. The absence of well validated measures of malnutrition is a central problem in field studies of malnutrition among children.

In considering the results of this research in Jamaica, I would first like to emphasise that they apply to boys followed up at ages six through ten who received good medical care after hospitalisation and good nutrition during convalescence. In all cases the malnutrition was during the first two years of life. Whether different results would have been obtained under other circumstances and conditions will have to be answered in other studies.

We did not take into account the possible effects of separation from family and the experiences of the child in hospital on his later development. It is also possible that the reduced physical activity, weakness and apathy of the boys which occurred during the period of malnutrition prior to hospitalisation may have altered the pattern of mother-child interactions with the child being less responsive to and initiating fewer responses from the mother and other caretakers. It was not possible, given the design of our study, to examine these issues.

Thinking has changed on the issue of critical periods when malnutrition may cause permanent damage since our study was designed. In recent studies of rats, Dobbing [13] has shown that, 'undernutrition need not be severe but it has to be prolonged, lasting throughout the major part of the brain growth spurt, if it is to have detectable effects on the physical brain'. In a study of human brain development Dobbing and Sands [14] showed that the brain growth spurt in the human is mainly a postnatal affair which begins in mid-gestation and lasts until at least the second birthday.

The design of our study does not permit an examination of this suggestion because none of the boys were hospitalised after two years of age, and all had a known period of good nutrition during convalescence.

Discussion

Returning to the two reviews with which the paper opened, our results give no evidence in support of the view that malnutrition is a major cause of mental retardation. Our findings are more in accord with the more cautious review that postnatal nutrition does have some effects on later development, but they are neither large nor easily detected, and further, that there is no evidence in support of permanent effects.

The suggestion that severe malnutrition leads to impairment of the central nervous system, which then causes intellectual impairment, is too simple. A more complex conceptualisation is needed which takes into account biological and social factors which influence the child's social and intellectual development. Our study has taken a first step in this direction. It will be necessary to employ more complex multivariate forms of analysis which take into account the interaction between variables.

There is an interesting parallel between studies of humans and animals in the history of research into the long term consequences of early malnutrition. The behaviour of animals who had been malnourished in infancy was compared with 'controls' who had not been malnourished. Differences found were attributed causally to malnutrition. It was only later that investigators with experience in animal behaviour pointed out the methods used to produce early malnutrition also produced differences in the forms of maternal rearing of their young, and that these differences had not been controlled in the experiments. For example, a method used for altering nutrition was to vary the litter size. It was not initially recognised that varying litter size also caused major changes in the maternal infant behaviour patterns. In both human and animal studies the primary focus on nutrition led to neglect of the role of behaviour and experience in the differences found at later ages and the neglect of these behaviour variables in designing studies. Good reviews of this issue are given by Plaut [15] and Fleisher, et al [16].

The more complex formulation of the issue of the effects of malnutrition have important social policy implications. As long as it was believed that malnutrition caused mental retardation, it was not unreasonable to try and solve the problem through the single appraoch of making food available. If our concern is providing children with the best opportunities for the development of their social and intellectual capabilities, then a far more complex set of actions are needed.

Acknowledgments

Support for this study was provided by the Foundation for Child Development, the British Medical Research Council, and the National Institutes of Health (HD00719) and (SO7RR05397/15).

References

1   Manocha, SL (1972) *Malnutrition and Retarded Human Development.* Charles C Thomas, Springfield, USA
2   Stein, Z, Susser, M, Saenger, G and Marolla, F (1975) *Famine and Human Development.* Oxford University Press, New York, USA
3   Dobbing, J (1964) The influence of early malnutrition on the development and myelination of the brain. *Proc. Roy. Soc. B., 159,* 503
4   Hertzig, ME, Birch, HG, Richardson, SA and Tizard, J (1971) Intellectual levels of school children severely malnourished during the first two years of life. *Pediatrics., 49,* 814–823
5   Richardson, SA, Birch, HG and Hertzig, ME (1972) School performance of children who were severely malnourished in infancy. *J. ment. Defic., 77,* 623–632
6   Richardson, SA, Birch, HG, Grabie, E and Yoder, K (1972) Behavior of children in school who were severely malnourished in the first two years of life. *J. Hlth. soc. Behav., 13,* 276–283
7   Richardson, SA, Birch, H and Ragbeer, C (1975) The behavior of children at home who have been severely malnourished during the first two years of life. *J. Biosoc. Sci., 7,* 255–267
8   Richardson, SA (1972) Ecology of malnutrition: Non-nutritional factors influencing intellectual and behavioral development. In. *Nutrition, The Nervous System and Behavior.* (Eds) D Picou, HG Birch and SA Richardson. Pan American Health Organisation, Proceedings of the Seminar, Mona, Jamaica, Publication Number 251
9   Richardson, SA (1974) The background histories of school children severely malnourished in infancy. In *Advances in Pediatrics, 21.* (Ed) I Schulman. Yearbook Medical Publications Inc., Chicago, USA. Pages 167–195
10   Richardson, SA (1976) The relation of severe malnutrition in infancy to the intelligence of school children having differing life histories. *Pediat. Res., 10,* 57–61
11   Richardson, SA, Koller, H, Katz, M and Albert, K (1978) The contribution of differing degrees of acute and chronic malnutrition to the intellectual development of Jamaican boys. *Early Human Development, 2/2,* 163–170
12   Waterlow, JC and Rutishauser, I (1974) Nutrition in man. *Swedish Nutrition Foundation Symposium on Early Malnutrition and Mental Development, Stockholm, Number XII.* (Eds) J Cravioto, L Hambraeus and B Vahlquist
13   Dobbing, J (1976) Food and human brain development. In *Food, Man and Society.* (Eds) DN Walcher, N Kretchmer and HL Barnett. Plenum Press, New York
14   Dobbing, J and Sands, J (1973) Quantitative growth and development of human brain. *Arch. Dis. Childh., 48,* 757
15   Plaut, SM (1970) Study of malnutrition in the young rat: Methodological considerations. *Developmental Psychobiology, 3,* 157
16   Fleisher, SF and Turkewitz, J (1979) Effect of neonatal stunting in the development of rats: Large litter rearing. *Developmental Psychobiology, 12,* 137–149

Addendum to Part V

The literature on the sequelae of generalized clinical malnutrition experienced in infancy is large and widely scattered. In his review, Lloyd-Still (1976, pp. 118-119; references, p. 121) provided a systematic, comparative, tabular analysis of 13 studies on the subject, published between 1963 and 1974. The information for two age levels—below and above five years of age at follow-up—pertains to the malnourished child's family (social class, IQ of parents—available for very few studies), details of birth (when available, and this happens very infrequently), sample size, the nature of malnutrition, controls, anthropometric characteristics of the children at the time of hospital admission, and data on follow-up (age at follow-up, tests used to measure a child's behavioral development and intelligence, the IQ level, days of hospitalization).

Tables IIA and IIIA in Galler's overview (1984a, pp. 80-82, 88-94) pick up some studies that were not considered by Lloyd-Still (Barrera Moncada, 1963; Botha-Antoun, Babayan, and Harfouche, 1968; Brockman and Ricciuti, 1971; Fisher et al., 1972; Hoorweg and Stanfield, 1972; Berglund and Rabo, 1973) and cover the publications that have appeared in the last 10 years. The information is analyzed in terms of the following categories: tests used, results, type of malnutrition, age studied, and study design. Strangely enough, Galler's bibliography fails to register Hoorweg's 1976 monograph. Without attempting to be exhaustive in the coverage, I wish to note some additional publications: Cravioto et al., 1969; Srikantia and Yoganda Sastri, 1971; Ghai et al., 1973; Parekh et al., 1974; and Bartel et al., 1978.

MALNUTRITION AND BEHAVIOR IN BARBADOS

The results of a follow-up study of 129 school boys and girls of Barbados (5 to 11 years of age) who were affected by marasmic malnutrition in the first year of life were reported in a series of journal articles (Galler et al., 1983a, b, c; Galler, Ramsey, and Solimano, 1984) and summarized in a book chapter (Galler, 1984b). Here we shall consider the effects of severe malnutrition in infancy on subsequent intellectual performance (Galler et al., 1983a) but focus on personal-social behavior (Galler et al., 1983b) assessed by using a questionnaire filled out by teachers who knew the children well but were not aware of the children's early nutritional history.

While there is a substantial amount of information on the effects of severe malnutrition in infancy on later cognitive functioning, there is a dearth of data on the sequelae of malnutrition in the personal-social area. This alone would fully justify, in this editor's view, a fairly detailed discussion of the study in this Addendum.

But there is another merit of the study that needs to be brought out (even though it has its roots in a limitation of the matching design basic to the present study): The work points the way to a critically important study (or a series of studies in different cultural settings) in research on the sequelae of infantile malnutrition. Let us first take a closer look at the study as it stands. Then we shall come back to its critique and constructive suggestions.

Background

In important ways, the Barbados population is relatively close to the Western standards. It has a very high literacy rate (95%) and school attendance rate (85%). Electricity is widely available. The authors note, but do not document, the island's socioeconomic homogeneity; if this is so, and if it applies to the samples studied in this investigation, the narrow range of variation would account, at least in part, for the low predictive power of the socioeconomic status shown repeatedly in the study. The population is ethnically fairly homogeneous, with 92% of the population being of West African origin. The island has its economic problems, with an unemployment rate of 15 to 20% of the labor force.

For several reasons Barbados was a good site for the study. For one, most of the children are born in facilities that keep records, and the children are routinely followed in local clinics. These materials were available to the investigators.

Second, the study was conducted in close association with the island's National Nutrition Center, founded in 1972. The center was carrying on its own longitudinal study of all the children who had experienced clinical malnutrition and who were treated at the Queen Elizabeth Hospital (cf. Ramsey, 1980). The children are being followed up to 12 years of age. Together with the siblings of malnourished children and children referred to the hospital by various agencies, the center sample exceeds an N of 2,000.

In the studies by Galler and co-workers, the index group (Exposed Series, $N = 129$) consists of children hospitalized in their first year of life for nutritional marasmus. They have been given routine medical care after discharge, including home visits by public health nurses. Their families have been provided with nutritional counseling and subsidized milk. Relevant biomedical information (birth weight below five pounds, prenatal and perinatal complications, history of convulsions, head injuries, loss of consciousness) used to eliminate the affected children from the study has been obtained by reviewing obstetrical records of the mothers and the perinatal records of all the children considered for inclusion in the study.

The control group (Unexposed Series, $N = 129$) met the same general criteria but was not hospitalized in infancy for malnutrition. The control subjects were matched with the index children by age, gender, and handedness. This is another important point of information since it touches on the very core of our criticism, spelled out later in greater detail, that these criteria were inadequate since they did not incorporate consideration of socioeconomic factors. As the data indicate, using schoolmates or neighborhood children in order to control for socioeconomic and other environmental differences did not assure comparability of the two samples called for in a study using a matching design. In principle, such a design requires effective matching on all the relevant variables, leaving the incidence of infantile malnutrition as the sole critical feature differentiating the control group from the index group. Such a requirement does raise some very difficult questions.

In the Barbados study the socioeconomic status of the families was assessed by using a 22-item schedule filled out by a staff member in an interview with the child's primary caretaker. By means of factor analysis the items were combined into four clusters. Three of the factors distinguished dependably between the index and the comparison group. They refer to conveniences available in the home (Factor 1—presence of a refrigerator, electricity, television, running water), the degree of crowding in the home (Factor 2—the number of bedrooms, beds, and rooms), and economic status (Factor 5—father works, type of work done by the father). As attested by scores on all the three factors, "the socioeconomic conditions in families from the *comparison group were advantaged* (Galler et al., 1983*a,* p. 13; emphasis added).

Results

Since the Verbal and Performance subscales of the Wechsler Intelligence Scale for Children and most of their components showed the same trend, only the Full Scale IQs will be considered here. The inferior performance of the index children, compared with the control group, was documented for males (mean IQs of 91.3 versus 100.1) as well as for females (90.5 versus 107.7).

For a given sequence in which the predictor variables were entered, the multiple regression analyses indicated that incidence of clinical malnutrition in infancy accounted for 17% of the IQ variance, with no additional significant contribution being made by the socioeconomic factors. An alternative analysis indicated that clinical malnutrition accounted for 12% of the IQ variance and the socioeconomic factors for 9%.

A telling naturalistic criterion of scholastic ability is the passing of the grades. There were 36 index children to 1 comparison child who were below the expected grade for age.

The children's behavior in school was characterized on the basis of a 30-item inventory, completed by the teacher and modeled after Richardson and co-workers (1972). The items were reduced to 7 factors. Statistically significant differences at the level of .01 or beyond were obtained between the index and the comparison group for Factor 1—Attention Deficit (short attention span, poor memory, distractability, restlessness), Factor 2—Ineffective Social Interaction (lack of ease in initiating conversation with teachers and peers), and Factor 3—Poor General Appearance (poor nutritional status, poor general health, sleepy in class). Some of these terms are the editor's.

The data indicated that the previously malnourished children had significantly more behavioral problems in school than the comparison group. These findings were confirmed when the statistical analyses werè repeated on a sample of the children who had IQs of 90 or above. Thus, the deficits in personal-social behavior are not limited to children with a lower IQ. Finally, the socioeconomic variables did not contribute to the variance of the criterion (in this case, measures of classroom behavior) except, marginally, for Poor General Appearance (Factor 3).

Critique and Suggestions

In controlled studies the keystone of the validity of the results is a definition of the proper control group and meeting the criteria in making up the control group in a particular investigation. In principle, the investigator has two choices:

1. He or she operates with random samples of the population of the index and control children, within the specified limits of age, socioeconomic characteristics, and sex. The investigator measures all the variables that are regarded as potentially relevant and uses statistical analytical techniques to arrive at the estimates of their impact, in terms of the percentage of the variance of the criterion (like IQ) explained by the predictors, singly and in combinations, pooling or separating their contributions.
2. The investigator endeavors to optimize the matching process.

Since the issue of the role of the socioeconomic variables is highly important, both theoretically and in practical terms, the cause of clarity and interpretability of the results of the Barbados study would have been served by including these variables in the matching process—if matching design is to be used and averages of outcome variables are to be presented. When the supply of the potential control subjects is large, as seems to have been the case in Barbados, an effective matching on a set of critically important variables is technically feasible.

An effective modification of the matching principle was introduced into the nutritional literature by S. A. Richardson whose article is reprinted in this volume (see Fig. 1 in Paper 17). While the sample size is small and an expansion and cross-validation of the study would be highly desirable, the data are internally consistent. They attest that we learn a great deal when we stop thinking in terms of an index group and a comparison group but compare subgroups sharing certain characteristics: When the index and the comparison children come from a relatively favorable social background and have relatively adequate nutritional history in preschool and school years (reflected in tall stature), the effect of the incident of clinical infant malnutrition on intellective functioning during school years is negligible. When stresses of poorer chronic nutrition (low stature) and less favorable social background are added, the level of intelligence decreases both in the comparison and in the index group, but—and this is a critical point—it decreases in the index group more markedly so that the differences between the comparison and the index group become progressively larger. In Richardson's data the differences are 2, 3, 7, and 9.

We welcome and appreciate the efforts and the achievements of Janina R. Galler and her colleagues. However, they owe the scientific community (and themselves) an explanation of why in their study the socioeconomic factors appear to fail to account for a part of the IQ variance (and of classroom behavior), which is in disagreement with the world literature on the subject.

REFERENCES

Barrera Moncada, G., 1963, *Estudios sobre Alteraciones del Crecimiento y del Desarrollo Psicológico del Síndrome Pluricarencial (Kwashiorkor),* Editora Grafas, Caracas, Venezuela, 377p.

Bartel, P. R., R. D. Griesel, L. S. Burnett, I. Freiman, E. U. Rosen, and J. Geefhuysen, 1978, Long-Term Effects of Kwashiorkor on Psychomotor Development, *S. Afr. Med. J.* **53:**360-362.

Berglund, G., and E. Rabo, 1973, A Long-Term Follow-up Investigation of Patients with Hypertrophic Pyloric Stenosis, with Special Reference to the Physical and Mental Development, *Acta Paediatr. Scand.* **62:**125-129.

Botha-Antoun, E., S. Babayan, and J. K. Harfouche, 1968, Intellectual Development Related to Nutritional Status, *J. Trop. Pediatr.* **14:**112-115.

Brockman, L. M., and H. N. Ricciuti, 1971, Severe Protein-Calorie Malnutrition and Cognitive Development in Infancy and Early Childhood, *Dev. Psychol.* **4:**312-319.

Cravioto, J., C. Piñero, M. Arroyo, and E. Alcalde, 1969, Mental Performance of School Children Who Suffered Malnutrition in Early Age, in *Nutrition in Preschool and School Age,* Symposium of the Swedish Foundation, vol. 7, Uppsala, Sweden, pp. 85-91.

Fisher, M. M., M. C. Killeross, M. Simonsson, and K. A. Elgie, 1972, Malnutrition and Reasoning Ability in Zambian School Children, *R. Soc. Trop. Med. Hyg. Trans.* **66:**471-478.

Galler, J. R., 1984*a,* Behavioral Consequences of Malnutrition in Early Life, in *Nutrition and Behavior,* J. R. Galler, ed., Plenum Press, New York, pp. 63-100.

Galler, J. R., 1984*b,* Study of Barbadian School Children, in *Nutrition and Behavior,* J. R. Galler, ed., Plenum Press, New York, pp. 101-111.

Galler, J. R., F. Ramsey, and G. Solimano, 1984, The Influence of Early Malnutrition on Subsequent Behavioral Development, III. Learning Disabilities as a Sequel to Malnutrition, *Pediatr. Res.,* **18:**309-313.

Galler, J. R., F. Ramsey, G. Solimano, G. Lowell, and E. Mason, 1983*a,* The Influence of Early Malnutrition on Subsequent Behavioral Development, I. Degree of Impairment of Intellectual Performance, *J. Child. Psychiatry* **22:**8-15.

Galler, J. R., F. Ramsey, G. Solimano, G. Lowell, and E. Mason, 1983*b,* The Influence of Early Malnutrition on Subsequent Behavioral Development, II. Classroom Behavior, *J. Child. Psychiatry* **22:**16-22.

Galler, J. R., F. Ramsey, G. Solimano, and K. Propert, 1983*c,* Sex Differences in the Growth of Barbadian School Children with Early Malnutrition, *Nutr. Rep. Int.* **27:**503-517.

Ghai, O. P., K. Ratna, K. Ramachandran, and J. S. Neki, 1973, Effect of Early Marasmic Malnutrition on Subsequent Mental Development, *Indian Pediatr.,* **10:**155-159.

Hoorweg, J. C., 1976, *Protein Malnutrition and Intellectual Abilities,* Mouton, The Hague, 148p.

Hoorweg, J. C., and J. P. Stanfield, 1972, The Influence of Malnutrition on Psychologic and Neurologic Development: Preliminary Communication, in *Nutrition, the Nervous System, and Behavior,* Pan American Health Organization Scientific Publication Number 251, Washington, D.C., pp. 55-63.

Lloyd-Still, J. D., 1976, Clinical Studies on the Effects of Malnutrition during Infancy on Subsequent Physical and Intellectual Development, in *Malnutrition and Intellectual Development,* J. D. Lloyd-Still, ed., Publishing Sciences Group, Littletown, Mass., pp. 103-159.

Parekh, U. C., P. M. Udani, P. A. Naik, and B. P. Sham, 1974, Mental Development of Children with Severe Protein Calorie Malnutrition in the Past and Present, *Indian Pediatr.* **11:**465-469.

Ramsey, F., 1980, *Protein-Energy Malnutrition in Barbados,* Macy Foundation, New York, 173p.

Richardson, S. A., F. Birch, E. Grabie, and K. Yoder, 1972, The Behavior of Children in School Who Were Severely Malnourished in the First Two Years of Life, *J. Health Soc. Behav.* **13:**276-285.

Srikantia, S. G., and C. Yoganda Sastri, 1971, Observations on Mental Development, *Indian J. Med. Res.* **59:**216-220.

Part VI

Generalized Subclinical Malnutrition: Descriptive Studies

Papers 18 Through 21: Commentary

18 CRAVIOTO, ESPINOSA GAONA, and BIRCH
Early Malnutrition and Auditory-Visual Integration in School-Age Children

19 POLLITT and RICCIUTI
Biological and Social Correlates of Stature Among Children in the Slums of Lima, Peru

20 GUPTA et al.
Impact of Nutrition on Intelligence

21 GRAVES
Cross-Cultural Comparisons of Mothers and Their Undernourished Infants in Asia

In some of the early studies on the psychological concomitants of chronic, subclinical malnutrition, height was used as a criterion of nutritionally induced growth retardation (later referred to as *stunting;* cf. Waterlow and Rutishauser, 1974; Waterlow, 1978). Thus, Cravioto, DeLicardie, and Birch (1966) compared the performance of Mexican rural children, 6 to 11 years of age, who fell into the upper and lower quartiles of the distribution of height. Paper 18 is a continuation and extension of these studies. The function that was studied was intersensory integration. In the 1966 study the recognition of the forms of objects involved visual-haptic, visual-kinesthetic, and haptic-kinesthetic comparisons. In Paper 18 the technique was extended to the comparisons of auditory and visual patterns. The earlier finding that short rural children tend to integrate less effectively the information presented through different sensory modalities was confirmed.

The 1966 report contains a critically important observation, limiting the usefulness of stature as a measure of chronic nutritional status. This measure is inappropriate for situations in which individual food intake is not controlled by socioeconomic factors: While in poor rural areas, in which generalized chronic malnutrition is endemic, marked differences in height were accompanied by differences in the capacity for intersensory integration, "for upper social class urban sample, the differences in height are not associated with differences in intersensory integrative competence" (Cravioto, DeLicardie, and Birch, 1966, p. 352).

Paper 19 raises and documents another related point bearing on the limitations of stature in research on malnutrition and behavior: Even within what appears to be a socioeconomically homogeneous area—the slums of the city of Lima, Peru, for example—stature is not a purely biological, simple variable since differences in height are associated with an array of biosocial variables. Thus, the shorter slum children tended to be progeny of shorter mothers. Furthermore, these mothers display characteristics indicative of social stress and disadvantage: more pregnancies, fewer years of schooling, and a greater number of marriages. The variable *stature,* intended to serve as an indicator of a child's nutritional background, may be confounded by possible genetic influences as well as biological and social factors that, on their own, may unfavorably affect the child's mental development.

The authors warn us (p. 746 in Paper 19) that:

> in most retrospective studies it would be virtually impossible to specify whether behavioral or intellectual differences between tall and short children are a primary function of nutritional factors, or of some of the factors associated with stature, or of some combination of these variables.

The appropriate solution is to measure both the nutritional and socioenvironmental variables and take them into account in the analyses of the data, as was done in some of the papers included in this volume, whether they dealt with the sequelae of clinical malnutrition (e.g., Richardson, 1980) or the effects of the supplementation of chronically undernourished children (Freeman et al., 1980).

Paper 20 reports on a study made in India on the effects of nutritional status (normal, subclinical, and three grades of severe undernutrition) and socioeconomic status (four classes, based on the income, education, and occupation of the guardian). For a given socioeconomic class, the average IQs decrease as the severity of undernutrition increases—that is, as the body weight, expressed as percentage of the reference value, decreases. Similarly, for a given level of nutritional status, the mean IQs decrease in parallel to the lowering of the socioeconomic status. It would be highly desirable to obtain this type of information for other geographical areas as well as for other behavioral functions than general intelligence.

In principle, few would challenge Super's comment that "culture may contribute to the manifestations of undernutrition" (Super, 1984, p. 327). In its title, Paper 21 addresses itself to this macroenvironmental feature of the samples studied in West Bengal and in Nepal. Unfortunately, the concept of culture is neither clearly defined nor made operational. In both samples the socioeconomic conditions are essentially identical, with most of the fathers of the study children working on the land and having some land and/or cattle of their own. What is it, specifically, in their culture that accounts for the high Activity scores and Distance Interaction scores of Nepalese well nourished and, although to a lesser degree, less well-nourished Nepalese children and their mothers in contrast to the Bengali sample? We are not being told. The author may have had such specific features of the culture in her mind when she was choosing the two locations, but the reader is not informed about such cultural differences. To the reader, the very concept of culture appears as a factor invented ad hoc to explain the behavioral differences established empirically between the two areas.

This is not to say that in research on malnutrition and behavior the concept of culture is not of fundamental importance for at least two cogent reasons:

First, motivation, a critical component of all performance, including cognitive performance, has its roots in culture. Second, most of the research in this field has been done in different parts of the Third World; this fact raises a host of issues, theoretical and methodological, that need to be examined in the perspective of cross-cultural psychology (Poortinga, 1977; Warren, 1977; cf. also Foster, 1966; Nerlove et al., 1974; Dasen, 1977; Irwin et al., 1977; Cole, 1981).

The principal reason for including Paper 21 is its behavioral methodology and an idea bearing on potential psychological mechanisms of mental retardation of malnourished children, involving a specific aspect of the infant-mother interaction.

The majority of the studies reported in the literature on the psychological concomitants of malnutrition used psychometric tools (tests) that vary widely in nature. This diversity is amply documented by the papers included in this volume. By contrast, in studies reported in Paper 21 the investigator relied heavily on direct observations of behavior in a standardized situation, with a focus on *exploratory behavior* and several categories of *attachment behavior* (distance interaction between the child and its mother, signals of distress, and close physical contact).

Activity scores were significantly lower in undernourished children studied in Nepal (but not in Bengal), reflecting the high average Activity scores of the well-nourished Nepalese children. Lower scores were consistently obtained in both areas for the combined score for attachment behaviors and, specifically, for Distance Interaction. Reduced reliance on communication at a distance (across space) may later be expressed in a lessened use of representational symbols, especially of words. In the author's view, "This would lead to underdevelopment of verbal skills and could well contribute to lower performance on measures of cognitive development, such as intelligence tests" (p. 105 in Paper 21).

Furthermore, while the concept of culture did not meaningfully contribute to the interpretation of the differences between the two areas (West Bengal and Nepal), considerations of the sociocultural setting are helpful in further clarifying the behavioral differences between the better nourished and the undernourished children. Two findings stand out: (1) There were dietary differences between the two groups, with the undernourished infants consuming animal protein less frequently, and (2) there was a difference in the educational level of the parents, the level being lower for the parents of the undernourished infants. The author concludes that "infant malnutrition may stem, in part, from parental ignorance of children's health and nutritional needs and, perhaps, from adherence to traditional beliefs and customs, discordant with the child's needs" (p. 106 in Paper 21). The assumptions call for empirical verification, in and out of Asia.

REFERENCES

Cole, M., 1981, *Society, Mind and Development,* Center for Human Information Processing Report 106, University of California, La Jolla, 40p.

Cravioto, J., E. R. DeLicardie, and H. G. Birch, 1966, Nutrition, Growth, and Neurointegrative Development: An Experimental and Ecologic Study, *Pediatrics* **38** (suppl.):319-372.

Dasen, P. R., 1977, Cross-Cultural Cognitive Development: The Cultural Aspects of Piaget's Theory, *N. Y. Acad. Sci. Ann.* **285:**332-337.

Foster, G. N., 1966, Social Anthropology and Nutrition of the Pre-School Child, Especially as Related to Latin America, in *Pre-School Child Malnutrition—Primary Deterrent to Human Progress,* National Academy of Sciences-National Research Council Publication Number 1282, Washington, D.C., pp. 258-266.

Freeman, H. E., R. E. Klein, J. W. Townsend, and A. Lechtig, 1980, Nutrition and Cognitive Development among Rural Guatemalan Children, *Am. J. Public Health* **70:**1277-1285.

Irwin, M., R. E. Klein, P. L. Engle, Ch. Yarbrough, and S. B. Nerlove, 1977, The Problem of Establishing Validity in Cross-Cultural Measurements, *N. Y. Acad. Sci. Ann.* **285:**308-325.

Nerlove, S. B., J. M. Roberts, R. E. Klein, C. Yarbrough, and J.-P. Habicht, 1974, Natural Indicators of Cognitive Development: An Observational Study of Guatemalan Children, *Ethos* **2:**265-295.

Poortinga, Y. H., ed., 1977, *Basic Problems in Cross-Cultural Psychology,* Swets and Zeitlinger, Amsterdam, 380p.

Richardson, S. A., 1980, The Long-Range Consequences of Malnutrition in Infancy: A Study of Children in Jamaica, West Indies, in *Topics in Pediatrics 2, Nutrition in Childhood,* B. Wharton, ed., Pitman Medical Publishing, Tunbridge Wells, England, pp. 163-176.

Super, C. M., 1984, Models of Assessment and Development, in *Malnutrition and Behavior: Critical Assessment of Key Issues,* J. Brožek and B. Schürch, eds., Nestlé Foundation Publication Series, vol. 4, Lausanne, Switzerland, pp. 327-336.

Warren, N., ed., 1977, *Studies in Cross-Cultural Psychology,* Academic Press, London, 212p.

Waterlow, J. C., 1978, Observations on the Assessment of Protein-Energy Malnutrition, with Special Reference to Stunting, *Courrier* **28:**455-460.

Waterlow, J. C., and I. E. H. Rutishauser, 1974, Malnutrition in Man, in *Early Malnutrition and Mental Development,* J. Cravioto, L. Hambraeus, and B. Vahlquist, eds., Symposia of the Swedish Nutrition Foundation, vol. 12, Uppsala, Sweden, pp. 13-26.

18: EARLY MALNUTRITION AND AUDITORY-VISUAL INTEGRATION IN SCHOOL-AGE CHILDREN[1]

J. Cravioto, C. Espinosa Gaona, and H. G. Birch

In a previous study (Cravioto, de Licardie, & Birch, 1966) we explored the effect of malnutrition on the neuro-integrative development of rural children living in pre-industrial cultures. In that study we found that children exposed to early malnutrition, as reflected in their height at school age, were significantly inferior to the taller children in the community in their ability to integrate visual, haptic, and kinaesthetic information.

In the present study we have extended these inquiries to consider another area of cross-modal integration: auditory-visual equivalence.

SUBJECTS AND METHOD

The children studied were enrolled in the primary school of a rural village in Southwestern Mexico. Assessment of their degree of exposure to early nutritional risk was based upon their height, since previous studies had demonstrated that differences in growth achievement, particularly at the extremes of growth distribution, are significant indicators of early exposure to primary or secondary malnutrition (Cravioto, 1963; Dean, 1960; Gruelich, 1958; Hiernaux, 1964).[2]

All children aged 7 through 12 were weighed and measured by a pediatrician especially trained in somatic measurement (Vega, Urrutia, & Cravioto, 1964), and on the basis of height two groups were identified, one representing the upper 25% of the height group for each age and sex and the other the lowest 25%. This resulted in a total group of 296 children, 141 boys and 155 girls. While general mental status has correlation with measures of auditory-visual integration, it was

[1] This work was supported in part by grants from the Association for the Aid of Crippled Children, New York, N.Y., the Nutrition Foundation, Inc., the Williams Waterman Fund for the Combat of Dietary Diseases, and the Gerber Baby Fund.

[2] *Primary malnutrition* is food deprivation deriving from ingestion of foods low in quantity and poor in quality. *Secondary malnutrition* is malnutrition which is a consequence of infection or parasitic infestation.

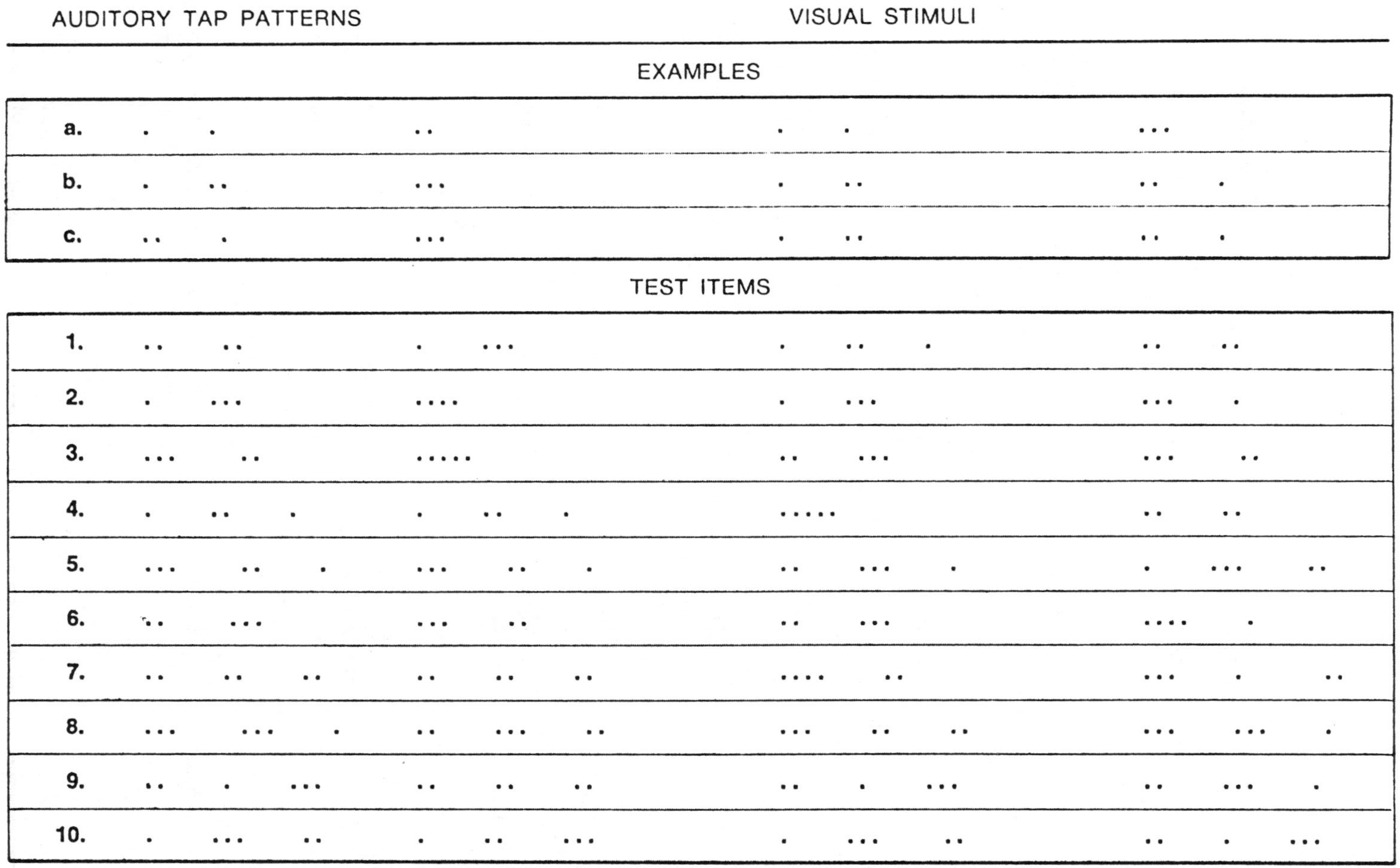

Figure 1. Auditory and visual test stimuli. Large and small spaces represent approximate time intervals of 1 second and 0.5 seconds respectively. Correct choices are not underlined on the test forms.

not taken into account as such in the present study.

The children's ability to integrate auditory and visual stimuli was individually studied by a method of equivalence (Birch & Belmont, 1964, 1965). The children were asked to identify visual dot patterns corresponding to rhythmic auditory patterns. The task therefore explored the ability to equate a temporally structured set of auditory stimuli with a spatially distributed set of visual ones. The auditory test items and the dot patterns from which selections were to be made are shown in Figure 1.

Sounds were tapped out with a half-second pause between taps for short intervals and a one-second pause for long intervals. The corresponding visual patterns from which the specific selections were to be made were presented immediately after the completion of the auditory stimulation. Each set of visual stimuli was presented on separate 5 by 8 index cards, and on any exposure only the specific set of visual dot patterns appropriate to the given auditory presentation was viewed.

The testing proceeded as follows:

The subject and examiner were seated at a table facing one another. The examiner said, "I am going to tap out some patterns. Listen." Using the edge of the table and a pencil, the examiner tapped out the examples A, B, and C shown in Figure 1, pausing from three to five seconds between examples.

The subject was then shown a few of the response cards containing the visual dot patterns and told, "Each pattern you hear is going to be like one of the dot patterns you see here." Examiner pointed to card. "Let me show you. Listen." The examiner once

again tapped out example A and this time showed the child the card containing the appropriate visual pattern. Then he asked the child, "Which one of these did you hear?" Simultaneous with the child's response and regardless of his choice, the examiner pointed to the correct selection and said, "It's this one."

For examples B and C the examiner said, "Listen again, and then show me which one you heard. Which one is it?" If the child made an incorrect choice, the examiner said, "No, it's this one," and pointed to the correct choice. Thus, the examiner indicated the correct choice for examples B and C only after the child made his choice. After presentation of three examples, the ten tasks of the test were given.

The subject was told, "Listen carefully and pick out the dots which look like the taps you hear." The sounds were then tapped out, and the specific multiple-choice card containing the visual pattern appropriate for the presented auditory pattern was shown to the child. During the test only first choices were accepted, and no changes in response were permitted.

RESULTS

Figure 2 (on the next page) indicates that for the children as a whole the ability to integrate auditory and visual information improves over the age span considered, with the most rapid improvement occurring between the ages of 9 and 11.

The relative ability of the short and tall children to integrate auditory and visual information over the age span may be considered in relation to data presented in Figure 3 (see over). Both groups show improvement with age, with the greatest rate of improvement occurring between the ages of 9 and 11. However, at each age level the

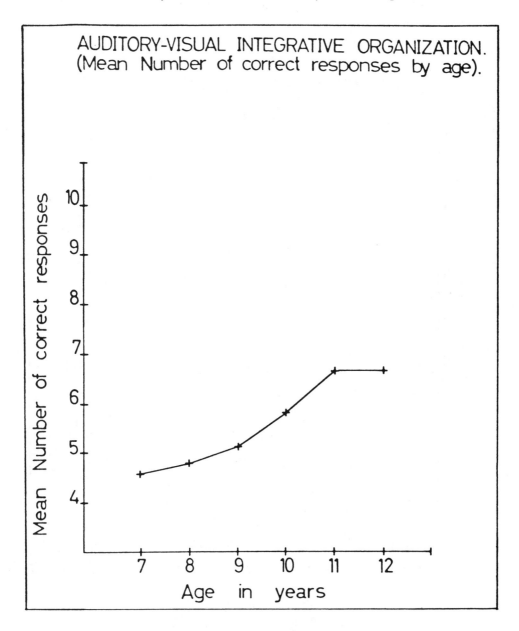

Figure 2

Auditory-visual integration in the
total group of rural children
as a function of chronological age.

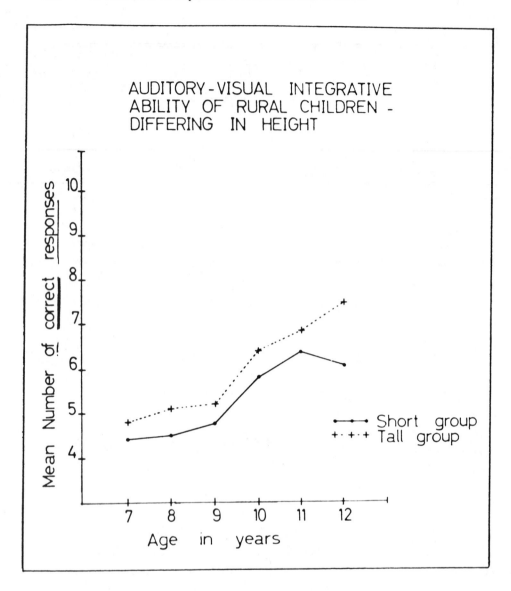

Figure 3

Relative ability of tall and short
rural children to integrate auditory and visual
information as a function of chronological age.

mean performance of the taller group is higher than that of the shorter. This difference is most striking at age 12, when the shorter group has a mean score of 6.1 correct responses in contrast to 7.5 correct responses for the taller children.

A more detailed view of the differences in performance in the two groups may be obtained from the cumulative frequency percentage curves presented in Figure 4. At all ages except age 9 the curve deviates to the right for the taller group. These data suggest that not only are the mean values for the two groups different but that these do not reflect a small number of extreme cases but rather characterize general differences in the groups as a whole. By the age of 8, 10% of the taller children are making eight or more correct judgments, whereas none of the shorter children are performing at this level. By age 12, 42% of the taller children are making eight or more correct judgments, with 30% achieving a perfect score of 10. In contrast, only 9% of the shorter children in this age group achieve scores of 8 or greater, with none making a perfect score.

DISCUSSION

The findings of the present study, which indicate that at each year of life the least adequately nourished children in our rural sample perform less well on a task requiring auditory-visual integration than do the better nourished children, are in general agreement with our earlier findings. In the earlier studies, which were based upon a different ethnic group with a different language background living in a different country, we noted that the least well-nourished of the school-age children in the rural population were consistently less able to integrate visual with haptic, haptic with kinaesthetic, and visual with kinaesthetic stimuli. The current finding that auditory and visual integration is affected by early malnutrition extends our knowledge of defective integrative functioning to include the teleoreceptor as well as the somatic senses.

The less adequate development of auditory-visual integration in the malnourished children has implications in two directions. In the first place, it suggests that the findings of neurologic changes in animals experimentally exposed to serious nutritional risk may well have their counterpart in human populations socially subjected to significant degrees of malnutrition. While such individuals need not reflect in full degree the failures in myelin formation reported by Davidson and Dobbing (1966) or the types of anatomic and electrophysiologic abnormalities found by Platt and his colleagues (Platt, Pampiglione, & Stewart, 1965), they do exhibit significant functional lags in the development of neuro-integrative capacities. The findings, therefore, raise the very important general question of the need to define nutritional requirements for adequate nervous system growth and development.

The second issue raised by our findings is more directly related to the functional significance of such neuro-integrative lags for the children at nutritional risk.

Learning to read requires the ability to transform temporally distributed auditory patterns into spatially distributed visual ones. Harris (1946) has suggested that for the beginning reader "reading is largely concerned with learning to recognize the symbols which represent spoken words" (p. 9). One of the characteristics un-

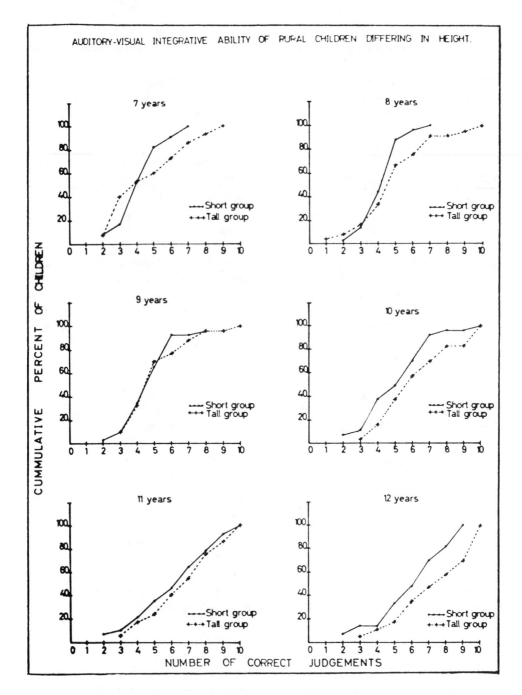

Figure 4

Cumulative percentage distribution curves
of tall and short rural children at different ages.

derlying reading readiness may be the development of the ability to make judgments of auditory-visual equivalence. A primary disturbance in the ability to integrate stimuli from the two critical sense modalities, hearing and vision, may therefore serve to increase the risk of becoming a poor reader.

The major findings of an earlier study (Birch & Belmont, 1965) was that judgments of auditory-visual equivalence tasks were significantly worse in retarded readers than in normal readers. The analysis strongly suggested that the ability to treat visual and auditory patterned information as equivalent was one of the factors that differentiated good readers from poor readers. Further, within each group, the auditory-visual pattern test performance did differentiate subjects with

lower from those with higher reading scores. These findings made more specific the suggestion of Rabinovitch (Rabinovitch, Drew, Dejong, Ingram, & Withey, 1954) that difficulties in integration are the major kinds of difficulty faced by children with primary reading retardation.

These data lead us to predict that the shorter children in our rural population, whose height is a reflection of their earlier and sometimes continuing malnutrition, will be educationally at risk. If this prediction is sustained, as field observations suggest, early malnutrition from either primary or secondary sources may be the starting point of a developmental path characterized by neuro-integrative inadequacy, school failure, and subsequent subnormal adaptive functioning.

References

Birch, H. G., & Belmont, L. Auditory-visual integration in normal and retarded readers. *American Journal of Orthopsychiatry*, 1964, 34, 852-861.

Birch, H. G., & Belmont, L. Auditory-visual integration. Intelligence and reading ability in school children. *Perceptual and Motor Skills*, 1965, 20, 295-305.

Cravioto, J. Application of newer knowledge of nutrition on physical and mental growth and development. A. J. P. H., 1963, 53, 1803-1809.

Cravioto, J. De Licardie, E. R./& Birch, H. G. Nutrition, growth and neurointegrative development: an experimental and ecologic study. *Pediatrics*, 1956, 38 (Supplement II), 319-372.

Davidson, A. N., & Dobbing, J. Myelination as a vulnerable period in brain development. *British Medical Bulletin*, 1966, 22, 40-44.

Dean, R. F. The effects of malnutrition on the growth of young children. *Modern Problems of Pediatrics*, 1960, 5, 111-122.

Gruelich, W. W. Growth of children of the same race under different environmental conditions. *Science*, 1958, 127, 515-516.

Harris, A. J. How to increase reading ability. (2nd ed.) New York: Longmans Green, 1946.

Hiernaux, J. Weight-height relationship during growth in Africans and Europeans. *Human Biology*, 1964, 36, 273-281.

Platt, B. S./Pampiglione, G./Stewart, R. J. C. Experimental protein-calorie deficiency. Clinical, electroencephalographic and neurophathological changes in pigs. *Developmental Medicine and Child Neurology*, 1965, 7, 9-26.

Rabinovitch, R. D./Drew, A. L./Dejong, R./Ingram, W./Withey, L. A research approach to reading retardation. In *Neurology and Psychiatry in Childhood*. Baltimore: Williams and Wilkins, 1954.

Vega, L./Urrutia, J. J./Cravioto, J. Estandarización de las mediciones de peso y talla en niños escolares. *Guatemala Pediátrica*, 1964, 4, 84-91.

19: BIOLOGICAL AND SOCIAL CORRELATES OF STATURE AMONG CHILDREN IN THE SLUMS OF LIMA, PERU

E. Pollitt and H. Ricciuti

Recent studies on the effects of malnutrition in early life on cognitive [4] and neurointegrative [5] development have used contrasts in stature as the sole procedure for contrasting nutritional background in children. This methodological practice is based on a substantial body of evidence indicating that nutritional conditions in early life greatly influence body size.[12] Despite the conclusive evidence that early nutrition affects stature, however, the use of stature as the sole index of nutritional background still involves serious methodological problems, especially in studies assessing the probable influence of nutritional background on psychological development. There is considerable evidence to suggest that children differing substantially in stature may well differ also in other biological

Submitted to the JOURNAL in February 1969.

DR. POLLITT was with Cornell at the time of this study. He is currently assistant professor of psychology in the Yale University School of Medicine.

* This research was supported in part by a U. S. Agency for International Development grant (AID cad–1209) to the second author and Dr. Richard Barnes, Graduate School of Nutrition, Cornell University.

and/or psycho-social variables which, independently of nutrition, could also affect psychological development. Groups of children of contrasting stature might show psychological differences resulting from nutritional factors, from other biological and psycho-social factors, or from the joint influence of various combinations of these factors. It would be misleading, therefore, to select nutrition as the only determinant of the psychological differences.

A recent illustration of a study in which such issues are raised is provided by the research of Cravioto, Delicardie, and Birch,[5] in which tall and short Guatemalan Indian children from 6 to 11 years of age, living in a rural village, were compared on a test of neurointegrative development (requiring matching of forms on the basis of information from different sensory modalities). The tall children performed significantly better than the short group, suggesting the possibility that nutritional deficiencies of the short children accounted for their poorer test performance. Aware of the fact that the stature differences might be associated with factors other than nutrition, these investigators attempted to evaluate the possible role of parental stature and of differences in rate of maturation. In addition, they were concerned with the possible influence of various socioeconomic, educational, and other environmental factors on intersensory test performance. In this connection, they also tested a control group of tall and short, upper-middle-class, urban children and obtained their parental heights. Moreover, information on the environmental background of the rural children was also obtained. Their results indicated that parental height was not significantly related to children's

height in the rural group, although there was a slight trend in this direction for fathers' height. In the urban upper-middle-class group, however, fathers' height was significantly related to children's height. This comparison was taken as suggesting that for the rural children variations in stature are determined more by nutritional variation than by genetic endowment, whereas the opposite is true in the urban upper-middle-class children. Since there were no significant psychological test score differences between the tall and short urban children, the case for nutritional influences on the contrasting test performance of the tall and short rural groups was seen as strengthened.

Most of the socioeconomic and environmental characteristics assessed in that study did not differ significantly between the tall and short village children. However, there was a rather marked difference in the amount of maternal education of these two groups, in favor of the tall children. While, as suggested by Cravioto et al., it is certainly true that the better educated mothers may have provided a better nutritional environment for their taller children, in the view of the present writers, they may well also have provided more psychological stimulation and opportunities for learning, which in turn may have positively influenced the test performance of their children. Thus, it is quite clear that one still can have no assurance that the relationship between stature and psychological test performance was mediated solely through nutritional differences.

There are a number of other correlates of stature, reported in a variety of different studies, which would need to be controlled or otherwise taken into account if one were to attempt to use stature as a measure of nutritional history, particularly in research on mal-nutrition and psychological development. In large-scale studies involving wide ranges of population variations, it has been found that stature, various indices of intellectual development, socioeconomic status, and general conditions of physical and mental health tend to correlate positively with one another.[9, 10, 16, 25] At the same time there is considerable evidence to suggest that among lower-class families, the factors of increased age, high parity, and poor physical condition of mothers are detrimental to the child's intrauterine and later physical growth.[7, 21, 26] Other research suggests that these same variables heighten the risk of central nervous system damage during fetal growth or at birth [3, 17] and that there is a relationship between birthweight, a measure of intrauterine growth, and later intelligence quotient scores.[6] Thus, the same prenatal or paranatal factors which tend to produce reduced physical stature may also affect intellectual development adversely, quite independently of any malnutrition which might occur subsequently.

It was the purpose of the present research to explore further some of the problems involved in the utilization of contrasting stature groups as a means of identifying children with different nutritional background, particularly in studies concerned with the influence of malnutrition on psychological development. More specifically, this research was concerned with the degree of association which might be found between extremes of stature and some of the biological and social factors associated with or capable of influencing intellectual development, within a sample of lower social class children from a population where malnutrition is endemic, namely the slums or "barriadas" of Lima, Peru. The variables of major interest included maternal height, age, and parity; medical attention at childbirth and birthweight of child; maternal education, family size, family stability, and financial income.

SUBJECTS

Two groups of 48 children from 6 to 53 months of age were selected from a population of 289 children attending seven day care centers in Lima. These centers, run by various charitable organizations, care for the preschool children of working mothers living in the slums. All centers provide adequate care for

Table I

MEAN AGE OF TALL AND SHORT CHILDREN BY SEX AND AGE INTERVALS

(age in months)

AGE	TALL			SHORT		
Intervals	Males	Females	Both	Males	Females	Both
6–17	10.67	11.67	11.17	12.16	12.00	12.08
18–29	23.67	23.33	23.50	23.50	24.16	23.83
30–41	36.00	35.00	35.50	35.33	35.33	35.33
42–53	48.00	47.50	47.75	47.50	47.14	47.33
TOTAL	29.58	29.38	29.48	29.62	29.67	29.65

Figure I

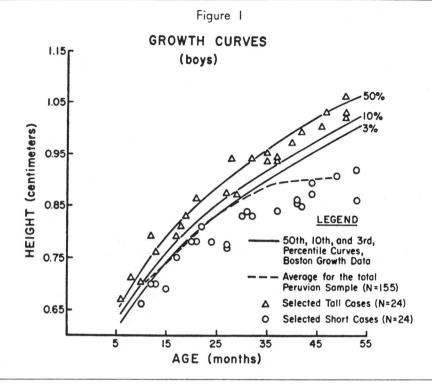

GROWTH CURVES
(boys)

LEGEND

——— 50th, 10th, and 3rd,
Percentile Curves,
Boston Growth Data

— — Average for the total
Peruvian Sample (N=155)

△ Selected Tall Cases (N=24)

O Selected Short Cases (N=24)

the children and give them two well-balanced meals a day.

The two groups of children, equally divided by sex, were selected to represent extremes in stature. In each sex subgroup, the samples of tall and short children were equally distributed into four 12-month age intervals, from 6 to 53 months, by selecting the six tallest and the six shortest children in each age interval.

TABLE 1 presents the mean ages for the four subgroups throughout the age intervals.

FIGURES 1 and 2 present the height-by-age curves for males and females for the total sample measured, as well as

the curves of the fiftieth, tenth, and third percentile of the Boston Growth norms from the Stuart and Meredith* data. The cases selected to represent the tall and short groups are also indicated.

PROCEDURES

The height measurements of all but 24 cases were obtained by one of the investigators. In one institution the measurements were obtained by the health nurse. The children were measured in supine position. Each child was measured twice; in case there was a discrepancy a third measure was obtained and all three were averaged.

The data on the biological and social

---

* Adopted by the Health Department, Milwaukee, Wisconsin. Anthropometric charts based on original data of H. C. Stuart and H. V. Meredith and prepared for use in Children's Medical Center, Boston.[27]

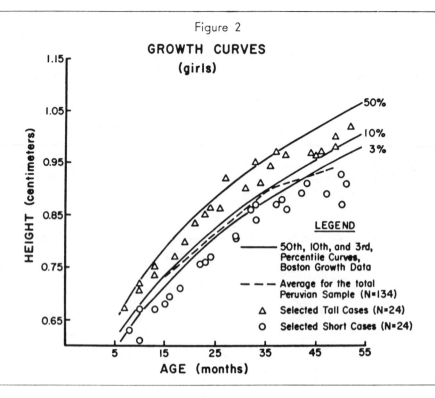

Figure 2

GROWTH CURVES
(girls)

variables were obtained by interviewing the children's mothers. The interview used was a modification of the form used by Cravioto et al.[5] in obtaining comparative information on the social, economic, and educational status of families from two rural height-contrasting groups of children. A section on general medical information, with data on parental height and a brief history of mother's pregnancy and child's birth, were added. The sections on cleanliness and housing conditions were eliminated because not all the mothers were interviewed in their homes.

PRINCIPAL VARIABLES ASSESSED

The main biological and social variables assessed may be listed and defined as follows:

I. PRENATAL VARIABLES

Maternal Height—height in centimeters, obtained by two measurements in a standing position. (All but three mothers were measured.)

Number of Pregnancies—all pregnancies including miscarriages, abortions, and stillbirths. (Target child's ordinal position among the children alive at the time of the interview was also recorded.)

Mother's Age—age at the time of the target child's birth.

II. PARANATAL VARIABLES

Birthweight—mother's report of the child's birthweight. (An attempt was made to obtain the birthweight of the children born in hospitals directly from the records but the hospitals' administration made this search impossible.)

Medical Attention at Childbirth—

mothers' reports regarding whether the target child was born at home with or without medical attention, in the field, medical post, or hospital.

III. SOCIAL VARIABLES

Maternal Education—number of years of schooling reported by mother. (In addition, an attempt was made to determine whether the women were literate or illiterate regardless of their reported years of schooling.)

Family Instability—(1) the number of men with whom the women had lived up to the time of the interview, and (2) the presence or absence of a father figure at the time the interview was carried out.

Family Income—monthly income of family in Peruvian soles. (one sol= .027¢)

Family Size—the number of people living in the house at the time of the interview.

Mother's Years of Residence in Lima —report on the number of years she had been living in Lima.

All interviews were done by one of the investigators (E.P.) and an assistant. Neither examiner knew if the woman interviewed was the mother of a tall or short child. All but three mothers were interviewed; in two of these three cases, the information was obtained from the woman taking care of the home and in the remaining case the father gave the information. An attempt was made to interview all the women in their home; however, many women spent most of their day at work. In these cases the interviews were done at the day care center or at their jobs.

RESULTS

I. PRENATAL VARIABLES

Maternal Height: As would have been expected on the basis of previous reports on the relationship between parents' and children's stature, the mothers of the tall children were significantly taller than the mothers of the short children, by five centimeters. TABLE 2 presents the

Table 2

HEIGHT OF MOTHERS BY AGE, SEX, AND HEIGHT OF CHILDREN
MEANS AND SUMMARY OF ANALYSIS OF VARIANCE
(height in centimeters)

	TALL CHILDREN			SHORT CHILDREN			BOTH		
	M	F	Both	M	F	Both	M	F	Both
YOUNG CHILDREN	151	152	152	146	149	148	149	151	150
OLD CHILDREN	150	152	151	142	146	144	146	149	147
TOTAL	151	152	151	144	148	146	147	150	

Source of Variation	MS	F	P
Age	.012	5.04	$<.05$
Sex	.016	6.66	$<.01$
Height	.065	27.12	$<.01$
Age x Sex	.001	<1.00	----
Age x Height	.006	<1.00	----
Sex x Height	.003	<1.00	----
Age x Sex x Height	.000	<1.00	----
Within Cells	.0024		

Table 3

MOTHERS' NUMBER OF PREGNANCIES BY AGE, SEX AND HEIGHT OF CHILDREN
MEANS AND SUMMARY OF ANALYSIS OF VARIANCE

	TALL CHILDREN			SHORT CHILDREN			BOTH		
	M	F	Both	M	F	Both	M	F	Both
YOUNG CHILDREN	3.25	4.08	3.67	4.00	5.08	4.54	3.60	4.58	4.10
OLD CHILDREN	3.75	4.00	3.88	4.66	5.00	4.83	4.20	4.50	4.35
TOTAL	3.50	4.04	3.77	4.33	5.04	4.68	3.91	4.54	

Source of Variation	MS	F	p
Age	1.55	<1.00	----
Sex	9.37	1.45	NS
Height	20.17	3.12	$<.10$
Age x Sex	2.66	<1.00	----
Age x Height	.04	<1.00	----
Sex x Height	.16	<1.00	----
Age x Sex x Height	.04	<1.00	----
Within Cells	6.465		

mean maternal height for all subgroups, and the summary of the analysis of variance in which height, age, and sex of the children were used as the independent variables.* The analysis shows that the difference between the maternal height for the tall (151 cms.) and short (146 cms.) children reached the 0.01 level of significance. Two additional significant findings, difficult to explain, were that the mothers of the females were significantly taller ($p < .01$) than the mothers of the males, and that the mothers of the younger children were taller ($p < .05$) than the mothers of the older children.

It was possible to obtain height measurements on 12 fathers from the tall and 10 from the short group. Both groups of fathers had exactly the same mean, namely 160 centimeters.

Number of Pregnancies: TABLE 3 presents the mean parity for the mothers of the different subgroups of children. On the average, the mothers of the tall children had had fewer pregnancies (3.77) than mothers in the contrasting group (4.68). Although this difference only reached the 0.10 level of significance, it is interesting to note that the direction of the difference was the same for each of the subcomparisons by age and sex. There were no age or sex differences.

Mothers' Age at Childbirth: In the case of this variable there were almost no differences between the two main groups. The mean age was 26.5 years for the mothers of the tall children, and 27.0 years for the mothers of the short group. Likewise, the difference between the age and sex subgroups were not statistically significant.

* Unless otherwise indicated the basic statistical model used has been a three-way analysis of variance, factorial design with equal number of observations per cell.[29] If there were three or less observations missing in the total sample, the respective mean of the group was used to cover each of the missing observations. Age, sex, and height of the children were used as the independent variables in the analysis. For the purpose of statistical analysis the children were divided into two age subgroups, young (6–29 months) and old (30–53 months).

II. PARANATAL VARIABLES

Birthweight: The mothers of 32 tall and 24 short children reported the birthweights of their respective children; the remaining mothers said that they did not remember or did not know their children's birthweight. The mean birthweight for the tall and short and for the male and female children are reported in TABLE 4. As expected, the re-

Table 4

CHILDREN'S BIRTHWEIGHT IN GRAMS BY SEX AND HEIGHT MEANS AND SUMMARY OF ANALYSIS OF VARIANCE [a]
(weight in grams)

	TALL (N=32)	SHORT (N=23)	BOTH
BOYS (N=25)	3,613	2,757	3,271
GIRLS (N=30)	3,676	3,201	3,470
BOTH	3,643	3,008	

Source of Variation	MS	F	p
Sex	0.866	1.87	NS
Height	5.905	12.80	<.01
Sex x Height	0.479	1.03	NS
Within Cells	0.461		

[a] A two-way analysis of variance with unequal observations per cell was used in this case: [29] Height and Sex of the children were used as independent variables.

ported birthweight of the tall children (3,643 grams) was much higher than that of the contrasting cases (3,008 grams), and this difference reached the .01 level of significance.

Medical Attention at Birth: According to the mothers' reports, a somewhat higher percentage of the short children (35%) were born without medical attention than was the case for the tall cases (25%); however, this difference was not statistically significant (p>.10).

III. SOCIAL VARIABLES

Maternal Education: TABLE 5 presents the reported number of years of schooling for all subgroups. One of the striking observations here is the small number of years of schooling for all cases. Despite this fact, however, mothers of the tall children had significantly more schooling (2.51 years) than the mothers of the short children (1.31 years) (p<.05). Moreover, this difference in schooling was consistent in each of the subgroup comparisons by age and sex. In addition, the information on illiteracy also yielded a considerable difference between these groups. Sixty percent of the mothers from the short group were illiterate in contrast to 38% of the tall group, and this difference also was consistent in each of the subgroup comparisons.

Forty mothers of the tall and 43 mothers of the short group provided information on their husbands' years of schooling. Parallelling the data on mothers, the fathers of the tall group had a higher average (4.40 years) than those of the short group (3.61 years); statistically, however, this difference reached only the .10 level of significance.

Family Instability: The number of women who had lived with two or more men differed rather sharply between the two children's height groups. While only 17% of the mothers of the tall children reported two or more "marriages," 42% of the mothers in the contrasting height group reported a similar experience. A chi^2 test showed that this difference reached a respectable level of statistical significance (p<.01). No differences were found in the comparisons involving presence or absence of a father figure.

Family Income: In contrast to what

Table 5

MOTHER'S MEAN YEARS OF SCHOOLING BY AGE, SEX AND HEIGHT OF CHILDREN
MEANS AND SUMMARY OF ANALYSIS OF VARIANCE [a]

	TALL CHILDREN			SHORT CHILDREN			BOTH		
	M	F	Both	M	F	Both	M	F	Both
YOUNG CHILDREN	2.91	2.83	2.87	1.41	1.08	1.25	2.16	1.95	2.05
OLD CHILDREN	1.50	2.83	2.13	0.83	1.92	1.37	1.16	2.38	1.72
TOTAL	2.20	2.83	2.51	1.12	1.50	1.31	1.66	2.16	

Source of Variation	X^2	df	p
Age	3.64	3	NS
Sex	1.20	3	NS
Height	8.71	3	<.05
Age x Sex	2.63	3	NS
Age x Height	6.48	3	<.10
Sex x Height	.07	3	NS
Age x Sex x Height	.38	3	NS

[a] The distribution of the mothers' years of schooling was negatively skewed. On this account a three-way nonparametric analysis of variance was used with the same three independent variables included in the other three-way model.[24]

might have been expected on the basis of previous findings, the reported monthly income for the families of the tall and short children did not differ significantly (Mean Tall=1,467 soles; Mean Short=1,376 soles; F<1.00). Likewise there were no age or sex differences in income between groups.

Size of Family: The average size of family was very similar for the two height contrasting groups. The averages for the tall and short children were 6.66 and 6.70 respectively. Likewise, there were no sex or age differences in family size.

Mothers' Years of Residence in Lima: It was found that the number of years of residence in Lima was quite similar for the mothers of the children in the tall and short groups, 15.83 and 14.39 respectively. Likewise, no appreciable differences were noted between sex and age subgroups.

As one might expect, there was some evidence that four of the five variables related to children's stature tended to constitute a cluster of interrelated factors: short maternal stature, lower educational level, more pregnancies, and more marriages tended to be associated with one another. On the other hand, birthweight was unrelated to the four variables just mentioned. TABLE 6 presents the rather low, but significant, contingency coefficients among the five variables that differentiated significantly between the tall and short children.

DISCUSSION

The main results of this study of correlates of stature in Lima slum children revealed that mothers of short children, in contrast with mothers of tall children, were significantly shorter (by 5 centimeters), had a reported history of more pregnancies, had significantly less education (1.3 vs. 2.5 years), and had been married significantly more often. In addition, the shorter children had significantly lower reported birth-

Table 6

CONTINGENCY COEFFICIENTS BETWEEN THE VARIABLES THAT PROVED TO BE
SIGNIFICANTLY DIFFERENT BETWEEN THE TWO HEIGHT GROUPS

	MOTHERS' PARITY	MOTHERS' EDUCATION	FAMILY STABILITY	BIRTHWEIGHT
MOTHERS' HEIGHT	0.24[a]	0.24[a]	—0.19	0.00
MOTHERS' PARITY	-----	—0.20[b]	—0.23[b]	0.00
MOTHERS' EDUCATION	-----	-----	0.00	0.00
FAMILY STABILITY	-----	-----	-----	0.00

[a] Significant at the .02 level.
[b] Significant at the .05 level.

weights. All of these relationships were quite similar and consistent when examined separately for boys and girls, and for the younger and older children. Moreover, the first four factors mentioned (exclusive of birthweight) tended to be associated with one another.

One of the most obvious first points of comparison evident here is that this cluster of biological and social variables associated with differences in stature closely resembles similar patterns of relationship found in previous studies of malnourished and "normal" children identified mainly on the basis of stature.[23] At the same time, the cluster of variables related to children's stature in this study parallels rather closely the pattern of biological and social factors frequently found to differentiate between so-called "culturally disadvantaged" and middle-class children in developed countries like the U.S.A. and Great Britain.[3, 10] What makes the results of the present study of particular interest is that maternal stature, education, number of pregnancies, and marital stability were so clearly related to children's stature within a lower socioeconomic or "disadvantaged" sample representing a relatively restricted portion of the total population range.

Let us now return to the central issue of the problems involved in the use of contrasts in stature as a primary index of contrasting nutritional background in children. The present research indicating a marked relationship between children's and mothers' stature suggests that one cannot disregard the possible genetic determinants of height. The contrast between this finding and the previously summarized research of Cravioto et al.[5] might indicate that the relationship between stature of parents and children varies from one type of "disadvantaged" sample to another. However, the existence of such height relationship in a low socioeconomic group like that of the present research points out that nutritional factors are not necessarily overriding and that genetic effects can confound the significance of using stature as a nutritional index.

In connection with the procedure of using stature specifically in studies of malnutrition and psychological development, the present research underscores significant methodological problems. For all five variables found to be related to stature in the present investigation, there is considerable evidence indicating that these variables are also related to intellectual development, and indeed may directly or indirectly influence such development. With regard to parental height, for example, as previously indicated, in large-scale studies there tend to be a positive relationship among factors such as stature, intellectual level, and socioeconomic status among adults as well as children. There is even some evidence suggesting possible relationship between parental size and children's psychological test performance within the same socioeconomic level.[12]

A number of further examples of these complicated relationships may be found in the literature. Many studies have shown that children clearly identified as mental retardates of a variety of different types are significantly shorter than equivalent aged children in the general population.[8, 18, 22] Again, while nutritional deficiencies may be involved here, it is obvious that a number of other factors play a significant role in the production of children who are both mentally retarded and of reduced stature. For example, there is considerable evidence to suggest that in large populations women of markedly reduced stature have a higher probability of being in poor health and nutrition, as well as a higher incidence of prenatal complications and premature births.[25, 26] Moreover, in women of low socioeconomic status increased parity is associated with a heightened probability of premature births, of neonatal mortality,[19] and of congenital malformations of the nervous system.[20] When severe enough, these various complications of pregnancy and birth have been shown repeatedly to be associated with impaired intellectual development, quite independently of problems of postnatal malnutrition.[17, 21] When one considers that the short children in the present study had shorter mothers, with

greater parity, and were of lower birthweight as compared with the tall children, the difficulty of relating possible intellectual deficiencies of the short children to postnatal malnutrition is made particularly clear.

Let us turn next to a consideration of the socio-environmental factors represented by maternal education and family instability in the present study. As previously indicated, there is a large body of evidence indicating a substantial positive relationship between socioeconomic level and children's intellectual status. Parental education, which is one of the main indices of socioeconomic level, has shown a particularly consistent relationship to children's intellectual development in early and later childhood, especially when the educational range represented is relatively broad, and to developmental quotients in the first few years of life.[1, 11, 15] In recent years research has been directed increasingly at the identification of those patterns of interaction between mothers and young children which play a significant role in fostering early learning and intellectual growth, and which may be quite different in families with different social and educational backgrounds.[2, 14] In regard to the present study, even though the educational differences between the mothers of the tall and short children were small and at the lower end of the educational scale (2.5 vs. 1.3 years of schooling, on the average), it is reasonable to assume that these mothers may well have employed different child-rearing practices, not only in regard to nutrition and health but also in the amount and kinds of psychological stimulation and opportunities for learning which they provided.

Marital or family instability is also

found more often in the lower socio-economic levels,[13] and thus may be viewed as part of the cluster of factors which have been found to be associated with lower intellectual levels in children. A related recent finding provides some additional information of interest on this matter. Werner et al.[28] reported that the intellectual development of children born under conditions of prenatal stress was significantly better if their home had been rated as "stable" (i.e. having less emotional stress) rather than "unstable."

In summary, the results of the present study are interpreted as confirming our concern that while differences in slum children's stature may reflect differences in nutritional background, they also reflect differences in a number of other biological and social factors associated with, or capable of influencing, intellectual development in children. Consequently, in most retrospective studies it would be virtually impossible to specify whether behavioral or intellectual differences between tall and short children are primarily a function of nutritional factors, or of some of the other factors associated with stature, or of some combination of these variables. Hence, in studies of undernutrition and psychological development it would be very unwise to use differences in stature as the principal index of previous nutritional history. Obviously, more direct measures of nutritional status and nutritional history would be considerably more desirable, but even this information is not always readily obtainable.

The problem of designing studies to assess the influence of malnutrition on psychological development in children involves a good many methodological difficulties, only a few of which have been discussed briefly in the present paper. While an adequate treatment of these difficulties in research design would require extended discussion which is beyond the scope of this report, it seems clear that retrospective studies are not likely to be very fruitful, particularly if stature differences constitute the main measure of nutritional background. It is the writers' contention that a more productive approach is likely to be found in prospective or experimental studies designed to permit an assessment of the interactions among known variations in nutritional status, dietary intake, parent-child relationships, amount and kind of stimulation for learning in the home, etc., as these factors jointly influence psychological development.

REFERENCES

1. BAYLEY, N., AND JONES, H. 1937. Environmental correlates of mental and motor development: a cumulative study from infancy to six years. Child Devel. 8:329–341.
2. BERNSTEIN, B. 1960. Language and social class. Brit. J. Soc. 11:271–276.
3. BIRCH, H. 1967. Health and the education of socially disadvantaged children. Paper presented at the Conference on Biosocial Factors in the Development of Learning of Disadvantaged Children. Syracuse, N.Y.
4. BROCKMAN, L. 1966. The effects of severe malnutrition on cognitive development in infants. Unpub. doctoral dissertation, Cornell Univ.
5. CRAVIOTO, J., DELICARDIE, E., AND BIRCH, H. 1966. Nutrition, growth, and neurointegrative development, an experimental and ecologic study. Pediat. 38, 11:319–372.
6. CHURCHILL, J., NEFF, J., AND CALDWELL, D. 1966. Birthweight and intelligence. Obs. and Gyn. 28:425–429.
7. CRUMP, E., ET AL. 1957. Growth and development. I. Relation of birthweight in negro infants to sex, maternal age, parity, prenatal care and socio-economic status. J. Pediat. 51:678–697.
8. CULLEY, W., JOLLY, D., AND MERTZ, E.

1963. Heights and weights of mentally retarded children. Amer. J. Ment. Defic. 68:233–235.

9. DOUGLAS, J., ROSS, J., AND SIMPSON, H. 1965. The relation between height and measured educational ability in school children of the same social class, family size and stage of physical development. Human Biology, 37:178–184.

10. DOUGLAS, J., AND SIMPSON, H. 1964. Height in relation to puberty, family size and social class. Milbank Memorial Fund Quarterly, 42:20–34.

11. FREEBERG, N., AND PAYNE, D. 1967. Parental influence on cognitive development in early childhood: A review. Child Development, 38:65–87.

12. GARN, S. 1966. Body size and its implications. *In* Review of Child Development, L. W. Hoffman and M. L. Hoffman (eds.): Vol. II, 529. Russel Sage Foundation, New York.

13. GOODE, W. 1964. The Family. Prentice-Hall, Englewood Cliffs, N. J.

14. HESS, R. D., AND SHIPMAN, V. C. 1965. Early experience and the socialization of cognitive modes in children. Child Development, 36:869–886.

15. HONZIK, M. 1957. Developmental studies of parent-child resemblance in intelligence. Child Development, 28:215–228.

16. JONES, H. 1954. The environment and mental development. *In* Manual of Child Psychology, L. Carmichael, ed.: 2nd Edit., 631. John Wiley & Sons, New York.

17. KNOBLOCH, N., AND PASAMANICK, B. 1966. Prospective studies on the epidemiology of reproductive casualty: methods, findings and some implications. Merrill Palmer Quar. 12:27–43.

18. MOSIER, H., GROSSMAN, H., AND DINGMAN, H. 1965. Physical growth in mental defectives. Pediat. 36, 11:465–519.

19. NEWCOMBE, H. 1965. Environmental versus genetic interpretations of birth order effects. Eugen. Quar. 12:90–101.

20. NEWCOMBE, H., AND TRAVENDALE, O. 1964. Maternal age and birth order correlations. Problems of distinguishing mutational from environmental components. Mutation Res. 1:446–467.

21. O'SULLIVAN, J., ET AL. 1965. Aspects of birth weight and its influencing variables. Amer. J. Obs. and Gyn. 92:1023–1029.

22. RUNDLE, A., AND SYLVESTER, P. 1963. Endocrinological aspects of mental deficiency. III. Growth and development of young males. J. Ment. Defic. Res. 7:10–15.

23. STOCH, M., AND SMYTHE, P. 1963. Does undernutrition during infancy inhibit brain growth and subsequent intellectual development? Arch. Dis. of Childhood, 38:546–552.

24. SUTCLIFFE, J. 1957. A general method of analysis of frequency data for multiple classification designs. Psychol. Bull. 54:134–137.

25. THOMSON, A. 1966. Adult stature. *In* Somatic Growth of the Child, J. J. Van der Werff Ten Bosch and A. Hask, eds. Charles C Thomas, Springfield, Ill.

26. THOMSON, A., AND BELEWICZ, W. 1963. Nutritional status, maternal physique and reproductive efficiency. Proceedings of the Nutritional Society, 22:55–60.

27. WATSON, E., AND LOWREY, G. 1954. Growth and Development of Children. Year Book Publishers, Chicago.

28. WERNER, E., ET AL. 1967. Cumulative effect of perinatal complications and deprived environment on physical, intellectual and social development of preschool children. Pediat. 39:490–505.

29. WINER, B. 1962. Statistical Principles in Experimental Design. McGraw-Hill, New York.

Senior author's address: Dr. Ernesto Pollitt, Department of Pediatrics, Yale University, New Haven, Conn. 06510

20: IMPACT OF NUTRITION ON INTELLIGENCE*

S. Gupta, D. C. Dhingra, M. V. Singh, and N. K. Anand

Introduction

Malnutrition is one of the major health problems of children in developing countries. Animal experiments in the last two decades have revealed that protein-calorie malnutrition (PCM) not only retards physical growth but also impairs serious aspects of mental faculties.[7-3]

Many studies have been done on children suffering from frank P.C.M., especially kwashiorkor and marasmus.[4-6] Similar work has been carried out in India.[7-9] Similar studies on sub-clinical malnutrition which is endemic in the country, however, have not been reported yet. The present investigation was, therefore, planned to study the impact of nutritional status on the intellectual potentialities in school children.

Materials and Methods

Two hunderd and four school-going children between 5 and 8 years of age were selected randomly from Municipal Corporation Schools and a Public School of Delhi. A thorough physical examination, with special reference to anthropometric measurements (height and weight), was carried out. A detailed history regarding the past illness and the family background was obtained. All the children were administered Stanford Binet Test of Intelligence (Hindi Version, 1953). Standard instructions for administration and scoring were followed.

Sample group was then classified in nourished and malnourished group using growth and development standards of Indian Council of Medical Research (1972). Children with a

* Read at the 14th International Congress of Pediatrics held at Argentina, during 3-9 October, 1974.

From the Department of Pediatrics, Maulana Azad Medical College & Associated Irwin and G.B. Pant Hospitals, New Delhi

standard below the expected weight for their age were grouped as malnourished. This group was further divided into subclinical, Grade I, Grade II type of malnutrition, using modified Gomez classification system. Children weighing 91 per cent and above for their age were classified as normally nourished, those between 75 and 90 per cent as subclinical, 61-75 per cent Grade I and 51 to 60 per cent as Grade II. There was no child weighing below 51 per cent of weight, which could be termed Grade III.

The above table has shown that all the groups with different nutritional status are matched for their age.

Table II shows that the different nutritional groups differed from each other as far as their socio-economic status is concerned.

Results

Table III shows that children from nourished group performed better as compared to the malnourished group on the Stanford Binet Test of Intelligence. All the children in former group had their I.Qs more than 90, whereas only 27.1 per cent children from the latter group obtained an I.Q. above 90.

Table IV shows that the mean I.Q. obtained by the nourished group is significantly higher as compared to the mean I.Q. of malnourished group (P>0.01).

The Graph shows that as we go down on the nutritional status of the children, there is lowering trend in the I.Q. distribution. Normal nutrition children have shown best performance and Grade II children have performed worst. Similar relative trend has been maintained by rest of the groups. All the 100 per cent boys of normal nutrition have obtained an I.Q. 90 or above with 50 per cent of superior or above average in intelligence. On the other hand, all the children from Grade II obtained an I.Q. below 81, with 84.2 per cent as mentally subnormal. Performance of children belonging to Grade I

Reprinted from *Indian Pediatr.* **12:**1079-1082 (1975); *Copyright © 1975 by the Indian Academy of Pediatrics.*

TABLE I—*Age distribution in relation to nutritional status*

Age, year	Normal nutrition	sub- clinical	Grade I	Grade II	Total
5 +	13	17	15	1	46
6 +	14	28	19	9	70
7 +	9	27	25	6	67
8 +	2	6	10	3	21
	38	78	69	19	204

$X^{2*} = 11.40$, df=9, p 0.05

The above table has shown that all the groups with different nutritional status are matched for their age

TABLE II—*Socio-economic status in relation to nutritional status*

SESS class*	Normal nutrition	Subclinical	Grade I	Grade II	Total
I	7	—	—	—	7
II	16	13	1	—	30
III	15	15	7	—	37
IV	—	50	61	19	130
Total	38	78	69	19	204

*Socio-economic status class on Kuppu Swamy SES Scale Urban (1956 which was based on the income, education and occupation of the guardian)

TABLE III—*I.Q. distribution of nourished and malnourished groups*

I.Q.	Nourished Group f	Nourished Group percentage	Malnourished group f	Malnourished group percentage
51 — 60	—	—	4	2.4
61 — 70	—	—	20	12.1
71 — 80	—	—	53	31.9
81 — 90	—	—	44	26.5
91 — 100	4	10.5	33	19.9
101 — 110	15	39.5	11	6.6
111 — 120	11	29.0	1	0.6
121 — 130	8	21.0	—	—
	38		166	

TABLE IV—*Mean I.Q. SD and level of significance*

Nutritional status	Mean I.Q.	SD	SEM	t value
Nourished group	110.50	9.40	1.53	14.24
Malnourished group	81.67	12.10		

Significant at 1 per cent level of confidence

TABLE V—*Mean I.Q. in relation to nutritional status and SESS class*

SESS	Nutritional group	N	Mean I.Q.	SD	t value
I	Normal nutrition	7	124.30	3.90	—
II	Normal nutrition	16	111.20	7.16	2.55**
	Subclinical	14	105.30	4.68	
III	Normal nutrition	15	105.30	5.31	6.17**
	Subclinical	15	95.30	3.48	3.22**
	Grade I	7	88.70	5.88	
IV	Subclinical	50	88.10	4.12	13.50**
	Grade I	61	76.60	4.60	8.76**
	Grade II	19	66.00	4.56	

** $P > 0.01$

Graph 1

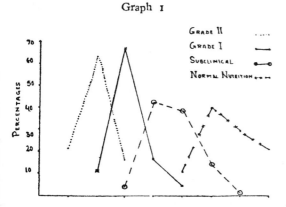

GRADE II ....
GRADE I — —
SUBCLINICAL •—•
NORMAL NUTRITION +—+

malnutrition was better than that of the Grade II group. In the same way subclinical group obtained higher I.Qs as compared to Grades I and II but lower than the normal nutrition group.

Table V shows that normal nutrition group of social class II, obtained significantly higher than mean I.Q. as compared to the sub-clinical group in the same social class. Similar results are obtained in social class III for these two groups. Subclinical group, when compared to Grade I group, also possessed higher mean I.Q. Exactly similar pattern has been observed for the subclinical, Grades I add II group in social class IV.

Discussion

The present series of investigations have revealed that the nourished group children performed better and obtained higher mean I.Q. as compared to the malnourished group. Severity of malnutrition is also found to be related to the performance of children on Binet Test of Intelligence. More severe the malnutrition the poorer the performance and hence lower the I.Q.

The results have also remained unchanged when the social class variable was controlled and the children of different nutritional status were compared to each other in the same social class. Though the impact of malnutrition along with the impact of poor social class was more marked on intelligence, the trend has been maintained when children of different nutritional status were isolated for their social class. Normal nutrition group scored highest I.Q. subclinical were 2nd highest followed by Grade I and Grade II groups, respectively.

The findings that malnutrition does have its impact on the intellectual functioning of the children has been strengthened by the present investigations. Our findings are in agreement to the findings of Stock and Symthe[4] Cabak and Najdanvic[5]; Cravioto *et al*[6]; Ghai *et al*[8]; Parekh *et al*[9]. We have gone a step further to say that even the degree of malnutrition is related to intellectual functioning. More severe the malnutrition, poorer the intelligence.

It can categorically be stated that improvement of the nutrition of young children and infant will ensure better intelligence or in other words better chances for the development of their innate intellectual potentialities.

Nutrition of the children is an important physical factor for the growth and development of this most important cognitive ability, which has a vital role to play in human life.

REFERENCES

1. Widdowson EM: Nutritional deprivation in Psychological development Studies in Animals. *Pan Am Health Org Tci Pub No.* 134: 27, 1966.

2. Novako V, Faltin J and Flandia N: Effects of early and late weaning on learning in adult rats. *Nature* 193: 280, 1962.

3. Dobbings J: The influence of early malnutrition on the development and myelination of the brain. *Proc Roy Soc Med* 159: 503, 1964.

4. Stock MB and Symthe PM: Does undernutrition during infancy inhibit brain growth and subsequent intellectual development. *Arch Dis Child* 38: 546, 1963.

5. Cabak V and Najdanvie R: Effect of under nutrition in early life on physical and mental development. *Arch Dis Child* 40: 532, 1965.

6. Cravioto J and Delicardie ER: Early malnutrition and mental performance in school age children. *Am J Dis Child* 120: 404, 1970.

7. Champakam S, Srikantia SG and Gopalan C; Kwashiorkor and mental development. *Am J Clin Nutr* 21: 844, 1968.

8. Ghai, OP, Ratna K, Ramchandaran K and Neki JS: Effects of early marasmic malnutrition on subsequent mental development. *Indian Pediatr* 3: 155, 1973.

9. Parekh UC, Udani PM, Naik PA and Shah BP: Mental development of children with severe protein calorie malnutrition in the past and present. *Indian Pediatr* 11: 465, 1974.

21: CROSS-CULTURAL COMPARISONS OF MOTHERS AND THEIR UNDERNOURISHED INFANTS IN ASIA

P. L. Graves

As a clinical psychologist, I have been impressed by R. Spitz's work (17) on psychogenic diseases in infancy, including a form of infantile marasmus--a physical wasting away in infants as a result of severe psychic trauma, such as emotional maternal deprivation. During a three-year stay in Southeast Asia between 1970-1973, I had the opportunity to study an obverse phenomenon--the potential impact of undernutrition on the psychological development of infants, with special reference to two aspects: the emerging capacity to explore the environment and the capacity to form trusting, secure ties with others, especially the mother. The sensorimotor investigation of the environment has profound developmental consequences since it influences later adaptability, learning, cognition, and social behavior (18). A secure attachment to the mother during the first years of life is important to the formation of ties to others, as stressed by Bowlby (3); in addition, it has been shown to promote exploration and, through it, cognitive functioning (13).

These two behavioral systems, exploratory behavior and attachment behavior, were selected as dependent variables for the purposes of the present study. Exploratory behavior was assessed from the fine and gross motor manipulation of objects (toys). Attachment behavior was assessed from behavior that promoted contact or proximity to the mother. Three categories of attachment behavior are particularly pertinent: distance interaction through which the infant establishes contact with the mother across a space (look, vocalize, smile, give toys); irritability, in the form of whimpering or crying, to signal distress; and close physical contact with the mother, indicating the child's preference to remain in the lap rather than to explore the surroundings.

An additional psychological variable, the maternal behavior, was studied to provide further information on the nature of the mother-infant tie. It included such characteristics as maternal readiness to initiate interaction or respond to the child's signals, or to interact with the child across a distance (look, smile, talk, give toys).

Moderate chronic malnutrition (undernutrition), characterized by food intake restricted both in quantity and in quality (15), constituted the independent variable. Cases of severe forms of malnutrition (marasmus, kwashiorkor) could be found but were not included in the study because chronic, not acute, undernutrition is the pressing worldwide problem (4).

Reprinted from pages 100-108 of *Behavioral Effects of Energy and Protein Deficits,* J. Brožek, ed., NIH Publication Number 79-1906, U.S. Government Printing Office, Washington, D.C., 1979, 370p.

SAMPLE

The studies reported here were conducted in West Bengal in India, and Kathmandu Valley in Nepal. Identical design and assessment methods were used to assess free-play activities and mother-child interaction in a standard setting among undernourished and adequately nourished infants. In both locations, the family settings were semi-rural: the study area in West Bengal, Singur District, was in close proximity to Calcutta, and the study area in Kathmandu Valley spread around the capital city Kathmandu. In both samples, the fathers were mostly farmers or farm laborers, and most of the families owned some land and/or cattle. When the two nutritional groups in each sample were compared with reference to their socio-economic status (income, cattle, or land owned), the ratings showed no statistically significant differences.

The children were randomly selected for study from among the mother-child pairs attending local well-baby clinics. The age range was from 7 to 18 months, and the two nutritional groups in each sample were matched for age. Three anthropometric criteria of nutritional status were used: body weight, related to international standards for age (9); an index, weight/length^2 x 100, developed in South India (14); and mid-arm/head circumference ratio (10). To be included in the study, an undernourished child had to have a weight between 60 and 70 percent of the standard weight for age, the South Indian index .14 or less, and the midarm/head circumference ratio below .280. A well-nourished child's weight was above the 85th percentile of the standard, the South Indian index .15 or above, and the midarm/head circumference ratio at or above .310. Following Gómez' classification (5) the undernourished were in the lower range of second degree of malnutrition; in terms of the classification based on midarm/head circumference ratios, they were within the range of moderate malnutrition. On the basis of a pediatric examination, all the children, including the undernourished ones, were judged to be free from disease.

The composition and size of the samples of well-nourished and undernourished children studies in the two areas are given in Table 1.

Table 1. The number and mean age of well-nourished and under-
          nourished children in West Bengal and Kathmandu Valley.

AREA	WELL-NOURISHED			UNDERNOURISHED		
	Mean Age (mos.)	Nos.	Total	Mean Age (mos.)	Nos.	Total
Bengal Boys	12.1 + 0.6	19	19	12.8 + 0.8	16	16
Girls						
Kathmandu	12.1 + 0.6		36	12.9 + 0.5		38
Boys		19			18	
Girls		17			20	

PROCEDURES

Only a brief description of the data collection will be given here; a more extensive account may be found elsewhere (6,7). The mother-child pairs were tested individually in a room adjacent to the clinics. The same seating arrangement was used for all mothers as well as the examiners (besides myself, a local assistant). The same toys (a rattle, two toy animals, and a ball) were distributed on the floor near the mother in a standard order. They were lifted on the table in front of the child after 90 seconds if the child stayed in the mother's lap. The child's free activities and the mother-child interaction were observed for twenty minutes. During this time, the mother was interviewed by the assistant since this helped mothers to be less self-conscious and more relaxed; otherwise she was to respond to her child as she would normally. The detailed observations, covering 30-second intervals, were later coded for statistical analysis.

Agreement between two observers (agreements as percentage of agreements plus disagreements) was assessed for ten randomly selected cases. The medians for observer agreements were exploratory behavior 93% (range 84-100), irritability 95% (70-100), attachment behavior 83% (68-90), and maternal behavior 77% (70-86).

The stability of behavior was assessed by observing 34 mother-child pairs twice, in the clinic setting, within three to seven days. Another group of 13 mother-child pairs was observed first at the clinic and, three days later, at home. The correlation coefficients indicating stability of observed behaviors in the same setting, and in the home and clinic settings were all positive and significant at or above .05 level; only irritability observed at the clinic and at home failed to reach a statistically significant level.

To assess coding reliability, two coders independently scored twenty randomly selected records of observation. Product-moment reliability coefficients ranged from + 0.93 to + 0.99 for child behavioral scores, and from + p.96 to + 0.98 for maternal scores.

While an infant intelligence test was also administered, this report is limited to the behavioral observations.

RESULTS

Since in West Bengal only a few undernourished girls could be contacted, the behavioral data were analyzed for boys only. The Nepali sample contained both boys and girls (Table 1).

The behavioral scores of the undernourished infants tended to be lower in both geographical areas, except for "crying" which was somewhat higher, but not significantly (Table 2).

Table 2. Behavior of well-nourished and undernourished children in West Bengal and in Kathmandu Valley. Mean scores for different categories of child behavior and significance level of the differences, based on the analysis of variance.

BEHAVIOR CATEGORY	WELL-NOURISHED		UNDERNOURISHED		SIGNIFICANCE	
	Bengal	Kathmandu	Bengal	Kathmandu	Bengal	Kathmandu
Activity	46.2	60.8	43.2	38.8	n.s.	0.01
Vigorous activity	6.0	3.6	2.7	1.6	0.05	n.s.
Crying	4.5	5.0	5.1	6.7	n.s.	n.s.
Distance interaction	11.6	20.4	6.7	14.6	0.05	0.05
Physical interaction	6.2	6.0	5.2	6.6	n.s.	n.s.
Approach	3.4	2.4	1.4	1.0	n.s.	0.05
All attach. behaviors	21.2	28.2	13.4	22.2	0.05	0.05

The undernourished children stayed more frequently in mother's laps (Table 3) and nursed with greater frequency during the period of observation.

Table 3. Behavior of well-nourished and undernourished children in West Bengal and in Kathmandu Valley. "Lap" refers to the number of children staying in the lap. "Feeding" denotes the frequency of nursing during the period of observation. For both variables the significance level is based on chi-square.

BEHAVIOR CATEGORY	WELL-NOURISHED		UNDERNOURISHED		SIGNIFICANCE	
	Bengal	Kathmandu	Bengal	Kathmandu	Bengal	Kathmandu
Lap	1	11	7	27	0.05	0.01
Feeding	4	13	9	31	n.s.	0.001

Bengali mothers tended to interact with undernourished children less vigorously than with the well-nourished children (Table 4). In the Nepali sample this difference was much less marked and it did not reach a level of statistical significance for any of the categories of maternal behavior.

It should be noted that in West Bengal mothers of well-nourished children reacted differently toward boys and toward girls (8).

Table 4. Behavior of the mothers of well-nourished and undernourished children in West Bengal and in Kathmandu
Valley. Mean scores for different categories of maternal behavior and significance level of the differences,
based on the analysis of variance.

BEHAVIOR CATEGORY	MOTHERS WITH WELL-NOURISHED CHILDREN		MOTHERS WITH UNDERNOURISHED CHILDREN		SIGNIFICANCE	
	Bengal	Kathmandu	Bengal	Kathmandu	Bengal	Kathmandu
Distance interaction	11.4	34.5	7.5	27.6	0.05	n.s.
Physical interaction	9.5	14.7	8.3	18.4	n.s.	n.s.
Initiated behavior	9.4	24.9	7.6	23.4	n.s.	n.s.
Response to non-cry	8.1	20.9	4.7	18.9	0.05	n.s.
Response to crying	1.0	1.5	0.6	1.3	0.05	n.s.
All maternal behaviors	21.1	52.4	15.8	49.8	0.05	n.s.

As a way of integrating and supplementing the tabular data,
let me present a composite picture of a typical well-nourished
child's behavior in the experimental setting. It arrived in the
room, carried by the mother, and briefly stayed in the lap to survey the scene. Very quickly, however, the infant made its way to
the floor and started an involved, concentrated exploration of the
toys. Both fine and gross motor movements were used extensively
to mouth, touch, pull, shake, bang, or throw the toys. The exploratory bouts were interrupted at times when the infant turned to
establish contact with the mother, primarily through interaction
across a distance. The interruptions were short and the infant
easily returned to manipulating the toys. If, while at play, the
infant maintained an interaction with the mother, it was done primarily via vocalizations, looks, smiles, or exchange of toys. A
typical well-nourished infant, then, was an active child for whom
the presence of the mother seemed to create a feeling of security
(1). This feeling enabled him to explore comfortably the novel
situation as well as to maintain rapport with the mother across
a distance.

An undernourished infant's behavior was different in several
crucial ways. Typically, the infant preferred to stay in the
mother's lap from where, leaning on her, it started to explore the
toys on the table. The manipulations had a markedly muted quality.

The activities with the toys were few, hesitant, and lacked vigor
(especially in the West Bengali sample). If the infant left the
lap, the play still retained its tentative, slow-paced nature.
The interaction with the mother had a similarly muted quality.
Exchanges across a distance (vocalizations, smiles, looks, giving
and taking toys) were infrequent; the main interactional mode was
through close physical contact. Frequently the infant left the
toys, turned to the mother, lifted the blouse, and started to
nurse. It appeared that the breast was used more frequently as a
pacifier rather than to meet the infant's nutritional needs. A
typical undernourished infant, then, was a rather inactive child,
who seldom left the physical safety of the mother's lap to explore
the environment. This way of relating to the mother was characteristic of younger infants, indicating a need for physical close-
ness and mothering. An impoverished mode in exploratory and attachment behaviors prevailed.

While the differences between the behavior of malnourished
and well-nourished infants were observed both in West Bengal and
in Kathmandu Valley, maternal behavior in the two cultural settings
was different. The Bengali mothers showed less interaction and
less reciprocity with the undernourished infants than with the
well-nourished infants. By contrast, among the Nepali mothers
the maternal behavior was less affected by the nutritional status
of the infants.

DISCUSSION

Four aspects of the findings may be of particular importance
for these children's later development. The first aspect concerns
the undernourished infants' reduced reliance on distance interaction with the mother. Sigel (16) has suggested that distancing,
that is, behaviors or events that separate the child cognitively
from the immediate behavioral environment, contributes to the
development of higher cognitive functioning, such as representational thought. In the present study it was not possible to test
this hypothesis. However, it is likely that the undernourished
children's reduced reliance on the distancing mode of communication would reduce also the need to use representational symbols,
such as words. This would lead to underdevelopment of verbal
skills and could well contribute to lower performance on measures
of cognitive development, such as intelligence tests.

The second aspect relates to the undernourished infants' reduced exploratory behavior. Such restriction of interaction with
the environment would interfere with the acquisition of information
needed for optimal cognitive growth and social-emotional development. The effects are akin to "functional isolation," a mechanism
suggested by Levitsky and Barnes (11): malnutrition "functionally
isolates" the infant from the environment and by doing so delays

those responses that are necessary to permit the infant to explore the environment and to learn, This mechanism would be another way of explaining the delays frequently found in the cognitive development of malnourished children.

Third, functional isolation of the infant may result in a different pattern of responses from the environment. Importantly, the infant may affect the caregiver's behavior (12), although we do not know much about these interaction patterns between the undernourished child and its parents. In societies like that of West Bengal, where the embedded cultural expectations influence maternal attitudes toward a non-thriving child, the effects will be very complex. That is, the culturally determined maternal attitudes and the undernourished infants' "functional isolation" may both contribute to qualitative and quantitative differences in parent-child interaction (6).

The fourth aspect involves the increased frequency of nursing found among the undernourished infants. In the present study it was not possible to determine whether this behavior was nutritive or non-nutritive in nature. However, infant and animal studies (2) suggest that increased suckling reflects a heightened motivational state of hunger. Among undernourished infants hunger may interfere with other motivational springs of behavior which would lead to exploration of the environment and establishment of social contacts.

As a final point, I would like to offer a tentative explanation for the causes of undernutrition in infancy. In both cultural settings two characteristics differentiated families of well-nourished and undernourished children. The first had to do with food habits. The analysis of the preceding day's diet indicated that the undernourished infants consumed animal protein less frequently than did the well-nourished infants. The second finding has to do primarily with parental level of education. In both samples, the parents of the undernourished children attained a significantly lower educational level than the well-nourished group's parents. These two findings suggest that infant undernutrition may stem, in part, from parental ignorance of children's health and nutritional needs, and, perhaps, from adherence to traditional beliefs and customs, discordant with the child's needs. If so, educational programs concerned with nutrition and geared to the village life style should be accorded a high priority.

REFERENCES

1. Ainsworth, M. D. S., Bell, S. M., Stayton, D. J. Individual differences in strange situation behavior of one-year-olds. In H. R. Schaffer, Ed. The Origin of Human Social Relations. London: Academic Press, pp. 17-57, 1971.

2. Ausubel, D. A. Theory and Problems of Child Development.
    New York: Grune & Stratton, 1958.

3. Bowlby, J. Attachment and Loss. Vol. 1: Attachment. New
    York: Basic Boods, 1969.

4. Food and Agriculture Organization of the United Nations.
    Production Year Book 1963. Rome: FAO, 1964.

5. Gómez, F. R., Galván, R., Cravioto, J. and Frenk, S. Malnu-
    trition in infancy and childhood, with special reference to
    kwashiorkor. Advan. Pediat., :131-169,1954.

6. Graves, P. L. Nutrition, infant behavior, and maternal char-
    acteristics: a pilot study in West Bengal, India. Amer.
    J. Clin. Nutr., 29:305-319, 1976.

7. Graves, P. L. Nutrition and infant behavior: A replication
    study in the Kathmandu Valley, Nepal. Amer. J. Clin. Nutr.,
    31:541-551, 1978.

8. Graves, P. L. Infant behavior and maternal attitudes in West
    Bengal, India: Early sex differences. J. Cross-Cult. Psy-
    chol., 9:45-60, 1978.

9. Jelliffe, D. B. The Assessment of Nutritional Status of the
    Community. (With Special Reference to Field Surveys in De-
    veloping Regions). WHO Monograph Series No. 53, 1966.

10. Kanawate, A. A. and McLaren, D. S. Midarm/head circumference
    ratio: A new technique to assess marginal protein-calorie
    malnutrition in a community. In P. G. Tulpule and K. S. J.
    Rao, Eds., Proc. First Asian Cong. Nutr., Hyderabad, India.
    India: Nutrition Society of India, pp. 786-789, 1972.

11. Levitsky, D. A. and Barnes, R. J. Nutritional and environ-
    mental interactions in the behavioral development of the rat:
    long-term effects. Science, 176:68-71, 1972.

12. Lewis, M. and Rosenblum, L. A., Eds. The Effect of the Infant
    on Its Caregiver. New York: Wiley & Sons, 1974.

13. Main, M. Exploration, play and cognitive functioning as re-
    lated to child-mother attachment. Unpublished doctoral dis-
    sertation. The Johns Hopkins University, 1973.

14. Rao , K. V. and Singh, D. An evaluation of the relationship
    between nutritional status and anthropometric measurements.
    Amer. J. Clin. Nutr., 28:83-93, 1970.

15. Read , M. S. Malnutrition, hunger and behavior. <u>J. Amer.</u>
    <u>Diet. Assoc</u>., 63:379-396, 1973.

16. Sigel, I. The distancing hypothesis: A causal hypothesis
    for the acquisition of representational thought. In M. R.
    Jones, Ed., <u>Miami Symposium on the Prediction of Behavior</u>:
    <u>1968: Effects of Early Experience</u>. Coral Gables, Florida:
    University of Miami Press, pp. 99-118, 1970.

17. Spitz, R. A. The psychogenic diseases in infancy: An attempt
    at their etiologic classification. <u>The Psychoanal. Study of</u>
    <u>the Child</u>, 6:255-275, 1951.

18. Weisler, A. and McCall, R. B. Exploration and play: Resumé
    and redirection. <u>Amer. Psychol</u>, 31:492-508, 1976.

Addendum to Part VI

ADDITIONAL READING

Prenatal malnutrition is discussed in articles by Als and co-workers (1976), Lester (1979), and Zeskind and Lester (1981). Ecology and undernutrition are covered by Chávez and co-workers (1972), Guthrie, Masangkay, and Guthrie (1976), and Pollitt (1969). Piagetian approach is discussed by Dasen and co-workers (1977). See Dasen et al. (1977) and Lavallée et al. (1979).

MALNUTRITION, ENVIRONMENT, HEALTH, AND INTELLIGENCE

There are different ways in which one may attempt to assess the joint and separate effects of nutritional, other biological, and social factors on intelligence. Mora and colleagues (1974) approached the issue in a cross-sectional study carried out in the early 1970s in Bogotá, Colombia, by using stepwise regression analysis.

First, let us consider a finding confirming what has been a generally held belief, at least in more recent times: The study documents quantitatively the idea that the environment of severe poverty, independent of inadequate nutrition, is potentially detrimental to cognitive development. Thus, while nonmalnourished younger siblings had an average general DQ of 100.9, the mean for the older siblings dropped to 95.1, using the Griffiths Mental Development Scale (Griffiths, 1970). The difference was statistically highly significant.

Our immediate concern is with the differences between the performance of better-nourished and malnourished children. In both age groups, younger and older, the malnourished children scored lower (with DQs of 100.9 versus 86.2 in the younger group and 95.1 versus 80.9 in the older age group); the differences are statistically highly significant.

It is important to note that the families of malnourished children scored lower on all the major indicators of socioeconomic status. Furthermore, there were differences in child-rearing practices, with the malnourished children receiving less attention from the mother. Finally, their morbidity was higher.

The stepwise regression analyses led to the conclusion that "the effects of malnutrition on intellectual performance could be isolated from the effects of social and health factors measured" (Mora et al., 1974, p. 233). Of the total variance of the Griffiths general developmental quotients, 19% was explained in the younger children by height and weight as measures of nutritional status, adjusting for the variance explained by social and health factors; for the older children the value was 14%. The social and health factors alone accounted for 16% and 17% of the variance (p. 221). Socioeconomic status was the single most important social variable in younger children (p. 223).

REFERENCES

Als, H., E. Tronick, L. Adamson, and T. B. Brazelton, 1976, The Behavior of the Full-term but Underweight Newborn Infant, *Dev. Med. Child Neurol.* **18:**590-602.

Chávez, A., C. Martínez, M. Muñoz, P. Arroyo, and H. Bourges, 1972, Ecological Factors in the Nutrition and Development of Children in Poor Rural Areas, in *3rd Western Hemisphere Nutrition Congress Proceedings,* Futura Publishing Company, Mount Kisco, New York, pp. 265-269.

Dasen, P., M. Lavallée, J. Retschitzky, and M. Reinhardt, 1977, Early Moderate Malnutrition and the Development of Sensori-Motor Intelligence, *J. Trop. Pediatr. Environ. Child Health* **23:**146-157.

Griffiths, R., 1970, *The Abilities of Young Children,* Child Development Research Center, London, 177p.

Guthrie, G. M., Z. Masangkay, and H. A. Guthrie, 1976, Behavior, Malnutrition, and Mental Development, *J. Cross-Cult. Psychol.* **7:**169-180.

Lavallée, M., P. Dasen, J. Retschitzky, M. Reinhardt, and C. Meylan, 1979, Subclinical Malnutrition and Sensorimotor Development in a Rural Area of the Ivory Coast, in *Behavioral Effects of Energy and Protein Deficits,* J. Brožek, ed., NIH Publication Number 79-1906, U.S. Government Printing Office, Washington, D.C., pp. 109-120.

Lester, B. M., 1979, A Synergistic Process Approach to the Study of Prenatal Malnutrition, *Int. J. Behav. Dev.* **2:**337-393.

Mora, J. O., A. Amezquita, L. Castro, N. Christiansen, J. Clement-Murphy, L. F. Cobos, H. D. Cremer, S. Dragastin, M. F. Elias, D. Franklin, M. G. Herrera, N. Ortiz, F. Padro, B. de Paredes, C. Ramos, R. Riley, H. Rodriguez, L. Vuori-Christiansen, M. Wagner, and J. F. Stare, 1974, Nutrition, Health and Social Factors Related to Intellectual Performance, *World Rev. Nutr. Diet* **19:**205-236.

Pollitt, E., 1969, Ecology, Malnutrition, and Mental Development, *Psychosom. Med.* **31:**193-199.

Zeskind, P. S., and B. M. Lester, 1981, Analysis of Cry Features in Newborns with Differential Fetal Growth, *Child Dev.* **52:**207-212.

Part VII

Generalized Subclinical Malnutrition: Interventions

Papers 22 Through 26: Commentary

The longitudinal studies on nutritional supplementation, with or without psychosocial stimulation, carried out in the 1970s at two sites in Colombia (Cali and Bogotá), in Guatemala, and in Mexico, occupy a unique position in the history of research on generalized subclinical (chronic) malnutrition. The designs, time schedules, samples, home diets, dietary supplements and their timing, and the nature of stimulation, if any, were described in detail elsewhere (Brožek, Coursin, and Read, 1977). The results were summarized by Pollitt (1980 and 1981, with an outline of the intervention programs on p. 264). Pollitt refers to these studies as "quasi-experimental" (cf. Campbell and Stanley, 1963) since only a part of the dietary intake of the participants was manipulated or closely monitored by the investigators.

The results of these intervention studies were presented in a large number of reports, many of them preliminary. Only the Mexican supplementation study was presented in the form of a monograph (in Spanish, Chávez and Martínez, 1979a; and in an English translation, Chávez and Martínez, 1982). In view of their complexity, final monographic accounts of the longitudinal Latin American studies would be highly desirable. In the context of the Berkeley Project on Education and Nutrition, the Guatemala data on diet, physical growth, verbal development, and school performance were analyzed by Wilson (1981), relying heavily on the technique of path analysis.

Papers 22, 23, and 24 are reports on supplementation without formal stimulation programs, while Papers 25 and 26 refer to studies incorporating such programs. Papers 22 and 23 deal with two different aspects (cognitive and social-emotional) and two different phases of the extensive, longitudinal Guatemalan study on the effects of nutritional supplements made available to four communities. Paper 22 reports data on cognitive performance of Guatemalan children from a rural area in which mild-to-moderate malnutrition is endemic. The study began in 1969, and the data collection terminated in 1977. It was anticipated that a monographic account of the study would be completed by 1979. Regrettably, however, the date came and passed.

Numerically, the Guatemalan sample studied longitudinally was the largest ever, with an N of well over 1,000. It included all the children in the four study villages who were less than seven years of age in 1969 and all the children born in these communities between 1969 and 1973; the latter group included 671 children. The fathers were, for the most part, poor subsistence farmers.

Daily supplements were provided in the local health centers and were freely available to pregnant and lactating mothers and to children. Intakes of the supplement were recorded individually for all children below seven years of age. In two of the villages, the supplement Atole contained calories (160 per cup) and protein (11 g per cup). The supplement called Fresco, served in the other two villages, contained some calories (60 per cup) but no protein. Both beverages contained vitamins and minerals. Only the information on the caloric supplementary intake was considered in Paper 22. As it turned out, this variable proved to be an ineffective predictor of mental performance. Interestingly enough, it did prove useful in the study of the social-emotional functioning (Paper 23).

In the Guatemalan study, mental performance capacity was characterized in terms of a composite test score (based on the tests constituting a Preschool Test Battery) as well as subscores on tests of language, memory, and perception. Our comment will be limited to the composite test score.

The socioenvironmental characteristics of the families, including the quality of the house, type of clothing worn by the mother, and the nature of the instruction received by the child at home were combined into a Social Factor Index. The relationships between the variables were characterized in terms of the coefficients or correlation. In some tables, coefficients of determination (squares of the coefficients of correlation) are reported, representing the percentages of the total variance of the dependent (predicted) variable accounted for by the independent (predictor) variable.

One of the most striking findings reported in Paper 22 is that the anthropometric indicator of Nutritional Status (based on stature and head circumference) was a much more effective predictor of cognitive competence than the amount of calorie supplement received by a child up to the time of testing. Thus, for the seven-year-old boys, the children's supplementary intake of calories yielded an $r = .08$, statistically not significant; for girls, an $r = .11$, statistically significant at the .05 level but accounting for a mere 1.2% of the variance of the composite test scores. By contrast, the anthropometric indicator of Nutritional Status yielded a statistically highly significant r of .22 for boys and .37 for girls, corresponding to 4.8 and 13.7% of the variance of the composite scores, accounted for by the predictor. For the Social Factor Index, the corresponding values were similar: rs of .21 and .36, equivalent to 4.4 and 13% of the variance explained.

By combining the Nutritional and the Social Indexes, the percentage of the variance explained increased to 7% in boys and 22% in the girls. By contrast, removing statistically the effect of the Social Factor reduces the predictive capacity of Nutritional Status to 3 and 9% of the variance. Similarly, when the effect of Nutritional Status is removed, the percentage of variance accounted for by the Social Factor decreases to 2 and 8% respectively. Thus, both sets of factors, nutritional and environmental, independently predicted mental performance and did so with similar effectiveness.

Paper 23 (cf. also Barrett, Radke-Yarrow, and Klein, 1982) is a milestone in the study of the psychological aspects of human malnutrition, marking a shift from years of concern with the children's cognitive development to social-emotional functioning. The innovative component is in the methodology, not in the awareness of the relevance of the social-emotional effects of malnutrition. The author reviews and presents in tabular form the relevant observations made in both the animal and the human studies, indicating that malnutrition alters the organism's attentional capacities, affect and emotional control, social responsiveness, and activity level. On this basis the author formulated hypotheses about possible effects of early undernutrition on selected dimensions of the social-emotional functioning of the older child.

The subjects were drawn from the sample participating in the longitudinal study described in Paper 22. Their age range, at the time of the Barrett study, was from six years, one month to eight years, three months.

Both general characteristics of behavior (across situations) and situation-specific behaviors were studied. The first category included interaction with peers, contact with adults, behavior in physical environment, level of activity, and affect. The situation-specific assessment involved the children's responses to four structured situations (novel environment, competitive game, frustrating problem, and impulse control game), described briefly in the text (p. 292 in Paper 23) and, in greater detail, in the Appendix. The situations formed a sequence of gamelike activities.

Three supplementation variables were considered: total supplementary energy (calorie) intake of the mother during pregnancy, of the child up to two years of age, and of the child from two to four years. On the basis of these data, the children were placed in one of two categories: Low Supplement and High Supplement, with 69 children in each category. Only the effects common to boys and girls and significant at the .01 level are noted here. The High Supplement children were more involved in group activities, were happier, were less anxious, displayed a higher energy level, were more involved in a competitive game, and used a greater number of strategies in tackling a frustrating task.

The proceedings of an international symposium in which Paper 23 was published contain two extensive comments on the paper. They present a "view from the bedside" (Frank, 1984) and a comment from the point of view of a cultural anthropologist (Super, 1984). Frank gives Barrett credit for two important advances in the field of research on child nutrition: (1) identification of social-emotional functioning as a sensitive behavioral criterion of the impact of early nutritional deprivation, moderate in intensity, and (2) development of a viable methodology for an objective assessment of that parameter complex.

She calls for a search for the biological and social mechanisms that mediate the association between early undernutrition and later social-emotional dysfunction.

Frank feels that Barrett's work has direct implications for clinical practice and stresses that in dealing with children who experience undernutrition early in life, "We must attend not only to their nutritional and medical needs, but [also] to their special educational and emotional requirements" (p. 324).

In Super's assessment, "the cultural issues faced by Barrett in his work are on the surface; they are more technical than theoretical" (p. 330). Super underscores that it is the cultural context that gives meaning to human activities and he insists that "children learn the structure and value of emotional responses no less than of morphemes" (p. 330). Not questioning the importance of Barrett's work, Super feels that it—like all truly innovative research—opens new lines of inquiry designed to clarify the question of what is behind the anxious expression and lower involvement of the less-supplemented Guatemalan children.

Paper 24 presents a facet of a multivariable, longitudinal study carried out in Tezonteopan, in the state of Puebla, a community typical of the poor rural areas of Mexico. There were two groups of mother-child dyads, with initial Ns of 20 each. The unsupplemented group of pregnant women was selected from 40 families in 1968. Using the same criteria (mother's height in the range of 136 to 152 cm, normal childbirth, birth weight of 2.5 kg or more), the group to be supplemented was constituted in 1970. Deaths and migration reduced the number of children to 17 in each of the two groups.

Beginning early in the pregnancy, the mothers in the supplemented group of 40 families received food supplements in the form of partly skimmed milk. The average supplement consumed daily during pregnancy was 205 cal and 15 g of protein; during lactation the supplement consumption rose to 305 cal and 23 g of protein per day.

Each day the children were offered one bottle of full-fat milk, beginning at three months of age. Over time the supplement was gradually increased and was continued through five years of age. The supplement provided calories and protein, plus minerals. While a variety of criteria were used in the study of the two groups of children when they attended the first grade of school (such as teachers' assessments and the results of a variety of tests), as in the study of the early phase of the children's lives (Chávez and Martínez, 1979b), the principal, novel, and important methodological feature of the study of the school children was a direct observation of behavior, using the technique of time sampling. A periscope made it possible for the investigators to make observations without the child's awareness of being observed. With two consecutive days of observation during three periods (at the beginning, in the middle, and at the end of the school year), two observation periods per day (90 minutes at the beginning and again at the end of the school day), and observations made very 20 seconds, a total of 3,240 observations were made per subject.

There were marked differences between the two groups in terms of their ability to pass the grade (6 out of 17 unsupplemented children failed) and their test performance. The average IQs differed in the predicted direction (75.8 for the unsupplemented, 80.4 for the supplemented children), but the difference was not significant statistically.

The direct observations of behavior indicated that the supplemented group was more active, more attentive, and less unhappy. Of particular interest were the changes in behavior from the morning to the afternoon session. While the previously supplemented children maintained alertness throughout, in the unsupplemented group the percentage of instances in which the children were found asleep rose from 1% in the morning to 8.5% in the afternoon.

Although very demanding as far as the observer is concerned, the procedure opens a whole new avenue to the study of very important problems involving the behavior of school children, such as the effectiveness of meals or snacks provided in the school, the effects of environmental variables, and various aspects of the school curricula, including the nature, duration, and placement of the exercise periods.

Paper 25 reports the results of a study of the effects in preschool children of nutritional supplementation, combined with stimulation in the form of a cognitively oriented educational program. The children came from a poor area of the city of Cali, Colombia. In 1970, 300 three-year-olds were selected from 800 families on the basis of low height for age (below the third percentile of the Harvard norms) and low weight for age (below the tenth percentile of the Harvard norms). Their families had very low incomes, and the average family size was 7.5 persons.

The study design is relatively complex. The combined program of nutritional supplementation, psychoeducational stimulation, and health care was provided to four separate age groups for four, three, two, and one years respectively. In each of these groups the initial N was 60. In addition, a group of the same size ($N = 60$), consisting of upper-class comparison children, was included without being involved in any intervention. Finally, three small groups (with $N = 20$ per group) received food supplementation and health care for three, two, and one years; during the final year they all participated in the combined (supplementation, stimulation, and health care) program.

The children participating in the comprehensive program attended a center in which they received food, psychoeducational stimulation, and health care. The supplement, consumed in the center, included mixed food and a high-protein (19%) mixture of soya and rice flour (*Colombiharina*). The goal of the supplementation program was to cover 100% of the children's protein needs and 80% of their energy needs.

The children not receiving psychoeducational stimulation did not attend the center. Their families picked up packages at the center that contained food supplements for the whole family, and the children ate the food at home. No record of the food intake of the individual nonstimulated children was kept.

Finally, an untreated group, comparable in its low socioeconomic status to the other groups, was tested at the end of the preschool period. This comparison group is not indicated in Figure 1 or Figure 2 of Paper 25. Its mean test score, obtained at seven years, three months, was lower than in any of the other groups. The value was not reported since it was felt that the depressed score may have been due, in part, to the fact that the group had not been tested since the neurological screening was done four years earlier.

The psychological variables were covered extensively in the Cali study. The 21 tests constituting the cognitive test battery are listed in an earlier report (McKay et al., 1978, p. 274). Each of these tests was used at two or more consecutive testing sessions out of the five measurement periods.

The data in Figure 2 of Paper 25 represent composite scores. At the final (fifth) testing session, the mean scores were lowest for the group that participated in the comprehensive program for one year. The score was highest for the group with four years of comprehensive treatment. The groups intermediary in the length of participation in the comprehensive program were intermediary also in their average test scores.

A possible alternate interpretation would postulate that the earlier in an undernourished child's life the treatment is instituted, the greater the overall gain in cognitive ability. Throughout, the rate of gain is highest during the first treatment period.

Paper 25 also addresses the issue of the durability of the gain beyond the treatment period. School performance, as measured by the grade level achieved by the fourth school year, parallels — though not rigorously — the duration of the comprehensive preschool intervention (Figure 6, p. 237 of Paper 25).

Paper 26 (cf. Herrera et al., 1980) is a product of the Bogotá Research Project on Malnutrition and Mental Development, initiated in 1973 and thus the youngest of the Latin American longitudinal studies. In this case, as in the Cali study (Paper 25), we deal with interventions, in the plural, not with a single intervention.

The design of the study is very complex since it involves six intervention schedules, corresponding to six groups of subjects:

1. Absence of supplementation and stimulation throughout;
2. Postnatal food supplementation for three years;
3. Supplementation during the last trimester of pregnancy and the first six postnatal months of the child's life;
4. Supplementation during pregnancy and postnatally for three years;
5. Stimulation from birth to the end of the third year of life;
6. Food supplementation beginning in pregnancy and continuing for three years, combined with stimulation for three years.

The intervention schedules are presented schematically in Figure 1 of Paper 25.

There were two basic issues: (1) What was the impact of the interventions on cognitive performance at the end of the child's third year of life? (2) What was the relative contribution of food supplementation and of psychological stimulation? The cognitive outcomes were measured by a battery of tests. Two of these tests, taken over from the Guatemalan battery (cf. Brožek, 1984) and involving Perceptual Analysis (embedded figures test) and Language (naming and recognition of pictures of common objects), were selected for the analysis reported in Paper 26.

In summary, supplementation affected significantly (at the .05 level) the scores in Perceptual Analysis, and stimulation had a highly significant effect on both Perceptual Analysis and Language. As concerns the indicators of Nutritional Status, both a higher body length and body weight were associated with higher scores in Perceptual Analysis and Language. Among the social measures, significant associations were ascertained between mother's education, family income, and per capita income and the scores on Perceptual Analysis and Language. Controlling the effects of other variables, in one of the analyses (Table 6A, p. 414 of Paper 26) the Nutrition Indicators accounted for 9.4% of the total variance of the scores for Perceptual Analysis and 8.4% for Language;

the corresponding variance percentages accounted for by the Social Scales were 8.3 and 10.6.

As we have seen in the Guatemala study (Paper 22), both nutritional and social inputs are relevant for some dimensions of cognitive functioning. Performance in a test of short memory correlated weakly with either the biological or social measures.

REFERENCES

Barrett, D. E., M. Radke-Yarrow, and R. E. Klein, 1982, Chronic Nutrition and Child Behavior: Effects of Early Caloric Supplementation on Social-Emotional Functioning at School Age, *Dev. Psychol.* **18:**541-556.

Brožek, J., 1984, Postscript, in *Malnutrition and Behavior: Critical Assessment of Key Issues,* J. Brožek and B. Schürch, eds., Nestlé Foundation Publication Series, vol. 4, Lausanne, Switzerland, pp. 175-176.

Brožek, J., D. B. Coursin, and M. S. Read, 1977, Longitudinal Studies on the Effects of Malnutrition, Nutritional Supplementation, and Behavioral Stimulation, *Pan Am. Health Organ. Bull.* **11:**237-249. (In Spanish, *Of. Sanit. Panam. Ból.* **33:**399-412.)

Campbell, D. T., and J. C. Stanley, 1963, *Experimental and Quasi-Experimental Designs for Research,* Rand McNally, Chicago, 84p.

Chávez, A., and C. Martínez, 1979*a, Nutrición y Desarrollo Infantil (Nutrition and Child Development),* Interamericana, Mexico, D.F., esp. pp. 78-122.

Chávez, A., and C. Martínez, 1979*b,* Behavioral Effects of Undernutrition and Food Supplementation, in *Behavioral Effects of Energy and Protein Deficits,* J. Brozak, ed., NIH Publication Number 79-1906, U.S. Government Printing Office, Washington, D.C., pp. 216-228.

Chávez, A., and C. Martínez, 1982, *Growing Up in a Developing Community: A Bio-Ecological Study of the Development of Children from Poor Rural Families of Mexico,* Instituto Nacional de Nutrición, Mexico, D.F., esp. pp. 84-131.

Frank, D. A., 1984, Malnutrition and Behavior: A View from the Bedside, in *Malnutrition and Behavior: Critical Assessment of Key Issues,* J. Brožek and B. Schürch, eds., Nestlé Foundation Publication Series, vol. 4, Lausanne, Switzerland, pp. 307-326.

Herrera, M. G., J. O. Mora, N. Christiansen, N. Ortiz, J. Clement, L. Vuori, D. Waber, B. De Paredes, and M. Wagner, 1980, Effects of Nutritional Supplementation and Early Education on Physical and Cognitive Development, in *Life-Span Developmental Psychology: Intervention,* R. R. Turner and H. W. Reese, eds., Academic Press, New York, pp. 149-184.

McKay, H., L. Sinisterra, A. McKay, H. Gómez, and P. Lloreda, 1978, Improving Cognitive Ability in Chronically Deprived Children, *Science* **200:**270-278.

Pollitt, E., 1980, *Poverty and Malnutrition in Latin America: Early Childhood Intervention Programs,* Praeger, New York, pp. 41-53.

Pollitt, E., 1981, Effects of Nutritional Supplementation on the Behavioral Development of Infants and Children, in *Textbook of Pediatric Nutrition,* R. M. Suskind, ed., Raven Press, New York, pp. 263-269.

Super, M., 1984, Models of Assessment and Development, in *Malnutrition and Behavior: Critical Assessment of Key Issues,* J. Brožek and B. Schürch, eds., Nestlé Foundation Publication Series, vol. 4, Lausanne, Switzerland, pp. 327-336.

Wilson, A. B., 1981, Longitudinal Analysis of Diet, Physical Growth, Verbal Development, and School Performance, in *Malnourished Children of the Rural Poor,* Auburn House Publishing Company, Boston, pp. 39-81.

22: NUTRITION AND COGNITIVE DEVELOPMENT AMONG RURAL GUATEMALAN CHILDREN

H. E. Freeman, R. E. Klein, J. W. Townsend, and A. Lechtig

Abstract: Women and children from four Guatemalan villages participated in a voluntary food supplementation program for seven years. In two of the villages, they received a vitamin and mineral fortified, high-protein calorie supplement. In the other two villages, the vitamin-mineral fortified supplement contained no protein and a relatively small number of calories.

Cognitive tests were administered regularly to children ages three to seven, and anthropometric measures obtained. In addition, measures of families' social milieu were collected at several points in time.

Using multiple regression analysis, we find that both nutritional and social environmental measures are related to various dimensions of cognitive competence. The results suggest that nutritional intake, independent of social factors, affects cognitive development. There is also some evidence that the children who receive the high-protein calorie supplement (and whose mothers received it during pregnancy and lactation) are more likely to score high in cognitive performance. Our results, while not diminishing social environmental explanations of differences in cognitive function, suggest benefits from nutrition intervention programs in rural areas of lesser-developed countries. (*Am J Public Health* 1980; 70:1277-1285.)

During the past 20 years, there has been a proliferation of studies of the effects of childhood malnutrition on physical and mental development.[1] The continued concern with the impact of malnutrition on physical and mental development is related to an inability to control population growth in lesser-developed countries, marginal food production on a world-wide basis, and inequitable food distribution even within our most industrialized countries. It is further stimulated by competition for the resources of governments, international agencies, and private foundations by advocates of nutrition intervention programs and those whose priorities lie in such other sectors as education and rural economic development. In addition to the press for findings to support policies and programs of nutrition intervention, the spate of investigation is an effort to extend and clarify animal studies of the relationship between malnutrition and neurological development, learning patterns, and other behaviors.[2-5]

Over the several decades of work, attention has shifted to a large extent from studies of the cognitive performance of severely malnourished children to investigations of those with mild and moderate protein-calorie deficiencies. An estimated three per cent of the world's children undergo one or more episodes of severe malnutrition prior to their fifth birthday.[6] In comparison, it is estimated that fully one-half of the pre-school children in lesser-developed countries are suffering from mild to moderate protein-calorie deficits, as well as a small, but critical, proportion of children in low-income families in industralized nations.[7]

Extrapolating the findings of early studies documenting a presumably causal link between children's severe nutritional deficiencies and their reduced cognitive development[8-12] to moderately and mildly nourished children has resulted in a continuing and intense scientific and policy debate. The controversy involves both the extent to which findings about severely malnourished children can be generalized to mild and moderate ones, and whether a causal relationship can be accepted on the basis of epidemiological data.

A causal linkage between mild and moderate malnutrition and intellectual development is challenged by findings of numerous investigations in both lesser-developed and industrialized countries. These range from broad investigations that find an association between children's social milieu and cognitive development[12] to specifically nutrition-focused studies, such as those of Evans and associates' South African investigation in which malnourished children and their healthier siblings achieved similar scores on cognitive tests.[13] Moreover, children in economically advantaged families have been found repeatedly to have larger anthropometric measurements on indicators commonly used to evaluate nutritional status. Thus, there is a strong argument that the relations between mild to moderate malnutrition and level of cognitive functioning is explainable by the covariation between socioenvironmental factors and nutritional status.

Adequate study of the competing explanations—nutritional status vs socioenvironmental factors—involves complex issues of conceptualization, design, analysis, and protection of human subjects. The immature state of the nutri-

Address reprint requests to Dr. Howard E. Freeman, Director, Institute for Social Science Research, University of California, Los Angeles, CA 90024. The other authors are all with the Institute of Nutrition of Central America and Panama (INCAP). Dr. Klein is Director of INCAP Division of Human Development and Drs. Townsend and Lechtig are senior staff members in this Division. This paper, submitted to the Journal June 16, 1980, was revised and accepted for publication August 20, 1980.

tional and behavioral sciences does not permit complete solutions to the major problems of method, including adequate operationalization and measurement of key variables (see Klein, *et al*, for an expanded discussion of this point[14]). Further, the number of variables that must be quantified and introduced into any reasonable design requires relatively large samples, collection and collation of data on extensive sets of variables and, consequently, sophisticated data analysis procedures.

The importance of the issue, however, and particularly the policy concern with nutritional interventions in lesser-developed countries, led to initiating a number of field investigations in the mid-1960s. These studies necessarily began with less than perfect designs, and are deficient to varying extents because of implementation difficulties that could not be fully overcome. Nevertheless, their results promise to refine knowledge about the causal impact of nutrition on cognition (see Klein, *et al*, for reports about these efforts, as well as a discussion of their methodological limitations[15]).

The data reported here come from a long-term longitudinal Guatemalan investigation of nutrition and mental development which began in 1968, and was recently completed by the Institute of Nutrition of Central America and Panama (INCAP).[16-18] In two earlier papers, we reported preliminary analyses of the contributions of nutritional and social factors to cognitive functioning.[14, 19]

The results of these early analyses suggested that both the nutritional and social domains are related to cognitive development among three and four year old children, and that the relative importance of nutritional and social factors depends on the particular cognitive dimension selected as the criterion variable. There were major sex differences in the amount of variance accounted for by the different social and nutritional measures included as independent variables. While findings had limited robustness, the results suggested that nutritional status had an independent, presumably causal, linkage to at least several of the important dimensions of cognitive functioning, as well as to a composite measure of mental development.

In this paper, we provide an analysis of the final data set on the contributions of nutritional and social factors to cognitive development. The analysis is expanded substantially: rather than having test scores at only ages three and four, we have data for children from ages three years through seven years. Furthermore, sample sizes, compared with the earlier reports, have increased.

The INCAP Study, Design and Methods

The study population consists of children from four small Spanish-speaking Guatemalan villages. In 1972, average family incomes were less than $300 per year. Most adults cannot read or write, almost no families have indoor sanitary facilities, and the water generally is contaminated with enteric bacteria. Corn and beans are the major diet, and animal protein is less than 12 per cent of total protein intake.[20]

TABLE 1—Number of Children Available for Analysis by Age and Sex

| Sex | Age at Time of Testing | | | | |
	3 years	4 years	5 years	6 years	7 years
Male	396	463	428	403	371
Female	341	397	405	388	368

Study Design

The study can most properly be described as a quasi-experiment.[21] In two of the villages, pregnant and lactating mothers and children were offered a protein-calorie supplement twice a day. In two other villages, a supplement containing no protein was provided. This supplement, a fruit-flavored drink, contains one-third of the calories (59 compared with 163 per ml) of the protein-calorie supplement. Both include vitamins, minerals, and fluorides limited in the home diet. In this paper the protein-calorie supplement will be referred to as the "high calorie supplement." Attendance at the supplementation program was voluntary, and there were no restrictions on how much could be ingested. A wide range of intake occurred.

The high-protein calorie supplementation in two of the four villages provides an overall study group that includes sufficient children and lactating mothers with an adequate calorie intake. Without "salting" the study group with supplemented children and mothers, the proportion malnourished in rural Guatemalan villages is so large it would not be possible to undertake the analysis. The impact of supplementation on physical growth is clear, with significant differences observed in anthropometric measures among children at birth and all ages.[22, 23]

The Subjects

The analysis includes 1,083 children, 671 born alive after the field work started in 1969, and 412 alive, and between three and seven years of age when data collection commenced.

Thus, at each age the number of children available for analysis consists of those of that age in the villages when the study began and first testing occurred, plus children who "grow up" to each age and were tested at that age-point. The number of children for which data are available at various ages also differs because there was mobility both in and out of the villages throughout the study. Also, sometimes children were unavailable in particular years for psychological testing and anthropometric measurement.

This point requires some additional amplification. When data are presented by age, the age designation refers to the information collected at a particular time point, e.g., information reported for age three, and then for age five, includes many of the same children in the two analyses, but the data differ by time point collected. The study group sizes by age and sex are reported in Table 1. The exact study group sizes for each analysis vary somewhat because of missing data; in general, subsequent tables contain about 95 per cent of the study groups size reported in Table 1.

Variables

In this paper we include four sets of data from the unusually large corpus of information available. The variables selected are the same as reported in the two earlier articles.[14, 19]

Dependent Variables

The cognitive measures used come from a specifically designed "preschool" battery. Three specific measures are employed, as well as a composite index.

Language Facility—The score is based on the child's ability to name and recognize pictures of common objects, and to note and state relations between orally presented verbal concepts.

Short-Term Memory for Numbers—The child's score is based on recall of increasingly long strands of numbers, read at the rate of one per second.

Perceptual Analysis—Scores of children are based on the ability to locate hidden figures imbedded in a complex picture.

Cognitive Composite—Results were first standardized and then added together on 12 tests to obtain the composite score. The cognitive composite summarizes the child's ability to memorize, recognize, perceive, infer, and verbalize.

Test-retest reliabilities differ somewhat by age, but are generally within the accepted .7 to .8 range when measures are obtained one month apart. The test-retest reliability of the cognitive composite battery so obtained was .88 for three year old children.

Socioenvironmental Measures

Although the villages are relatively "flat" in stratification, nevertheless there is evidence of structural and lifestyle variation. After attempts to develop a range of scales, it was decided to obtain family data repeatedly on three measures. The data used here were obtained in the third (1974) survey:

Quality of House—Rating based on the type of construction, interior design, and condition of dwelling. (Test-retest reliability = .80.)

Mother's Dress—Rating based on whether or not the mother possessed specified items of commercially manufactured clothing. (Test-retest reliability = .65.)

Task Instruction—Rating based on family members' reports of teaching the child to perform household tasks and to travel to a nearby town. (Test-retest reliability = .50.)

The first measure, quality of house, is conceived as a social-economic stratification measure. The second, mother's dress, reflects modernity as well as income. The third, task instruction, is viewed as an indicator of the parents' efforts to provide adult modeling and purposeful learning opportunities. Reliability of the two stratification measures is reasonably high, particularly the quality of house measure. The task instruction measure's reliability is border-

line. Reliability of measures is increased by pooling the three scores. The composite measure is referred to as the "social factor index." The test-retest reliability of the social factor index is .85.

Nutritional Data

The child's head circumference and total height are used as indices of nutritional status. Both variables presumably reflect the child's history of protein-calorie intake, although genetic background and illness experience also influence them. Height is generally the best indicator of extended nutritional deficiency; head circumference is most sensitive to malnourishment before the age of two years.[24] Extensive field trials conducted as part of the INCAP program argue for the utility of anthropometric measures as indicators of nutritional status. As previously reported, INCAP field surveys have found that in villages in which children receive an annual intake of more than 20 liters of the high calorie food supplement, their physical growth velocities are similar to those recorded for children in the United States.[14] In villages receiving the low-calorie supplement, these velocities are significantly lower. The height and head circumference measures are combined into a *Nutrition Index* by first standardizing and then adding the values together.

Supplementation Data

Children and their mothers received and drank the supplements under supervision, with careful recording of amounts. Three different measures are used in this analysis: the caloric intake of mothers during gestation, their intake during lactation, and the total calories consumed by the children from birth until seven years of age.

In the two villages receiving the high calorie supplement during both pregnancy and lactation, mothers consumed at least twice as many calories as in the villages receiving the low calorie supplement. Children in the high calorie villages, depending upon the age point studied, received anywhere from two to six times the number of calories (see Table 2).

Results

Separate multiple regression analyses with the data pooled for the four villages were undertaken by age and sex. A large number of repeated analyses were performed. First, in order to estimate the independent and joint effects of variables in the several domains of measures, they were "forced" into the analysis in different orders (for example, social factors first and then nutritional measures).

Second, analyses were undertaken with individual measures and with composite indices. While indices minimize the number of variables, conserve the degrees of freedom, and simplify interpretation and presentation of findings, the amount of variance explained may be reduced since the components in the composite indices are not highly correlated with each other.

Third, analyses were undertaken with and without taking into account interaction effects between variables. There

TABLE 2—Average Total Supplement Consumed (Kcal × 100) by Age of Child

	3 years		4 years		5 years		6 years		7 years	
	Age									
	Type of Supplementation Children Received*									
	H	L	H	L	H	L	H	L	H	L
Mothers during Gestation	138	95	120	80	74	61	42	26	15	9
Mothers during Lactation	232	51	197	42	150	35	121	26	56	14
Male Children	1180	193	1533	362	1797	572	1986	740	2069	920
Female Children	1004	166	1452	334	1652	507	1984	656	2069	904

*H = High Protein Calorie Supplement (11g of protein and 163 Kcal/180 ml.)
 L = Low Calorie (No Protein) Supplement (59 Kcal/180 ml.)

were no interaction effects important enough to include in this report. The variance explained by them was not statistically significant and was outweighed by the loss of degrees of freedom. Finally, a further refinement was to adjust correlations for estimated reliability of measures. Again, this procedure does not modify the results.

Nutrition and Cognitive Performance

In Table 3, we present the zero-order correlations of the nutritional measures and the psychological test scores. The R^2 of the two nutrition variables, height and head circumference, and the psychological test scores are included.

TABLE 3—Correlations between Nutritional Status and Cognitive Measures

		Language		Memory		Perception		Composite	
		M	F	M	F	M	F	M	F
Nutritional Index	Age 3	.27**	.28**	.12*	.31**	.13*	.24**	.22**	40**
	4	.23**	.37**	.04	.22**	.15**	.07	.21**	.34**
	5	.30**	.34**	.15**	.23**	.20**	.20**	.29**	.32**
	6	.38**	.34**	.10	.13*	.16**	.22**	.29**	.29**
	7	.32**	.36**	−.03	.22**	.13*	.32**	.22**	.37**
Height	Age 3	.30**	.26**	.17**	.28**	.14**	.19**	.26**	.32**
	4	.26**	.32**	.11*	.19**	.15**	.04	26**	.29**
	5	.29**	.27**	.19**	.18**	.17**	.20**	.28**	.26**
	6	.27**	.28**	.10	.11*	.15**	.13*	.23**	.23**
	7	.24**	.30**	.00	.20**	.12*	.28**	.15**	.33**
Head Circumference	Age 3	.17**	.24**	.03	.25**	.08	.23**	.10	.36**
	4	.12*	.32**	−.05	.18**	.10*	.06	.10*	.30**
	5	.21**	.31**	.07	.22**	.15**	.13**	.20**	.29**
	6	.35**	.28**	.06	.10	.11*	.23**	.25**	25**
	7	.28**	.29**	−.05	.16**	.10	.25**	.21**	.29**
R^2 of Height and Head Circumference	Age 3	.09**	.08**	.03*	.10**	.03*	.06**	.07**	.16**
	4	.07**	.14**	.02*	.06**	.02*	.00	.07**	.13**
	5	.10**	.12**	.04**	.06**	.04**	.05**	.09**	.11**
	6	.15**	.11**	.02	.02	.03*	.06**	.09**	.08**
	7	.11**	.13**	.02	.05**	.02	.10**	.06**	.14**

*P < .05; **P < .01

The overall conclusion is clear. Both independently and taken together either as a summated index or in terms of a multiple regression result, nutritional status is related to cognitive competence. The results are striking in the case of both language and the cognitive composite measure. The two nutrition variables taken together explain at all ages approximately 10 per cent of the variance in language scores and, at all ages, at least 7 per cent of the variance in cognitive composite scores.

Memory results are less consistent, particularly for males; relations between the nutrition measures and perception are somewhat more consistent and higher for older female children than for older male children. It is difficult to explain the spottiness of the correlation values for the memory variable. The low values at four years for the perception measure is accountable by the design of the test. At age four, the test was made more difficult in order to avoid ceiling effects (it would have probably been better to increase the level of difficulty at age five rather than four). The level of diffi-

culty of the test accounts for the reduced amount of variance explained.

The variations in the correlations of height and head circumference may be explained by the age-ceiling on head circumference; most of the variation takes place by 24 months of age. In contrast, height is sensitive to health and nutritional insults throughout childhood. In any event, consistent with epidemiological studies of nutritional status and intellectual development and our previously reported analyses, there is in general, a clear association between nutritional status and cognitive measures.

Social Factors and Cognitive Scores

Socioenvironmental factors as well as nutritional status are related to cognitive scores. In Table 4 we report zero-order correlations for the three individual measures—quality of housing, mother's dress, and task instruction—and for the social factor index. With respect to language, the three individual variables, as well as the social factor index, are signif-

TABLE 4—Correlations between Social Measures and Cognitive Scores

	Language		Memory		Perception		Composite	
	M	F	M	F	M	F	M	F
Social Factor Index								
Age 3	.20**	.13*	.13*	.01	.11*	-.01	.18**	.05
4	.19**	.19**	.15**	.08	.13**	.04	.23**	.19**
5	.31**	.22**	.18**	.18**	.10*	.08	.34**	.20**
6	.24**	.28**	.22**	.24**	.16**	.09	.27**	.31**
7	.26**	.34**	.13*	.24**	.10	.18**	.21**	.36**
House Quality								
Age 3	.07	.14*	.05	-.02	.01	.02	.05	.08′
4	.05	.16**	.05	.09	.03	.02	.08	.17**
5	.15**	.17**	.11**	.16**	.06	.07	.18**	.18**
6	.13*	.22**	.14**	.15**	.14**	.04	.13*	.23**
7	.15**	.29**	.13*	.14**	.05	.20**	.14**	.32**
Mother's Dress								
Age 3	.19**	.06	.15**	.00	.08	-.04	.20**	.02
4	.22**	.17**	.19**	.09	.13**	.04	.26**	.17**
5	.26**	.17**	.10*	.12*	.07	.02	.27**	.15**
6	.22**	.19**	.14**	.18**	.12*	.11*	.23**	.26**
7	.20**	.25**	.09	.19**	.07	.09	.16**	.27**
Task Instruction								
Age 3	.17**	.05	.08	.03	.14**	-.01	.14**	-.00
4	.16**	.08	.08	-.03	.13**	.03	.17**	.05
5	.27**	.13*	.18**	.11*	.10*	.08	.29**	.09
6	.18**	.18**	.18**	.19**	.08	.06	.24**	.19**
7	.21**	.20**	.05	.22**	.09	.09	.17**	.18**
Multiple R²								
Age 3	.05**	.02	.02	.00	.02*	.00	.05**	.01
4	.06**	.04**	.04**	.02	.03**	.00	.08**	.04**
5	.11**	.05**	.04**	.04**	.01	.01	.12**	.12**
6	.07**	.08**	.05**	.06**	.03*	.01	.09**	.10**
7	.07**	.12**	.02	.07**	.01	.04**	.05**	.14**

*P < .05; **P < .01

icantly correlated with test scores. The amount of variance explained by the three measures, depending upon age, ranges from 4 to 10 per cent. There is some trend, although not marked, for the measures to explain an increased amount of variance when children are older, particularly among females.

These social measurements are also strong predictors of memory scores, at least for ages five and six, and for females at age seven. The three social variables also predict perception scores, although many of the values are not significant or borderline in significance. The overall cognitive composite measure is quite consistently predicted by the three

social factor measures, particularly at later ages for females. The combined amount of variance explained is considerable. Certainly the general direction of the correlations is consistent and strong enough to suggest a link between socioenvironmental differences and psychological performance.

Independent Impact of Nutrition and Social Factors

The data presented suggest that both domains of variables are related to psychological test performance. The issue is whether or not a statement can be made about the unique contributions of nutritional status and social factors to mental development. To put it another way, do the nutri-

TABLE 5—Proportion of Variance Explained by Nutrition and Social Factor Measures

	Test							
	Language		Memory		Perception		Composite	
	M	F	M	F	M	F	M	F
Nutrition Index Alone								
Age 3	.06**	.11**	.01*	.10**	.02*	.06**	.05**	.16**
4	.04**	.14**	.00	.05**	.02**	.00	.05**	.12**
5	.10**	.09**	.02**	.05**	.04**	.04**	.08**	.10**
6	.14**	.11**	.01	.02*	.03**	.05**	.09**	.08**
7	.10**	.14**	.00	.05**	.02*	.10**	.05**	.14**
Social Factor Index Alone								
Age 3	.04**	.02*	.02*	.00	.01*	.00	.03	.00
4	.04**	.04**	.02**	.01	.02**	.00	.05**	.03**
5	.10**	.05**	.03**	.03**	.01*	.01	.11**	.04**
6	.06**	.08**	.05**	.06**	.03**	.01	.07**	.10**
7	.07**	.11**	.02*	.06**	.01	.03**	.05**	.13**
Nutrition and Social Factor Index Combined								
Age 3	.08**	.12**	.03*	.10**	.03**	.06**	.06**	.16**
4	.07**	.14**	.02*	.05**	.03**	.00	.08**	.12**
5	.16**	.11**	.04**	.07**	.04**	.05**	.16**	.12**
6	.16**	.16**	.04**	.07**	.04**	.05**	.12**	.15**
7	.12**	.21**	.03*	.08**	.02**	.11**	.07**	.22**
Nutrition Index with Social Factor Index First Removed								
Age 3	.03**	.10**	.01	.10**	.01*	.06**	.03**	.02**
4	.03**	.11**	.00	.05**	.01*	.00	.03**	.10**
5	.05**	.07**	.01*	.05**	.02**	.04**	.04**	.09**
6	.11**	.07**	.00	.00	.01*	.04**	.06**	.04**
7	.07**	.09**	.01	.02**	.01	.08**	.03**	.09**
Social Factor Index with Nutrition Index First Removed								
Age 3	.02**	.01	.01	.00	.01	.00	.02*	.00
4	.02**	.01	.02*	.00	.01*	.00	.03**	.01
5	.06**	.01*	.02*	.01	.01	.00	.08**	.01
6	.02**	.04**	.03**	.05**	.01*	.00	.03**	.06**
7	.03**	.07**	.02**	.04**	.01	.01*	.02**	.08**

*P < .05; **P < .01

tional measures predict cognitive functioning after all of the variance that can be attributed to social factors is first removed, and vice-versa?

Multiple regressions were undertaken in which the social factors were forced first, followed by the nutritional terms, and then by the interactions between these measures. In other regressions, the nutritional measures and the height X head circumference interaction were first forced, followed by the social variables. The analyses were undertaken using the composite indices, as well as separate variables.

In Table 5 we show the proportion of variance explained when the composite, nutrition and social factor indices are regressed on the psychological measures. The results are substantially the same when the individual nutrition and social factor measures are used, although the amount of variance explained when the composite indices are used is somewhat lower.

In two-thirds of the regressions, the amount of variance explained by the nutrition index for the three specific psychological measures is statistically significant even when the social factor effects are first taken into account. In the case of the composite measure, all of the regression values are statistically significant. When the procedure is reversed, i.e., when the social factor index is forced in subsequent to removing variance explained by the nutrition measures, there continue to be a number of significant regressions. There are, however, proportionately fewer significant values than when social factors are first removed, and the magnitudes of the values, in general, tend to be lower.

Reasons for the sex differences in regression values and for the variations by test are difficult to explain. Study group sizes for the analyses provided here are large enough to minimize sample size fluctuation as the explanation. With the exception of the already discussed level of difficulty problem of the perception test at age four, there seems little reason to believe that the psychometric properties of the different tests explain the variations in correlation values. It seems clear that both nutrition and social factors independently contribute to cognitive performance, the results being most consistent for the language variable and the cognitive composite measure.

Impact of Supplementation

As in the previous analysis, based only on the children at younger ages and partial study groups, the data presented up to now in this paper make a substantial case for the view that inadequate nutrition is associated with lower cognitive performance. Statements of a causal nature, however, are risky from essentially correlational data. Fortunately, the information on intake of supplementation is available and provides, albeit limited, support for the causal character of the association between nutritional cognition.

In Table 6, the findings on supplementation and cognitive performance are shown. For each of the three psychological tests and the cognitive composite, zero-order values are shown between test scores and the amount of supplement consumed during gestation and lactation, and during the child's participation in the study. In addition, R^2 values

are shown for gestation and lactation taken together, and also for gestation, lactation and child-consumed supplement.

Ideally it would have been desirable to have measures of home diet intake as well. Home nutrition surveys were regularly undertaken. They are not precise enough for use here, although they do provide evidence that the interventions are true supplementations and not substitutes for food normally eaten by the children.

Almost one-half of the multiple regressions that take into account supplementation of the child are statistically significant. In general, the language measure shows the most profound impact of the supplement, with enough significant relations with memory and perception to support an overall generalization that nutrition impacts on cognition. Although the amount of variation is low, the cognitive composite variable also supports this contention.

There are further internal comparisons that support the contention of a causal link between nutrition and cognition. Supplementation for children trails off as they become older because of the design of the study. Specifically, children who were older when the study began (for example, age six) had the least opportunity to participate in the supplementation intervention. Children conceived when the study was first implemented had maximum opportunity, through mother's supplementation and the child's own participation, to receive extra calories. Children who were four years at the study's termination, if continually exposed to the supplementation, and whose mothers also received supplementation, on the average would have consumed more than twice that of the seven-year-old group. The higher values between amount of supplement consumed and test scores at early ages, a consequence of the design of the intervention, provide an additional hint that nutritional status is causally linked to psychological competence.

Further, analyses were undertaken in which social factors were controlled first and then supplementation correlated with test scores. However, there are few significant correlations between social factor scores and supplements ingested; whenever there are significant correlations between these variables they are *negative*. Thus, social factors have no impact or slightly raise the correlational values shown in Table 6.

The data just presented require revising one finding disseminated from earlier INCAP analyses,[14, 25] namely that the relations identified between nutrition, supplementation, and cognitive scores were mainly due to the impact on the nutritional status of pregnant and lactating mothers, rather than on children after weaning. The data in Table 6 suggest that, if anything, it is the amount of supplement consumed by the child that is correlated with cognitive scores. This is most clear in the case of memory, and also with respect to cognitive composite results.

Discussion

This field study is hardly an ideal randomized design, and there are problems of validity of many of the variables, and of reliability with some of them—particularly the social

TABLE 6—Correlations between Supplementation and Test Scores

	3 years		4 years		5 years		6 years		7 years	
Test	M	F	M	F	M	F	M	F	M	F
Language										
During Gestation	.09	.10	.11*	.11*	.09	−.02	.03	.03	.06	.04
During Lactation	.08	.14*	.12*	.17**	.05	.08	.07	.04	.08	.10
R^2 (G+L)	.01*	.02*	.02**	.03**	.01	.00	.00	.00	.00	.01
Of Child	.14**	.10	.16**	.20**	.11*	.12*	.15**	.14**	.11*	.18**
R^2 (G+L+C)	.02**	.02	.03**	.04**	.02	.02*	.02*	.02*	.01	.03**
Memory										
During Gestation	.05	−.00	.03	.04	−.04	−.07	−.04	−.05	−.09	−.04
During Lactation	.02	.15*	−.03	.09	−.07	−.05	−.06	−.03	−.03	−.04
R^2 (G+L)	.00	.01	.00	.01	.00	.00	.00	.00	.01	.00
Of Child	.12*	.13*	.02	−.01	−.00	−.11*	.01	−.16**	−.03	−.08
R^2 (G+L+C)	.02	.04*	.01	.01	.01	.01	.01	.03**	.01	.01
Perception										
During Gestation	.06	.05	.02	.02	.08	.08	.07	−.01	.08	.08
During Lactation	.05	.03	.11*	.06	.08	.01	.07	−.03	.04	.03
R^2 (G+L)	.00	.00	.01	.00	.01	.00	.00	.00	.00	.00
Of Child	.04	.06	.13**	.09	.11*	.12*	.11*	.09	.05	.13*
R^2 (G+L+C)	.00	.01	.02*	.01	.01	.03*	.01	.02	.01	.02*
Composite										
During Gestation	.14**	.12*	.14**	.09	.11*	.02	.04	−.01	.04	.05
During Lactation	.09	.12*	.12**	.12*	.03	.08	.01	.02	.01	.09
R^2 (G+L)	.02**	.02*	.02**	.02*	.01	.00	.00	.00	.00	.01
Of Child	.11*	.10	.19**	.10*	.13**	.07	.15**	.03	.08	.11*
R^2 (G+L+C)	.02*	.02	.04**	.02	.03**	.01	.03**	.00	.01	.02

*P < .05; **P < .01

measures. Furthermore, we are at a loss to explain some of the findings. For example, it is puzzling that the effect of nutrition is greater for language, essentially a nondynamic cognitive variable, than for memory which requires focused attention and cognitive strategy. Finally, and most important, we may be accused of not having measured all of the dimensions of the child's social environment and that, if we had done so, the amount of variance explained by nutritional measures after forcing social measures in first would have been substantially reduced.

The INCAP evaluation, despite costs and implementation difficulties in undertaking large-scale field studies, should be followed by additional research in order to deal with some of its problematic issues. Nevertheless, the analysis persuasively suggests that there is a causal linkage between nutrition and cognition competence. Follow-up of children into school and efforts to validate the cognitive tests by obtaining indigenous rankings of intellectual performance demonstrate that the test measures are not idle scores. Children with higher cognitive composites do better, attend school in greater proportions,[18] and are ranked as more intelligent by adults in the villages in which they live.[26]

There are a number of plausible explanations for the relationship between nutritional status and cognitive development. Either a lack of adequate total calories or a deficiency of protein may impede the development of the neurological system. Another possibility is that the poorly nourished child, pre- and post-partum, has insufficient energy to take advantage of opportunities for social contacts and learning. Finally, it may be that adults and older children treat the larger child as a more mature individual, which leads to increased social learning opportunities. Clearly, the state of knowledge in neither the nutritional nor the social sciences is sufficient to suggest a single, primary explanation.

It bears emphasis that the findings do not diminish social environmental explanations of difference in cognitive functioning. The generally persistent correlations between the social factor variables and cognitive functioning support the reasonableness of various views about the consequences of deficient family milieux. Moreover, the fairly systematic findings on the amounts of variance explained by nutritional and social measures from one cognitive dimension to the next suggest that the social and nutritional inputs into a child's life have different magnitudes of importance in determining performance on various cognitive dimensions.

Nevertheless, as we noted in our 1977 preliminary report, at least in rural Guatemala, nutrition intervention programs are relatively easy to implement in comparison to most other social action efforts. In terms of the human and economic resources required for broad-scale, sustained social milieu interventions, and the political and cultural barriers to their rapid implementation, there is sound reason to stress nutrition intervention efforts in the formulation of social and community development policies for rural Guatemala—and perhaps for other lesser-developed countries as well.

REFERENCES

1. Brozek J (ed): Behavioral effects of energy and protein deficits. Proceedings of the International Nutrition Conference, November 30-December 2, 1977. National Institute of Arthritis, Metabolism, and Digestive Diseases, DHEW, NIH Pub. No. 79-1906, August 1979.
2. Chase HP, Lindsley WFB, O'Brian D: Undernutrition and cerebellar development. Nature 1969; 221:554-555.
3. Dobbing J: Effects of experimental undernutrition on the development of the nervous system. IN: Scrimshaw NS and Gordon JE (eds): Malnutrition, Learning and Behavior. Cambridge, MA: MIT Press, 1968, pp 181-203.
4. Barnes RH, Moore AU, Pond WG: Behavioral abnormalities in young adult pigs caused by malnutrition in early life. J Nutrition 1970; 100:149-155.
5. Dobbing J, Smart JL: Clinics in Development Medicine. London: Heinemann Radical Publications, 1972.
6. Behar M: Prevalence of malnutrition among preschool children in developing countries. IN: Scrimshaw NS and Gordon JE (eds): Malnutrition, Learning and Behavior. Cambridge, MA: MIT Press, 1968, p 30.
7. U.S. Department of Health, Education, and Welfare, National Center for Health Statistics: Height and Weight of Children: Socioeconomics Status. Vital and Health Statistics Series 11- No. 119. DHEW Pub. No. (HSM) 73-1601, 1972.
8. Cabak V, Najdanvic R: Effect of undernutrition in early life on physical and mental development. Archives of Disease in Childhood 1965; 40:532-534.
9. Cravioto J, DeLicardie ER, Birch HG: Nutrition, growth and neurointegrative development: An experimental and ecologic study. Pediatrics 1966; 38:319-372.
10. Monckeberg F: Effects of early marasmic malnutrition on subsequent physical and psychological development. IN: Scrimshaw NS and Gordon JE (eds): Malnutrition, Learning and Behavior. Cambridge, MA: MIT Press, 1968, pp 269-278.
11. Stoch MB, Smythe PM: Undernutrition during infancy and subsequent brain growth in intellectual development. IN: Scrimshaw NS and Gordon JE (eds): Malnutrition, Learning and Behavior. Cambridge, MA: MIT Press, 1968, pp 278-289.
12. Hess RD: Social class and ethnic influences on socialization. IN: Musse PH (ed): Carmichael's Manual of Child Psychology, Vol. 2. New York: Wiley, 1970, pp 457-559.
13. Evans DE, Moodie AD, Hansen JDL: Kwashiorkor and intellectual development. S A Med J 1971; 45:1413-1426.
14. Klein RE, Freeman HE, Kagan J, et al: Is big smart? The relation of growth to cognition. J Health and Social Behavior 1972; 13:219-225.
15. Klein RE, Read MS, Riecken HW, et al (eds): Evaluating the Impact of Nutrition and Health Programs. New York, NY: Plenum Press, 1979.
16. Klein RE, Irwin M, Engle PL, Yarbrough C: Malnutrition and mental development in rural Guatemala: An applied cross-cultural research study. IN: Warren N (ed): Advances in Cross-Cultural Psychology. New York: Academic Press, 1977, pp 92-121.
17. Klein RE, Arenales P, Delgado H, et al: Effect of maternal nutrition on fetal growth and infant development. Pan American Health Organization Bulletin 1976; 10:301-306.
18. Irwin M, Engle PL, Yarbrough C, et al: The relationship of prior ability and family characteristics to school attendance and school achievement in rural Guatemala. Child Develop 1978; 49:415-427.
19. Freeman HE, Klein RE, Kagan J, Yarbrough C: Relations between nutrition and cognition in rural Guatemala. Am J Public Health 1977; 67:233-239.
20. Mejia-Pivaral V: Caracteristicas economicas y socioculturales de cuatro aldeas ladinas de Guatemala. Guatemala Indigena, Vol. VII, No. 3, Instituto Indigenista National, Guatemala, 1972.
21. Rossi PH, Freeman HE, Wright SR: Evaluation—A Systematic Approach. Bevery Hills, CA: Sage Publications, Inc., 1979.
22. Monckeberg F, Tisler S, Toro S, et al: Malnutrition and mental development. Amer J Clin Nutr 1972; 25:766-772.
23. Lechtig A, Habicht JP, Delgado H, et al: Effect of food supplementation during pregnancy on birth weight. Pediatrics 1975; 56:508-520.
24. Yarbrough C, Habicht JP, Martorell R, Klein RE: Physical anthropology and mild to moderate malnutrition: A definition of the problem. Wenner-Gren Foundations/Fels Research Institute, NY, 1974.
25. Klein RE, Lester BM, Yarbrough C, Habicht JP: On malnutrition and mental development: Some preliminary findings. IN: Chavez A, Bourges H, Basta S (eds): Nutrition, Vol. 2. Switzerland: S. Karger Basel, 1975, pp 315-321.
26. Klein RE, Freeman HE, Spring B, et al: Cognitive test performance and indigenous conceptions of intelligence. J of Psychology 1976; 93:273-279.

ACKNOWLEDGMENTS

This report, prepared as part of a program of collaborative research on Uniform Measures of Social Competence by H. E. Freeman, J. Kagan, R. E. Klein, and A. K. Romney, was supported by the National Science Foundation (Grant GS-33047).

[*Editor's Note:* The core study from which the data were drawn was supported during the seven-year investigation by grants from the National Institute of Child Health and Human Development, National Institutes of Health.]

23: MALNUTRITION AND CHILD BEHAVIOR: CONCEPTUALIZATION, ASSESSMENT AND AN EMPIRICAL STUDY OF SOCIAL-EMOTIONAL FUNCTIONING

D. E. Barrett

Abstract

Until quite recently, researchers examining the behavioral effects of undernutrition tended to focus on the consequences with respect to cognitive development. There have been very few studies which have examined the effects of malnutrition on children's social and emotional functioning. There is reason to believe that the social and emotional characteristics of the child are significantly affected by a history of undernutrition. Both the literature on the effects of malnutrition in animals and the studies on the behavior of undernourished human infants link malnutrition with important functional alterations, including apathy, poor attention, reduced social responsiveness, and difficulty in regulating state and behavior. Thus, there is a need for studies which examine the effects of malnutrition on child behavior and development in the social and affective domains. In the present chapter the author first selectively reviews research on the behavioral effects of malnutrition in animals and human infants and suggests the types of behavioral functions which may be affected in the young (i.e., preschool or school age) child. Next, he addresses the question of how we should conceptualize and measure social-emotional functioning when examining the effects of malnutrition on behavior. In discussing assessment, characteristics of different methodologies are presented and contrasted. An illustration of an approach to the conceptualization and assessment of social-emotional functioning is provided. Specifically, the author reports the methods and results of a recent study on the effects of prenatal and early postnatal energy supplementation on child behavior at school age, with particular attention to the procedures used for studying children's behavior in naturalistic situations. Finally, the question of behavioral assessment in cross-cultural research is raised, and some of the problems which may occur when one carries out behavioral studies in non-US populations are considered.

Key words: assessment of children's behavior – ecological validity – emotional characteristics – Guatemala – malnutrition – small group observations – social behavior – social interaction

Reprinted from pages 280-306 of *Malnutrition and Behavior: Critical Assessment of Key Issues,* J. Brožek and B. Schürch, eds., Nestlé Foundation Publication Series, vol. 4, Lausanne, Switzerland, 1984, 656p.; *Copyright © 1984 by the Nestlé Foundation.*

1. Introduction

In the period from 1960 to 1975, a large number of studies were carried out which examined the effects of malnutrition on children's behavioral development. Reviews of these studies (cf. POLLITT and THOMSON, 1977) show that almost all were concerned primarily with cognitive development and that the great majority focused on performance on standardized intelligence tests.

In recent years, however, researchers have become more interested in the effects of malnutrition on children's social and emotional development. There are several reasons for this shift in emphasis.

First, cognitive test performance is highly dependent on motivational factors including attention, persistence, and self-confidence (cf. ZIGLER and BUTTERFIELD, 1968). It has become increasingly recognized that it is difficult to interpret data on the effects of malnutrition on cognitive development unless there are data on how malnutrition affects motivational characteristics.

Second, researchers have begun to re-examine their decision to focus on the cognitive sequelae of human malnutrition to the exclusion of the social and emotional aspects in light of the empirical data on the effects of malnutrition on animals (RICCIUTI, 1981; BARRETT, RADKE-YARROW and KLEIN, 1982). The research on malnourished animals identifies an array of behavioral characteristics which are affected by malnutrition. Some of these behavior dimensions (described in greater detail later in the chapter) are activity level, emotional control, attention to novel stimuli, and social responsiveness. The animal research leads us to consider the consequences of malnutrition in human beings with respect to social and emotional functioning.

Third, there is a body of research accumulating which suggests that social and emotional capacities may be more vulnerable to chronic environmental insult than cognitive functions (RUTTER, 1979). Longitudinal studies of children deprived of maternal child-rearing and peer experiences (TIZARD and REES, 1974; TIZARD and HODGES, 1978) show that lasting behavior problems may result from social deprivation, even when cognitive functioning is not impaired. There is interest in exploring the relative vulnerabilities of cognitive and social functions to different types of social environmental deficits (cf. BAKEMAN and BROWN, 1980), one of which is chronic undernutrition. The latter is a particularly interesting type of environmental deprivation, because (a) infant feeding occurs within an interactive context, thus constituting a type of social stimulation in and of itself, and (b) interferences with infant feeding could logically be expected to result in decreased interaction with the physical and social environment, thus resulting in a general reduction of environmental stimulation.

Finally, the issue of the social and emotional consequences of malnutrition has taken on increased importance with the shift on the part of educators and psychologists from cognitive to social competence as the major criterion for evaluating the psychological functioning of children (SCARR, 1982) and, in particular, as the criterion for studying the effectiveness of intervention programs aimed at improving children's ability to profit from school and other learning experiences (ZIGLER and TRICKETT, 1982).

2. Overview of the chapter

In this chapter, four issues bearing on the study of the effects of undernutrition on children's social and emotional functioning will be discussed.

(1)   What are the theoretical and empirical bases for studying the behavioral effects of malnutrition? What is the evidence that malnutrition *per se* may be causally related to social and emotional characteristics?

(2)   How should we (a) conceptualize and (b) assess social and emotional functions when we study the behavioral effects of malnutrition in children? There are many aspects to children's psychological adjustment: interaction with peers, group problem solving, coping with frustration, relations with adults. What should be the constructs of interest? How do we measure these functions in field studies of malnutrition and behavior?

(3)   Is there evidence that the types of social behaviors and emotional characteristics which are suggested, in this paper, as the proper criterion variables for study are in fact related to malnutrition? Will the strategy presented here for studying behavioral effects of malnutrition enable us to identify nutrition-behavior relationships? In this section, findings will be presented which show that the child's early nutritional history may be significantly related to important aspects of the child's social behavior and emotional characteristics at school age.

(4)   How can we determine whether our measurement procedures are valid for different cultures and/or social groups within a culture? An approach to this issue will be suggested in our cross-cultural research.

3. Theoretical and empirical bases for research on social and emotional consequences of malnutrition

There are two lines of research which converge to suggest a number of dimensions of social and emotional functioning which may be influenced by a history of undernutrition. There are, first, the studies on the behavioral characteristics of malnourished animals. Although there are a number of important reasons why we cannot extrapolate hastily from animals to humans (including issues relating to type and severity of the nutritional deprivation, differences between species in rate of central nervous system development, and differences in the social contexts of the nutritional insult), the findings from the animal research link malnutrition to important functional disorders, and these relationships allow us to generate hypotheses about the possible effects on humans. Second, there is recent research on human infants with a history of prenatal undernutrition. This research, which includes both non-experimental, comparative studies of adequately nourished and malnourished infants and experimental studies of the effects of prenatal maternal nutritional supplementation on the behavior of infants otherwise at risk for undernutrition, provides us with further evidence that malnutrition may disrupt the social and emotional development of the child.

3.1. Animal research

While a complete review of the literature on the effects of malnutrition on animal behavior is beyond the scope of this chapter, a brief summary is given. *Table 1* gives a listing of major studies on the behavioral effects of nutritional deprivation in animals, identifying the investigators, animal species that was studied, type of nutritional deprivation, and behavioral outcomes. It is clear from the table that malnutrition in animals is associated with poor attention, lack of social responsiveness, emotionality, avoidance of new stimuli, and poor behavior organization. For example, STROBEL and ZIMMERMAN (1971) found that experimentally malnourished monkeys per-

Table 1: Animal studies on protein-energy deprivation

Investigator	Animal	Behavior Alteration
PLATT and STEWART (1967)	dog[a, b]	Aggressiveness, unpredictable behavior, little play
FRAŇKOVÁ and BARNES (1969)	rat[a, b]	Emotionality, heightened activity
BARNES, MOORE and POND (1970)	pig[a]	Emotionality
STROBEL and ZIMMERMAN (1971)	monkey[b]	Lack of interest in problem-solving
STROBEL and ZIMMERMAN (1972)	monkey[b]	Fear of new stimuli
ZIMMERMAN et al. (1972)	monkey[b]	Low on social approach and responsiveness
FRAŇKOVÁ (1973)	rat[a, b]	Few social contacts, little play, aggressiveness, little exploration
ZIMMERMAN et al. (1974)	monkey[b]	Reduced attention on discrimination task
LEVITSKY and BARNES (1975)	rat[b]	Poor exploration of maze

[a] Pre-weaning deprivation
[b] Post-weaning deprivation

formed less well than controls on a manipulative puzzle after repeated presentations, apparently due to loss of interest in the problem. The same investigators also found (1972) that malnourished monkeys showed avoidance of a novel manipulative task. When familiar materials were used, their performance declined with repeated testing. FRAŇKOVÁ (1973), studying pre- and post-weaning protein-calorie deprivation in rats, found that malnourished rats were more aggressive, engaged in less grooming, were more negative in response to approaches from other animals than control rats, and showed withdrawal and inhibition of exploration. Other studies have documented such characteristics as nonpurposive behavior (FRAŇKOVÁ and BARNES, 1968), excitability under stress (BARNES, MOORE and POND, 1970), and unpredictable aggression (PLATT and STEWART, 1968). In sum, across a variety of species and procedures, there is evidence that severe protein-energy deprivation in animals is related to attentional impairments, poor behavior control, and lack of interest in the social and physical environment. These studies lead us to examine a similar complex of behaviors as they relate to malnutrition in humans.

3.2. Human studies

The human studies which have examined the «non-cognitive» effects of malnutrition on behavior have tended to focus on human infants, rather than children, but the findings are consistent and have clear implications for children's development. The results of the studies are shown in *Table 2* which summarizes findings from both the non-experimental and the experimental (supplementation) studies. As shown in the table, prenatal undernutrition results in attentional impairments, reduced social responsiveness, poor state control, and poor stimulus modulation. Infants with a history of undernutrition have difficulty tolerating frustration, have low activity levels, and lack initiative and independence. Thus we see the same complex of behavioral characteristics associated with undernutrition in human infants that we saw in the animal research: reduced social responsiveness, altered affect, diminished involvement, and difficulty in stimulus regulation.

I will elaborate on these studies, for they provide insight into some of the processes whereby early undernutrition may affect the child's later behavior. The studies by ALS et al. (1976) and BRAZELTON et al. (1977) which were carried out in Boston and Guatemala, respectively, compared low birthweight and presumably prenatally undernourished infants with normal birthweight, well-nourished controls in the first month of life. The investigators found that, on the BRAZELTON neonatal examination, the undernourished infants showed little vigor of movement, moved more slowly into

Table 2: Infant studies on behavioral effects of undernutrition

Investigator	Site	Age at Assessment	Behavior Alteration
LESTER (1975)	Guatemala	one year	Diminished orienting response
ALS et al. (1976)	USA	first 10 days	Poor motoric processes, low social responsiveness
BRAZELTON et al. (1977)	Guatemala	one month	Poor motoric processes, poor at eliciting social responses, lethargic, difficult to arouse
MORA et al. (1978), HERRERA et al. (1980)	Colombia	15 days	Irritability, poor frustration tolerance, slow visual habituation[a]
CHÁVEZ and MARTÍNEZ (1979)	Mexico	one year	Frequent crying, clinging, high dependency
		18 months	Low activity, infrequent playing
RUSH, STEIN and SUSSER (1980)	USA	one year	Short duration of play Slow visual habituation
ZESKIND and RAMEY (1981)	USA	three years	Withdrawn, anxious[a]

[a] These studies also showed significant effects on measured intelligence at age 3.

higher states of arousal, and had difficulty orienting toward visual stimuli. The infants were underdemanding and poor elicitors of maternal response. LESTER (1975) examined the cardiac orienting response, a measure of central nervous system integrity, in one-year-old Guatemalan infants. The index group was 55–75 percent of average weight-for-age, while the control group was of average weight. LESTER administered pure tone stimuli to the infants and used heart deceleration as a measure of the orienting response. While the well-nourished infants showed the expected heart rate deceleration on the first trial after a new tone was presented, the poorly nourished infants did not show any effects over trials: there was a diminished orienting response, no indication of habituation over trials, and no dishabituation following the introduction of a new tone. The results indicated an attentional impairment. Two studies on the effects of prenatal supplementation were carried out in Bogotá, Columbia (MORA et al., 1979; HERRERA et al., 1980) and in Mexico (CHÁVEZ and MARTÍNEZ, 1979). In the Bogotá study, food supplements rich in protein, calcium, vitamins and iron were administered weekly to families at risk for undernutrition. Supplementation began at 6 months of pregnancy and continued through the child's third year. In comparison to supplemented children, non-supplemented infants showed heightened reactivity to aversive stimuli at 15 days of age and apathetic behavior at 4 to 8 months of age. The most recent follow-up studies at 3 years of age show lower scores on a standard measure of personal-social competence, as well as poorer cognitive and linguistic functioning (WABER et al., 1981). CHÁVEZ and MARTÍNEZ administered a protein-energy supplement to women beginning at six weeks of pregnancy and continuing through lactation, and to their children beginning at 3 months of age. By 8 months of age, supplemented children were more active than non-supplemented children. By one year, supplemented children spent less time crying and clinging, and at 18 months were significantly more independent than non-supplemented children: they were carried less, spent more time out of doors, and played more. The investigators found that the supplemented children were more demanding than the non-supplemented children and were more successful at eliciting both maternal and paternal responses, qualities which appear to have resulted in their being fed more often. Two other studies involved nutritional supplementation but differed from the others in that (a) they studied United States populations and (b) they focused upon somewhat different types of research questions. One of these studies was carried out by RUSH, STEIN and SUSSER (1980) in Harlem, New York. The purpose of this study was to examine the effects of provision of a high protein supplement, a low protein supplement, or no supplement at all to undernourished pregnant women with respect to their children's growth and development. The effects of supplementation on growth were complex, depending on whether or not the child was premature, and on the timing of the supplementation as well as on the type of beverage (high vs. low protein). Effects on child behavior were more readily interpretable: high protein-energy supplementation was associated with better performance at one year on measures of attention, persistence and visual habituation. A final study, by ZESKIND and RAMEY (1978; 1981), was concerned with evaluating the effects of a nutritional, medical and educational intervention (beginning in infancy) on the cognitive development of children who were born with a low ponderal index (PI), a measure of weight-for-length which is an indicator of prenatal undernutrition. The most recent report of the study shows that, by 3 years of age, the low PI children who did not receive the intervention showed more anxiety and withdrawn behavior than normal PI children or children receiving the intervention, in addition to performing more poorly on a standardized intelligence test. In summary, the research on human infants provides further support for the hypothesis that malnutrition has important implications for the child's behavioral development, and suggests the need to study in depth the social and emotional consequences in the post-infancy years.

4. Conceptualization of social-emotional functioning

The findings from the animal and infant studies on behavioral effects of malnutrition indicate that malnutrition alters the organism's attentional capacities, affect and emotional control, social responsiveness, and activity level. Consideration of the developmental implications of such impairments enables us to formulate hypotheses about the undernourished child's future course of behavioral development. More specifically, by considering the ways in which undernutrition might affect the child during infancy, and the way such behavioral effects might influence the child's experiences with the caregiving and peer environments, we are able to arrive at a formulation which identifies dimensions of behavioral functioning in childhood which might be affected by malnutrition, and then, begin to operationalize these variables.

Let us consider, then, the behavioral dimensions we have identified: social responsiveness, activity level, affect, and interest in the environment. It seems reasonable to surmise that an infant who shows impairments in any or all of these characteristics becomes a different type of stimulus both to caregivers and peers. We know from the previously cited work that caregivers tend to respond to undernourished children less often and with less enthusiasm than to better nourished children. We would expect that the young child who does not successfully elicit responses from others would learn to withdraw from social interaction situations and would not learn the social skills which are normal in infants who have developed adequate relationships with principal caregivers (cf. BRAZELTON, KOSLOWSKI and MAIN, 1974, for a description of parent-child reciprocal interaction in infancy). Further, we should expect that disruptions of the caregiver-child relationship would influence the child's interactions with peers in the toddler and preschool periods. There is evidence that it is the secure attachment to the mother which provides the emotional base which allows the child to begin to explore and interact with the environment (AINSWORTH, 1979). The child who has not been successful in the earliest social interactions with the caregiver is likely to fail in interpersonal interactions with peers and non-familial adults. The cumulative effect of such interactive failures would, we may assume, be a lowered self-esteem, avoidance of new persons and situations, and general inability to handle routinely stressful social situations, including group problem-solving situations. In addition, we should expect affective withdrawal and lowered physical activity.

Thus, at the childhood stage, we can begin to identify specific dimensions of behavior which could be influenced by the child's nutritional history. One conceptualization, developed from our research on malnutrition (BARRETT, RADKE-YARROW and KLEIN, 1982) considers the child's social-emotional competence in terms of two types of characteristics. First, the child's general social interaction characteristics (i.e., across situations). These include: (1) interaction with peers, (2) behavior towards adults, (3) response to the physical environment, (4) affect, and (5) activity level. Second, the child's characteristic responses to specific types of situations, and, in particular, to routinely stressful or pressured situations. These would include responses to: competition, frustrating problems, physical stress or discomfort, another person in distress, an unfamiliar environment, and demands to control impulses (e.g., situations calling for delay of gratification or resistance to temptation).

This formulation has heuristic value for two reasons. It encompasses almost all of the social behavioral characteristics which have been considered under the rubric «social competence» (see ZIGLER and TRICKETT, 1978). Importantly, each of the categories can be conceptualized in terms of specific aspects of function which we would hypothesize to be related to undernutrition. For example, consider the five broad categories of general social interaction characteristics. For each of these categories, we can think of a number of variables which might be sensitive to differences in nutritional history. For example, for interaction with peers, we would make predictions of less frequent social initiations toward others, less sensitive responding to cues from others, more passive or submissive behavior, and less physically active play in undernourished children. In terms of responses to adults, we would expect children with a history of undernutrition to show more dependent behavior, and, in particular, more attention seeking. With regard to the response to the physical environment, we might expect less adequately nourished children to show less sustained involvement with materials and with group activities, more wandering, greater susceptability to distraction from task-irrelevant events, and less careful handling of materials. For affect, we would predict less outward show of expression (happy, angry, concerned), a generally flat affect, and more frequent emotional outbursts. Finally, we would expect less well-nourished children to have difficulty modulating activity, resulting in generally low activity level with periods of uncontrolled activity.

In the specific situations, all of which involve some type of routine stress or challenge, we would expect the less well-nourished children to show the following characteristics: In group situations involving competition, we would expect lower levels of participation and perhaps a tendency to withdraw. In group problem solving situations (for example, a puzzle or real-life dilemma), we might predict a tendency to give up easily and failure to attempt a variety of strategies. For response to physical stress, we would expect greater emotionality. For response to another person in distress, we would expect a tendency to fail to notice the other's cues (for example, facial expression), more uncertainty when (or if) distress cues are noticed, and less overt helping. For response to an unfamiliar environment, we would expect less curiosity (fewer materials explored and lower levels of involvement), and a tendency to withdraw from the situation. Finally, in impulse control situations, we would expect a general inability to inhibit rapid responses – for example, a difficulty in delaying gratification or resisting an opportunity to obtain an immediate reward in the face of a rule or prohibition.

In summary, a useful approach to the conceptualization of social emotional functioning is to identify general categories of behavior which encompass the most salient features of children's activity and which include dimensions of behavior which are relevant to our hypotheses about the behavioral effects of undernutrition. It is suggested that we consider both situation-general and situation-specific aspects of behavior, and that within each of these general categories, we identify classes of behavior for assessment.

5. Assessment of social-emotional functioning

Having identified the dimensions of child behavior in which we are interested, the next step is to operationalize the behavior variables. If we wish to assess the child's «general» behavioral characteristics (i.e., across situations), the most frequently used approaches are (1) to collect and score «time-samples» of behavior, and (2) to make «global» ratings of behavior. Using the first method, the investigator observes the child's behavior in a variety of situations and, utilizing a systematic coding system, assigns scores to the behaviors of interest in each situation. The scores are aggregated across situations, thus providing a summary score (i.e., for each variable) which describes the child's «central tendency» with respect to the behavior of interest. Using the second method, the coder makes ratings of the child's behavior on the characteristic of interest, but does so on the basis of general knowledge of the child, rather than on the basis of how the child behaved in a specific situation. Ratings are generally made by persons who are familiar with the subjects – for example teachers or parents – although the research investigators may also be in a position to make ratings (for example, in the study which I will describe, the observer made general behavior ratings after all time-sampling assessments were completed). The strengths and weaknesses of the two approaches have been thoughtfully described by CAIRNS and GREEN (1979), who pointed out that the two methods have somewhat different objectives and yield different information. Briefly, the naturalistic observation approach is sensitive to contextual influences on behavior; that is, it will «pick up» behaviors which are both situation-general and situation-specific. Thus, whenever we are attempting to arrive at scores which reflect the child's general behavioral characteristics or traits, this is a useful method only if we can sample widely across situations and periods. Otherwise, the individual measurements will reflect short-term, situational influences (in which we are presumably not interested) and this will limit generalizability. The rating approach is in some ways less precise than the naturalistic assessment approach because it is based on a summary judgment about the child, made «after the fact» – that is, after the child's behavior (in a variety of situations and occasions) has occurred. It is highly influenced by a number of factors that do not influence the time-sampling observation: for example, the rater's personal «concept» of the variable of interest, the rater's selective memory, and the rater's bias with regard to the subject. However, because it is not influenced by situational factors, since it represents a judgment which transcends time and place, the rating constitutes an assessment of the child's enduring (i.e., situation-general) behavior tendencies with respect to the variable of interest. It is for this reason that given carefully trained raters, ratings made of children's behaviors are often more predictive than time-sampling observations of the child. That is, because the rating is made with the understanding that situational or temporal variations in the child's behavior are to be overlooked and scores assigned on the basis of what the rater sees as the child's general response tendencies, there will be a greater likelihood of showing a significant relationship with some other (presumably, also situation-general) personality characteristic.

When we are interested in describing a child's typical response to a particular type of situation, rather than to situations in general, either time-sampling observations or ratings may be used. In either case the observations are made with the understanding that the variable of interest is a specified behavior under specified conditions, and relations are sought between the independent variable(s) of interest and the measure of situational responding.

In our research on malnutrition and behavior, we studied both classes of behavior: situation-general and situation-specific behavior. To assess the situation-general behaviors using a time-sampling procedure, we studied each behavior of interest in a variety of situations and obtained an average frequency count of the behavior per specified time interval (i.e., behavior rate) across situations. Subsequently we asked raters to make «global assessments» across a number of behavior dimensions based on their overall impressions of the children (i.e., after having observed the children in the variety of activities). To obtain scores on the situation-specific variables, we created structured situations for the subjects and observed their responses, making behavior ratings «on the spot». Thus, although in general the assessments took the form of ratings rather than frequency counts, the approach was similar to the time-sampling assessments in that we recorded behaviors at the moment of observation and in the situation of interest.

I will now describe the specifics of the measurement paradigm and coding methods.

5.1. General observation paradigm

Children are observed in social interaction in groups of six. The assessments cover a period of two days. On each day, the children are observed in a number of situations which provide the opportunity to code both their interpersonal behaviors and their non-social behaviors on a time-sampling basis. The activities include clay construction activities, painting a mural, free play in a relatively new environment (after an initial familiarization period), and play with «physical» materials such as balloons, balls, large blocks and wagons. In addition, the children are observed in a number of problem solving situations in which we examine their responses to particular problems (described below under «Specific Situations»). The situations are organized so that together they comprise a coherent sequence of gamelike activities.

5.2. Time-sampling assessments

Across the variety of activities, each child is observed for a series of two-minute periods which are divided into 30 second intervals. Behaviors are coded in 5 classes: Interaction with Peers, Contact with Adults, Behavior in Physical Environment, Level of Activity, and Emotions. The specific categories are shown in *Table 3*. For each behavior category, each child receives a score representing the average number of occurrences of that behavior per two-minute interval. Thus, we obtain, for each child, a set of scores, representing the rate of each of a number of theoretically relevant behaviors across a variety of situations.

5.3. Global ratings

Following the two days of observations, each observer rates each child on a number of behavior dimensions which we have hypothesized to be related to undernutrition. On scales of 1 to 5, subjects are rated for energy level, work orientation, attention (to the group activity), communication skills, disposition, obedience to adult directions, and self-confidence.

5.4. Situation-specific assessments

Data are collected on the child's responses to the following structured situations described in greater detail in the Appendix:

Table 3: Behaviors coded on time-sampling basis in small-group activities

A. *Interaction with Peers*	3. Destructive with materials
1. Friendly interaction	4. Wanders
2. Helps, shares, comforts	5. Physical play alone
3. Physical aggression	6. Imaginative play
4. Verbal aggression	7. Distracted by outside events
5. Rough and tumble play	8. Only watching
6. Intrudes, interferes	9. Inactive
7. Dominates, asserts self	
8. Seeks help	D. *Level of Activity*
9. Submissive	1. Low
10. Defends self	2. Moderate
11. Positive response to bid	3. High
12. Negative response to bid	4. Very high
13. No interaction	
	E. *Emotion*
B. *Contact with Adults*	1. Happy, laughs, smiles
1. Seeks attention	2. Anxious
2. Seeks physical contact	3. Angry, hostile
3. No interaction	4. Sad
	5. Loses control
C. *Behavior in Physical Environment*	6. No emotion shown
1. Involved in group activity	
2. Plays with materials	

1. Novel Environment
    a. Latency to first contact with toys (rating of 1 to 4)
    b. Number of materials touched (number from 0 to 5 or more)
    c. Level of involvement with individual toys (rating of 1 to 3)
2. Competitive Game
    a. Level of task involvement (rating of 1 to 3)
    b. Positive affect (rating of 1 to 4)
    c. Sense of competition (presence or absence)
    d. Fearfulness about popping balloons (rating of 1 to 3)
3. Frustrating Problem
    a. Number of strategies used to solve the problem (number from 0 to 7)
4. Impulse Control Game
    a. Number of errors of commission
    b. Number of anticipatory responses
    c. Number of errors of omission

5.5. Evaluating observer agreement

To obtain information on observer agreement, we instruct each of three observers to watch 3 children per activity. In the time sampling assessments, children are watched one at a time, in sequence, for two-minute periods. Since there are 3 observers and 6 children, we are able to obtain matching observational records and thus determine inter-rater agreement (on a given child's behavior). The data are analyzed for observer agreement using the intraclass correlation (BARTKO, 1966) which indicates what percent of variance in scores for a group of subjects is due to «subject variance» as opposed to «rater variance». For global ratings and for ratings of responses to specific situations we compute coefficient weighted kappa (CO-HEN, 1968) which indicates the degree of agreement between raters, correcting for chance agreement. Weighting is linear; for example, a disagreement of 2 scale points is weighted twice as heavily as a disagreement of 1 point. Intraclass correlations and kappa statistics obtained in our research are reported in the following section of the chapter.

I have presented an approach to the conceptualization and assessment of social and emotional functioning in examining relationships between malnutrition and child behavior. We may now ask if there is empirical evidence that this can be a fruitful approach for studying the effects of malnutrition on children's behavior.

6. Report of an empirical study

The present research was carried out in Guatemala to examine the effects of energy supplementation – prenatal and early postnatal – on the behavior of school age children from a population in which undernutrition was endemic. Our subjects were selected from among former participants of the IN-CAP longitudinal study and were between the ages of 6 years, 1 month and 8 years, 3 months when the present study was carried out. There were 78 boys and 60 girls.

6.1. Design of the study

The design of the INCAP study has been described in detail (KLEIN et al., 1977), as have the characteristics of the study villages (NERLOVE et al., 1974). Nonetheless, a brief description is given here, since the justification for the use of the supplementation paradigm to make inferences about the effects of malnutrition on behavior depends on showing that (a) the study population was deficient in the nutrient used for supplementation and (b) supplementation was administered in such a way that differences in behavior related to differences in supplementation could be interpreted as due to the effects of improved nutrition and not to other related factors.

The study villages are located 30 to 60 kilometers from Guatemala City. They are agricultural. The literacy rate is approximately 50 percent and the mean *per capita* income $ 500 per year. On the basis of both anthropometric and dietary criteria, the study population was chronically malnourished. At the beginning of the INCAP study in 1968, 80 to 85% of preschool children were classified as at least mildly to moderately undernourished according to the GÓMEZ classification (1956) based on weight-for-age. Mean daily diet calories were below requirements at all age levels, with pregnant women receiving about one half the recommended allowances and preschool children ¾ of recommended allowances. Protein intakes were also below recommended levels for women (mean intake was approximately 40 g per day) but were at or above safe levels for children. Thus, the population may be considered energy deficient.

In the original INCAP study, the investigators wished to determine the effectiveness of a protein-energy supplement in improving the physical growth and cognitive development of chronically malnourished children. Four study villages were selected, matched on a number of number of social-environmental and epidemiological variables (KLEIN, 1979). Two villages received a protein-energy supplement, the others an energy-only supplement. The protein-energy supplement (Atole) consisted of a vegetable protein mixture, dry skim milk, and sugar, while the energy-only supplement (Fresco) contained only sugar and flavoring. One cup (180 ml) of protein-energy supplement contained 11.5 grams of protein and 163 calories. One cup of energy-only supplement contained 59 calories. Both supplements contained essential vitamins and minerals.

Supplements in the form of a drink, were made available at central food stations in the villages that were being studied. Attendance was voluntary. Daily supplement intake was recorded for all women during pregnancy and for all children under seven years.

6.2. Independent variables

From the INCAP data, we constructed three supplementation variables; these were the total supplement energy intake of the mother during pregnancy, total supplement energy intake of the child from birth to two years, and total supplement energy intake of the child from age two to four years. Children were placed into the Low Supplement (LS) Category if the supplemental calorie intake during any of the three periods was equal to or greater than one standard deviation below the mean for that period. All other children were placed into the High Supplement (HS) Category. There were 69 subjects in each category.

6.3. Dependent variables (behavior measures)

Assessments were made of children's social and emotional functioning, based on observations of groups of six children each. All observations took place at a central location in the village and were made on two consecutive mornings. There were three observers/testers, all Guatemalan women who had participated in the longitudinal study as test administrators. Three types of behavioral data were collected: (1) Time-sampling assessments of children's interactions with peers and the environment; (2) ratings of children's responses to specific structured situations, including an unfamiliar environment, a competitive game, a frustrating problem, and an impulse control game; (3) global ratings of personality. After all observations were made, observers rated the children on a number of dimensions of personality and behavior.

Measures of inter-observer reliability and level of agreement were computed. For time-sampling assessments, median intraclass correlations for each of the five major categories were .81 for interaction with peers, .59 for behavior with adults, .84 for interaction with the environment, .71 for activity level, and .66 for emotion. Median values of weighted kappa were .40 for the global ratings and .84 for responses to specific situations. The data on social-emotional functioning of the children were analyzed using a 2 × 2 analysis of variance, with supplementation (High, Low) and sex (Boy, Girl) as factors. Earlier we reported (Barrett, Radke-Yarrow and Klein, 1982) the results of a multiple regression analysis which yielded results similar to those reported here.

6.4. Results

Results of the analysis of variance for all social-emotional measures are summarized in *Tables 4, 5* and *6*.

6.4.1. Supplementation effects

Main effects for supplementation occurred for several of the behaviors measured on the Interaction Record. HS children had higher rates of behavior than LS children on Involved in Group Activity ($F_{1,134} = 4.53$, p < .001), Moderate Activity Level ($F_{1,134} = 5.59$, p < .04), Very High Activity Level ($F_{1,134} = 5.59$, p < .02) and Happy Affect ($F_{1,134} = 10.86$, p < .001). HS children had lower rates of behavior on Anxious ($F_{1,134} = 7.90$, p < .01), Distracted ($F_{1,134} = 3.02$, p < .09) and Wanders ($F_{1,134} = 3.77$, p < .06). On global ratings, HS children had higher Energy Level ($F_{1,128} = 7.48$, p < .01) and more Self-Confidence ($F_{1,128} = 3.40$, p < .07). They had higher rat-

Table 4: Mean scores (frequency per 2-minute interval) and results of analysis of variance for effects of supplementation, sex, and supplementation x sex interaction on children's behavior: Time-sampling assessments

Variable	Means for Boys		Means for Girls		Significant Effects
	Low Supp.	High Supp.	Low Supp.	High Supp.	
Verbal Aggression	.000	.007	.007	.001	Int.**
Rough and Tumble Play	.016	.122	.073	.054	Int.*
Seeks Help from Peer	.184	.207	.108	.148	Sex**
Negative to Bid from Peer	.022	.020	.206	.163	Sex**
Involved in Group Activity	1.62	2.24	1.48	2.05	Supp.***
Talks to Adult	.037	.059	.107	.053	Sex*, Int.*
Wanders	.013	.005	.048	.013	Supp.*, Sex*
Distracted	.119	.121	.232	.106	Supp.*, Int.*
Moderate Activity Level	2.34	2.57	2.17	2.63	Supp.**
Very High Activity Level	.032	.147	.051	.051	Supp.**, Sex**, Int.**
Happy	0.93	1.50	0.89	1.17	Supp.***
Anxious	.298	.054	.323	.067	Supp.***

Note: Supplementation effects are indicated by Supp., Interaction effects by Int., Sex effects by Sex. Significance levels are based on F tests with 1,134 d.f., except for the variable Verbal Aggression, for which d.f. are 1,110.
* $p < .10$ ** $p < .05$ *** $p < .01$

Table 5: Mean ratings on a five point scale (1–5) and results of analysis of variance for effects of supplementation, sex, and supplementation x sex interaction on children's behavior: Global ratings

Variable	Means for Boys		Means for Girls		Significant Effects
	Low Supp.	High Supp.	Low Supp.	High Supp.	
Energy Level	2.71	3.41	2.82	2.96	Supp.***, Int.*
Anger.......................	1.12	1.34	1.07	1.19	Supp.*
Good Disposition	2.82	3.41	3.03	2.94	Int.**
Non-Compliance	1.10	1.63	1.10	1.32	Supp.**
Self-Confidence	2.79	3.24	3.00	3.17	Supp.*

Note. Supplementation effects are indicated by Supp., Interaction Effects by Int., Sex effects by Sex. Significance levels are based on F tests with 1,128 d.f.
* $p < .10$ ** $p < .05$ *** $p < .01$

Table 6: Mean scores and results of analysis of variance for effects of supplementation, sex, and supplementation x sex interaction on children's behavior: Structured situations

Variable	Means for Boys		Means for Girls		Significant Effects
	Low Supp.	High Supp.	Low Supp.	High Supp.	
Novel Environment					
No. of Materials Touched[a] ..	1.45	1.82	1.40	1.57	Supp.**
Level of Exploration[b]	1.83	2.29	1.53	1.75	Supp.**, Sex***
Competitive Game					
Level of Involvement[b, c]	1.78	1.14	1.59	1.28	Supp.***
Frustrating Task					
No. of Strategies Used[a]	1.97	2.56	2.15	2.64	Supp.***
Impulse Control Game					
Anticipates Responses[a]	.038	400	.000	.000	Supp.**, Sex***, Int.**
Error of Commission[a]	.730	.900	.434	.400	Sex**
Error of Omission[a]	1.23	0.32	1.00	0.60	Supp.*

Note. Supplementation effects are indicated by Supp., Interaction effects by Int., Sex effects by Sex. Significance levels are based on F tests with 1,134 d.f. (for Novel Environment, Competitive Game, and Frustrating Task) or 1,113 d.f. (Impulse Control Game).

[a]Scores represent raw frequencies   * $p < .10$
[b]Scores are based on a rating scale   ** $p < .05$
[c]Low score indicates high involvement   *** $p < .01$

ings on Anger ($F_{1,128} = 3.61$, $p < .06$) and were lower in Compliance ($F_{1,128} = 4.03$, $p < .04$).

With respect to responses to specific situations, HS children had higher scores than LS children on Number of Materials Touched ($F_{1,134} = 6.28$, $p < .02$) and Level of Involvement with Toys ($F_{1,134} = 4.72$, $p < .04$) in the Novel Environment; scored higher on Level of Task Involvement in the Competitive Game ($F_{1,134} = 13.89$, $p < .001$) and used a larger number of strategies ($F_{1,138} = 7.52$, $p < .01$) on the Frustrating Problem. In the Impulse Control Game, they made more Anticipatory Responses ($F_{1,110} = 4.76$, $p < .04$) and made fewer Errors of Omission ($F_{1,110} = 2.88$, $p < .10$).

6.4.2. Sex effects

For the Interaction Record Measures, boys had higher rates of behavior than girls on Seeks Help from Peer ($F_{1,134} = 5.06$, $p < .03$), and Very High Activity Level ($F_{1,134} = 4.55$, $p < .04$). Girls scored higher on Negative to Bid from Peer ($F_{1,134} = 6.39$, $p < .02$), Talks to Adult ($F_{1,134} = 3.12$, $p < .08$) and Wanders ($F_{1,134} = 3.41$, $p < .07$). There were no sex differences on the global ratings. On responses to structured situations, boys scored higher than girls on Level of Involvement with Toys in the Novel Environment ($F_{1,134} = 7.51$, p < 0.1) and made more Errors of Commission and more Anticipatory Responses ($F_{1,110} = 6,21$, p < .02 and $F_{1,110} = 7.00$, p < .01, respectively) on the Impulse Control Game.

6.4.3. Supplement x sex interactions

Of the variables assessed using the Interaction Record, interaction effects were identified for Verbal Aggression ($F_{1,110} = 6.00$, p < .02), Rough and Tumble Play ($F_{1,134} = 3.68$, p < .06), Talks to Adult ($F_{1,134} = 3.25$, p < .08), Distracted ($F_{1,110} = 3.30$, p < .09) and Very High Activity Level ($F_{1,134} = 6.21$, p < .02). Examination of the means shown in *Table 4* indicates: a) Supplementation level was positively related to Verbal Aggression and to Rough and Tumble Play for boys, but negatively related for girls; b) Supplementation was positively related to Very High Activity Level for boys, while there was no relation for girls; c) Supplementation was unrelated to Distracted for boys but negatively related for girls; and d) Supplementation was positively related to Talks to Adult for boys and negatively related for girls. On global ratings, there were two interaction effects. High supplementation was related to high energy level and positive disposition for boys only ($F_{1,128} = 3.32$, p < .08 and $F_{1,128} = 4.98$, p < .03, respectively).

There was one interaction effect with respect to structured situations. On the Impulse Control Game, the supplementation effect for Anticipates Response was specific to boys ($F_{1,110} = 4,76$, p < .04).

6.4.4. Summary of results

As we had hypothesized, the child's nutritional history was significantly related to a number of important dimensions of the child's social and emotional functioning at school age and, specifically, to interest and involvement in the peer group's activity, activity level, and affective characteristics. Children who had received a higher level of supplementation were more involved with peers, showed more positive affect, were less often anxious, and were more frequently characterized by a moderate activity level than were the less well-supplemented children. In addition, they showed the predicted superiority to poorly supplemented children in responses to moderately stressful situations. They showed more exploration of a novel environment, more persistence on a frustrating task, more involvement in a competitive game, and greater alertness and better motor control on an impulse control game. In addition, a clear pattern emerged of supplementation-behavior relationships which were significant only for boys. Supplementation increased physical, aggressive and high-activity behaviors for boys, while there were negligible or negative effects of supplementation on these behaviors for girls. These differential outcomes are portrayed in *Figures 1* and *2,* which illustrate the major supplementation effects (i.e., across sexes) and supplementation x sex interactions, respectively, with respect to children's social interaction and emotional characteristics.[1] In addition, sex differences in social-emotional behavior, and supplementation x sex interactions with respect to other classes of behavior variables were identified.

We hypothesize that (a) the general effect of supplementation on later behavior is to increase the child's ability to seek out stimulation and respond to environmental stimuli, but that (b) the specific behavior patterns that emerge will depend to some extent on the child's social and cultural milieu, including the physical environment, available role models, and behavior norms and expectation. The present findings support this hypothesis, since they show that boys and girls, who are socialized differently and for whom there are markedly different behavior norms and expectations, are differentially affected by early nutritional supplementation. As one might predict, the «masculine-type» behaviors – physical, aggressive, assertive – appear to be enhanced by supplementation for boys. The data suggest that improved supplementation among girls may increase their ability to control their behaviors, so that that «inappropriate» behaviors (i.e., aggression) are inhibited.

The results demonstrate the utility of the approach described here for studying children's social and emotional competence in studies which examine the sequelae of early malnutrition. Considered in conjunction with other developmental outcomes, measures of social behavior and affective characteristics help to provide a more complete picture of the child's capacity to learn from and enjoy social experiences.

7. Cultural appropriateness of assessment procedures

The issues of reliability and construct validity of assessments will be considered briefly. Measurement procedures must be sufficiently appropriate to the study population so that we can hope to obtain a range of codable, interpretable and reliable responses. The interested reader is referred to JOHNSON and BOLSTAD (1973) and MITCHELL (1978) for in-depth treatments of the more general issue of reliability in field research. A description

---

1 The interaction for Angry Affect, although not statistically significant, is illustrated in *Figure 2* because of its theoretical relevance to the other interaction effects which are shown. It should be noted that multiple regression analyses (BARRETT, YARROW and KLEIN, 1982, p. 551) showed a significant relationship between child calorie supplementation from birth to 2 years and Angry Affect ($F_{1,67} = 8.22$); $p < .01$) for boys, and no relationship for girls.

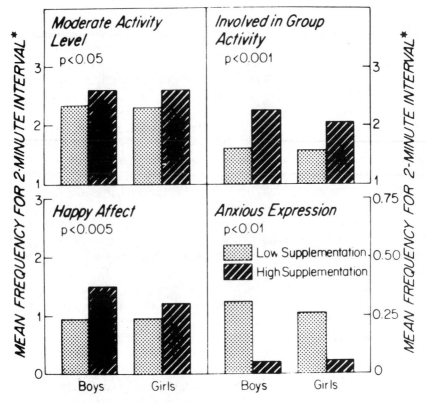

*Each 2-minute interval was divided into
4 30-second intervals. Minimum
Score = 0. Maximum Score = 4.

Figure 1: Variables for which Effects of Supplementation are Consistent Across Sexes

of an empirical, factor analytical approach to construct validation in cross-cultural research was given by BRISLIN, LONNER and THORNDIKE (1973). In the context of nutrition research the problem was examined by LEIBEL et al. (1982). BARRETT (1982) has indicated some of the pitfalls of a strictly empirical approach to cross-cultural validation and suggested alternative, theoretical approaches.

Let us return to the issue of cultural appropriateness of the behavioral assessment procedures. When procedures are developed in one population and then applied to another, the researchers may find that the procedures do not work as expected, and that changes in procedures are necessary if they are to elicit the types of responses they were designed to assess. To illustrate this, I will give examples of two play situations which we developed

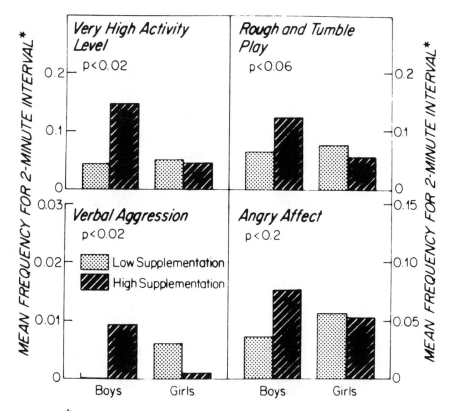

Figure 2: Variables for which Effects of Supplementation Differ for Boys and Girls

in the US with non-Hispanic populations as a means of eliciting child activity but which we had to modify to make them appropriate for rural Guatemalan children.

(1) We wished to see whether differences among children in their capacities to become positively involved in a playful group activity could be related to nutritional history. We structured a relay race game in which children, playing in three-person teams, had to run to the end of a room, pop a balloon, and return to their line to touch their team-mate, who would then take his or her turn. The game was to end when all balloons were popped. When we first devised the task, we told the children they could not pop the balloons with their hands, but had to use some other part of their body. We did this to make the game more novel and exciting and to increase

the range of individual responses to the task. When we were pretesting these procedures in Guatemala with preschool children, we found that, unlike the US children, the children were extremely timid about popping the balloons. So afraid were they of the sound of the «pop» and getting close to the balloons that they invariably stomped on the balloons with their feet, shying away as they did so. As a result, the balloons flew all about, there was general chaos, and the game could not proceed. We decided, therefore, to tell the children that they *had* to pop the balloons with their hands. In this way, there would still be tension and excitement in the game, but the goal of the game could be achieved and our assessments could progress. This modification was successful, and, indeed, there were significant nutrition effects with respect to our measures of performance on this task. (These are described in the previous section.)

(2) A second area of study was impulse control. We designed a task to study children's alertness, and their ability to inhibit motor responses. At first we used the usual instructions given in «Simon Says» types of games. All behaviors were modelled and the children were directed to imitate the model's movement if the model said: «Simon says do this!», and not to imitate if the model said only: «Do this!». When we tried the game in Guatemala, a very interesting thing happened. *All* children imitated *all* modelled actions, regardless of the verbal directions. In short, there was no variability of response. In thinking about this problems, we considered two facts. First, that the culture we were studying is very traditional and authoritarian, more so than the urban, US populations we had studied. Second, and related to the first point, children at this age level were trained in their school rooms to imitate adults' actions. Much of the classroom activity involved repeating of adult actions and words (singing, marching, reciting the alphabet), and the children were probably not used to situations in which an adult demonstrated a behavior and they were expected *not* to perform it. So again we changed the situation. Instead of providing visual cues for the children, we asked them only to respond differentially to verbal cues, which, we reasoned, would exert less «pull» on the subjects. The new directions were: If the model said «one-two-three-yes», the child was to clap. If the model said «one-two-three-no», the child was to refrain from clapping. This task worked beautifully. There were wide individual differences, and, as described earlier, we found that there were significant relationships between speed and accuracy of responding and nutritional history.

These illustrations should convey the importance of familiarity, on the part of the investigator, with the study population. In conducting cross-cultural research, the investigators must be sufficiently flexible so that procedures which may have been originally developed for one population can be modified so that they are appropriate to the population now under study. Only in this way will the assessment procedures be effective.

8. Conclusions

There are many aspects of child behavior which are likely to be affected by a history of undernutrition. After many years of research on the effects of malnutrition on cognitive development, researchers have begun to shift their attention to the social and emotional sequelae of malnutrition.

There are four reasons for the increased research interest in examining the social and emotional consequences of undernutrition: (1) Recognition of the need to study the processes which may mediate relationships between malnutrition and mental development; (2) recognition, from animal research, of the probable links between malnutrition and behavioral function; (3) interest in the issue of social and emotional functions as particularly vulnerable to a range of social-environmental deprivations, including malnutrition; (4) a general shift in focus from cognitive to social competencies as criteria for evaluating the effectiveness of intervention programs designed to improve children's mental health and psychological well-being.

In this chapter the author has provided a conceptual framework for investigating the effects of malnutrition on child behavior, suggested procedural approaches to the assessment of children's social and emotional functioning, and presented a summary of his recent findings on the effects of chronic malnutrition on child behavior in the early school years. The need for thoughtful consideration of the appropriateness of the assessment procedures for the particular population under study has been emphasized.

Appendix

Brief Description of Structured Situations

1. Novel Environment
   Objective: To examine the quality of the child's response to a new situation, including the child's involvement with materials and responses to persons.
   Procedure: Novel play materials (Surprise Box, pinball machine, colored balls, tunnel, stacking toys) are located in accessible places for the children's use. The experimenter tells the children that they will be playing games but that before beginning, they may do whatever they wish in the playroom.

2. Competitive Game
   Objective: To examine the child's capacity for becoming positively emotionally involved in play; to examine the child's response to a competitive situation.

Procedure: Children are given instructions for a «3 against 3» relay race. In the race they must run to a balloon, pop the balloon – using their hands – and run back to their line to touch the hand of their team-mate.

3. Frustrating Problem

   Objective: To study the child's approach to and persistence in a situation that presents a challenge or problem.

   Procedure: Children are each given a plastic container, containing a small «prize». The container is sealed so that it is very difficult to open; however, it gives the appearance of being fairly easy to open. Children are told that if they can open the container they can have the prize. (At the end of the activity, the containers are pried open and children are given the prize).

4. Impulse Control Game

   Objective: To examine the child's ability to attend to directions and control motor responses, and, specifically, to initiate or inhibit motor responses depending on a verbal signal.

   Procedure: Children are asked to stand in a line, approximately two arms lengths apart. The experimenter, facing the children, tells them that when s/he says «One-two-three-yes» they are to clap, but when s/he says «One-two-three-no», they are not to clap. There are 10 clap commands and 5 no-clap commands, all interspersed. The game is played three times.

Acknowledgement

The original research reported in this chapter was carried out when the author was a Research Psychologist at the Laboratory of Developmental Psychology, National Institute of Mental Health.

References

Ainsworth, M.D.S.: Infant-mother attachment. Am. Psychol., *34*, 932–937 (1979).

Als, H.; Tronick, E.; Adamson, L.; Brazelton, T.B.: The behaviour of full-term but underweight newborn infant. Dev. Med. Child Neurol., *18*, 590–602 (1976).

Bakeman, R.; Brown, J.V.: Early interaction: consequences for social and mental development at three years. Child Dev., *51*, 437–447 (1980).

Barnes, R.H.; Moore, A.U.; Pond, W.G.: Behavioral abnormalities in young adult pigs caused by malnutrition in early life. J. Nutr., *100*, 149–155 (1970).

Barrett, D.E.: An approach to the conceptualization and assessment of social-emotional functioning in studying nutrition-behavior relationships. Am. J. Clin. Nutr., *35*, 1222–1227 (1982).

BARRETT, D.E.; RADKE-YARROW, M.; KLEIN, R.E.: Chronic malnutrition and child behavior: effects of early caloric supplementation on social-emotional functioning at school age. Dev. Psychol., *18*, 541–556 (1982).

BARTKO, J.J.: The intraclass correlation as a measure of reliability. Psychol. Rep., *19*, 3–11 (1966).

BRAZELTON, T.B.; KOWLOWSKI, B.; MAIN, M.: The origins of reciprocity: the early mother-infant interaction. In: The Effect of the Infant on Its Caregiver, M. LEWIS, L.A. ROSENBLUM (Eds.). Wiley, New York, NY, 1974.

BRAZELTON, T.B.; TRONICK, E.; LECHTIG, A.; LASKY, R.E.; KLEIN, R.E.: The behavior of nutritionally deprived Guatemalan infants. Dev. Med. Child Neurol., *19*, 364–372 (1977).

BRESLIN, R.W.; LONNER, W.J.; THORNDIKE, R.M.: Cross-cultural Research Methods. Wiley, New York, NY, 1973.

CAIRNS, R.B.; GREEN, J.: How to assess personality and social patterns: observations or ratings? In: The Analysis of Social Interactions, R.B. CAIRNS (Ed.). Lawrence Erlbaum, Hillsdale, NJ, 1979.

CHÁVEZ, A.; MARTÍNEZ, C.: Consequences of insufficient nutrition on child character and behavior. In: Malnutrition, Environment, and Behavior. Cornell University Press, Ithaca, NY, 1979.

COHEN, J.: Weighted kappa: nominal scale agreement with provision for scaled disagreement or partial credit. Psychol. Bull., *70*, 213–220 (1968).

FRAŇKOVÁ, S.: Effect of protein-calories malnutrition on the development of social behavior in rats. Dev. Psychobiol., *6*, 33–43 (1973).

FRAŇKOVÁ, S.; BARNES, R.H.: Effect of malnutrition in early life on avoidance conditioning and behavior of adult rats. J. Nutr., *96*, 485–493 (1968).

GÓMEZ, F.; RAMOS-GALVÁN, R.; FRENK, S.; CRAVIOTO, J.; CHÁVEZ, R.; VASQUEZ, J.: Mortality in second and third degree malnutrition. J. Trop. Pediatr., *2*, 77–83 (1956).

HERRERA, M.G.; MORA, J.O.; CHRISTIANSEN, N.; ORTIZ, N.; CLEMENT, J.; VUORI, L.; WABER, D.; DE PAREDES, B.; WAGNER, M.: Effects of nutritional supplementation and early education on physical and cognitive development. In: Life-span Developmental Psychology, R.R. TURNER, F. REESE (Eds.). Academic Press, New York, NY, 1980.

JOHNSON, S.M.; BOLSTAD, O.D.: Methodological issues in naturalistic observation: some problems and solutions for field research. In: Behavior Change: Methodology, Concepts, and Practice, M.A. HAMERLYNK, L.C. HANDY, E.J. MASH (Eds.). Research Press, Champaign, IL, 1973.

KLEIN, R.E.: Malnutrition and human behavior: a backward glance at an ongoing longitudinal study. In: Malnutrition, Environment and Behavior, D.A. LEVITSKY (Ed.). Cornell University Press, Ithaca, NY, 1979.

KLEIN, R.E.; IRWIN, M.; ENGLE, P.L.; YARBROUGH, C.: Malnutrition and mental development in rural Guatemala. In: Studies in Cross-cultural Psychology, N. WARREN (Ed.). Academic Press, New York, NY, 1977.

LEIBEL, R.L.; POLLITT, E.; KIM, I.; VITERI, F.: Studies regarding the impact of micronutrient status on behavior in man: iron deficiency as a model. Am. J. Clin. Nutr., *35*, 1211–1221 (1982).

LESTER, B.M.: Cardiac habituation of the orienting response in infants of varying nutritional status. Dev. Psychol., *11*, 432–442 (1975).

LEVITSKY, D.A.; BARNES, R.H.: Malnutrition and the biology of experience. In: Proceedings of the IXth International Congress on Nutrition, A. CHÁVEZ, H. BOURGES, S.S. BASTA (Eds.). S. Karger, Basel, Switzerland, 1975.

MITCHELL, S.K.: Interobserver agreement, reliability, and generalizability of data collected in observational studies. Psychol. Bull., *86*, 376–390 (1979).

MORA, J.O.; CLEMENT, J.; CHRISTIANSEN, N.; ORTIZ, N.; VUORI, L.; WAGNER, M.: Nutritional supplementation, early stimulation, and child development. In: Behavioral Effects of Energy and Protein Deficits, J. BROŽEK (Ed.), pp. 255–269. DHEW, NIH Publ. No. 79–1906, Washington, D.C., 1979.

NERLOVE, S.B.; ROBERTS, J.M.; KLEIN, R.E.; YARBROUGH, C.; HABICHT, J.P.: Naturals indicators of cognitive development: an observational study of rural Guatemalan children. Ethos, *2*, 265–295 (1974).

PLATT, B.S.; STEWART, R.J.C.: Effects of protein-calorie deficiency on dogs. Reproduction, growth and behavior. Dev. Med. Child Neurol., 10, 3–24 (1968).

POLLITT, E.; THOMSON, C.: Protein-calorie malnutrition and behavior: a view from psychology. In: Nutrition and the Brain, R.J. WURTMAN, J.J. WURTMAN (Eds.), Vol. 2. Basic Books, New York, NY, 1977.

RICCIUTI, H.N.: Developmental consequences of malnutrition in early childhood. In: The Uncommun Child, M. LEWIS, L. ROSENBLUM (Eds.). Plenum Press, New York, NY, 1981.

RUSH, D.; STEIN, Z.; SUSSER, M.: A randomized controlled trial of prenatal nutritional supplementation in New York City. Pediatrics, 65, 683–697 (1980).

RUTTER, M.: Maternal deprivation, 1972–1978. New findings, new concepts, new approaches. Child Dev., 50, 283–305 (1979).

SCARR, S.: Testing for children: assessment and the many determinants of intellectual competence. Am. Psychol., 36, 1159–1166 (1981).

STROBEL, D.A.; ZIMMERMAN, R.R.: Manipulatory responsiveness in protein-malnourished monkeys. Psyconomic Sci., 24, 19–20 (1971).

STROBEL, D.A.; ZIMMERMAN, R.R.: Responsiveness of protein deficient monkeys to manipulative stimuli. Dev. Psychobiol., 5, 291–296 (1972).

TIZARD, B.; HODGES, J.: The effect of early institutional rearing on the cognitive development of eight-year-old children. J. Child Psychol. Psychiatry, 19, 99–118 (1978).

TIZARD, B.; REES, J.: A comparison of the effects of adoption, restoration to the natural mother, and continued institutionalization on the cognitive development of four-year-old children. Child Dev., 45, 92–99 (1974).

WABER, D.P.; VUORI-CHRISTIANSEN, L.V.; ORTIZ, N.; CLEMENT, J.R.; CHRISTIANSEN, N.E.; MORA, J.O.; REED, R.B.; HERRERA, M.G.: Nutritional supplementation, maternal education, and cognitive development of infants at risk of malnutrition. Am. J. Clin. Nutr., 34, 807–813 (1981).

ZESKIND, P.S.; RAMEY, C.T.: Fetal malnutrition: an experimental study of its consequences on infant development in two caregiving environments. Child Dev., 49, 1155–1162 (1978).

ZESKIND, P.S.; RAMEY, C.T.: Preventing intellectual and interactional sequelae of fetal malnutrition: a longitudinal, transactional, and synergistic approach to development. Child Dev., 52, 213–218 (1981).

ZIGLER, E.; BUTTERFIELD, E.C.: Motivational aspects of changes in IQ performance of culturally deprived nursery school children. Child Dev., 39, 1–4 (1968).

ZIGLER, E.; TRICKETT, P.K.: IQ, social competence, and evaluation of early intervention programs. Am. Psychol., 33, 789–798 (1978).

ZIMMERMAN, R.R.; GEIST, C.R.; STROBEL, D.A.; CLEVELAND, T.J.: Attention deficiencies in malnourished monkeys. In: Early Malnutrition and Mental Development, J. CRAVIOTO, L. HAMBRAEUS, B. VAHLQUIST (Eds.). Almquist and Wiksell, Uppsala, Sweden, 1974.

ZIMMERMAN, R.R.; STEERE, P.O.; STROBEL, D.A.; HAM, H.L.: Abnormal social development of protein-malnourished rhesus monkeys. J. Abnorm. Psychol., 80, 125–131 (1972).

24: SCHOOL PERFORMANCE OF SUPPLEMENTED AND UNSUPPLEMENTED CHILDREN FROM A POOR RURAL AREA

A. Chávez and C. Martínez

Most of the literature on nutrition considers, as a demonstrated fact, that malnutrition renders learning difficult and, therefore, limits children's achievement in school. Nevertheless, in spite of these opinions and in spite of so much money being spent on school lunch programs, there is no definitive proof that better nutrition directly helps the child in the learning process. This is due to the fact that nutrition forms a part of a complex situation which may be defined as "social deprivation". This means that children in a poor medium lack food and suffer malnutrition; at the same time, though, they are deficient in health, stimuli, ambition, motivation as well as in other collateral abilities. This has made it difficult to design a research project that can isolate the factor of malnutrition and, consequently, show that this is the principal causal factor(1).

It is known that a more intense and, especially, an earlier presence of malnutrition affects brain function to a greater degree(5). From this fact it may be concluded that insufficient nutrition can affect school achievement in two ways: on a long term basis as a consequence of early malnutrition and on a short term basis as a consequence of deficiencies at the moment of learning. This study was designed to measure the impact of food supplementation during life time to a group of children from a poor town in which malnutrition is prevalent.

Reprinted from pages 393-402 of *Nutrition in Health and Disease and International Development: Symposia from the XII International Congress of Nutrition,* Alan R. Liss, Inc., New York, 1981; *Copyright © 1981 by Alan R. Liss, Inc.*

MATERIAL AND METHODS

The material of this study is made up of two similar groups of seventeen children each, that were followed longitudinally from the time of their birth up to the present time. One was observed without any kind of intervention and the other was supplemented with good food since early pregnancy, the experimental design has been presented in previous publications(2).

The first group has been called non-supplemented or malnourished and the second group supplemented or wellnourished. The main difference between them has been the single variable introduced:a better diet(4).

Several methods were used in evaluating the school achievement of both groups:

1. The grades given by the teachers themselves on final examinations.

2. The grades given by a teacher who was member of the program staff but who knew nothing of the experimental design.The following tests were considered:

a) national examinations(official examinations for all schools in the country)

b) international tests from a developed country(the Detroit-Engel test),given at the beginning and at the end of the course

c) grades on international tests of a developing country(the ABC test of Lorenco Filho)

3. Reading and writing tests,applied by a neurologist who was a specialist in language.

4. Observation of the behavior of the child in the school.This was done through the method of time sampling,with an observation every 20 seconds for consecutive periods of 90 minutes A kind of periscope was designed for this purpose so that the

child would not know that he was being observed.
Each child was observed during the first hour and
a half in the morning(early) and during the last
hour and a half before leaving school(late),on two
consecutive days,and three times during the school
year(at the beginning,at the middle,and at the end
of the course). Therefore,in spite of the fact that
the number of cases in this study is small,the number of observations is large: 3,240 per case and
55,080 per comparative group.

Since this phase of the study was planned it
was supposed that little child activity would be
found,based on previous knowledge of the community
problems and on measurements made during the standar
dization of the procedure.The final results,however,
far surpassed predictions;deficiencies among the tea
chers as well as among the students are much greater
than expected.This seems to be characteristic of the
rural schools.The fact that all children are wasting
time and not participating, seems to be of no import
ance to the teachers.

RESULTS

Table 1 shows the results of the different
school tests that were applied during the first year,
differences between both groups are clearly shown.

TABLE I
PERFORMANCE ON THE DIFFERENT TESTS

TYPE OF TEST	WHEN GIVEN IN COURSE	NON-SUPPL	SUPPL.
School exam*	End	6.5±1.9	8.1±0.5
National exam*	End	6.3±1.2	8.6±0.9
Detroit-Engel*	End	6.2±1.0	7.9±0.7
Detroit-Engel**	Start	12.8±3.4	25.2±3.2
ABC-Filho**	Middle	8.8±1.4	13.3±0.9
Detroit-Engel**	End	19.4±2.5	36.1±3.1

  * Exams in scale 0 to 10.
 ** Scores(total number of correct answers).
    All differences between supplemented and non-
    supplemented are significant. The exams at
    level of 0.01 and scores at level of 0.001.

Among the poorly nourished children, 35.3%
(6 out of 17) failed on the end-of-course exams
while among the better nourished none went as low
as even a marginal grade.The poorly nourished group
in average was barely above six while the better
nourished achievemed eight or higher.The differences
between both groups are very significant in spite of
the small number in each sampling.

The test that are shown as number of correct
answers(there was no experience in grading)showed
much more significant differences between the two
groups.The supplemented children gave almost twice
as many answers as did the non-supplemented children.
The tests that were given during the first week of
classes showed even greater differences.The poorly
nourished had difficulty in answering only one fourth
of the questions and the supplemented answered twice
as many items(that is,half of them).None of them had
had any formal prior education.

The possibility of comparing the two groups was
lost during the second school year since more than
one third of the poorly nourished failed and so had
to repeat the first year.There was a clear differen
ce between the tests administered by the program per
sonnel and those administered by the regular teacher.
For instance,in accordance with the national exams
administered by the program personnel,both groups
would have done much worse.In average the poorly nou
rished,even considering the ones in the second try
of first year would have dropped,according to natio
nal standards,from an average grade of 6.3 to 5.3
(the school teachers graded them better, 7.4). The
supplemented group,all in second grade,also would
have dropped from 8.1 to 6.4(the teachers graded
them about the same as the previous year, 8.3).

Regarding the tests relative to the ability of
the children to read and write,the results were im-
portant.As for the ability of basic reading and writ
ing no significant differences between groups were
found, although the supplemented group had better
scores on all the tests.

When the tests became difficult, it began to
become evident that the non-supplemented children
had difficulty especially with the written language.
For example, in regard to retarded writing, which
functions basically through specific short term me
mory, there already appeared differences in tests A
(auditive) and Vv(visual verbal)(Graph 1).

GRAPH I

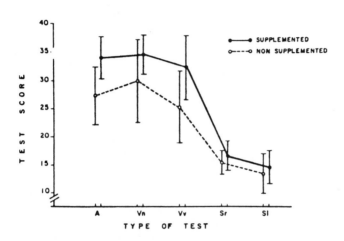

Graph 1. Delayed writing. Measures
mainly specific immediate memory.

In the writing test using the left hand,which
requires interhemispheric transmission of information the differences are even more marked. This test
could indicate the possibility that even upon reaching school age there is still present part of the
brain damage found at earlier ages.

GRAPH 2

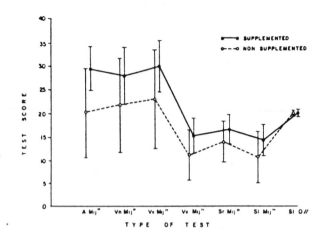

Graph 2. Left hand writing. Measures mainly specific interhemispheric transmission.

The Terman-Merrill tests showed differences that were of little importance and non-significant. The IQ of the non-supplemented group was in average 75.8 ± 5.2 while that of the supplemented group was slightly higher, 80.4 ± 3.6. The differences are greater when the children enter school and, as the children spend more time in school, tend to diminish. This is due in part to the fact that the IQ's of the supplemented children tend to drop with time. At the age of seven these children have an IQ of 85.9 ± 5.1, which drops slowly. At the same time the poorly nourished maintain and even improve a little their level at school.

The most interesting findings in this study are in the area of observations of behavior done through time samplings. These are shown in Table 2.

TABLE 2

BEHAVIOR OF NON-SUPPLEMENTED AND SUPPLEMENTED CHILDREN IN SCHOOL

3240 observations per child during the first year

ACTIVITIES OBSERVED	EARLY OBSERVATIONS NON-SUPPL.	EARLY OBSERVATIONS SUPPL.	LATE OBSERVATIONS NON-SUPPL.	LATE OBSERVATIONS SUPPL.	TOTAL OBSERVATIONS NON-SUPPL.	TOTAL OBSERVATIONS SUPPL.
LOOKING AT TEACHER	5.1%	11.4%	1.2%	8.7%	3.1%	10.0%
OBEYING INSTRUCTIONS	1.9%	3.4%	0.7%	1.7%	1.3%	2.6%
ASKING QUESTIONS	0.3%	1.3%	0.0%	1.3%	0.1%	1.3%
TALKING	4.1%	5.5%	1.5%	3.7%	2.8%	4.6%
PLAYING	4.6%	12.6%	2.6%	12.8%	3.6%	12.7%
OUT OF SEAT	1.8%	7.7%	0.7%	6.6%	1.3%	7.2%
ASLEEP	1.0%	0.0%	8.5%	0.0%	4.7%	0.7%
FIGHTING	0.1%	0.7%	0.8%	1.3%	0.4%	1.0%
CRYING	6.3%	2.2%	3.0%	1.4%	4.7%	0.6%

The differences between the two groups are very marked.The supplemented are more active,shown by the fact that they are out of their seats more often,and they are also more attentive to what is going on in the class.They participate more,they obey the teacher more,and they answer questions more often.They are also more playful.On the other hand the poorly nourished spend more time either crying or sleeping.

Another clear difference is that the poorly nourished tire more since they show very marked dif ferences between the observations made early in the morning and at noon.Their activity,attention,and par ticipation drop,their drowsiness increases a great deal and their nervousness also seems to increase, since they increment the time spent in fighting.

COMENTARIES

There is no doubt that the sampling is small and disproportionate to the great importance of the matter being dealt with,but the methodology used does not allow for greater numbers.Several of the results are quite demonstrative.The poorly nourished children come to school in a very disadvantageous condition.They do very poorly on the first test that is given to them,and they went through the whole year at an average level which was at the minimal limit. The supplemented children also did poorly on the first test,but were able to improve significantly with the first teachings since they ended the year quite well.These results make evident the differen ces in learning capacity between the two groups.

To a great degree,the learning differences seem to be related to their behavior.The time sampling tests show the malnourished to be very inactive,ti mid,passive,and distracted.All these characteristics were found at early ages through observations in their homes and in open field tests(3).In the same manner,in this age and at that time they cry exces sively,this apparently being to be linked to a feel ing of insecurity.These results indicate that the behavior previously described as a "chipil child" (crybaby)are still present at school age,although not in so obvious and in so constant way.

In the same way, there continue to exist certain differences between the two groups in the neurological tests, especially in the area of language. The same is true, but to a lesser degree, regarding IQ. These differences are present to a more subtle degree, demonstrable only through the use of more refined tests.

Consequently, just as at ages prior to school age, it seems that three mechanisms that limit learning operate in the poorly nourished child: 1) a certain degree of brain damage, organic or only functional, which, at these ages at least, seem to be of little importance, 2) an inadequate behavior which reduces the possibilities of receiving stimuli and information; this is directly due to malnutrition, and include such factors as inactivity, lack of concentration, passivity, insecurity, timidity, and, perhaps, a certain degree of tension. This behavior seems to be the main factor in the lack of capacity toward learning and, therefore, the lack of capacity in performance on the exams, and, 3) the social factors, which operate on both groups, especially during the second school year, due to the lack of interest on the part of the teachers and the conformism throughout the school, and especially due to the lack of motivation toward study; the low degree of a competitive attitude because of cultural factors; and, of course, non-compliance on the part of the teachers.

In consideration of the great importance that this line of research has and of the possibilities that this combined methodology has in being able to more precisely clarify the dynamic of the process, the sampling is currently being extended. We now have a larger group of children who have been supplemented since infancy, and they are currently under observation. Some of the methods are being refined, especially those that will allow to get further down to the root of the problem. For example, more attention is being given to the possible role of language and memory in the deficiencies as well as to define the importance of some behavior characteristics.

REFERENCES

1) Barnes, R.H.: Dual role of environmental depri
vation and malnutrition in retarding intellectual development. Am.Jour.Clin.Nut. 29:912,1976

2) Chávez, A. and Martínez, C.: Nutrition and Dev-
elopment of Children from Poor Rural Areas.
Reprints of papers published in Nutr.Rep. Intern.
Monograph L-37,División de Nutrición,1979

3) Chávez, A. and Martínez, C.: Consequences of
Insufficient Nutrition on Child Character and
Behavior. In Levitsky(ed)(1979). Malnutrition
Environment and Behavior. Ithaca, N.Y.:Cornell
Univ. Press.

4) Chávez, Z., Martínez, C. and Yaschine, T.:
Nutrition, Behavioral Development, and Mother-
Child Interaction in Young Rural Children.
Fed. Proc. 34:1574,1975

5) Winick, M.: (Ed)(1979). "Nutrition pre- and
postnatal development". New York: Plenum press

25: RESPONSE OF MALNOURISHED PRESCHOOL CHILDREN TO MULTIDISCIPLINARY INTERVENTION

L. Sinisterra, H. McKay, A. McKay, H. Gómez, and J. Korgi

We have reported the design, progress, and initial results of a quasi-experimental longitudinal study that began with more than 500 children in 1970 (2,3,4), and continues today with over 350 children now 10 years of age. Children from stable families of both the highest and the lowest socio-economic status to be found in the city of Cali, Colombia were included. The purpose was to establish the degree to which preschool children having the poorest nutritional and socio-economic status would improve in mental and physical growth given multi-disciplinary treatment. The treatment program included nutritional supplementation, educational and social activities, and health care for varying lengths of time, from ten months to three and a half years prior to entering primary school.

Cali, Colombia's third largest city, is an industrial and agricultural center with a million inhabitants, located in a large valley at 1000 meters above sea level in the southwest part of the country, near the equator. During the past 20 years, Cali has experienced continuous heavy immigration which has resulted in large numbers of unskilled, marginally employed men and women, and families living in small makeshift dwellings on the periphery of the city. As a consequence of the poor economic and housing conditions, the low educational level of community members, and the large family size, a high proportion of the children in these families endure chronic undernutrition during the first years of life and at school age (7 years); are small for their age (in our sample, 2 years behind normal); have lowered capacity for physical work (6); have a history of frequent episodes of illness; and are far below normal levels of **intellectual** abilities. These are, of course, conditions found in the large urban centers of many developing countries in the tropical zones of the world.

The present longitudinal study grew out of several years of work with malnourished children and their families in and around Cali, and two more years of pilot study, stimulated by the 1967 MIT conference (5).

At the end of the pilot study, and before the beginning of the longitudinal experimental study, we had come to a major conclusion: for the vast majority of the preschool children with mild to moderate malnutrition found in urban poverty areas, nutritional supplementation alone was unlikely to produce significant improvement in cognitive ability. Although increased general activity was observed to result from a nutritional supplementation program, we came to believe that cognitive abilities would be

Reprinted from pages 229-238 of *Behavioral Effects of Energy and Protein Deficits.* J. Brožek, ed., NIH Publication Number 79-1906, U.S. Government Printing Office, Washington, D.C., 1979, 370p.

positively affected only if the improved food intake would be sustained over a longer period of time concurrently with improved learning opportunities.

Another conclusion we reached quite early was that, with the population we had chosen, significant improvement in physical growth could be achieved only with an aggressive program of supplementation that provided considerably more than 50% of the child's daily protein-calorie requirements, in addition to food received at home. The question remained as to whether the gains in growth would be permanent or only temporary, disappearing after the improved intake ended. There was no information in 1969 to guide us in this respect. In fact, even information about the short-range effects of nutritional intervention upon physical growth among groups of undernourished preschool age children is still fragmentary.

Finally, the pilot study indicated that malnourished children significantly increased their cognitive capacity through participation in a program of educational activities accompanying the nutritional supplementation. That these increases could be sustained once treatment ended was in considerable doubt; as had been shown clearly, in the United States at least, that gains in intellectual ability among "disadvantaged" preschoolers enrolled in educational enrichment programs faded out within two years of primary school (1). What had not been studied adequately up to then, however, was the quantitative relationship of treatment duration or intensity to response duration. We adopted the hypothesis that a longer education intervention would produce more enduring cognitive ability gains, especially if accompanied by improved nutrition.

With this background, we launched a longitudinal study combining the known but inadequately quantified primary effects of nutritional supplementation (improved physical growth), and educational activities (improved cognitive ability), and the possible additional or secondary effects of improved nutrition in order to produce maximal benefits to undernourished preschoolers. It was expected that not only might there be effects of nutrition upon cognitive growth, but also that there might be effects of the educational program on physical growth due to, for example, the transfer of hygienic behaviors learned at the treatment center to the home, or more assertiveness by the child with respect to food portions at home.

DESIGN, SUBJECT SELECTION AND TREATMENTS

The design, as originally conceived (Figure 1) included the four groups receiving one, two, three, and four 10-month periods of combined intervention (groups T1 to T4); three subgroups receiving one, two, and three periods of nutritional supplementation at home, prior to a period of combined intervention (groups Tla, Tlb, and Tlc); and a high socio-economic level group (group HS) receiving no intervention. All groups were measured at the same time throughout the study, approximately every 10 months

In order to have 60 children available for each primary treatment group, approximately 7500 families living in two of the city's lowest-income areas were visited, and all children with birth dates between June 2 and November 30, 1967 were identified.

			experimental design				
		NUTRITION HEALTH AND EDUCATION PRESCHOOL PROJECT CALI COLOMBIA					
GROUPS	N. 1971	treatment years					N. 1974
		1971	1972	1973	1974		
T4	60	enh	enh	enh	enh		53
T3	60		enh	enh	enh		50
T2	60			enh	enh		51
T1	60				enh		50
HS	60	UPPER	CLASS	COMPARISON	GROUP		52
T1(a)	20	nh	nh	nh	enh		16
T1(b)	20		nh	nh	enh		17
T1(c)	20			nh	enh		16
	360						315

e = EDUCATION

n = NUTRITIONAL SUPPLEMENTATION

h = HEALTH CARE

Figure 1. Schematic of Cali project design. All the components of intervention for Groups T4 through T1 were provided in a treatment center while Groups Tl(a,b,c) received nutritional supplementation at home and health care (medical examination and treatment) in the center. Group HS children, constituting the upperclass comparison group, received no treatment but were measured periodically in the same times as the treated undernourished children; at the beginning of the study, the means on measures of physical and cognitive development and socio-economic well-being for Group HS were between 1.5 and 3 standard deviations above those of children selected for treatment.

These birth dates coincide with primary-school entry in 1974. During a second visit to 733 families with children having the desired birth dates, invitations were extended for medical examinations of the children. The families of 518 children accepted and each child received a clinical examination, anthropometric assessment, and screening for serious neurological dysfunctions. During a third visit to these families, interviews and observations were conducted to determine living conditions, economic resources, age, and education and occupation of family members. As a result of the interviews, observations, and initial screening, 69 children were not considered for further study because of errors in birth date, serious neurological or sensory dysfunctions, rejection of further participation, or because the child no longer lived in the area. This reduced the number of potential study subjects to 449.

In view of the anticipated subject losses, 333 children were selected for the study to assure the participation of 300 at the beginning of treatment (301 were still available at that time; 53% males). Children selected for the study from among the 449 candidates were those having the lowest height and weight for age, the highest number of clinical signs of malnutrition, and lowest per capita family income. The second and third criteria were employed only where differences among children in weight and height were judged by the medical staff to be too small to have biological significance.

The group of 116 children (group T0, not indicated in Figure 1), not selected for the study because their height and weight for age, clinical signs, and economic resources put them in the upper part of the distributions, were left untreated and were not measured until four years later. At that point, the 72 children of families still living in the area and willing once again to collaborate were incorporated into the longitudinal study. Their physical growth and cognitive development were measured at the same time as that of the selected children, beginning at 7 years of age.

The high socio-economic level group (HS) was included in order to provide a set of local reference standards for normal growth and development, and to enable us to attempt to assess the social significance of the effects of intervention, not just their statistical significance. We wanted not only to evaluate the effects of treatment on the basis of the difference between treated and untreated children from the same neighborhood but also to be able to say what this represented in terms of progress toward normality, represented by this upper class group.

The 333 subjects selected for intervention were assigned to treatment groups in subgroups of 13 to 19 children living in a geographical area. The assignment of the children by sectors, in-

stead of by individuals, was done to minimize social interaction
between different treatment-group families and to make daily transportation more efficient.

During the preschool phase of the study there were four 10-
month periods between the beginning of 1971 and the end of 1974,
each period corresponding roughly in length to a school year in
Colombia. This yielded about 170, 360, 550, and 730 treatment
days, respectively. An average day of combined treatment consisted
of six hours of integrated health, nutritional and educational activities, with four hours dedicated to education and two to health,
nutrition and hygiene. A more complete description of the treatment is reported elsewhere (4).

Clinical health examinations, body measurements, and tests of
cognitive development were scheduled at the end of one or the beginning of the next treatment period during the preschool phase,
and during the initial months of each school year in the follow-
up phase.

EFFECTS OF TREATMENT

During the preschool phase the integrated treatment resulted
in significant gains in general cognitive ability. Figure 2 shows
the progress of cognitive development in the different experimental
groups and the upper-class comparison group. In this graph, the
data for group Tl are combined with those for groups Tl(a,b,c)
since they participated in only one period of integrated treatment
(see Figure 1). Several facts emerge:

1) The effects of the treatment periods, varying in number
from one to four, are cumulative: The greater the number of the
treatment periods, the higher the average level of cognitive ability at the end of the preschool period (87 months of age).
2) The major changes in the velocity of cognitive development
occur in the first treatment period.
3) The earlier in the child's life the integrated treatment
is provided, the larger are the effects during the first treatment
period. Physical growth shows the same tendency but less clearly.
4) After the first treatment period, the gap between the mean
performance scores of the children of the comparison group HS
(high socio-economic status, untreated) and the experimental groups
(low socio-economic and nutritional status, treated) has been widening.

Figure 3 portrays cognitive development during the first two
years of school, following the cessation of experimental intervention at the end of the preschool period. The experimental groups
(Tl to T4) maintain their position to each other but there is a

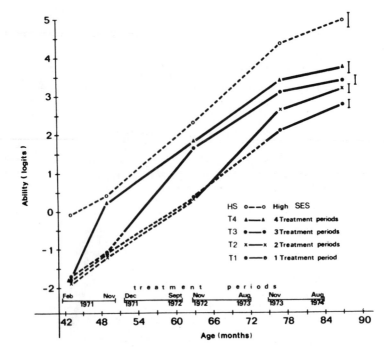

Figure 2. Growth of general cognitive ability of study children
from 43 months of age to 87 months, the beginning of
primary school. Ability scores are scaled sums of correct test items. Solid lines represent periods of treatment. Brackets to the right of the curves indicate plus
or minus one standard error of the corresponding group
means at the fifth measurement point (from Ref. 4).

leveling of intellectual performance, while the HS group exhibited
continued growth. The gap between the children of high and low
socio-economic status became still wider.

Group T0 (low in socio-economic status, untreated), first
tested at the end of the preschool period, has the lowest performance level. The score at 87 months may be depressed, in part,
because they had no prior experience in taking tests. By 112
months of age this initial disadvantage has probably been overcome.

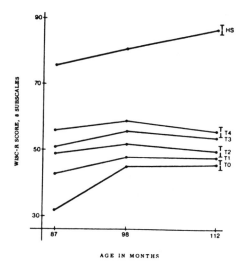

AGE IN MONTHS

Figure 3. Progress of cognitive development of experimental and comparison groups in the period following preschool intervention. Scores are based on 8 scales from the Wechsler Intelligence Scale for Children (7): design, Picture arrangement.
Brackets at right of curves represent approximately plus
or minus one standard error at 112 months of age.

The fact that these were, at least initially, the healthiest and
physically most normal children, and yet show scores lower than the
least treated group, leads us to conclude that strong obstacles to
normal cognitive growth in the urban poverty environment exist
even when nutritional conditions are not grossly inadequate.

Contrary to the evidence from other studies, the effect of
intervention does not disappear in the absence of continued treatment, although it is reduced. The same tendency was found in physical growth as well, with a lessening of treatment effects and a
progressively widening gap between these children and those from
the higher socio-economic group.

The reduction of cognitive ability is not of the same magnitude for all the subtests represented in Figure 3. In tests involving logical processes (Figure 4) the treatment effects remain
fairly strong, although here too there has been a regression and
a widening of the gap between socio-economic levels.

In two of the subtests which reflect acquaintance with concepts (Vocabulary, Information), the reduction in cognitive ability

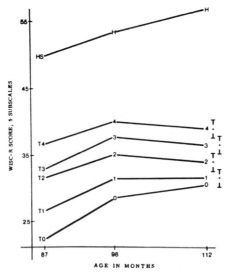

Figure 4. Cognitive development of experimental and comparison
groups in the period following preschool intervention.
Scores are based on five subtests from the Wechsler
Intelligence Scale for Children: Arithmetic, Mazes,
Similarities, Block Design, Picture Arrangement.
Brackets at right of curves represent approximately
plus or minus one standard error at 112 months of age.

is marked and the persisting effects of integrated preschool treatment are substantially smaller (Figure 5). This demonstrates the
difficulty of sustaining cognitive gains in the setting of extreme
poverty. The home, the community in general and, unfortunately,
also the schools have become increasingly less adequate providers
of stimuli necessary for what could be considered normal intellectual growth.

Further evidence of the effect of the integrated preschool
intervention is primary school achievement. Figure 6 shows the
grade level reached at the beginning of the 1977-78 school year.
Although the differences are small among the groups, the tendency
is clear: longer preschool treatment yields higher grade levels.
It should be noted that the public schools these children are attending are crowded, with few materials for the students or teacher
and schedules limited to four hours per day.

Finally, achievement tests of reading and arithmetic, designed
by the public school teachers, show the same positive relationship
between the amount of preschool experience and test performance.

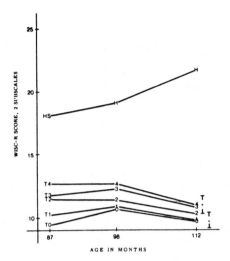

Figure 5. Cognitive development of experimental and comparison groups following preschool intervention. Scores based on two subtests from the Wechsler Intelligence Scale for Children: Vocabulary and Information. Brackets at right of curves represent approximately plus or minus one standard error at 112 months of age.

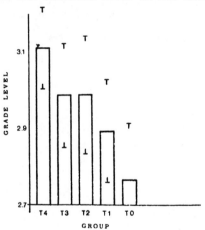

Figure 6. Grade level achieved by the study cnildren in 1977. Brackets above and below top of bar represent plus or minus one standard error.

REFERENCES

1. Bronfenbrenner, U. Is Early Intervention Effective? DHEW Publication No. (OHD) 76-30025, Washington, D.C., 1974.

2. McKay, H.,McKay, A. and Sinisterra, L. Behavioral intervention studies with malnourished children: A review of experiences. In D. Kallen, Ed., Nutrition, Development and Social Behavior. DHEW Publication No.(NIH) 73-242, Washington, D.C., pp. 121-145, 1973.

3. McKay, H.,McKay, A. and Sinisterra, L. Intellectual development of malnourished preschool children in programs of stimulation and nutritional supplementation. In J. Cravioto, L. Hambraeus, and B. Vahlquist, Eds., Early Malnutrition and Mental Development. Uppsala: Almqvist and Wiksell, ppl 226-233, 1974.

4. McKay, H., Sinisterra, L., McKay, A., Gómez, H. and Lloreda, P. Improving cognitive ability in chronically deprived children. Science, 200:270-278, 1978.

5. Scrimshaw, N. S. and Gordon, J. E., Eds., Malnutrition, Learning and Behavior. Cambridge, Mass.: M.I.T. Press, 1968.

6. Spurr, G. B., Barac-Nieto, M. and Maksud, M. G. Childhood undernutrition: Implications for adult work capacity and productivity. In L. J. Folinsbee, J. Wagner, J. Borgia, B. Prinkwater, J. Gliner and J. Bedi, Eds., Stress: Individual Human Adaptation. New York: Academic Press (to be published).

7. Wechsler, D. WISC-R: Wechsler Intelligence Scale for Children—Revised. New York: The Psychological Corporation, 1974.

26: NUTRITION, SOCIAL ENVIRONMENT AND COGNITIVE PERFORMANCE OF DISADVANTAGED COLOMBIAN CHILDREN AT THREE YEARS[1]

J. O. Mora, M. G. Herrera, S. G. Sellers, and N. Ortiz

INTRODUCTION

The intervention approach has been the most commonly used for the longitudinal study of the relationship between malnutrition and mental development (1). The approach is based on the idea that, through specific interventions, it is possible to broaden the range of variation naturally occurring in nutritional status, while modifying as little as possible other confounding variables, thus facilitating the assessment of the relationships between nutritional manipulations and changes in cognitive performance.

The Bogota Research Project on Malnutrition and Mental Development was a randomized intervention study of families and children at risk of malnutrition living in a poor urban area. Some major findings of this study are hereby reported regarding the relationships of nutrition, social variables, and the experimental interventions to cognitive performance of the children at 36 months of age, the end point of the interventions.

The analyses were aimed at answering the following questions: Were there differential effects of the interventions on cognitive performance of children at 36 months ? What was the relative contribution of nutritional and non-nutritional factors to cognitive performance ?

(1) Supported in part by the Colombian Institute of Family Welfare, NICHHD Grant No. HD06774, The Ford Foundation Grant No. 740-0348, and the Fund for Research and Teaching, Dept. of Nutrition, Harvard School of Public Health.

Reprinted from pages 403-420 of *Nutrition in Health and Disease and International Development: Symposia from the XII International Congress of Nutrition,* Alan R. Liss, Inc., New York, 1981; *Copyright © 1981 by Alan R. Liss, Inc.*

RESEARCH DESIGN

The basic research design was a classical two-by-two
factorial with nutritional supplementation and home education for infant stimulation as intervention programs. The
study sample consisted of 456 low income families with malnourished children and the mother in the first or second
trimester of pregnancy.

Families volunteering to participate were randomly assigned to six experimental groups, as seen in Figure 1. Data
used for this report belong to the four groups of the factorial design (Figure 2). Randomization was effective in
creating initially comparable groups, as indicated by several major social variables. All study families were offered free health care services. Families, mothers during
pregnancy, and their offspring were observed longitudinally
by repeated measurements of social variables, morbidity,
nutritional status and cognitive performance. The period
of intervention extended up to 36 months of child's age,
but periodic measurements continued throughout the post-in-
tervention follow-up period up to 6 years of age.

Nutritional supplements were common foods (powder skim
milk, enriched bread and cooking oil) provided for all members of the family; commercial iron and vitamin A were also
given to the target children. Supplements were delivered
weekly to be taken home in rations containing about 620 calories and 30 g protein per person/day. No systematic nutrition education was imparted, but the families were constantly encouraged to use the supplements in addition to
and not to replace food items in their regular diet. Unexpected home visits and periodic dietary surveys were used
to monitor and measure supplement use. Supplementation
substantially increased the child's intake of protein and,
to a lesser extent, of calories (2).

The"stimulation"intervention consisted of home education to the mothers and other child caretakers, by means
of two weekly home visits by primary school teachers especially trained. It was intended to teach the mother, through
demonstrations with her own child, practical means to improve the level of psychosocial stimulation provided to the
infant (3). The aim was to modify the patterns of mother's
behavior and interaction with the child, encouraging physical and emotional contacts to enrich sensoriomotor stimula-

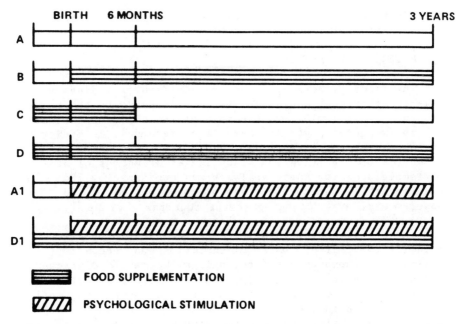

Figure 1. Intervention schedule for the experimental groups.

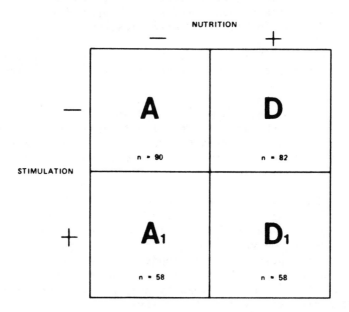

Figure 2. Experimental design.

tion. Each home visitor was assigned seven families from the
child's birth until he was 36 months.

MATERIAL AND METHODS

The findings here reported include data periodically
collected through a social survey questionnaire to the mothers, and the following measurements of the children: anthropometry (weight, length and head circumference), morbidity
over the first three years as reported by the mothers, and
the scores of cognitive tests applied at 36 months of age.
The sample used for these analyses was conformed by 184
children having the complete set of the above mentioned
measurements, and belonging to the four basic groups.

The social survey questionnaire recorded information
on family composition, parental education and occupation,
family income, expenses and belongings, household characteristics, family social participation, and mother's emotional
status and attitudes, beliefs, and practices regarding child
rearing. All anthropometric measurements were taken by the
same observer, using standard techniques. The morbidity
data were collected through biweekly home visits using a
check list of disease symptoms, and it was coded monthly as
days and episodes of disease categories.

An extensive battery of cognitive tests was applied at
36 months, three of which were selected for the present report:

1. Perceptual analysis (Embedded figures test). It
is based on the ability of the child to analyze 18 increasingly complex visual arrays and to locate hidden figures embedded in a large background. The score indicates the total
number of correct answers.

2. Short-term memory. This test was given in two
parts: the first scored the child's recall of 18 increasingly long (from two to six) series of numbers read to him
at the rate of one per second; in the second part, the child
was asked to repeat 18 increasingly long sentences (from 2
to 10 word) read at him at a standard speed. The maximum
amplitude of response attained by the child on the corresponding series was used in the analyses.

3. Language. It measures the child's ability to name

and recognize 41 pictures of common objects. The total number of correct answers was scored for the two components of the test (naming and recognizing).

These tests were selected from the psychometric battery used by the INCAP study on malnutrition and mental development in rural Guatemala (4). All were applied by primary school teachers appropriately trained and standardized over three months and periodically thereafter. For all tests, intertester and test-retest correlations above .80 were obtained in standardization sessions carried out with children in day care centers, before they were applied to the study children. The tests were applied in a single session of about 75 minutes beginning with the Griffiths test and following with the three cognitive tests in the order described above.

While some social variables were used as single items in the analyses, others were reduced to a number of composite scales, as follows:

Mother's and father's education. Each of these two scales is composed of items referring to years of schooling and reading habits (frequency and amount of newspaper reading, and magazine reading). The scale for the mother includes two more items referring to reading and writing ability as observed by the interviewer.

Mother's unhappiness. This scale scores cumulative points over time for answers to the following questions: Would you like your life to continue as it is or change considerably ? In recent weeks have you felt dissatisfied or bored at times ? The higher the score on this scale the more the mother has felt unhappy or dissatisfied.

Household sanitary environment. This is an ordinal scale reflecting sanitary conditions of the household: availability and source of water supply, sewage and garbage disposal systems.

Negative attitudes toward child rearing. This scale mostly reflects mother's expressed negative attitudes about the child and some observations of negative behavior: this is crybaby, he is too much of a bother, he bothers too much at night, children are a bother, this child does not let her get anything done around the house; mother uses to hit or punch the child.

Mother teaches child. Summation of positive answers
to questionning whether the mother uses to teach the child
numbers, colors, the alphabet, opposite concepts, and new
words, as well as whether she reads to the child and plays
with him daily.

Physical contact. The four items of this scale denote
affectionate physical contact between the mother and child:
pampering the child, lulling the child with cooing sounds,
carrying the child frequently, and picking him up and carry
him when he cries.

Change income and income instability during the study
period. These two indices were calculated by regressing
the deflated total family income on time, taking the slope
as the linear change of the family income and the residual
variance as the degree of income instability. While the
scores of change income (slope) are higher for increasing
incomes, those of income instability reflect the amount of
instability above and below the linear regression.

The following statistical procedures were used. First,
analyses of variance (ANOVA) of the cognitive scores by
treatment group were done to assess the effects of the interventions on specific cognitive dimensions; these analyses
were also done by levels of weight and length at 36 months
above and below the third percentile of the WHO reference
standards (5). An intercorrelation matrix was also computed
for the cognitive scores and independent variables of either
social or nutritional nature. Finally, using cognitive
scores as dependent variables, separated multiple regression
analyses were undertaken with the data pooled for the four
treatment groups. Three repeated analyses were performed
per test: first, using the step-wise option in which independent variables were left to enter the regression equation
without a pre-specified order, and then two hierarchical al-
ternatives forcing either the social or the nutritional variables first.

RESULTS

Mean cognitive scores at 36 months by intervention
group and the results of the corresponding analyses of variance are shown in Table 1. The intervened groups tended

Table 1.   Mean cognitive scores by intervention group.

Intervention Group	Perceptual Analysis (n=184)	Short-Term Memory		Language (n=184)
		Digits (n=173)	Sentences (n=171)	
Control	10.4 ± 2.9	1.9 ± 0.9	2.8 ± 1.9	23.7 ± 6.8
Supplemented	11.3 ± 3.1	2.0 ± 0.9	3.1 ± 1.8	24.4 ± 6.1
Stimulated	11.1 ± 3.4	2.1 ± 1.0	3.0 ± 2.1	26.9 ± 6.2
Supplemented and Stimulated	12.8 ± 2.6	2.1 ± 0.9	3.3 ± 2.0	27.5 ± 5.3
All Groups	11.3 ± 3.1	2.0 ± 0.9	3.0 ± 1.9	25.2 ± 6.3

ANOVA (p values)

1. Supplementation	<.05	N.S.	N.S.	N.S.
2. Stimulation	<.025	N.S.	N.S.	<.001
3. Interaction 1 x 2	N.S.	N.S.	N.S.	N.S.

NS = Non significant

Table 2.   Mean cognitive scores by nutritional status.

Nutritional Indicators	Perceptual Analysis (n=182)	Short-Term Memory		Language (n=182)
		Digits (n=171)	Sentences (n=169)	
Weight				
Normal	12.0 ± 3.0	2.0 ± 0.9	3.1 ± 2.0	26.2 ± 5.9
Sub-normal	10.2 ± 2.9	2.0 ± 0.9	3.0 ± 1.8	23.6 ± 6.8
p *	.002	N.S.	N.S.	.045
Length				
Normal	12.7 ± 2.4	1.9 ± 1.0	3.1 ± 2.1	28.2 ± 4.9
Sub-normal	10.9 ± 3.1	2.0 ± 0.9	3.0 ± 1.9	24.3 ± 6.5
p *	.001	N.S.	N.S.	.001

p * =   probability level in analysis of variance by weight or length category.

N.S.=   Non significant.

to score higher in the four tests, but the effects were significant only for supplementation on perceptual analysis (p <.05) and for stimulation on perceptual analysis (p ⊲025) and on language (p <.001). The interaction effects were not statistically significant, even though the group with the combined intervention scored higher in all tests. There were no significant intervention effects on the memory tests.

Mean cognitive scores by levels of nutritional status (weight and length), irrespective of treatment group, are given in Table 2. There were significant differences between normal and subnormal levels of physical growth in perceptual analysis and language, but not in the memory tests.

Correlational analyses are displayed in Tables 3 and 4. Significant correlations were found between perceptual analysis scores and weight, length, supplementation, diarrheal morbidity in the preceeding month, mother's education, mother's unhappiness, household sanitary environment, total family income, per-capita income, change in income over the study period, and stimulation. Language scores were significantly correlated with weight, length, mother's education, mother's teaching of the child, total and per-capita income, and stimulation. Few significant correlations were found between the memory tests and other variables. There were significant correlations between the cognitive scores: perceptual analysis and memory (r=.15 and .12), and language (r=.47); language and memory (r=.22), and between memory tests (r=.57).

The results of multiple regression analyses are summarized in Tables 5 and 6. A relatively small proportion of the variance (less than 10%) in the memory tests could be explained, thus only the results of perceptual analysis and language are presented. About 25% of the variance in perceptual analysis and 27% of that in language was accounted for by the independent variables. In both cases, five variables explained above 1% of the variance each, when left to enter the regression equation without a pre-specified order. As much as 21% of the variance in perceptual analysis was explained by weight, per-capita income, the interaction between supplementation and stimulation, mother's education and head circumference. Similarly, five variables accounted for 24% of the variance in language scores: the interaction between supplementation and stimulation, mother's education, child's weight, per-capita income and head cir-

Table 3.   Correlations between nutritional indicators, morbidity measures and cognitive scores.

Nutritional Indicators and Morbidity Measures.	Perceptual Analysis (n=182)	Short-Term Memory		Language (n=182)
		Digits (n=171)	Sentences (n=169)	
Birth weight	.041	.044	.026	.080
Weight	.290 **	-.009	-.034	.160 *
Length	.295 **	.064	-.030	.273 **
Head Circumference	.116	.078	.034	.088
Supplementation	.200 **	.056	.054	.074
Respiratory Illnesses, last month	.034	.001	.040	.078
Diarrhea, last month	-.159 *	-.159 *	-.029	-.078
Total Illnesses, last month	-.003	-.026	.052	.061
Cumulated Respiratory Illnesses, 36 months	-.034	-.044	-.008	.019
Cumulated Diarrheas, 36 months	-.075	-.046	.084	-.006
Cumulated Total Illnesses, 36 months	-.023	-.020	.019	.020

* p < .05
** p < .01

Table 4. Correlations between social measures and cognitive scores.

Social Measures	Perceptual Analysis	Short-Term Memory		Language
		Digits	Sentences	
Family size	-.036	-.036	-.075	-.009
Mother's Education	.183 **	-.035	.010	.145 *
Father's Education	.039	-.033	-.156 *	-.013
Mother's Unhappiness	-.119 *	.008	.044	-.025
Household Environment	.145 *	.072	-.185 *	.095
Childrearing Practices	-.012	-.034	-.153 *	.027
Mother Teaches Child	.072	.030	.061	.159 *
Physical Contact	.071	.139	.129	.035
Family Income	.186 **	.011	-.057	.152 *
Per-capita Income	-.209 **	.055	.007	.189 **
Change Income	.150 *	.014	-.038	.095
Income Stability	-.025	-.121	-.090	-.080
Stimulation	.201 **	.071	.070	.243 **

* p < .05
** p < .01

Table 5.   Step-wise multiple regressions of perceptual analysis and language scores on nutritional and socio-environmental variables (1).

Independent Variables	R Square	R Square Change	F	BETA
PERCEPTUAL ANALYSIS			
Weight	.083	.083	11.11**	.311
Per-capita income	.132	.049	6.87**	.164
Supplementation by Stimulation	.181	.049	7.23**	.201
Mother's Education	.198	.017	2.60*	.123
Head Circumference	.210	.012	1.86	-.120
LANGUAGE			
Supplementation by Stimulation	.081	.081	10.84**	.151
Mother's Education	.145	.064	9.15**	.187
Weight	.180	.035	5.22**	.287
Per-capita Income	.210	.030	4.43**	.560
Head Circumference	.240	.030	4.81**	.184

(1) Only variables accounting for more than 1% of the variance are reported.

* $p < .05$

** $p < .01$

Table 6.   Proportion of variance in perceptual analysis
and language scores explained by nutritional
indicators and social variables forced in alternate orders.

Independent Variables	Perceptual Analysis	Language
A. Supplementation	.036	.022
Nutritional Indicators	.094	.084
Morbidity	.006	.002
Stimulation	.011	.051
Supplementation by Stimulation		
Interaction	.014	.008
Social Scales	.083	.106
Total	.244	.273
B. Stimulation	.021	.066
Social Scales	.076	.104
Morbidity	.008	.004
Supplementation	.010	.004
Supplementation by Stimulation		
Interaction	.068	.034
Nutritional Indicators	.061	.061
Total	.244	.273

cumference (Table 5).
Independent variables were also forced to enter the regression equation in two different orders, so as to ascertain the independent contribution of nutrition, morbidity, the interventions and their interactions, and social factors to the variance in cognitive scores, after controlling for the effects of the others (Table 6). Both nutrition indicators and social variables, as well as the interventions, contributed significantly to the variance in either cognitive test.

When supplementation, nutrition and morbidity indicators were forced to enter first, they accounted for 13.6% of the variance in perceptual analysis and 10.8% in language; in this case, stimulation and its interaction with supplementation explained an additional 2.5% and 5.9% of the variance, respectively, while the social scales contributed 8.3% and 10.6%. When the order was reversed, stimulation and social variables contributed 9.7% and 18.0%, and the nutritional indicators still contributed 6.1% to the variance of either cognitive test. When the interventions were forced first, supplementation accounted for a larger proportion of variance in perceptual analysis (3.6%) while stimulation contributed more to language (6.6%).

DISCUSSION AND CONCLUSIONS

We have elsewhere shown from past cross-sectional studies, that infant calorie-protein malnutrition was associated with low performance in general I.Q. measures such as the Griffiths test, and that both nutritional indicators and social variables contributed significantly to the variance in I.Q. (6,7). More recently we have reported, from the same longitudinal study used for the present paper, significant effects of food supplementation on motor development and of stimulation on the speech and language subscale of the same I.Q. test (8,9).

It has been asserted that tests of specific cognitive abilities usually have higher stability of performance from infancy into adulthood and may be better predictors of later I.Q. than aggregate measures of intelligence (10,11). We have used tests of perceptual analysis, memory and language because they are among the basic universal cognitive functions of children, and are supposed to be a constant part of intelligence throughout the different de-

velopmental levels (11, 12). The embedded figures test is
also a measure of attentional maturational processes required for analytical thinking. The present study was
aimed at ascertaining the unique and joint contributions
of nutritional indicators, social variables and targeted
interventions aimed at their modification, to variation
in the scores of those three specific cognitive tests. The
tests were considered separately since they have been shown
to be differentially associated with nutritional and social
indicators (4, 13, 14).

Physical growth retardation was associated with significantly lower cognitive scores in perceptual analysis and
language, and nutritional supplementation significantly
increased performance in perceptual analysis, but not in
language. Short-term memory was not related to physical
growth nor affected by supplementation or stimulation. One
possible explanation is that the activation of the cognitive strategies required for verbal memory is associated
with a certain level of maturation which is achieved at
older ages than that needed for visual memory. It is interesting, however, that short-term memory was just the
only cognitive domain resistant to the effects of a comprehensive nutrition, health and psychosocial intervention
from 3 to 7 years on multiple deprived children in Cali,
Colombia (15).

Both socioenvironmental factors and physical growth,
as well as their experimental manipulations, made some independent contribution to variation in cognitive performance, and their relative importance depended on the particular cognitive domain. Nutritional indicators and supplementation were associated mostly with perceptual analysis;
conversely, language was more affected by social variables
and the stimulation intervention enriching the social environment. The morbidity variables used in the analysis did
not substantially contribute to the variance in test scores.
On the other hand, short-term memory was not sensitive to
the effects of either set of indicators.

The results of this study, though do not contradict
other reports using the same cognitive tests, clearly indicate stronger correlations and greater proportions of
variance attributable to socio-environmental variables.
In the present study not only a more efficient research
design was used which allowed the selective manipulation of

either nutrition or social-environmental stimulation, but also the measurement of social factors went far beyond the limited scope of others including only gross social stratification indicators taken at a given time. Besides some demographic family characteristics, more specific features of the child's functional environment were included as measured by variables likely to reflect social-environmental stimulation over time.

The inclusion of a more extensive array of social variables and specific social domains related to the child's early experience, could have resulted in greater contribution of social factors to cognitive performance than it has been reported from other studies. The significance of the nutrition variable may depend on the number of relevant social variables entering the equation and covarying with the nutrition variable that explain part of the variance in test scores (11). The physical growth parameters used as indicators of nutritional status have been constant in most studies: weight, as an overall measure of body built; length or height, as a reflection of linear growth; and head circumference, supposedly related to brain size.

What are the possible mechanisms by which nutrition, nutritional supplementation, social factors and psychosocial stimulation affected the specific cognitive domains ? As far as nutritional supplementation is concerned, the effect on perceptual analysis may have been mediated by increased alertness and attention span facilitating the expression of maturational processes related to the child's ability to analyze and correctly respond to a problematic situation; impaired attentional processes have been described as part of a consistent pattern of behavioral disturbances in malnourished infants (16). The effect of mild to moderate malnutrition on cognitive development of children would then be indirect, decreasing motivation and arousal levels, and affecting behavioral performance rather than underlying cognitive structures. It appears that tasks which require the capacity to elicit and sustain attention may be particularly affected by malnutrition. Wellnourished children may differ from those malnourished and otherwise socially deprived, in their ability to attend to, or concentrate on, as well as in their motivation to become engaged in a task rather than in their cognitive capacities. If this is true, then prospects for behavioral remediation and reversibility should be more helpful, as it has been shown (12,15,17).

Social stimulation is likely to affect language development through increased motivation and greater familiarity with strangers and with the testing situation; language ability is known to be particularly sensitive to social environmental influences. It may well be that changes in cognitive performance associated with stimulation are only partly cognitive in nature and reflect, to a large extent, changes in the child's motivation resulting from repeated contact with the stimulation personnel; this may be the case with the language test which is heavily based on verbal instructions.

The present study represents an important contribution to the understanding of the relationships between nutrition, social environment and cognitive development; it should be recognized, however, that it has limitations inherent to the state of the art in the conceptualization and measurement of nutritional status, functionally relevant socio-environmental inputs and cognitive functioning. A further limitation arises from the wellknown difficulties in determining the nature of field interventions which, in practice, cannot be implemented in isolation and free from unintended collateral effects.

The practical implications of the findings here reported certainly depend on both the functional significance of the cognitive dimensions measured by the tests and the persistance of the intervention effects over time once the treatments are suspended. Although short-term evaluations of some early childhood intervention programs have been disappointing because of the apparent vanishing of the cognitive gains soon after the treatment is withdrawn, there is some recent evidence, from long-term evaluations of such programs in USA, of enduring positive results in measures of school achievement (18,19).

As a general conclusion, our findings support the contention that social and nutritional inputs have different magnitude of importance in determining performance on various cognitive dimensions of children. There are independent contributions of nutritional and other environmental factors, especially social stimulation, and the child's ultimate intellectual development is the resultant of those specific effects. Therefore, as Ricciutti contends (20), to bring about a substantial enhancement of the mental development of poor children at risk of malnutrition, amelio-

ration of the several adverse social, economical and environmental influences is required, and not only improved dietary
intake and nutrition.

REFERENCES

1. Brozek J, Coursin DB and Read MS. Longitudinal studies
   on the effects of malnutrition, nutritional supplementation, and behavioral stimulation. Bull. Pan Amer. Hlth.
   Organ. 11: 237-249,1977.
2. Sellers SG, Mora JO, and Herrera MG. (1981) The effects
   of nutritional supplementation and home education on
   children's diets. Prepublication draft.
3. Super CM, Clement J, Vuori L, Christiansen N, Mora JO
   and Herrera MG. Infant and caretaker behavior as me-
   diators of nutritional and social intervention in the
   barrios of Bogota. In: T. Field et al (eds) Culture and
   Early Interaction. Hillsdale, N.J.: Earlbaum (in press
   1981).
4. Klein RE, Freeman HE, Kagan J, Yarbrough C and Habicht
   JP. (1972) Is big smart ? The relation of growth to cognition. J. Health and Social Behavior 13: 219-225.
5. WHO (1978) A growth chart for international use in maternal and child health care. Guidelines for primary
   health care personnel. World Health Organization Non-
   Serial Publication, Geneva.
6. Mora JO, Amézquita A, Castro L, Christiansen N, Clement
   J, Franklin D, Herrera MG, Ortiz N, Pardo F, de Paredes
   B, Ramos C, Riley D, Rodriguez H, Vuori L, Wagner M,
   and Stare FJ. Nutrition, health and social factors related to intellectual performance. World Review of Nutrition and Dietetics 19: 205-236 (1974)
7. Christiansen N, Vuori L, Clement J, Herrera MG, Mora JO,
   Ortiz N (1977). Malnutrition. social environment and
   cognitive development of Colombian infants and preschoolers. Nutr. Rep. Intern. 16: 93-102.
8. Mora JO, Clement J, Christiansen N, Ortiz N, Vuori L,
   Wagner N.(1979). Nutritional supplementation, early stimulation, and child development. In: Brozek J (ed.)
   Behavioral effects of energy and protein deficits. Proceedings of an International Nutrition Conference USA,
   DHEW, NIH Publication No. 79-1906, pp. 255-269, Wash.
9. Waber DP, Vuori L, Ortiz N, Clement J, Christiansen N,
   Mora JO, Reed RB and Herrera MG (1981). Nutritional supplementation, maternal education and cognitive development of infants at risk of malnutrition. Am.J.Clin.Nutr.
   34: 807-813.

10. Mc Call RB, Hogarty PS and Hurburt N. (1972) Transitions in infant sensori-motor development and the prediction of childhood I.Q. Amer. Psychol. 27:728-748.

11. Pollitt E and Thompson C. (1977). Protein-calorie malnutrition and behavior: a view from Psychology. In: Wurtman RJ and Wurtman JJ (eds.) Nutrition and the brain, Vol. 2, New York: Raven.

12. Kagan J, Klein RE (1973) Cross-cultural perspectives on early development. Amer. Psychol. 28: 947-961.

13. Freeman HE, Klein RE, Kagan J, Yarbrough C. (1977) Relations between nutrition and cognition in rural Guatemala. Am. J. Public Hlth. 67: 233-239.

14. Lasky RE, Klein RE, Yarbrough C, Engle PL, Lechtig A, and Martorell R, (1981) The relationship between physical growth and infant behavioral development in rural Guatemala. Child Development 52: 219-226.

15. McKay H, Sinisterra L, McKay A, Gomez H, Lloreda P, (1978). Improving cognitive ability in chronically deprived children. Science 200: 270-278.

16. Lester BM (1975). Cardiac habituation of the orienting response in infants of varying nutritional status. Developmental Psychology 11: 432-442.

17. Winick M, Meyer KK, Harris RC (1975). Malnutrition and environmental enrichment by early adoption. Science 190: 1173-1175

18. Darlington RB, Royce JM, Snipper AS, Murray HW, and Lazar I (1980). Preschool programs and later school competence of children from low-income families. Science 208: 202-204.

19. Weikart DP, and Schweinhart L, (1981). Lasting effects of preschool training on children from low-income American families. Paper presented at the International Seminar on Relations between Preschool and Primary Education. Bogota, Colombia, May.

20. Ricciutti H (1980). Effects of adverse environmental and nutritional influence on mental development. A summary of current knowledge, with implications for programs and policies aimed at prevention and remediation. Working paper prepared for a meeting on the Impact of Malnutrition and related environmental factors on mental development. Pan American Health Organization, PAHO/WHO, Washington, D.C., May.

Addendum to Part VII

Nutritional interventions, with or without stimulation, are the nerve center of community-oriented nutritional research. The importance of the topic is reflected in the five papers reprinted in Part VII and is also considered in the Addendum to Part VIII.

In the formulation of Guthrie and colleagues (1984):

> The ultimate hope of everyone who studies any aspect of malnutrition is to find better ways of preventing or remediating malnutrition. But attempts at alleviation can also provide a rich source of insight into the factors that cause and maintain malnutrition. We come to understand the biosocial processes as we try to alter them. (p. 502)

Nutritional interventions may do more than teach us about the phenomena of malnutrition, their etiology, and their consequences by serving as "planned programs of action intended to improve the nutritional status of a target population" (Celedón, Colombo, and López, 1984, p. 476). They may constitute a rapid response to a nutritional emergency situation while, applied in a more deliberate fashion, they may serve as a research tool that provides information relevant to social planning and as testing grounds for nationwide nutritional programs.

With Celedón, Colombo, and López (1984) we may classify nutritional interventions in terms of the target groups (preschool children with mild to moderate malnutrition or pregnant women suffering from iron deficiency) and program types (food distribution or nutrition education). Another classificatory criterion is provided by the level of prevention and remediation: primary—targeted at asymptomatic individuals, secondary—directed to cases of incipient malnutrition detected early, and tertiary—aimed at the rehabilitation of severely malnourished individuals. Specific problems differ according to the point of view of the individuals who are concerned with a nutritional intervention: the persons responsible for and actively involved in carrying out a project (the manager—typically an interdisciplinary team), the evaluators, the policymakers, and last but not least, the group that is all too frequently overlooked, the participants in the program.

Here we shall consider three projects dealing with different aspects of interventions relevant to malnutrition and behavior.

MATERNAL SUPPLEMENTATION AND INFANT
BEHAVIOR—RURAL TAIWAN

The Taiwan study was initiated by the late Bacon Chow of Johns Hopkins University (Joos et al., 1983). The study meets the criteria of the classical studies on nutritional supplementation, specified by Joos and Pollitt (1984). Their criteria for inclusion of a study into their review were fourfold:

1. A large sample ($N > 100$); in the Taiwan study, $N = 198$;
2. Supplementation of the mother begun during gestation (third trimester of pregnancy in Taiwan);
3. Good control over the delivery of the supplement (intake monitored by nurses in the Chow study);
4. Systematic and longitudinal data collection.

The women recruited for the Taiwan study were 19 to 39 years of age and in good health, had delivered one normal male child, came from a poor family, and had a protein intake estimated at less than 40 g/day. The nutritional supplements were supplied to the women in the form of canned beverages during pregnancy and lactation. The supplement was provided twice daily, and the amount actually consumed was recorded. The average supplementary intake was estimated at 600 kcal and 30 g of protein/day. The control group received a liquid supplement yielding an estimated daily intake of 6 kcal/day for the first three years and 80 kcal/day subsequently. The individuals were assigned randomly to the two treatment groups. The infants received no direct supplements. The progenies were tested only once, around the eighth month of life, using the Bayley Scale of Infant Development, with a mental and motor subscale.

As summarized by Joos and Pollitt (1984),

> In the Taiwan group, no treatment differences were present in the original Bayley mental and motor scores. The analyses were repeated for modified scales from which all items with low response variability were dropped. . . . Using these modified scales, there were still no treatment group differences in the mental scores. There was a marginally significant difference in the mean motor scores ($t = 1.89$, $p = 0.06$), although the magnitude of the difference was small. (p. 515)

REINFORCING COMPLIANCE IN THE PHILIPPINES

In comparison with nationwide interventions (cf. Celedón, Colombo, and López, 1984), the study by Guthrie and co-workers (1982; cf. 1984) would appear, indeed, to be a small-scale intervention. With an N of about 150 mother-infant dyads in three upland villages (*barangays*), the present editor would prefer to speak of an intervention of a medium-range scale. The critical issue, however, is not the terminology but the fact that the mothers were seen every month; consequently, the term *personalized intervention* might be appropriate.

The heart of the project and its distinguishing feature was the investigators' endeavor to maintain the mothers' feeding behavior that would bring about, under the given conditions of poverty, a good or at least improved nutritional status of the child and to do so by using effectively the foods produced in or near their community. The authors saw the need not for adding to the mothers' information about what constitutes a good diet for a toddler but for enhancing the mothers' compliance with what they have been taught in the local health center. This model (or creed) had four points:

1. Maintain breastfeeding for at least a year.
2. Supplement breast milk adequately, beginning at about the fourth month of the child's life.
3. Plant green, leafy vegetables near the home (and use them).
4. Strive for a weight gain every month.

The mothers who participated in the project were to return to the health center every month so that a check could be made on the health, diet, and progress of the child, including its weight gain. The "secret weapon"—the critical tool—of the investigators was positive reinforcement of the mothers for compliance with the steps specified in the model of good nutritional behavior plus returning to the center for a monthly checkup on the child. Compliance was rewarded by giving each mother an appropriate number of tickets (referred to euphemistically as health coupons) every month for a local lottery. The drawings were made every three months, and sacks of corn or rice were given out as the prizes.

The design of the study included two other groups of mothers. In the first comparison group, Kodacolor prints of the picture of the mother and the baby were given out as reinforcers to mothers who maintained the child's weight within the normal band for three succeeding months or who succeeded in raising the baby's weight to the next higher level of nutritional status (classified on the basis of the baby's weight as normal or as mild, moderate, or severe undernutrition). The second comparison group received nutritional education but no reinforcements for compliance with the steps specified in the model.

In summary (Guthrie et al., 1982, p. 632), ". . . we have not stamped out malnutrition. We have succeeded in changing mothers' feeding habits enough to make a clinically as well as statistically significant improvement." The authors emphasize that these results were achieved without offering food supplements (except for a few children who slipped into the third-degree, severe undernutrition), so that the approach did not involve an extensive infusion of food into the communities from outside sources. The two systems of reinforcement were about equally effective. The cultural influences, in the form of traditional beliefs and practices concerning the causes of illness of the child and of poor child growth, frequently clashing with the nutritional model, receive detailed considerations.

SOCIOECONOMIC SPILLOVER EFFECTS OF
INTERVENTIONS—BOGOTÁ

Paper 26 provides information on the effects of an intervention program, put into action in Bogotá, Colombia, on the cognitive performance of three-year-old children. Christiansen (1984) addresses himself to the unintended spillover effects of the program.

The study sample was selected from poor barrios on the edge of the city of Bogotá, characterized by all the typical features of Third World urban poverty, including unstable working conditions, overcrowding, and poor sanitation. Three forms of intervention were used, singly or combined:

1. Health care: The families that received health care alone served as control for the groups that received additional forms of treatment.
2. Nutritional supplementation: The families participating in this facet of the intervention program received food supplements for the whole family in the form of powdered skim milk, enriched bread, and cooking oil. The supplements were calculated to provide about 600 kcal and 30 g of protein for each member of the family above one year of age. The supplement of the pregnant and lactating mothers was, roughly, 200 kcal and 10 g of protein higher. The mothers were encouraged to breastfeed, but if breast milk became insufficient, an infant formula was provided in quantities appropriate for the child's age, up to one year. All infants, beginning at three months of age, received a locally produced weaning food made of corn, rice, soya, and dry milk. The food supplements were collected by the families every week at a distribution center.
3. Home stimulation program: The mother-child pairs were visited by a staff member of the project twice a week. The visitors played with the child and encouraged the mother to do so, to teach and observe the child, and to meet its needs.

Periodically, mostly at 6-month intervals, beginning in the sixth month of pregnancy, social surveys of the families were carried out. The last of these surveys was made when the children were 36 months old. This final survey provided the principal data for Christiansen's paper. Statistically significant effects of the interventions, other than health care alone, were observed in five areas.

Summarizing:

> Supplementation programs decreased the amount of money spent for food in the family. Both home stimulation and supplementation increased the use of contraceptive methods, the supplementation effects being demonstrable only within the higher income segment. Both supplementation and home stimulation were associated with a higher level of maternal employment, the supplementation effects being present only in the lower income segment. Supplementation led to migration of families to better neighborhoods, particularly among the group with inferior housing, and home stimulation resulted in lower reported heavy drinking by husbands. [Christiansen, 1984, p. 520]

CLOSING COMMENT

The range of strategies involved in interventions is wide—from increased food production and food distribution through nutritional supplementation to measures aimed at improving sanitation, education, and the purchasing power of the poor families. Celedón, Colombo, and López (1984, p. 488) view nutritional interventions as necessary—in certain circumstances—palliative measures but insufficient to solve the problem of hunger. They believe that economic growth, generating new jobs and sources of income in underdeveloped countries, is essential. Without disagreeing with their point, the editor wishes to underscore that, in his view, all these efforts will fail unless the excessive growth of many populations of the world can be effectively checked.

REFERENCES

Celedón, J. M., M. Colombo, and I. López, 1984, Nutrition Interventions, Research, and Social Change, in *Malnutrition and Behavior: Critical Assessment of Key Issues,* J. Brožek and B. Schürch, eds., Nestlé Foundation Publication Series, vol. 4, Lausanne, Switzerland, pp. 476-489.

Christiansen, N., 1984, Social and Economic Effects of Supplementation and Stimulation, in *Malnutrition and Behavior: Critical Assessment of Key Issues,* J. Brožek and B. Schürch, eds., Nestlé Foundation Publication Series, vol. 4, Lausanne, Switzerland, pp. 520-530.

Guthrie, G. M., H. A. Guthrie, T. L. Fernandez, and N. O. Estrera, 1982, Cultural Influences and Reinforcement Strategies, *Behav. Ther.* **13:**624-637. Guthrie, G. M., H. A. Guthrie, C. V. C. Barba, T. L. Fernandez, and N. O. Estrera, 1984, Small-scale Interventions in the Philippines, in *Malnutrition and Behavior: Critical Assessment of Key Issues,* J. Brožek and B. Schürch, eds., Nestlé Foundation Publication Series, vol. 4, Lausanne, Switzerland, pp. 502-506.

Joos, S., and E. Pollitt, 1984, Comparison of Four Supplementation Studies, in *Malnutrition and Behavior: Critical Assessment of Key Issues,* J. Brožek and B. Schürch, eds., Nestlé Foundation Publication Series, vol. 4, Lausanne, Switzerland, pp. 507-519.

Joos, S., E. Pollitt, W. H. Mueller, and D. L. Albright, 1983, The Bacon Chow Study: Maternal Nutritional Supplementation and Infant Development, *Child Dev.* **54:**669-676.

Part VIII

Malnutrition in the United States

Papers 27 Through 30: Commentary

The author of Paper 27 coined, in 1933, the term *psychodietetics,* intended to designate the field of study of the relationships between diet and behavior, defining it as "the science of the feeding of an individual in sickness and health, with particular reference to the mental aspect" (p. 181). In Fritz's conception, the term was to apply not only to the impact of nutrition on behavior (in the editor's symbolization, N→B) but also to the psychological determinants of food intake (N←B), like food habits. Several diseases, nutritional in origin (like pellagra), symptoms accompanied by psychological symptoms, are noted and some early animal studies on the effects of the depletion of vitamin B complex are cited. Fritz (1932) is the author of one of these early studies. He also compiled the first bibliography of psychodietetics (Fritz, 1934).

Paper 28 is a report on female Korean infants adopted by American middle-class families. The adoption represents a complex environmental enrichment. Prior to adoption the infants had been classified as malnourished on the basis of height and weight (below the third percentile of Korean norms), moderately nourished (third to twenty-fourth percentile), and well nourished (above the twenty-fourth percentile). At the time of the follow-up, when the children attended elementary schools, all three groups surpassed the median values of the children living in Korea in both height and weight. In mean IQ and in scholastic achievement, they reached or exceeded the mean values of their U.S.-born peers.

The results of this "social experiment" indicate clearly that placing disadvantaged children at an early age in an enriched home environment brings about good physical growth and mental development. At the same time, the three critical variables (height, IQ, and scholastic achievement) continued to show statistically significant mean differences between the children initially classified as malnourished and well-nourished. Why?

Paper 29 has a distinctive place in the literature on malnutrition and behavior (and in this volume) because it deals with the behavioral sequelae of prenatal—rather than postnatal—malnutrition and because the children manifesting at birth the features of intrauterine growth retardation (the index group) were followed up to the age of 14 years. A control group of infants who grew normally during the prenatal period was studied in parallel.

In both groups the psychometric evaluations were made on six different occasions, using a wide variety of scales and tests. Here we shall refer only to measures of behavioral development and of intellectual functioning in the preschool period and in the early teens.

At the age of three years, the DQs (Gesell Scales) were significantly lower in the index children for the Full Scale as well as for the Adaptive and Language subscales. The mean DQs for the Gross Motor and Fine Motor subscales were also lower, but the differences did not reach a level of statistical significance. At the age of 12 to 14 years, the results obtained using the age-appropriate Wechsler Intelligence Scale confirmed the presence of a long-term deficit in intellective functioning for the Full Scale as well as for the Verbal and Performance subscales.

Paper 30 was presented in the closing session of an international conference on behavioral effects on energy and protein deficits (Brožek, 1979), entitled "Look into the Future." The authors are thoroughly familiar with the U.S. scene. The four theses around which their paper is built are as follows:

1. To understand better the effects of malnutrition on behavior, it will be essential to examine the nature and the dynamics of the socioeconomic factors operating in the various U.S. settings.
2. Evaluation of the U.S. food supplementation programs would profit from a critical assessment of the nature and magnitude of their broader impact on the caregivers and the children participating in such programs (and the communities at large), beyond the immediate, specific goals of the program.
3. In addition to the generalized (energy-protein) malnutrition, the effects of an inadequate intake of micronutrients—vitamins and minerals, especially iron—should receive attention.
4. Our approach to the assessment of cognitive functioning must become more sophisticated, rooted more deeply in psychological theory.

In their closing comments, the authors stress the critical need for a comprehensive, coherent, theoretical framework relating nutrition (and malnutrition) to behavior. They believe that—in the final analysis—extensive matrices of the coefficients of correlation between nutritional, socioeconomic, and behavioral variables advance little our understanding of the "web of causes and consequences" (Margen, 1984; cf. Balderston et al., 1981).

REFERENCES

Balderston, J. B., A. B. Wilson, M. E. Freire, and M. S. Simonen, eds., 1981, *Malnourished Children of the Rural Poor: The Web of Food, Health, Education, and Agricultural Production,* Auburn House Publishing Company, Boston, 204p.

Brožek, J., ed., 1979, *Behavioral Effects of Energy and Protein Deficits,* NIH Publication Number 79-1906, U.S. Government Printing Office, Washington, D.C., 366p.

Fritz, M. F., 1932, Maze Performance of the White Rat in Relation to Unfavorable Salt Mixture and Vitamin B Deficiency, *J. Comp. Psychol.* **13:**365-390.

Fritz, M. F., 1934, A Classified Bibliography on Psychodietetics, *Psychol. Monogr.* **46**(2):1-53.

Margen, S., 1984, Energy-Protein Malnutrition: The Web of Causes and Consequences, in *Malnutrition and Behavior: Critical Assessment of Key Issues,* J. Brožek and B. Schürch, eds., Nestlé Foundation Publication Series, vol. 4, Lausanne, Switzerland, pp. 20-31.

27: THE FIELD OF PSYCHODIETETICS*

M. F. Fritz

Although physicians, physiologists and biochemists have, in recent years, given a great deal of consideration to diet and nutrition, psychologists have given this field but little attention. Less than a half dozen reports are to be found in strictly psychological journals, if drugs and fasting are excluded. Most of the psychological observations have been made incidentally by specialists in other fields whose interests were primarily physiological rather than psychological. In the vast body of literature which has grown up on the question of diet we may find many suggestions of important problems which need to be investigated from the psychological angle. Valuable contributions to knowledge can be made by those who are thoroughly trained in the scientific approach to behavior, and whose interests would be fixed upon the psychological aspects. Dietary studies have rapidly assumed increasing importance and because of the popular appeal it should be possible to enlist public support for investigation. It is to be hoped that psychologists with a good background of training in biochemistry will turn their attention to this field and develop the psychological phases until they compare favorably with the contributions made by other investigators.

It would seem desirable to have some term which would refer to the psychological phases of dietary situations. To meet this need we may coin the term *psychodietetics*. Wood and Weeks (8) define dietetics as "the science of the feeding of an individual in sickness and in health." Using this as a basis, we may define *Psycho*-dietetics as "the science of the feeding of an individual in sickness and in health with particular reference to the mental aspect." This definition clearly designates the field which concerns the relationship between diet and mental life. Broadly speaking, the term psychodietetics may be used to cover not only those cases where diet is a factor in the direct causation of mental

* Paper read before the Section on Clinical Psychology of the American Psychological Association, The University of Chicago, September 12, 1933.

Reprinted from *Psychol. Clin.* 22:181-186 (1933/1934); *Copyright © 1934 by The Psychological Clinic Press.*

phenomena but also where behavior has a dietary expression as, for example, in the case of food fads due to peculiar notions on the part of the individual.

Among the diseases now definitely attributed to dietary defects or deficiencies are certain ones which involve mental or neurological symptoms. Pernicious anemia, pellagra, sprue, nightblindness and beriberi are diseases which have dietary significance and are accompanied by symptoms of particular interest to the psychologist. Perhaps the most outstanding example is pernicious anemia. Mental symptoms were mentioned by Addison who first described the malady in 1855. Almost every writer, in giving a description, mentions symptoms suggesting a psychopathological condition as a part of the syndrome. A long array of symptoms have been mentioned by various writers but no constant psychopathological symptomatology has been worked out. However, there seems to be rather general agreement that at least 80 per cent of the patients will show definite mental involvement. It is possible that the incidence is even higher as might be discovered by more accurate methods of diagnosis. It is claimed that the mental symptoms may precede the blood picture by months or even years. These considerations point to the fact that pernicious anemia may have important legal implications, as in the case of wills. This problem has already arisen in the courts and if a case of pernicious anemia can be proved, there would seem to be good reason for setting aside the will (4). It is clear that a scientific consideration of this disease from the psychological angle, particularly with respect to the higher mental processes, would be very valuable. The etiology of pernicious anemia cannot be taken up at this time, except to say it is very doubtful that defective diet is the cause, although diet does seem to be the cure.

Pellagra, one of the deficiency diseases, is found mostly in the Southern states where it is sufficiently prevalent to constitute an important problem. It has been referred to as the disease of the three D's—diarrhœa, dermatitis and depression. Although a variety of mental symptoms have been reported, they do not seem to present any clinical uniformity with the possible exception of depression. The disease terminates in a psychosis with a rather high degree of frequency. It has been argued that pellagra does not directly cause but merely uncovers the psychosis, but if this is true it would seem to be a rather efficient agent for uncovering psychoses. This malady awaits a thorough investigation from the psychological angle. Concerning the question of the etiology of pellagra, it seems that a vitamin G deficiency is the most favored hypothesis at the present time. It is interesting to note that almost from the very beginning of the study of this disease, it has been thought to have some close connection with diet and treatment has nearly always been dietary.

Sprue is a disease which was formerly thought to be a purely tropical disorder. In recent years cases have been reported in the United States. Investigators have reported that it bears certain resemblances to both pellagra and pernicious anemia and that it is sometimes confused with these two maladies. The alleged presence of mental symptoms makes sprue a disease of psychological interest.

Nutritional nightblindness, to be differentiated from idiopathic nightblindness or retinitis pigmentosa, is a disorder which was known to the ancients and, what is even more interesting, they knew the cure for it—the eating of liver. Spence (7) reports that this cure is handed down as tribal lore among the Eskimos and other primitive races. Nightblindness, attributed to defective diets, has been observed in China, Newfoundland, Labrador and other places. Administration of cod liver oil is said to result in a decided improvement within twenty-four hours. The effectiveness of liver and cod liver oil as therapeutic agents points rather forcibly to a vitamin A deficiency. This factor, along with exposure to strong light, seems to offer the most plausible etiological explanation. Recent experimental work on rats supports this hypothesis. If nightblindness can be produced or cured almost at will by dietary methods, it would offer interesting possibilities for the psychological investigation of certain visual phenomena.

Beriberi, now commonly attributed to a lack of vitamin B in the diet, is characterized by peripheral nerve degeneration which results in anesthesia, paresthesia and disturbed reflexes. There have been relatively few observations of disturbance of the higher mental processes. However, several reports of neural degeneration in the spinal cord and brain suggest the possibility that some mental effects might be found, were a careful psychological investigation made.

Acrodynia is a children's disease which has come to occupy the attention of pediatricians in recent years. The patients are said to present such a picture of abject misery that a case once seen will never be forgotten. Fortunately, acrodynia does not seem to be very common. Besides the evident pain and misery, there is photo-phobia and paresthesia. Some investigators have considered diet an important factor both in causation and treatment but this is not accepted by all clinicians.

Migraine is an old affliction and few disorders have had so many etiological explanations. That it is a neurosis has been suggested but apparently this hypothesis has not greatly aided in its treatment. In recent years the supporters of food allergy have claimed that in many cases it is possible to secure great benefit or even a complete elimination of the paroxysms by means of dietary control. The symptoms of migraine should make it of considerable psychological interest. The most prevalent and essential feature is a periodic headache, generally though not always unilateral, which may vary from a short attack hardly to be noticed to complete prostration lasting for days. Sometimes there are visual phenomena, vertigo, nausea and a feeling of dullness. Although the victims report that an attack means considerable shock to the body, there does not seem to be any deterioration of mentality as in the case of epilepsy. It is even a prevalent idea that only individuals of superior intellect are subject to migraine but this has been sharply challenged. Psychological tests should prove to be of value in settling this point.

The mental features of epilepsy are familiar to psychologists and so will not be given special consideration. This disease, known since antiquity, has provoked a great variety of treatments directed toward supposed causes ranging from spirits to physical pathology. In recent years, one more method of treatment has been added to the list and that is the ketogenic diet. For this reason it becomes necessary to consider epilepsy in a discussion of psychodietetics. The ketogenic diet is enthusiastically supported by some, who explain failures on the grounds that the subjects either did not adhere rigidly to the dietary schedule or else were confirmed institutional cases. It is claimed that cases of petit mal and newly developed cases are most successfully treated. Those who support food allergy as a causal factor maintain that the particular food or foods to which the individual is sensitive are accidentally withheld in the ketogenic diet. If the belief, strongly held by some, that epilepsy is a disorder of metabolism is correct, then we may have some hopes that dietary treatment will be of benefit. It seems to be widely accepted that brain lesions may lead to epileptic seizures, in which case diet could hardly be expected to have any influence. The suggestion has been made that infantile convulsions might be controlled by eliminating offending proteins from the diet and in this way avoiding future cases of epilepsy. On the whole, it may be said that dietary control in the early stages of epilepsy looks promising but much work still needs to be done.

Balyeat (1) reports that allergic children have a higher mental rating than non-allergic children which he suggests may be due to greater nervous sensitivity on the part of the allergic children. The nervous sensitivity would be considered a part of the greater general tissue irritability which manifests itself as a food allergy. If this hypothesis can be verified it would open the way for studies on a possible relationship between personality and food. It is evident that there are excellent opportunities for cooperative research to be carried on by allergists and psychologists.

Maurer and Tsai (5, 6) report pronounced bad effects upon the learning ability of white rats when vitamin B is withheld during the nursing period only. These findings do not necessarily conflict with those of Fritz (3) who found but little effect on mature rats even with a combination of salt defectiveness and vitamin B deficiency. That vitamin B deficiency results in nervous degeneration is hardly open to question, but what the psychological effects may be has received little attention.

It has been supposed for a number of years that intestinal toxemia is responsible for a great many alarming symptoms including profound mental effects. Some physicians, and no doubt the majority of the public, believe thoroughly in the horrible effects of intestinal toxemia. A few have flatly challenged these beliefs. Studies on voluntary constipation (2) suggest that the bad effects are reflexive and due to a packing of the colon with fecal material rather than a toxic condition. The difficulty of stating exactly what is meant by intestinal toxemia and how it would be produced, along with the scarcity of well-controlled experimental investigations, still leaves this field a "free for all." However, if it is as prevalent as is generally thought and the nervous and mental symptoms are as profound as it is often claimed, then there can be no doubt that scientific information would be of the greatest practical value.

It seems very probable, judging from rather careful experimental work, that vitamin B deficiency will result in anorexia. Clinically, it is found that feeding infants a high vitamin B diet stimulates appetite.

It is not possible at this time to take up all of the situations which should receive consideration in a discussion on psychodietetics. Some of these can only be mentioned. Neurasthenia, hyperexcitability, "nervousness," sexual virility and fatigability are found by some to be related to diet. Racial vigor and temperament have not been clearly established as a function of food although this interpretation has been strongly defended. Instinct as a guide to food has received experimental consideration and the results would seem to point to an ability of both animals and humans to select food according to nutritional requirements.

In conclusion, it may be stated that perhaps the findings in the field of psychodietetics should, for the most part, be considered tentative. One of the conspicuous faults in most of the reported observations is the complete absence of control groups. While it is certainly true that in many cases it would be difficult, if not impossible, to secure a control group, we can hardly lower our standards of scientific accuracy because of this. The clinician must act according to the most plausible hypothesis and he can scarcely withhold treatment just to find out what will happen. It must be recognized that the clinician is treating to cure and not performing an experiment. More laboratory work is needed and a partial solution may lie in the experimental use of animals.

Only a few specific references to literature have been made in this paper since a review and fairly complete bibliography on psychodietetics up to 1933 will be published later.

REFERENCES

1. BALYEAT, R. M. The general health and mental activity of allergic children, *Amer. J. Dis. Child.*, 1929, 37, 1193–7.
2. DONALDSON, A. N. Relation of constipation to intestinal intoxication, *J. Amer. Med. Asso.*, 1922, 78, 884–8.
3. FRITZ, M. F. Maze performance of the white rat in relation to unfavorable salt mixture and vitamin B deficiency, *J. Comp. Psychol.*, 1932, 13, 365–90.
4. HULETT, A. G. The psychological and medicolegal aspects of pernicious anemia, *Med. J. and Rec.*, 1928, 127, 1–6.
5. MAURER, S., & TSAI, L. S. Vitamin B deficiency and learning ability, *J. Comp. Psychol.*, 1930, 11, 51–62.
6. MAURER, S., & TSAI, L. S. The effect of partial depletion of vitamin B complex upon learning ability in rats, *J. of Nutrition*, 1931, 4, 507–16.
7. SPENCE, J. C. A clinical study of nutritional xerophthalmia and night-blindness, *Arch. Dis. in Childhood*, 1931, 6, 17–26.
8. WOOD, B. M., & WEEKS, A. L. Fundamentals of dietetics, W. B. Saunders Co., 1930.

28: MALNUTRITION AND ENVIRONMENTAL ENRICHMENT BY EARLY ADOPTION

M. Winick, K. K. Meyer, and R. C. Harris

Numerous studies conducted in several different countries have demonstrated that malnutrition during the first two years of life, when coupled with all the other socioeconomic deprivations that generally accompany it, is associated with retarded brain growth and mental development which persist into adult life (1 3). What is not clear is the contribution of the malnutrition relative to that of the other social and cultural deprivations. When malnutrition has occurred in human populations not deprived in other ways the effects on mental development have been much less marked (4). Animal experiments have shown that early isolation results in the same type of persistent behavioral abnormalities as does early malnutrition (5). A stimulatory environment has been shown to counteract the untoward behavioral effects of early malnutrition in rats (6). These observations have led to the hypothesis that malnutrition and environmental deprivation act synergistically to isolate the infant from the normal stimulatory inputs necessary for normal development (6). In addition, they suggest that enriching the environment of previously malnourished children might result in improved development. To test this hypothesis, we have examined the current status of a group of Korean orphans who were adopted during early life by U.S. parents and who had thereby undergone a total change in environment.

Experimental Sample

The sample was drawn from records of children who had been admitted to the Holt Adoption Service in Korea between 1958 and 1967. The following criteria were established for inclusion in the sample:

1) The child must be female. This was decided in order to eliminate sex differences; and because many more female than male infants were brought to the agency they provided a larger adoptive sample to choose from.

2) Date of birth and results of physical examination at the time of admission to Holt care, including height and weight, must be available on the records.

3) The child must have been less than two years old when first admitted to Holt care and less than three years old when adopted.

4) The child must have been reported to be full term at birth.

5) The physician's examination at time of initial contact must have revealed no physical defect or chronic illness.

6) The child must have been followed by the adoption service for at least six years and must be currently in elementary school (grades 1 to 8).

7) The child must have a current mailing address in the United States.

From 908 records chosen at random 229 children were found who met all these criteria.

Table 1. Number of cases in each group.

Group	Total number	Number measured for			
		Current height	Current weight	IQ	School achievement
1	42	41	41	36	40
2	52	50	51	38	38
3	47	47	47	37	37

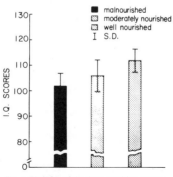

Fig. 1. The IQ's of the three nutrition groups means and standard deviations (S.D.).

- ■ malnourished
- ▨ moderately nourished
- ▨ well nourished
- I S.D.

We divided these 229 into three groups, as follows, on the basis of how their height and weight at time of admission to Holt related to a reference standard of normal Korean children of the same age (7): group 1, designated "malnourished" below the 3rd percentile for both height and weight; group 2, "moderately nourished" from the 3rd through the 24th percentile for both height and weight; group 3, "well-nourished" or control at or above the 25th percentile for both height and weight.

There were 24 children, randomly distributed through the three groups, whose height and weight were not in the same percentile grouping. These were eliminated from the sample. The remaining 205 consisted of 59 children in group 1, 76 in group 2, and 70 in group 3.

A letter was sent by the Holt Adoption Service to the parents describing the general objectives of the study and asking their cooperation. It was followed by a letter from us explaining the study in more detail and asking for permission to request information about the child from the school. Where possible, the parents were called by telephone so that any questions they had about the study could be answered. For various reasons, 64 children could not be followed 17 in group 1, 24 in group 2, and 23 in group 3. Most of this loss resulted from inability to reach the parents, from an inadequate response, or from parental refusal. The final sample thus consisted of 141 children 42 in group 1, 52 in group 2, and 47 in group 3.

Information on health, growth and nutrition, and family socioeconomic background was obtained from the families of these 141 children by means of a checklist questionnaire (8). Information about scores on standardized tests of intelligence and school performance for the years 1971 to 1973 was requested from the schools on a mailed form constructed for this purpose.

The outcome data presented here consist of current height, which was obtainable for 138 children; current weight, obtainable for 139; current IQ (9), for 111; and current achievement scores, for 115. Table 1 shows the number of children in each group about whom these data were obtained.

Results

As may be seen in Tables 2 and 3, all three groups have surpassed the expected mean (50th percentile) for Korean children in both height and weight. There is a tendency for the children in groups 1 and 2 to be smaller and lighter than in group 3, but the differences are statistically significant only between the mean heights of children in groups 1 and 3 (Table 2). Although all three groups are heavier and taller than would be expected if they had remained in Korea, their means all fall below the 50th percentile of an American standard.

The mean IQ of group 1 is 102; of group 2, 106; and of group 3, 112 (Fig. 1). Only the difference between groups 1 and 3 is statistically significant ($P \leq .005$). All the groups have reached or exceeded mean values of American children. When the data are converted to stanines (Table 4) the results are the same as with the IQ scores.

Results for achievement scores (Table 5) are similar to those for IQ's. All the groups have achieved at least to stanine 5 (the mean for U.S. school children of the same age). There is a highly statistically significant difference between group 1 and group 3 ($P \leq .001$). Differences in achievement between groups 1 and 2 just reach the level of statistical significance. All the groups are doing at least as well as would be expected from an average U.S. population.

Discussion

In the studies referred to earlier which showed persistent retardation in children malnourished during the first two years of life (1–3), after successful nutritional rehabilitation the children were sent back to the environment from which they came. Even by comparison with nonmalnourished siblings or other children from similar socioeconomic environments their growth and development were retarded (3). Thus severe malnutrition itself during the first two years of life appears to exacerbate the developmental retardation that occurs under poor socioeconomic conditions. What happens to the child from a high socioeconomic background who becomes malnourished early in life? In the few such cases that have been studied (children with cystic fibrosis or pyloric stenosis) the children have shown a much smaller degree of retardation in growth and development and have tended to catch up with time (4). What has not been determined yet and what is a much more important practical problem is the fate of a malnourished child from a poor socioeconomic background who is subsequently reared in the relatively "enriched" environment of a higher socioeconomic stratum.

In a few instances attempts have been made to modify the subsequent environment either by keeping the child longer in the hospital in a program of environmental stimulation or by sending the child home but enrolling him or her in a special preschool program designed to provide a variety of enriching experiences. Improvement in development has been noted with both these approaches but there have been reversals as soon as the special program was discontinued (10). The data suggest that if a severely malnourished child is subsequently to develop adequately, any program of environmental enrichment must be of long duration. In the present study, severely malnourished children were compared with moderately malnourished and well-nourished children after all had undergone a radical and permanent change in their environments by being adopted into primarily middle-class American homes. (The adoptive parents had no knowledge of the previous nutritional status of the child, and the distribution of these children into their adoptive homes was entirely random.) The results are in striking contrast to those obtained from similar groups of children returned to the environments from which they came (1, 2). Even the severely malnourished adopted Korean children have surpassed Korean norms of height and weight. Moreover, the marked initial size differences between the malnourished and the well-nourished infants

Table 2. Current height (percentiles, Korean reference standard): comparison of the three nutrition groups. F prob. is the probability that the calculated F ratio would occur by chance.

Group	N	Mean percentile	S.D.	F prob.	Contrast groups	t-test	
						t	P
1	41	71.32	24.98	0.068	1 vs. 2	1.25	0.264
2	50	76.86	21.25		1 vs. 3	2.22	0.029*
3	47	82.81	23.36		2 vs. 3	1.31	0.194
Total sample	138	77.24	23.41				

*Statistically significant.

Table 3. Current weight (percentiles, Korean reference standard): comparison of the three nutrition groups. F prob. is the probability that the calculated F ratio would occur by chance.

Group	N	Mean percentile	S.D.	F prob.	Contrast groups	t-test	
						t	P
1	41	73.95	24.60	0.223	1 vs. 2	1.24	0.218
2	51	79.94	20.78		1 vs. 3	1.61	0.111
3	47	82.11	22.66		2 vs. 3	0.49	0.624
Total sample	139	78.91	22.68				

Table 4. IQ stanines: comparison of the three nutrition groups. F prob. is the probability that the calculated F ratio would occur by chance.

Group	N	Mean percentile	S.D.	F prob.	Contrast groups	t-test	
						t	P
1	37	5.25	1.32	0.005	1 vs. 2	1.42	0.160
2	38	5.74	1.62		1 vs. 3	3.45	0.001*
3	37	6.46	1.66		2 vs. 3	1.91	0.061
Total sample	112	5.82	1.61				

*Statistically significant.

Table 5. Achievement stanines: comparison of the three nutrition groups. F prob. is the probability that the calculated F ratio would occur by chance.

Group	N	Mean percentile	S.D.	F prob.	Contrast groups	t-test	
						t	P
1	40	5.07	1.51	0.002	1 vs. 2	2.12	0.038*
2	38	5.79	1.47		1 vs. 3	3.60	0.001*
3	37	6.48	1.89		2 vs. 3	-1.80	0.080
Total sample	115	5.76	1.72				

*Statistically significant.

have almost entirely disappeared, leaving only a small difference in height. None of the groups reach mean values for American children of the same age. This may reflect either genetic size differences between Korean and American children or the effects of chronic undernutrition extending for several generations in developing countries such as South Korea.

Perhaps even more striking and less in accord with previously reported experience is the fact that the mean IQ of the severely malnourished children is 102 and slightly skewed to the right. It is about 40 points higher than that reported in similar populations that were returned to their early home environments (*1, 3*). In addition, achievement in school for the severely malnourished group is equal to that expected of normal U.S. children. However, the stigmata of malnutrition had not entirely disappeared by the time these children were studied. There are statistically significant differences between the previously malnourished and well-nourished children in IQ and achievement scores. Whether these are permanent differences it may be too soon to judge. It should be noted, however, that the initially well-nourished children attained a mean IQ and achievement score higher than that of middle-class American children. It may be that these attainments (and those of the other two groups as well) reflect the select character of adoptive parents and of the environment they provide to their adopted children.

In this study all the children came to their U.S. homes before the age of three — the mean age was 18 months. Thus they spent a major portion of their early developmental years in their adoptive homes. It would be important both theoretically and practically to determine whether adoption at later ages produces similar results. Such studies are being planned.

References and Notes

1. M. B. Stoch and P. M. Smythe, *Arch. Dis. Child.* **38**, 546 (1963); H. G. Birch, *Am. J. Public Health* **62**, 73 (1972).
2. J. Cravioto, E. R. De Licardie, H. G. Birch, *Pediatrics* **38**, 319 (1966).
3. M. E. Hertzig, H. G. Birch, S. A. Richardson, J. Tizard, *ibid.* **49**, 814 (1972).
4. J. D. Lloyd-Still, paper presented at the annual meeting of the Society for Pediatric Research, San Francisco, May 1974; P. S. Klein, G. B. Forbes, P. R. Nader, *Pediatrics*, in press.
5. S. Levine, in *Stimulation in Early Infancy*, A. Ambrose, Ed. (Academic Press, London, 1969), p. 21; V. Denenberg, *ibid.*, p. 62.
6. D. A. Levitsky and R. H. Barnes, *Science* **176**, 68 (1972).
7. Chang Yu Hong, *Pediatric Diagnosis and Treatment* (Yongrin, Korea, 1970).
8. A publication showing the questionnaire is in preparation.
9. Results of only four tests of mental ability, all of them group tests, were used in this study: Lorge-Thorndike Intelligence Test, Otis-Lennon Mental Ability Test, Cognitive Abilities Test, and California Test of Mental Maturity. Each of these tests has a mean of 100 and a standard deviation of 15; they were chosen, on the advice of two consulting educational psychologists, because of their equivalency. Results of the following achievement tests were used: California Achievement Test, California Test of Basic Skills, Metropolitan Achievement Test, Stanford Achievement Test, and SRA Achievement Series. To facilitate comparison of ability and achievement scores both were converted to stanine scores, the former by chronological age, the latter by school grade. In stanine scores 9 is high, 1 is low, and the mean is 5. The conversion to stanine scores was done by two educational psychologists who had no knowledge of the nutrition group assignments.
10. D. S. McLaren *et al.*, *J. Ment. Defic. Res.* **17**, 273 (1973); H. McKay and A. McKay, paper presented at the Western Hemisphere Conference, Mayaguez, Puerto Rico, October 1970.
11. Acknowledgment is made to the Agency for International Development and the Grant Foundation for support of this research. We thank J. Justman and M. Sontag for consultations on how to evaluate the school data, L. Burrill for help with converting the IQ and achievement scores into standard stanines, B. Miller for technical assistance with the sampling and mailing, and G. Raabe and B. Milcarek for computer programming.

29: THE IMPACT OF INTRAUTERINE MALNUTRITION ON THE DEVELOPMENTAL POTENTIAL OF THE HUMAN INFANT— A 14-YEAR PROGRESSIVE STUDY

R. M. Hill, W. M. Verniaud, G. Rettig, T. Zion, and A. Vorderman

During the early part of this conference we have learned of the efforts of several groups to study the behavioral effects of protein malnutrition using animal models. This morning we have heard accounts of studies on psychological sequelae of protein malnutrition occurring during the first years of life, combined with adverse environmental factors. Now I would like to present the results of a developmental follow-up, since 1963, of 33 white children who were born in the United States and manifested intrauterine malnutrition at birth (IM) and of 13 well nourished (WN) control infants.

The newborn demonstrated no evidence of chromosomal abnormalities or intrauterine infections. At the time the infants were selected for study the Colorado Intrauterine Growth Grid (3), presently used to assess intrauterine growth, was not available. Figure 1 indicates the birth weight of the infants, retrospectively plotted on the grid. Forty-five percent of the infants assessed clinically as being malnourished had birth weights above the 10th percentile.

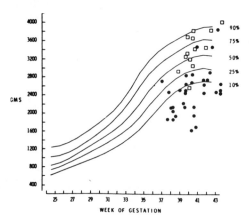

Figure 1. Intrauterine growth retrospectively plotted from birth weights (gm) of malnourished (circles) and well-nourished (squares) infants. Data is plotted on the Colorado Intrauterine Growth Grid.

Reprinted from pages 199-206 of *Behavioral Effects of Energy and Protein Deficits,* J. Brožek, ed., NIH Publication Number 79-1906, U.S. Government Printing Office, Washington, D.C., 1979, 370p.

The physical finding used in clinical assessment of intrauterine malnutrition was a lack of subcutaneous tissue, usually
most evident in the inguinal area. The skin lays in folds on
the legs, arms and back. Figure 2 shows a typical malnourished
infant. The skull is firm, the umbilical cord was small in cali-
ber, and the skin is mature in appearance. The WN infants had
normal amounts of subcutaneous tissue and lacked evidence of excess maturing. Twenty-six percent of the IM infants were post
dated (>42 weeks) compared to 15% of the WN infants. None of the
infants was born after less than 37 weeks of gestation. Sixty-
four percent of the IM infants and 46% of the WN infants were
males. All of the parents came from a middle to high socio--eco-
nomic strata and were similar somatically. Their mean level of
education was 14 years. Table 1 contains the somatic characteristics of the IM and WN infants.

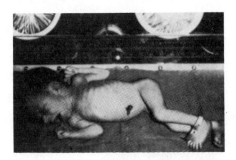

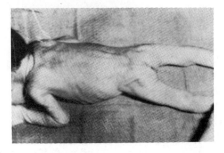

Figure 2.   Examples of infants selected for
            study who demonstrated evidence of
            intrauterine malnutrition.

Additional information regarding pregnancy events is given in a separate publication (2). Here we shall present only the psychological data and some of the neurological information which is normally noted when evaluating the developmental level of a child.

On the average, both groups received 6 psychometric evaluations during the 14-year period. Between 9 months to 3 years of age the Knobloch-Pasamanick modification of the Gesell test was administered. From 4 years through 6 years the Wechsler Preschool and Primary Scale of Intelligence (WPPSI) was utilized; from 7 to 11 years, the Wechsler Intelligence Scale for Children (WISC); and from 12 to 14 years of age, the Revised Wechsler Intelligence Scale for Children (WISC-R). The Vineland Test of Social Maturity, the Goodenough Draw-a-Man Test and the Bender Gestalt Test were also utilized. The two psychologists who administered the tests did so without prior knowledge of the child's nutritional status at birth.

Table 1. Means and ranges of somatic characteristics, at birth, of infants malnourished in utero (IM) and of well-nourished infants (WN). BW = Body weight, FOC = Frontal-occipital head circumference.

Somatic Characteristics	IM	WN
BW (grams)	2466 (1616-3856)	3419 (2552-4181)
Length (cm)	47.7 (41.0-56.0)	51.0 (48.0-53.5)
FOC (cm)	33.0 (30.0-40.0)	34.5 (32.5-36.5)

RESULTS

Psychological Findings

Figure 3 provides a comparison of the results obtained in psychometric tests in the first 3 years of life for the IM and WN infants. The IM infants performed at a lower level, throughout. At 9 months of age their performance was significantly lower on the scale of fine motor skills and on the Full Scale. By 3 years of age, it was significantly lower on all the scales ($p < 0.05$) except for gross and fine motor skills.

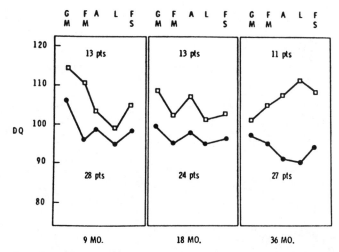

Figure 3.   Gesell Developmental Quotients (DQ) at 9-36 months
of age for children malnourished in utero (IM,
circles) and for well-nourished children (WN, squares).
FS = Full Scale DQ. Subscales : GM = Gross Motor;
FM = Fine Motor, A = Adaptive, L = Language. pts =
patients (subjects).

At 4 years of age, 3 of the 27 IM infants could not be
tested with the WPPSI test. Even at older ages (Figure 4), the
IM infants had consistently lower IQ's. The differences were
statistically significant at 4, 8 and 12-14 years (p < .05). The
results for two of the 3 IM infants who were educable mental retardates (Full Scale IQ's of 62 and 53) are not included in the
psychometric data after 18 months of age.

At 12-14 years of age, the 26 IM infants had a mean Full
Scale IQ of 104±15, the WN, 121±13 (p < .01). The mean verbal
IQ of the IM infants was 105±18, the WN, 119±13 (p < .05). The
mean performance IQ for the IM infants was 100±16, the WN, 119±14
(p < .01). At 12-14 years of age there was no statistically significant difference in the test profiles of the IM infants whose
birth weights were <10th percentile or >10th percentile. The
mean Full Scale IQ of the infants with birth weights <10th percentile was 106±17, >10th percentile, 101±13; the mean verbal
IQ, 108±21 and 101±15; the mean performance IQ, 100±20 and
100±11, respectively.

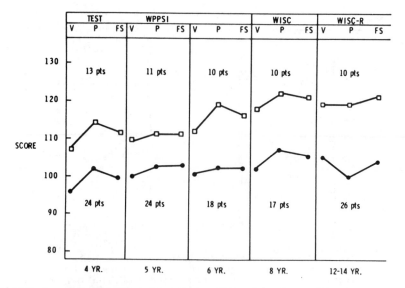

Figure 4.   Intelligence Quotients (IQ), based on different tests
(WPPSI, WISC-R) administered at ages 4-14 years, for
children malnourished in utero (IM, circles) and for
well-nourished children (WN, squares). V = Verbal,
P = Performance, FS = Full Scale. pts = patients.

Utilizing the last Full Scale IQ obtained for each infant,
it was found that 42% of the IM infants scored <101, compared to
8% for the WN infants; and 12% of the IM infants scored >121,
compared to 38% of the WN infants. Twenty-four percent of the
IM infants had Full Scale IQ of <90 while none of the WN infants
scored that low.

Eighteen percent of the IM infants required structured educational assistance (special education) in order to learn. By
contrast, none of the WN infants were identified as having such
non-compensated learning disability. Fifteen percent of the IM
and the WN infants were found to have a compensated learning disability; however, the mean Full Scale IQ in the IM group was 8
points lower, the mean verbal IQ, 10 points lower, and the mean
performance IQ, 3 points lower. Specific learning disabilities
were present in 24% of the IM infants and 15% of the WN infants.

Neurological Findings

Asymmetry of muscle tone was present with equal frequency in both groups of infants (IM, 78%; WN, 76%). In one-fifth of the infants in both groups the asymmetrical tone persisted beyond 4 years of age.

Nine percent of the IM infants developed hand dominance before 12 months of age while none of the WN infants did. Significant language problems, such as failure to develop patterns of speech and communication beyond 3 years of age, were seen in 18% of the IM children. One IM child at 14 years of age still had unintelligible speech.

Although visual problems such as strabismus, inability to converge, and the necessity for glasses **were seen with almost** equal frequency in the two categories of subjects, the severity of opthalmological problems was greater in the IM infants. One infant required surgical correction of a divergent **strabismus. A severe** visual problem (tunnel vision) occurred in another IM infant.

Twenty-four percent of the IM infants were noted to have a short attention span. The inattentiveness was most obvious in children 3 years of age or older. Hyperactivity was present in 4 IM infants (12%) and in one WN infant (8%); the IM infants but not the WN infant required medical treatment.

One IM infant (3%) had spastic diplegia. Five IM infants (15%) had seizures between 12 months and 6 years of age compared to one WN infant (8%). Seizures in the IM infants were most frequently associated with fever but three of the **five IM infants** had prior seizures in the neonatal period. Two IM infants (6%) still require anticonvulsant therapy. One WN infant had a single seizure associated with trauma.

DISCUSSION

Physicians have come to consider only those infants whose somatic measurements are 2 SD below the mean of the reference population (or below the 10th percentile on accepted growth grids) as deviating from normal growth and thus being neurologically at risk. McLean and Usher (4) and Miller (5) have long cautioned that anthropometric measurements do not adequately identify the malnourished infant and in particular, do not reliably distinguish the malnourished infant from an immature infant.

Fitzhardinge (1) reported that small-for-date infants showed elevated incidence of neurological handicaps. Table 2 compares Fitzhardinge's findings (in babies whose birth weights were below 2 SDs from the mean **for nursery of origin) and those in our IM** infants. The trend in neurological morbidity and sequelae is similar even though 45% o f the IM infants would today not be consi-

dered to suffer from intrauterine malnutrition, utilizing conventional growth grids (3,6).

We urgently need more effective methods to identify infants
who become malnourished during intrauterine development. In the
past the opinion was held by many that the poor mental performance
and neurological sequelae seen in prenatally malnourished infants
were due to their poor ability to withstand the many complications
surrounding labor and delivery and the immediate postnatal days.
With improved methods for prevention of anoxia and biochemical
abnormalities during labor and delivery and the immediate neonatal
period, we may find that neurological handicaps seen at a later
date had origin prior to labor and delivery. In the present study,
36% of the infants who manifested malnutrition at birth exhibit
neurological handicaps in the form of mental retardation, learning disabilities, cerebral palsy or permanent seizure disorders.

Since the advent of amniocentesis and ultrasound, the human
fetus is no longer an inaccessible passenger on a 9-month voyage
on an unknown, treacherous sea. The fetus in jeopardy of intrauterine malnutrition must be identified in utero. If there is
evidence that the fetus has lungs which can function properly in
an extrauterine environment, then the pregnancy should be terminated
and proper nutrients should be provided. If the lungs are immature and extrauterine survival is not possible, then supplementary nutrients required for proper fetal growth must be given.

Table 2. Comparison between the neurological morbidity observed
in small-for-gestational-age infants (Fitzhardinge)
and prenatally malnourished infants (Hill).

NEUROLOGICAL MORBIDITY FACTORS	Fitzhardinge (N = 96)	Hill (N = 33)
Year Selected	1960–66	1963–66
Duration of Follow-up	8 yrs.	14 yrs.
Criteria for Selection of Infants	Birth weight 2 SD below mean (6)	Clinical malnu-trition (3)
Gestation	38 weeks or greater	37 weeks or greater
Morbidity		
Mental Retardation	1%	9%
Convulsions after Neonatal period	6%	15%
Delayed or Absent Speech	4%	9%
Learning Disability	25%	33%
Cerebral Palsy	1%	3%
Mean Full Scale IQ	93–101	104
School Failure IQ > 100	33%	3%
IQ > 90	*	6%
Special Education	*	18%

*Not stated.

ACKNOWLEDGEMENT

The research reported in this paper was supported by the MacDonald Fund and the Doris Hebbard Knapp Grant; the Linda Fay Halbouty Premature and Newborn Research Unit, St. Luke's Episcopal Hospital; and the Blue Bird Circle for Pediatric Neurology, Methodist Hospital.

REFERENCES

1. Fitzhardinge, P. M. and Steven, E. M. The small-for-date infant. II. Neurological and Intellectual Sequelae. <u>Pediatrics</u>, 50: 50-57, 1972.

2. Hill, R. M., Verniaud, W. M., Rettig, G. M., Zion, T., Kellaway, P., Vorderman, A., Helms, P., McCulley, L., Tennyson, L., and Singleton, E. The effect of intrauterine malnutrition on the human infant - a 14-year study. Submitted for publication.

3. Lubchenco, L. O., Hansman, C., and Boyd, E. Intrauterine growth in length and head circumference as estimated from live births at gestational ages from 26 to 42 weeks. <u>Pediatrics</u>, 37: 403-408, 1966.

4. McLean, F. and Usher, R. Measurements of liveborn fetal malnutrition infants compared with similar gestation and with similar birth weight normal controls. <u>Biol. Neonate</u>, 16: 215-221, 1970.

5. Miller, H. C. and Hassanein, K. Diagnosis of impaired fetal growth in newborn infants. <u>Pediatrics</u>, 48: 511-522, 1971.

6. Usher, R. and McLean, F. **Intrauterine growth of live-born** Caucasian infants at sea level: Standards obtained from measurements in 7 dimensions of infants born between 25 and 44 weeks of gestation. <u>J. Pediat.</u>, 74: 901-910, 1969.

ERRATUM

In Figure 4 "SCORE" should read "IQ."

30: U.S. NEEDS AND PRIORITIES IN RESEARCH ON BEHAVIORAL EFFECTS OF NUTRITIONAL DEFICIENCIES

E. Pollitt, D. Greenfield, and R. Leibel

In this communication we endeavor to identify priority issues for U.S. research on the links between malnutrition and behavior, taking into account work done abroad, especially in Latin America (1,4,7). We shall advance four propositions. It should be noted that some of these propositions go beyond protein and energy deficits.

PROPOSITION ONE

There is a complex web of interactions between socio-economic factors and malnutrition affecting the mental development of children who live in poverty. The nature of these factors and their interaction vary as a function of geographic, demographic, cultural, and economic circumstances (9). In order to understand the effects of malnutrition on behavior in the U.S., it will be necessary to consider the nature and dynamics of these variables in various U.S. settings.

An example of the kind of variables relevant in the United States is provided by a study conducted in Cambridge, Massachusetts, on social characteristics of 19 undersized, underweight children, 2 to 6 years old, who had no evidence of organic derangement as a cause for their small size (10). These children were contrasted with a set of normally growing children matched for age, sex, and color of the skin. The groups were compared on variables characterizing the economic conditions and history of the families, marital adjustment of the parents, dietary habits, patterns of child care and mother-child interaction. Through a discriminant-function analysis, 16 children in each of the groups were correctly assigned to the respective anthropometric group solely on the basis of three social variables: (1) ratings of the quality of the mother-infant interaction, (2) the amount of aid mothers received in caring for their children, and (3) an aggregate family economic indicator.

A problem we encountered in the Cambridge study (and one that will reappear in future research endeavors aimed at understanding the interactions among malnutrition, the social environment, and mental development) is the selection of social factors of potential importance. This problem is aggravated by the fact that currently no theory exists that would relate the contributions of the social environment to the onset of malnutrition and to the mental development of children. No organized conceptual system is at hand from which to deduce relevant hypotheses.

Reprinted from pages 314-325 of *Behavioral Effects of Energy and Protein Deficits,* J. Brožek, ed., NIH Publication Number 79-1906, U.S. Government Printing Office, Washington, D.C., 1979, 370p.

However, a few guidelines may be obtained from recent studies of the changes in the structure of the American family and from health analyses conducted in a sociological context. Let us briefly review some of these data to clarify this point.

Demographic data included in a 1976 report on National Policy for Children and Families (8) show that there has been a marked increase in the number of single-parent families in the U.S. Figure 1 presents the number of single-parent families expressed as percentage of all families with children under 18, under 6, under 3, and from 6 through 17 years of age. An upward trend is evident for all categories but it is most steep for single-parent families with children under 6 or under 3 years of age. They almost doubled between 1968 and 1975. The contributing factors include increases both in the illegitimacy ratio and in the number of divorces without remarriages.

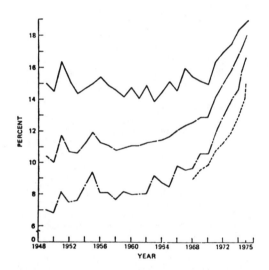

Figure 1. Single-parent families as a percentage of all families with children of different ages (1948-1975). Symbols: ———— 6-17, — — — under 18, —————— under 6 (includes those under 3), ———————— under 3 years of age.

The number of low-income, single-parent families headed by females--young and poorly educated--is rising rapidly

(Figure 2). In 1974, the median income for single mothers under 25 years of age was $3,021, and there were about 500,000 women in this category.

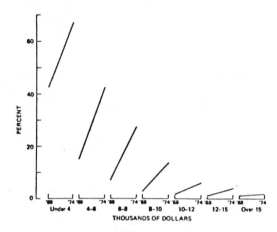

Figure 2.   Female-headed families as a percentage of
             all families in which the head of the house-
             hold is under 65 and the children are under
             18 years of age, by income in the previous
             year (1968-1974).

Figure 3 breaks down the percentage of single-parent families (1959-1975) with children under 18 years of age according to education of the head of the household. It shows that the less schooling a mother has, the more likely she is to be a single parent.

These data on family changes in the United States are of particular interest in the context of demographic information concerning health status. A recent study relating differences in the birth weights of infants and the social characteristics of their families in 326 health districts of New York City (12) is illuminating. The rate of low birth weight was defined in this study as a ratio of the number of children born alive between 1958 and 1962 who weighed under 2501 grams, divided by the total number of children born alive during that same period. The overall prevalence of low birth weight was 93 infants per thousand live births, with a range of 41 to 175. This variable was then examined in relation to income, familial, and race characteristics.

A hierarchical correlational analysis indicated that overcrowding
and low income accounted for 64% of the variance of low birth
weight while separation and divorce added 16% to the statistically
explained variance. Thus, 80% of the variability in low birth
weight could be accounted for statistically by demographic
characteristics that are on the increase in the U.S.

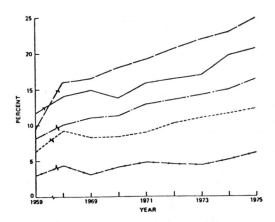

Figure 3. Percentage of families with children under
18 years of age headed by a single parent,
by education of head of household (1959-
1975). Symbols: — ·— — elementary school,
————— some high school, —·——·—· completed high school, --·--····--- some college,
—·— -·— -·— completed college.

Consequently, it seems to us, it would be pertinent to examine the potential association between current alterations in the
patterns of child care in the U.S. and nutritional deprivation,
at different points in a child's life and within a matrix of rural
and urban samples differing in ethnic composition and cultural
setting.

PROPOSITION TWO

The effects of nutrition intervention programs aimed at preventing deficits in child growth and development are generally
broader than their specified goals. In the caregivers and in the
children themselves, they modify behavior related to health and
nutrition (by treatment co-variants or treatment-context

actions); this may have greater preventive impact than the intervention itself (11). However, little is known about the exact
nature or true magnitude of this impact. Evaluations of food
supplementation programs in the U.S. would, therefore, profit
from assessments of these broader effects on health and malnutrition.

For a discussion of this proposition in the U.S. context we
shall selectively focus on the Federal WIC (Women, Infants and
Children) Program, a $250,000,000 per annum USDA-sponsored pro-
gram for low-income pregnant and lactating women, infants, and
children up to 5 years of age. WIC now operated through state
health departments in 49 states as well as Puerto Rico and the
Virgin Islands. About one million individuals received food
through this program in fiscal year 1977. It began in 1974 as
an effort to provide specific foods (formula, milk, cheese, eggs,
fruit juices and cereals) to segments of the population at "nutritional risk" by virtue of socio-economic status, age, pregnancy, medical state or dietary practice. In time the scope of this
program has been deliberately widened to include mandated nutrition education for its recipients. The educational portion of
the program represented approximately 5% ($12.5 million) of the
total expenditures in fiscal year 1977.

The medical evaluation of the early phase of the WIC Program
(2) indicated that there was accelerated somatic growth including increased head circumference, as well as augmented hemoglobin
concentration in participating infants and children. Pregnant
women were found to gain more weight and to have longer gestation
periods and larger infants; there was also a reduction in the rate
of anemia in these women. Although the apparently unavoidable
lack of suitable controls renders these studies suspect in detail,
it should be noted that others have reported similar changes in
individuals exposed to comparable feeding programs in this country (6). Furthermore, studies conducted on the gravida/child
population of Cambridge, Massachusetts (Leibel, R., unpublished
data), before and after the institution of a WIC Program, have
demonstrated reduction in the prevalence of both lead poisoning
and iron-deficiency anemia, as well as a decline in the percentage
of full-term births in the 5 lb.- 5 lb. 8 oz. category, without
concomitant shifts in the incidence of prematurity. This is the
weight range in which one might anticipate the greatest impact of
a maternal feeding program.

One may reasonably ask whether the modest anthropometric and
biochemical changes associated with such programs are biologically
significant,and if so, whether they are in fact worth the cost
in dollars and efforts. The complex, and as yet poorly understood interactions between nutritional input, other environmental
factors, and individual biological characteristics make it likely
that, beyond a certain point (and most U.S. citizens are beyond
it), augmented calorie and/or protein intake alone will provide

diminishing returns if enhanced psychosocial performance is the goal. WIC, however, may ultimately prove to be beneficial not because it provides additional calories and protein to what are usually, at worst, marginally malnourished individuals, but because it involves legislated access to medical care and makes available a captive population for nutrition and health indoctrination.

Programs such as WIC provide an opportunity to practice the preventive-medicine approach, tacitly implied in much of the current public health literature on nutrition. The assumption is that a prudent and scientifically sound diet, wedded to a medical program of health maintenance, will prolong life, improve its quality and, at the same time, reduce the cost to society of so-called "diseases of choice" (5). Yet even allowing for the probable validity of this assumption, we do not have the knowledge to produce the requisite behavioral changes in the population; we know more about the influence of nutrition on behavior than the converse. Before committing large amounts of money to "nutrition education," we need to investigate the efficacy of our current methods in that field. There is reason to believe that much of the money now being spent to evaluate such programs as WIC is not being used efficiently or effectively (13). We need, first of all, to demonstrate that nutrition-related behavior can be significantly altered by education, in the broadest sense of the word; and then examine in detail the ideal program content, target group(s), and methods for educating the U.S. population in practical nutrition. Undoubtedly, much could be learned regarding the latter issue from the advertising industry.

The long-range impact of medically administered supplemental food programs like WIC is more likely to be reflected in the educational than in the gross somatic effects. Accordingly, in research we should focus our attention not on the short-range physical effects, but on the actual and potential capability of such programs to produce long-term salutary changes in the health-related choices and activities of the target populations. Rather than continuing to search for small increases in head circumference, stature, weight, and hemoglobin (which may or may not be attributable to supplementary feeding), their broader potential impact on health status and health-related behavior should be studied. Only through the development of such an admittedly complex socio-medical approach shall we be able ultimately to assess the real impact of such programs and to make wise decisions regarding the disposition of health-care dollars.

PROPOSITION THREE

Vitamin and mineral deficiencies may often be partly responsible for the behavioral alterations noted in energy-protein malnutrition. Data already available suggest that iron deficiency, in particular, affects specific behavioral functions, such as the

maintenance of attention. Iron deficiency is frequent in the
United States and should be studied systematically for possible
behavioral impact.

In Cambridge, Massachusetts, we have been conducting a prospective study regarding the effects of iron deficiency on attention, memory, and learning. Our sample consisted of 23 children
who were iron-deficient at the time of initial testing, and 23
matched controls. Activity level and intelligence were also assessed. At present, only preliminary data are available.

In terms of serum iron (SI) related to total iron-binding
capacity (SI/TIBC), iron deficiency was defined as a saturation
of 17% or less. The hemoglobin values of the control children
exceeded 11g% (g/100 cc), and the SI/TIBC values exceeded 20%.
Each iron-deficient child was matched with a child of the same
sex, race and age. Each group consisted of 17 boys and 6 girls.

Table 1 summarizes the characteristics of the two groups at
the time of initial testing. As the table shows, the two groups
were similar in height and weight, identical in age, but differed
significantly in some aspects of their hematologic status. It
should be noted that the mean hemoglobin and hematocrit values
for both groups were high, indicating that the children who were
iron-deficient (in terms of SI/TIBC) were only mildly, if at all,
anemic (in terms of hemoglobin and hematocrit).

Table 1. Status of iron-deficient and normal
groups at initial testing.

| Variable | Iron-Deficient | | Normal | | P < |
	Mean	S.D.	Mean	S.D.	(t-test)
Hemoglobin (g/100cc)	11.5	0.9	12.1	0.5	0.025
Hematocrit (%)	32.9	2.8	34.1	1.4	0.05
Serum iron (SI) (µg/100 cc)	35.0	10.0	77.7	17.1	0.001
SI/TIBC (%)	13.4	3.3	29.0	6.9	0.001
Age (months)	45.4	8.6	44.9	9.0	N.S.
Height (cm)	101.2	6.9	100.8	6.4	N.S.
Weight (kg)	16.7	3.5	17.0	2.5	N.S.

Each child received a complete physical examination and two consecutive days of behavioral testing. Each session was approximately one hour long. Before the beginning of the first testing session, the experimenter spent about 10 minutes playing with the child and establishing rapport. The experimenter had no knowledge of the hematologic status (anemic, iron-deficient, normal) of the child during the administration of the behavioral tests.

Following this initial phase, all anemic children (Hb < 11; SI/TIBC < 20) and half the children with iron deficiency but no anemia (SI/TIBC < 20; Hb ≥ 11) were treated for 4 months with oral iron (either as drops or syrup) at a dose of 3 to 4 mg of elemental iron per kilogram of body weight per day. After a 4-month period, all children, regardless of iron status or treatment condition, were given a second physical examination and 2 days of behavioral testing. Again, the experimenter had no knowledge of the hematologic status of a child.

The tests were designed to assess "structural" and "control" characteristics of attention, memory, and learning (3). The "structural" features deal with permanent capacity whereas the "control" processes regulate momentary fluctuations in the processing of information. These concepts will be discussed at greater length in PROPOSITION FOUR.

On measures of structural features, no differences appeared between the two groups at either testing period. However, iron-deficient children performed less well than the normal children on three of five measures of control processes at the time of initial testing. The iron-deficient children were less able to attend selectively to relevant information, used less appropriate rehearsal strategies when their memory system was overloaded, and responded to salient stimuli less frequently than children who were not iron-deficient. All these deficits were eliminated once the iron status was restored to normal.

Although there have been studies pertaining to the possible impact of iron deficiency on behavior, none has approached the problem with the degree of rigor that we have been able to achieve in our study. Moreover, we are not aware of any published information documenting the existence of specific cognitive alterations associated with iron deficiency, per se, rather than with iron-deficiency anemia. We strongly feel that this area of research needs further expansion in the United Sates.

Although this study demonstrates an impact of iron deficiency on aspects of behavior one would assume to be important for learning, the overall contribution of such a deficiency to scholastic performance might be small. The study's major importance may consist in the development of a methodology for studying the behavioral impact of micronutrient disturbances in men. An expansion of projects investigating the behavioral effects of specific nutritional deficiency states is, in our opinion, a high-priority item.

PROPOSITION FOUR

Energy-protein and micronutrient deficits may alter different neurophysiological systems and functions. Importantly, contemporary theories of cognitive processing should be incorporated into the theoretical framework for research on malnutrition and behavior. This proposition is particularly relevant to the United States where operational facilities and techniques exist that are required for the application of sophisticated theories of mental function.

Although the fact is generally recognized, it may be useful to emphasize that a global, conglomerate measure of cognitive development, such as an IQ test, may yield differences between groups that are difficult to interpret. The differences may be due to a number of factors, including deficits of motivation, memory, learning, or language. Furthermore, if only one of these processes is affected by the nutrition variable in question, the lack of differences on the remaining variables comprising the conglomerate measure may mask this difference.

Conversely, if the test battery consists of a loose collection of behavioral tests, not fitting into a theoretical framework, significant differences obtained for some of the tests may also be difficult to interpret. Are the differences spurious? Do several differences reflect the same process? How do these differences relate to the function of the central nervous system?

To illustrate this point, let us use as an example the study on stores of body iron and behavior that we are conducting in Cambridge. The battery of psychological tests was based on a theory (3) considering attention, memory and learning in the development of preschool children. As noted earlier, the theory distinguishes between "structural features" and "control processes."

The structural features of cognitive functions may be compared to the hardware of a computer: they will determine how much information can be attended to and processed within a given time, and how much information may be stored in memory. Control processes, on the other hand, are analogous to computer software. Like computer programs, they are modifiable; they determine how a particular set of data will be processed at a given time. For example, regardless of the size of a memory system, an individual may or may not remember the information presented, depending upon whether or not he pays attention to what he sees and whether or not he rehearses the information in memory. Both the capacity for processing information and the choice of processing strategy will determine what is learned. Thus, although both structural deficits and processing deficits can lead to behavioral deficits, differentiating between these two aspects is most important if the aim is to disentangle the nutrition-behavior relations. The theoretical model we adopted enables us to do just that.

CONCLUSION

Anyone who has had the temerity to attempt to untie the Gordian knot that binds nutrition to behavior will encounter a substantial amount of frustration. The number of variables involved and their interrelations defy current methods of data collection and analysis.

We have presented four propositions which we believe will help to begin to unravel this complex problem. Although the web of interactions between socio-economic factors and malnutrition is tightly spun, we have indicated what we believe to be promising guidelines for the selection of factors that are likely to exert significant influences. We have also indicated the pressing need for the evaluation of nutrition intervention programs and the expansion of investigations on the relationship between nutritional deficiencies and behavior. We are now beginning to get a glimpse of the fabric that will result from the interweaving of the various threads of relevant information.

The final point we wish to make is that a comprehensive, coherent theoretical framework permitting workers in a wide variety of disciplines to formulate hypotheses and design experiments relating nutrition to behavior is conspicuously absent. In the final analysis, gigantic correlational matrices do little to advance our understanding of the interaction between nutrition, socio-economic and cultural environment, and behavior. Although the information on which to base such a theoretical structure is admittedly limited, without such a structure the data gathered will be of little value.

ACKNOWLEDGMENT

The work on which this paper is based has been supported in part by the National Institutes of Health Grant No. 1R22 HD09228; the Department of Health, Education and Welfare; and the Ford Foundation.

REFERENCES

1. Chávez, A., Martínez, C. and Yaschine, T. The importance of nutrition and stimuli on child mental and social development. In J. Cravioto, L. Hambraeus, and B. Vahlquist, Eds., <u>Early Malnutrition and Mental Development.</u> Uppsala: Almquist & Wiksell, pp. 221-225, 1974.

2. Ediozien, J. C., Switzer, B. R. and Bryan, R. B. <u>Medical Evaluation of the Special Supplemental Food Program for Women, Infants and Children (WIC). Summary and Conclusions.</u> Department of Nutrition, School of Public Health, University of North Carolina, Chapel Hill, N.C, 1976.

3. Fisher, M. A. and Zeaman, D. An attention-retention theory of retardate discrimination learning. In N. R. Ellis, Ed., <u>International Review of Research in Mental Retardation</u>, Vol. 7. New York: Academic Press, pp. 171–257, 1973.

4. Freeman, H. F., Klein, R. W., Kagan, J. and Yarbrough, C. Relations between nutrition and cognition in rural Guatemala. <u>Am. J. Publ. Health</u>, 67:233-239, 1977.

5. Jacobson, H. N. Current concepts in nutrition diet in pregnancy. <u>New Engl. J. Med.</u>, 297:1051- 1053, 1977.

6. Kafatos, A. G. and Zee, P. Nutritional benefits from federal food assistance. <u>Am. J. Dis. Child.</u>, 131:265-]69, 1977.

7. Mora, J. O., Paredes, B., Wagner, M., Navarro, L., Suescun, J., Christiansen, N. and Herrera, G. M. Nutritional supplementation and the outcome of pregnancy. I. Birthweight. <u>Am. J. Clin. Nutr.</u> (in press).

8. National Research Council--National Academy of Sciences. <u>Towards a National Policy for Children and Families.</u> Washington, D.C.: National Academy of Sciences, 1976.

9. Pollitt, E. Nutrition and behavior of infants and toddlers: Review of data from quasi-experimental studies in Latin A-America. In R. Suskind, Ed., <u>Pediatric Nutrition</u>. New York: Raven Press (in press).

10. Pollitt, E. and Leibel, R. Biological and social correlates of failure to thrive. In L. Greene and F. Johnston, Eds., <u>Social and Biological Predictors of Nutritional Status, Physical Growth and Behavioral Development.</u> New York: Academic Press (in press).

11. Pollitt, E. and Thomson, C. Protein malnutrition and behavior: A view from psychology. In R. J. Wurtman and J. J. Wurtman, Eds., <u>Nutrition and the Brain, Vol. 2.</u> New York: Raven Press, pp. 261-306, 1977.

12. Struening, E. C., Rabkin, J.G., Cohen, P., Raabe, G., Nuhlin, G. L. and Cohen, J. Family, ethnic and economic indicators of low birth weight infants and infant mortality: A social area analysis. <u>Ann. N.Y. Acad. Sci.</u>, pp. 87-107, 1973.

13. The Urban Institute. <u>Toward Efficiency and Effectiveness in the WIC Delivery System.</u> Washington, D.C.: The Urban Institute, 1976.

Addendum to Part VIII

We shall note but not comment on U.S. studies of fasting, early (Langfeld, 1914; Marsh, 1916) or recent (Pollitt et al., 1982/1983); the reports of studies on the relations between body dimensions and measured intelligence, summarized by Paterson (1930) and yielding coefficients of correlation that were close to zero; an early paper on nutritional improvement of child mentality (Kugelmass, Poull, and Samuel, 1944); monographs on thiamine supplementation of the diet of children living in an orphanage (Harrell, 1943, 1947); a flurry of reports on the sequelae of infantile malnutrition due to gastrointestinal disorders (Lloyd-Still et al., 1974; Klein, Forbes, and Nader, 1975; Beardsley et al., 1982); and supplementation in pregnancy (Rush, Stein, and Susser, 1981).

SEQUELAE OF CLINICAL MALNUTRITION

The overwhelming majority of studies on the sequelae of infant malnutrition requiring hospitalization was carried out in the industrially less developed countries. A paper by Chase and Martin (1970), reporting observations and measurements made in Denver, Colorado, is one of the rare exceptions.

In this study, the age at which an infant was hospitalized proved to be an important factor: Infants in whom undernutrition was corrected before the age of four months had a normal DQ when examined 3.5 years later, with a mean DQ of 95 versus 99 for the controls. By contrast, for children hospitalized after four months (and thus in whom severe undernutrition persisted probably for a longer time), the mean DQ was 70. The assessment was made with the Yale Revised Developmental Examination Schedule.

The Denver study is also of interest in that the child-parent interaction was assessed, using Caldwell's (1967) Home Stimulation Inventory Scale, and the social conditions of the family were characterized on the basis of the San Mateo County Social Functioning Scale (Chope and Blackford, 1963). With a score of 50 as the normal reference point, the index mothers scored significantly more poorly (42) than the control mothers (48). The biosocial risk factors included poorer health of the family, parental separation, alcohol-related problems, inadequate finances, large families, and high frequency of unwanted pregnancies.

THEORY AND METHODOLOGY

There is no lack of models linking a web of determinants to the behavioral effects of malnutrition (Brožek, 1984), but they are, for the most part, too general. The macromodels must be supplemented and stregthened by micromodels of limited sectors of the web.

Tucker and Sandstead (1984) gave consideration to theoretical models that aim to clarify the role of nutrients in neuropsychological development. Such endeavors call for taking into account the altered metabolic processes, anatomical specificity of nutritional insults, impairment in the transmission of nervous impulses and in the regulation of cortical arousal and attention, and the translation of neurophysiological processes into behavior, including cognition.

Tucker and Sandstead note that:

> The need for a clearer formulation of hypotheses concerning the way nutrients participate in the metabolic processes is fully recognized, while the importance of clear and explicit psychological theory in research on malnutrition and behavior is not as widely appreciated. [1984, p. 353]

Tucker and Sandstead view cognition as a function of the brain involved in the handling of information requisite to cope with the demands of life—information input, processing, storage, and output. While the brain-as-a-computer model is considered useful, it has severe limitations in the search for the links—biochemical, neurophysiological, and neuropsychological—between nutrient intake and behavior.

A related but different issue is the use of an information-processing paradigm in the development of test batteries for research on the effects of malnutrition on cognitive functioning. The approach was described in a chapter on methods for behavioral assessment of the consequences of malnutrition (Pollitt, 1984, pp. 190-200) and used in the study on the effects of iron deficiency in preschool children in Cambridge, Massachusetts (Pollitt, Leibel, and Greenfield, 1983). Pollitt et al., (1984) expanded their concern to the possibility of using a test battery, derived from a theoretical model proposed by Fisher and Zeaman (1973), in different cultural settings. The battery taps attention, conceptual learning, and memory processes. In addition to Cambridge, the tests were administered in two Guatemalan villages. The authors interpret the data as "strongly supporting the validity of process-oriented research in cross-cultural studies" (Pollitt et al., 1984, p. 186).

FROM THEORY TO PRACTICE: NUTRITIONAL SUPPLEMENTATION

Critical discussion, even controversy, facilitates the progress of science. For this reason it would have been useful to reprint in this volume a whole series of recent exchanges dealing with the effectiveness of early nutritional supplementation: the initial principal paper (Hicks, Langham, and Takenada, 1982), an editorial comment (Rush, 1982), the authors' rejoinder and discussion (Hicks, Langham, and Takenada, 1983), a comment by Pollitt and Lorimer (1983), and a closing response by the author of the initial editorial (Rush, 1983). We shall provide a brief summary as an inducement to the reader to examine critically the original publications.

Rush (1982, p. 1103) viewed the paper by Hicks and his associates (1982) as "an important first step in addressing possible effects of WIC participation [Special Supplemental Food Program for Women, Infants and Children] on cognition and behavior." However, he continued, "This study needs extension, replication and elaboration because, although [it is] of moderately sound design, there are limitations in accepting the dramatic findings as generally applicable." Rush is quite specific and points out that the sample is small, there are questions about the appropriateness of the control (comparison) subjects, the assessor was aware of a given child's status as index case or control, and the magnitude of the positive effects (termed *dramatic* by Rush) is larger than might be expected from the past studies. Rush's closing comment is constructive: The study is a challenge to look further at the behavioral and cognitive effects of the WIC feeding program.

Hicks, Langham, and Takenaka (1982) studied pairs of siblings. While the Late Supplement siblings began to participate in the supplementation program after the first year of life and continued in the program for 30.8 months, the younger siblings, constituting the Early Supplement group, began supplementation in the last trimester of pregnancy and participated in the program for 56.1 months.

At the time of testing, the older (Late Supplement) group averaged 106 months of age, and the younger (Early Supplement) group averaged 75.9 months of age.

The results indicated large differences in IQ, in favor of the younger (Early Supplement) group. To illustrate, the means of the Full Scale IQ in the Wechsler Intelligence Scale for Children were 73.4 for the older group (Late Supplement) and 86.4 for the younger (Early Supplement) group. The difference between the mean IQs (13 IQ points) is statistically highly significant.

Pollitt and Lorimer (1983) compare the improvement reported by Hicks and his colleagues (1982) to four well-controlled studies on the effects of nutritional supplementation on mental development. The mean scores on developmental scales, obtained in children tested at ages of 4 to 18 months, are presented in tabular form. Additional data are cited for children studied in preschool and early school years. The critics conclude that "the magnitude of the effects reported by Hicks et al. are inconsistent with those found in more controlled studies" (Pollitt and Lorimer, 1983, p. 696). They consider a number of factors that could account for what appears to be an anomalous finding. Oversimplifying, one may question whether using older siblings for comparison with the younger ones is appropriate since, in economically impoverished populations, the IQ of the children tends to decrease with age, perhaps reflecting a cumulative deficit in the environmental factors supporting mental development.

This factor could certainly account for a part of the difference. However, it is not likely to explain away the positive effect. Let us take a closer look at the figures reported in Pollitt and Lorimer's (1983) table. While it is true that in the New York study no positive effect of supplementation on intellective performance could be demonstrated, in the Bogotá study the differences in favor of the supplemented children ranged, in infants of different age, from 1.0 to 3.7 DQ points. In Guatemala the High Supplement group exceeded the Low Supplement group by 4.0 points on the mental scale at the age of 6 months; at the age of 15 months the values were 73.8 versus 62.9, yielding a mean difference of 10.2

points. The difference is not dramatically distinct from the figure reported by Hicks and his associates.

Thus, the true value of gain is likely to be less than Hick's 13 IQ points but more than the zero effect observed in the New York study. How much more? This issue calls for additional analyses, including the age effect on the decrement in measured intelligence in the age range of the children in the study by Hicks and co-workers.

IRON DEFICITS

Over the last 25 years the psychological concomitants of nutritional iron deficiency, particularly its milder forms, have attracted more attention in the United States than the deficits of any other single micronutrient. In 1968 a team of nutritionists, biochemists, and behavioral scientists initiated at Tulane University a series of studies on the effects of iron deficits, as reflected in low levels of hemoglobin (Sulzer, 1971). In summarizing, Smith, Sulzer, and Goldsmith (1975, p. 428) stated that "Children with high hemoglobin levels showed better performance in the Kahn Intelligence test and, in the younger group, in simple and disjunctive reaction time tests." They concluded that "Nutritional intervention through diet or micronutrient supplementation can improve performance in tasks demanding attentiveness."

In the early 1970s Webb and Oski (1973) reported that young black adolescents with iron deficiency anemia, especially males, had significantly lower scores on a battery of school achievement tests than did the nonanemic fellow students. In a follow-up study (Webb and Oski, 1974), 38 anemic and 36 nonanemic male subjects were selected on the basis of a hematological survey of 1,800 high school students living in an economically depressed, virtually all-black section of Philadelphia. Using the Behavior Problem Checklist (Peterson, 1961), English teachers unaware of the hematological status of the students provided observational ratings. No statistically significant mean differences were obtained on the rating scales labeled Personality Disturbances and Inadequacy-Immaturity, while Conduct Problems tended to be severer in the anemic 13-year-olds, and the difference became statistically highly significant for the 14-year-olds.

A milestone in the history of research on iron deficiency was a conference held in 1981; the proceedings appeared in print the next year (Pollitt and Leibel, 1982).

In 1983 Pollitt, Leibel, and Greenfield, utilizing sophisticated behavorial methodology, established the presence of significant differences in the test performance of preschool children who were iron deficient and the matched nondeficient controls. Treatment of the deficient group with an oral iron preparation for four to six months, with a dosage of 4 to 5 mg of iron per kilogram of body weight, normalized the iron status of the previously iron deficient children. At that time the initial differences in test performance were eliminated. Thus the study demonstrated that alterations in cognitive function observed in mildly iron deficient children, three to six years old, are reversible.

REFERENCES

Beardsley, W. R., P. H. Wolff, I. Hurwitz, B. Parikh, and H. Shwachman, 1982, The Effects of Infantile Malnutrition on Behavioral Development: A Follow-up Study, *Am. J. Clin. Nutr.* **35:**1437-1441.

Brožek, J., 1984, Why Theories? in *Malnutrition and Behavior: Critical Assessment of Key Issues,* J. Brožek and B. Schürch, eds., Nestlé Foundation Publication Series, vol. 4, Lausanne Switzerland, pp. 338-347.

Caldwell, B. M., 1967, Descriptive Evaluations of Child Development and of Developmental Settings, *Pediatrics* **40:**46-54.

Chase, H. P., and H. P. Martin, 1970, Undernutrition and Child Development, *New Engl. J. Med.* **282:**933-939.

Chope, H. D., and I. Blackford, 1963, The Chronic Problem Family: San Mateo County Experience, *Am. J. Orthopsychiatry* **33:**462-469.

Fisher, M. A., and D. Zeaman, 1973, An Attention-Retention Theory of Retardate Discrimination Learning, *Int. Rev. Res. Ment. Retard.* **6:**169-256.

Harrell, R. F., 1943, Effect of Added Thiamine on Learning, Columbia University Teachers College, New York, 55p.

Harrell, R. F., 1947, *Further Effects of Added Thiamine on Learning and Other Processes,* Columbia University Teachers College, New York, 102p.

Hicks, L. E., R. A. Langham, and J. Takenaka, 1982, Cognitive and Health Measures Following Early Nutritional Supplementation: A Sibling Study, *Am. J. Public Health* **72:**1110-1118.

Hicks, L. E., R. A. Langham, and J. Takenaka, 1983, Interpretation of Behavioral Findings in Studies of Nutritional Supplementation, *Am. J. Public Health* **73:**695-697.

Klein, P. S., G. B. Forbes, and P. R. Nader, 1975, Effects of Starvation in Infancy (Pyloric Stenosis) on Subsequent Learning Abilities, *J. Pediatr.* **87:**8-15.

Kugelmass, I. N., L. E. Poull, and E. L. Samuel, 1944, Nutritional Improvement of Child Mentality, *Am. J. Med. Sci.* **208:**631-633.

Langfeld, H. S., 1914, On the Psychophysiology of Prolonged Fast, *Psychol. Monogr.* **16**(5):1-50 (plus appendixes).

Lloyd-Still, J. D., I. Hurwitz, P. H. Wolff, and H. Shwachman, 1974, Intellectual Development After Severe Malnutrition in Infancy, *Pediatrics* **53:**306-311.

Marsh, H. D., 1916, Individual and Sex Differences Brought Out by Fasting, *Psychol. Rev.* **23:**437-445.

Paterson, D. G., 1930, *Physique and Intellect,* The Century Company, New York, 304p.

Peterson, D. R., 1961, Behavior Problems of Middle Childhood, *J. Consult. Psychol.* **25:**205-209.

Pollitt, E., 1984, Methods for the Behavioral Assessment of the Consequences of Malnutrition, in *Methods for the Evaluation of the Impact of Food and Nutrition Programs,* D. E. Sahn, R. Lockwood, and N. S. Scrimshaw, eds., The United Nations University, Tokyo, pp. 179-203.

Pollitt, E., and R. L. Leibel, eds., 1982, *Iron Deficiency: Brain Biochemistry and Behavior,* Raven Press, New York, 214p.

Pollitt, E., and R. Lorimer, 1983, Effects of WIC on Cognitive Development, *Am. J. Public Health* **73:**698-700.

Pollitt, E., R. L. Leibel, and D. B. Greenfield, 1983, Iron Deficiency and Cognitive Test Performance in Preschool Children, *Nutr. Behav.* **1:**137-146.

Pollitt, E., N. L. Lewis, C. Garza, and R. J. Shulman, 1982/1983, Fasting and Cognitive Function, *J. Psychiatr. Res.* **17:**698-700.

Pollitt, E., D. B. Greenfield, C. Saco-Pollitt, and S. Joos, 1984, A Validation of Attention-Retention Tests in Studies of Malnutrition in Two Cultures, in *Malnutrition and*

Behavior: Critical Assessment of Key Issues, J. Brožek and B. Schürch, eds., Nestlé Foundation Publication Series, vól. 4, Lausanne, Switzerland, pp. 186-202.

Rush, D., 1982, Is WIC Worthwhile? (An Editorial), *Am. J. Public Health* **72:**1101-1103.

Rush, D., 1983, In Response to Hicks et al., *Am. J. Public Health* **73:** 700-701.

Rush, D., Z. Stein, and M. Susser, 1981, *Diet in Pregnancy: A Randomized Controlled Trial of Nutritional Supplement,* A. R. Liss, New York, 200p.

Smith, J. L., J. L. Sulzer, and G. A. Goldsmith, 1975, Prevention of Vitamin and Mineral Deficiencies Associated with Protein-Calorie Malnutrition, in *Protein-Calorie Malnutrition,* R. E. Olson, ed., Academic Press, New York, pp. 415-429.

Sulzer, J. L., 1971, Effects of Iron Deficiency on Psychological Tests in Children, in *Extent and Meaning of Iron Deficiency in the U.S.: Summary of Proceedings,* Food and Nutrition Board, National Academy of Sciences, Washington, D.C., pp. 70-76.

Tucker, D. M., and H. Sandstead, 1984, Nutrition and Brain Function, in *Malnutrition and Behavior: Critical Assessment of Key Issues,* J. Brožek and B. Schürch, eds., Nestlé Foundation Publication Series, vol. 4, Lausanne, Switzerland, pp. 348-356.

Webb, T. E., and F. A. Oski, 1973, Iron Deficiency Anemia May Affect Scholastic Achievement in Young Adolescents, *J. Pediatr.* **87:**827-829.

Webb, T. E., and F. A. Oski, 1974, Behavioral Status of Young Adolescents with Iron Deficiency, *J. Spec. Educ.* **8:**153-156.

Part IX

Overview

Papers 31 and 32: Commentary

31 RICCIUTI
*Developmental Consequences of Malnutrition in Early
Childhood*

32 BROŽEK
Many Faces of Nutrition

Malnutrition and Human Behavior provides a selective portrait of twentieth-century research on the behavioral effects of malnutrition, quantitative (involving a reduction in the food intake) and qualitative (referring to deficits of specific nutrients). Both the clinical (acute) and subclinical (chronic) forms of generalized malnutrition are considered. The volume deals only with human studies.

One of the early outlines of this volume called for centering it around systematic, published reviews. This would have enhanced the continuity of the story, broadened the coverage of the literature, and provided additional information. A temptation to reprint overviews was successfully resisted in the body of the book. The volume will close with two review-type papers.

Paper 31 supplements some of the recent, extensive reviews of the literature on malnutrition and behavior, cited in the opening part of the paper, by a synthesis of the major research strategies, and considers, in a broader perspective, current research developments and needs. This topic has been examined with specific reference to the United States in Paper 30.

Paper 31 focuses on three subtopics: the interaction between malnutrition and the social environment (cf. Brožek, 1981), mechanisms through which malnutrition may affect cognitive functioning (cf. Brožek and Schürch, 1984), and the effectiveness of nutritional and behavioral interventions in enhancing cognitive development (cf. Celedón, Colombo, and López, 1984). The author closes with the encouraging thought that properly conceived intervention research

> should add significantly to our basic understanding of the influence of malnutrition and early experience on behavioral development, while at the same time strengthening the knowledge base required for planning effective social programs aimed at prevention and remediation of suboptimal development. [p. 170 of Paper 31]

Paper 32 is a review of an armful of book-length publications, supplemented in the Addendum by comments on the most recent arrivals. The aim is to round out the portrait of psychodietetics (psychonutrition) and to bring the reader up-to-date in regard to the nonperiodical literature.

REFERENCES

Brožek, J., 1981, Malnutrition, Environment, and Behavior, in *Nutrition in Health and Disease and International Development,* Symposia from the 12th International Congress of Nutrition, A. R. Liss, New York, pp. 372-382.

Brožek, J., and B. Schürch, eds., 1984, *Malnutrition and Behavior: Critical Assessment of Key Issues,* Nestlé Foundation Publication Series, Lausanne, Switzerland, pp. 337-473.

Celedón, J. M., M. Colombo, and I. López, 1984, Nutritional Intervention, Research, and Social Change, in *Malnutrition and Behavior: Critical Assessment of Key Issues,* J. Brožek and B. Schürch, eds., Nestlé Foundation Publication Series, vol. 4, Lausanne, Switzerland, pp. 476-489 (with Addenda and Comments on pp. 490-506).

31: DEVELOPMENTAL CONSEQUENCES OF MALNUTRITION IN EARLY CHILDHOOD

H. N. Ricciuti

The past ten years have witnessed a heightened and continuing concern with malnutrition as a serious public health problem which constitutes a threat to the normal growth and development of many thousands of poor children in various regions of the world, including the United States. Malnutrition tends to occur primarily in poor families confronting the adverse socioeconomic and environmental conditions typically associated with poverty, including poor housing and sanitation, exposure to infectious and parasitic disease, inadequate health care, large family size, very limited educational and occupational opportunities, poor feeding and child care practices, etc. Under such circumstances, it is well known that malnutrition may lead to increased early childhood mortality and morbidity, and to substantial impairment of physical growth and brain development, particularly if the nutritional deficits are early, severe, and long-lasting without treatment. The possibility that malnutrition may also result in a significant and long-lasting impairment of the development of intellectual and social competence, and of adaptive behavior generally, has been a matter of continuing widespread concern during the past ten years. This issue is obviously not only a matter of substantial scientific importance but one with tremendous social and public-policy implications as well.

In the late 1960s and early 1970s in the atmosphere of heightened

Reprinted from pages 151-172 of *The Uncommon Child,* M. Lewis and L. A. Rosenblum, eds., Plenum Publishing Corporation, New York, 1981; *Copyright © 1981 by Plenum Publishing Corporation.*

public concern about malnutrition as a public health problem in this country and elsewhere, there was a rather widespread tendency to assume somewhat uncritically that there was a direct causal relationship between early malnutrition and impaired learning and intellectual development, leading in some instances to irreversible mental retardation (Ricciuti, 1970; Scrimshaw & Gordon, 1968). This assumption was based in large part on human as well as animal studies indicating retarded brain development and brain function resulting from early malnutrition (Dobbing, 1968; Winick & Rosso, 1969), and on the frequent observation that children having suffered obvious malnutrition tend to show reduced levels of intellectual functioning and school achievement. During the past few years, however, it has become increasingly recognized that the relationships between nutritional deprivation and psychological development in children are quite complicated ones which are methodologically difficult to investigate and are not yet clearly understood.

A substantial body of research has shown quite clearly, for example, that it is extremely difficult, if not impossible, to make a meaningful evaluation of the independent effect of malnutrition *as such* on mental development in children, apart from the influence of various adverse social and environmental conditions typically associated with malnutrition, and capable of having a substantial impact on children's behavior and intellectual development in their own right (Pollitt & Thomson, 1977; Ricciuti, 1977). There has been a tendency, therefore, to move away from the assumption of a direct causal relationship between early malnutrition, altered brain development, and impaired intellectual functioning, toward a focusing of greater attention on the following issues:

(a) More systematic analysis of the ways in which the child's nutritional status and aspects of his social environment and early experience may interact in jointly influencing the course of psychological development, with more precise assessment of nutritional status as well as behavioral outcomes.

(b) A fuller understanding of the mechanisms through which altered nutritional status may affect behavior and psychological development.

(c) Evaluation of the effectiveness of systematic efforts to prevent or ameliorate the potentially adverse behavioral consequences of early malnutrition.

Since there have been a number of recent extensive reviews of the substantial research literature on malnutrition and behavioral development (Brozek, 1978; Pollitt & Thomson, 1977; Latham, 1974), this paper will not attempt to present another exhaustive review of this literature. Rather, it will endeavor to critically summarize and evaluate the present state of our knowledge in this area, and to delineate in some detail some of the major research issues and priorities which currently represent topics of prime concern to a good many investigators in the field. Attention will be focused primarily on protein–calorie malnutrition, the most common nutritional problem occurring worldwide in poor populations. Space limitations preclude discussion of such issues as iron deficiency anemia, and the problem of obesity, which is generally considered the most widespread nutritional problem in this country.

We turn first to a brief discussion of the nature of protein–calorie malnutrition and how it is typically assessed, followed by an overview of the major research strategies that have been employed in studies of malnutrition and psychological development.

Protein–Calorie Malnutrition

Definition and Assessment

The major concern of this paper is with malnutrition resulting essentially from an insufficiency of protein and calories in the child's diet, commonly referred to as "protein–calorie malnutrition" (PCM), although more recently alluded to under the generic rubric of "protein and energy deficits". Protein–calorie malnutrition includes the conditions of *nutritional marasmus*, or starvation, usually beginning in the earliest months of life and continuing for an extended period, producing infants whose physical growth and motor development are grossly impaired; and *kwashiorkor*, due primarily to an insufficiency of protein, typically occurring as a rather acute illness toward the end of the first year or in the second year of life, frequently after the birth of a younger sibling. Many combinations or mixtures of these two conditions are found in practice, and they vary greatly in severity and duration (Scrimshaw, 1963).

The most severe clinical forms of marasmus or kwashiorkor typically occur in combination with various infectious or parasitic diseases, and require hospitalization and treatment to ensure the child's survival. Although early and severe malnutrition occurs with considerable frequency in the poorer populations of developing countries (up to 20% in some instances), the most widespread type of malnutrition is that of mild-to-moderate chronic undernutrition, which is most readily noted in some retardation of physical growth and development.

One of the important methodological problems in this area is that it is difficult to secure accurate assessments of nutritional status in children, particularly if one is concerned with measurement throughout a broad range of nutritional variation and not simply with clinically obvious and severe malnutrition. Three types of measures are usually employed: assessment of food intake from detailed dietary information; clinical or physical evaluations, including various anthropometric measures, particularly height, weight, and head circumference; and biochemical evaluations of specific nutrients from blood and urine samples. The interpretation of such measures is considered quite difficult, particularly if one attempts to judge the adequacy of an individual's nutritional status from a single index, and many nutritionists feel that these assessments are most valid when used in combination with one another (Ten State Nutrition Survey, 1972).

A final definitional comment has to do with the importance of distinguishing between hunger and malnutrition. The schoolchild who frequently misses breakfast or lunch may perform poorly because of inattentiveness and distractability associated with hunger. However, these potential influences on school performance and learning, about which we know very little, clearly need to be differentiated from those effects which are the result of long-term protein–calorie malnutrition. Many severely malnourished children are characterized by apathy, withdrawal, and loss of appetite, rather than by the increased activity and restlessness associated with hunger (Cravioto, DeLicardie, & Birch, 1966).

Major Research Strategies

Most studies of protein–calorie malnutrition have been based on samples of children from poor populations in Latin America, Asia, and Africa. The general strategy has usually involved a comparison of developmental or intelligence test scores, school performance, or other behavioral assessments of children with a known or presumed history of malnutrition, with those of children from the same general population but with a more favorable nutritional history. In the case of early malnutrition serious enough to warrant hospitalization or special treatment, comparative assessments of behavior and development status have sometimes been made during treatment and recovery, as well as a number of years later when the children are of school age. Most studies of school-age children have been retrospective, involving a comparison of children with and without a history of hospitalization for severe malnutrition in the first two or three years of life.

Studies of the more common mild-to-moderate, chronic malnutrition have usually employed anthropometric indices of growth, such as stature or head circumference, as indices of the preschool or school-age child's nutritional history, and correlated these indices with various behavioral outcome measures.

A second research strategy which has been employed more frequently in recent years involves the use of various types of experimental intervention. Children considered at risk of malnutrition are provided with added health care and nutritional supplementation, and an evaluation is made of the behavioral consequences of such intervention, along with the effects on physical growth, nutritional status, and health. More recently, we are beginning to see various forms of environmental stimulation included as an added intervention aimed at promoting behavioral development and physical growth.

A third strategy, less common but potentially extremely valuable, involves the ecologically oriented, detailed longitudinal study of the growth and development of samples of children from birth, in settings where chronic malnutrition is endemic. This approach is best illustrated by Cravioto's recent studies in a rural Mexican village (Cravioto, Birch, DeLicardie, Rosales, & Vega, 1969). The assumption underlying this approach is that the natural variation occurring in such a population will make it possible to study prospectively those conditions which lead to the development of malnutrition in some children and not in others in the same environment.

Studies of Severe Malnutrition

There have been a number of studies indicating that infants examined during and shortly after rehabilitation from severe protein–calorie malnutrition requiring hospitalization in the first several years of life, are substantially retarded in physical growth and motor development, and show appreciably reduced performance on developmental and cognitive tests (Cravioto & Robles, 1965; Chase & Martin, 1970; Brockman & Ricciuti, 1971). The severity of the malnutrition and the associated developmental delay involved here is reflected in the fact, for example, that many of these children might have body weights when hospitalized for treatment at 5 or 6 months of age which are no greater or even less than their birthweights, and have made little or no gain in length; or, they may have body weights at 10 months which are no greater than that of a normal 1-month-old. At the same time, these children may have Developmental Quotients on standard infant tests that are well below 60. Preschool and school-age children 5–11 years of age having experienced severe malnutrition in the first 2 or 3 years of life have also frequently been found to perform substantially less well than controls on a variety of intelligence and perceptual–cognitive tests and do less well in school (Cravioto &

DeLicardie, 1970; Hertzig, Birch, Richardson, & Tizard, 1972; Champakam, Srikantia, & Gopalan, 1968).

It is interesting to note that a number of the investigators reporting these results caution against uncritical interpretation of the findings as evidence of a direct causal relationship between malnutrition and mental subnormality, since the same socioenvironmental factors which contribute to the development of marasmus or kwashiorkor in some children and not in others in the same environment may well contribute directly to the reduced intellectual performance observed (Chase & Martin, 1970; Champakam *et al.*, 1968). Moreover, those children who continue to manifest subnormal levels of intellectual functioning six to ten years after treatment for early, severe malnutrition have typically returned to the same adverse environments which contributed to the severe malnutrition in the first place, and which may be a major determinant of the child's current intellectual functioning.

The importance of variations in the quality of the home environments among very poor families is illustrated in recent work by Richardson (1976) in Jamaica, indicating that children with early, severe malnutrition whose families scored relatively high on several social-background factors showed only a minimal reduction in IQ at six to ten years of age relative to comparison cases. On the other hand, children whose families were characterized by more adverse social conditions showed a substantially greater IQ reduction. Thus, the potential effects of even severe early malnutrition on intellectual functioning in the early elementary school years may be considerably attenuated by relatively more favorable social-background conditions in the generally very poor families. Somewhat more dramatic evidence of the potential for amelioration of long-term effects of severe, early malnutrition is suggested in the recent work of Winick, Meyer, and Harris (1975). Korean orphan girls with a history of malnutrition, as judged by retarded physical growth at two to three years of age, shortly before adoption by primarily middle-class American families, were found to have IQs and school achievement within the normal range for American children when followed up in grades 1 to 8.

In summary, then, there is reasonably good evidence that severe protein–calorie malnutrition in the first several years of life may have substantial adverse effects on children's intellectual development. The effects appear to be more marked the more severe the nutritional deprivation, and the longer it continues without treatment. If nutritional treatment and rehabilitation occur early in the first year, the chances of recovery of normal or near normal intellectual functioning appear quite good. There is some evidence, although not entirely consistent, to suggest that severe malnutrition beginning in the second year of life or later, often taking the form of kwashiorkor, appears to produce effects which are not as severe and seem to be more amenable to treatment and remediation. It is still not clear whether malnutrition *as such* is the primary determinant of impaired intellectual functioning, since it is so inextricably intertwined with adverse social and environmental circumstances. Recent studies suggest that the potential long-term effects of early, severe malnutrition may be greatly attenuated, or virtually eliminated, by favorable developmentally supportive later environments, or compounded by less favorable environmental conditions. Considerable effort is being made to understand more clearly the mechanisms through which severe malnutrition may exert its influence on behavior and development, as well as to determine which psychological processes are more vulnerable to its potential impact. These topics will be discussed more fully somewhat later in the paper.

Studies of Mild-to-Moderate Chronic Malnutrition

There have been a good many studies of the intellectual development of children who have presumably experienced the very widespread mild-to-moderate chronic malnutrition which is endemic in many poor populations, as judged primarily on the basis of some physical growth retardation, particularly in height, weight, or head circumference. While these shorter children often tend to show somewhat reduced levels of intellectual function, these findings are particulary difficult to interpret because of the problems involved in using simple anthropometric indices like height or head circumference as the principal indices of nutritional status and history. It is well known, for example, that while variations in height may well reflect children's nutritional histories, particularly under conditions of nutritional adversity, these height variations may also reflect a variety of other social characteristics of the environment, or biological characteristics of the individual (including genetic factors), which are themselves capable of influencing the child's intellectual development (Ricciuti, 1977; Pollitt & Ricciuti, 1969).

Several studies of the intellectual competence of tall and short children in Latin America illustrate these interpretive difficulties. In a study of 6- to 11-year-old children living in a Guatemalan village, for example (Cravioto et al., 1966), tall children tended to make fewer errors than short children in identifying geometric forms on the basis of integrating visual, haptic, and kinesthetic information. Although the tall and short children came from families with generally equivalent socioenvironmental backgrounds, maternal education was markedly higher in the case of the tall children, who may thus have had substantially more intellectual stimulation and opportunities for learning. Similarly, in a Chilean study of 1- to 5-year-old poor children considered at risk of mild-to-moderate malnutrition (Monckeberg, Tisler, Toro, Gattas, & Vegal, 1972), a substantial correlation was found between mothers' IQ and the children's growth in height ($r = .71$). Thus, the lower IQs found in the shorter children may well be attributable to genetic factors or to reduced levels of intellectual stimulation provided by the less competent mothers.

A number of more recent studies of mild-to-moderate malnutrition have endeavored to evaluate the relative influence of social or environmental factors, and the nutritional variations reflected in physical growth measures, with the use of correlational and multiple-regression analyses. In a Guatemala study of 3- to 6-year-old village children, for example, Klein, Freeman, Kagan, Yarbrough, and Habicht (1972) found that physical growth measures and a composite of social factors showed generally equivalent correlations with tests of language and memory (mostly .20 to .40). On the other hand, insofar as the development of perceptual competence is concerned, their data suggest that nutritional background (height and head circumference) may play a somewhat greater role than social experience (r's were .33 vs. .18 for boys, and .33 vs. .25 for girls).

Working with considerably younger children in Bogota (6–30 months), Christiansen, Vuori, Mora, and Wagner (1974) found that Griffiths Developmental Quotients (DQs) were substantially more highly correlated with physical growth (multiple R for height and weight $= .57$) than with a composite socioeconomic index (multiple R $= .43$). Moreover, the predictability of DQs from height and weight alone was increased by only .05, from .57 to .62, when the social factors were added. Klein, Yarbrough, Lasky, and Habicht's study of 24-month-old children (1974) also suggests a somewhat greater influence of nutritional or growth factors rather than social factors on developmental test scores, particularly with regard to motor development.

On the other hand, in Richardson's (1976) previously mentioned study of 6- to 10-year-old Jamaica boys who experienced severe malnutrition early in life, a composite family social background index was much more predictive of IQ levels than was the occurrence of the previous history of severe malnutrition. These and other studies indicate that it is very difficult to arrive at any firm, consistent estimates of the magnitude of the independent contributions of nutritional and associated socioenvironmental influences to the growth of intellectual competencies. As will be argued more fully somewhat later in this paper, a more fruitful approach would involve a closer examination of the potential interactions between these two major sources of influence, as they jointly shape the course of intellectual development.

In summary, when we consider the chronic, mild-to-moderate malnutrition which is endemic in many economically disadvantaged populations, the research evidence suggesting adverse effects on children's psychological development is substantially weaker and less clear than that dealing with early and severe malnutrition. Generally speaking, the reserch thus far suggests that mild-to-moderate malnutrition appears to play a relatively minor role in determining children's intellectual development, in comparison with the substantial ifluence exerted by various social and environmental factors.

CURRENT RESEARCH DEVELOPMENTS, NEEDS, AND PRIORITIES

Having briefly reviewed some of the major findings of recent research bearing on the relationship between malnutrition and behavioral development in children, we turn next to a somewhat more analytical consideration of contemporary research issues and priorities which appear to this reviewer to represent important directions for continued investigation.

As indicated in the foregoing summary, there is a large body of literature indicating that malnutrition tends to be associated with reduced levels of intellectual functioning in children. In my view, there would be very little to be gained by additional studies which again simply showed that malnourished children perform less well on various intellectual tests than adequately nourished children from the same general population, or even from families with approximately equivalent educational backgrounds. Generally speaking, what is needed at present is a much sharper delineation and analysis of these relationships, with more precise assessments of nutritional status as well as behavioral outcomes. More specifically, as mentioned at the outset, we need to direct our efforts toward a fuller understanding of how malnutrition and other environmental influences interact in combination to influence development, a more complete explanation of the mechanisms or channels of influence through which variations in nutritional status may affect the course of mental development and cognitive functioning, and further studies of the effectiveness of various forms of experimental interventions, including health care, nutritional supplementation, enrichment of the child's social and learning environment, etc. In the long run, these lines of inquiry should not only substantially enhance our understanding of the basic scientific issues involved, but at the same time provide a sounder knowledge base on which to build systematic and effective field programs of prevention and remediation.

In the paragraphs which follow, research issues and needs which seem to this reviewer to be of particularly high priority in each of the three areas just mentioned will be discussed briefly, along with suggested research strategies.

Analyses of Patterns of Interaction between Malnutrition and Socioenvironmental Influences

As mentioned in the initial summary, in recent years there has been an increased recognition of the significant role played by various social and environmental conditions typically associated with malnutrition as important determinants of psychological development in children. Various research and analytic strategies have been employed in an effort to evaluate the relationship between nutritional status and intellectual competencies, independent of those socioenvironmental influences associated both with malnutrition and behavioral outcomes. These efforts have sometimes taken the form of comparing the performance of malnourished and better nourished children from the same neighborhoods or general socioeconomic levels. Such a strategy, however, does not take into account the likelihood that those poor families whose children are better-nourished may also be living under less adverse socioeconomic circumstances than the experimental families, and may be providing a social and learning environment which is more facilitative of their children's intellectual development (Monckeberg *et al.*, 1972). Other investigators have employed somewhat more refined but still relatively simple indices of variations in family and home environment (type of housing, income, education of parent) and incorporated them in partial correlation or regression analyses aimed at determining how much of the variance in cognitive performance can be accounted for by nutritional status alone, by socioenvironmental variations alone, and by the two combined (Klein *et al.*, 1972; Christiansen *et al.*, 1974).

From this reviewer's perspective, these kinds of analyses are heuristically useful up to a point, but they are of rather limited value in advancing our understanding of the interactive influences of nutritional and socioenvironmental variations on intellectual development. First, the indices of nutritional status and of the family and home environment are typically quite simplistic and hence may be capturing only a small portion of the developmentally relevant variations in each domain. Moreover, obtained estimates of the independent contribution of nutritional versus socioenvironmental factors will vary greatly depending on various characteristics of the samples employed (such as age, homogeneity or heterogeneity with respect to environmental and nutritional variation), and also depending on the particular outcome measures utilized (Ricciuti, 1977). Most studies employing this analytic approach typically find that simple indices of nutritional status (ht., wt., h.c.) and of socioeconomic background are positively correlated (r's in the .20s to .30s), with correlations of about the same order of magnitude being found between each of these predictors and measures of intellectual competence. Regression analyses tend to show that both social factors and nutritional history make some independent contribution to intellectual competence, with the percentages of variance presumably attributable to each source of influence varying substantially from study to study (e.g., 29% for social factors vs. 5% for severe early malnutrition in the previously mentioned study of 6- to 10-year-old Jamaican boys [Richardson, 1976]; 18% vs. 32% in a study of 6- to 30-month-old Colombian children [Christiansen et al., 1974]).

At this point in time, there would appear to be little value in further studies concerned primarily with the question of *how much* of the variation in intellectual competence can be attributed to nutritional status alone or to socioenvironmental factors alone. Rather, we need to go beyond such analytic strategies and systematically direct our research at increased understanding of how malnutrition and the child's social environment *interact* in jointly influencing the development of intellectual competencies, employing more refined measures of nutritional status, as well as more precise and detailed analyses of relevant features of the social and physical environment in the home, neighborhood, or community.

The potential value of this line of approach is strongly suggested by several recent studies indicating that within very poor populations where children are known to be generally at risk of early malnutrition, variations in particular features of the child's home and family environment may either increase or reduce substantially the likelihood of severe malnutrition occurring in specific families (DeLicardie & Cravioto, 1974; Richardson, 1974). It is important to note also, that these features of the child's social environment associated with the occurrence of malnutrition include environmental influences which can have a substantial direct effect on the child's mental development (e.g., mother's competence, degree to which child-care practices provide nurturance and support for psychological development). For example, in a longitudinal study of several hundred infants born in a poor rural Mexican village (DiLicardie & Cravioto, 1974), those children who experienced severe malnutrition in the first three years of life were found to have lower IQs than controls at five years of age, and tended to come from homes which, as early as the first year of life, were observed to be lower in the quantity and quality of social, emotional, and cognitive stimulation provided to the child. Moreoever, these same features of the early home environment were also related to IQ at five years of age among children without a history of severe malnutrition.

In the present context, it is particularly important to note, as mentioned earlier, that once a child has suffered from early malnutrition, even of the severe type, the risk of subsequent impairment of mental development will also depend very much on the quality of the child's home and family environment. On the basis of both human and animal studies, it has become increasingly apparent that a developmentally facilitative social environment may substantially attenuate or even prevent the potentially unfavorable consequences of early, severe malnutrition (Richardson, 1976; Winick *et al.*, 1975; Lloyd-Still, Hurwitz, Wolff, & Shwachmann, 1974; Levitsky, 1979).

The studies just summarized clearly emphasize the importance of our directing more systematic attention toward more precise evaluations of those aspects of the family environment or family functioning which make some families less vulnerable to the occurrence of severe malnutrition than others in the same "at risk" population, and also more capable of "buffering" or attenuating the potentially adverse behavior effects of malnutrition when it does occur. The approach suggested here involves going beyond the well-known demographic indicators of increased biosocial stress and risk such as maternal age or health history, family size, parental education, income, exposure to infections or parasitic disease, accessibility of health care, etc. What is needed is a more refined analysis of the coping strengths and strategies used by families, as well as their capacity to provide developmentally facilitative child care or child-rearing environments which are supportive of both physical growth and psychological development, in the face of generally adverse socioenvironmental circumstances. The identification of these intrafamilial strengths or vulnerabilities should certainly enhance significantly our basic understanding of important interactions between nutritional and socioenvironmental influences on growth and development. At the same time, from the perspective of prevention and remediation, this added knowledge should provide helpful guidelines or avenues of approach in the development of effective programs of intervention and support for families coping with adversity.

Another example of important interrelationships between malnutrition and salient aspects of the child's social environment or early experience is reflected in the growing evidence that the infant or young child's altered nutritional status, as reflected in physical appearance and behavior, may affect the manner in which primary caregivers respond to or care for the child, thus potentially altering his early experience in developmentally significant ways (Chavez, Martinez, & Yachine, 1975; Graves, 1978). Further systematic investigation of these interrelationships should shed additional light on the question of why some children in a given family are severely malnourished while siblings are spared. As our knowledge concerning these developmentally significant patterns of child care and parent–child relationships expands, we should better be able to plan effective preventive or remedial approaches to families where the risk of malnutrition is particularly high.

While the emphasis in the discussion thus far has been upon the interaction of malnutrition and *social* factors in the child's experience and environment, it would similarly be very important to examine more carefully the manner in which malnutrition of various types and degrees of severity might combine with other biological risk factors, such as low birth weight, prematurity, congenital or genetic anomalies, etc., adversely affecting the development of intellectual competecies.

Identification of Mechanisms through Which Altered Nutritional Status May Affect Intellectual Competencies

One of the most important research questions still confronting us in this field is the problem of specifying the mechanisms, or channels of influence, through which malnutrition might exert its impact on the development of various behavioral competencies. In human studies, this problem is being approached in part by efforts to assess a wider array of potential behavioral outcomes of malnutrition in order to determine whether various specific perceptual–cognitive, learning, or motivational processes might be particularly vulnerable to the impact of nutritional deficits (Klein, 1979; Hoorweg, 1976; Pollitt, Greenfield, & Leibel, 1978). The same general approach is being followed in much of the recent animal research, where investigators have also been able to manipulate experimentally the conditions of nutritional deprivation, recovery, and treatment (including added experience) (Levitsky, 1979; Frankova, 1974).

When the concerns about malnutrition as a possible major cause of mental retardation reached a peak in the late 1960s and early 1970s it was assumed by many that the brain changes produced by malnutrition led directly to an impairment of learning ability and thus to retarded intellectual development, which was often irreversible. On the basis of much human as well as animal research since that time, however, most investigators have tended to discard this view in favor of the hypothesis that malnutrition may exert its major influence on behavioral competencies through dysfunctional changes in attention, responsiveness, motivation, and emotionality, rather than through a more direct impairment of basic ability to learn. In short, the malnourished child's interaction with his environment may be altered in ways that make him less likely to seek out, utilize, and respond to opportunities for learning and social interaction available in his environment. This state of events would imply quite hopeful prospects for reversibility or remediation, since it may be possible to manipulate the environment so as to make the child's interaction with it more intellectually facilitative (to be discussed more fully later in this review).

This general problem of more precise identification of the mechanisms through which the behavioral effects of malnutrition might be mediated certainly deserves much more systematic attention with human subjects at different age levels, and with different types and severity of nutritional deficits. As indicated earlier, one approach to this problem is to broaden our behavioral assessments so as to include measures specifically intended to determine which psychological processes or competencies are particularly vulnerable to various kinds of malnutrition. Although a good many recent studies have indeed gone beyond general IQ or DQ assessments, particularly with preschool or school-age children, it is difficult to find consistent patterns of differential nutritional vulnerability for various perceptual–cognitive functions across studies. Much of this inconsistency is to be expected, since the particular competencies or skills which seem most affected by malnutrition are likely to vary with the age of the children, the severity of the malnutrition, the particular tests used, the degree to which sociocultural or environmental influences on performance have been controlled, etc.

Nevertheless, perhaps the most common suggestion derivable from much of the research, but particularly from studies of early and severe malnutrition, is that the nutritional deficits seem to alter the child's attentional competencies and responsiveness to the environment. For example, the commonly reported clinical observations of reduced activity or apathy in severe early malnutrition, particularly of the marasmic type, are supported by recent experimental studies indicating reduced alerting or orienting responses to simple auditory stimuli (Lester, Klein, & Martinez, 1975). On the other hand, while these malnourished infants or toddlers seem less responsive to low or moderate levels of stimulation, they appear to be hyperreactive to higher stimulus levels that are more "intrusive." Nonsupplemented young infants, for example, responded more irritably to a moderately stressful stimulus than did supplemented infants (Vuori, de Navarro, Christiansen, Mora, & Herrera, 1978), a finding paralleling reports of heightened "emotionality" and difficulty in extinguishing conditioned responses in malnourished animals. It is interesting to note that this same pattern of reduced attention to moderate stimuli and hyperreactivity to more intense stimuli is also being found in very recent studies of premature or low-birth-weight infants in this country (Rose, Schmidt, & Bridger, 1976). Accompanying this pattern of altered responsiveness in children with early malnutrition are reports of reduced curiosity and exploratory behavior in infants and toddlers (Chavez et al., 1975; Graves, 1978).

Although the data are much less consistent and clear, there are some suggestions from studies of preschool and school-age children that tasks which require the capacity to mobilize and sustain attention may be particularly affected by malnutrition—e.g., simple tasks of short-term memory, or tasks in which incidental learning is possible. These suggestive findings, which need much more systematic replication, come both from studies of mild-to-moderate malnutrition (Klein, 1979; Irwin, Klein, et al., 1979; McKay, McKay, & Sinisterra, 1974), as well as a recent study of teenage children with history of clinical malnutrition in the first two years of life (Hoorweg, 1976). The importance of further systematic research directed at the impact of malnutrition on the child's attentional and motivational competencies is also supported by recent reports of altered work styles, or responses to cognitive demands shown by preschool children having experienced early clinical malnutrition (DeLicardie & Cravioto, 1974), as well as less favorable performance on tasks requiring sustained attention by Boston children with iron deficiency (Pollitt, Greenfield, & Leibel, 1978).

Virtually all the research just discussed has involved behavioral assessments of children performing in structured test or experimental situations. There is great need to extend systematically the beginning efforts that have been made recently to examine the potential consequences of malnutrition on various adaptive, intellectual, or learning competencies manifested in various real-life settings (Hoorweg, 1976; Nerlove, Roberts, Klein, Yarbrough, & Habicht, 1974; Richardson, Birch, & Hertzig, 1973). Assessments of functional competence based on observations of performance in these natural settings would complement the more common test or laboratory assessments in important ways, not the least of which would be to shed some light on the ecological or functional validity of these more controlled measurements. It is interesting to note that current early-intervention research in this country strongly reflects a similar movement away from a heavy dependence on psychological tests or laboratory observations, toward more utilization of evaluations of competence manifested in natural situations.

Effectiveness of Nutritional and Social Interventions in Fostering the Development of Intellectual Competence

The systematic utilization of experimental intervention strategies represents one of the most potent research approaches in this field. The hospitalization and treatment of clinically ill children with severe malnutrition obviously represents a basic and widely used form of intervention, which could be more fully exploited for systematic behavioral research purposes than it has been thus far. It is encouraging to note that in the past few years there has been an increasing utilization of nutritional intervention as a research strategy, particularly in connection with efforts to prevent malnutrition in populations where the problem is a chronic and endemic one. Because such studies are carried out within a longitudinal, prospective framework, they provide the opportunity to follow the physical growth and psychological development of children whose nutritional histories have been systematically influenced through the provision of added health care and nutritional supplementation, beginning prenatally in some instances (Irwin *et al.*, 1979; Brozek, Coursin, & Read, 1977). One of the major advantages of the intervention strategy is that changes or contrasts in children's dietary intake and nutritional status can be monitored prospectively as they occur, along with concurrent social and environmental factors, so that their relationships to contemporary or subsequent developmental outcome measures can be more meaningfully evaluated. This contrasts rather sharply with the situation characterizing many retrospective studies of malnourished children, in which information about previous nutritional and developmental histories is often very limited and unclear.

A few recent nutritional-intervention studies have begun to incorporate procedures for enrichment or enhancement of the child's social and learning environment as components of the intervention program, along with nutritional supplementation and health care. This intervention has sometimes been provided as an enrichment of experience, or "stimulation" during treatment for severe malnutrition, sometimes as a preschool program for children typically exposed to chronic undernutrition, and sometimes in the form of a home visiting program to support the mother as a caregiver and promoter of her infant or toddler's development (Brozek *et al.*, 1977). In my view, this general strategy represents an extremely important approach since it recognizes the fact that the child's health and nutritional status, and his opportunities for learning and social development represent integral components of developmentally supportive child-care or child-rearing environments.

Let us briefly consider some of these recent intervention studies in somewhat more detail. With regard to severe and early malnutrition, as previously mentioned, it has been apparent for some time that the earlier the treatment and rehabilitation, the less the risk of severe developmental impairment (Pollitt & Thomson, 1977). Also, ensuring that the child is not deprived of adequate social and physical stimulation during treatment and rehabilitation, or providing added experiences during this period, seems to offer some facilitation of the recovery process (McLaren, Yaktin, Kanawati, Sabbagh, & Kadi, 1973; Monckeberg & Ruimallo, 1979). The long-term benefits of these early treatments and interventions, of course, are very much influenced by the nature of the enduring environments to which the children return after hospitalization. As indicated earlier, the importance of the later developmental environments of children having experienced early and severe malnutrition is emphasized by recent findings indicating that if these environments are favorable and supportive of development there may be a substantial recovery of both physical growth (Winick et al., 1975; Graham, 1972), as well as intellectual development (Winick et al., 1975; Lloyd-Still et al., 1974).

Insofar as mild-to-moderate malnutrition is concerned, research thus far suggests that the provision of freely available nutritional supplementation to children and families at risk of mild-to-moderate undernutrition in rural Guatemalan villages has relatively little impact on the enhancement of mental development, particularly when compared with the role played by socioenvironmental influences (Klein, 1979; Irwin et al., 1979). In an experimental intervention study with urban poor families in Bogota, during the first 18 months of life children who had received either nutritional supplementation or home visiting to promote maternal encouragement of intellectual development showed rather slight advantages in developmental-test scores over control children receiving only health care (Mora, Christiansen, Ortiz, Vuori, & Herrera, 1979). Children who received both treatments showed somewhat more favorable gains in both physical growth and developmental-test performance.

While the results just summarized and a few other behavioral advantages reported for supplemented infants early in the first year of life can be considered somewhat promising, they represent quite modest effects, considering the scope and cost of the interventions involved. On the other hand there may be more subtle but important effects on the families provided with the combined health-care, supplementation, and home-visiting program, which have not yet been fully assessed.

The recent report from the Cali, Colombia project (McKay, Sinisterra, McKay, Gomez, & Llorenda, 1978) indicates that some facilitation of cognitive functioning can apparently be produced by a highly structured, cognitively oriented all-day preschool program, which also provides health care and nutritional supplementation. As is the case with many preschool intervention programs in this country, it is not clear at this point to what extent these apparent benefits will be maintained when the children continue on in the public school system, particularly if no systematic efforts have been made to enhance the continuing environment of the home and family.

In considering the general implications of these recent intervention studies one is inclined to conclude, on the other hand, that the results thus far are mildly promising, at least in the case of the studies which have included social or environmental intervention as well as health care and nutritional supplementation. At the same time, however, these studies also reflect the difficulties of designing and implementing effective early-intervention programs which can be shown to produce functionally meaningful enhancement of intellectual competencies. Nevertheless, this reviewer remains convinced that more of our research efforts must be aimed directly at the issue of intervention strategies for optimizing the growth and development of children who live in adverse environments and are at risk of both malnutrition and suboptimal intellectual development, or have already experienced severe malnutrition. Obviously, in the long run the most effective forms of "intervention" would involve major improvements of the developmentally threatening economic, social, and physical conditions under which large populations of the poor live. Short of these long-term political, social, and economic changes, however, and working within the framework of resources potentially available in the immediate future, we need to continue to develop and systematically evaluate the effectiveness of various forms of intervention which could eventually be incorporated into realistic, ongoing social programs.

It seems highly possible that the most effective intervention strategies are likely to be those which are simultaneously concerned not only with nutritional and health needs, but also with ensuring necessary socioenvironmental supports for optimal psychological development. Our major research goal, then, should be to determine how best to combine these elements in programs which meet the special needs of particular groups of children and families, given our goal of facilitating cognitive development. It seems reasonable to assume, also, that intervention is most likely to be effective, as well as more feasible economically, if it can be focused so as to reach particularly those children and families considered to be at greatest biological or socioenvironmental risk of impaired development.

SUMMARY AND CONCLUSIONS

It is quite clear that protein–calorie malnutrition represents a significant threat to the normal growth and development of many thousands of children living under the adverse conditions associated with poverty in many regions of the world. While protein–calorie malnutrition may produce substantial retardation of physical growth and brain development, there is relatively little evidence thus far that it has a direct and independent effect in producing intellectual or learning deficits in children, apart from the adverse social and environmental conditions typically associated with malnutrition. Nevertheless, severe and extended malnutrition beginning in the first two years of lfe may well be implicated as one important determinant of suboptimal development, particularly if combined with a developmentally unfavorable social and learning environment in the home. Even in such instances, however, it appears that the long-term effects of severe malnutrition may be substantially attenuated or minimized by a more favorable, developmentally supportive later environment. Mild or moderate malnutrition appears to play a relatively minor role in determining children's intellectual development, in comparison with the substantial influence exerted by various social and environmental factors.

Much current research is quite properly directed at a fuller understanding of the interactions between malnutrition and specific features of the child's social and physical environment in the home and neighborhood, in order to determine how these two major sources of potential influence may combine to produce either heightened or attenuated risk to normal psychological development. At the same time, considerable research has been focused on a better understanding of the mechanisms through which malnutrition may exert its influence on behavior, through both human and animal studies. Considerable evidence thus far suggests that malnutrition may alter the child's attentional strategies and competencies, responsiveness to the environment, and emotionality, rather than directly impairing the basic ability to learn.

There has also been a substantial increase in experimental intervention studies concerned with evaluation of the effectiveness of broadly based nutritional-supplementation and health-care programs in enhancing both physical and mental development. Some of these programs have begun to incorporate efforts to provide added enrichment or enhancement of the child's early social and learning environments as well. While the results of these efforts to enhance children's intellectual development have not been particularly encouraging so far, continued research along these lines is very much needed. Such intervention research should add significantly to our basic understanding of the influence of malnutrition and early experience on behavioral development, while at the same time strengthening the knowledge base required for planning effective social programs aimed at prevention and remediation of suboptimal development.

References

Brockman, L.M., & Ricciuti, H.N. Severe protein–calorie malnutrition and cognitive development in infancy and early childhood. *Developmental Psychology*, 1971, *4*, 312–319.

Brozek, J. Nutrition, malnutrition, and behavior. *Annual Review of Psychology*, 1978, *29*, 157–177.

Brozek, J., Coursin, D.B., & Read, M.S. Longitudinal studies on the effects of malnutrition, nutritional supplementation, and behavioral stimulation. *Bulletin of the Pan American Health Organization*, 1977, *11*, 237–249.

Champakam, S., Srikantia, S.G., & Gopalan, C. Kwashiorkor and mental development. *American Journal of Clinical Nutrition*, 1968, *21*, 844–852.

Chase, H.P., & Martin, H.P. Undernutrition and child development. *New England Journal of Medicine*, 1970, *282*, 933–939.

Chavez, A., Martinez, C., & Yachine, T. Nutrition, behavioral development, and mother–child interaction in young rural children. *Federation Proceedings*, 1975, *34*, 1574–1582.

Christiansen, N., Vuori, L., Mora, J.O., & Wagner, M. Social environment as it relates to malnutrition and mental development. In J. Cravioto *et al.* (Eds.), *Early malnutrition and mental development*. Uppsala: Almquist and Wiksell, 1974, pp. 186–199.

Cravioto, J., & DeLicardie, E.R. Mental performance in school age children. *American Journal of Diseases of Children*, 1970, *120*, 404.

Cravioto, J., & Robles, B. Evolution of adaptive and motor behavior during rehabilitation from kwashiorkor. *American Journal of Orthopsychiatry*, 1965, *35*, 449–464.

Cravioto, J., DeLicardie, E.R., & Birch, H.G. Nutrition, growth and neuro-integrative development: An experimental and ecologic study. *Pediatrics*, 1966, *38*,319–372.

Cravioto, J., Birch, H.G., DeLicardie, E., Rosales, L., & Vega, . The ecology of growth and development in a Mexican pre-industrial community. *Monographs of the Society for Research in Child Development*, 1969, *34*, 1–65.

DeLicardie, E.R., & Cravioto, J. Behavioral responsiveness of survivors of clinically severe malnutrition to cognitive demands. In J. Cravioto *et al.* (Eds.), *Early malnutrition and mental development*. Uppsala: Almquist and Wiksell, 1974, pp. 134–153.

Dobbing, J. Efects of experimental undernutrition on development of the nervous system. In N.S. Scrimshaw & J.E. Gordon (Eds.), *Malnutrition, learning and behavior*. Cambridge: Massachusetts Institute of Technology Press, 1968, pp. 181–202.

Frankova, S. Interaction between early malnutrition and stimulation in animals. In J. Cravioto *et al.* (Eds.), *Early malnutrition and mental development.* Uppsala: Almquist and Wiksell, 1974, pp. 202–209.

Graham, G. Environmental factors affecting the growth of children. *American Journal of Clinical Nutrition,* 1972, *25,* 1184–1188.

Graves, P.L. Nutrition and infant behavior: A replication study in the Katmandu Valley, Nepal. *American Journal of Clinical Nutrition,* 1978, *31,* 541–551.

Hertzig, M.E., Birch, H.G., Richardson, S.A., & Tizard, J. Intellectual levels of school children severely malnourished during the first two years of life. *Pediatrics,* 1972, *49,* 814–824.

Hoorweg, J.C. *Protein–energy malnutrition and intellectual abilities.* The Hague/Paris: Mouton, 1976.

Irwin, M.H., Klein, R.E., & others Effects of food supplementation on cognitive development and behavior among rural Guatemalan children. In J. Brozek (Ed.), *Behavioral effects of energy and protein deficits.* Bethesda: Department of Health, Education and Welfare (NIH), 1979, pp. 239–254.

Klein, R.E. Malnutrition and human behavior: A backward glance at an ongoing longitudinal study. In D.A. Levitsky (Ed.), *Malnutrition, environment, and behavior: New perspectives.* Ithaca: Cornell University Press, 1979, pp. 219–237.

Klein, R.E., Freeman, H.E., Kagan, J., Yarbrough, C., & Habicht, J.P. Is big smart? The relation of growth to cognition. *Journal of Health and Social Behavior,* 1972, *13,* 219–225.

Klein, R.E., Yarbrough, C., Lasky, R.E., & Habicht, J.P. Correlations of mild to moderate protein–calorie malnutrition among rural Guatemalan infants and preschool children. In J. Cravioto *et al.* (Eds.), *Early malnutrition and mental development.* Uppsala: Almquist & Wiksell, 1974, pp. 168–181.

Latham, M.C. Protein–calorie malnutrition in children and its relation to psychological development and behavior. *Physiological Review,* 1974, *54*(3), 541–565.

Lester, B.M., Klein, R.E., & Martinez, S.J. The use of habituation in the study of the effects of infantile malnutrition. *Developmental Psychobiology,* 1975, *8,* 541–546.

Levitsky, D.A. (Ed.). *Malnutrition, environment, and behavior: New perspectives.* Ithaca: Cornell University Press, 1979.

Lloyd-Still, J.D., Hurwitz, I., Wolff, P.H., & Shwachmann, H. Intellectual development after severe malnutrition in infancy. *Pediatrics,* 1974, *54,* 306–311.

McKay, H., McKay, A., & Sinisterra, L. Intellectual development of malnourished preschool children in programs of stimulation and nutritional supplementation. In J. Cravioto *et al.* (Eds.), *Early malnutrition and mental development.* Uppsala: Almquist and Wiksell, 1974, pp. 226–233.

McKay, H., Sinisterra, L., McKay, H.G., Gomez, H., & Lloreda, P. Improving cognitive ability in chronically deprived children. *Science,* 1978, *200,* 270–278.

McLaren, D.S., Yaktim, U.S., Kanawati, A.A., Sabbagh, S., & Kadi Z. The subsequent mental and physical development of rehabilitated marasmic infants. *Journal of Mental Deficiency Research,* 1973, *17,* 273–281.

Monckeberg, F., & Ruimallo, J. Psychomotor stimulation in recovery of early severe marasmic malnutrition: Experience in recovery centers. In J. Brozek (Ed.), *Behavioral effects of energy and protein deficits.* Bethesda, Md.: Department of Health, Education and Welfare (NIH), 1979, pp. 121–130.

Monckeberg, F., Tisler, S., Toro, S., Gattas, V., & Vegal, L. Malnutrition and mental development. *American Journal of Clinical Nutrition,* 1972, *25,* 766–772.

Mora, J.O., Christiansen, N., Ortiz, N., Vuori, L., & Herrera, M.G. Nutritional supplementation, early environment, and child development during the first 18 months of life. In J. Brozek (Ed.), *Behavioral effects of energy and protein deficits*. Bethesda: Department of Health, Education and Welfare (NIH), 1979, pp. 255–269.

Nerlove, S.B., Roberts, J.M., Klein, R.E., Yarbrough, C., & Habicht, J.P. Natural indicators of cognitive development: An observational study of rural Guatemalan children. *Ethos*, 1974, *2*, 265–295.

Pollitt, E., & Ricciuti, H. Biological and social correlates of stature among children living in the slums of Lima, Peru. *American Journal of Orthopsychiatry*, 1969, *39*, 735–747.

Pollitt, E., & Thomson, C. Protein–calorie malnutrition and behavior: A view from psychology. In R.J. Wurtman & J.J. Wurtman (Eds.), *Nutrition and the brain* (Vol. 2). New York: Raven Press, 1977, pp. 261–306.

Pollitt, E., Greenfield, D., & Leibel, R. Behavioral effects of iron deficiency among preschool children in Cambridge, Massachusetts. Paper presented at the 62d Annual Meeting of the Federation of American Societies for Experimental Biology, Atlantic City, New Jersey, April 1978.

Richardson, S.A. The background histories of school children severely malnourished in infancy. In I. Schulman (Ed.), *Advances in pediatrics, 21*. Chicago: Yearbook Medical Publications, 1974, pp. 167–192.

Richardson, S.A. The relation of severe malnutrition in infancy to intelligence of school children with differing life histories. *Pediatric Research*, 1976, *10*, 57–61.

Richardson, S.A., Birch, H.G., & Hertzig, M.E. School performance of children who were severely malnourished in infancy. *American Journal of Mental Deficiency*, 1973, *77*, 623–632.

Ricciuti, H.N. Malnutrition, learning and intellectual development: Research and re-mediation. In *Psychology and the Problems of Society*. Washington, D.C.: American Psychological Association, 1970.

Ricciuti, H.N. Adverse social and biological influences on early development. In H. McGurk (Ed.), *Ecological factors in human development*. Amsterdam: North Holland Press, 1977, Chapter 12.

Rose, S.A., Schmidt, K., & Bridger, W.H. Cardiac and behavioral responsivity to tactile stimulation in premature and full-term infants. *Developmental Psychology*, 1976, *12*, 311–320.

Scrimshaw, N.S. Malnutrition and the health of children. *Journal of the American Dietetic Association*, 1963, *42*, 203–208.

Scrimshaw, N.S., & Gordon, J.E. (Eds). *Malnutrition, learning and behavior*. Cambridge: MIT Press, 1968.

Ten State Nutrition Survey 1968–1970. Department of Health, Education and Welfare Publication No. (HSM) 72-8131, 1972.

Vuori, L., de Navarro, L., Christiansen, N., Mora, J.O., & Herrera, M.G. Food supplementation of pregnant women at risk of malnutrition and newborn responsiveness to stimulation. Unpublished manuscript. Harvard School of Public Health, Dept. of Nutrition, Boston, 1978.

Winick, M., & Rosso, P. Head circumference and cellular growth of the brain in normal and marasmic children. *Journal of Pediatrics*, 1969, *74*, 774–778.

Winick, M., Meyer, K., & Harris, R.C. Malnutrition and environmental enrichment by adoption. *Science*, 1975, *190*, 1173–1175.

32: MANY FACES OF NUTRITION

J. Brožek

Books Reviewed: *Pre- and Postnatal Development,* Human Nutrition: A Comprehensive Treatise, vol. 1, M. Winick, ed., Plenum Press, New York, 1979, 516p.; *Nutrition and Growth,* Human Nutrition: A Comprehensive Treatise, vol. 2, D. B. Jelliffe and E. F. Patrice Jelliffe, eds., Plenum Press, New York, 1979, 472p.; *Macronutrients,* Human Nutrition: A Comprehensive Treatise, vols. 3A and 3B, R. B. Alfin-Slater and D. Kritchevesky, eds., Plenum Press, New York, 1979, 308p. and 443p.; *Metabolic and Clinical Applications,* Human Nutrition: A Comprehensive Treatise, vol. 4, R. E. Hodges, ed., Plenum Press, New York, 1979, 500p.; *Ernährungspsychologie (Psychology of Nutrition),* 2nd ed., by J. M. Diehl, Fachbuchhandlung für Psychologie, Federal Republic of Germany, 1980, 211p.; *Malnutrition in Southern Africa,* R. D. Griesel, ed., University of South Africa, Pretoria, 1980, 313p.

The topic of nutrition and behavior is complex. This complexity is reflected in the books under review. Diehl's volume focuses on industrially developed countries where overnutrition rather than undernutrition is likely to be a serious public-health concern. The multivolume treatise considers both types of deviations from the "norm," that is, deficits as well as excesses, whereas the South African colloquium addresses itself to malnutrition or, to be more precise, to energy-protein malnutrition.

Inadequacy of nutrients absorbed by a given child represents a final link in a long chain of antecedents, including geographical, socioeconomic, and political factors. Complex also are the effects of malnutrition, perceivable at the level of cells, tissues, organs, and organisms operating in a social context. The study of malnutrition calls for a multidisciplinary approach in which psychology is one of the participating disciplines. At the same time, human nutrition is an area rich in promise and challenge to a broad range of specialities within psychology: physiological, developmental, social, clinical, even industrial psychology. It poses challenges to psychometrics as well.

As used by Diehl, the term *nutritional behavior* (*Ernährungsverhalten*) covers all forms of behavior that involve nutrition, including *co-determinants* of food intake (such as food preferences, food aversions, or food fadism), psychological *concomitants* of the process of eating (including the alleged "softening" of clients by salesmen who prefer to talk things over in a restaurant), and psychological *consequences* of deviant food consumption.

At times, as in anorexia nervosa or in obesity, the situation is more complex. Thus, hyperphagic responses (B_1) to stress may be relevant to the *etiology* of obesity. In turn, the resultant abnormal nutritional status ("nutriture," N) may affect a person's feelings of well-being and personality (B_2). Furthermore, typically, an obese individual is affected by discriminatory attitudes and actions of its social environment (B_3). Thus, we could write, in first approximation: $B_1 \rightarrow N \rightarrow B_2 \leftarrow B_3$.

Although Diehl gives due consideration to the development of food-related behavior and food habits from infancy to adolescence, he focuses his attention on the adults and on the factors (sociocultural, situational, and personal) affecting "normal" food intake. In separate chapters the author takes up breakfast habits (including data on children and adolescents) and the complex problem of obesity, with emphasis on factors (physiological, psychological, social) affecting body weight. Brief reference is made to therapy. The potential psychological side effects of weight reduction are noted (e.g., "dieting depression"), as are the predisposing factors, such as a long history of overweight and long, unrelieved weight reduction.

Diehl only touches upon the effects of chronically inadequate intake of nutrients, encountered in many parts of the Third World, and on the effects, if any, of vitamin supplements, widely used in industrially developed countries—a geographic area that is of primary concern to the author.

The extensive bibliography (pp. 150–208) is a welcome feature of this valuable, critical addition to the world literature on "psychonutrition."

In Volume 1 of the treatise on human nutrition a substantial amount of space is devoted to "malnutrition and behavior." *Malnutrition* refers primarily to the effects of dietary deficits of energy (calories) and protein, except for the chapter on iron deficiency. In that chapter studies on animal learning are considered briefly, and the author places emphasis on the examination of possible adverse effects of iron deficiency in humans, from infants to adults.

In Volume 4, an author touches on food preferences in connection with the relationships between nutrition and health in old age. Fads are considered in reference to vitamins, especially a high consumption of vitamin C. It is noted that dietary deprivation of thiamine may result in disturbed function of the central nervous system (encephalopathy) as well as of peripheral nerves (polyneuropathy); disturbance of memory is a distinct feature of the Wernicke-Korsakoff syndrome. In deficiency of vitamin B_{12}, early neurological manifestations are symptomatic of the
· involvement of peripheral nerves and spinal cord; at a more advanced stage of the disorder the psychological symptoms may range "from apathy, depression, irritability, and paranoid ideation to marked confusional state and frank dementia" (p. 6). The psychological symptoms of pellagra, involving a dietary lack of niacin (a B-complex vitamin), and its precursor, tryptophan (an amino acid), are described as follows:

In the early stages, patients may be depressed and apathetic or apprehensive and morbidly fearful. They may complain of insomnia, dizziness, and headache. As the disease progresses, a florid psychosis characterized by confusion, delusion, disorientation, hallucinosis and delirium may develop. (p. 73)

Obesity is discussed in the context of the nutrition of infants (Vol. 1, including a warning against overfeeding the infant by bottle and against premature introduction of solid foods); young children (Vol. 2, emotional factors in etiology of obesity and emotional effects of obesity); adolescents (Vol. 2, briefly mentioning behavior modification in reducing energy intake); and adults (Vol. 4, with a discussion of the use of behavior modification in the treatment of obesity). The critical and unsolved problem is the long-term maintenance of the changes in life-style with respect to eating behavior and physical activity.

Multifactorial etiology of obesity is stressed throughout (e.g., "Humans are vulnerable to many neurological, metabolic, and psychological disturbances which alter the mechanisms for appetite, satiety and physical activity" [Vol. 3A, p. 85]).

Psychonutrition: N ← B and N → B
The colloquium on "Malnutrition in

Southern Africa," racially integrated in regard to both speakers and audience, was held at the Institute for Behavioural Sciences, University of South Africa, Pretoria, in July 1979. Although due attention was given to the etiology and prevalence of malnutrition and to a variety of measures designed to counter malnutrition, in this comment we shall limit ourselves to matters psychological.

The underlying general schema, N ⇌ B, refers to the fact that the interaction between nutrition (N) and behavior (B) is a two-way street.

Behavior—as attitudes, habits, and practices—is involved in the causation of malnutrition; as information acquisition, it is relevant to the combating of malnutrition. This is the N ← B part of the story, considered primarily in the section on "Psycho-social Factors," with special reference to taboos and food preferences on the one hand and to breast-feeding habits on the other hand.

The body of the proceedings addresses itself to the impact of malnutrition on brain function and behavior, that is, to the the N → B part of the equation. The scope is broad. Included are considerations of the early South African human and animal research, some of it going back to 1955; more recent human studies—in Africa's South, West, and East; and a brief look at "the tasks for the visible future."

Behavioral effects at time of follow-up
The centerpiece of the section entitled "More Recent Studies" is a pair of follow-up investigations and a 20-year developmental study of children who experienced clinical malnutrition in infancy. In both follow-up studies the energy-protein malnutrition was of the kwashiorkor ("wet") variety, characterized by the presence of edema, and the children were hospitalized, for the most part, in their second year of life. In the retrospective study, reviewed in detail in CP (1978, 23, 257–259), the index children were selected on the basis of the records of patients treated at Baragwanath Hospital, serving the community of Soweto near Johannesburg; at follow-up, with the ages ranging from 6 to 14 years, the behavioral characteristics of the group of the index children did not differ significantly from the two control groups (siblings and yard mates).

The prospective, 15-year follow-up study involved the Cape's "coloured" population. The mean age of the index children at follow-up was 16.8 years; the age of siblings who grew up under the same socio-

economic conditions but never suffered from kwashiokor, 17.2 years. Again, no differences between the groups could be demonstrated. The study brings out the hazards of prospective studies in populations in which the socioeconomic and health conditions are undergoing rapid changes. Thus over a period of some 20 years, the infant mortality rate (number of deaths under 1 year per 1,000 live births) for the Cape's "coloured" population decreased from 90 to 25, which is close to the level for whites.

Of particular interest are the comments on an intervention study in which dietary supplements, provided during the first 2 years of life, assured normal rate of physical growth of the infants at risk of malnutrition. Whereas upon cessation of supplementation the height and weight regressed to the values typical of the population, 7 years after the return to the habitual diet the IQ of the initially supplemented children was higher than the IQ of the siblings (means of 84 vs. 71). Over the next 4 years, the IQ level of the initially supplemented children was well maintained (mean 82), whereas in the siblings it decreased (mean of 62). The reported phenomenon calls for verification.

In the discussion (pp. 145–146) it was brought out that the supplemented children altered their social environment. Specifically, the social worker who regularly visited the homes of the study children observed that the fathers of the supplemented children would come home early and play with the cheerful, smiling child, so strikingly different from the typical apathetic, crying, and miserable infants. Similar observations were also reported, independently, by Adolfo Chávez and Celia Martínez (1979).

The sample of the index children examined in a longitudinal study, conducted in Cape Town, is small—9 boys and 11 girls— but the study holds the world record for length of the observation period. The last measurements were taken when the subjects were about 21 years old. In contrast to the two follow-up studies referred to above, the infants became "grossly undernourished" during the first year of life and suffered from nutritional marasmus—the "dry," protracted form of clinical energy-protein malnutrition. Both the difference in the age at hospitalization and nature of malnutrition are important, and may have contributed to the "positive" findings, including smaller head circumference, deficits in visual-motor functioning (Bender test), and higher incidence of EEG abnormalities. It is stated (p. 74) that the data obtained for the index subjects were compared with the results obtained for "twenty better nourished control infants matched for sex, age, socioeconomic status and ethnicity" (p. 74). However, the editors of the proceedings in which the earlier report of this study appeared (Scrimshaw & Gordon, 1968) noted that there were differences in the social circumstances of the index and the control groups (e.g., in housing, marital status, and employment of fathers). The authors of the study do not address themselves to this critical issue. However, there is other evidence that marasmus tends to affect behavior more profoundly and for longer periods of time than does kwashiorkor.

The syntheses required (yet difficult to obtain)

In closing, let us take a brief look at the past and peek around the corner of the future, focusing on the effects of dietary deficits.

Field research on the behavioral aspects of energy-protein malnutrition in its severe, clinical forms was initiated in the mid-1950s in Mexico, Uganda, and South Africa. The decade of the 1960s was a period of world-wide exploration, continuing into the 1970s. This period witnessed a shift of interest to subclinical, chronic malnutrition and the growing awareness of the role of socioeconomic macro-environment and, eventually, of the micro-environment of the family. Importantly, the 1970s were the times of longitudinal investigations, without and with intervention. In turn, the interventions varied widely in terms of the

age at which they were applied and in their nature—from the provision of nutritional supplements through a combination of nutritional supplementation with behavioral (psychoeducational) stimulation to a broad "intervention" in the form of adoption of Korean female infants by American families. Throughout, human research was paralleled by (and at times, although altogether too rarely, did interact with) animal investigations.

What are the prospects and tasks for the 1980s? One thing appears certain: It will be a row harder to hoe. The largess of the funding bodies characteristic of the 1960s and 1970s is a phenomenon of the past. This is a critical point because field studies are inescapably expensive, especially when they are longitudinal in nature.

The National Institute of Human Development, providing much of the financial support for research on malnutrition and behavior in the 1960s and 1970s has shifted the direction of its interests. This is true also of the Malnutrition Panel, operating in the context of the U.S.–Japan Cooperative Medical Research Program.

One of the prerequisities of any "grand design" for the 1980s is a critical synthesis of the available, large, but widely scattered information: (a) a synthesis across the *disciplines* relevant to the topic, from concern with macroscopic and microscopic structures, metabolism, and organ function to the behavior of the organisms considered singly and in interaction with their sociocultural environment; (b) a synthesis across *species*, from the lowly rodents through subhuman primates to humans; (c) a synthesis of the data obtained at different *stages* of man's ontogenetic development;

(d) a synthesis across *nutrients* the deficits of which importantly affect behavior, including not only the deficits of energy and protein but also of minerals, such as iron and iodine, and vitamins, such as vitamin A and vitamins of the B complex; (e) a synthesis across different *parameters of behavior*, from intraorganismic phenomena, especially those characterizing the CNS, through sensory functions and motor performance in its various aspects (general activity, strength, speed, coordination, endurance) to intellective functions and personality; and last but not least (f) a synthesis across *cultures* and geographic space, paying careful attention to the similarities and differences of diet and environment in the countries of the Western hemisphere, especially of Central and South America, in various parts of Africa, and in Asia.

It is unfortunate that one of the potential facilitators of the multiphasic process of synthesis, the Committee on Nutrition, Brain and Behavior (Food and Nutrition Board, National Research Council–National Academy of Sciences) was terminated in 1980 "because of lack of funding for proposed projects" (Assembly of Life Sciences, 1980).

References

Assembly of Life Sciences, National Research Council, Report 1979/80. Washington, D.C.: National Academy Press, 1980, p. 37.

Chávez, A., & Martínez, C. *Nutrición y desarollo infantil*. Mexico, D.F.: Interamericana, 1979, pp. 106–107.

Scrimshaw, N. S., & Gordon, J. E. (Eds.), *Malnutrition, learning, and behavior*. Cambridge, Mass.: MIT Press, 1968, pp. 288–289.

Addendum To Part IX

A SYSTEMATIC ACCOUNT

The final (fifth) volume of the comprehensive treatise on human nutrition, edited by Janina R. Galler, is devoted to nutrition and behavior. Thus, this note directly supplements Paper 32 in which the first four volumes of the treatise were reviewed.

The volume covers both wings of psychonutrition. Part 1, entitled "Nutritional Deficiencies or Excesses Modifying Behavioral Outcomes," is more directly relevant to this book since it covers the N→B issues. Part 2, entitled "Behavioral Determinants of Food Intake and Nutritional Status," refers to the N←B processes and thus complements, in important ways, the present anthology.

In Part 1, the behavioral consequences of malnutrition in early life are examined by the editor, who summarized the evidence from human studies on the concurrent, intermediate, and long-term effects of malnutrition (pp. 64-100). Particular attention is given to a study of Barbadian school children (pp. 101-109) in which Galler was involved as senior investigator and that was reported in a series of journal articles (see Addendum to Part V in the present volume).

Galler's account is supplemented in an important way by David Rush's chapter on the behavioral consequences of generalized (energy-protein) nutritional deprivation and the effectiveness of cognitive stimulation and nutritional supplementation (pp. 119-157). Separate chapters are devoted to the behavioral consequences of vitamin deficiencies (and excesses) in adults and to the practical issue of nutritional therapy in children. Three chapters are oriented theoretically: (1) a chapter on the mechanism of nutrient action on brain function, with special reference to the chemical transmission of information within the nervous system; (2) a thoughtful analysis of the complex issue of validity in the context of research on behavioral effects of malnutrition; and (3) critical assessment of the use of animals for understanding the effects of malnutrition on human behavior (cf. Smart, 1984).

Part 2 of Galler's volume takes up the psychological (perceptual) and sociocultural factors affecting food intake and examines the role of mother-infant interaction in nutritional disorders. Separate chapters are devoted to the two principal eating disorders: severely restricted food intake (anorexia nervosa) and excessive food intake (bulimia) leading to obesity.

The frequent use of tabular summaries of the literature facilitates the reader's orientation in such complex issues as brain size and the concurrent electrophysiological effects of malnutrition, DQs in malnourished children, mother-infant interaction, intellectual performance of children recently recovered from malnutrition and their home environment, long-term effects of early malnutrition on electrophysiologically characterized brain function and on intellectual performance, intersensory integration, and school performance.

CRITICAL ASSESSMENT OF KEY ISSUES

A critical assessment of selected key issues in the area of malnutrition and behavior was the goal of an international symposium—a symposium at a distance, by mail—that took place in the years 1982 and 1983 (Brožek and Schürch, 1984). The extensive proceedings of the symposium cover the following six topics:

1. Forms and quantitative characterization (with emphasis on anthropometry) of generalized malnutrition;
2. Assessment of functions (electrophysiological, cognitive, motor, socioemotional);
3. Mechanisms, including social factors and sex, interaction of organisms with the environment, and impairment of the interaction by malnutrition. The advantages and limitations of animal models are examined;
4. Interventions under conditions of subclinical, chronic malnutrition and rehabilitation following clinical malnutrition;
5. Research design and data analysis, including the role of comprehensive data banks;
6. Criteria of significance (dependability, magnitude of the changes induced by malnutrition, impact) taking into account issues such as human capital, productivity, and other social outcomes.

A distinctive feature of the proceedings are the comments and addenda following a large number of the primary papers. The aim of the symposium was to cover in greater depth a selected number of topics. Perhaps another symposium can take up some of the remaining major issues including metabolic links between inadequate nutrient intake and brain function and behavior, and the cross-cultural aspects of research on malnutrition and behavior.

NUTRITION AND DEVELOPMENT

The proceedings of an international workshop held in Baroda, India (Rajalakshmi, 1983), in January 1982, contain 62 papers, of which 4 report animal studies on malnutrition and behavior and 4 other papers deal with malnutrition in children. Of the latter, 2 are reviews (interaction of adverse environmental and nutritional influences by H. N. Ricciuti, and nutritional and nonnutritional factors in human behavior by R. Rajalakshmi); 1 concerns behavioral methodology (use of Piagetian techniques by P. Dasen and E. Colomb); and 1 discusses effective strategies for early interventions (B. M. Caldwell).

A WEB OF CAUSES AND CONSEQUENCES

Web is an effective metaphor for referring to problems in which the factors are many and the relationships between them are multidirectional, such as the etiology and the effects of malnutrition (Margen, 1984). The term is used to designate the complex of issues examined in a monograph entitled *Malnourished Children of the Rural Poor* (Balderston et al., 1981), the subtitle of which reads *The Web of Food, Health, Education, Fertility, and Agricultural Production*. The body of the volume consists of four separate studies based on the data collected in the years 1969 through 1978 by the staff of the Institute of Nutrition of Central America and Panama (INCAP) in four Guatemalan villages and, in 1974 to 1975, by the personnel of the RAND Corporation. The authors' contribution consists of the analysis (or reanalysis) of the data and the writing of the four reports bearing the following titles:

"Longitudinal Analysis of Diet, Physical Growth, Verbal Development, and School Performance," by Alan B. Wilson;
"Determinants of Children's School Participation," by Judith B. Balderston;
"Education and Agricultural Efficiency," by Marie E. Freire;
"Education, Family Economic Production, and Fertility," by Mari S. Simonen.

The chapter entitled "The Guatemalan Experiment—The Villages and the Data" is the result of the collaborative effort of the members of the Berkeley Project on Education and Nutrition and provides information on the setting and the nature of the INCAP longitudinal study on the effects of supplementation of preschool children and pregnant and lactating women (cf. Papers 22 and 23). J. B. Balderston wrote the introductory chapter ("Investigating the Web of Poverty—The Need for Research") and the closing chapter entitled "Synthesis of Findings and Policy Implications."

A novel feature of the analyses carried out at Berkeley involved relating the information on early growth and development to effectiveness at tasks met at later stages of life—specifically, school participation and performance, economic (more specifically, agricultural) activities, and control of family size. In disentangling the web of disadvantaging factors associated with generalized (energy-protein) subclinical, chronic malnutrition and their effects, heavy reliance has been placed on the technique of path analysis, including schematic verbal outlines of the relationships (path diagrams) and the calculation of structural coefficients.

We shall illustrate the conclusions of Wilson's (1981) study with reference to two criteria:

1. Performance on verbal tests: Taller children perform better; girls perform better than boys.
2. School performance: Children with high verbal proficiency are more likely to enroll in school and to perform well; children having higher current energy intake perform in school better than children with low energy intakes.

Special attention is given to the issue of combining interventions involving nutrition, public health, education, rural development, and family planning.

GROWING UP IN POVERTY IN MEXICO

The title of the English translation of the monograph on a longitudinal supplementation study—*Growing Up in a Developing Community* (Chávez and Martínez, 1982)—is an interpretation, not a literal rendition of the Spanish original: *Nutrition and Child Development* (Chávez and Martínez, 1979*b*).

The original (Spanish) edition was reviewed, in English, in diverse media and from different points of view (Brožek, 1981*a*, 1981*b*, 1981*c*). Consequently, our comment here may be brief. In the present context the critical chapters are Chapter 7, "Neurological Maturation and Performance on Mental Tests," and Chapter 8, "Effects of Insufficient Food on Child Behavior." The essential information on the design of the study was provided in the comment on Paper 24, reprinted in Part VII.

A distinct methodological feature of the study of the infants was the heavy emphasis on direct, objective, and quantified observations of behavior (cf. Chávez and Martínez, 1979*b*). The authors measured characteristics such as the amount of time the study children were carried on their mothers' backs, spent crying, were in physical contact with the mother, or stayed outside the house. The observations referring to the parents' behavior included the percentage of the observation time during which the mothers smiled at, talked to, or played with the children; the number of sentences per hour directed at the child by the mother and the father; the number of different categories of behavior the fathers exhibited in interacting with the young children; and the number of the types of stimulation provided by the family members to the study children. The changes, with age, in the number of positive and negative complex behaviors of the children (like biting the mother) were also recorded.

The results may be illustrated by the behavior of the unsupplemented and the supplemented children in the open field test in which the child was placed in the center of a square that was divided by lines into 100 units. Mother was located in the middle of one side of the field, and toys were placed at the opposite side of the field. Observers, stationed at the center of the other two sides of the field, traced the movements of the child in the field.

In the test situation children behaved differently. Thus, after having been placed in the center of the field, the undernourished children would go toward their mother, cry and demand to be picked up and taken away; they were afraid of the setting and did not become interested in the toys. By contrast, "The better nourished children . . . felt more confident, frequently went toward the toys, picked them up and carried them to the mother and to the observers, and moved all around the quadrilateral" (Chávez and Martínez, 1982, p. 126).

The authors are not blind to the social injustices prevalent in the poor communities of most rural areas of Mexico. However, in the spirit of realism, they do not call for transforming the poor rural communities into a paradise but for instituting a minimal "package of actions" that will ensure that the conditions of life will not be "physically, mentally, and socially limited by chronic malnutrition" (Chávez and Martínez, 1982, p. 147).

POVERTY, MALNUTRITION, AND SOCIAL POLICY

Pollitt (1980) has devoted a monograph, in English, to the early interventions targeted at poverty and malnutrition in Latin America. The 1982 volume, in Spanish, picks up these themes: Part I, poverty and cognitive development; Part II, malnutrition (light to moderate as well as severe) and mental development; Part III, nutritional interventions, including nutritional supplementation and psychosocial stimulation; and Part IV, nutritional interventions and social policy.

Pollitt (1982, p. 123) is highly skeptical of the effectiveness of narrow, monophasic (e.g., nutritional or educational) interventions and pleads for broader changes in the social and economic organization and dynamics of Latin American society. His aim is the creation of a "world that will be more just to the child" *(un mundo que sea más justo para el niño)*.

SEVERE MALNUTRITION AND CHILD DEVELOPMENT

It was a tragedy, for Chile and for the world, that—as a result of an airplane accident—José Miguel Celedón, one of the promising young men on the nutritional scene of Latin America, did not see the publication in 1983 of the volume he edited and to which he contributed two important chapters: an extensive, informative introduction outlining the economic, sociocultural, psychological, and medical features of extreme poverty as the setting for malnutrition during infancy, and a chapter, neurological in focus, on the effects of malnutrition on the central nervous system. Of the remaining five chapters, two are of central interest in the present context: one on neurological, psychomotor, and mental development of children treated for severe malnutrition, and one on mental development and the affective ties between the severely malnourished infant and its mother in the setting of extreme poverty.

ENERGY INTAKE AND ACTIVITY

Apathy, manifested in part as reduced activity, is a consistent finding in children and adults suffering from severe, clinical malnutrition. A reduction of general physical activity and, in children, a reduction of exploratory activity as well, has been attested also under conditions of less severe deficits of energy and protein. Thus in adults studied under laboratory conditions, the loss of one-fourth of body weight was associated with the decrease of 24-hour calorie expenditure for general activity from 46.5 to 30.0% of the total energy output (Keys et al., 1950, p. 371). Chávez and Martínez (1982, p. 104) observed marked differences in the rate of physical activity between the supplemented and unsupplemented infants during the second year of life.

The amount of quantitative data on the effects of malnutrition on physical activity is limited due, in large measure, to the methodological difficulties. Readers concerned with functional consequences of calorie and protein deficits will be interested in the proceedings of a conference on energy and activity held in May 1983 (Pollitt and Amante, 1984).

Pollitt and Amante's volume opens with a section on energy balance in populations living under conditions of a low energy intake. In the closing chapter of the book, G. H. Beaton (pp. 395-403) returns to the vexing issue of adaptation to chronically low energy intake, noting glaring inconsistencies between the estimates of the food intake and the calculated energy requirements. He points out that either our concept, understanding, and method of calculating energy requirements is wrong or the data on food intake are incorrect.

Beaton sees a way of clarifying the matters by differentiating between two classes of mechanisms by which the actual expenditure of energy may be reduced: the physiological adaptations such as the lowering of the basal metabolic rate (cf. Keys et al., 1950, p. 335), and behavioral compensatory accomodations involving activities outside the essential economic (work) activities (see Paper 2). The ultimate concern is with the human cost of subsistence on a low energy intake. This is a complex issue, calling for pooling of resources and methods of the biological, behavioral, and social sciences.

In the proceedings, the methods for the assessment of physical activity are considered separately for adults and for children. The section on the results obtained in field studies also includes R. Malina's overview of the literature on physical activity and motor development (performance) of children with moderate and severe energy-protein malnutrition (Pollitt and Amante, 1984, pp. 285-302), an issue also considered in a chapter by Chávez and Martínez (pp. 302-321). Reutlinger (pp. 377-394) addresses himself to policy implications of research on energy intake and activity levels.

NUTRITION AND EDUCATIONAL ACHIEVEMENT

Pollitt (1984) provides an appropriate setting for the consideration of inadequate nutrition as a risk factor in the educational process by stressing the individual, social, and economic benefits to be derived from effective participation in that process:

> Schooling as a formal educational system is one of the most potent socializing agents. . . . It has beneficial effects on psychosocial development and on the acquisition and utilization of knowledge, contributing to the economic and social development of individuals and society, both in developed and developing countries. . . . The general direction of the available information, despite a few controversial findings, supports the conclusion that schooling is an instrument of individual and social change, increasing the probabilities of general well being. (p. 7)

The author's basic proposition is that "nutrition, in particular, and health, in general, need to be considered as key determinants of school progress and achievement, and that they are amenable to changes through relevant social and educational policies" (p. 5).

In the present anthology, Paper 24 attests that malnutrition—even a "mild-to-moderate" malnutrition—during infancy and the preschool years may affect school achievement negatively and contribute to "educational wastage" by increasing the chances that a child will have to repeat grades. Pollitt (1984) provides a critical, selective review of the literature on this socially, highly important issue.

Actually, the subject matter of the monograph is broader than the title indicates, since both school achievement and intellectual functioning are taken into account as dependent variables. Nutrition—the independent variable—is examined in separate chapters that deal with malnutrition in infancy and the preschool years, nutritional status at school age, and nutritional interventions. As is done in Part II of the present volume, Pollitt (1984) considers both the effects of energy-protein malnutrition and the deficits of three micronutrients of major social significance—iron, vitamin A, and iodine.

Pollitt concludes with a descriptive summary (pp. 30-32) and tabular presentation (pp. 35-42) of 14 studies on the effects of early malnutrition on subsequent intellectual functioning and school progress, 6 studies on the relationship between the students' current nutritional status and their school progress, and 4 studies on educational consequences of nutrition intervention programs. In the three tables the information is presented under the following headings:

1. Author and Place of the Study;
2. The Number and Description of the Nutritional Condition of the Experimental Subjects;
3. Age at Time of Hospital Admission of the Experimental Subjects (when relevant);
4. The Number and Description of the Comparison Subjects;
5. Age of Experimental and Comparison Subjects at Evaluation;
6. Tests Used and Type of Measure Obtained;
7. Results.

The evidence reviewed in the monograph (Pollitt, 1984) leads the author to conclude (p. 32) that it is imperative (especially in regard to many of the developing countries and to underprivileged segments of the population of the industrially developed countries) to include nutrition as a co-determinant of school performance and achievement. Early malnutrition, as well as poor nutritional status during the school years, tend to have adverse effects on school progress. On the positive side, "the protection of the child's nutritional status during the early formative years and during the school period will result in a better student, and will significantly decrease the human and capital costs of school wastage" (p. 32).

REFERENCES

Balderston, J. B., A. B. Wilson, M. E. Freire, and M. S. Simonen, eds., 1981, *Malnourished Children of the Rural Poor: The Web of Food, Health, Education, Fertility, and Agricultural Production,* Auburn House Publishing Company, Boston, 204p.

Brožek, J., 1981a, Review of "Nutrición y Desarrollo Infantil" by A. Chávez and C. Martínez, *Nutr. Plann.* **4**(1):4-6.

Brožek, J., 1981b, Review of "Nutrición y Desarrollo Infantil" by A. Chávez and C. Martínez, *Ecol. Food Nutr.* **11**:65-67.

Brožek, J., 1981*c*, Review of "Nutrición y Desarrollo Infantil" by A. Chávez and C. Martínez, *Food Nutr. Bull.* **3**(2):35-37.

Brožek, J., and B. Schürch, eds., 1984, *Malnutrition and Behavior: Critical Assessment of Key Issues,* Nestlé Foundation Publication Series, vol. 4, Lausanne, Switzerland, 656p.

Celedón, J. M., ed., 1983, *Nutrición e Inteligencia en el Niño (Nutrition and Intelligence in the Child),* Ediciones de la Universidad de Chile, Santiago, 263p.

Chávez, A., and C. Martínez, 1979*a, Nutrición y Desarrollo Infantil (Nutrition and Child Development),* Interamericana, Mexico, D. F., 148p.

Chávez, A., and C. Martínez, 1979*b,* Behavioral Effects of Undernutrition and Food Supplementation, in *Behavioral Effects of Energy and Protein Deficits,* J. Brožek, ed., NIH Publication Number 79-1906, U.S. Government Printing Office, Washington, D.C., pp. 216-228.

Chávez, A., and C. Martínez, 1982, *Growing Up in a Developing Community,* Instituto Nacional de la Nutrición, Mexico, D. F., 155p.

Galler, J. R., ed., 1984, *Nutrition and Behavior,* Human Nutrition: A Comprehensive Treatise, vol. 5, Plenum Press, New York, 514p.

Keys, A., J. Brožek, A. Henschel, O. Mickelsen, and H. L. Taylor, 1950, *The Biology of Human Starvation,* University of Minnesota Press, Minneapolis, 1385p.

Margen, S., 1984, Energy-Protein Malnutrition: The Web of Causes and Consequences, in *Malnutrition and Behavior: Critical Assessment of Key Issues,* J. Brožek and B. Schürch, eds., Nestlé Foundation Publication Series, vol. 4, Lausanne, Switzerland, pp. 20-31.

Pollitt, E., 1980, *Poverty and Malnutrition in Latin America: Early Childhood Intervention Programs,* Praeger Press, New York, 162p.

Pollitt, E., 1982, *Desnutrición, Inteligencia y Política Social (Malnutrition, Intelligence and Social Policy),* Librería Studium, Lima, Peru, 135p.

Pollitt, E., 1984, *Nutrition and Educational Achievement,* United Nations Educational, Scientific, and Cultural Organization (UNESCO), Nutrition Education Series Issue 9, Paris, 42p.

Pollitt, E., and P. Amante, 1984, *Energy Intake and Activity,* Alan. R. Liss for the United Nations University, New York, 418p.

Rajalakshmi, R., 1983, ed., *Nutrition and the Development of the Child,* Biochemistry Department, M.S. University of Baroda, India, 447p.

Smart, J. L., 1984, Animal Models of Early Malnutrition, in *Malnutrition and Behavior: Critical Assessment of Key Issues,* J. Brožek and B. Schürch, eds., Nestlé Foundation Publication Series, vol. 4, Lausanne, Switzerland, pp. 440-459 (followed by comments by L. S. Crnic on pp. 460-468 and G. Turkewitz on pp. 469-473).

Wilson, A. B., 1981, Longitudinal Analysis of Diet, Physical Growth, Verbal Development, and School Performance, in *Malnourished Children of the Rural Poor: The Web of Food, Health, and Education, Fertility, and Agricultural Production,* J. B. Balderston, A. B. Wilson, M. E. Freire, and M. S. Simonen, Auburn House Publishing Company, Boston, pp. 39-81.

AUTHOR CITATION INDEX

SUBJECT INDEX

About the Author

JOSEF BROŽEK received the Ph.D. in philosophy, specializing in psychology, from Charles University, Prague, in 1937. He became interested in the effects of dietary factors in human behavior in 1938 when, as industrial psychologist in a large shoe factory in southeastern Moravia, Czechoslovakia, he encountered in a group of applicants for employment the phenomenon of a low-measured intelligence that appeared to be nutritional in origin. It turned out that the men came from a nearby mountain area where iodine deficit in the diet was documented by the presence of cretinism and deaf-mutism.

Following postdoctoral studies in applied psychology at the University of Pennsylvania (1939-1940) and the University of Minnesota (1940-1941), Dr. Brožek joined the Laboratory of Physiological Hygiene, directed by Ancel Keys and associated as a research and teaching unit with the School of Public Health, University of Minnesota. The Laboratory was preparing for interdisciplinary experimental studies on the effects of controlled nutrient intake on broadly defined "fitness"—a topic that fitted Brožek's professional interests. The studies were concerned with vitamins (especially those of the B complex), food deficits (varying in degree, duration, and nutrient composition), and (to a limited extent) restricted intake of water. The largest of these studies dealt with the effects of six months of severe food restriction ("semistarvation").

In 1956 Brožek organized a symposium on nutrition and behavior, the first part of which was concerned with the impact of diet on behavior, and he served as co-editor and co-author of the proceedings of a 1957 symposium on performance capacity. In a variety of ways, Brožek continued to be active in the field after his move to Lehigh University in 1959. This included the organization of a worldwide conference held in 1977 on behavioral effects on the dietary deficits of energy and protein, and an international symposium on key issues in research on malnutrition and behavior (1982-1983). Dr. Brožek has collaborated with many other specialists in his field and their publications include *The Biology of Human Starvation* (1950, University of Minnesota Press), *Symposium on Nutrition and Behavior* (1957, National Vitamin Foundation), *Performance Capacity: A Symposium* (1961, Quartermaster Food and Container Institute for the Armed Forces), *Behavioral Effects of Energy and Protein Deficits* (1979, U.S. Government Printing Office), and *Malnutrition and Behavior: Critical Assessment of Key Issues* (1984, Nestlé Foundation). Dr. Brožek is also author of "Soviet Studies on Nutrition and Higher Nervous Activity" (1962, *N.Y. Acad. Sci. Ann.*).